AN IRISH HISTORY OF CIVILIZATION

Volume Two

AN IRISH HISTORY OF CIVILIZATION

Book 1   Downpatrick Is the Butterfly Capital of the Universe

Book 2   Kings of the Wild Frontiers?

Book 3   Half the Globe's Our Home

Book 4   America's Century

An Irish History of Civilization

Volume Two

Comprising Books 3 and 4

DON AKENSON

McGill-Queen's University Press
Montreal & Kingston

© Donald Harman Akenson 2005
ISBN 0-7735-2891-1

Legal deposit first quarter 2005
Bibliothèque nationale du Québec

Published in Great Britain by Granta Books

Printed in Canada on acid-free paper

McGill-Queen's University Press acknowledges the support of the
Canada Council for the Arts for our publishing program. We also
acknowledge the financial support of the Government of Canada
through the Book Publishing Industry Development Program (BPIDP)
for our publishing activities.

Library and Archives Canada Cataloguing in Publication

Akenson, Donald Harman–
    An Irish history of civilization/Don Akenson.

    Includes index.
    Contents: bk. 1. Downpatrick is the butterfly capital of the
    universe – bk. 2. Kings of the wild frontiers? – bk. 3. Half
    the globe's our home – bk. 4. America's century.
    ISBN 0-7735-2890-3 (v. 1) – ISBN 0-7735-2891-1 (v. 2)

    1. Irish – History. 2. Ireland – Emigration and immigration.
    3. Ireland–History. I. Title.

DA925.A365 2005   941.5   C2003-905373-3

This book was typeset by Dynagram Inc. in 10/13 Palatino.

To the memory of

Sir Walter Raleigh,
who should have known better,

and in honour of

Eduardo Galeano,
who certainly does.

Contents

Preface   ix

BOOK THREE   HALF THE GLOBE'S OUR HOME

God's Lethal Spur. Famine 1845–1852   1

An Old World Becoming New? Ireland 1852–1900   27

Not Far, But Not Home. England 1845–1900   75

Nearly Normal. Australia 1845–1900   113

Earnest Accommodation. New Zealand and Outer Polynesia 1845–1900   187

Mourn The Wild Colonial Boys? 1845–1900   257

Land of the Terminally Victorian. Upper Canada 1845–1900   291

The Advent of the Belated Irish. The USA 1845–1898   323

BOOK FOUR   AMERICA'S CENTURY

The Road Home. Ireland 1900–1923   385

Ever Farther. Australasia and Polynesia 1900–1969   437

Still the Cavaliers Ride 1900–1969   481

The Lord Has Mersey, and Lots More. England 1900–1969   523

So Far, So Fast, So So Far. Ireland 1922–1969   555

The Creation of the American Century 1898–1969   603

Recessional 659

Postlude 667

Index: Personal Names 673

　　　Story Titles 689

Preface

As in the case of the two supernal Talmuds, the Yerushalmi and the Bavli, nothing original is proposed in these volumes, only respectful commentary on what Sages have said, or should have.

Everything in them, I have read, heard from somebody, or talked about to myself; or the reader has creatively imputed new meanings to old words. For all of these voices, I am grateful. Where I have directly quoted someone, it is pretty clearly marked.

Against my inclination, my publishers have insisted that to aid librarians and bookstore owners in putting these volumes on the right shelves I label clearly what they are.

Like all human lives, this is a collection of fictive short stories or, if you prefer, of Aggadah: very little in the way of Halachah here.

Some of the stories are accurate; all of them are true. Of course, as Church dogma teaches, if any thing is not true, then no thing is. Still, as far as mere accuracy is concerned, not all seeming errors in the text are accidental. Sometimes even the immortal Homer only pretended to nod.

Taken together, this Irish history of civilization is a micro-Talmud of humankind: for, ultimately, we are all of the one stock, and what we learn of one of us tells us something about each of us. I am confident that Irish readers will be generous and will permit their culture's experience of world history to be presented in this Jewish form. After all, the Irish rarely forget a debt.

DA

AN IRISH HISTORY OF CIVILIZATION

Book Three

Half the Globe's Our Home

GOD'S LETHAL SPUR.
FAMINE
1845–1852

The Partitionings of Ireland (1)

Starvation, typhoid, typhus, dysentery and a hundred unnamed scythes of death kill at least one million people. This is the worst famine caused mostly by nature in modern history. That's if you judge it according to the proportion of the population that it kills – one out of eight, roughly – and exclude from your comparison famines caused by wars or by governments starving unruly parts of their own populace to death.

One map is never drawn by chroniclers. This is the death rate townland-by-townland throughout the countryside. Too hard to do, they say.

Were it to be drawn, that map would show that in two swathes the death rate was lowest. One of these was the diversified farming areas south of Dublin, running through Wicklow down to Wexford. Nobody is too fussed about this area, though it's worth asking why this is the area where the 1798 Rising became a local civil war.

What has to be stared at unblinkingly is a second set of contours. They follow, like an exercise in topology, the border that in 1920 was made to partition Northern Ireland from the rest of the country. You see, the partition of modern Ireland into two sharply different worlds had begun in the later eighteenth century with the diversifying of the economy first into linen, and then, other textiles. The ratification of that partition was the Famine. Yes, the northeast suffered, but nothing like the rest of the country. Catholics and Protestants of the north carried a hatred of each other into the high Victorian era, but they did not share with the rest of Ireland the full woundings by the knife-of-a million-cuts.

The Liverpool Machine in Operation (1)

The thousands and thousands who pour across the Irish sea to Liverpool have little perspective. Unlike the spalpeens who are accustomed to rattling sea trips that sometimes take up to thirty hours, few of those fleeing Ireland for the first time have ever before been on a boat. The steamers that take them to England are a vast improvement over the old sailing ferries because they can sail against the wind, or across the wind and tide. And that, indeed, is the trouble: the winds and tides running between Ireland and Britain usually come at the ferries at an awkward angle. The ships jump about unpredictably, half-roll, half-pitch, completely ill-making. How can anyone have perspective when every breath of below-deck air is pervaded by the miasma of nausea and every inch of deck space is made slippery by sputum and uncontrolled evacuation of bodily wastes?

The ferry passengers of the Famine years are a mixture of still-solvent families who are banded together in below-deck "cabins." They are on their way to North America and have luggage and money in hand. The less fortunate, single women and men, young families with babes-in-arms and only pennies in their pockets, are crowded into steerage or made to travel on deck where there is only standing room. They all are being transported by the first arm of the Liverpool Machine, and they can be forgiven if they do not understand the economic flywheel that keeps this instrument in balance: they are being transported out of Ireland so cheaply – ten pence to two shillings a head or so – because they are poor, generally. And because they are poor and can pay little for the voyage, they must be packed like mackerel in a can: seventy-two below-deck passengers were suffocated in one notorious voyage from Sligo to Liverpool in December 1848.

Does anyone expect these people to accept the economists' brass-necked tautology that they are made miserable because of their immiseration?

LIMERICK. 11 APRIL 1846

An Economy of Truth

Some words of Edmund Burke stay with the commissary-general of Limerick.

Burke, who had the handicap of seeing everything equally clearly, had written *Thoughts and Details on Scarcity* in 1795 in response to a bad harvest in Britain. It began: *Of all things, an indiscreet tampering with the trade of provisions is the most dangerous, and it is always worst when men are most disposed to it, that is, in the time of scarcity.* Decades ahead of most of his political counterparts, Burke had assimilated the belief in economic laws and, being Burke, gave to these laws divine sanction. *It is not in breaking the laws of commerce, which are the laws of nature, and consequently the laws of God, that we place our hope of softening the Divine displeasure …*

Sir Robert Peel, the United Kingdom's prime minister, had spent his second premiership removing obstacles to free trade, but he read the reports from the Irish constabulary and he was a man of large heart, if rigid demeanour. On his own responsibility, Peel in November 1845 purchases £100,000 in maize from the USA and has it shipped to Ireland to relieve the worst starvation. It seems to work. Three-quarters of the potato harvest had survived in the autumn of 1845, and Peel's aid saves thousands of lives and appears to ameliorate the crisis.

That was the problem: the problem seemed soluble. The crop would not fail again, surely, and playing against economic laws was immoral. The commissary-general of Limerick writes to Charles Trevelyan who has ably directed the relief efforts. *I am so thoroughly persuaded of the general truth of the principles laid down by Burke in his Thoughts and Details on Scarcity that I have always sought to excuse rather than commend the interference of the government on this occasion.*

Repeat: *excuse rather than commend.* This from one who saw the outstretched hands each day.

Limerick's commissary-general put his signature to this letter in a large, confident scrawl: Edward Pine Coffin, a name beyond irony.

THE NORTH AMERICAN SEABOARD. 1846–47

Advance Guard

They look messy. Smell bad. Speak strange English. But the advance guard of the Famine migration from Ireland to North America still holds some crucial commonalities with its pre-1846 predecessors: about half of the emigrants still land in British North America – Quebec City, St. John, Montreal. And they still come mostly in family networks – not always the nuclear family, but often cousins, aunts, uncles. And, poor though they now are, they had in Ireland more resources than average: they have paid for a transatlantic ticket. People of real poverty starved; those with only a few pence made their way to England.

These are the quick people.

Remember, they do not know what we do; moreover, some important things they think they know are very wrong. Never in Ireland has there been a complete failure of the potato two years running. They do not believe that the main food of the nation could fail completely two years out of four and, in some areas, four years straight. Even so, they know the world outside Ireland is a better place to live: almost any world.

They are alighting in this New World in massive numbers – a quarter of a million in 1847 – with their heads held higher than those who will soon follow.

To call them lucky would be an insult. Yet, truly, they leave Ireland before the Angelus of doom has fully struck all of its notes.

THE ENGLISH-SPEAKING WORLD. 1846–52

The Partitionings of Ireland (2)

When Sir Robert Peel – having just achieved the repeal of the corn laws, the last inhibition on the importation of food into the British Isles – was voted from office it was on an Irish coercion bill: more law and order for Ireland. The Irish nationalist MPs, led by Daniel O'Connell, voted to have him gone and celebrated when the result was announced. For O'Connell there was every excuse: he was an old man nursing a younger man's grievance: in 1825, when Peel was chief secretary for Ireland, he and Peel had agreed to fight a duel. This being prevented, he never lost the desire to drive a stake into Sir Robert's heart. The other Irish MPs should have known better. In helping to dump Peel they were replacing the one big person on the stage, the only one who would break the newly-declared economic laws, in order to help Ireland. Thus the representatives of the Irish people help to set the stage for Lord John Russell's six years of sensible, heartless Whiggery.

If the Famine partitioned the home island into two separate mentalités, it did so even more sharply in the Irish diaspora. Here it was a case of small changes having large and unintended consequences.

Before the Famine, between 1842 and '44, Peel's government had enacted a schedule for reducing and eventually abolishing the duties on squared timber. So? These duties had exempted British North America, meaning that it was very profitable to fill a ship that had brought over emigrants with timber on the way home. Each migrant to the Canadas or the Maritimes was invisibly subsidized by this system and fares to British North America were lower than to New York, Boston, Philadelphia, Baltimore. Even taking into account the migrants who used the Canadas as a gateway to the States, a good guess at the distribution of Irish migration from 1830–45 is as follows: British North America, 50 percent; USA, 25 percent; Great Britain 20 percent; other places, 5 percent.

This held through 1845 and early 1846. But the fare-patterns had been changed by Peel's earlier administration and by 1847 every emigrant knew that the passages to the USA now were cheaper than to the Canadas. And, on top of this, in 1848 the Canadian government began requiring shipowners to post bonds to guarantee the health of their passengers. This diverted more traffic to the USA. So, just at the time the biggest flash-flood in the history of the Irish diaspora was occurring, the flood gates in North America were being cranked around so as to divert most of the roiling wash of humanity to the USA. There was nothing planned about this or nothing "natural" (most Irish people could have found land and place in British North America). It was unintentional. Yet real: we're dealing with roughly one million Famine emigrants. This massive Famine migration, 1845–51, probably was divided as follows (nobody knows for certain): USA, 60 percent; Great Britain, 30 percent; the rest of the English-speaking world, 10 percent. And for the continuing emigration of the next half century that ordinal ranking remained.

Accidentally, the Irish diaspora was partitioned, and along memory-lines. The USA, alone among the countries of the Irish diaspora, has the communal memory of the Irish as an ethnic group washed over and permanently dominated by the Famine. In the Canadas, Newfoundland, Australia, New Zealand, the Famine has only a tithe of this effect. In those places, as in Great Britain, the roots and folk memory go back to earlier days. The Famine's partitioning of the Irish diaspora forms a wall, permeable but substantial, between the Irish in the USA and everywhere else.

BOSTON, MASS. MARCH 1847

The Liverpool Machine in Operation (2)

Herman Melville, making notes for *Redburn*, remembers Liverpool from a seaman's perspective. For someone who has voyaged the earth, it remains one of the wonders of the world, a mixture of mechanical genius and social control.

Melville recalls with still-fresh awe the vast row of wet-docks on the Mersey. For miles he had walked along the front, looking at immense maritime fortresses, each forming a massive "U" and enclosing fifteen to twenty acres. Each of these machines – which Melville compares favourably to the merely immobile obelisks of Luxor – has its own port of entry, a water gate. Ships can only enter or leave the big docks at high tide, when the level of the estuary rises twenty feet and coincides with the level of the water that has been kept inside the dock by the watergate. Suddenly, when that equivalency is reached, hundreds of ships of all sizes and configurations, standing above the quayside with their masts resembling a burned-over forest, leave through their various watergates at once, and then newcoming vessels race to get inside the dockage before the tide starts to ebb and the water gates have to be closed.

Melville is equally impressed with the discipline enforced by the Liverpool harbourmasters. Outside the quays, hovels, dead-end lanes, beggars, thieves, whores might prevail, but the harbour itself, if frantically busy, is tightly ordered. Take the matter of ship's wastes: the bilge usually is full of effluent, the galley has buckets of rubbish, and dirt and dunnage lie all over most vessels after a long voyage. Unlike every other major port Melville has experienced, it is illegal to throw the least thing overboard into the wet dock, even bits of old rope, and the law is strongly enforced. The ships do not float in encrusted sewage as they do in most harbours. And the populace is kept out of the docks. When, at noon, the crews of hundreds of ships go off for their dinner, they run a gantlet of the deformed, the desperate, and the depraved. But inside the wharves, property is fairly safe, and the gravel of landlocked humanity is not allowed to wear away the gears of the efficient Liverpool machine.

COUNTY GALWAY. MARCH 1847

A Keen Sense

John Mitchel has a keen sense of smell, and he is puzzled. Something in the air is missing.

He is making a tour of the far west of Ireland. Mitchel has become accustomed to the bare, nearly hedgeless landscape that the potato-world has become. Only on steep hills, above the line of possible cultivation, does natural vegetation grow, clinging to cliffs and eroding moraines. Everywhere else, outside of landlords' enclosed demesne lands, are pitiful cabins, often so close to each other that, were this a city, it would be called a slum. Many of the cabins are made of mud and they appear half-melted by rainfall. The patches of land around each cabin are almost entirely filled by the ridges of the previous year's potato crop. The pattern is higgledy-piggledy as the rigs of one family run into those of their surrounding neighbours. From a height, the land appears to be a quilt pieced together by an astigmatic lunatic. There are no songbirds in this overcultivated, hedgeless desert, only scavengers, birds that wear black.

Mitchel finally realizes what is missing: he cannot smell smoke. In this packed landscape, smoke should curl from chimneys or through holes in the roofs. The aroma of turf fires should be omnipresent. Mitchel dismounts and enters a cabin. He quickly remounts and goes to another and another. In each, he discovers a cold hearth, an empty home. He knows not where the people have gone – to a New World or to the Other Land. All he knows for certain is that they have left forever.

THE UNITED KINGDOM OF GREAT BRITAIN
AND IRELAND. 24 MARCH 1847

Brethren, Pray without Ceasing

Although it is mid-week – Wednesday – commercial and industrial England is closed. So too is lowland Scotland and the commercialized portions of Ireland, around Belfast and Dublin.

Churches are full.

It is the Day of National Humiliation, a fast day. Long sermons are preached explaining why the Lord has visited the tragedy of the Famine upon the Nation. That the portions of the "nation" in question that are suffering comprise Ireland and highland Scotland is convenient, for it allows more scope for explaining why God's providence should treat the potato-people so harshly. Explanations run from the governmental grant made to Maynooth College in 1845 to intemperance (English and Scottish as well as Irish), Sabbath-breaking, and neglect of philanthropy. This providential ill-fortune, the Famine, is held up as a divine generosity, for it provides an opportunity for repentance.

More than £170,000 is raised at church doors to relieve Irish distress.

In Ireland, only around Dublin, where gentle old Archbishop Daniel Murray is in charge, do the Catholic churches participate.

Elsewhere in the country the people have been praying without cease for nearly two years and for them volitional fasting is out of the question.

IRELAND. 1847–52

Not So Mysterious a Fact

Prescient observers remark on the phenomenon, and more than a century after the Famine, demographers puzzle over it: the fact that boys and men were more vulnerable to the Famine and its diseases than were girls and women. Oh, one can argue about the degree of difference, but the material is unmistakable: males in Ireland in the mid-nineteenth century succumbed more readily, females hung on.

Convoluted, almost Baroque, explanations are put forward, involving everything from biological dimorphism to imagined male chivalry.

The real explanation is so simple that it hurts. In Ireland in the immediate pre-Famine years, boys got the first crust, girls the last; men ate first, ate most, women last and least.

Hence, before the Famine, Ireland had been harrowed of its weakest girls, its most debilitated females. Soft boys, weak men had been kept alive by the scrapings and morsels that females surrendered.

Pre-Famine Ireland was one of the worst places in the world to be a peasant woman. The weakest had already been deleted from the living before the Famine. Men died more often in the Famine because the Apocalypse's third horseman reduced men to the level of scarcity their wives and daughters already had visited.

GROSSE ÎLE, QUEBEC CITY, AND NEW YORK CITY. 1847

Two-Way Traffic (1)

The cruelest end, they say, for a shipwrecked person, is to die within sight of land.

In the summer of 1847, nearly 105,000 Irish managed to catch sight of a Canadian port, most of them landing at Grosse Île quarantine station. Twelve thousand, or more, of their fellow travellers had died along the way. In this, the first year of the great Famine migration, typhus was the big killer. Shipping fever it was called. The authorities on Grosse Île are so deluged that they can no longer segregate in two separate zones the healthy from the diseased. Lazarettos and fever hospitals spring up among the tents set aside for the healthy. Five thousand, five hundred Irish migrants die on Grosse Île. Another 6,000 end their days on Pointe St. Charles, Montreal, an overflow centre for the quarantine station. This last band had not only caught sight of the promised land, but had touched it, and then were buried in it.

William Hume Blake and his wife (and, truth be told, cousin) Catherine Honoria Hume Blake travelled to New York City and then boarded a sailing vessel. They were visiting their homeland, Ireland, and in the right way, they felt: not in the modish new steam-powered vessels, but by sail. This was to remind them of their original journey to the Canadas, in 1832.

Such a pleasant journey it had been! Some one of their clever circle had suggested they all migrate together and not do so in any of those vessels that contained tiresome labourers and that sort. Why, it would be terrific fun to charter our own vessel! and so they did. They could afford it. William's family, the Blakes, were a branch of the wealthy County Galway family that had kept its money and lands intact by turning Protestant in the eighteenth century; and both Catherine and William also were part of the County Wicklow gentry clan, the

Humes. Now, in their expansive and prosperous middle years they thought a voyage to Ireland would be a restorative, for Upper Canada was so tiring, don't you know.

Honoria keeps a journal, the usual shipboard sort. She and William take in the sights of Liverpool on a selected scale and then by steamer go to Dublin, and thence to the rural places they had known in their youth.

There, her journal ends, not because she did not keep it well, but because she kept it too well. She could not bear the thought of her children or grandchildren reading the details of anything so terrible as the sights she witnessed in the homeland. She erased all record of her journey, from the moment she caught a glimpse of the hill of Howth.

MONTREAL. 1847

Two-Way Traffic (2)

Colonel James FitzGibbon surveys the human misery being unloaded on the wharfs of Montreal. He cannot long watch: he turns away. Although he is now an embittered and self-pitying shadow, he still has some nerve-endings. At age sixty-seven, he still is every inch the soldier in physique and bearing. He is deeply disillusioned with Upper Canada. He had saved the province's existence not once but twice and look what he had to show for it: a handful of political jobs and £3,000 in debts, no assets, no dreams remaining.

He cannot view the bedraggled men, women, children disembarking, mostly on their way to Upper Canada – not, not, not because of their pain. It is because of their hope. These people look terrible, but he knows they are not broken. They are going to a better future, just as he had done, when, forty-five years earlier, as a young soldier he had been posted to the Canadas.

A man with a large past, but small future, must envy those whose future has a broad horizon.

When Colonel FitzGibbon finally embarks for Liverpool, he spends the first four days in his cabin. He does not wish to see any hint of the in-comers, the people-of-hope whose vessels are moving through the Gulf of St. Lawrence.

He does not return to his native Ireland. He settles in lodgings near Buckingham Palace. He reads, walks about, and is introduced to Jane Strickland, the third of the Strickland women. In her late forties, she has just completed her latest children's novel, *The Orphan Captive or Christian Endurance. A Tale of Shipwreck and Slavery of an Ambassador's Daughter*, an heroic narrative FitzGibbon greatly admires. They become close acquaintances. She loves his anecdotes; he thrives on female attention; and they both agree that Susanna Strickland Moodie, whom FitzGibbon knows distantly and whom Jane no longer bothers writing to, is a very dreary item. With Jane Strickland's encouragement the old soldier publishes a book on early childhood education, a topic about which he knows less than Miss Strickland does about shipwrecks, slavery, or ambassadors' daughters.

Hope returns.

And luck, in small pieces.

In 1850, Lord Seaton, who had been lieutenant-governor of Upper Canada, obtains for FitzGibbon a lifetime appointment as one of the Knights of Windsor. He is one of a dozen-and-a-half deserving former soldiers who are given apartments in Windsor Castle, splendid uniforms, and finally, a peaceful end: at age eighty-three in his case.

THE EASTERN SEABOARD, USA. 1848–52

The Second Wave

The second wave of Famine-caused migration to the U.S. changes forever both America and the Irish diaspora. Over 100,000 persons a year come down the gangplanks and most of them have the dispirited air of prisoners who do not understand the sentence that has been handed to them. They are surprisingly silent about the Starvation, benumbed, rather than enraged, puzzled that God would punish them thus: not sure of what they are being punished for. Nor do they demonstrate overtly their awareness that they are fortunate to survive, for many of them do not believe this is good fortune, only the prolonging of bad fate.

The Famine migration continues long after the Starvation is ended and the land is once again producing enough food to sustain the Irish people. The outpouring to the USA continues in spate into the mid-1850s and in big numbers, more than 50,000 annually, into the 1870s.

To-the-USA, that is the key. In 1848, British North America raises its port health standards and the sick and weak now are passed on to U.S. ports. There those sad wretches stay alive only long enough to die.

Roughly 90 percent of these migrants to the USA are Roman Catholic and that is why they are frightening to the locals, the more so as they, in contrast to the pre-1848 immigrants, pile up for years in the seaport cities, unable to move inland and find work. The 10 percent who are Protestant are not negligible, but in the massive flow they are lost, for they fit in fairly quickly in Protestant America.

The belated Irish are quadruply different from the bulk of the American-Irish. They are Catholics; their origins are not mostly in the north and east of Ireland, but in the south and west; they are post-Famine, and they think they are the only Irish who exist. They are a people who were saturated in the intoxicating rhetoric of Daniel O'Connell: when the Liberator used the word Irish, he meant the Catholic people.

That's what these new arrivals believe. Benumbed at first, they acquire eventually the hubris that characterizes the USA, making it culturally irresistible and imperially unstoppable – so they convince themselves and many of their friends around the world that the only Irish diaspora is that of people like themselves, the dispersal of the Catholic people of a holy island: a small comfort and a forgivable self-deception.

BALLINGARRY, CO. TIPPERARY. JULY 1848

Before the I.R.B.

As the constabulary surround the quixotic rebels of 1848, Terence Bellew MacManus distinguishes himself by doing some real fighting. He fights furiously because he is truly furious. Not solely at the constabulary: given the opportunity, he would not mind strangling a handful or two of his alleged allies.

As a Liverpool merchant-forwarder, MacManus knew the port of Liverpool as if it were an Irish townland. And he was well-connected in Irish circles. He had his middle class friends (such as Charles Gavan Duffy) and his contacts in the borderlands of south Ulster where he had been a merchant. So why is he in the cabbage patch?

Pure frustration. Terence Bellew MacManus understood, as few Young Irelanders in the Old Country did, that Ribbonism had migrated across the Irish Sea and that with proper leadership, Lancashire Ribbonmen were an army in waiting. In the back parishes and roadless spaces of Ireland, Ribbonism was a creature with a thousand claws, but no head. In one place it would be solely an anti-landlord conspiracy, in another, a political guild. All secret, all lacking coordination. The compacting of so many thousands of Irish people within a half-mile of the curve of the Liverpool docklands meant that Ribbonism could break out of the old rural parish mould. Somewhere between thirty and forty secret clubs – named for heroes such as Patrick Sarsfield – could mobilize up to 4,000 serious revolutionaries: so estimated both MacManus and the Liverpool police.

MacManus had promised that when the flag was raised, he would provide transport for weapons that were to be seized from Chester Castle in England and taken to Wexford. And, he assured Gavan Duffy, if plans were well made, the Irish Catholic community of Liverpool, led by the New Model Ribbonmen would turn the entire docklands into a torch.

He did his part: he chartered three small steamboats to carry the arms to Ireland.

And then, informants running through the entire Young Ireland apparatus like worms in a Stilton, ended the dream.

MacManus, though he knows that the '48 Rising must fail, takes himself to Ireland and fights with an anger that comes from being part of a failure.

"For all we did," he later tells William Smith O'Brien, "we might'st as well shipped to Australia."

BOULAGH COMMONS, BALLINGARRY,
COUNTY TIPPERARY. 29 JULY 1848

Martyred for Their Beliefs

Unlike Terence Bellew MacManus, most of the Young Irelanders of 1848 were a Dublin-based band of gentry and haute bourgeoisie, with a few followers among the more fashionable of the Catholic clergy. In the countryside, not one person in a hundred-thousand had heard of them. Emboldened by the revolutionary chic of the Paris revolution of February 1848, they decided to stage an Irish one, a national rising in the countryside.

In the actual event, in July 1848, 100 peasants turn out, 40 police and a slightly pitched battle (actually more tipsy than pitched) is fought for control of the Widow McCormack's house.

The gentry leaders of the '48 Rising were martyred by being transported, in first-class staterooms, to Tasmania, where they had household servants, freedom of movement and, if they wished, their families joined them.

The gentry rebels of '48 were martyred for their beliefs. They believed that the peasants would show up and the police wouldn't.

OKLAHOMA. 1848

Famine Relief (1)

Of all of the Amerindian nations, the Choctaw had the most to dislike about the Irish. An American-Irish president and cavalry officers had driven them along the Trail of Tears into Oklahoma.

There they hear from their Indian agent of the terrible suffering across the water. They cannot envisage the land; they can understand the hunger.

The Choctaw scrape together their pennies and, with a few dollars from the white administrators of their lands, they manage to send $170 to the Quakers. This is forwarded to Ireland to help feed those in need.

BOSTON, MASSACHUSETTS. 1848

Famine Relief (2)

Henry David Thoreau is polishing some poems and selections from his journal. He is working hard at introducing some spontaneity into the journal and for him that is very demanding work. He works indoors, at a large leather-padded desk in a Boston mansion, for the outdoors is distracting and should be avoided by an outdoor writer as much as possible.

The section that gives him most trouble deals with an Irish couple who have arrived at Walden and made ripples on the Pond and upon the mirror-like reflectiveness of Thoreau's consciousness. These people just do not act right. They work too hard, spending most of their days in heavy labour for local farmers, when all they have to do to eat is to let a line drop limpidly into the water, as does the writer. Because the Irishman and his young son do heavy labour, they wear heavy clothes and heavy boots, twice as expensive as the light gear that Thoreau sports. And they pay too much for rent. Why, if they just lived like Thoreau, they might in a month or two *build a palace* of their own. The problem is all cultural, of course. This Irish family eats a lot because they work hard, whereas they could work less hard, eat less, and save the money. Sadly, *they fight at an overwhelming disadvantage ... alas! without arithmetic, and failing so.*

Having given them so much good advice, and seeing that it is not taken, Thoreau can only shake his head when he considers the head of this Irish family, *with his horizon all his own, yet he, a poor man, born to be poor, with his inherited Irish poverty or his poor life, his Adam's grandmother and boggy ways, not to rise in this world, he nor his posterity, 'till their wading webbed bog-trotting feet get talaria [wings] to their heels.*

That's poetry, really: "wading webbed bog-trotting feet."

LIVERPOOL, ENGLAND. 1848

Without Resources

Despite their stiff collars and civil service ways, the United Kingdom's Commissioners of Emigration care. They are particularly worried about Irish emigrants who are bilked in Liverpool and end up in New York City. They worry about the New York bound because New York, Dublin, and Liverpool itself are the world's three cities with the most Irish-born people and problems on one point of the triangle mean trouble at all three.

Emigrant runners: *They generally call themselves agents of some transportation or forwarding bureau and endeavour to impress the emigrant who intends going farther than New York with the belief that it is for his benefit, and in the highest degree desireable, to secure his passage hence to the place of his destination before he leaves Europe.*

Instances have come to the knowledge of the Commissioners, where the difference amounted to three dollars a person.

But this is not all. The cases are by no means rare, in which the tickets prove **entirely worthless.** *They bear the name of offices which never existed ... or the offices whose names they bear will be found shut up ... or the emigrants are directed to parties refusing to acknowledge the agent who issued the tickets.*

And in all these cases the emigrant loses the money paid for them.

DUNGANSTOWN, COUNTY WICKLOW. OCTOBER 1848

Not Without Resources

As he begins his journey by foot to New Ross, and thence by boat to Boston, Patrick Kennedy carries a cloth satchel, balanced on a pole that cuts into his shoulder and he is fully aware of it every step he takes. He is a shrewd man and he is aware of some things he is bringing with him that do not weigh anything, but that are more important than the extra pair of boots and the half-dozen tradesman's tools that he has in the satchel. He has a lot in his head.

He knows a surprising amount about the east coast of North America. Migrants, even famine migrants, from Counties Wicklow, Wexford and Waterford have that advantage. Since the later seventeenth century an annual flotilla had gone from southeastern Ireland to the Newfoundland fisheries, returning each autumn with money and stories and knowledge. By the early eighteenth century, many of the seamen were staying for years, and increasingly, living permanently in Newfoundland. Gradually they filtered their way down into Nova Scotia, and then to what they later call "the Boston States." Patrick Kennedy has harvested the oral knowledge that flowed back to Wicklow-Wexford and he has a shrewd idea how and where to find a start.

Kennedy, twenty-five years of age, never had a prayer of making a living by farming in Ireland: his parents have three sons and only a holding large enough for a single family; but they – and the maritime requirements of Wexford – have given him the means of making a sure livelihood in the Boston States. For he was given a trade. He is a rough cooper: not a master cooper, but he knows how to shape staves into the mysterious elliptical forms that makes a watertight barrel. Next to being a wheelwright, being a wet-cooper is one of the most skill-demanding jobs of the early industrial era. If you doubt it, take some cardboard and try to find the precise shape, that, when multiplied ten or twenty times, will form a container that has the same radius at top and bottom, but will bell outward in the middle. Then consider doing that in oak or other hardwood, and reckon how to put at least three iron bands around that container. These must have enough strength to hold the vessel together when it is full of liquid and yet not be so forceful as to cave in the cask when it is empty. Oh yes, all this has to be done to watertight standards and somehow a circular top or bottom has to be inserted.

Patrick Kennedy can do most of those things at a rough level, and that is why there is a clinking sound every step he takes. A man with tools is like a knight with armour: he is protected. And so, in East Boston, Kennedy becomes a journeyman cooper, making whiskey barrels.

LIVERPOOL. JANUARY 1849

Inhale/Exhale

The Swedish Nightingale sings with a clarity of diction that can only be obtained in a second or third language, never in one's first. So crystal clear are the melancholy standards that Jenny Lind sings, that a crowd of the dispossessed, gathered outside the theatre, can hear each line and can shed tears in synchrony with the quality of Liverpool who listen within. The charity concert is for Liverpool's hospitals, choked with cholera and typhus victims, mostly Irish.

Charity, yes, and admirable: yet in the years 1845 through 1854, Liverpool ships to Ireland more than 66,000 paupers, men and women who have no right of settlement under the poor law and can be settled back in Ireland where their future is as bleak as is their past.

ORMSKIRK, LANCASHIRE. 1849

Small Problems

Big cities receive most of the attention, but the Irish Famine spilled into the English countryside.

Ormskirk, a Lancashire market town of 4,900 in 1841, had lost its Quarter Sessions status as long ago as 1817; its rural character had degenerated into the tatterdemalion commercialism of an exurb; its economy was unsteady, stumbling along like a town drunk veering unsteadily homeward. Small trades, such as basketweaving, silk-making, malting, prevailed and the mouths fed almost exactly equalled the work produced.

So, the rise of 1,300 inhabitants, though small in absolute number, Famine Irish with no resources, was overwhelming. The local vestry and poor law guardians could not cope. Orsmkirk had almost no covered sewage drains, a situation that was all right for a sleepy market town, but now they clogged. The new population crammed itself into every attic room and Irish labourers slept in basements on dryish straw for a penny a night. The town's main drain was situated only five feet away from Ormskirk's water pump. A town with amenities suitable for 1801 cracked in 1851.

Across the mid-section of England the same thing was happening to hamlet and village, each in its own unrecorded way.

BOSTON, MASSACHUSETTS. 1849

Tourist

Like many English visitors to North America, Major John Thornton is an expert the moment he arrives and, ah, he writes a book about his travels. The volume is a mixture of his wisdom and vignettes of the Americans.

Major Thornton: Here, sir. Do you not think that the deportation of the Niggers might well solve your slavery problem?

Proper Bostonian: Perhaps. However, sir, the deportation of the Irish would be preferable.

LONDON. 1849

A Rare Sense of Humour

Employing an old, but still useful trick, Thomas Carlyle writes an anonymous article for *Fraser's Magazine*. Entitled, "Occasional Discourse on the Negro Question," it is arch, but not satirical. He'd like to follow in the footsteps of Jonathan Swift or of Richard Whately, whose anonymous *Historic Doubts* about the existence of Napoleon Buonaparte was the hit of the late Georgian era. Carlyle, though, lacks the ability to say the opposite of what he really means, so that instead of undercutting his opponents' position by satire, he simply speaks his own ideas in a virulent manner.

He is unhappy that British workers are having to pay too much for sugar and that former slave planters are going broke: the former slaves just won't work hard enough. The black: *sunk to the ears in pumpkin, imbibing saccharine juices, and much at his ease in the Creation, he can listen to the less fortunate white man's 'demand' and take his own time in supplying it. Higher wages, massa – till no conceivable opulence of cane-crop will cover such wages.*

Political economists have suggested bringing in free labourers from Africa. *If the new Africans, after labouring a little, take to pumpkins like the others, what remedy is there? To bring in new and ever new Africans ... til the country is crowded with Africans; and black men there, like white men here, are forced by hunger to labour for their living. That will be a consummation. To have emancipated the West Indies into* **Black Ireland**. *'Free' indeed, but in Ireland, and black!*

In case no one gets the point, Carlyle expands the article and publishes it in 1851 as *Occasional Discourse on the Nigger Question*.

CORK CITY. AUGUST 1849

The Partitionings of Ireland (3)

To raise morale in Ireland, Queen Victoria, no longer young but still handsome at age thirty, makes a flying visit to Ireland. One of her stops is the almost-completed Queen's College, Cork, one of the three colleges – in Belfast, Galway, and Cork – being built to benefit the Irish middle class, especially the Catholics.

The architect, Sir Thomas Deane, has arranged a surprise for her. As she enters the central grounds, she sees herself being raised to the gable of the tallest building: herself in the form of a statue.

She smiles. She rather likes seeing herself swathed in the medieval garb that the sculptor had chosen for her. These university colleges in the leading Irish provincial towns are a very good idea, she decides.

Two-and-a-half years later the Irish Catholic bishops promulgate a set of decrees drawn at their Synod of Thurles: these condemn the Queen's Colleges as godless. More importantly, they condemn all "mixed education" of Catholics and Protestants and at every level, from elementary schools through universities.

Keep apart.

Later, the man most responsible for the synod's decrees, Archbishop Paul Cullen, proudly states that he has never dined with a Protestant.

Queen Victoria, frozen in time as a thirty-year-old in garments 600 years older, survives at University College, Cork until the Irish revolution of the twentieth century is complete. Then the college authorities have her discreetly buried, awaiting the statue's resurrection in a more tolerant age.

SKIBBEREEN, COUNTY CORK;
LAWRENCE, MASSACHUSETTS. 1850

Dirty Pictures

Famine-porn: a genre that develops in the later 1840s. The leading purveyor is *The London Illustrated News*. There's a worldwide demand for engravings of half-clad wretches, bones projecting at odd angles from beneath their rags, vacant faces on the quick and the dead alike, carts heaped with corpses, skeleton-thin dray horses stumbling as they pull their ghoulish loads through an endless necropolis.

The public love it.

Skibbereen is the feature-town in this porn form, and if much of the art work is accurate, the consumer's desire for it is not entirely understandable. Undoubtedly, some buyers are genuinely touched by what they see and give liberally to Famine relief. But is this not in part because of the guilt they feel at letting their pulse race quickly as they stare at these dirty pictures? A century later, there will be collectors of similar pictures of the Nazi atrocities and not all the voyeurs then, any more than in the 1840s, will be persons of pure and generous spirit.

Behind the hideous depiction of Skibbereen is an heroic aspect. The survivors, privately, raise themselves from the slough. One Simon Dailey, a local man of immense character, somehow charters a boat in 1850 and fills it with people who wish to reach the USA. Some few can pay in advance. From the rest, he takes bits of precious metal, promissory notes signed with an X, and oaths sworn on the lives of men and women's children.

That is all ritual: it is run on trust and a prayer. He is repaid.

The Skibbereen people settle on a corner of south Lawrence, Massachusetts that is called "Simon Dailey's Boat." There, for fifty years, every shop has a Skibbereen family's name above the door. Not names from even as far north as Macroom. Skibbereen.

That's where they truly live; not in the glossy pages of a dirty English magazine.

IRELAND. 1851

Blessed Amnesia

By the beginning of 1851, it is becoming clear who will have survived and who not.

What does not survive is memory. The patterns that remain in the survivors' minds are bare and twisted, like the girders of an overcrowded hotel after a fire. That is a blessing, for the survivors could not remember full and true and remain sane.

Later, within a decade, a service industry begins. It tells the Irish people what they should remember concerning the Famine and thus relieves them of the need to carry the weight of individual memory. Professional rememberers take over: politicians, writers (of whom John Mitchel is the most successful artistically), gombeen men, priests, and, later, oral historians and then academic chroniclers. They all make their own way forward in life, profiting and walking far on others' wounds. The children and grandchildren and subsequent generations learn a stylized story, one that has the most jagged and ugliest points sanded smooth. Certain kinds of pain are universally ruled rememberable: others not.

The amnesia that settles on the survivors comes like an evening mist settling on a declivity in the land. It blurs everything. Only the outlines of the familiar and the acceptable remain visible and all else is obscured from mind.

Hideous as the Famine was, its survivors do not permit themselves to remember the worst: *throughout the Famine the Irish killed their own*. Historical terms such as "excess mortality" hide the thousands of mothers who, in a grief beyond words and thank-God beyond memory, kill their own infants. Sometimes it was the withdrawn breast, other times a quiet shove of the bairn into a cold corner for the night. Who can judge – much less who should dare judge – whether a woman's saving her own life was a sin. On the edges of survival, the fierce priorities of human biology make such a query moot.

Despite the stylized pictures in *The London Illustrated News* of the time of the Famine family huddled together, evicted from their cabin, as often the real family picture was of fighting over bits of food. Of men, women, children watching each other warily, ready to snatch any scrap that falls from others' hands or lips.

So often, the strong simply abandon the weak.

The strongest, the young men and women who leave their parents and infants brothers and sisters behind, tell others, and tell themselves, that they are on their way to Dublin, to Liverpool, to New York, with their parents' blessing. And some are, and all come to believe that they are. Yet in their tens of thousands, they have sentenced their parents and brothers and sisters to die. That is what biological survival demands.

For months in some locales, years in others, a black cowl covers the face of Ireland: the social order breaks down. Family does not count; kinship counts even less; friendship does not exist; theft is a virtue and honesty a path to starvation. So many human bodies are left unburied, not because the people are too weak to scrape a piece of shallow ground, but because the survivors, no less than the dead, have ceased to be human.

This no one wants to remember, for no one can remember and remain ambulatory. The survivors of the Famine are able to move about: that is their common characteristic, a way of walking that makes them seem to be automatons. They never lose it and, a decade later, intelligent observers can tell Famine survivors from those who did not go through the terror, simply by picking out the ones who shuffle, as if shackled as members of a vast chain-gang.

The chapels of Ireland are full of Famine survivors and an army of priests tries, unsuccessfully, to explain to them the nature of God's Will. Unlike their practice in pre-Famine times, these survivors go frequently to confession.

Yet they can never tell their priests what is really eating at their souls: for, truly, they cannot remember.

THE CURRAGH OF KILDARE. 1852

In-Gathering of the Souls

When the million-plus who have starved in the Great Famine or died in ancillary diseases meet, they are pleasantly surprised, at first.

For Holy Mother Church is wrong. The infants are there. They are not consigned to the *limbus infantium*, the everlasting uneasiness of unbaptized babies who are innocent of personal guilt, but suffer from the stain of Original Sin, the sin of Adam carried in the marrow of all humanity. Yes, the babies are present, no longer crying, but occasionally gurgling: wistfully, as is possible outside the mortal plane.

And plain mortals are present and are not in torment. There is no Purgatory through which all but the most holy must pass: ten, one hundred, one thousand years of torment before those who have led a good life are permitted passage to friendlier fields. From the dogma of St. Thomas Aquinas, that the smallest pain in Purgatory is greater than the greatest pain on earth, this generation of Irish has been exempted. Young men and women, struck down in their prime, now stand together; they move listlessly, pushed back and forth by some unseen force; they move like ranks of reeds in a slow-washed estuary. They feel no pain.

Nor do the unredeemable sinners, the unbelievers or the Protestants or the Dissenters. Hell has closed its doors.

The hard sinners remember the fierce, freedom-giving recoil of whiskey.

The young men recall how meat tasted, the few times they had chewed it.

The women look at the babies who, when they ruckle in their sleep, are recalling the before-words exultation of discovering a breast that has not yet run dry.

AN OLD WORLD
BECOMING NEW?
IRELAND
1852–1900

Big Faith

Fr. John Henry Newman dislikes Dublin intensely. He spends as little time in it as possible, but as the president of the not-yet-extant Catholic University, he has to leave the prayerful quiet of the Birmingham Oratory and enter the bearpit of Irish ecclesiastical politics. In Dublin, he takes to the streets infrequently, and when he does, he skittles from place to place, head down, moving with the jerky, irregular pace of a cockchafer.

He is especially afraid that he will come face-to-face with his Protestant past. That danger is most likely to be encountered near Stephen's Green, where the Protestant archbishop of Dublin, Richard Whately, has his archepiscopal offices. Newman does not wish to be reminded that he is one of Whately's many protegés, distinguished though that cohort is. When young John Newman, then a keen Anglican evangelical, had been elected a Fellow of Oriel College, Oxford, he was assigned to Whately to have his mind and manners brought up to scratch. And then, in 1825, when Whately became principal of St. Alban's Hall, Newman went along with him to serve as vice-principal. They were close, and if Newman eventually turned against the liberalism (as he saw it) of Whately and of Oxford, he could not deny that the man who was now the Protestant archbishop of Dublin had formed his mind, taught him to reason tightly and, however unintentionally, thus made possible his conversion to Catholicism.

Some debts are impossible of repayment and painful of remembrance.

Nor does Newman enjoy his everyday consciousness that he owes his appointment as president of the soon-to-be university to Archbishop Paul Cullen. He distrusts Cullen and with reason. Capturing Newman – the most famous convert from Anglicanism in the English-speaking world – for the Irish Catholic church was a coup for Cullen. Yet, even though he signed-on Newman in mid-1851, he has not had the appointment ratified by the bench of Irish bishops or by Rome. Newman is, therefore, on probation, and he actually is rescued from this indeterminate state (a theological construct he knows only too well) only by a papal brief in 1854.

Yet now, in 1852, despite his vulnerability, John Henry Newman gives the most heroic sets of lectures in Irish history, *Discourses on the*

Scope and Nature of University Education, and one of the least success-ful. He sets out to explain to the Irish bishops what a university is, a work of supererogation, since none of them has ever been to one; jun-iorates and seminaries have been their places of training, and there si-lence and obedience are the required mode of behaviour.

Father Newman has big faith. He actually believes what most of the Irish prelates only mouth: that all human knowledge is part of God's plan. Of course any real university has to include theology as a form of knowledge, but there are other forms, and God will use them to His glory. *I have said that all branches of knowledge are con-nected together, because the subject-matter of knowledge is intimately united in itself, as being the great Creator and His work.* As bishops' chaplains, sent to take notes and report on Newman's plans for the new Catholic University shift uneasily in their seats, he presents an argument that has about it a whiff of something they have been warned about. *Knowledge is capable of being its own end. Such is the constitution of the human mind that any kind of knowledge, if it be really such, is its own reward. And if this is true of all knowledge, it is true also of that special philosophy, which I have made to consist in a comprehensive view of truth in all its branches* ... It sounds like the sin of liberalism, something the listening clerics have been warned about incessantly. *I speak of knowledge which is its own end, when I call it liberal knowledge, or a gentleman's knowledge, when I educate for it, and make it the scope of a university.* Oh dear, just what the men in soutanes fear. A gentle-man's education? a liberal one? for Catholics? *Catholics who aspire to be on a level with Protestants in discipline and refinement of intellect have recourse to Protestant universities* ... *Robbed, oppressed, and thrust aside, Catholics in these islands have not been in condition for centuries to at-tempt the sort of education which is necessary for the man of the world, the statesman, the landholder, or the opulent gentleman.* Oh, so he is propos-ing a Protestant education for our young laymen! At least we can guard against moral perils by supervising the young closely. *When a multitude of young persons, keen, open-hearted, sympathetic, and obser-vant, as young persons are, come together and they freely mix with each other, they are sure to learn from one another, even if there be no one to teach them; the conversation of all is a series of lectures to each, and they gain for themselves new ideas and views, fresh matter of thought and dis-tinct principles for judging and acting, day by day.*

Newman's plan yields collective shudders that rumble through the episcopal palaces of Ireland. His scholarship is so surely based on orthodoxy, his argumentation so tight, that he cannot be caught out in error. Yet, what he proposes goes so strongly against the experience of all of the Catholic bishops that they know it has to be wrong. Newman's prestige and the Vatican's wishes mean that he has to be given his head for a time, but the bishops will watch closely and, like the slow-moving stones of a massive grain mill, will eventually grind the Rev. Mr. Newman extremely finely.

COUNTY KERRY. 1853

Stringent Self-Control

When the very logical, very well-meaning, very unsmiling agent on the Lansdowne estates in Kerry introduces a system of population control, he is resisted publicly by most of the peasantry, but quietly supported by the Catholic clergy and many of the older people who had survived the Famine and begun to understand why it had happened. Of course a Protestant land agent was not to be embraced, especially if he meddled in family matters, but William Steuart Trench had a simple prescription for preventing future famines and an ingenious, if heartless, mode of enforcement. No sub-division of land was permitted on the Lansdowne estate, only consolidation of holdings: that meant an escape from potato cultivation as the sole source of nutrition. And – here Trench was as harsh as a Puritan – any tenant whose son or daughter married without his permission was to be evicted. If no land was available, then no marriage.

Trench was only making explicit a system of unwritten family law that the Irish small farmers and their clergy embrace after the Famine. Like a spreading spill of ink on a blotter, the ascetic model moves across Ireland and, a generation after the Famine, it is the rule. Tenant farmers no longer break up their lands; only one family member can marry and receive the family holding. The rest must leave or, if they stay, remain unmarried.

As the century *after* the Famine is played out, Ireland's population drops by more than one-third. Emigration does some of this, but Ireland's birth rate does not come up to its death rate, and that means a natural decline in population even without emigration. That happens elsewhere. What is unique is that post-Famine Ireland is the only country ever to reduce its numbers by having fewer births than deaths entirely through natural means (no birth control) and without having undergone a war or debilitating epidemic.

William Steuart Trench was only distinguished by his rebarbarative mixture of tactlessness and prescience. In sexual matters, Ireland after the Famine becomes the most controlled society ever recorded. No sex outside marriage. No land, then no marriage. And, no land, then no living: instead, leaving.

And over the decades, hundreds of thousands of young people are squeezed out of Ireland. Their immense good fortune is that this occurs when there are still New Worlds that need their skills, their minds, their strength.

NEW YORK CITY. 12 AUGUST 1853

Finding the Hook

Both Karl Marx and Frederick Engels make walking-around-money by writing for Horace Greeley's *The New York Daily Tribune*. Greeley's only demand on them is that they send him pieces that are deeply depressing. This restriction was especially hard on Marx who, in the 1850s, was leading a happy life and enjoyed watching pretty girls as they walked in and out of the British Museum.

Marx's usual regimen when he had to send something to Greeley was to immerse himself in several of the parliamentary Blue Books. For his August column, however, Karl Marx meditates on the life of Jonathan Swift. To Marx the most revealing point in Swift's career as a moral gyrfalcon was that he bequeathed his fortune to found Ireland's first true lunatic asylum. Thus inspired, Marx wrote for his American audience:

If the social melioration of the Irish people is making such progress, how is it that, on the other hand, insanity has made such terrific progress among them since 1847, and especially since 1851? Look at the following data from "the Sixth Report on the District Criminal and Private Lunatic Asylums in Ireland:"

1851 sum total of admissions in Lunatic Asylums	*2,584*
1852	*2,662*
March 1853	*2,870*

And this is the same country in which the celebrated Swift, the founder of the first Lunatic Asylum in Ireland, doubted whether 90 madmen could be found.

"CASTLE ROBIN," NR. LISBURN, CO. ANTRIM. 1854

St. Patrick's Well

Members of well-off families as well as the poor emigrated and when they did so they took an endowment with them.

The Cullen family of Castle Robin had a tradition of giving a tooth to family emigrants in need of special protection.

Not just any tooth.

It came from a jaw bone that the family kept in a silver box. It was, they believed, the jawbone of St. Patrick.

By 1854, when inquisitive antiquaries inventory this precious shrine, poor St. Patrick is down to one double tooth.

The shrine is passed on to St. Malachy's College, Belfast for safe keeping. Thus, once again, St. Malachy assumes responsibility for keeping St. Patrick's legacy safe.

DUBLIN. 15 JANUARY 1856

Pet Seminary

Although one would never know it from his public demeanour, Paul Cullen, now translated from the archbishopric of Armagh to that of Dublin, loves gossip. He has a delicious feline sense. If he uses gossip as a means both of entertainment and as a way to reach his own imperial goals, so be it: low means to higher ends and all that.

Cullen wants John Henry Newman, whose Catholic University now is up-and-running, either to be a tame pet or to be gone. Indeed, if it weren't for the animated agitation of Cullen's own bête noir, John MacHale, the archbishop of Tuam, against the Catholic University, Cullen would have driven Newman out a week after classes had begun.

For the moment Cullen contents himself by writing to his friend and satellite Tobias Kirkby, rector of the Irish College in Rome.

Dr. Newman expended a very large sum on billiards. Few short stories have started better. *There is also a hired man to mark the throws: "a marker."* Nice touch that, as if Cullen did not know that one does not throw a billiard ball. *I suppose such things are done in Oxford but here it is really too bad for us to throw away the money of the poor on such trifles.* Splendid rhetorical turn, from tittle-tattle to righteousness: *Dr. Newman has the Oxford system in view. He wishes to leave young men to themselves.* Unlike, say, to the Christian Brothers? *This will not do in Ireland. The people do not wish to have their children exposed to corruption. They wish to have them under discipline.*

BELFAST. 13 JULY 1857

Something to Count On

It's a cartographer's dream.

The first of Belfast's serious urban riots begins and runs for seven days. Rural religious fights in Ulster have been common, but since the Famine, Belfast is the only city in Ireland that is prospering: growing as part of the British industrial revolution and increasing in population at three to four percent per year. It pulls in population from the countryside – one out of three, roughly, is Catholic – and the new urban working class segregates itself by religion.

After the last day of rioting, the exact location of the fault lines in this new culture can be mapped simply by charting where the paving stones are missing.

A mapping of the 1857 riots (they start again in September) is not a historical artifact, but a medium of prophecy. It will tell you where the riots will be when next they occur: 1864, 1872, 1886 ... 1969.

DUBLIN. 17 MARCH 1858

The Divine Right to Rule

In nineteenth-century tradition, St. Patrick's Day was a dreary day in honour of the Patron Saint's having had so much trouble over water.

It was a misty and cold Patrick's Morning in 1858 and the old ones who went to early mass wrapped their shawls tightly around themselves. Later in the day, those who had put off doing their religious duty in the hope of better weather were chastized by heavy showers. They returned to their lodgings to shake themselves like spaniels.

The day suited James Stephens, a prodigious drawer of diagrams and drafter of constitutions and inventor of secret codes and conjurer of pantomime recognition-signs. The gloomier the day, the sooner night would come and with it the founding of the Irish Republic.

Stephens was assembling those men of Dublin who would become the centre point of a nationwide secret organization. Of course they would! He had a set of diagrams, rolled up like a set of building plans showing how a secret cell in each parish, its members known only to each other, would join at the county level and finally nationally, all interlocking; but at each level every unit was to be sealed, knowing only its own members, not those next parish over. Stephens' diagrams were well done. Before joining the 1848 Rising, and subsequent escape to Paris, he had been an apprentice railway engineer. He loved neatness.

His chosen operatives were well known to himself, but to instill a tone of urgency and discipline, he insisted that each one approach the meeting place by a circuitous route and that they each execute a manoeuvre that identified them as actually being the right individuals: men in dark overcoats on dark nights were easy to mistake and who knows what Dublin Castle knew?

The route prescribed involved a check-point: the Metal Bridge over the Liffey, a pedestrian structure that once had been a toll bridge. It could easily be watched by a confederate leaning against the wall of the Merchants Arch. The recognition ritual Stephens prescribed caused a bit of crumbling. Each potential conspirator was to stand on the crown of the arch and check to see if he was being followed. To do this he was to urinate against the gas lamp that surmounted the arch, something common enough among nighttime drunks that it would not cause comment, and then was to look around anxiously, as men do when caught short in public. Assuming no spies skulking, the man was to walk off the bridge whistling "Lillibulero," a Protestant tune. That two dozen men, in sequence peeing on a lamp post and then whistling the same irritating air did not arouse any complaints, speaks well for the tolerance of the Dublin populace.

An entire night passed in listening to Stephens discuss his beloved diagrams and then in debating the constitution of the Irish Republic, an instrument that Stephens, like the blind harper, just happened to have with him. In its original form the Republic's constitution left cloudy what the new network of patriots was to be called.

The Supreme Council of the Organisation is declared to be the sole government of the Irish Republic.

For several succeeding years the network is called either the Organisation or the Brotherhood until, finally, Irish Republican Brotherhood is agreed upon. The American counterpart, called Clann na-Gael, has a head who loves the ancient Irish mythological cycles and the idea of the "Fianna," the band of heroic Celtic warriors, and it becomes common for enthusiasts to refer to the republican brotherhood as Fenians.

The Head of the Organisation shall be in law and in fact the Head of the Irish Republic.

Whatever the wobbliness of terms for the Organisation, its pivotal claim is that it is the sole legitimate government of Ireland. This does not require elections, for it is intuitively obvious, following from the Republic's being the morally superior form of government for the Irish people.

The Supreme council of the Organisation, being the government of the Irish Republic retains the right to make treaties and declare war and negotiate terms of peace.

By the time the sun rises on a clear morn, James Stephens is well satisfied. The Irish Republic has come into existence and he has a secret army in embryo.

His men return to their dwellings in the full confidence that they are the true and only embodiment of the Irish people. Some of them walk over the Metal Bridge and they laugh; they are made momentarily joyful by the knowledge that in the new Ireland just born, they, the rulers, can piss when and wherever they wish.

BRAY. 3 AUGUST 1858

The Wages of Win

I think that my letters must have shown you that I am suffering very much. For some time I have spent sleepless nights and days full of anxiety. Paul

Cullen, well on his way to being the most powerful churchman in the English-speaking world, is feeling low. He has forced John Henry Newman out of Dublin, and the Catholic University now is in Cullen's hands. Yet, success triggers depression, for Cullen is one of those persons who must always feel oppressed and hard done by and who is unsettled by a clear win. *I feel greatly dejected,* he tells his confidant Tobias Kirkby, *and fear everything. The condition of the University and the troubles likely to arise cause me great anxiety ... I am broken down in health ... I have come out to Bray, nine miles from Dublin to try to sleep, but I have not slept for the last two nights.*

Meanwhile, John Henry Newman, home in England, sleeps very well at night. But each morning he awakes and, like a prize fighter knocked senseless by a superior opponent, he shakes his head, and it takes him a minute or two to remember exactly where he is.

ULSTER, 1859; IRELAND 1850–70

The Psychologies of Religious Experience

Everyday there is less devil and more Jesus.

Case One. The Holy Spirit rolls through Presbyterian Ulster in 1859. This is a rural revival that begins in a small congregation in County Antrim. Waves of conversions sweep through the small towns and surrounding farmsteads, into County Down and out to Londonderry and Armagh. At church services, men and women are suddenly seized by the Spirit and cast to the floor, often in convulsions, sometimes in catatonic paralysis. Others are taken with paroxysms of tears as they realize their own sinful state and then are consumed with immense joy as they realize that Jesus has taken away their sins. The sudden sense of being free is entirely new to most of these people. They have been regular churchgoers, steady workers, good farmers, but always weighted down. Now, for a moment, they are walking without a load upon their shoulders.

The contours of the revival follow exactly the lines of Scottish Presbyterian settlement in Ulster in the seventeenth and eighteenth centuries. Anglicans and Methodists take part on the edges, but overwhelmingly it is Presbyterians. There is no attempt to proselytize Catholics, though a few are so attracted by the bouts of religious ecstasy that they join in.

The revival of 1859, though keyed by a revival in rural America in 1856–58 that especially affected rural Ulster Scots, is a domestic matter. The laity are in charge. Much of the preaching is done by newly-saved, Spirit-inspired men and women; formerly silent souls who scarcely spoke to a person on their own threshold now share their experience of meeting God with a volubility that sometimes runs for hours.

The revival of 1859 is the flywheel of a revolution in Ulster Presbyterian psychology. Calvinism, with its implied sense of accepting the inevitable, is relegated to a few islands of theological abstraction populated by the haute bourgeoisie. Of course a revival cannot go on forever (one runs out of people to convert) but its social effects ripple onward. Between 1798 and 1912, the revival of 1859 involved in a shared experience more Ulster Protestants than any other event, religious or political.

Case Two. As soon as the effects of the Famine begin to diminish, the Catholic church in Ireland begins to change radically and between, roughly 1850 and 1870, a revolution equal to that of the Presbyterians occurs. It too involves a quantum increase in religious intensity, but there the similarity ends. The Catholic revolution is led from the top, not the demos; it has the professionally religious fully in charge; and it involves an increase in discipline, a near-abolition of local enthusiasms and eccentricities.

Even as now-empty mud-cabins are being allowed to dissolve back into the landscape, in small towns the thatch is being replaced on chapels, bells are being added, interiors are being washed white with lime. In the larger towns, new churches arise, with slated roofs, steeples, and altar windows of stained glass. Diocesan colleges expand and new senior seminaries come into service. The number of priests in the countryside increases rapidly and there is a surplus to send overseas to care for Irish emigrants. In this, the Irish Catholic equivalent of the Industrial Revolution, discipline is everything and Paul Cullen, first as archbishop of Armagh and then of Dublin, stamps out irregularities with remarkable efficiency. Like the machines of Birmingham and Manchester, the Catholic churches of Ireland now deliver a single standard of service throughout the nation.

This revolution is possible because of the Famine, sad as that is to say. The Famine blasts away the very poor, who were a terrible weight on the church. Now, the rural bourgeois, the rising tenant farmers, are the backbone of the church. They have a little surplus wealth and some of it goes to build chapels and colleges; and they have surplus children, and the ablest of them become clerics. And the daughters of the strong farmers and Catholic gentry are welcome in convents, as they bring dowries with them.

The deepest impact of this revolution is in the chapels. The Irish Catholics before the Famine had not been a church-going people. Most did their religious duty once or twice a year and mixed their Catholicism with scraps of Celtic folklore and magic. The new church demands regular attendance and disciplined devotion, and has the clerical manpower to enforce these demands.

Two generations are required for the full Catholic revolution to be completed: Catholic Ireland will enter the twentieth century with a distinction that it is to maintain throughout that century. It has the highest level of weekly religious attendance of any country in the Christian world.

Interpretive query. Is Ireland after the Famine, where both Protestants and Catholics are more religious in practice and more devout in heart, more likely to be at peace?

"REDESDALE" NR DUBLIN. SEPTEMBER-OCTOBER 1863

Post-Rationalism

The most rational person ever to be an Irish cleric approaches the terrors of his own impending death with the methods of necromancy. Richard Whately, the greatest English logician of the first one-third of the century, the inventor of social sciences in Ireland, sensible theoretician of emigration, proponent of religious amity, fighter against souperism, enthusiast of universal education for the Irish people, views his legacy calmly enough: he knows that as a liberal he is despised by most Anglican clergy and as a Protestant, his work will go unappreciated by the Catholic populace. That is a logical result he can accept, for it is a conclusion that follows directly from valid premises.

Whately has no fear of eternity, but while waiting for it to arrive he is achingly lonely. His wife has died and his family is dispersed. The archbishop takes to conversing with those already dead through spiritualism. A lady clairvoyant becomes resident in the archepiscopal residence and one of Whately's last acts before taking to his death bed is a session of table-turning and spirit-rapping.

He is dying painfully. An ulcer on his leg has bothered him for two years and now has turned gangrenous. As a philosopher and logician, he has always distrusted scientific medicine and now that distrust precludes his relying on it for relief. Instead, he engages a homeopathic practitioner who gives him doses of drugs so minuscule as to be irrelevant. Thus Archbishop Whately spends his last days sitting in a wheelchair, his infected leg extended and in excruciating pain. He is a brave man but several times he passes out from sheer agony. He will not waver, however, and transferred to his death bed, he refuses the opiates and antiseptics of rational medicine. On the eighth of October he is finally allowed to go to the world where he belongs: one in which all syllogisms are sound, the geometry is Euclidean and argument is a means to agreement, not separation.

DUBLIN. 9 DECEMBER 1864

Inside the Laager

Archbishop Cullen is happiest and most effective as manager of the Irish church when he feels he is surrounded by evil. That way, his sword-strikes in any direction are justified. When his enemies won't encircle him, he stitches them together in his mind.

His pastoral letter for St. Patrick's Day, 1864, denounces Fenianism, and he asks Rome that it be formally condemned. He has great fears of any oath-bound secret society, especially a patriotic one, for it is a rival of the church for the allegiance of the people.

He is right about that, but he needs more enemies.

So he writes to his old friend Tobias Kirby with a fantasy so bizarre it is clinically diagnostic. *I fear our Fenians are spreading. I have no doubt they are encouraged by those who wish to keep up the Protestant Church.*

BELFAST. 26 JULY 1866

Last Ties

Quietly, in no pain, Mary Anne McCracken prepares to meet her friends, the Belfast radicals of 1798. She is ninety-six years of age.

Since 1815, when she and her sister ceased to run their own textile business, she has been a full-time philanthropist of the hands-on sort. Relief of the poor of Belfast has been her mission.

Now, slipping into rest, she remembers Major Bunting and the Belfast harp festival and recalls the time when the leading Presbyterian men of commerce were radicals and democrats. She recalls running messages during the '98 Rising and weeps a dry tear for her brother, Henry Joy McCracken, executed. And she laughs silently when she thinks of the *Belfast News-Letter*, founded in 1737 by her forebear, Francis Joy. Even in Mary Anne's lifetime the paper was well on its way to being the oldest daily paper in the British Isles.

She laughs to herself because grandfather had begun the rag as a radical broadsheet. "Now who would ever guess that?" she asks the approaching angel.

LONDON. 1867

Karl Marx Assesses the New Brigade

James Stephens promised a rising. Some of his fellow Fenians began to worry, however, when in 1863 he founded a newspaper, *The Irish People*, not a traditional tool of a revolutionary society, certainly not one that was intended to be totally secret. Nor, when he declared "Sixty-Five will be the Year for Action," was it prudent or customary to print this motto under the masthead on the paper. In fact, as his IRB comrades increasingly realized, Stephens was so in love with his diagrams, with the pristine architecture of his cell-constructed organization (partly imagined, partly real), that he could not bear the thought of anything making them tumble down. Stephens kept finding excuses for putting off a rebellion until in December 1866 he abandoned it entirely. He quickly hied off to Paris, and in the spirit of sensible self-preservation remained an exile there until 1891, when his old colleagues finally permitted him to return to Dublin.

Several small risings are attempted in Ireland in 1867 and one in Chester, England. When captured IRB men are held in Manchester, the Brotherhood tries to free two of them from a police van and unintentionally kill an unarmed police sergeant. Five Fenians are quickly condemned to death, and three of them, Michael Larkin,

William Allen and Michael O'Brien are executed. They become the "Manchester Martyrs."

Marx surveys the scene and tells Engels that it is best to "behave diplomatically," by which he means they should not condemn the Fenians for being ineffective. He added, in a reply to a note from Engels, "As regards the Fenians you are quite right. The beastliness of the English must not make us forget that the leaders of this sect are mostly asses and partly exploiters and we cannot in any way make ourselves responsible for the stupidities which occur in every conspiracy. And they are certain to happen."

When a Fenian escape-attempt in London, intended to break Fenian prisoners out of Clerkenwell gaol, kills several civilians, Marx is livid. *The stupid affair in Clerkenwell was obviously the work of a few specialised fanatics ... In particular, there has been a lot of bluster in America about this blowing up and arson business, and then a few asses come and instigate such nonsense. Morever these cannibals are in general the greatest cowards ... And then the idea of liberating Ireland by setting a London tailor's shop on fire!*

LONDON. 1868

Prophecy (1)

The trouble with having been tutored by his demanding father was that John Stuart Mill, having mastered Latin, Greek, and mathematics through calculus by the time he was fourteen, had a lot of time on his hands. Editing Jeremy Bentham's more abstruse works and becoming the premier logician of the mid-nineteenth century still left Mill with too much empty time. In an effort to fill the void, Mill became a Gladstonian MP for a while (1865–68) and a prophet. Not a bad seer, actually, as an excerpt from his *England and Ireland* (1868) shows:

What if there were a civil war between the Protestant and Catholic Irish, or between Ulster and the other provinces? Is it in human nature that the sympathies of England should not be principally with the English Protestant colony, and would not she either help that side, or be constantly believed to be on the point of helping it? For generations it is to be feared that the two nations would be either at war, or in a chronic state of precarious and armed peace, each constantly watching a probable enemy so near at hand that in an instant they might be at each other's throat. By this state of their relations it is almost superfluous to say that the poorer of the two countries would suffer most. To England it would be an inconvenience: to Ireland a public calamity ...

THE WELSH MAIL. 27 SEPTEMBER 1868

Prophecy (2)

Whenever he wished to needle Karl Marx, Frederick Engels would ask, in German, "Are you absolutely certain that you are not a Lutheran?" He would continue, in English, "You seem so solemn. Maybe it's that you're a Presbyterian. Yes, that's it. But my friend, I know what will cure you: a good Irish peasant bint."

This was a sore point with Marx. He spent many hours in Bedford Square trying to pick up Irish serving girls, and never with any success. In contrast, Engels had a succession of Irish-born slum girls whom he acquired and discarded as if they were industrial-seconds. Finally, he had married one, Lizzie Burns, but that did not stop his frequently taking the temperature of the Irish working class in London.

Engels is returning from an investigative trip to Ireland, conducted with his wife Lizzie and Karl Marx's youngest daughter, Eleanor. The trip worried Marx, the more so because he knew that his youngest daughter was truly free of bourgeois inhibitions. So Engels writes to Marx, needling him a little, but letting him know that his daughter is safe and has not yet run off with the gypsies. Engels tells Marx that he has been reading William Steuart Trench's *Realities of Irish Life* and he approves of Trench's statement that if he were an Irish peasant, he too would be a Ribbonman, a revolutionary.

Engels adds,

The worst about the Irish is that they become corruptible as soon as they stop being peasants and turn bourgeois. True, this is the case with most peasant nations. But in Ireland it is particularly bad.

He concludes:

That is why the press is so terribly lousy.

DUBLIN. NOVEMBER, 1870

Vintage Year

As the Advent of a new religious year approaches, Paul Cullen reflects that, as God's vintner in Ireland, he has had a year suitable for the production of a *grand cru*. Oh, so much still to be done, but the mission moves forward so well. Needing to be alone in the episcopal palace, Cullen dismisses his chaplain and retreats to his private apartments. There he stands in front of a mirror and, as he often does when in residence in Dublin, takes out his red hat, the badge of his worthiness before God, and reverently places it on his head. He recreates with his own hands the tactile sensation that the Supreme Pontiff's divine touch had engendered when Cullen had been invested a cardinal. Not just any cardinal: the first Irishman, ever. Cullen often went over in his mind the Irish hierarchy as it would exist in heaven. Now, he knows with certainty that he takes precedence over St. Patrick.

The year 1870 was Cardinal Cullen's year of miracles. On the twelfth of January, Pius IX had decreed the condemnation of the Fenians, the band of atheistic-Protestant-Italian guttersnipes, supported by the devil and the dross of the Irish nation now lodged in America (Cullen had complex views), who were attempting to wrestle the souls of the Irish people away from Holy Mother Church. Thank you, Supreme Pontiff.

Then, through the hard spring and hot early summer of 1870, Cullen had returned the favour, and more. He had fought with immense energy and equal cunning at the Vatican Council for the adoption of the new doctrine of Papal Infallibility. It was a battle of diplomacy, bribery, theology, sophistry and, ultimately, faith, conducted in stilted Latin, animated Italian and self-conscious English. Cardinal Cullen had set down the formula of Infallibility that Cardinal Bilio rewrote and put forward successfully. Cullen was sincere in his beliefs, for he had spent his career in Ireland turning the Irish Catholic church into a pyramid. And what held for Ireland certainly should hold for the Christian world.

Cullen knew from his confidants in Rome that many members of the Curia were mentioning him as a possible successor to Pius IX. If the call came, he was resolved not to shirk his responsibility to God, humanity, and Ireland.

Still wearing his cardinal's hat, Cullen takes out a missal and reads Psalm 9, his favourite:

> *As my enemies are driven back,*
>   *They shall fall and perish at Thy presence.*
> *For Thou hast maintained my right and my cause,*
>   *Thou art set on the throne,*
>   *Thou who judge rightly.*

He reads the psalm twice, and he contemplates with enthusiasm the next victory over his enemies that the Almighty has promised to him: at the beginning of the next secular year – 1 January 1871 – the Church of Ireland will no longer be the Established Church of Ireland. It will become just another of the yelping curs of Protestantism. The public humiliation that the puffed-up Protestant bishops and archbishops are even-now undergoing gives immense pleasure, and it is a pure pleasure, for the vengeance upon them is God's, not man's.

Paul Cullen, Cardinal Archbishop of Dublin, seized by the wonder of this time of miracles, dances. Awkwardly, but with quickly-increasing facility, he does as he had seen others do, in his youth before he was cut off from the Irish people. He dances a jig and with so much energy that his red hat falls off and he does not notice.

DERRY CATHEDRAL. 1 JANUARY 1871

Evensong

A lugubrious hymn, but authentic:

> *Look down, Lord of Heaven, on our desolation!*
> *Fallen, fallen, fallen, is now our Country's crown,*
> *Dimly dawns the New Year on a churchless nation,*
> *Ammon and Amalek tread our borders down.*

This, the writing of Mrs. Alexander (she was permitted no other name), wife of the Anglican bishop of Derry. It was written for the service of mourning that marked the Church of Ireland's first day as a disestablished church. Many members of the congregation wore black, as if in mourning for a family member.

> Lord. we have sinned. Kneeling down before Thee
> Make we full confession, the people and the priest.
> In our day of plenty little fruit we bore Thee,
> Oh, the fast forgotten! Oh, the songless feast!

Across Ireland, the Anglican community reorientates itself quickly: laymen (and, later women), now choose their own priests; bishops are diminished; democracy slides rapidly into the fissures left by retreating authority. And the church worries. Will it survive financially? Can the split between Ulster (where most of the members are urban or rural working class) and the rest of the country (where the Anglicans are middle-class or gentry, mostly), be prevented from deepening. And, really, is there any future for Protestantism in Ireland south of the Black Pig's Dyke?

> Oh, the songless feast!

LONDON. MARCH 1872

Editor's Choice

All right! I agree. No doubt, yes, yes, yes. Completely correct.

Yes, it is true that Engels could not quite complete his history of the Irish problem because of outside interferences: the Franco-Prussian War, the Commune, and the International. As he said, they got in the way.

True, though he might not have been a publisher's dream (can you imagine him on a book promotion tour? urban insurance rates would skyrocket). Still, yes, I completely agree with you that the book's not being published in the English-speaking world until 1965 was hard on the old darling.

But, really, isn't it possible he hexed himself, called down the charge of hubris from the gods he did not believe in? Engels must have angered some deity when he wrote to Sigisimund Borkheim, languidly stating, *however simple the Irish problem may be* (that's where he caught the guardian's attention), *it is nevertheless the result of a long historical struggle and hence has to be studied.* Then he made his modest book-proposal. *A manual explaining it all in about two hours does not exist.*

Jesu Bambino!

ULSTER. 1870ff

Code

Within the perimeter, thousands of women speak in terms that, to an outsider, are meaningless:

Reeler.

Doffing mistress.

Lying week.

Hackler.

The women, a mixed sorority of Catholics and Protestants, are the main work force of the seventy or so spinning companies that run factories in Ulster. These are not tiny enterprises: 600-700 employees are found in each operation. Ulster by the early 1870s has become the largest linen-producing region in the world, and there is cotton spinning besides. The strength-demanding jobs (hackling the scutched flax into threads) and the very best (plant managers) are held by men, but the middle range is overwhelmingly female.

Wiping down.

hannel-holer

band-tier

heddle-heuk

The firms are scattered around Ulster, with Belfast – now as big as Dublin and growing faster, and much richer – the centre. Still, the dispersal is wide and the ownership is both Protestant and Catholic, though Protestant firms predominate. The key is that if one puts all the Catholic firms on the same map as the Protestant ones, the dots on the map provide a pattern weirdly similar to the map of bawns – the turreted and high-walled defensive structures that defended the farmsteads of the English plantation and Scottish infiltration of the seventeenth and early eighteenth centuries. What the bawn was to the seventeenth century, the textile manufactory is to the nineteenth: the architectural marker of a social and economic order different in significant ways from that of the rest of Ireland, and in this case it is a regional, not merely a sectarian difference.

> *Don't ye ken the difference:*
> *Factory is for weaving,*
> *Mill is for spinning,*
> *and stitching is in the wardroom.*

Usually all the finishing crafts are done in a single building, the men hackling fibres into line on the ground floor, women spinning on the second and third, and a mixed, but mostly female force, weaving damasks or plain linens, on the fourth. A four-storey building: four-square or rectangular in shape, like a bawn, but with a big difference – the workers inside are religiously mixed. A few owners hire only their own, but they are the exception. Overall, Protestants are apt to be in the factory and paid more than the mill girls, mostly Catholic, but each room has some of each. Trouble sometimes. The same song, ends in two contrasting ways:

> *And we'll make them curse the Pope,*
> *On the Twelfth of July in the morning.*
>   or
> *And we'll cut King William's throat*
> *On the Twelfth of July in the morning.*

So, most owners ban party-songs and most mills and factory are civil places, if not exactly ecumenical covens.

Girls enter the textile trades at age thirteen or fourteen. Usually someone says a good word for them. The best recommendation is from someone who's worked for the owner in the past and been a good worker. Political or clerical endorsements are not much use: the textile trade is a ruthless international competition and owners want workers, disciplined ones. The women work a twelve-hour day with two hours out for meals. That five days a week. Saturday is a half-day.

Dark Satanic mills? Not if you ask the women. Yes, the air of the wet-spinning room is fetid and working bare-foot in flax slime is no pleasure. Yes, weaving is ceaseless, and, like almost all jobs, done while standing on a hardwood floor. But it's not machine-paced. It's piece work. The reward is directly related to the effort. And, the women say, it is *ours*.

That's the tune. In post-Famine Ireland, where most young women either find a male with a farm and join him, or must emigrate to England or the New World, this is an alternative. An independent living, and quite a good one. The best damask weavers earn as much as joiners, some as much a cabinet makers, the aristocrats of the working class. That's why the photographs and paintings and sketches of mill and factory girls so often show happy women, proud, not broken, not beholden.

These Ulster women have an alternative to emigration and to marriage. They can support themselves if they wish or, as is the usual case, when they decide to marry in their late twenties, they have their own nest egg and can be choosey. No arranged matches here. They have escaped the tyranny of a rural world in the throes of constriction.

Several generations of these women: tens of thousands over nearly a century: women with attitude: women who take the attitude back to their homes and communities: unionists, nationalists, Catholics, Protestants. Knowing of their lives helps to explain something that smacks the observers of Irish society in the face. That in political and religious matters (especially the education of their children), Ulster working-class women, from the late Victorian age onward, are much more assertive, and walk with their heads higher than do those in the rest of the country.

Not dark Satanic mills at all.

THE ROTUNDA, DUBLIN. NOVEMBER 1873

The Horseman Passes By

Many an heroic struggle for life has been won in the Rotunda. If a birth is so difficult that it cannot be a home-delivery, this is the place to be. And the hospital's attached meeting rooms, rented out for the support of the medical work, are the right places to start a political independence movement. The neighbourhood, with its grand houses on Cavendish Row, gives an air of importance to anyone who enters the Rotunda's main meeting hall, and the life-or-death ambience of a hospital lends solemnity.

There, in mid-November 1873, the Home Rule League of Ireland is founded. Within a year, Home Rule is the most-debated topic in Westminster politics, and remains so until the beginning of World War I.

One Irish MP passes by the Rotunda several times during the founding meetings. He does so from a closed carriage, for this allows him to peer from between drawn curtains. He is assessing things the way a point-to-point rider assesses the course before a race.

Arthur McMorrough Kavanagh, formerly MP for County Wexford, now sits for County Carlow. Like most of the front bench of Home Rule MPs, he is Protestant and, given that he rides to the hounds with ferocious brilliance, he would be Anglo-Irish by definition: except that he traces his own lineage to the Kavanagh kings, and regards the Anglo-Irish as recent blow-ins.

He would be a perfect addition to the party. He has all the right gentry credentials – lineage, money, (important in an era when MPs are unpaid), a record as a progressive landlord (he has designed and constructed cheap labourers' cottages that won a national architectural competition), and possesses an admirable record as an adventurer (among other things, as a despatch rider for the East India Company in the troubled Aurungabad district). As an MP he would be particularly helpful, as he possesses a large bass voice and, nevertheless, does not speak often in the House. In the party of Charles Stewart Parnell, willingness to serve as a member of a disciplined chorus was to be essential.

Arthur Kavanagh, MP, does not take the leap. He remains a conservative. He is still mourning the loss of the Established Church in Ireland, an allegiance his deeply religious mother, a daughter of the rectory, had ingrained in him.

But what a loss for the Home Rule side! for Kavanagh was among the most cheerfully heroic parliamentarians of Victoria's reign.

Arthur McMorrough Kavanagh was born with neither arms nor legs, merely tiny stumps, barely long enough to qualify as appendages. In an age before prosthetics developed, he nevertheless turned into a handsome, confident, notably happy person. He rode brilliantly (and with endurance, across Egypt, Palestine, Persia), wrote long, loving letters to his family (using a pen held in his mouth), and was a leading long-distance yachtsman. To make his life as an MP easier, he travelled to parliament on his own boat and was permitted to berth near the Palace of Westminster. There he would be rowed to the Speaker's Steps and carried on his servant's back into the House. An heroic man, happy to be alive and willing to take big risks.

So it is not cowardice that makes him pass by.

Later, in 1880, the cruel necessities of politics set him against Parnell's party, and he loses.

Kavanagh was too big of spirit to understand the inevitable harshness of Irish politics. A comment he had once made in Hyderabad indicated that his heart was too gentle for the real world: *A few words of thanks could prevent a whole revolution. If the English had said "thank you" more often to the Irish, that country would not be in its present plight.*

Years later, his eldest son, Walter, with a more realistic eye, surveyed the Irish situation and declared for Home Rule and ran as a nationalist candidate for County Carlow.

And for that he was forced to resign from the Kildare Street Club, the tackroom of the Protestant-on-a-horse.

KILKENNY. 1876

Trouble, Right There in River City

The Most Reverend the Bishop of Ossory is on his way to becoming the Cardinal Archbishop of Sydney, Australia, but it's well that he does not know this, for he has sufficient troubles, right here in Kilkenny. Someone wants to polka and that rhymes with Tolka and that'll start a row.

The trouble is the daughters of the Catholic gentry and rising middle class. So many of them just won't listen. Or, if they do, they giggle and try to hide their impudence behind their hands. The children of prosperity are all potentially licentious, the bishop believes. The daughters of small farmers and of agricultural labourers, they're fine. They've mostly taken to sexual abstinence, repetitive religious ritual, and admirable silence, but these cosseted daughters of the rising class, the new merchants and newer landlords and old-line gentry, they seem to think like Protestants. They wish to dance obscene foreign dances and wear dresses that display their, their ... female ... their breasts, and it has to stop. Here, now, in Kilkenny, or tomorrow all Ireland will be awash with white flesh and flailing limbs and the daughters, the flowers of the new Ireland, will all be acting like heretics. Sometimes the bishop longed for the penal laws.

The only comfort Patrick Francis Moran has is that the full array of the Irish church is behind him. He and his fellow bishops have recently met in synod at Maynooth and have warned their flocks against "the improper dances which have been imported into our country from abroad, to the incalculable detriment of morality and decency."

Bishop Moran sits in his study and stares at an invitation, passed to him by the decent and respectful father of one of the girls. A ball is being held at Kilkenny Castle by Lady Ormonde. Several daughters of Moran's flock have been invited. He holds the card by a corner, as he would a shroud of a plague victim. It meant, he knew, décolletage and waltzes and worse: polkas.

Moran's clergy feared him, but some of the older ones, the parish priests who remembered the bad old times, saw him as too narrow. He was a tall dark man with, some said, a touch of the sepulchre abut him. Whenever he interviewed his priests, he made them stand before him and he, perched on a high-backed chair that served as a throne, leaned backward, spine erect, as if one of them might jump forward and, like a leper, touch him. Moran lived a life of quiet self discipline and bodily mortification and he could not understand why the rest of the world did not follow his example.

Though at first the bishop condemned attendance at Lady Ormonde's ball, a pair of older priests worked out a compromise. Scuttling back and forth between the bishop and the guardians of Ireland's daughters, like the diplomats at the Treaty of Vienna, they came to an agreement. The girls could attend the ball, but they could not do fast-dances – the polka and the waltz, where their crinolines might flare out and show some ankle or worse yet, the bare white of a shin. Shins, the Lord Bishop of Ossory knew, had been the moral undoing of pure Irish young men in numbers greater than could be counted in the sheaves of all County Kilkenny.

And the parents also had to promise that the "V" at the neck of each girl's ball gown would display only a patch of neck, nothing more.

And, make no mistake, polkas and waltzes would be a mortal sin.

Ah, the bishop. The girls arrive at Kilkenny Castle in shawls up to their chins. They promptly toss them to a maid, reveal their half-covered breasts, danced the fast-dances, incite young Irish Catholic gentlemen to lust and thus, ultimately, help to multiply the growing Catholic haute bourgeoisie.

KILKENNY. 1880

The Clear Eye

One of the more experienced and liberal priests of Bishop Moran's diocese of Ossory intently observes Charles Stewart Parnell. *He came to a Land League meeting which was held on the Parade at Kilkenny, the platform being erected outside what was then called the Athenaeum.* Parnell is president of the Irish National Land League, a nationwide organization that had sprung from the recesses of the agricultural depression of the late 1870s. It invented "boycotting" in 1880 on the estate of Charles Cunningham Boycott, and in a hundred other ways pushed landlords to lower their rents. *Mr. Parnell was on the platform before the speeches began, very handsome, faultlessly dressed, reserved, almost haughty, listening but speaking little.* Parnell is also head of the Home Rule party. Although not himself keen on land reform, he takes over leadership of the land agitation because he wishes to harness its energy for the Home Rule cause. Otherwise, land reform will replace national independence as the people's goal. *When called upon to make his speech, he took off his overcoat; and, as I was near him – a little behind and at his right, so that I could see his eye – I had a good opportunity of studying him while he spoke. He was very nervous; not, however as if he were afraid of the audience or doubtful of his own powers, but as if he were one seething mass of energy, striving to burst into violent eruption, but kept under firm control.* Parnell, by force of his own will, held virtually all of Irish nationalism under his control, a feat of tiger-taming not seen in Ireland either before or since. *He spoke a good deal with clenched right hand, and one could see the nails digging into the flesh, while up along the back his tightly fitting frock-coat showed the muscles playing as an instrument.* Parnell's power was not that of fire, but of ice. *There was no great volume in Mr. Parnell's voice, but it was so distinct and cut so sharp that it could be heard all over the parade, as one could see by the attention of the people who filled the place. While he spoke I could see his eye, which glinted with a cold blue-green light, not a flame, but like the glint of a bayonet.* In Parnell's presence, one either accepted his dominance or left quickly, desperately trying not to hear his conquering chant, and, above all, not letting his eyes capture your soul. *Parnell's eye when he spoke that day, did not flash or blaze, much less twinkle: or, if it did flash, it was not sheet lightning, but the true forked kind, blue-grey, cold and steely. It showed a devil in the man, and made you fear him.*

KILMALLOCK, COUNTY LIMERICK. 1881

The Land League Priest (1)

His parishioners kneel as Father Eugene Sheehy is led past. The local Royal Irish Constabulary sergeant is extremely uncomfortable in arresting Fr. Sheehy, but the orders are clear: the priest is for Kilmainham Gaol. Taken from the curate's house, Fr. Sheehy is marched to the police barracks. As he passes, the people ask for his blessing.

Sheehy, a distant relative of the martyr of 1766, Fr. Nicholas Sheehy, is a bishop's nightmare. He is not one of the grovelling curates thrown up by the Famine, but from a family that had maintained its status, and much of its wealth, all through the penal era. He is a gentleman and, despite his clerical vows, has the right to independent thought and action that status confers. Despite the Irish bishops' ban on political action by priests, he has joined the Irish Land League in its fight for a peasant proprietorship of agricultural land. Worse, in 1880 he had accompanied Charles Stewart Parnell on a tour of the United States to raise funds for the League. And, worse still, in October 1881, when the government outlaws the League, Fr. Sheehy shows no signs of giving over his enthusiasm. He is staunch.

Fr. Sheehy stops to bless each of his kneeling congregants. The sergeant does not interfere. Fr. Sheehy places a hand on the heads of the babes-in-arms and says a brief prayer.

When he is past, the people rise from their knees and curse the police and the government in words so strong that they border on mortal sins.

IRELAND. 1881–85

Tout Court

During the 1880s, French journalists swarmed over Ireland, as if the Irish had something to teach the Cultural Metropole about confusion. Fascinated by Irish protest movements, the scribblers write hundreds of despatches and almost always get it wrong. They miss the basic point: most Irish protest movements are not essays in lawlessness, or anarchy, but of exactly the opposite: the big movements, such as the Land War, are exercises in alternative law and alternative systems of order.

Take the boycotting of landlords or the punishing of tenants who paid their rents to the landlords. Secret courts give warnings, in the form of ill-spelled notices in legal language. Tenants who pay their rent are "charged" by the courts, and punishment is in the form of a sentence, carried out by delegates of an invisible judiciary. Boycotted landlords find the gates of their estates and the walls of shops where they did their marketing plastered with notices signed "by Order." Often by Order of Captain Moonlight, but it is the phrase that counts, *by Order*. The legal form is crucial, for the Irish are among the world's most ethically concerned revolutionaries: they need both moral law and legal institutions, even if self-made, on their side.

And, equally, the visitors miss the fact that Irish mass movements ebb not when they are crushed by coercion, but when their supporters are seduced into accepting governmental law as being superior to that of the invisible courts. Again, take the Land War. When, in 1881, William Ewart Gladstone creates local land courts to fix fair rents, allows free sale by a tenant of any improvement the tenant has made to the property, and fixity of tenure as long as the rent is paid. When that law passes the Westminster parliament, the former land-warriors flock to the governmental courts. This despite Parnell, Michael Davitt, and the leadership of the Land League telling them to hold out for a better deal. Better? Parnell and his colleagues are trampled in the peasants' rush to the courts.

The French journalists shake their heads. They are mystified. Parnell, though, learns his lesson: give the Irish people law. They won't buy any revolution, social, cultural, political, unless it is housed in legal architecture, and is decorated by court notices, writs, and appeals to the past – preferably the distant and therefore pure past – as precedent.

DUBLIN. 1883

Alien Abduction

The middle level officials in Dublin Castle are mystified when the results of the 1881 census of the United Kingdom becomes available.

Something has happened in Ireland that they had not foreseen and which they cannot now understand. Though anyone with two eyes and living outside of Dublin long knew what was going on.

The enumeration forms for Ireland, collated by hand by dozens of eye-shaded employees with steel-nibbed pens and mental arithmetic, show that the Irish agricultural labourer is half-way to being extinct. The labourer: the man with no land, who supported himself and, sometimes, a wife and children, by working for a tenant farmer, is disappearing fast. An entire social class is becoming vestigial. By 1901 it will be down to one-tenth of its numbers before the Famine. Now, the 1880s is its most noticeable point of decline, for the Depression of the 1870s has driven hundreds of thousands of men who formerly worked in the Irish countryside, to England and to America.

They will not be back.

The Irish small farmer rises after the Famine, becomes a larger and larger farmer. The landless are abducted, pulled ineluctably to an alien world where they can work, eat meat, and are permitted to marry and create life.

DUBLIN. 16 JUNE 1885

Hedge-Bet

Commodity traders call it a straddle and it's illegal in some places and unethical in all.

Until recently, William Butler Yeats, just twenty, has been spending much of his spare time with the bearded fifty-five-year-old romantic, John O'Leary. Yeats's head is full of stories of O'Leary in 1848 and later as a courier for the Fenians, an exile in Paris, and now a lion returned to Dublin.

Young Yeats has other interests as well, and in mid-June 1885 he founds in TCD the Dublin Hermetic Society, which puts him and his friends in touch with not only a larger world, but an invisible one.

Yeats is preparing for his lifelong task of subsuming the story of the Irish people into his own personal history. Eventually, like the writers of any scripture, he becomes larger than his subject.

Working towards that moment, young Yeats covers both worlds, the invisible past and the invisible hermetic. He is the link.

Later in the year, he becomes the only man in a bow-tie ever to take the oath of the Irish Republican Brotherhood. Of course, he scrupulously honours one of the requirements of that oath: to deny he ever swore it.

CORK, 21 JANUARY 1885; BELFAST, 22 FEBRUARY 1886

Large Mammals Fighting

They paw the ground and snort, pose for their admirers, strut, kick dust. Show. Yet not merely show, for these beasts' combat eventually kills thousands of onlookers.

Charles Stewart Parnell, sleek, controlled, lethal, makes in Cork City the most uncontrollable speech of his life. It is a demand for Home Rule for Ireland. *We cannot ask for less than the restitution of Grattan's Parliament.* Fair enough, 1782 was a good year in Irish constitutional history. *We cannot under the British constitution ask for more than the restitution of Grattan's Parliament **but no man has the right to fix the boundary of the march of the nation**.* In his dust-stirring, pre-rut ritual, Parnell is uttering words that he cannot later control. *No man has a right to say to his country: "Thus far shalt thou go and no further," and we have never attempted to fix the* ne plus ultra *to the progress of Ireland's nationhood, and we never shall.*

Within the year, Parnell has nearly achieved his dream: after a general election his party has eighty-five seats and controls the balance of power in the United Kingdom's house of commons. Parnell works mightily to call back his words: he and his party will settle for Home Rule as a permanent settlement for Ireland: there *is* a boundary to the march of the nation.

Parnell's pawing the earth, his "ne-plus-ultra" speech, his electoral success, calls forth in opposition a mastodon, a remarkably fit and intelligent one: Lord Randolph Churchill, the rising figure in the English conservative party. He has heard Parnell and takes him seriously. No diminution of the Union for him. He has already added one phrase to the political phrasebook by stating that when William Ewart Gladstone, liberal leader, went for Home Rule, *the Orange card will be the one to play.* After Gladstone becomes prime minister and commits himself to Home Rule for Ireland, Churchill is speaker-of-honour in February

1886 at an anti-home rule rally in the Ulster Hall, Belfast and there he all but promises that English Tories will support anything the Ulster Protestants do. The speech is memorable, but more so because later Churchill adds a phrase that most unionists place in their memory as if he had uttered it in the Ulster Hall: *Ulster will fight and Ulster will be right*. And in the short-run he indeed is right: sufficient members of Gladstone's own party abandon him and Home Rule does not pass the commons.

The trumpeted battle cries of these larger-than-life mammals

– No man has the right to fix the boundary to the march of the nation ...

– Ulster will fight and Ulster will be right ...

do not merely echo, nor do they diminish. Long after each man has become a wraith, large herds, virtual armies, hundreds of thousands strong, blunder blindly through a jungle of saw grass, swamp, cypress, head-high cane and tiny, false-hope savannahs, trying to find and engage each other, searching for moments of primal mammalian combat.

Occasionally they come so close that their grunts and chants spiral, loop, and intermingle:

If
Ulster
has the right
To fight
the fixed boundaries
of no man.
Then
Will
The march of the
Nation
for no man
be right?

BELFAST. JULY, 1886

The Map Read Rightly

Even before he turns to the morning post, at his breakfast table Dr. John McCaw reads the newspaper reports of the returns of the 1886 election.

McCaw has a private practice, but his real love is his work at the Belfast Hospital for Sick Children, Queen Street. There he works without pay and works small miracles. A mother brings him a child with a gamy foot, and he fashions an orthopedic shoe and then works on the disease that really crimps the lad's future: poverty, ultimately, and diet immediately. He arranges for free milk for the household and keeps his eye open for a wee job for the mother.

He, like many of the Belfast professional class, remains a Gladstonian liberal, both in homage to their freethinking ancestors of the 1790s, and in hope of a quiet Irish future.

After the papers, Dr. McCaw reads his mail and takes pleasure in a letter from his brother in South Africa, a mining engineer. The brother's letters are alway full of good stories about camp life and interesting sketches of technical problems that he has had to solve at the diggings. He often twits Dr. McCaw about the provincialism of the Ulster people and, for that matter, everyone in the northern hemisphere. Frequently he closes his letters with a quick sketch of the way the world really exists: he draws the globe in a perfectly sensible manner: with the north pole on the bottom and all the arrogant Europeans holding on for dear life to avoid falling off.

Dr. McCaw smiles and then reassesses his morning paper's electoral map of Ireland. Parnell has swept Ireland for the second time, winning eighty-four of the country's 103 parliamentary seats. McCaw spins the paper's map upside down and stops smiling.

Charles Stewart Parnell has not won Ireland.

He has lost most of Ulster. Solidly. Perhaps permanently.

Dr. McCaw decides to attend his surgery, where he knows rickets and yaws are but temporary afflictions, and that the world, however painful, will not be turned upside down.

TULLAMORE, KING'S COUNTY. 1887–88

The Land League Priest (2)

All winter long, David Sheehy, younger brother of the Land League Priest, Fr. Eugene Sheehy, was in Tullamore Gaol. He and his fellow prisoners, mostly members of the Irish Republic Brotherhood, refused to wear prison clothes. That was for criminals and they saw themselves as political prisoners. So they spent the winter naked, dragging bits of blanket around on their shoulders, and being fed bread and water.

For David Sheehy, sitting out the damp winter with his ballocks hanging out was harder than for most of the men. He was from a prosperous family and, like his priestly brother, had been schooled in Paris. He owned a succesful grain mill near Templemore, County Tipperary and, in the great Parnellite sweep of 1885 had become MP for Galway South, a seat he now held. Though, in Tullaghmore Gaol, he mostly tried not to sit, for the iron bedsteads were the only furniture and they were shocking cold.

Down in Limerick, Fr. Eugene Sheehy delivers a homily required annually before collecting "Peter's Pence," the yearly offering of the faithful for the maintenace of the fabric of the Vatican and, particularly, the daily estate of the Pope. Father Sheehy begins by describing the conditions of the Tullaghmore Gaol: dripping roof, broken windows, squalid sanitary conditions. He tells what all that does to his brother who, while maintaining his dignity, is going noticeably deaf in one ear. He is eating less, Father Sheehy says, than a monk on Skellig Michael and those were Irish saints, not prisoners of the British.

Father Sheehy pauses a long time.

"Nevertheless, be of good cheer my children!" He smiles broadly. "I can personally assure you, from having visited St. Peter's myself and from having seen the apartments of the Holy Father, that he has servants in-plenty, fine foods, and is free to come and go whenever he pleases."

"So unlike Tullaghmore Gaol."

He closes quickly. "In the name of the Father, the Son, and the Holy Ghost. Amen."

The year's parish offering for the Vatican raises sixpence, if one counts an American penny that has a big nick out of it.

BRUREE NATIONAL SCHOOL, COUNTY LIMERICK.
7 MAY 1888

The Land League Priest (3)

The priest of a rural flock carries a terrible burden: he knows their secrets, while they only know their rumours.

Father Eugene Sheehy, now parish priest in charge of Bruree, is manager of the local primary school: he appoints and dismisses teachers, admits new pupils, and deals with the most difficult discipline problems. He knows that the law requires a child to begin primary education at six years of age and, within the vagueness on such matters of chronology characteristic of country people, he enforces the rule. Now he formally signs the admission form for Edmund de Valera.

Actually, young de Valera is eight years and some months of age and Fr. Sheehy knows this full well. He has heard confession from his guardians, young de Valera's uncle and aunt, and several other locals involved in the benign deception. "I have a fine tall lad for you," he tells the schoolmaster. "Treat him fairly. I have no doubt he will grow to be a giant."

Edward de Valera's mother Catherine (familiarly, Kate), a maid at the house of the local landlord, Thomas Aitkinson of Glenwilliam Castle, Ballingarry, Co. Limerick, had suddenly left for New York in October 1879. She was twenty-two and had been serving in the Aitkinson house since she was seventeen. The squire, Thomas, was famous well beyond County Limerick as a procreator of prodigious abilities. He was a tall, elegant, spare man, very Protestant-looking in the way people of the time took that term. Father Sheehy's view was that the man should be neutered.

Kate Coll (that was her family name) delivered her baby in New York and went to work as a maid. Employment was easily found, for she was well trained; but paying friends to care for the bairn took all her resources. Her salvation, so it seemed, was a Spanish-Cuban sculptor, now turned guitar-teacher, Juan Vivion de Valera. He did not make much money, but he had a rich father and, besides, he was an agreeable, handsome little man. Kate had laughed hysterically when she discovered that Juan, being only 5'8" or 5'9", and wishing to be more imposing, sometimes wore women's platform boots.

Juan was not the sort of man who married, but he enjoyed Kate's body and he was kinder to Kate's wee bastard than most men would have been. In mid-October 1882, Juan and Kate produced a child of their own, whom, on 10 November 1882, they named in the State of New York registry as George de Valero. The baby was called after the patron saint of England. He died shortly thereafter.

Kate, clever in a practical way, sees this not as a tragedy but as an opportunity to begin to clear up her problem with young Edmund. In the whirl of New York in the early 1880s, it was not unusual for a priest to be only vaguely acquainted with those who called on his services, or at all uncommon for children to go unbaptized for several years. So, the son of Kate Coll and Thomas Aitkinson, is baptized on 3 December 1882 in St. Agnes's parish, New York. He is named "Edmund De Valeros," after Edmund the Confessor, an English saint, and his baptismal certificate makes him appear almost two and a half years younger than he really is. And, crucially, he has a father-of-record, the diminutive Spanish-Cuban music teacher.

Why should this deception be held against the lad? Fr. Sheehy has asked himself. He understands the cruelty of tight rural societies and knows that if young Edmund is publicly branded a bastard, his chances in life will be nil. No decent woman will be given to him in marriage, no job except the lowest be open to him. It's a hard society. Father Sheehy is the only person in the community with the power to certify the de Valera lie, and he does so with a slightly uneasy conscience. He does not believe the sins of the parents should be visited upon their children, but lying about procreation is no minor sin for a priest to engage. Nevertheless, he presses on and the moment he tells the schoolmaster "He'll be turning six soon now, so enroll him," the world of Bruree has to accept this as being the truth. Thus, Edmund de Valera is declared legitimate and has a future in Ireland.

Later, when confessing and meditating on the matter with his own spiritual adviser, Fr. Sheehy says by way of explanation, "It was the mother, that's what turned me. Such a hard woman, no love in her for anyone or anything." He shifted uneasily.

"Yes Father?"

"She came back once, you know. To get her own baptismal lines. She was still a spinster in the eyes of Holy Mother Church and needed the lines to marry some Englishman she'd met in America, fellow of the name Wheelwright. Proper name for a coachman which is what he was. Strange that she was so keen on marrying in America in the True Church; Wheelwright is a Protestant."

"Often that's the way of it. Had she not been married by a priest, her family would never have spoken to her."

"No."

"By-the-by, Father, what happened to the Spaniard?"

"Kate Coll – she's Mrs. Wheelwright now I suppose – is very vague and has no real knowledge. He drifted off to Minneapolis or to Denver, she can't remember, and she hasn't heard from him and thinks he may be dead. That's what she told everyone here: 'my husband is dead.' I don't think she cared one way or another."

"But at least she brought young Edmund home to her people."

"In a manner of speaking. He was cramping her style. Three or four years ago she paid for her brother Ned to come over to New York and pick up Edmund. Ned Coll. Solid. Did the whole trip though he was only seventeen years at the time."

"When was it that Kate Coll came back home to fetch her baptismal lines from you?"

"Just this winter past."

"Ah. When, Father, did you decide to tell your lie about Edmund de Valera's age?"

"After his mother returned to New York. I thought about what she'd told me and what she had not told. Mostly, though, I reflected on her treatment of Edmund. She had hardly a word for him, poor lad. He would sit silently, following her with his eyes, never wavering. He was like a puppy, starved for love. All he wanted was a pat on the head. And she ... she spent most of her time in Limerick at dressmakers and parties. I don't doubt she was prospecting for a possibly-better husband than Wheelwright. Hard woman. When she was in Bruree she ignored Edmund entirely. You could see it carving out his soul, poor lad. He had not cast eyes on his mother for three years and she was as cold to him as if he was a leper."

"So ..."

"So, I prayed and it came to me that Our Lord had shown in his miracles that no one need be a leper for life. And Holy Mother Church teaches that everyone can be healed of their sins by God's grace. Then who was I to sentence this child to Purgatory here on earth?"

"And you meant this in your heart, not just as a convenient argument?"

"Completely. Did I sin?"

"No. A mere and accidental act of omission."

"Thank you, Father."

"You did well. And, actually, Fr. Sheehy, our Faith has reason to be generous to persons of unusual parentage."

OXFORD UNIVERSITY. SPRING, 1889

Deathstar

William Butler Yeat sits in the Bodleian Library and carefully copies out one of the manuscripts of a man whose mind, he believes, is almost as large as his own. William Blake's *Book of Thel* absorbs his attention almost completely. Taking Blake into his own almighty consciousness is important because he believes that Blake was an Irishman.

Almost simultaneously, in Kent, at the other end of the park from the home of Mrs. O'Shea, mistress of Charles Stewart Parnell, death creeps in. The wealthy aunt of Mrs. O'Shea dies, full of years and with a very full purse. The large Georgian House, "The Lodge" is quickly closed up and a large black velvet bow on the front door announces mourning. At age ninety-six, the grand old lady left almost her entire fortune to Parnell's mistress.

Not benefiting much from the legacy, Mrs. O'Shea's husband, who has long colluded in his own cuckolding in hopes of cashing-out big when the old aunt died, now is free to bring a suit for divorce on the grounds of adultery.

COUNTY LIMERICK. 30 DECEMBER 1889

Faith and Works

Rolling in the mud in a desperate attempt to avoid the kicks and sticks of a band of Limerick pig dealers, David Sheehy swears that when the moment comes, he will himself take a stick to Parnell.

Sheehy has been a nationalist MP since 1886, and having giving up his Fenianism, had served Charles Stewart Parnell with the same loyalty to him as if he had sworn a secret oath to the man. That's why Sheehy had had no trouble in believing Parnell's denial of his having had an affair with the adulterous Mrs. O'Shea. With the utmost confidence and grace, Parnell had called his most trusted MPs into his private office at Westminster and had given the matter all the airing the Uncrowned King felt it needed. "Gentlemen," he said, languidly leaning against the mantelpiece, "Could you believe that of me?" That was enough of a denial for Sheehy and he became one of Parnell's most zealous defenders: "All an English plot," was Sheehy's standard comment.

Near year's end Sheehy is making a speech defending Parnell in Limerick on market day, when a stop-press edition of the *Freeman's Journal* appears. "PARNELL SUIT UNDEFENDED!" scream the news-hawkers and everyone knows immediately what this means: Parnell has been lying to all of us for months and deceiving us for years.

The Limerick pig-buyers, famous for their high moral standards, emerge from the crowd that has been listening to David Sheehy declare Parnell innocent and they start to shove him about. They're not entirely sure what adultery is, but it can't be anything good if Parnell could only do it in England. Sheehy takes some whacks from the pig-sticks and a hob-nailed boot catches him in the calf and he falls down. Soon he's in real trouble, and would have been seriously injured, had not one of the buyers called out, "Stop it now boys! his brother's a priest."

David Sheehy requires six sutures to patch up his forehead, but the heaviest damage is to his sense of honour. Parnell, whom he had trusted as much as God himself, has lied to him. When the reckoning comes, he will turn on Parnell with the hard-toe vigour of those Limerick men's boots.

BRIGHTON, ENGLAND. 6 OCTOBER 1891

Epic Modesty

Charles Stewart Parnell dies of a "rheumatic heart," but the diagnosis could have been of hubris, of a prideful soul serrated by the punishments of the gods. His now-wife, the former Mrs. O'Shea, proclaims that his last words were "Kiss me, sweet wife, and I will sleep a little," and perhaps they were. More reliably, the last words any third party heard him utter are reported to have been a feverish muttering, "the Conservative Party."

"The modern literature of Ireland ..." William Butler Yeats later lectured at the Royal Academy of Sweden, *"... began when Parnell fell from power in 1891. A disillusioned and embittered Ireland turned from parliamentary politics; an event was conceived; and the race began ..."* Yeats, in 1923 has been named Nobel Laureate in Literature and he is explaining how he, Douglas Hyde, and a few others created Ireland. *"Dr. Hyde founded the Gaelic League, which was for many years to substitute for political armament a Gaelic grammar, and for political meetings village gatherings, where songs were sung and stories told in the Gaelic language.*

"Meanwhile I had begun a movement in English, in the language in which modern Ireland thinks and does business ..." Meticulously, Yeats chronicles the cultural movement that he believes created Ireland, telling his earnest Swedish auditors what he had done on each day of Creation.

LARNE TO BELFAST. OCTOBER, 1892

Dr. Hyde and Miss Jackel

For one of the few times in his life, Dr. Douglas Hyde (LL.D., TCD) is in a second-class railway carriage and he finds the experience unsettling. He has been up the Glens of Antrim, checking variant versions of Gaelic language stories that he will eventually use as exhibits in his *Three Sorrows of Storytelling* (1895). He is not in the first-class carriage because it was sold out to a party of Presbyterian elders who were returning home from interviewing clerical licentiates of Edinburgh University for admission to pulpits in the Synod of Ulster. Hyde had watched them march solemnly from the Stranraer ferry to the first-class carriage and he wondered at first if they were a congerie of morticians, so universally black in dress and morose in manner were they.

The Belfast and Northern Counties Railway ran only to its station at York Street and Dr. Hyde would have to take a Clarence cab or, worse yet, a jaunting car, to the Great Northern Railways station at Great Victoria Street. Only then could he escape Belfast, which he loathed, and return to Dublin.

Before his second-class carriage filled up, Hyde had pulled from his travelling case a sheaf of papers headed "The Necessity for De-Anglicizing Ireland." It is a lecture that he is to give in the next month to the National Literary Society, a new organization founded as a satellite of William Butler Yeats's Irish Literary Society of London. Over the mild objections of the poet, Dr. Hyde was elected president: Yeats would have preferred the old Fenian, John O'Leary. As president, Hyde was expected to give a stirring address. In any case, it was a good opportunity for self-advertisement, as Hyde was seeking an academic post in the USA and some eloquent pro-Gaelic oratory would help his cause.

Within the last ninety years we have, with an unparalleled frivolity, deliberately thrown away our birthright and Anglicised ourselves. Strong sentence: Hyde tinkers with it for a minute and decides to keep it. He works on versions of a phrase whose sense is right, but hard to complete: *the greatest stroke of all in our Anglicisation, the loss of our language.* Hyde is justifiably proud of his own mastery of all the regional dialects of the Irish language.

Just before the train finally starts, the carriage door is opened by a breathless young woman in her early twenties, working class, and, to Hyde's dismay, an incessant chatterer. She's Miss Jackel from Doagh she says and has been at some sort of a school and is making her first visit to Belfast and … and despite her talking incessantly all the way down the Antrim coast to York Street, Dr. Hyde cannot understand much of her language. When she says that she has been to larn to larn it takes him most of the journey to realize that she has been to Larne to learn, in this case to a knitting school for textile apprentices. He never does discern that lag is one of her two pedal extremities, that knack attaches one's head to one's body, or that water is boiled in a cattle. Her words go by so quickly and the grammatical formations she employs are certainly not those of the English language.

Dr. Hyde keeps in check his irritation at having his thoughts interrupted: he twirls the ends of the massive mustache that he has grown to make himself look older and wiser. When he finally is in a first-class carriage taking him from Belfast to Dublin he returns to his manuscript. *I have no hesitation at all in saying that every Irish-feeling Irishman, who hates the reproach of West-Britonism, should set himself to encourage the efforts which are being made to keep alive our once great national language.* Hyde, a zealous adherent of dichotomous thinking, immediately dismisses from his mind the chattering girl with the strange manner of speaking that he could not crack. He knows that there are only two languages in Ireland, English and Irish, only two cultures, and only two ways of thinking. The poor girl must have been somewhat retarded mentally, or even dangerous, he concludes. Yes, he agrees with himself, that's the only explanation.

BELFAST. APRIL-MAY 1893

Wisdom?

When William Ewart Gladstone's second Home Rule bill receives its second reading in the house of commons, the Belfast Protestant shipworkers explode. They drive the Catholic workers out of the yard and mills. This accomplished, like a small army, they march homeward through North Street, past Carrick Hill and finally to the Shankill. They are armed with rivets small enough to make handy missiles and with iron bolts large enough to be head-splitting coshes. The police have seen this sort of thing before and know how to deal with it if they are so minded: and this moment they are, since the elected government of the United Kingdom is solidly behind Home Rule. The police form into a straight line, raise their batons, and charge the Shankill men, breaking heads with the joyful abandon of a puppy cracking eggs in a henhouse. The rioting ends quickly.

Two weeks later, the Rev. Dr. R.R. Kane, grand master of the Loyal Orange Order for Belfast, declares that any man who would demand separate treatment for Ulster in a Home Rule bill deserved to be in a lunatic asylum. Orangemen would not allow the Protestants of the south to be cut off from their brothers in the north. And, Dr. Kane added, he could not see that Catholics in the south would allow the Catholic minority in the north to be separated. Partition, the Worshipful Master said, defied common sense.

LONDON. FEBRUARY 1894

Dining Out

Late in the afternoon of a wet February, a barrister is crossing the Strand. He is in a hurry for the law is only his second job. He practises because he is an MP and that is a gentleman's occupation and assumes private means. He is MP for Trinity College, Dublin and he is late.

As he cuts across traffic, a two-horse carriage narrowly misses him. It stops and the barrister expects acrimony to ensue. Instead, a moderately friendly and very loud voice calls out, "Is that you, Ned Carson?"

"Indeed, and who …" A large man, even taller than Carson, steps down from the cab. He and Carson could scarcely be dressed more differently: Carson in a tight-fitting black topcoat, celluloid collar rising stiffly beneath, almost to his chin. "Well. Hullo Ned Carson, how are you?" Oscar Wilde, wrapped in a huge overcoat with a Persian

Lamb collar, somehow sports a large white flower in his lapel. It rests against the black, curly lapel as if it is a misplaced hors d'oeuvre. The two men chat briefly and Wilde promises to have Carson to dinner some night soon.

Oscar Wilde and Edward Carson have long known each other. Their parents were acquaintances and as children the two had played together at the seashore. They had attended TCD together, but then had not met until today, twenty years later. Wilde was the most fashionable of London's playwrights, *The Importance of Being Earnest* now running. Carson, having become the Irish bar's most successful barrister, had entered politics, and just now was beginning to practise in England. They could not be more different, especially now: Carson was lonely, financially pressed as he waited for English briefs, and dead tired from parliamentary overwork. Wilde was almost never alone, was making and spending a small fortune, and was dead tired from playing too hard. Carson speaks with a heavy Dublin accent that he never attempts to lose; Wilde in a Dublinless accent he had created for himself.

"Yes, we have to have a meal together, Oscar. Soon. Let me know when you have a free moment."

Edward Carson, a clean lawyer in a world of dirty attorneys, had two distinguishing characteristics: he took only one case at a time and concentrated all his legal attention on it; and he never took a case against anyone who was a friend or even anyone who had treated him as one.

Sadly for Oscar, he forgot Carson entirely: for if he had remembered the dinner invitation he never would have seen the inside of a prison.

BRUREE, COUNTY LIMERICK. 1896

The Future Prince

Edmund de Valera does well in the national school, very well. He is remarkably swift for his declared age, and no one dares bully him: he is a big lad. He has ambitions. As much as living with his uncle in one of the new government-built labourers' cottages is a prestige-item in Bruree, it leads nowhere and the lad is smart enough to do his sums.

Emigration aside, the only way out of Bruree is by obtaining an ex-hibitionship in some secondary school that will either yield entry to the church or produce a decent job in the civil service. There's a big gap, however, between Bruree National School and a real secondary school where the exhibitionships give entry to a future of white pa-per, black ink, and working indoors. The nearest bridge to Edmund de Valera's future is in Charleville, seven miles away, where the Christian Brothers have a school.

It costs more than Uncle Ned will provide, however.

"Why not write to your mother in America?" Father Sheehy sug-gests. "She and her husband have good jobs now."

Accidentally, Fr. Sheehy has started Edmund de Valera on his path to becoming the Irish Machiavelli.

For Edmund writes a letter that the Prince himself would have ap-proved. He tells his mother of the need for money for the Christian Brothers' schooling, and could she spare it?

And – clearly the lad had an intuitive genius for the Irish heart – he suggests to her that, alternatively, she should send funds so that he can come and join her in America.

Remittance for the school fees comes from America by telegraphic post, and Edmund de Valera is on his way to being a master of Irish diplomatics.

LARNE, CO. ANTRIM. 1897

The Irish Renaissance

Auctioneering Agents of Satan
Bands of Assumptionists
Clay Crabs of Corruption
Drunken Ignorant Dross

These are a few of the steam calliope of terms that the author has for nay-saying literary critics. It is a private list, but it could be shared with any of the lions of the Irish renaissance. Each of them was bruised by unfair hits from all sides: low-foreheaded clergy, dirty-booted nationalists, pursed-lipped bank managers, Philistine Protes-tants-on-horses.

Egotistical Earth Worms
Frequent Fosterers of Falsehood
Genius Scathers
Hogwashing Hooligans

The author's first novel, *Irene Iddesleigh*, has been ill-received. Her later *Delina Delaney* fares worse, and makes difficult the publication of her mature works, such as *Helen Huddleson* and her inimitable *Poems of Puncture*. The latter deals mostly with lawyers she dislikes and a few of the clients who have engaged them: such as one Susan Crawford, upon whose death the poet wrote: "No more we'll hear her lieing din./ Her tongue's now thick."

Ingenious Ingots of Iniquity
Jape-sniping Jackals
K ... (here she ran out of alliteratives)
Loitering Louts of Literacy

Amanda McKitrick Ros was the wife of the station master of Larne, a big amiable red-bearded man whom everybody called by his first name. In her time, she was widely recognized as the worst novelist in the English-speaking world, an Irish giant to equal the Scottish poet McGonagall. Her monumental awfulness produced a cult following, including Aldous Huxley who in an essay of 1923 pleaded with publishers to make her work more accessible. And they did. Still, she was never satisfied. No great artist is.

Mushroom Class of Idiots ...
Random Roughs ...
Vicious Vandals
Worms

DUBLIN. 1898

Remember '98

Maud Gonne has been selected to unveil a plaque in memory of Lord Edward Fitzgerald, martyred hero of 1798. She is a good choice for a ceremony of sentiment, for the sentimental eye that reigns at such moments sees her as the stunning aquiline beauty she once was. This day, a cold-eyed observer would see a tall woman in her early thirties, overweight, awkward, looking at least forty.

In a cape that she dramatically sweeps over her shoulder, like a cavalier before a duel, she steps from her carriage and somehow misses the ground, mostly.

If only she would permit herself to wear spectacles, just occasionally. Her arm is broken by the fall and she is carried from the field of battle, an injured warrior.

She takes to her divan and William Butler Yeats ministers to her as if she had suffered an amputation. During the course of the convalescence they work more and more on their cosmic affinities. By year's end they have travelled together astrally, a much safer mode of transport as Miss Gonne is enabled to miss the ground, entirely.

BRUREE, COUNTY LIMERICK. 1898

The Land League Priest (4)

Serving mass for Father Sheehy was not an easy ride. His politics may have been free swinging, but his liturgics were tight. Don't miss a step, lads, or you'll have a clip on the ear after service. Mass was the most important dance that humanity ever performed, he told his altar boys, and God would never forgive their failure to reverence his altar properly.

The altar boys were the Land League priest's favourites, in an era when that had no bad overtones: it's something every village lad wanted to be. It placed one in the immediate presence of the Host. And, in Bruree, it gave them the presence of Fr. Sheehy and his deep devotion: to two Gods, that of the altar and that of the Irish nation. The deities were intertwined. Father Sheehy trained his acolytes of a Saturday afternoon, and he made certain they knew what they were doing – pass me the ciborium *before* I move across the rail, you rascal! – and why. They learned the dance of Christianity.

Liturgics for Fr. Sheehy moved easily into politics. Of a Saturday afternoon, he told the altar boys of Irish heroes of the far past – the ancient Fianna and Patrick Sarsfield of Jacobite times, and of the near past: including Michael Davitt and of Fr. Sheehy's own brother, still an MP. Among the lads who listened was Edmund de Valera who, late in life, wrote "He taught me patriotism."

He did more, much more than de Valera knew, for Fr. Sheehy was himself a master of ecclesiastical string-pulling, albeit strictly limited by his own radical politics.

The de Valera lad had a future, Sheehy knew, if only it could be unlocked. He tried to gain Edmund's admission to the up-nose County Limerick secondary schools, St. Munchin's and Mungret Colleges, but they were too close to home: the prefects of admission looked at Edmund de Valera's family history – "raised by an uncle: curious, that" – and rejected him.

Father Sheehy understood: the farther from Bruree young Edmund is proposed, the more apt he will be to be accepted. And, Fr. Sheehy has a useful marionette, his own curate, Fr. James Liston, who had made the acquaintanceship of the president of Blackrock College, Dublin. So, Fr. Sheehy has his curate act as catspaw, putting forward Edmund de Valera for admission. The curate is instructed to suggest in his letter of recommendation that an unknown benefactor will pay £20 a year towards the annual fee of £40, if the college will grant an exhibitionship of £20.

Thus does Edmund de Valera escape into the future Irish ruling class. And each year the Holy Ghost Fathers receive anonymously four of the large £5 notes that Irish banks issue – so large they have to be folded to fit into a banker's till – with a hand-written note saying, "For the Education of E. de Valera, Esq."

DUBLIN. 1899–1900

More Renaissance

Few historians pay attention to the real Irish cultural renaissance.

In June 1899, the Catholic Truth Society is formed. It is to Irish twentieth-century culture what Propaganda was to the church in the seventeenth. As a publisher, it produces more titles than any other house in Ireland: 424 penny throwaways in its first ten years, with a circulation of over five million copies, plus prayer books and other substantial publications. Readers are encouraged, once they have read them, to leave the publications on buses and trains.

On the first of September 1900, the gombeen heart of the resurgent small-farmer, small-businessman class found its perfect expression in the *Leader*, edited by D.P. Moran. Three hundred years of resentment welled up in Moran, who still waxed wrathful about the battle of Kinsale in 1603, and he found an immediate audience that predicted what post-independence Ireland would be like. No time, none, for the Irish literary renaissance: it was loaded with Protestants and its Catholic exponents were corrupted. The Irish national party in parliament was derided as the creation of a Protestant adulterer, and the mouthpiece of West Britons. *Shoneen* was Moran's favourite abuse-term, and it applied to anybody who read a British newspaper, attended the Abbey Theatre, or visited the Continent except to worship at selected shrines. Moran's program was simple, even if his rhetoric was complex: Ireland and the Irish people should keep themselves distinctive and this meant having as little as possible to do with outside cultural influences and all their fopperies and pretensions. Thus would Irish ethnicity be cleansed. An added advantage from the viewpoint of the small farmers with children to place, was that it promised that when Ireland became a state the civil service posts, and the teaching appointments, and the cultural prizes would go to their children: the right sort of faithful.

Moran publishes weekly for thirty-six years and when death silences his squeaking quill, he need not be replaced, for his views have become the policy of the independent Irish state. Thus, as late as the 1950s, Patrick Kavanagh, who should have known better, could contemptuously pitch into a corner a book that labelled Yeats, Joyce and Shaw as "three great Irishmen," damning it "a journalist's lie!" Two out of the three were Protestants and thus not really Irish and the third had abandoned holy Ireland for the brothel of Continental culture.

A nation once again.

NOT FAR, BUT NOT HOME.
ENGLAND
1845–1900

The Liverpool Machine As Portcullis

The Liverpool machine could not change the course of Irish emigration by itself, any more than a sea wall could change solely by its own position the course of the ocean. Yet, as an expression of social forces and as an instrument of the public policy of nations, the enormous machine was the instrument of the realignment of the Irish world.

No one knows how many Irish men, women, children, came to Liverpool; how many left, or exactly where they went: did they stay in England? or return eventually to Ireland? out-migrate quickly to some New World or labour for years in England before moving onwards, sometimes back home, other times to the USA, Canada, Australasia? In the peak years of 1846–51, up to a million entrances and exits a year are conceivable, given all these possibilities.

We do know that, like a portcullis, the Liverpool machine re-ordered the priorities of Irish out-migration. Before 1846, British North America was the first choice of long-term Irish emigrants, England second, the USA third. By 1851, the flow has been redirected: the United States is the prime destination, England still second, and Canada now third. This new order holds until World War I.

Liverpool in 1851 is second only to Dublin and Belfast in the number of Irish-born inhabitants.

Some machine. Necessary. No one loved Liverpool, but if the devil had not invented it, some god would have had to.

The Boyne Paradox

Although he deplored permitting uncontrolled Irish migration into England, Dr. James Kay-Shuttleworth believed if the Irish could not be sent back to Ireland then they had to be turned into civilized beings in England. (Dr. Kay had contracted an advantageous marriage in 1842 and added the second name by royal licence.) Kay-Shuttleworth had been in charge of popular education in England since 1839. This activity was run out of a sub-committee of the

Privy Council and it granted operating aid to Anglican and Non-Conformist schools on the basis of minimal inspections.

Quietly in 1847 the special committee begins to give grants to Catholic schools. By 1870, 103,000 children are in the state-aided Catholic schools. Thereafter, as the school system of England evolves, Catholic schools receive less than do state schools (but not much less), and a full ecclesiastically-dominated Catholic school system emerges, mostly paid for by the English state. The bishops complain, of course, but the slightly-lower grants are a reasonable price to pay for not having a bunch of laymen interfering in the daily running of the schools, good Catholics though they may be.

Thus the paradox: the two jurisdictions in the Irish diaspora where overt anti-Catholic rhetoric is most acceptable and Orangeism most flourishes – England and what is later called "Ontario" – are also the two places in the diaspora where the church is treated most generously on the one issue it cares about most: the provision of a Catholic education for children of the faith.

VATICAN CITY. 12 APRIL 1850

Brand Names

Pius IX sullenly re-enters Rome. He is under the protection of the French army as the Italians have shown little enthusiasm for his reign. He is conducted to his private chapel and there, after prayer, he vows to devote the rest of his life to restoring the grandeur of the papacy.

Earlier, in February, he had appointed Paul Cullen as archbishop of Armagh, an intelligent move equal to appointing Wellington a field general.

In late September, with Cullen's enthusiastic support, His Holiness makes one of his first dramatic gestures: he re-establishes the Roman Catholic hierarchy in England. This is something the English Catholics long have desired: since the Reformation they have been under the care of Vicars Apostolic, which is not organizationally crimping, but is down-market ecclesiastically. Now the church in England will have a full bench of bishops and archbishops and, if they are lucky, a red hat or two.

English Catholics understand that this benison occurs only because of the Irish presence among them. The English need the Irish in the church, the same way that officers need foot soldiers. The English Catholic church has grown rapidly. There are 520,000 Irish immigrants in England and, roughly 800,000 first- and second-generation (including Protestant Irish). Nobody knows for sure. And there are probably 800,000 nominal Roman Catholics in England. Again, no census designer thinks to ask: actual churchgoers are about 250,000. But a simple formula – four-fifths of the Irish, first and second generation, are Catholic and four-fifths of Catholics in England are Irish – is the reality understood by the authorities of the Catholic church in England.

And not just the Catholic authorities. The re-establishment of the Catholic hierarchy in England, with its hordes of Irish foot soldiers, brings out a potent blend of anti-Irish, anti-Catholic feeling, and produces a bizarre product: the Ecclesiastical Titles Act of 1851, the only new penal measure framed in the nineteenth century. There is actual rioting about "Papal Aggression" (always capitalized), and parliament prohibits the use of territorial titles (such as "Canterbury") throughout the United Kingdom by Catholic prelates and cathedral deans. It's a matter of keeping the brand names for the Church of England.

For the Irish hierarchy, the measure is redundant (they were prohibited by a clause in the Catholic Emancipation Act from using territorial titles) and unenforceable (they had done so anyway). For the English bishops it is an indignity: they gracefully choose territorial titles (a violation of the law), but don't use those already taken by the Anglicans.

So silly is the law that it is never enforced and in 1871 is repealed as part of W.E. Gladstone's dealing with the Irish church question.

In 1890, Cardinal Manning estimates that eight-tenths of the Catholics in England are of Irish background and that there are a million of them.

Earlier, in 1882, he had implicitly declared Pius IX to have been victorious in his worldwide campaign to restore the Vatican's glory. "I remember saying," the cardinal recalled, "that I had given up working for the people of England to work for the Irish occupation of England."

He continued. "But that occupation is a part of the Church throughout the world – an Empire greater than the British."

LIVERPOOL. 1850–58

Liar's Dice

Henry Boyd, an Anglo-Irish shipping merchant from Ardee, County Louth, made an honest living in a dishonest business. Mostly he dealt in goods, but as part of the charitable network set up by his family friend Vere Foster, he helped families and women of good character to emigrate from Ireland, via Liverpool, to one of the several New Worlds open to them. "Good character" was not a code phrase for Protestant (a common Liverpool usage of the time), but in this philanthropy meant women and men with at least one trustworthy character reference who were not likely to be a charge on the public funds in their new land.

Information and help in avoiding being cheated: Boyd's benevolence was practical, for without honest guidance any Irish person trying to migrate to North America by way of Liverpool was vulnerable to being caught up in a bankrupting game of liar's dice. Touts met every ship from Ireland, and spying those passengers with the heavy trunks of the long-distant migrant, gave them gratuitous advice on which ships were sailing soonest and which were the cleanest and had the best captain. Once they had the arm of a migrant, these leeches could hardly be dislodged. They were paid on commission to sell tickets; by the early 1850s, most of the long-distance trade was in the hands of brokers, rather than ships' owners or masters, so a family could be sold a berth on one ship and then find themselves shoved onto another. Other runners sold lodgings and still others practised a range of confidence tricks. Over the years, tens of thousands of men and women came to Liverpool with resources sufficient to carry them to North America and were swindled in various ways and ended as part of the vagrant flux of Irish, constantly on the move in England, never comfortable, never at rest.

Henry Boyd did nothing heroic. He simply helped men, families and, especially, women to choose solid ships, avoid certain captains, be sure to take enough food, and to look for a berth on a three-masted vessel that had an auxiliary steam engine to drive a screw propeller, not side paddles: weeks of ocean travel could be saved that way. The enterprise made him only a nominal profit.

Vere Foster's scheme, in which Boyd was a small cog, was endorsed by such diverse persons as Abraham Lincoln and Horace Greeley. It was particularly concerned with protecting emigrant women – Ireland, uniquely among European countries, sent as many women as men abroad – and it was clean: no complaints were ever made about the propriety with which the women were treated.

Henry Boyd was buried back home in Ireland in 1858. He had been an ordinary decent man. Come to think about it, not all that ordinary.

LONDON, LIVERPOOL, MANCHESTER. 1850–70

Such a Damp Desert

The thirst is the same in every new industrial city, in every newly-packed tenement, and most residents do not think it a paradox that they are living in a land of puddles and encircling damp, yet they have to treasure a cup of water as if they were in the salt barrens of Utah.

Almost every expanding city in England is running dry. Natural wells are few and they could serve the eighteenth-century populace, not the nineteenth. Septic ground water seeps into those wells that still work efficiently and these become the centre of the great Commune of the English city: the commune of shared bacilli.

By means of hollowed-out logs, private companies and, later, responsible municipalities, water is delivered from country streams and reservoirs to the parched rookeries. Delivery is erratic and often only for a total of three-quarters of an hour a day. Water thieving is a recognized criminal form and water-begging by children is a duty for the youngest in many families.

Each cup of water is used over and over in ways that are ingenious and extremely unhealthy. Good advice is never to look into the liquid one is drinking.

When water services are finally developed, in most municipalities these depend upon leaden pipes.

As a change from the swamp ooze they have been enduring, most people find the change a startling pleasure. The flaking bits of lead that spiral down the pipes provide a clean tang that the people quite like.

STOCKPORT, LANCASHIRE. 1852

Scorecard

Lord Derby, Tory prime minister, neither liked nor disliked Catholics. However, he always made a point of saying *Roman* Catholics, and usually he meant something more precise: Irish Roman Catholics. That, certainly, was his meaning when on 15 June 1852 his cabinet forbade Catholics to hold processions on the streets of England if these involved any symbols of their faith.

A general election was three weeks away and the police were worried about thirty or so towns where there was a dangerous number of Catholics, and thus, the chance of Protestant-Catholic riots.

The annual Sunday School procession of the Catholics of Stockport was already scheduled for 27 June and the local priests made certain that the celebration was discreet: no crosses or statues and the clergy did not wear full canonicals.

Score at the end of the next day, when the rioting was finished: twenty-four Catholic homes burned, one dead body (a Catholic who may have been killed by a fellow Catholic in a side incident), two Catholic chapels burned.

Most tellingly: ten English Protestants and ten Irish Catholics were sent to Chester for trial for riot.

Three Englishmen guilty.

Ten Irishmen guilty.

DR. TUKE'S ASYLUM, LONDON. APRIL 1853

What Counted

"How many Commandments are there, Sir?"

Feargus O'Connor is being interviewed by a Lunacy Commission. It consists of three very serious men. It is not often that a former member of parliament comes into their orbit.

"There are 613," O'Connor replies. He smiles confidently.

The three assessors look at each other significantly. Two of them think they have noticed a confirmation of O'Connor's lunacy. The third clears his throat and says, "Gentlemen. Perhaps we should confer." They withdraw to a corner, while O'Connor sits back in his chair and counts the tin ceiling tiles. They return, sit opposite him at a long mahogany table. "Yes," their chairman agrees, "yes, technically you are right. But, we aren't Jews now are we, heh-heh?"

"No."

"Thus, sir, how many Christian commandments are there?"

"Oh, you mean the Top Ten commandments?"

"Indeed."

"Fifteen or sixteen," O'Connor offers. "Depends on how you count coveting your neighbour's ass."

The commissioners look at each other in a slightly worried fashion. They are here to confirm Feargus O'Connor's continuing need for mental hospitalization and they are supposed to be in charge, not he. Best get to an unambiguous test of reality.

"Sir, can you tell us how many points are in the Chartist programme? The movement you so ably … ah, led?"

"Not six."

Each one makes a notation immediately. O'Connor observes this and says angrily, "Not six, I said, and not-six it is."

"Ah, please explain how …"

"Everyone has always had that wrong. Original Charter, 1838, had nine points. The one we presented to parliament in 1839 had five. Chartist petition of 1842 had nine. And included, I am proud to say …" his voice rises.

"Mr. O'Connor, do not excite yourself in this way."

"… I am very proud to say, included eight points of democratic reforms of parliament *and* the Repeal of the iniquitous Union of Britain and Ireland!"

O'Connor slumps back into his seat and withdraws into his own world of memory, where things counted and counted rightly. He, who now has to put up with three mental embalmers, once addressed crowds of tens of thousands. His voice had been loud, coming from his massive chest like a bass trill on a pipe organ. More importantly, he had known how to speak to crowds who mostly could not hear him: give them a speech they can give to each other, was his secret. So he repeated himself, used rhyming phrases, and talked with his body. In the early 1840s, he always wore the fustian cloth suit that distinguished the ordinary working man from his well-woven betters. And he used hand and facial gestures that could not be mistaken even from 500 yards away. If only the Royal Navy had possessed such gifted signalmen! And O'Connor did theatre. He was a natural mimic and did turns that were retailed in pubs across the country. He was especially good at doing Protestant clergymen and his best act was a skit on Henry Brougham, the false-radical the Chartists used as a bogey. Oh, you'd pay to see "Fear-Goose," as the crowd lovingly called him. Seeing him work was better than any theatre.

"Sir ... sir." The investigators were tapping on the window of his mind, bringing him back. "Now, sir, another question, if you please."

"Ah, to be sure." O'Connor mixed apparent gentility with an implied accusation that the lunacy commissioners were merely confirming in their notebooks their pre-purchased prejudice against him.

"How many children do you have, sir?"

"Damned if I know. No wife, but a big handful of children, or so I am told. Of course all that's why I'm here."

This time there was no mixed meaning, just an unstated one. Feargus O'Connor was suffering from a form of syphilis that he himself understood in those moments when the disease fell into temporary remission. "Can't have women without having children, can a man? And, come-now, you're doctors, can't have women without having illnesses. Count on that, can't you?"

"That is as the Lord provides," one of them answered without much enthusiasm.

Silence for a moment. "Do you remember, sir, why you were expelled from the House of Commons?"

This time Feargus does not want to remember. He wished to erase from his mind knowledge that after being unexpectedly called to represent Nottingham in 1847, he had taken to wearing clothes based on those of his own father: nankeen breeches, buckle shoes and a blue coat with brass buttons, an Anglo-Irish rig that, though worn in Cork in the early nineteenth century, had hardly been seen in England since the eighteenth. And Feargus hated to remember that, driven by some unknown force, he had taken to weird horseplay: sitting in the seats of other MPs, even setting himself on the Speaker's chair. And, that, though he got away with slapping Lord Palmerston, his punching Sir Benjamin Hall was one step too far. The sergeant at arms of the Commons had Feargus arrested, and that is how he came to be in Dr. Harrington Tuke's genteel lunatic asylum.

No, those things did not count and he absolutely refused to remember them. Correctly, the commissioners of lunacy left O'Connor in care. His syphilis took an epileptic form and by 1855 he was completely helpless. He died on 30 August, pain tormenting his body, but his mind far away, counting the crowds.

Patronage

Like a lot of people who have no sense of humour, Nathaniel Hawthorne smiled a lot. He licked his lips frequently and that, combined with his rictic smile, made him look perpetually hungry. Hawthorne was in the diplomatic business for pelf: although *The Scarlet Letter* and *The House of the Seven Gables* had made him America's biggest author at a moment when authors were becoming big in America, he still had too little money for his liking. His good fortune was that Franklin Pierce, an old college chum from Bowdoin, had just become president of the United States and Pierce took care of his friends: especially Hawthorne who in 1852 had written a shameless campaign biography of Pierce: warts not at all.

Liverpool, the second largest city in England, was the most lucrative post in the American diplomatic service, even if played honestly and there was no reason to do that. Besides the usual consular duties – ranging from aiding destitute American travellers to receiving rich travellers who came with letters of introduction from their state's senators – the real job was to sign a warrant for each shipment of U.S. goods that left Liverpool for the USA. The consul received $2.00 for his signature on each piece of paper and that was on top of the table: backhanders were whatever the traffic would bear. Hawthorne, who had previously spent some time in the U.S. customs service, was not at all embarrassed about this patronage appointment. He calculated that if he could tolerate Liverpool for four years, he could keep on writing and still save $30,000 to take home. He was overly optimistic in each case, but he knew a patronage plum when he saw it.

If only he could accept patronage without being patronizing.

Alas, Hawthorne had the Boston disease. In common with many cultured Americans from New England and New York, he viewed the expansion of midland England as a raw and running sore, a cultureless wasteland of bad manners, vulgar styles, and wealth without breeding. Americans can be such snobs about the English.

And Liverpool, he truly hated. He moved across the Mersey to Rock Ferry in the Wirral as soon as possible and then to Southport, which bored him to death.

One Saturday, travelling to Rock Ferry, he met a group of English workers having a day's holiday. It's something he has never before encountered. *The women were the most remarkable; though they seemed not disreputable, there was in them a coarseness, a freedom, and – I don't know what, that was purely English. In fact, men and women here do things that would at least make them ridiculous in America. They are not afraid to enjoy themselves in their own way, and have no pseudo-gentility to support.* Thus observes the genteel American. At the Rockport Ferry Hawthorne sees a group of charity children being taken from the work-houses to be trained as household servants. *A countless multitude of little girls, in coarse blue gowns, who, as they landed, formed in procession and walked up the dock ... I should not have conceived it possible that so many children could have been collected together, without a single trace of beauty or scarcely of intelligence in so much as one individual; such mean, coarse, vulgar features and figures betraying unmistakably a low origin, and ignorant and brutal parents. They did not appear wicked, but only stupid, animal, and soulless. It must require many generations of better life to wake the soul in them. All America could not show the like.*

LIVERPOOL. 1854

Duty

"What is the date of your birth?" Nathaniel Hawthorne is attempting to aid an American sailor who has lost his seaman's ticket and needs documentation so that he can ship home to New York.

"The twenty-second of December."

Hawthorne's consulate is in the Washington Buildings, a five-storey pile of stone that turns dismal black whenever it rains. His own office is only twelve-by-fifteen feet, but his vice-consul and two assistants have their own space. Most of the daily paperwork is organized by the staff and Hawthorne gets through it in an hour a day. The special cases, though, such as U.S. citizens who have lost their documents, are Hawthorne's own responsibility.

"What year?"

"Every year."

Hawthorne sighs. He can hear the assistants in the next room laughing, but he is not amused. He puts on his thin-lipped smile and patiently enquires of the seaman, "I mean sir, in what year were you born?"

When the seaman is gone, Hawthorne stands, puts his hands in his pockets and balefully observes the decorations of his office: a map of the United States and one of Europe; several small portraits and pictures of American naval battles, always tactful to have on hand in England; a lithograph of the Tennessee Statehouse, and a life-sized, hand-tinted engraving of General Taylor. It would require a very spiritual man, Hawthorne reflects, to be at home in these surroundings.

He is preparing himself to receive an Atlanta businessman and his wife who have a letter of introduction from their state governor. First, however, he has to deal with one of the several dozen vagrant and mendicant Yankees who cross his threshold each month, pleading for funds to get themselves home or, failing that, to some place in England where they claim a job is waiting for them. He is not usually generous and his questioning is harsh. Today, his spirit is not up to a full interrogation of a fey man in his twenties who claims to know that he is an American citizen but suffers from intermittent amnesia.

"Intermittent?"

"Yessir."

"In what way does it affect your memory?"

"I forget."

This time the vice-consul and assistants can be heard outright laughing.

Nathaniel Hawthorne smiles rigidly and gives the man half a crown to be gone.

SOUTHPORT, NR LIVERPOOL. 12-14 NOVEMBER 1856

Benign Difference

Herman Melville's brief visit to Nathaniel Hawthorne's home was one of the few times during his Liverpool internment that Hawthorne was truly happy. As old friends, he and Melville could disagree without having to worry that their arguings would shake their fundamental friendship. They spent a day walking up and down the sand and grass of the desolate beach and charting the intellectual heavens the way astronomers discuss the celestial.

Hawthorne's greatest act of instinctive and admirable character in life had been to champion Melville when he had little reputation as a writer – *Moby Dick* is dedicated to him – and now that the novel has proved such a failure with the American public, he has twice tried to find writerly jobs for Melville: first as editor of Commodore Perry's papers and then as a consular appointment with the U.S. government. Both efforts fail, but these are failures of effect, not of faith.

The friends talk about everything. How, asks Hawthorne, does Melville travel with only a carpet bag, when he cannot himself take even a fortnight in London without requiring a separate carriage for the family luggage? Is there a place in modern literature, Melville worries, for someone who does not have a Transcendent base, much less a belief in religion? Hawthorne worries that he will not be able to write well again after his stint in government service, and he brings up, as he has several times in their friendship, his concern about being descended from one of the judges of the Salem Witch trials. Will the sins of that generation be visited upon his own?

They talk about the Liverpool Machine, and though it's of little consequence to their friendship, they disagree entirely. To Melville's surprise, Hawthorne has spent long hours walking through the warrens of alleyways and tenement closes that Melville had known as a visiting merchant seaman. He has watched hundreds of thousands of Irish migrants being shipped off to become the new working stock of America. He is well informed, and not unpleasant about these things: they simply do not excite any passion in his austere New England soul. Melville tries to explain the wondrous maritime machinery of Liverpool, how it bestraddles the commerce of the entire Atlantic, but Hawthorne cannot hear; nor can he remember more of the housing and life of the slums, people than that the smells were so noisome as to require a change of morning coats when he had returned to his consulate.

Dear friends, but at heart Melville is an appreciater of the world, Hawthorne an evaluator. Hawthorne looks down upon the world and especially upon England. London he has come to approve a bit. "It is much pleasanter than stagnating in this wretched hole," he says in comparing it to Liverpool.

As for the English upper classes, "a week or two might pass very agreeably in an English country-house, provided the host and hostess and the guests were particularly pleasant people. Otherwise I would rather possess myself in a hotel."

MANCHESTER AND LIVERPOOL. 1859

Sing Us Another One

It's the original urban-and-western music: topical, scab-picking, heart-bleeding, I-been-done-wrong music. Irish urban ballads. They're the same all over the diaspora. In England, it's Liverpool and Manchester that are music-city.

> *It was a dark and dreary day*
> *When I left old Ireland.*
> *The boys and girls seemed so gay*
> *As they shook me by the hand.*

This is a small man's business, this music. Two sorts work at it. The really skilled ones write songs about any topic of the day – executions, shipwrecks, bloody battles, suicides are especially good – and sing them a few times near the docks or in pubs or at the markets. If they work, they have copies immediately printed by a job-printer, and by nightfall they are selling broadsheet copies of a song they composed that very morning: song-writing, singing, selling, all in the one day.

> *In the present year of '59, our hero General McMahon,*
> *Did deeds of arms that were sublime, upon the Italian land.*

(That for a French general of Irish extraction who fought for Napoleon the Third.)

The second sort of song flogger was more industrialized. A small printer would pay a few shillings to a song-writer, print up a ream, and then send loud-voiced balladeers into the streets and pubs, to sing a verse or two and sell the broadsheet. The songs are less topical, either lachrymose or staunchly patriotic, or both.

> *You surely will find that Paddy his aid will always lend*
> *And he be ready to assist you if e'er you want a friend,*
> *For true hospitality no matter where I've been,*
> *There's no place like ould Ireland, my native land so green.*

The Irish shared the Victorian English taste for a good deathbed scene, an execution, a wrenched and broken heart; the only difference was that instead of three-volume novels they preferred to engage their therapeutic clichés in public.

> *Poor Pat is often painted*
> *With a ragged coat and hat,*
> *His heart and hospitality*
> *Has much to do with that.*

GAWTHORPE HALL, NR BURNLEY, LANCASHIRE. 1860

Pedagogy

What a pleasant way to spend a Sunday afternoon, elevating the people. The gentleman who opens the grounds of Gawthorpe to the public for three or four hours of Sunday afternoon has come a long way from being Dr. James Kay and spending his time ankle deep in the ooze of the Manchester slums. His unremitting assertion of the need to civilize the populace had led to his being the first civil servant in charge of English mass education (as secretary to the Committee of the Privy Council for Education).

Every time he has moved up the social ladder his name has become longer. First, in 1842 when he had made an advantageous marriage to the sole offspring of a good estate and become James Kay-Shuttleworth by royal licence. Then, in 1849, upon retiring to the countryside to permit others to civilize the industrial beast that was festering in England's belly, he was knighted. Sir James Kay-Shuttleworth was pleased with himself and only disappointed that he did not himself receive a peerage and thus a really nice long name. (His son, James Kay-Shuttleworth, created Baron Shuttleworth of Gawthorpe, had that pleasure.)

This Sunday the good doctor is walking amidst the several hundred proletarians and artisans who have taken up his offer of fresh air and clear vistas. Gawthorpe Hall is close by industrial settlements, an oasis. Sir James has a few simple rules: no nipping the buds; no picnicking, and civility.

The latter is most important. If he passes a group of young men who keep their hands insolently in their pockets, rather than at their sides as is proper, he becomes upset. And if a man or boy wears a cap and does not touch it to him in respect, Sir James corrects him. His usual method is gentle enough. He turns and catches up with the offender or, more often, three or four lads; he bows deeply before them in the most formal fashion, all without saying a word. Awkwardly, the hands will come out of the pocket and the caps are raised in respect.

Sir James often tells himself that he is a natural educator.

SYDNEY AND MELBOURNE, AUSTRALIA;
MANCHESTER, ENGLAND. 1862-63

More Famine Relief

Mrs. Elizabeth Gaskell of 46 Plymouth Grove, Manchester, never set eyes on the Sydney, New South Wales *Morning Herald*, and she would not have been pleased if anyone had meretriciously said that its prose closely resembled hers. This, though, was different, and it is a pity that she could not have seen how close instinctive generosity could bring divergent literary styles.

The common point was their immediate reaction to the Cotton Famine. The Irish Potato Famine had been something else entirely: another country's problem and an intractable one; and this one ... this one was taking place in *England*.

Several hundred thousand textile workers in Manchester, Preston, Blackburn and, to a lesser extent in Liverpool and south Lancashire generally, were on the edge of starvation. The Union side in the American Civil War blockaded the cotton ports of the south and effectively blockaded the English cotton industry. Every operative was affected one way or another – but pity especially those unlucky Irish immigrants who had found a niche in the textile trade and now were facing extreme destitution once again.

Instinctively, Mrs. Gaskell writes to her friends, and she receives money by return mail to help her local Manchester committee ameliorate the pain.

Simultaneously, societies are formed in Sydney, Melbourne, Adelaide and Launceston, to aid the destitute of Lancashire. Well over £20,000 is collected.

The scheme almost comes to disaster, it must be admitted, when the unctuous Sir James Kay-Shuttleworth proposes from the English end that the whole amount be given over to public education rather than to reducing destitution; fortunately the Australians are not fooled by his sanctimony about schooling being such a much longer-lasting gift than mere food.

CHESTER AND LIVERPOOL. 1867

Information Received

"Lies, lunacy, and conundrums, that's all we've ever received from those informing chancers," the head constable of Liverpool, Major J.J. Greig, told his sergeant. He was especially vexed because he now had to report to the Liverpool Watch Committee on his latest bit of detecting. The police had received a strange, but compelling, series of anonymous letters telling them that the Head Centre of the whole Fenian Brotherhood was hiding in Toxteth Park: not exactly Sherwood Forest, but all tips were gratefully received. Greig handled the case himself – what a trophy to collect if this were true! – and he was half-convinced by a second letter that told him that in an emergency the Head Centre would be moved to the crypt of St. Patrick's Roman Catholic church. That, to a convinced anti-Catholic (the Liverpool police force voted Tory and prayed Protestant), was a true-sounding detail. And a further anonymous note from the same source added the clinching detail: the head of the IRB was to be concealed in the crypt in a specially made coffin that had a breathing apparatus. Just the sort of thing those cunning devils would think of, Greig concluded: "Plans probably came from the Vatican," he had told his sergeant.

Now, he was starting the new year having to explain to the Watch Committee why he had been convinced that a notorious villain had been secured in a shabby chapel in the equivalent of a diving bell. Greig had to talk very fast to keep his job.

Head Constable Greig actually was doing better than he thought. Something was going on and the melange of paid informers, anonymous tipsters, and robustly-interrogated prisoners agreed on that, though they were weak on details. In fact, 1867 became the Irish Republicans' year of action in England, running from an attempt to seize Chester Castle and its arms in February, through the Manchester actions of March and September, and finally, the London bombing in Clerkenwell in December.

That lay ahead. What Greig did know for certain in early January was that Irish-America was striking back at England. Organizers from the USA, Irish-born or the offspring of Irish parents, were working their way through Lancashire and London setting up terrorist cells (not a word Greig would have used, but accurate). As a front, the IRB in Liverpool (but, curiously, not in Manchester), used the National Brotherhood, a mostly-above-board political pressure group that had been publicly launched in Dublin in July 1861. This was a very public event indeed, for it was announced at the funeral of Terence Bellew MacManus, whose body was now back from the USA, freed both from his exile and his alcoholic torments, still doing service to the cause of Irish freedom.

Desperate for more information – something *was* going on – Greig chose the most thick-knuckled of his detectives to re-interrogate the Irish suspects in his custody. This was a long and tiring job, since half of the drunks and petty thieves in the lock-up were Irish, and the detectives took to wearing gloves to keep their hands from turning blue with contusions. The most promising prisoner was a young bank clerk who gurgled out something about Chester Castle. Unhappily, he died overnight, perhaps from the interrogation, perhaps because one of his cell-mates stopped him from talking further. It had been a mistake, the interrogators realized, to put him back in the big holding cell. The only information they received from his associates was that not only did they know nothing but, in fact, when a person dies in his sleep he doesn't know about it himself until the next morning.

Behind the curtain of misinformation, James McCafferty, born in Sandusky, Ohio, of Irish parents, was putting together a scheme of raiding Chester Castle, seizing the small arms and ammunition stored there, and transporting them to Holyhead, where vessels would take the cargo to Ireland and there the real business would begin. McCafferty was no näif. He had been a captain in the Civil War and knew tactics and how to assert authority. Like many Irish immigrants and Irish-Americans of the second-generation, he had not much cared about which side he fought on – slavery being what blacks were good for, right? – and his service was on the Confederate side. Some measure of Captain McCafferty's ability was that he engaged 1,200 Lancashire Fenians in the plan and still the police could not crack it.

Finally, on 11 February, Head Constable Greig and his associates in the Cheshire constabulary received a decent tip. The 54th Regiment was alerted to protect the castle and the whole event ended ignominiously. McCafferty and the other leaders received prison sentences.

Perhaps it all would have failed – 1,200 Fenians casually making their way from all around Lancashire to Cheshire, whistling patriotic tunes, seems a bit optimistic, as does their taking the castle while armed only with revolvers, as does their travelling by train to Holyhead – but Head Constable Greig cannot have been at all pleased to discover that the IRB could call up over 1,000 men. Nor, had he known it, would he have been happy to find that the hard men among the Irish in England were losing their trust in "Irish Yankees" and were resolving to do things on their own.

LONDON. MAY 1868

More Calculations

Michael Barratt stepped steadily up the ladder that led to the scaffold, an admirable bit of biometric calculation on his part, given that he was double-bound, ropes tightly cinched about his hands and his arms. He was on the verge of celebrity: he would be the last person publicly executed in England.

Barratt's brief rise to eminence was the product of a deficient exercise in mental arithmetic. In December 1867, he had been part of a plan to rescue two Fenian prisoners. A barrel of explosives was placed against the wall of Clerkenwell prison with the intention of blowing out the wall of the exercise yard. The calculation was wildly off: that day the prisoners were forbidden their exercise and when Barratt set off the explosion it was so excessive that sixty persons in the street outside were either killed or injured.

As the date of Michael Barratt's execution approached, the supreme council of the Irish Republican Brotherhood met in Manchester and calculated how to limit damage to the Brotherhood. A Message-to-the-Irish-People was framed. The Clerkenwell explosion was declared an act of Monstrous Brutality, Done Without Authority. *And were the perpetrators within our control ... their punishment would be commensurate with our sense of justice.* Meaning: we would hang them if the English were not doing the job already.

Not, certainly, calculated to show potential recruits that the organization would be steadfastly with them, even to death.

Penal law reformers are pleased when the Barratt execution is over, for they calculate that the deterrent effect of a hanging is greater if it is conducted in secret, in the yard of a prison, with only government officials as witnesses. Nicer, too, some of them suggest.

PRESTON. 1868

A Terrible Weight of Fear

Peter Mangan, from Cootehill, County Cavan, is an innocent victim of the Fenian attacks on England. He and his wife have built up a nice little drygoods shop by dint of his working in the textile mills by day while she minds the shop, and his keeping shop in the evening while she attends evening classes. They are on their way up: then their English custom begins to tail off as the Fenian bombings cast a shadow on the reliability of all Irish immigrants. And, as the Mangans ruefully note, the English are the only customers who pay on time and fully.

The background fear of all Irish women and children of the peasantry in Ireland or working class immigrants in England was that their male breadwinner would disappear. Peter's own father, an illegal distiller, had died doing a gaol term, and his stepfather had refused to support young Peter, so that from age eight he was on his own, scavenging a living in County Cavan, and finally being allowed to join his mother and stepfather in their new home in Drogheda. That was at age twelve when he was old enough that his presence in the family was a break-even proposition; Peter had a fulltime job in a cotton mill.

When his drygoods shop failed, Peter Mangan, like so many Irish males of his generation, has a choice: go on the road and eventually reassemble his family, or go on the road and forget them forever. The latter choice was frequent and is the now-repressed memory of their descendants. Irish families in the wash of the Great Famine were not all warm and loyal. Mostly they were hard, Darwinian little cockpits.

Five children and a wife are left behind by Mangan as he goes to the USA to repair his fortune, and no one thinks it unnatural. In fact, Peter's leaving the family with six months' support money was a rare bit of generosity. His wife will support and raise the children until he can reassemble the family. She must live with the knowledge, gnawing at her constantly, that many, many Irish men just disappear.

On her own, she exhausts the family savings, and returns with the children to Ireland to live on the charity of her own parents and to pray constantly that Peter will someday send for them.

Peter Mangan is a lucky and a good man. He works in the Boston area and in fifteen months has enough money to send for his family. He spends the rest of his life moving from job to job in New England, often living away from home, but he takes care of his own.

His eldest son goes to Holy Cross College, a gift of loyalty and love from his family much greater than the son could ever fully appreciate.

LONDON. 1869

Caveat

Daniel Joseph Kirwan is one of the best descriptive journalists in the world. His masterpiece is a set of articles for the *New York World* that describes London to the New York public. He can do crime stories that make readers shiver, but without the gore that would keep the newspaper from a proper sitting room; he can describe a brothel without using that word, and can give decent family men a sense of illicit excitement without making their wives upset. And he details the odd and ungainly without the pointing of the freak-show barker. He really understands his audience. Americans want to know about London, now 3 and ½ million people and rivalling the North as England's economic engine. Kirwan gives them everyday details of the lives of sewer-scroungers, Billingsgate fishwives, scarlet women in flash houses, successful courtesans, Jews in the used-rag trade, and the topographical confusion of men and women whose two pints daily of gin leave them circling towards their nightly doss like a blind gull seeking its nest.

Kirwan knows that most of his New York readers are "Americans," in the sense of being as parochial as the wide ocean can make them, but he has one special set of readers who, in their own way, are worldly: his compatriots of Irish background and every now and then he slips them a sentence, or even a full paragraph.

For: the Irish around the world are great ones for reading about each other, and they expect to hear that things are worse there (wherever "there" may be) than "here." And they want to learn that immoral as every far world is, the Irish people in it are not quite as lost as is the run of humanity.

So, the life of the costermongers – "peddlars" he explains – is detailed. They are up at the New Cut in Lambeth by four or five in the morning, buying game, whelks, nuts, ginger beer, anything to sell on their barrows. After a quick breakfast they're on the streets by 7:00, and they keep hawking until well after dark, sometimes to midnight, and then start all over again, a life of half-pennies and half-legalities. At most, police tell Kirwan, ten percent of the costermongers are married, though they cohabit like burrowing rodents. *A marriage certificate in a costermonger's den would, indeed be a curious and unusual relic, as would also the marriage ring.* Kirwan, having written those words, catches himself. *Mind, I am now speaking of the English costermonger, for with the Irish costermonger, both male and female, who are still lower in the social scale as far as the goods of the world go, it is different.* Kirwan assures New Yorkers that Irish costermongers are ever-welcoming to their priests, believe in the sanctity of marriage, do not have illegitimate children, and always have a few pennies to give to the priest to help those less fortunate than themselves.

Caveat Emptor.

LONDON. 1869

Eternal Verities

Since the time of Roman consuls in Gaul and the British Isles, some things have not changed and Daniel Joseph Kirwan understands this.

He has just visited the Carlisle Arms in Soho, a hideaway for hack journalists, illustrators and never-finish novelists. Now, he discovers *there is another resort of the higher class of writers, authors, and artists, in the neighbourhood of the theatres, and this place is known to those who frequent it as the Albion.*

A good place indeed. *At the Albion there is an excellent restaurant, and well-cooked viands and wines of the best quality may be obtained there at reasonable prices.*

Although, to be frank, the price is not all that important as the individuals who frequent it do not pay. *Choice little dinners, illuminated by wit and humour, are given here by journalists to each other.*

The term may have changed since Roman times, but not the fact: everyone who has any real wit is on expenses, and Mr. Kirwan in his turn, eats and treats there very often. He puts these down in his reports to New York as "investigative honoraria."

STAFFORD. 1870

School Leaving Certificate

Ben Tillet, rising ten years of age, leaves the elementary school in Stafford swathed in temporary glory.

Tillet, destined to become one of the century's greatest labour leaders, has been working full-time since age seven: first as a clay cutter for a brickmaker and later as a circus acrobat. An elder sister grabbed him from the circus and took him to be schooled.

Not for long. His accent, a mixture of Bristol-Irish and circus slang, irritated the school master immensely. Disciplined by having his knuckles cut by the teacher's ebony ruler, Ben became a berserker. He jumped at the teacher and knocked the unprepared tyrant flat. His comrades, following his example of resistance, pelted the teacher with ink pots and dart-sharp pens.

Ben Tillet completed his valediction by doing back-flips from one wrought-iron school desk to another.

LIVERPOOL. 1870

The Gentry

Styling themselves the Brothers of St. Mary's Conference of the Society of St. Vincent de Paul, the righteous males of Catholic Liverpool visit the homes of impoverished Irish families with the same impunity that a landlord's agent scrutinized a peasant's cabin in the Old Country. And that's why they're called "the gentry" by their petitioners; these dispensers of philanthropy to the neediest of the Liverpool Irish, those who huddle around St. Mary's Church, Highfield. "The gentry" are laymen, but they identify closely with the clergy, and they take the priest's suggestions as to who, and what sort, of person should be eligible for Catholic charity just as a private soldier would take an order from an officer.

These men mean well, mostly, but their invasion of a tenement – almost always that of a woman whose husband has levanted or is on a tramp for work or is a spendthrift drunk – is humiliating and inevitably produces nearly as much resentment as it does gratitude. In return for a chit that provides for shoes for a child, or a food ration, or a few shillings to keep the landlord at bay, they look around the packed dens of poverty, all but holding handkerchief-to-nose. And they demand answers to questions:
– where's your husband at, so?
– will you take work if it is offered?
– is it the drink that we detect upon your person?
– when were you last at mass?
– are your childer in the heretic schools? or are they receiving a good Catholic schooling?

Mothers break down in front of their children and sob out their need for food for the babbies; or they keep silent dignity until the black-coated men leave, and then call down curses upon the dirty-minded craw-thumpers who only want to see a female's misery and a little bit more if they can.

These men actually are lower-middle class at best and, distasteful as they are, they represent the future, the first step up for formerly-impoverished Irish immigrants in England. They have made it out of the worst poverty and they have not bolted: they are sticking with their fellow Catholics. They are proud, irritatingly so, of the way they are able to raise the moral standards and increase the social control of their own people.

What makes their closely-pared generosity bearable is that the best of them learn. They are given a direct look at the home conditions and daily problems of Irish immigrant women that the English social reformers rarely see, and that Irish revolutionaries openly disdain.

The best of them learn that these women's fight for simple respectability among the swill that surrounds them requires more character and courage than to go on a holy mission to some dark land.

LONDON. MARCH 1871

Resurgence

The resurrection of the Grogan family from their problems of 1798 is well in train.

A royal warrant is granted. Not as wine merchants, their first step back to high respectability, but better: as surveyor general of houses and buildings for the Duchy of Lancaster. That is, the Queen's estate agent.

This is a new generation of Grogans. Nicholas, of the illiterate wife, had done well in wines, and his ablest son, William, had started a Mayfair estate agency in 1849: the Irish peasantry may have been abandoning their land, but the English gentry were buying anything near Hyde Park, Green Park, St. James's Park and, like all good land, no more of it was being made.

William Grogan's big break was being engaged to sell the Carlton Gardens house of William Ewart Gladstone, now chancellor of the exchequer. Gladstone was doing a bit of profit-taking and was on the rise even faster than were the Grogans.

Like so many Victorian men of "thrust," – the term of the time – William Grogan wore out women. His wife bore thirteen children and died on Christmas Eve, 1868. Gladstone, now prime minister, sent condolences.

Five years later, Grogan, possessing his royal warrant and as much thrust as ever, is smitten by a woman twenty-two years his junior.

Their first child is given the Christian name of "Ewart." His godfather, who has just resigned as prime minister, attends the christening and gives the infant Ewart Grogan a silver mug, an extremely appropriate present.

DUBLIN. 1872

Parental Confusion

Irish parents are often confused by offspring who move to England. Those who take long journeys to New Worlds won't be back, though their remittances will, please God, and they can be expected to become Americans or Australians or whatever. The confusing ones are those who go to England. There is no general pattern. Some go forever, as if they had journeyed to Antarctica. Most, though, keep in touch, send money home, or, more often, come home with gifts, stay for a while and then return to England. And they bring along grand-children who act like little English gits, with fast new words and clever attitudes, and yet say that they don't like the English. It's con-fusing indeed for the old people.

The *Nation*, a Dublin weekly that attempts to revive the glories of the 1840s, sends a reporter, Hugh Heinrick, to England to survey and explain these Irish in England to their parents in Ireland. Heinrick ends up as confused as when he started, but that does not keep him from writing sixteen articles, notable both for their insight and con-tradictory character, a possible sign of accuracy.

Liverpool seems to him to be where the Irish have done the best. *Indeed, everything considered, the Irish people in Liverpool have attained to a degree of prosperity and power eminently creditable to their industry and force of character* … He has a nice turn of phrase: *In nine cases out of ten, even the educated Irishman on coming here had to undergo a novici-ate of toil* – there, the folks in Ireland will understand that lapidary lark in the clear air – *noviciate of toil before entering on the comparative ease of superior employment* … Heinrick makes no attempt to explain why Liverpool, once hell for the Irish, is now a good place. He misses the obvious point that the way to make any ethnic group rise is simple: reduce the number of new recruits and that's what has happened in Liverpool. By the mid 1850s new migration from Ire-land was down to 5,000 or so a year; because the Liverpool econ-omy was on a gradual ramp downward (dropping palm oil prices, the American Civil War, etc.), and most new Irish migrants passed through Liverpool inland and increasingly moved south. So of course the Liverpool Irish look comparatively good. They now were mostly second generation and soon the third and fourth generation would be dominant and these people had an employment profile that was not much different from the general English population, save at the very top.

But are they still Irish? Heinrick worries, as do their relatives in Ireland. Yes and no is the answer. He is worried about the *Tablet*, official organ of the Catholic church in England, for it tries *to con-vince us that we ought to forget differences of nationality and only re-member that we are English Catholics*. He reassures their relatives that their children in England will never be weaned from their Irish ways or acknowledge themselves to be English. That is, he bets against Holy Mother Church's turning them into English Catholics.

London, in contrast to Liverpool, is a deep worry. It's now the chief destination of young Irish workers. Heinrick understands London a little. He realizes that, despite its size, it still is a series of distinct villages, increasingly sprawling into each other, and that the Irish are not found in any single self-protective enclave. Yes, in Whitechapel and Bethnal Green there are big pools of the very poor, but most live among the everyday English and that, parents of Ireland, is the trouble. *Our people are in every moral attribute infinitely superior to the race among whom their lot is cast ... but poverty, more than any other social cause tends to the moral degradation of the Irish people in the English towns, and particularly in London.* There are perhaps a quarter of a million Irish persons in London. The new emigrant, *he comes poor, he has to settle amongst the poor of the English towns – that is, amongst the most vicious of the worst classes in English society – where his generous and impressionable nature too readily assumes the mask and manner of his surroundings.*

That explains things pretty clearly: London vice conquers Irish virtue.

In case, however, they haven't heard the pure Christian narrative lately, the one where deicide triumphs, Hugh Heinrick reminds the parents of Ireland that real vice emanates from the Hebrews – in this case the Jews of Spitalfields and Whitechapel are *the chief employers of the unsophisticated Irish girl when she arrives in London. She is strong and willing, goes for low wages, and not over fastidious in matters of food and accommodation, and hence she becomes the prey of the mercenary and immoral classes ... The virtuous Irish girl is ruined. She is degraded in her own estimation, and sinks to lower depths still, till, in the end, the bright and blooming Irish girl who left her native village pure as the breeze on the heather of her native hills, with the benediction of the old priest who counselled and guided her from childhood on her head, and the fond wishes of generous friends and devoted parents following her in the land of the stranger, sinks broken-hearted and lost beneath the burden of her sin.*

Apparently, none of this would have happened if those Jewish employers who gave the girls their first job had put out a sign saying No Irish Need Apply.

LONDON. 1876

A Good Irish Boy

For this constantly descending Anglo-Irish family the 1870s were an especially hard time even though they found the Great Depression of the 1870s more galling than depressing. George Bernard Shaw was raised from age three onwards in a *ménage à trois* that included his drunken legal father, his possible biological father (a Catholic singing teacher named Lee) and his musically gifted mother. She had the emotional strength of a matron in a cavalry barracks.

With a nice sense of timing – it was the twenty-first anniversary of her marriage – Shaw's mother left for London to teach singing. George was seventeen and stayed in Dublin with his stocious father. Having had a job-trot education that ended at age sixteen – acquired at the Wesleyan Connexion School and, briefly, in a Catholic institution – he was ashamed for the remainder of life of his lack of proper schooling. Thus, he became one of the world's massive intellectual snobs.

For four years he worked in an estate agent's office, first as a junior clerk and errand boy and then as the firm's cashier. No future.

Realizing that he needed help, he did what every good Irish boy should do and turned to his mother. He wrote an inveigling letter to her, pleaded love and need in equal quantities. She permitted him to move into her London home, a good address in Kensington.

ENGLAND. 1880–1920

Bruderbund

Big numbers squash small realities.
So, look at the following list:
Journalists
Lawyers
Medical doctors
Church of England rectors
Catholic priests
Police

What do they have in common? All right, it's easy enough.

Each of them is part of a worldwide network, one that is strongest between Ireland and England, but is resilient throughout the diaspora.

Each profession places men, and a very few women, from Ireland in their specific professions all over the world. It's a pattern lost in the big numbers of family migration, in the chains of movement from one region to some favourite sector of a New World and, especially, in the mass swirl of bodies from Ireland to England. But take the directories of the professions (the concept of profession is only firmly established in the latter part of Victoria's reign) and you'll find that a filigree of professional chain migration exists: tiny, as compared to the mass Irish exodus, but, like a thin necklace of white gold among clumps of gaudy beads. These are the working aristocracy of the Irish diaspora.

Crockford's clerical directory, lists of the Royal College of Surgeons of Ireland, the Law Registry, alumni directories of TCD and of the Queen's Colleges, table-books of the Irish Inns of Court, duty registers of the RIC, the annual register of the Catholic Church, old mastheads from Irish newspapers, the clerkship registers of Quantity Surveyors and of Chartered Accountants, all show the same thing: that one-quarter to two-thirds of the young professionals trained in Ireland take their skills outside of Ireland, to the imperial civil service, to North America, and most often to England.

This is not a Freemasonry, where one brother takes care of another, but it is a *bruderbund* of information and of shared self-interest: it is in the interest of each to have Irish qualifications (or at least Irish experience) recognized as widely as possible. Hence, they support each other collectively even though they may dislike each other personally.

In the form of skilled professionals, Ireland is exporting its intellectual capital. When this occurs between Ireland and England, it is a case of one of the poorest nations in Europe sending capital to the richest, an arrangement that on the surface seems preposterous. Economists, however, explain that the poor nation's supporting the rich in such a matter is a natural occurrence and will continue indefinitely, unless someone interferes with the Laws of Economics.

WESTMINSTER. APRIL 1883

Textual Analysis

Sir William Harcourt, home secretary, and William Ewart Gladstone, prime minister, sat opposite each other at a large mahogany table, heads bowed. Each was reading a text, and both were experienced hands at textual analysis: Harcourt's commentaries had been a staple of the *Saturday Review* and he was an expert on international law. Gladstone was an exegete of biblical and classical texts.

Both men are appalled at today's text.

"The Explosives Act, 1875."

It defines an English liberty very liberally: all citizens have the right to apply for a licence to hold up to two hundredweight of gunpowder, five hundredweight of explosives and two hundredweight of fireworks. Or, if they prefer, up to sixty pounds of mixed explosives, such as dynamite and nitroglycerine. And the privilege is presumptive: the local authorities have no right to refuse a licence, even to a convicted felon.

"Dear God," said Harcourt, looking up.

"Dear me," said Gladstone, looking down.

Their attention had been drawn to the Explosives Act because they had recently learned that six Irish emigrants to the USA had come to England and acquired over 400 pounds of nitroglycerine in its most unstable form. Under the canny directorship of Dr. Thomas Gallagher, this was a joint operation of the U.S.'s Clann na Gael and the Irish Republican Brotherhood. The bombers had collected the nitro in Birmingham and then, in lots of eighty to two hundred pounds had moved it to London. The task was more than a little dangerous and was made more so by the team's being short of stout rubber bags to hold the thick, oily liquid. One part of the shipment had to be brought along in rubber wading stockings used by fly fishermen. The warriors had easily enough explosives to level a wing of the houses of parliament, their first choice, but were willing to settle for easier targets nearby.

"We can be thankful, Harcourt, for the RIC. Though it seems strange to have Irish police seconded to England."

"A temporary expedient, I promise you."

On the fifth of April, in a total of only one and a half-hours, the House of Commons unanimously passes Harcourt's new Explosives Bill,

and the Lords quickly follows. It's now two to fourteen years for ille-
gally possessing explosives, fifteen pounds is the personal limit for
legal items, and local authorities now can say "no."

Thus ended the reading: and thus was the Irish-Americans' "Dynamite War" of the 1870s and 1880s contained.

PARIS. FEBRUARY 1884

The Word

Terror as a means to a religious, political or ideological goal has only
one articulated justification, and it stays the same no matter what language expresses it.

The Chester Castle mastermind, American-Irish Captain John Mc-
Cafferty, out of prison on amnesty, continues his campaign. His methods are now more ruthless.

He is the untraceable "No. 1" who puts together The Invincibles.
Their hacking to death of T.H. Burke and Lord Frederick Cavendish
in the Phoenix Park in May 1882 was intended to be the start of a program of political assassinations in Ireland and England. They would
bleed the enemy like a butcher sticks a squealing pig. Cut short after
the Invincibles' first mission leads to his operatives being caught, Mc-
Cafferty coolly slides away, and leaves a bogus "No. 1" in his place.
As far as the authorities are concerned, McCafferty no longer exists.

Yet, in Paris, planning and raising funds, he gives an interview to
The Irishman.

"Terrorism," McCafferty declares, "*is the lawful weapon of the weak
against the strong.*"

THE LONDON-DUBLIN COACH. JUNE 1885

Three Men in a Tub (1)

Three gentlemen share a first class carriage. Their conversation is
stilted. Only one of them, Charles Stewart Parnell, knows exactly
what is going on. T.P. O'Connor, MP for Galway City, has no idea, but

does not mind, for he has blind faith in Parnell and, in any case, is one of God's natural optimists. The third, Captain William O'Shea, wants nothing more than to be a Liberal member of parliament and, failing that, some kind of Irish nationalist member. He has an air of knowing everything, even the silent thoughts of Parnell.

As the train approaches one of its platform stops, Captain O'Shea points out a particularly pretty girl and says drily, "They're a much overrated pleasure, you know."

Parnell makes no reply.

Later in the journey, Parnell and O'Connor talk politics. Parnell has decided that O'Connor, who has been serving as Home Rule's missionary to the Irish in England – he is president of the National League of Great Britain and remains so for forty years – will contest the Liverpool South seat in the upcoming general election. "It's even safer than my seat," he has told O'Connor with complete accuracy. Liverpool South is an island of first and second generation Irish Catholics in Liverpool's Orange sea and, in the actual event, returns T.P. O'Connor from 1885 until his death, past age eighty, in 1929: that is, the seat was so safe that he held it long after Home Rule itself was dead.

That was future. Now, willing to aid Parnell in any way, O'Connor gives his best attention to his monarch: "Do you think the Captain has a chance of taking one of the other Liverpool seats?" Parnell asks O'Connor with one of his rare smiles.

"No. Not a hope." O'Connor is emphatic. He knows the Liverpool Irish and they won't wear an officer, especially one who openly despises them.

Thus O'Connor, innocent of Parnell's rich personal life, is surprised when in the middle of the 1885 campaign, Parnell arrives in Liverpool and announces that Captain O'Shea will be the Irish nationalist candidate for Liverpool Exchange. He loses by fifty-five votes to the conservative candidate, and in the general election that quickly follows in 1886, Parnell has no choice but to put O'Shea into the Galway City seat now vacated by T. P. O'Connor. His caucus can barely stomach this manoeuvre, but no one dares ask Parnell the reason for it.

T.P. O'Connor goes to his grave believing that if Captain O'Shea would have received a miserable fifty-six more votes in Liverpool Exchange in 1885, then all subsequent Irish history would have been different: that Parnell would not have been unmasked as an adulterer and Gladstone would have carried Home Rule. No partition, no violence, no civil war.

THE UNITED KINGDOM. 1885–86

Interior Decoration

When William Ewart Gladstone embraced the cause of Home Rule for Ireland, he not only broke apart the Liberal Party, but reoriented the decoration of peasant cottages in Ireland and Irish Catholic working class lodgings in Great Britain.

Now, to the fading mezzotint of Daniel O'Connell, fixed on one wall, was added a lithograph of the English prime minister. In places where the Devotional Revolution had done its work, this new addition often led to late-night debates. Newly re-Catholicized Irish families were not sure whether the print of the Sacred Heart of Jesus, the equivalent of "Priest-Approved Home," should be moved to make space for the One Decent Man in all England. And if they did not move it, was it against the Faith to have Gladstone, a Protestant, on the same wall as the Sacred Heart?

The court of St. James required no such physical refurbishing. Queen Victoria and her courtiers added Gladstone to their list of gargoyles that should be covered with black velvet and not viewed by polite persons. The leading English intellectuals of the age, always willing to add a new specimen to their personal bestiaries, declared Gladstone to be a lunatic or, worse, a demon incarnate: Matthew Arnold, Alfred Lord Tennyson, dozens of others, who really should have known better.

WESTMINSTER. 1887

Three Men in a Tub (2)

When the *Times* of London publishes its libellous and wildly inaccurate charges that Charles Stewart Parnell was in an approving correspondence with a band of Irish assassins, the text was a projective test: one's immediate reactions to the letter produced by the gutter-boy Richard Pigott told who you were and what you were made of.

T.P. O'Connor had one look at the text and knew it was a forgery. Mostly this was because he was so loyal that no other conclusion was possible. But more: he knew that Parnell was costive to the point of paranoia with his own signature and would never sign a letter to a murder gang. O'Connor, more than most members of the Home Rule party, had spent long hours in Parnell's company, sometimes in working evenings, other times over a chop and a pint of white wine. Parnell liked O'Connor. He was easy company, had no ambitions to high office and, being based in Liverpool, was outside the gossip circle of most Irish MPs. What O'Connor had observed when sitting across from Parnell in the Members' Library was that his leader occasionally was to be seen signing the very top line of a piece of blank paper and placing it in an envelope. "That is for an autograph hunter," he once explained. Parnell gave no one a chance to insert anything over his name.

Captain William O'Shea, MP was called to serve as a witness before a three-judge commission on Parnellism and Crime. He was the picture of straightforward officerdom. When shown the damning letter ascribed to Parnell, he modestly pointed out that he was no expert on handwriting. Honest chap that. But would he please hazard an opinion? O'Shea looked at the paper for a long time and shifted it about so that the light would fall on it fully. Then he pronounced: he had seen a lot of Parnell's signatures and this certainly seemed to him to be genuine.

Charles Stewart Parnell, as always, acted exceedingly strangely. He took to hanging about a public house near Leicester Square. This was a cave for a band of Fenians whom Parnell believed wanted him brought down and he thought O'Shea was consorting with them. So, muffled up like a Bedouin in a sand storm, he stood in doorways halfway through the night, watching for the hated O'Shea. Sometimes his private secretary spelled him, but mostly he watched for himself. Long hours alone, accompanied by demons that did not know even their own names.

LONDON. 12 AUGUST 1889

Hybrid Vigour

Two dockers knock at the door of Ben Tillet's house. Members of a tiny union, the Tea Operatives, of which Tillet is steward, they have been working on London's South Docks and are being cheated. It's a matter of the "plus," a bonus that is paid if a given cargo is off-loaded in less than a standard time. Sometimes this "plus" runs as high as 40 percent of a casual labourer's pay, so missing it hurts. Tillet, who still has the confidence and dexterity of the ten-year-old acrobat who had flattened his oppressive schoolmaster, decides that he can close down the entire Thames.

Ben Tillet is everything the middle class abhors. Cheeky, dapper, self-educated (naval and merchant marine service had taught him literacy and he was an omnivorous reader) and, worst of all, a believer in "mixing." In the sense, certainly, of mixing-it-up in a brawl, but in a second sense that is totally un-Victorian. That is, Catholic priests, Anglican parsons, rabbis, Dissenting clergy all preach against the mixing of people of one religious sort with another. Mixed education and mixed marriages are horrors to be avoided. Social arbiters set down lines of class differentiation and one does not mix outside one's own class. Culturally, lines of demarcation are tight: Hebraism and Hellenism are ruled to be immutable categories, national languages something to be preserved from mixing with nasty foreign words. Political nationalism, the smallpox of the last thirty years of the Victorian era, spreads from the Continent and the British Isles. Europeans carve up Africa into European-defined satrapies. That's the spirit of the times.

Using his small union as a lever, Ben Tillet enlists the Amalgamated Society of Dock Companies' Servants and General Labourers. They had convinced the Stevedores, who have an Irish-descended secretary at their head, to march under his flag. Already that mixes classes of labourers, those with regular daily jobs and the casual men who queue up every morning and every afternoon for the hope of a day or half-day of heavy lifting in cramped and filthy conditions. Tillet closes down the South Docks, an achievement in itself but, more impressive, by the third day of the strike he has pickets on a front of fifty miles. Fifty miles. The port of London was shut.

Part of the secret of his success is to use Irish labourers, who are the least secure of the casual labourers, as the colporteurs of the strike, the carriers of the banner and the cadgers with the collection boxes for relief of strikers' families. This is a revolution, as compared to the old Manchester system, where Irish workers were used to break English strikes. Here Tillet mixes the Irish, first and second generation, and the English and, as in his own personal make-up, hybrid vigour is the result. Bonding the casual and the regular labourers, the English and the Irish, into one social class action is new: new in that, though it has been tried before, this is the first real success and, indeed, the most important expression of working class unity until the General Strike of 1926.

Cranes, gantries, and jibs ceased to move. They bowed over, as if broken in spirit. A minimum of 16,000 pickets were on duty at any one time. The wharf firms and dock owners buckled: 6d as a minimum hourly wage and no man was to be employed for less than four hours a day.

Not a revolution, perhaps, but the replacement of dozens of little unions with a single port organization of 18,000 workers was something as feared by bishops as by capitalists: they all feared the mixing, and then the bonding of persons whom they preferred to control as separate and isolated particulants.

LONDON. 1898

Affirmative Action

He should be a grumblesome, self-pitying old man.

Approaching age seventy he is nearly blind, is broken physically, and has little to think about other than the memories of an Irish immigrant who arrived at Euston Station, London, in 1852 and made his way through a life that he found infinitely fascinating, and challenging, and not unpleasant. He refuses to be a victim.

Instead, Justin McCarthy, who had begun his career as a journalist covering the 1848 treason trials of William Smith O'Brien and Thomas Meagher for the *Cork Examiner*, remembers in the gloaming of his increasing blindness the amazing people he has met and the pleasure engaging with them has given him. John Bright. Richard Cobden. George Eliot. Lord Randolph Churchill. Cardinal Manning. Not a bad run for a lower middle class, largely self-taught Irish lad.

Charles Stewart Parnell he remembers with pain, but not hate. Parnell had chosen him, now an English journalist, to sit for Louth in 1879 and had made him vice-chairman of the Irish nationalist party. He revered Parnell, but had headed the anti-Parnellite party after the adultery scandal.

The man he knew well and almost worshipped was William Ewart Gladstone. Integrity. Devotion to Irish justice. Moral purity, apparently. If only Parnell had possessed these traits in equal abundance.

Justin McCarthy looks back with his Tiresias-becoming eyes and summarizes his life in England. No drama. Neither his Catholic religion nor his Irish background have been leaden weights, impeding his progress.

"I may say," he dictated to his secretary, "that I had on my first visit no friends in London who could be of much use to me in my attempts at a literary career." He pauses, as much because he has emphysema as because he is reflecting. "And I was handicapped, in the opinion of many of my friends at home, by the fact that I was a Catholic by religion and an ardent Irish nationalist in politics."

Here he stops, silent, for so long that it make his secretary shift uncomfortably. Then, in his House of Commons voice, Justin McCarthy declares, "1 never found either of these conditions to interfere in the slightest degree with my way in journalism or in literature here in England."

NEARLY NORMAL.
AUSTRALIA
1845–1900

Nearly Normal

The effects of Ireland's Great Famine of 1845–48 barely reached Australian shores. The tide of humanity that flooded into Great Britain and North America reached the Antipodean colonies as a mild ripple: Australia was just too far and too expensive to be a place of relief.

Only one notable band of Famine refugees fetched up in Australia: shiploads of "workhouse orphan girls," paid for by governmental authorities. Often as not, they were not orphans in the technical sense, but rather children deserted by their parents. This, in the Famine years was frequently a merciful, not a cruel, act: if the parents could not provide for them, leaving the children with the poor law guardians at least kept them alive. Eventually 4,175 girls 14-18 years of age were landed in the three main cities of the Australian colonies (and five dozen somehow ended up in South Africa). These were not the cream of Irish society. At best they had lived a brutal existence, alternating between extreme physical deprivation when living outside the workhouses and extreme social deprivation within. Some were frauds: lunatics, whores, whom the parishes loaded onto this London-created scheme (the one unalloyed positive achievement of Sir Charles Trevelyan, assistant secretary of the treasury), but most were decent girls, willing to work hard if told clearly what to do. Mostly, they were Roman Catholics, and that brought out the bigotry in the Australian middle class, always looking for someone to look down upon.

As they came down the gangplanks in Sydney, Melbourne, Adelaide, the girls made a curious impression. They were clothed in dresses of drab fulled cloth, but wore tartan shawls and straw hats, too warm for the climate, but respectable garb, undeniably. Each carried a stout wooden lock-box. This chest contained petticoats, stockings, an extra pair of shoes, two gowns and a Bible and a prayer book or missal. Standard-issue. The chests were awkward, their heavy rope handles being fixed to each end, so that the girls came off the ships with the rolling gait and extended arms of a deliveryman carrying a parcel one size too big for his person. Both at embarkation at Cork (or Plymouth for the Dublin girls) and in their new world the girls struck most observers as being unusually shaped: short, stout for their age, waistless creatures with wide shoulders and, apparently, unusual physical strength.

These mostly were the great-stout-Irish-girls of musical legend. At first most of them were tried as indoor servants, but they left a lot to be desired: they came out of the Famine workhouse, not a Swiss boarding school. Eventually, most of them married men of Irish background and became what they could not become in Ireland: spouses of men who acquired land, farmed, or ranched, or were stockmen. This New World, Australia, provided Irish women and men the chance to continue a rural life, to maintain, in an altered but basically similar form, the life of the countryside.

At this same moment, Australia was becoming normal: transportation to New South Wales (including the district that later became Victoria) ceased in 1840; to Norfolk Island in the mid 1840s; to Van Diemen's Land in 1853 and to Western Australia in 1868. By mid-nineteenth century, the bulk of the population was non-penal in origin and a massive influx, keyed by a gold rush, was soon to begin four decades of heavy migration from the British Isles. Crucially, about 80 percent of the migrants were "assisted" in some way: meaning that they were recruited and selected by representatives of the Australian colonies and their travel was subsidized. They were not a gentry elite, but the selection process meant that the least-able were excluded.

Big winners: the Irish generally and Irish women in particular. Women make up half of Irish emigration in the second half of the nineteenth century, much more than for the Scots or the English. Roughly 200,000 Irish migrate to the Australian colonies in these years. It's women who understand the system best: about one-half of the Irish men were "assisted," but 90 percent of the Irish women were.

And it's women who give the Irish as an ethnic group an advantage over others: for there are enough women to allow continuation of the Irish family in a New World. And all the evidence shows that women are most responsible for keeping chain migration going: bringing over sisters, brothers, informing them of Australian opportunities and in letters home telling them how the various colonial assistance schemes operate.

Timing is perfect: just as Australian society goes over the big watershed – from a culture dominated by a penal mentality to a robust self-confidence – the Irish flood in, led by women.

Actually, the regiment of stout workhouse girls of 1848–50 was the unlikely advance guard of a conquering force.

EN ROUTE TO VAN DIEMEN'S LAND. JULY-OCTOBER 1849

Singing Against the Beat

The *Swift* was a man-of-war, a full-sailed, fast-moving vessel of the sort the four state prisoners deserved. Quality for the Quality, so they joked.

Four men, sentenced to be hanged, drawn and quartered for high treason, but then reprieved and sent to Van Diemen's Land, not as ordinary criminals but as state prisoners: William Smith O'Brien, Thomas Francis Meagher, Terence Bellew MacManus, and Patrick Denis O'Donoghue. These men, and another eight who will join them by other routes of punishment, have been Young Irelanders, romantic nationalists in one of Europe's most politically romantic eras. In the lubricious days of the 1848 French Revolution, they had attempted a revolution of their own.

Though they had been in tune with European ideas, they are completely out of phase with the Australian colonies. None of the dozen men transported in the late 1840s intends to have a life or a career in Australia, and only one actually does. Most of them plan on leaving Australia as soon as possible. Dramatic escape is their preferred method, for they all intend continuing careers as heroes, either in the USA or Ireland.

Already in Ireland and the USA the "1848 Exiles" (their name in public print) are considered martyrs, for they are going to Van Diemen's Land, that harsh purgatory of a prison. And as political prisoners.

The shipboard regimen, though, is not that of early Irish convicts. The four state prisoners share a common drawing room, roughly twelve feet by twelve feet. And off this common room they each have a private cabin with a berth, lockers for their personal items (such as MacManus's backgammon set and his battery of fishing gear). After a bit of barracking of the *Swift*'s captain (they are very good at the "now-see-here-my-good-man" business), they receive a daily meat meal and two glasses of wine with it. William Smith O'Brien, who has long prided himself on his ability to be indifferent to creature comforts, swears to make-do and he does: for the first time in his life he makes his own bed.

Conversation is good on the voyage, for these are educated men. Smith-O'Brien, the second son of Sir Edward O'Brien, and the holder of an estate in his own right, was educated at Harrow and Trinity College, Cambridge. The elder statesman and sometime leader of the group, he is forty-five years old. He had entered the pre-1832 unreformed parliament at the age of twenty-five and has had dinner with almost every powerful liberal in London. He has loads of entertaining stories. Thomas Francis Meagher is only twenty-five and he is voluble. The Jesuits at Clongowes Wood and at Stonyhurst College, and the benchers at the Dublin Inns of Court have made him outspoken beyond his years. He is proud to be known as "Meagher of the Sword," for a speech he made in 1846 that attacked Daniel O'Connell's peaceful tactics. Terence Bellew MacManus spent his youth in Ireland and then became a successful Liverpool businessman, earning £1,000 annually. And Patrick O'Donoghue was a Dublin law clerk, slightly less educated than the others, and the only one who does not have sufficient independent financial resources to make his exile comfortable.

The four martyrs talk about their colleagues. Two especially. One, who was arrested early, before the revolution was actually attempted and who is on his way to Van Diemen's Land by way of Bermuda: John Mitchel, a physical-force firebrand who had broken with them and sought a full-scale peasants' rising, with *jacquerie* and all the bloodshed beloved by the late Jacobins. They'll see him soon and they hope that he has calmed down. And they discuss another ally who also was arrested early, but managed to survive five rigged state trials: Charles Gavan Duffy, who had been defended by Isaac Butt, the best lawyer of his time. Will Duffy stay with the cause?

Even on the longest evenings, the four exiles avoid one big topic, but it sits in the corner of the room, a hard-eyed demon whom they cannot quite obscure by their heavy pipe smoking. It is the question: why were we not hanged? Why were we made state prisoners and sent away in a gilded cage? Each of them knows the reason: their Rising had been so ridiculously ill-planned and unsuccessful – the battle of Widow McCormack's Cabbage Patch, near Ballingary, Co. Tipperary – that no London government could put them to death for high treason. Forty ill-trained police had defeated them.

As they sat and smoked of an evening, they remembered, perhaps with pride, that William Smith O'Brien had insisted on shaking hands with each of the policemen to whom he surrendered. A real Irish gentleman.

EN ROUTE, BERMUDA TO CAPE TOWN.
11 SEPTEMBER 1849

A Revolutionary Agrees
with the Protestant Archbishop

The only thing that John Mitchel and Archbishop Richard Whately had in common was that both of them understood transportation to be a failure and for the same reason. Other than that, they were both Protestants (Unitarian and Anglican, respectively), but that was no bond. One was an extreme physical-force radical, the other the sort of enemy that revolutionaries hated even more than they did conservatives: a compassionate liberal.

John Mitchel passes the endless hours between Bermuda and South Africa by writing furiously in his "Jail Journal." Mostly he is thoroughly furious, for not only did the Irish peasantry not follow the detailed plans for a guerilla uprising that he had published weekly in the *United Irishman*, but when he came to the dock, his confident belief that his corrupt trial would lead to an immediate national rising was dashed. National silence, even from his former Young Ireland colleagues, was the only reaction. Mitchel, an extremely talented writer in the florid Victorian mode, fills his Jail Journal with denigration of all of his and of Ireland's enemies and, more deliciously, of all his friends.

Occasionally, he waxes reflective:

But if this transportation turns out to be no punishment at all to the criminal population generally, it is, on the contrary (and partly for that very reason) a far too severe punishment – far worse than the cruellest death – to the unhardened and casual delinquents, who have sometimes, for one moment of mad passion and sore temptation to dree this rueful doom. No punishment but a shure and comfortable establishment for all the tribe of professed rascaldom – but utter, final shipwreck of soul and body to the poor wanderer who might be taken by the hand and led from the devil's path, if only the laws were made and administered by any others than the devil's servants.

Doubtlessly Archbishop Whately would have shuddered at that last line, but the main point is agreed – transportation is too beneficial to the truly criminal and too hard on everyone else. Mitchel's Jail Journal is later published in the USA in 1854 as a newspaper series. Then it was reprinted as a book. It has never since been out of print.

VAN DIEMEN'S LAND. NOVEMBER 1849

The Prisoner's Regimen

Thomas Meagher – "Meagher of the Sword" – begins his punishment in Van Diemen's Land. He is delivered from the guard boat to a coach that takes him from Hobart to Campbell Town. It is just a large village, and he has it mastered in twenty minutes. He decides to stay in the main hotel, that of a Mrs. Kierney whose establishment is adorned with pictures of Daniel O'Connell, Brian Boru and other Irish national heroes. Meagher briefly projects his own portrait into the phalanx of heroes, and then decides, no, he deserves better than this.

Meagher cannot take the tedium of Campbell Town, so after three days he hires a gig and goes off to Ross. This hamlet – forty houses – is so small that it affords him privacy. He tries to imagine that he is on a spiritual retreat. He settles into a hotel owned by a devout Wesleyan couple.

Life is very quiet indeed, and although the penal district he is confined to is over 500 square miles in extent, he finds it confining. Thomas Meagher concludes that the real purpose of his being transported is to bore him to death.

PITCAIRN ISLAND. JANUARY 1850

A Real Missionary

Although technically Christmas was past on the western calendar, Hugh Francis Carleton decides that the locals should have the pleasure of celebrating Orthodox Christmas as well. They clearly need cheering up; they are almost sepulchrally pale of skin and hatchet-faced, and seem to be remembering something they can't quite articulate. Some of them seem malnourished.

Carleton, the son of a large landowner in Cork and Tipperary, had taken up world travelling as his business, and dabbling in business as his hobby. But his real love in life was a passion that had gripped him during his formative years at Eton and Trinity College, Cambridge: he was besotted with choral music.

So, instead of fretting about having been blown off course on his way to trade in San Francisco, he takes this visit to Pitcairn as an opportunity. He passes the time by teaching the islanders part-singing and they celebrate a magnificent Orthodox Christmas.

This alleviates the islanders' depression for a time, but in 1856, about 200 islanders, the entire population, are transferred of their own free will to Norfolk Island, the former location of the harshest of all of the penal colonies.

HOBART, VAN DIEMEN'S LAND. APRIL 1850

Modesty Forbids

To my utter amazement. I had a letter today from Patrick O'Donoghue, who has been permitted to live in the city of Hobart ... John Mitchel is writing furiously in his journal. He is in Hobart himself, as a prisoner under very loose supervision. ... *informing me that he has established a newspaper called the "Irish Exile"* ... This is a good thing for O'Donoghue, as he is the only one of the leading prisoners of '48 who does not have independent means and cannot live comfortably in exile. ... *Herein is a marvelous thing. How happens it that the convict authorities permit him to conduct a paper at all? Or what would be the use of such a publication here, even if he were competent to manage it? The thing is a hideous absurdity altogether* ...

Mitchel imagines that he is looking into a mirror and that he is able to blush. ... *The "Irish Exile" is bepuffing me now most outrageously. God preserve me from organs of opinion! Have I sailed round the terraqueous globe, and dropped in here in a cove of the far South Pacific, to find an 'able editor' mounted stiltwise upon phrases tall, and blowing deliberate puffs in my face? Gladly I would bare my brow to all the tornadoes and "ouragans" of the West Indies, to the black-squalls of the tropics, to the heavy gales of the British Channel and the typhoons of the China Seas, rather than to the flattering flatulence of these mephitic airs.*

VAN DIEMEN'S LAND. 6 NOVEMBER 1850

A Question of Values

Gentleman to a fault, William Smith O'Brien at first refuses a ticket-of-leave because one of the conditions is that he not try to escape.

And it is his knightly duty to attempt escape. The other prisoners of '48 take the ticket. O'Brien is sent to Maria Island, off the coast of Van Diemen's Land. He lives in a cottage no larger than that of a fifteen-acre farmer at home in Ireland. Not only has he to make his own bed (he has become quite adept at that) but to wash his own dishes. His shoes and boots are cleaned for him by a servant only once a week.

After two months of near-solitary exile, he is allowed to mix with the superintendent of the small island and his family. He is observed by police constables (who keep watch on him through telescopes) dallying beneath the skirts of the thirteen year-old daughter of the superintendent. He denies everything, but apologizes chivalrously.

Then he tries escape, unsuccessfully and equally chivalrously. Placed in tight supervision at Port Arthur, he still is given his own cottage and freedom to garden and to order his days as he pleases. He complains a lot, not chivalrously.

John Mitchel, now living in the middle of Van Diemen's Land, does not agree with William Smith O'Brien that here a gentleman cannot live on only £80 a year.

Mitchel's wife and children have joined him and the air is good, he finds.

The notion of gentlemanhood has always seemed rather vague to me. And it has grown more confused than ever to me since I came to this place, but I find that I can live as I please, take as much as I like of the best society of the place, ride a good horse, and occasionally (in conjunction with Meagher, Martin etc) see some little company at the Lakes – and all for £80.

William Smith O'Brien changes his mind and applies for a ticket-of-leave and late in November 1850 it is granted. Thus is honour served.

PORT PHILLIP DISTRICT, NSW. 11 NOVEMBER 1850

Patriotic Messages

He cannot not help appearing like a caricature of one of the Irish wee folk and, frankly, he does not mind. Edmund Finn, the best newspaper reporter in his corner of New South Wales, is a tiny pilgarlic of a man, barely 5 feet in height. Quick-witted, slightly malicious, unexpectedly erudite, given to speaking in Latin or in Irish or, with drink taken, both. He is one of the founders of the St. Patrick's Society of Port Phillip and as the longtime general reporter on the *Port Phillip*

Herald, he knows where all the bodies are buried, socially speaking.

Glorious News! Separation at Last! We lose not a single moment in communicating to the public the soul-stirring intelligence that Separation has come at last!!!

Finn, from Tipperary, shares the radical streak of so many Tipperary emigrants and, like most of them, he is of more-than-one-mind when it comes to the practical world. So, his reaction to the intelligence that he discovers in one of the papers-from-London is energetic, but confused, for the colonial Port Phillip District and his old home, Tipperary, are the same to him, but different, of course.

The long-oppressed, long-buffetted Port Phillip is at length an Independent Colony, gifted with the Royal Name of Victoria, and endowed with a flourishing revenue and almost inexhaustible resources.

Separation, yes, but scarcely republicanism, or even colonial nationalism.

Colonists, 'Now is the day and now is the hour!' For this act of justice to Port Phillip and every other good gift, may God bless the Queen.

CALIFORNIA AND VICTORIA. JUNE 1851

Opposite Directions

Terence Bellew MacManus, former Liverpool businessman and forever Young Irelander, arrives in San Francisco on the fifth of June 1851. He is the first of the martyrs of 1848 to escape and he has done so without violating honour: his ticket-of leave had been revoked by the authorities for his roving about Van Diemen's Land too freely. No violence was involved: he did a successful runner and is welcomed in San Francisco by an Irish-American reception committee that includes the city's mayor, a senator, and every Irish person with money, quite a few in the era of gold.

For a time MacManus is a local California hero. Dinners are held in his honour, with plenty of Ireland-forever speeches, and a local doss house, featuring a fifty-bed communal loft, is named "The Mac-Manus Rest."

Almost simultaneously, gold is discovered in New South Wales and Victoria. Americans, especially California-experienced miners, stream to Australia. Britons and Irish appear in droves a year or so later: most of the Irish are provided with assisted passages by the colonial governments. They all are preceded by Australians, of course, and an especially large contingent from Van Diemen's Land. Most of these are emancipists, but many are ticket-of-leave men whose sentences are not yet served-out. The newly-separated colony of Victoria receives so many of these former-felons that it passes a law fining ships' captains who carry any ex-convict from Van Diemen's Land to Victoria unless the passenger has an absolute free pardon. Magistrates or police meet incoming ships.

Despite his business experience in Liverpool, England, Terence MacManus finds it hard to make a living. He tries several businesses and ranching, with indifferent results. Success in the American republic is a slippery eel indeed.

Melbourne, within a year of the first gold strike has a population of 39,000, larger than San Francisco's. In a decade, New South Wales's numbers double, to 350,000, and Victoria rockets from 75,000 to 550,000. One-third of the world's gold production comes from Victoria. That in 1861.

On 15 January 1861 Terence Bellew MacManus dies in California in near-poverty. Nevertheless, the newly-formed Fenian Brotherhood has use for him. While new immigrants are venturing west, his corpse is sent east. He is given a funeral mass in St. Patrick's Cathedral in New York, and Archbishop Hughes preaches the funeral sermon on the theme: an oppressed people have the right to struggle for their liberation.

Then MacManus's body is shipped to Dublin where the Fenians try for another patriotic mass. They are baulked by the new Archbishop of Dublin, Paul Cullen, who remembers only too vividly what 1848 had meant to the Holy See: Pius IX had been forced to flee Rome.

Still, MacManus was honoured. The patriotic procession behind his coffin as it was taken to Glasnevin cemetery stretched for miles.

VAN DIEMEN'S LAND. 1845–52

Scorecard

Read the silences.

Habitual drunks, highway padders, peter-biters, mug-hunters, petticoat-merchants, fences, rum-dubbers, sodomites, barrack hacks, rapists, mock-auction swindlers.

The Dublin newspapers report the activities of them all. The sheets use varying degrees of circumlocution (the *Freeman's Journal* is positively prissy, more Victorian than Queen Victoria), and they garb the more sensational stories in the courtroom language of the prosecuting attorney. Then, as now, the courts are the stage where the pornography of the age is put on public display.

One criminal set is almost entirely missing. At most it is referred to in curt reports of sentences handed down, details missing: women who kill their babies.

Infanticide by desperate women: older mothers grieving for a puling death-sick infant; unmarried girls who lose all hope of escaping permanent poverty if they are themselves known to have a child; women in their twenties driven mad by poor nutrition, howling children, absent futures; women in their early thirties abandoned by their husbands while pregnant with their sixth, seventh, eighth child.

The largely unspoken, and thus publicly unknown, crime: yet, female infanticide is probably the most frequent form of mortal felony in Ireland in the hideous dozen years that begin with 1840, run through the Famine and then the trauma-stunned aftermath, when everyone who is ambulatory wants out.

Of the forty-two Irish women sentenced in the years 1850–52 to Van Diemen's Land for committing murder, seventeen were killers of their own children.

VAN DIEMEN'S LAND. 3 JANUARY 1852

Not Quite Cricket?

During the previous week, Thomas Francis Meagher decided to escape. On the third of January he writes a letter to the authorities throwing in his ticket-of-leave and telling them that after twenty-four hours have passed he will feel himself to be free of his parole. It's all part of the game of soldiers the men of 1848 play and Meagher later, in America, has to undergo a pseudo-court martial (which of course vindicates him), for John Mitchel charges that Meagher cheated: that a letter was not enough and that honour required him to do a face-to-face with the authorities before scarpering. Not cricket.

What was actually *tref* was the real reason Meagher escaped when he did. It was not because he was so compellingly sick of exotic parrots, of living in a lakeshore cottage, of eucalyptus trees, of fishing and riding whenever he pleased, that he could not take another moment. No, the problem was domestic. A year earlier he had married Catherine Bennet, a dead-common girl who had been born in Van Diemen's Land, which is to say that she was the daughter of a common criminal. The men of '48 agreed that she was socially unsuited to a man of their class, although Terence MacManus had possessed the decency to show up (in heavy disguise) at the wedding.

Now Meagher's wife is in advanced pregnancy and Meagher knows that if he does not escape immediately, he won't be able to leave without taking his family and that's a difficult escape.

Meagher's domestically unencumbered escape is clean and efficient and he arrives in New York City, via South America, 26 May 1852. There he is a celebrity and Irish hero.

His infant son dies in Van Diemen's Land on the eighth of June.

Meagher has his wife Catherine, twenty-years old, shipped to Waterford, Ireland. There his family has property: his father is a former Lord Mayor and former member of parliament, and a successful merchant.

Catherine is permitted to visit Meagher in New York City, but she is then sent back to Waterford where she dies, having served her purpose, on 9 May 1854.

Then Thomas Francis Meagher marries an American woman of property.

NORFOLK ISLAND. MARCH, 1852

The One Remaining Hulk

The one remaining place of hideously hard time in the once-ferocious Australian penal system, Norfolk Island, is visited by the Roman Catholic bishop of Van Diemen's Land, the English-born R.W. Willson. He is not naive. This is his third visit and he is not shocked to find that things are bad (this he expected) but that they are becoming worse. Using his own flock as an example, he finds that of the 270 Catholic prisoners – mostly Irish – who attend mass, 218 are in chains. On the island there are 130 cells of solitary confinement and each has an occupant, most with thirty-six pound weights attached.

Flogging is still extreme and sadistic – twenty-nine, or was it thirty-nine, men had just been flogged in a mass punishment.

Bishop Willson writes a thirty-page letter, a damning indictment of the failing prison island, and sends it to the lieutenant-governor of Van Diemen's Land. Copies go overseas. His description of the "living skeletons" he has encountered is more than the Victorian sensibility can stomach.

The colonial government in Australia and the Colonial Office in London begin the run-down of the island. In 1856 it is given over to the Pitcairn islanders, descendants of the *Bounty* mutineers.

HOLYHEAD, WALES. 22 AUGUST 1852

Swarming

He's Protestant, but that's hardly unusual: so too are about one-quarter of the Irish migrants to the Australian colonies in the 1850s. He's from a family that was well enough off to have avoided the Starvation, but were far from rich and, besides, lots of toffs and gents, never mind members of the middle class, made the Australian trip.

As he boards the *Great Britain* at Holyhead, John Sadleir, still in his teens, is distinguished only by his having an unblinking knowledge that he is part of a massive ruck – he has an image in his mind that informs his entire Australian career. He is, he believes, part of an impulse that vibrates subsonically throughout Ireland: the "impulse to swarm off from the old hives."

He marches aboard the *Great Britain* with his brother who is also making the journey. The two young men are fundamentally similar to the tens of thousands of other Irish young people who have learned of opportunities in Australia from a relative who settled there earlier. The Sadleirs are not seduced by the gold rush directly, but by the climate of opportunity. The relative who preceded the Sadleir boys was thought of as something of a degenerate and a loafer when he was in Ireland; yet, now he has more than 100,000 sheep and his biggest problem is finding shepherds and shearers. If he can succeed, we can scarcely fail, the brothers tell each other.

The Sadleirs' trip was unusual only in that it was on the maiden voyage to Australia of a steamship. So recent is this innovation that coal is sent ahead to St. Helena and to the Cape of Good Hope, in case the vessel has need. The run to Melbourne takes only eighty-two days, half the usual time.

John Sadleir scouts for opportunity and finds it exactly where thousands of young Irishmen do, all over the Empire: he joins the police force.

MELBOURNE, VICTORIA. 22 DECEMBER 1852

Exit Visa

The man tapping lightly, but insistently, on the backstreet door in Melbourne is Patrick Denis O'Donoghue. A deep-draught alcoholic, he needs a drink; more than that, he needs a friend.

O'Donoghue is the next of the Young Ireland martyrs to go against the tide of the Irish people, leaving Australia just as thousands of Irish migrants pour in – but then the Young Irelanders never really were attuned to the popular will. As the only one of the state prisoners not to have independent means, O'Donoghue has had the hardest imprisonment. He spent some time in confinement and was badly thumped in a fight with another prisoner. He'd had to work for a living, running a newspaper. Given his social class, none of his fellow state prisoners censure him for breaking his parole and stowing aboard a vessel from Launceston to Melbourne: honour is for gentlemen, like MacManus, Meagher, Mitchel, and William Smith O'Brien.

Dear Lord, he needed a drink. Getting this far had been harrowing, although not as difficult a feat as O'Donoghue's fragile nerves make it seem. More than 2,600 sea-going vessels anchored in Melbourne in 1852, and immigration control was stretched beyond its capacity. Later investigations showed that from Van Diemen's Land more than 5,000 pardoned felons had entered Victoria and more than 2,000 who were only on conditional pardons. In that septic flow, O'Donoghue was only one more floating item.

Thank God! The door opens, and O'Donoghue is wrapped in a blanket of patriotic affection that cocoons him in food, safety, drink, and security. Friends of the Irish-cause place him on an American barque and this takes him to San Francisco. From there he makes his way to Boston.

Patrick Denis O'Donoghue can find no purchase in the patriot-industry that thrives in Boston. He is too drunk and too ordinary and as a competent newspaperman he has a long memory and a disabling belief that facts exist. O'Donoghue comes to public notice only twice in his American career. The first time, he attends an 1853 birthday celebration held in honour of Thomas Meagher by the local patriots. Vainglorious puppy, young Meagher! who gulls his supporters. So O'Donoghue believes, and when at the public birthday party he attempts to make a speech that comes too close to actual, not romantic, facts, he is silenced by the chairman. The next day O'Donoghue challenges the man to a duel and they both are put in jail until they cool down.

O'Donoghue moves to Brooklyn, New York, and there he again makes the papers. According to his obituary, he died while awaiting his family's arrival from Ireland. And according to the newspaper, he died of a shattered nervous system and of diarrhea.

BOTHWELL, VAN DIEMEN'S LAND. 3-5 JANUARY 1853

Critical Awareness

Kangaroo hunting is one of the best diversions to be had in Van Diemen's Land. A brace or small pack of dogs, especially trained to the task, are walked through the rocky hillsides and the tree-denuded gullies. They jump prostrate trees that have yet to be hauled away and cast about for a scent. Their masters follow slowly on horseback, for either the cut-over land is pockmarked and dangerous, or the remaining bush is thick and impossible to ride through quickly. Eventually, the dogs scent or see a kangaroo and tear off after it, baying all the time. Finally there is silence and the dogs either return frisking victoriously, or hangdog, having lost their quarry. Sometimes the canines are wounded, for a cornered kangaroo rises on its hind legs and slashes with its claws.

John Mitchel celebrates the New Year with two days of kangaroo hunting. He is fascinated by the behaviour of one female that the dogs run down. She was large, at least fifty pounds, and surprisingly, after the dogs had killed her, she was found to have left a little joey in her pocket. Usually the females, when they spy an aggressive enemy, take the young from the pouch and hide it in a safe place. She had not done so. She lay in a pool of blood, her head almost torn off.

Mitchel slings her over the saddle.

Next day, John Mitchel goes back to saving the hay on his small holding. He has two felons working for him. *I am prosecuting my hay-harvest diligently, with the aid of two or three horrible cut-throats, all from Ireland.* He really does not like the Irish proletariat very much, especially this set, who have been transported for the act of seizing arms, an activity Mitchel had once recommended to the entire Irish peasantry. *This is considered, amongst these fellows, a respectable sort of offence. The rascals can earn ten British shillings per diem, at harvest time; and they live all the year round like Irish kings, not to speak of Irish cut-throats. They don't like to work too hard and require a good deal of wine.*

For all that, he finds that they are law-abiding in Van Diemen's Land, because of the savage punishment for minor crimes. ... *For nearly three years, during which time I have been in Van Diemen's Land, for most part in a lonely cottage, with windows all round close to the ground, and quite unsecured, and with two or more prisoner-servants always about the place, my family have felt as secure, and slept as peacefully, as ever they did in Banbridge.*

He adds, *and save one double-barrelled gun, nothing was ever stolen from me.* He sees nothing incongruous in a state prisoner, such as himself, being issued convict servants and permitted to own firearms.

HOBART, VAN DIEMEN'S LAND. FEBRUARY 1853

Humane Relations

The people of the Australian colonies learn that Lord Derby's government has announced the end of transportation as criminal punishment. This is confirmed by the Aberdeen coalition that follows Derby late in 1852.

The system runs down. Van Diemen's Land becomes "Tasmania" in 1855 and receives "responsible government," meaning control of its own local affairs.

Western Australia, which needs labour, keeps receiving prisoners until 1868, and it is two decades more before they are all out of the system.

As for the prisoners in Van Diemen's Land in 1853, they can either wait until they fall out of the crumbling pipeline or, if they wish, they still have time to effect an heroic escape.

BOTHWELL, VAN DIEMEN'S LAND. 9 JUNE 1853

Critical Success

John Mitchel has been unswervingly critical of all the other exiles of '48, so he not only has to escape in a proper and chivalric manner, but with dramatic success. With Van Diemen's Land being run down as a penal colony there is every chance that he will be given a pardon and allowed to stay with his wife and six children on the farm that he has purchased. That would be disaster.

He walks into the office of the magistrate of his district and hands him a note that is dated the previous day (for reasons never adequately explained). He is renouncing his ticket-of-leave, and withdrawing his parole. He offers to be taken into custody: "If you can catch me," is the invisible sentence on the page. He is starting a game of hare and hounds, with himself as the blameless prey.

Mitchel's tactical problems should not be understated. To serve honour, he has to be sure that his wife and six bairns (who are free persons), make their exit in phase with his penal escape. No dumping them. And Mitchel is handicapped, like a hare with a bad leg: in his case he is extremely near-sighted. Either he must wear thick spectacles (which, in his era are rare enough to be a police-identification item) or he bumps into things and approaches the wrong people. Friends and foes can be sorted out only at a distance of ten feet.

On the positive side of the ledger, he has the help of Patrick J. Smyth, an Irishman most recently from New York. Smyth, the son of a wealthy Dublin tanner, has come to rescue Irish political prisoners. He arrives in Van Diemen's Land wearing a long frock coat, a cloak that he sweeps around himself like a villain in a melodrama, and a full mustache and chin whiskers. He is twenty-five years of age and has spent some time in South America. Mitchel assigns him the name "Nicaragua," as preferable to the prosaic "Smyth."

When Mitchel hands the note to the local magistrate's office, Smyth is right behind him, which is just as well, as Mitchel, who refuses to wear his spectacles for this scene, starts to give the renunciation-of-parole to the constable of the barracks. Smyth nudges Mitchel's elbow and directs him to the police clerk about whose literacy there is no doubt. Mitchel's note does not garner much response, so he has to repeat aloud several times that he no longer considers himself in custody. Finally, the police take in the situation and move to arrest him.

Satisfying: Mitchel and Smyth, with pistols tucked into belts and waistcoats, run for their horses and disappear. This is great stuff and its success is made more likely by Mitchel's previously having purchased the best horse in the neighbourhood for £80, an amount he once said one could live on for a year as a gentleman. Deft touch: the horse had belonged to the police magistrate.

After a month of hiding, Mitchel boards a ship at Hobart destined for Sydney. He is disguised as a very near-sighted priest, which, as a very far-sighted Unitarian, pleases him. Given his good Protestant education, he is able to exchange Latin tags with several of his fellow passengers. With less than shrewd planning, "Nicaragua" has booked Mitchel's wife and six children on the same vessel. It speaks volumes either about Mitchel's ability as an actor, or his debility as a parent, that none of his children recognize him.

From Sydney, it was easy to ship to America, one would think: but here the real world briefly intervened in Mitchel's drama. Not only was the outside world pouring into Sydney and Melbourne, but the gold fever was so seductive that it was commonplace for ships' crews to desert and try their hand at the diggings. Ship owners grew so desperate for crew that they placed advertisements for seamen in the newspapers. Mitchel's vessel was deserted by its crew and he was almost apprehended when police came around to protect the now-empty vessel. Finally, however, he made California, where he was honoured at a dinner given by the governor, and then he and his family made for New York City.

He is a hero and in January 1854 he begins the serial publication in the New York *Citizen* of his "Jail Journal." A ballad is written about him and his harsh imprisonment. Its last stanza:

> Adieu! Adieu! to sweet Belfast, and likewise Dublin too.
> And to my young and tender babes; alas what will they do?
> But there's one request I ask of you, when your liberty you gain:
> *Remember John Mitchel far away, a convict bound in chains.*

Though a hard man to please, John Mitchel liked that.

GEELONG, VICTORIA. JANUARY 1854

Short Similes

"Friend, severe work."

"Very, very, Friend, the prisoners hate it."

Sixty-four years old, Foster Fyans is working on his memoirs. He has had a varied life: born just outside of Dublin, baptized Church of Ireland, served as a junior officer in the Peninsular War. Later he fought in the Burmese War and when his regiment was sent to the Australian colonies he was acting-commandant of Norfolk Island. This at the time of the 1834 convict uprising. Captain Fyans presided over courts martial whose results were that thirteen convicts were hanged: but only after they had dug their own graves.

"Friend, that is sufficient for Friend Walker."

"Friend, I want no more!"

Fyans is with pleasure recording the period, 1836–37, when he was commandant of the Moreton Bay penal settlement, near Brisbane, a colony for hard cases. According to his lights, he had run it well. He recalls an inspection visit by a group of Quakers:

The Friends visit the magnificent wind mill which was in full operation, grinding maize for the use of the convicts. From this mill a great shaft turns the tread mill by a shifting bar ... Therefore, when many defaults, say four to ten, they were punished on the mill. To the number of one hundred and fifty men could be at once employed, or to so low a number as two.

Fyans has no time for the softness of character that led to the phasing out of penal colonies, nor for the professional do-gooders and God-botherers who prattle on about human dignity and internal reformation of character and the like. He knows that sound punishment works. He recalls with pleasure his having given the sanctimonious Quakers a taste of real work:

I kept them for some time, telling them that the idlers were always worked harder by the power of the wind mill, when immediately the bar was shifted and away it went at full speed. After giving the Quakers a good heat of ten minutes, the mill was stopped, and the Friends came off with thanks, blowing, puffing, and short similes.

BEECHWORTH, NORTHEASTERN VICTORIA.
FEBRUARY 1854

Dip

John Sadleir, now a police constable, meets and becomes friends with one of the most famous Irishmen in Australian history, the doom-laden Robert O'Hara Burke. Burke is thirteen years senior to Sadleir and is his superior in the Victorian police. They're both Irish, how-ever – Burke from a gentry family in County Galway – both Protes-tants, and both men of considerable courage.

Despite having been an officer in an Austrian cavalry regiment and an officer in the Royal Irish Constabulary, Burke was gloriously un-military in detail, though heroic in posture. He would drill mounted policemen while dressed in a slouch hat, an open sac coat, no shirt or vest over his hairy chest and expanding stomach, and wearing carpet slippers. All this on horseback. His men loved him, but outsiders thought him mad.

Worried about his increasing weight, Burke for a time ordered his housekeeper to spend no more than sixpence a day on food.

Sadleir would visit Burke of an evening and frequently he was re-ceived in a massive tub, cut into the solid rock near the police bar-racks: twelve feet on each side and ten feet at its deepest. Only about two feet of water accumulated there. In the long evenings, Burke would splash about for a time with his retriever and then stretch out and read a book, covering his head with a pith helmet of the African sort, surmounted with mosquito netting.

VAN DIEMEN'S LAND. MAY 1854

Sunset

Word filters to the prisoners that they are to receive conditional par-dons: William Smith O'Brien, the few remaining men of 1848, and a handful of Chartists, Englishmen who had been transported for being politically dangerous.

For O'Brien and his comrades there are modest celebrations in Hobart and later on the Australian mainland. At those events a stout effort is made to maintain face. Speakers repeatedly point out that the '48 Exiles had not petitioned for their pardons. And, in any case, they are still martyrs, for the condition on the pardons is that they not return to Great Britain or, tragically, Ireland.

An agreed opinion is that the government of the United Kingdom pardoned the remaining '48 exiles because it would help recruiting for the war in the Crimea with Russia. No one points to what they all know: that the Irish peasantry, from whom foot soldiers of empire were to be drawn, had scarcely heard of William Smith O'Brien and his remaining colleagues and could not have cared less. Nor does anyone wish to note that the imperial authorities were running down the entire Australian penal system and that hundreds of prisoners were receiving their conditional pardons.

Yet William Smith O'Brien is now past illusion: he knows that he is being released for bureaucratic convenience and because neither he nor his views are a threat to the government.

O'Brien travelled slowly to Paris, his new place of exile, and then in 1856 he received an absolute pardon. When he returned to Ireland it was quietly. No bands played. He published two volumes of lucubrations on government that he had written in Van Diemen's Land. The two volumes were thick enough to stop a bullet, but that was their only possible connection with revolution.

When he returned to his estate, "Cahirmoyle," O'Brien found that his wife was tolerant, if distant, but that his children (five sons and two daughters) viewed him as a returned lunatic. They had no time for his views. Perhaps John Mitchel was right, O'Brien reflected, I should have brought the wife and children with me into exile.

When his wife dies in 1861, William Smith O'Brien is heart-rendered and, simultaneously, alienated from his children. In a gentlemanly way, of course. Because he had placed all his property into trusts for his children before he went into exile, the trustees now are in charge and they block his attempts to regain control of his own estates. So, mournfully, O'Brien settles with his eldest son: the son acquires the house and lands and the father receives a pension of £2,000 a year from his offspring.

Occasionally William Smith O'Brien returns to "Cahirmoyle," but he always considers himself a mere visitor. He spends most of the time before his death in 1864 at Killiney, south of Dublin, watching the eastward sea, grateful that from such a location he can not fully see the sun set.

BALLARAT, VICTORIA. OCTOBER-DECEMBER 1854

Obtaining Licence

"Have your licence, digger?"

"I've had it since Julius Caesar was a pup."

The only successful Irish Rising of the nineteenth century did not take place in Ireland, but in Australia; it was spontaneous and simple, rather than a complex event masterminded by the political intelligentsia; it was ethnically inclusive, and in that sense not only Irish; Scots, Englishmen and all sorts of Europeans threw in their lot with Irish leaders; and, unlike every other nineteenth-century rising, whether in Ireland or abroad, it was successful in the long run; instead of increased repression, it brought a widening of the Australian colonial polity.

"Digger. Your licence now or you're up before the magistrate."

"Oh, by Christ your honour, I was just on my way to buy the licence, so I was."

Efficient government has caused as many revolutions as has inefficient, that is one of history's cynical lessons. The authorities of the Australian colonies had learned a good deal from the unregulated horrors of the California gold rush and they were determined to keep order. So, each miner had to purchase a monthly licence, at a cost of thirty shillings, and had to keep it to hand and produce it immediately when braced by the mining police. This was bad enough financially: many diggers could barely scratch that amount out each month. But being under the surveillance of the mining police constantly humiliated men whose spirit was proud. Usually, a cash-poor miner could get away with not having the licence for the first ten days of the month or so, because the mining administrators were busy taking the thirty shillings from the diggers as they came into town and were up to their ankles in paperwork. After that it became tough: skint diggers took to working only at night, or to sharing a single certificate with a mate, mining only alternate days. Trouble was, early in 1854, a new administration introduced real efficiency and more licence enforcers. Diggers were stopped, every day, all month, sometimes three or four times a day. The sport of "digger-hunting" became a nasty game, the government hounds chasing the unlicensed hares. Like so many games humanity plays, the game really was one of dominance vs. submission.

"That will be fifteen pounds or two months gaol."

"That's as dirty as Liverpool weather."

"And that will be three months. Next case."

Even so, the Eureka Rising probably would not have occurred save for the gratuitous face-grinding of the miners by the local establishment. Ballarat was a massive town for its time and place: perhaps 40,000 residents of one form or another, a wide main street lined with buildings that sported the lace-work verandas of gold-rush wealth, big hotels, expensive bars, and off the main drag all the supply, assay, and pawn shops that a mining town needed, and then, in concentric circles, shebeens, low-end brothels, shacks cramped with in-town miners, and finally satellite settlements on the diggings, canvas worlds of men, tools, hope, anger.

The nastiest part of the local establishment was run by ex-convicts from Van Diemen's Land, and the most successful of these was James F. Bentley who ran the Eureka Hotel, the biggest drinking shop in town. Early one morning, after closing, he was counting the day's takings, when a pair of drunk miners tried to obtain a nightcap. The door was locked and they gave it a good kick, called out that Bentley's wife was a whore, and went away. Enraged, Bentley followed them out, along with his wife, two of his own mates and the hotel's bouncer. One of the miners, a Scot, was kicked to death. The local coroner and a stacked jury exonerated Bentley and his pack. One of the jury members was a close friend of Bentley and the coroner had been drinking at his hotel until shortly before the killing occurred.

"I've seen fairer drops at a hanging."

"And bigger teats on a bull."

Outraged miners took to the streets for several days. Watching, with a studiousness that contrasted with their agitation, was Peter Lalor, from Queen's County, which he always called County Laoise. He was a tall, darkly handsome man, with command written all over him. He and one of his brothers had arrived in Victoria in 1852 with twin resolutions: to get rich and to stay away from politics. He fit Australia well, for this was an era when one could, if one possessed talent and resources, move freely without much regard for social boundaries. Peter Lalor and his brother worked railway construction for a time, then opened a provision-wine-spirits house in Melbourne. They had a bit of family money and their construction savings. The mercantile business did well, but Peter's brother decided to go back to Ireland, where eventually he became a member of Parliament for Laoise and an ardent Parnellite. Peter moved shop for a time to Ballarat and then sold up the business (he had more than £1,000 in wine and tobacco alone), and took to digging. His own claim was near that of the Scotsman who had been kicked to death by the Bentley bunch.

"A vote for every miner."

"Secret Ballots!"

"Fair electoral districts."

"No property qualifications."

"Annual goddamn elections."

A district judge, frightened at the furore, reviewed the Bentley case. He was as tainted as the coroner and coroner's jury had been, for the judge owned a stake in the Eureka Hotel. He gave the killers an honourable discharge.

Then the town went up. Three to five thousand miners took to the streets and as they did so, they moved from simple justice to politics. English miners intermixed the program of the Chartists – universal suffrage, the secret ballot and the like – with the miners' general grievance, and Irish diggers liberated the fuckyouenergy that generations of alienation from state power provided. A fund was raised to prosecute the corrupt governmental officials and Peter Lalor was one of the seven diggers appointed to an executive committee. He might be trying to escape politics, but he was in, like it or not. When government troops arrive to protect the Eureka Hotel, that is the spark. The miners burn the place.

Peter Lalor went back to his claim at Baker's Hill. He and his Scottish mate had dug a shaft 140 feet below ground and were bringing up enough paydirt to be among the more successful of the diggers: not crazy-rich, but doing well. Lalor really was quite happy to be a miner.

"On the green banks of Shannon, when Sheelagh was nigh,

No blithe Irish lad was so happy as I;

No harp like my own could so cheerily play,

And wherever I went was my poor dog Tray."

Popular songs of his day: Peter Lalor loved them, and he sang aloud underground, a strange and wonderful experience: the soil and gravel refused all pleas for resonance and Lalor heard only his own naked voice and the sound of his pick and shovel. He imagined that was the way God heard humanity, no distortion, no self-magnification.

Peter Lalor's whole life before Australia had been a training in just the opposite, a life-long education in the art of self-magnification, of using the individual to move the mass. In County Laoise, his father, a strong farmer, had led the 1831–32 Tithe War against the Established

Church, and then sat for the county in the House of Commons 1832–35. He followed Daniel O'Connell as a campaigner for the Repeal of the Union of Great Britain and Ireland. The elder Lalor had eleven sons, and one of them, James Fintan Lalor, was the most radical of all the men of '48. It was he who had taught John Mitchel the doctrine of peasant insurrection and in the *Irish Felon* mapped out the practical aspects of rural guerilla war, and the ultimate need for peasant ownership of the land, something approaching agrarian socialism. Arrested for his writings, James Fintan Lalor was in too bad health to play a part in the '48 Rising and in fact died in 1849. His example had taught Peter Lalor one thing: that Irish politics were not for him. Peter, having completed his studies at the highly respectable Carlow College (the secondary school of choice of Catholic strong farmers), had trained as a civil engineer and then hied off to Australia, far from Irish revolution.

Gentlemen, I find myself in the responsible position I now occupy, for this reason. The diggers, outraged at …

Despite all of his resolution, Peter Lalor found himself cast as a rebel leader. The authorities had charged three of the diggers who had burned the Eureka Hotel and in response the miners had turned their association into the Ballarat Reform League whose principles were one-half Chartist and one-half aimed at alleviating miners' specific grievances, such as the licensing arrangements. The authorities used licence-hunts as a way of breaking the men, checking a man several times a day, and when transgressors were caught, they would be roped to eucalyptus trees until several were snared, and then marched off to court, like slaves going to a market.

… The diggers, outraged at the unaccountable conduct of the Camp officials in such a wicked licence-hunt at the point of the bayonet, as the one of this morning, took it as an insult to their manhood, and a challenge to the determination come to at the monster meeting of yesterday …

Lalor here was lapsing into Irish idiom. "Monster meetings" were what Daniel O'Connell had held in his successful Catholic Emancipation campaign.

The diggers rushed to their tents for arms and crowded on Bakery Hill. They wanted a leader. No one came forward, and confusion was the consequence. I mounted the stump where you saw me and called on the people to "fall in" into divisions, according to the firearms they had got and to choose their own captains out of the best men they had among themselves. My call was answered with unanimous acclamation and complied to with willing obedience. The result is that I have been able to bring about order, without which it would be folly to face the pending struggle like men.

Lalor has no military experience, but he is a trained engineer and, more importantly, he has in the back of his mind the tactics for peasant insurrection that his late brother, James Fintan Lalor, had published in Ireland, half a decade earlier. Therefore, he forms on Baker's Hill ("always take the high ground") a stockade that keeps one's own often-fractious guerillas inside and under discipline, and forces the enemy to attack in force and to do so across an open space. That the Redcoats, well-armed and supported by a scratch cavalry, would win eventually was likely. Yet, Lalor had several hundred hard men on his side, and some Irish captains who would run through hell for him: Timothy Hayes, Patrick Curtin, John Manning, plus some very clever, tough Europeans, Scots, and English Chartists.

The password for entry into the stockade was "Vinegar Hill."

Shrewdly, on the third of December, the Redcoats hit early in the morning when many of the rebels had gone back to their tents to replenish supplies. At that time only 120 to 150 men were in the Eureka Stockade, beneath their flag, the Southern Cross. About twice that number of soldiers and police attacked. Thirty miners and five police and soldiers were killed. Lalor was shot in the arm. He stayed to the end, as he had promised he would do, but when he collapsed from loss of blood, he was hidden by his remaining followers, and eventually smuggled out: his arm had to be amputated, and he came to consciousness while it was being cut. "Work on, boys," he said, before collapsing again.

A Success? Yes. The authorities charged thirteen men with treason, then dropped one charge, and the remaining twelve were acquitted by juries. The message was clear: no jury in Victoria would convict the men of Eureka.

A commission investigated conditions in the gold fields, the licence system was virtually abolished and, crucially, miners received the vote. Now, even though a miner might not have any real estate of his own, if he paid an annual fee of £1 he had all the voting, legal, and political rights of any property-owning citizen. And the legislative council was expanded to contain representatives of the goldfields.

Peter Lalor, though still having a price on his head, was voted by his fellows a memorial of 160 acres of good land near Ballarat. He came out of hiding. The government withdrew its reward and he was let live in peace. He married the woman who nursed him after his arm's amputation, and was elected to the legislative council as a representative of Ballarat in 1855. He sat in parliament almost continuously into the late 1880s and was several times a cabinet member.

He refused to be labelled a democrat, if that meant republicanism; he supported a free press, widespread landholding, liberal institutions, and a well-ordered society. His Irish Rising of 1854, like all of the (few) successful anti-imperial efforts between the American Revolution and the creation of the Irish Free State, was successful by measure of its yielding an improvement of English-model institutions, not their abolition. Peter's brother, James Fintan Lalor, would have hated to observe that.

MELBOURNE, VICTORIA. 1855

Good Catholic

Charles Gavan Duffy was a good Catholic and that is why on his emigration voyage to Australia he had an interview with the captain of the *Ocean Chief*. A bell had been rung on Sunday morning and the first-class passengers assembled in the saloon, where the captain read passages from the Book of Common Prayer.

Afterward, Duffy asked the skipper, a Nova Scotian of Irish descent, "Is there an Established Church decreed for this ship?"

"Certainly not."

"Well, have the goodness to have the bell rung again," Duffy demanded. "I will read the prayers for the Irish Catholics in the second class and steerage."

And so it was.

Duffy, founding owner and editor of *The Nation*, Young Ireland's broadsheet, too rarely received credit for his faith. John Mitchel vilified him for having been acquitted for high treason in his five harrowing trials. And those men of '48 who made it to America and lived off their former heroism downplayed Duffy's steadfastness.

Then, when Duffy entered parliament as a member for New Ross in 1852 and tried to create a truly independent Irish political party, he ran into the disapproval of Archbishop Paul Cullen, who saw him as "another Mazzini." Duffy was not sycophantically ultramontane enough for the archbishop, but few human beings were.

Baulked, heartsick, Charles Gavan Duffy quit politics and quit Ireland. He was received in Melbourne as a godsend and was immediately elected to the legislative assembly for Victoria. Less than fifteen years later he served a brief term as prime minister. Subsequently he was knighted and was named speaker of the assembly.

AUSTRALIAN COLONIES. 1850–90

Fair Dinkum

Dust. It's the first thing that imprints on Irish immigrants as they enter at Sydney or Melbourne. There, and wherever the migrants go inland, it's always dusty. They have been forewarned in letters from earlier migrants about the heat, but no one mentions the dust. Unless it's rained recently, little whirlwinds of grit make breathing an irritation. After half an hour outside on a breezy day, faces feel as if they are sandpapered, and that's one reason colonial men take to wearing beards that make their faces as full and round as pumpkins. Dust is one thing that all the Irish migrants have in common. Most of them share another; their own swirling path to Australia has been paid in large part by the colonial governments. Even so, the cost to the migrant is greater than the cost of sailing from Ireland to North America. Among Irish emigrants, the ones with least resources go to Great Britain, especially England; the next least-able go to the USA. Australia gets a better cut: its Irish migrants have been less affected by hard times and, also, have been weeded by the assisted-passage rules. They are not the dust of the Irish diaspora.

Flies. Some emigrants have been told about the creatures in letters from brothers, sisters, cousins, but the way that flies swarm around every table, and fall into the tea and the gravy is not something they foresaw. Thousands of the creatures alight on any thing that is not moving. At night, they do their death-dances on bedroom floors, upside down, wings flailing frantically, sounding out a maddening threnody, like a band of jaw-harps all resonating off-pitch. Sleep is not easy. The Irish migrants descend upon Australia not as a plague, but as a benison. Roughly 10 percent of the people who leave Ireland in the second half of the nineteenth century come to Australia. By the census of 1861, men, women, children of Irish ethnicity are a quarter of the population of the Australian colonies and they are the same proportion at the close of Queen Victoria's reign. Australia becomes the second-most-Irish jurisdiction in the world (only Ontario, sometimes called "Upper Canada" has a higher proportion).

Land. The Irish are not all the same: about one-quarter are Protestants. And among both Catholics and Protestants there is a big social range, from squeaky-poor loners to gentry "capitalists" (the word for anyone with a thousand pounds or more in pocket). Yet, universally, they come from a home country that had not enough land and most of them are affected, one way or another, by land hunger. Once they have stopped rolling – rid themselves of gold-fever or spent their time being domestic servants or draymen in the cities – they migrate rural-ward and there, in small towns and on stations, they eventually settle. The Irish are a rural people. Only in the twentieth century do they move city-ward, and that in concert with the rest of the Australian population. Even so, it's well after World War I that they become (like everyone else) mostly urban or suburban. These Irish, the outflow that follows the Great Famine, are people of the land.

Skills. The learning curve is incredibly steep. Irish migrants learn their way to the land by taking jobs they have never done before. Sawyers, stockmen, miners, shepherds, fossickers, drovers among the men; hotel maids, boarding house owners, house maids, among the women. They learn to use tools they have never even touched in Ireland: American axes, saddles and bridles, wheat-harvesting sickles, sheep shears, guns. Even migrants who had been raised on strong farms in the Old Country had to retrain themselves: everything here grows differently and few of the agricultural arts are entirely familiar. The new migrants move about constantly, each cast of the dice for a better bit of fortune is also another chapter in the book of New World skills. Many fail many times. Job-jumpers are the bane of the whole labour-starved country: men who take a job they know nothing about, get paid in part or full, and then skive off, the task half done. But most learn, become skilled, act decently.

Home. The restless search for a purchase, for a rural base, throws up a series of homes. When finally on land they call their own, even if it is a small unfenced run, they begin with a house without a hearth, a shelter covered with strips of bark peeled from local trees, sheets nine or ten feet long and two to three feet in width. These organic walls start out wrapped snugly around the house posts and rafters, but, being green, they soon warp into every shape save a Mobius strip: winter draughts find little obstacle. Next, the migrants build a frame house around a stone and daub chimney and, if they are prospering, construct walls of planks: edge-slabs from large logs are used and the chinks filled in with mud. And on and on. What would look to a later visitor as white-trash-heaven is nothing of the sort for its inhabitants. These new homes and lands are a vast improvement over life in the Old Country. These Irish migrants talk a lot about Ireland, but there is no doubt where, for them, home now is: here.

THE "UNITED STATES HOTEL," BALLARAT, VICTORIA.
17 FEBRUARY 1856

A Nice Irish Girl

"*Will you attack a damsel?!*" She used that word as self-description, though she was thirty-eight years old, becoming a bit chunky, and had to slap a lot of pancake to cover the eruptions on her face. The actress was conducting a battle with the editor of *The Ballarat Times* who had given her previous night's performance a less-than-enthusiastic review. His weapon of choice had been words, but she was using a horsewhip and going for his face. He had merely pointed out that her famous "Spider Dance" was immoral and awkward. Perhaps, but the miners loved it and threw gold nuggets on to the stage. The best part of the dance as far as they were concerned was when she arched backwards, hands and feet on the floor, her pelvis pumping towards the ceiling. An arachnid, but not one to avoid: she moved slowly in a circle until her splayed legs were open directly in front of them. That's the art that had made her famous.

Ouch! Beast! So you will indeed attack a defenceless woman. The actress had chosen the wrong man to bully: Henry Seekamp, who had been one of the stalwarts of the diggers' cause at the Eureka Stockade and who had spent three months imprisonment for backing them. When he heard that the actress was looking for him, and with a stock whip, he had not hesitated. He went to see her: with a horsewhip of his own in hand. Usually the actress encountered more pliant males. She was well past bigamy: into husband four or five, no one knew for sure, and certainly not she. And, some of her paramours had lived suspiciously shortened lives: her present manager-lover would, six months later, mysteriously fall overboard near Fiji as she and he sailed towards San Francisco; two years earlier, a German doctor who was named as a co-respondent in the divorce action of one of her husbands, was mysteriously shot; there were others.

Henry Seekamp whacks her hard on the shoulder, avoiding her face.

How dare you attack me in your filthy little paper? In her twenties she had been distractingly beautiful and, trained in Spanish dance, given to performing on stage in a manner that caused the male members of her audience to place their evening coats on their laps. She was also one of the great fucks of Europe: ask the wraiths of Franz Liszt, Alexandre Dumas, and Alexandre Dujarier, each of whose mistress she was, sequentially, mostly.

Will you abuse me again, animal? This time she cuts the editor's face severely, just missing an eye, and he does not have any courtly inhibitions: he punches her in the mouth and also gets in a whack on her cheek with his own whip. So unlike the actress's most devoted admirer, Ludwig I of Bavaria, who had created her Countess Marie von Landsfeld and depended on her advice for making and breaking government ministers. Oh, if only those dreadful students and young revolutionaries in 1848 had not rioted against her influence! Oh, and of course if those nasty politicians had not told King Ludwig that she was sleeping with at least four other men, and oh, dear dear, if it had not been true. Still, the king was courtly: he abdicated his throne because of his folly, and that's something for a girl to remember, isn't it?

Won't some gentleman save me? The actress has wisely inferred that her opponent intends to continue returning cut for cut, blow for blow. Immediately half a dozen diggers, who had been enjoying the duet almost as much as they liked the actress's Spider Dance, pulled Seekamp away and, save for a moment of mutual hair-pulling when Seekamp broke from his captors, that was that.

Just an average day for Lola Montez of County Limerick, the daughter of a junior naval officer and a Spanish mother.

She was only six years away from a pustulant death of tertiary syphilis, no end for a nice Irish girl.

NORFOLK ISLAND. MAY 1856

Animal Magnetism

The poor horse! The Pitcairn islanders have never seen one before and they are amazed to discover that they can ride a mammal other than each other. The overseer's horse, from the prison-days of Norfolk Island still, briefly, survives. On their first day ashore, the islanders are shown how to sit on the old thing and make it carry them around their new island and they all take turns. Almost all. The horse dies from exhaustion before the last of them has been permitted to clamber aboard.

The Pitcairn people walked about Norfolk Island like Goths in ancient Rome. Reverent Goths, mind you. Cells, barracks, punishment-triangles, overseers' houses, everything was still there. The breath of the previous inhabitants, tubercular, hate-filled, toxic, remained, but nary a human being, save a handful of official welcomers. The islanders spent days going over the new island, letting fall through their hands soil – dear Lord, they had been forced to make soil on their home island!

One big unhappy family from their earliest days, the Pitcairn islanders silently split into two camps: those who see this new home as release from the grey-green-black cloud that has hung over them from earliest times, and those who believe that they have wrongly moved over the edge of the earth. So attuned are the 200 Pitcairners to each other that they know, within families, within cousinships (and there is nothing else) who feels which way. No words.

The government is generous. Who is the government? They know not. They had written to Victoria Regina, Queen Empress of the Empire, and this was the result. Are these stone buildings not royal castles left for them by Her Majesty? And the provender, how good Her Majesty is! No less than 45,500 lbs of biscuits, rice, maize. Twenty-two horses, 16,000 lbs of hay, which they have never seen before and it has to be explained to them; ten pigs, a flock of domestic fowl bigger than they had ever encountered, straw, everything.

Yet some feel deeply suspicious. The black-coated clergy and the governmental officials are people they have been trained to fear and the words of those blackcoats, their soft hands that are pressed together in palm-congratulating obsequiousness, are somehow wrong, and ill-boding.

The Pitcairners bury an infant, Phoebe Adams, aged five months, who is the first of their tribe to be interred on Norfolk Island.

BUCKLAND, VICTORIA. MARCH 1857

Moderation

It's like a kangaroo drive, only no dogs are used. More than a thousand "European" miners are engaged in a scheme they have hatched secretly for months. Strung out in a line, they are driving the Chinese ahead of them. They have waited for this moment: all the police save one constable have been called to Beechworth, sixty miles away. The diggers will cleanse the Buckland diggings of the Chinese, who work day and night like ants, rarely spend money with local shopkeepers, and speak a secret language and refuse to use English.

"European" is the term of the time, but the diggers are mostly English and Irish, with a few Americans and continental Europeans among them. In their frantic retreat before the advance of European civilization, several of the Chinese fall into the Buckland River gorge and are drowned: running across narrow log bridges is dangerous when one is nearly blind with terror. The lucky ones scamper into the bush, there to gnaw roots and search for water.

News comes to the police barracks at Beechworth and an excitable magistrate issues a sheaf of blank warrants: he intends the police to charge with a felony anybody who took part in the drive. Robert O'Hara Burke says no, that might be good law, but the result would be a full-scale war between the diggers and the police and, ultimately, the military. Instead, Burke stuffs the warrants into his pocket and rides with a handful of men to Buckland. He inquires carefully, looks before he leaps, and arrests only men who actually kicked, beat, shot Chinese. He is surgically accurate and when he comes to arrest the miners, their mates do not interfere, for they know Burke is right.

GALONG, NSW. MAY 1858

Discreet Silence

The social distinction in wider society that the Gaelic chieftain Ned Ryan never was able to achieve is assumed easily by his Irish-born-and -educated son, John Nagle Ryan. John is quietly rich, a gentleman in the Anglo-Irish style, not a Celtic warrior.

John Nagle Ryan begins a circuit, visiting all of his neighbours who have votes. A year later, the seal on his acceptance as a civil leader is his election for the Lachlan Pastoral District to the New South Wales legislative assembly.

He is twice re-elected.

During his three terms of office, he rarely speaks. One report is that his only utterance was to ask that a window be closed.

An alternative report suggests that he frequently raised questions, but on only a single issue: "When will the railway be taken to Boorowa?"

BEECHWORTH, VICTORIA. 1858

Night Watchman

John Sadleir, now an imposing figure in his police uniform, solid, a man one does not push, spends his off hours keeping an eye on his superintendent, Robert O'Hara Burke. Sadleir reveres his superior and in a brotherly fashion also feels some responsibility for him. Burke, lately, has ceased being a daunting eccentric and has turned into a loopey, lovesick teenager.

A buxom, sixteen-year-old burlesque singer and comedian, Julia Matthews, has been playing the dust-and-flies circuit of inland Victoria. When she played Beechworth, Burke listened to her pert English accent and watched her kicking up her heels in a parody of "Richard the Third," and his Arthurian streak was kindled. Like a line of gunpowder, it crackled along, working towards its unavoidable, albeit thoroughly illogical conclusion.

As often as he can, John Sadleir accompanies his superior to the performances, where they sit conspicuously in the front row. Soon, however, Burke takes to following Miss Matthews's *opera bouffe* company from town to town and back to Melbourne. He presses his case, but she will have nothing to do with the bulky, shambling policeman with upper-class manners and only a policeman's salary.

Hopelessly in love, Burke draws the Camelot conclusion: he must perform a truly noble deed if he is to win the hand of the clever little Cockney princess.

ADELAIDE, SOUTH AUSTRALIA;
HUNGERFORD, QUEENSLAND. 1860

Minor Ideas

It's only a tiny idea: most important ones are.

Robert Torrens, an ill-tempered, slightly fanatical law reformer has resigned from the South Australia assembly where, briefly, he had been premier. He intents to fight the legal profession and force passage of a bill he had introduced whilst premier. He comes of a stiff-necked County Cork family: his father a full colonel, his wife a niece of the legendary African explorer, Mungo Park. Torrens's idea is tiny and very simple: do away with all uncertainty of land titles. Instead of the execution of title deeds, which are easily lost and which, unless they are skilfully drawn, are ambiguous and lead to litigation, simply have all land ownership put on a public register. Once properly registered, the government guarantees title and anyone buying a piece of land can do so knowing that the title is safe. Torrens first convinces the South Australian government to adopt the system and then evangelizes other colonies and nations. The "Torrens system" underwrites most land titles today in the English-speaking world.

It's only a tiny idea: most really bad ones are.

Thomas Hungerford, son of a captain in the South Cork Militia, tries to work out ways of becoming a bigger and bigger grazier. In 1847 he had introduced the swinging-gate for sorting out cattle on his Queensland run. Now he develops a system of land-clearing that requires no moving parts. He introduces ring-barking on a systematic and massive scale. Trees dessicate and tumble in their hundreds and hundreds of thousands. He clears 20,000 acres of his own, but his real impact, like that of Robert Torrens, is through demonstration. Other owners of big stations follow his example, the first step in turning an arid land into a saline salt pan that, ultimately, cannot support agriculture.

It's an undignified idea, but many good ones are.

Edmund FitzGibbon, son of Gibbon Carew FitzGibbon of Cork, claims to be the heir to the title of the White Knight of Kerry, and it's a serious claim, even though it is recognized only within the colony of Victoria. He is the town clerk of Melbourne, and runs the day-to-day administration of a large city.

He is an unceasing advocate of a single idea: instead of road metal, use asphalt paving for the streets. That, later, makes public transportation, based on trams and light railways, possible.

MELBOURNE, VICTORIA. 20 AUGUST 1860

A Big Idea

"At an early hour crowds of eager holiday folks, pedestrian and equestrian, were to be seen hieing along the dusty ways to the pleasant glades and umbrageous shade (a warm breeze, the first of the season, was blowing from the north-east) of the Royal Park. A busy scene was there presented. Men, horses, camels, drays, and goods were scattered here and there amongst the tents, in the sheds, and on the greensward in picturesque confusion – everything premised a departure." So the Melbourne *Herald* reported the next day.

Robert O'Hara Burke was beginning his Arthurian quest. Financed by a grant from the Victoria colonial government and by public subscription, he would be the first to cross the Australian continent vertically, from south to north. The *Herald*'s reporter did not know that the previous evening Burke had left his party as final arrangements were being made and gone into central Melbourne to throw this bouquet, the conquest of a continent, at the feet of the perky Julia Matthews. Unlike the Arthurian chronicles, the actress had her own script: no hand wringing and, frankly, Mr. Burke, I am not impressed.

The *Herald*'s reporter did know, however, but tactfully avoided mention that the assembly point for Burke's expedition was in a park next to the Melbourne General Cemetery.

The expedition was entirely successful, if one discounts the fact that seven men, two dozen camels and an unknown number of horses perished. Yet one man did indeed make the trek to the Gulf of Carpentaria and back.

Not Burke, but his third-in-command, John King, an ex-soldier in his early twenties, who already had completed more adventures then most men desire, being a veteran of the Indian Mutiny of 1857.

"Mr Burke has taken with him everything necessary for making signals in case any of the party should become separated in the bush ..." the *Herald* noted. "He has a large Chinese gong, two Union Jacks, and an ample supply of rockets and blue lights."

The heart of Burke's quest was a march from a base camp at Cooper's Creek to the Gulf, roughly 1,500 miles. Yes: march. Although he was well supplied with camels (a special purchase from India), he thought it an offence against the game to ride them too much, so mostly the camels carried packs and the men walked. Four men left base camp for the Gulf of Carpentaria, three made it. Virtually: Burke, his second-in-command John Wills, Charlie Gray and John King, yet they never actually saw open water or even heard the sea. The bush was too thick to penetrate and they were satisfied to taste brackish water that ran upstream at high tide.

The trip back was a cascade of errors, all made by Robert O'Hara Burke and accepted loyally by Wills and King (Gray dies early of dysentery and beri-beri). Refusal to take full advantage of Aboriginal hospitality. Bungled liaisons with relief companies. Abandonment of base camp. The choice of an improbable route south.

All those things the sole survivor, the loyal, stunned, stubbornly literal John King could recite for newspaper reporters when he was brought into Melbourne in November 1861. The journalists never asked him the real question that would haunt him the rest of his life: having touched the holy grail, did Robert O'Hara Burke really intend to survive? Wasn't he seeking the holy end that he found? Dressed in the clothes of a gentleman, his pistol in his right hand, he lay down on the earth. He instructed John King not to bury him and, with open eyes welcomed the morning sun that he believed would witness his immortality.

MELBOURNE. 1861

A Truly Daft Idea

The perfectly-professorial looking man is the son of the professor of medicine at Queen's College, Galway and is himself the foundation professor of natural science at the University of Melbourne, a post he assumed in 1855. He's a dab palaeontologist, but that hardly explains why he spends so much time with birds, game fish, and mammals from the British Isles. These he imports, looks after, and has released into the wild. Professor (eventually Sir) Frederick McCoy is a leading light in the Acclimatisation Society. It has nothing to do with adjusting Europeans to Australian reality, but quite the reverse: to turning Australia into a European forest park. So the society imports from the northern hemisphere dozens of song birds, game fish, deer and, in a word, introduces ecological disaster. Professor McCoy is a true believer. He thinks the grain-eating flocks of English sparrows are lovely and that the acclimatization of the rabbit (which the society did not itself import), was an example to be followed.

The introduction of alien species into the fragile Australian landscape was not solely an Irish predilection, yet one is struck by the coincidence that, in 1878, the prime mover in the South Australian Acclimatisation Society was Richard Minchin, Tipperary-born son of an Anglican rector and eventually the highly successful director of the Adelaide zoological gardens.

LAMBING FLATS, NSW. 1861

Attention to Detail

Most white miners were like waterbugs, skimming the surface of their world and flitting unpredictably from one site to another. The Chinese, because they were so often attacked, kept working at a site if it was secure from violence. At Lambing Flats this paid off. The white miners found a bit of gold, but not enough to hold their attention and, having marked the field, they skittered off. Chinese miners worked systematically and found plenty.

Not an unalloyed success: when the Europeans learned of the Chinese paydirt, they flooded back to Lambing Flats, claiming that the Chinese had stolen gold that was rightly theirs. Soon they outnumbered the Chinese and drove them to a sub-field, half a dozen miles distant.

Still, the Chinese did well. One bunch of whites, known as the Tipperary Mob, terrorized everyone in the diggings, and was especially violent when the Chinese were concerned. They ploughed a set of furrows around the new Chinese site and any yellow person found outside that enclosure knew his life was in danger. Pigtail collecting was a favourite Tipperary sport.

The semi-respectable voice of the white miners was the Miners' Protective League. James Torpy, Irish publican and a league leader, said it clearly, concerning the Chinese. "The instinct of self-preservation impels us to oppose their coming here."

Sunday, 30 June 1861, at least 3,000 white men collected in "Tipperary Gulch" and, with a German band leading the way, playing selections from Handel, they moved on the Chinese miners. Twelve hundred of them, roughly, were corralled and beaten, their belongings stolen, their shanties burned.

It took the government of New South Wales a month to restore order and only by using soldiers and marines was it able to do so. A Chinese Immigration and Goldfield Regulation Act, passed in 1861, gave the colony the right to refuse mining privileges to all Chinese. It stayed on the books for only six years; it was an interesting case of blaming the victims for the crime.

Like the Chinese miners, James Torpy of the Miners' Protective League paid attention to details. In the midst of all the racial attacks on the Chinese, he and a few friends quietly sold their rights to a high yielding claim to a Chinese syndicate.

The Chinese, mindful of diplomatic necessity, gave a banquet to honour the sellers, one long table holding European food, another Chinese. Eating heartily, Torpy decreed, "better to make a profit from an enemy than a loss."

KILMORE, VICTORIA. JULY 1862

Clear Start

The lad was eight and he perjured himself like a trooper. His Uncle James was up for cattle rustling and the lad and his mother provide an alibi, that he was with them when the crime occurred.

Perjury, no doubt whatsoever.

The court does not buy it and Uncle James is sentenced to three years.

Ned Kelly.

DUBLIN. 1862

Harbinger

The Rev. Patrick Bermingham, co-priest of the parish of Yass, New South Wales in the heartland of prosperous Irish-Australian farmers, is on an overseas mission.

His goal is to discredit the two ranking Australian ecclesiastics, who are in regular orders: Archbishop John Bede Polding, a Benedictine of English background, and Bishop James Goold, an Augustinian from Ireland. Previously, in 1859, Bermingham had written to Paul Cullen, archbishop of Dublin, and to the Vatican, urging that the Australian church be investigated.

Now, he reads a lengthy memorial to Cullen and to his secretary and nephew, the Rev. Patrick Moran. The Catholic people of Australia can only be saved by the replacement of all English-born bishops with Irish-born prelates. And secular clergy should be the backbone of church extension, not clergy in regular orders: the church militant in the colonies needed to be controlled, as was the Irish church, by a strict pyramid of authority.

This is music to Cardinal Cullen, who wishes his clerical empire to embrace the entire globe. To Archbishop Polding, however, it is such rank treason that he forbids Bermingham to return to Australia.

AVENEL, VICTORIA. 1865

Alternate Futures

"The lad's a proper hero, and should have an honour."

Ned Kelly, in his eleventh year, had acted with instinctive heroism and saved a six-year-old schoolmate from drowning. The boy's parents had a specially embossed sash made and presented to Ned at the local school.

Ned, now in the fourth grade, was already better educated than his parents, both of whom were illiterate. His father was a Tipperary pig-stealer who had been transported and had completed his sentence in 1848.

In October, Ned, who kept failing geography and English grammar, ended his formal education.

Family Force

As part of the scheme of Archbishop Cullen of Dublin to create a globe-circling ecclesiastical empire, Irishmen, when appointed to colonial sees, always took with them several priests. That way the new bishops could take control of a diocese quickly and impose proper order.

Father Daniel Murphy, who arrives in Tasmania to be installed as bishop, takes invasion tactics one step farther. He brings with him, as chaplain, his nephew. Then five months later, another clerical nephew and his own sister, Mother Superior Frances Murphy, arrive along with four Presentation Sisters under her direction. Later, two more nephews who are priests are appointed to serve in Bishop Murphy's diocese.

An autocrat in his diocese, as Cullen desired, and an obedient servant of his religious superiors, Murphy makes certain that his priests teach clearly the new doctrines of the age: the Immaculate Conception of the Virgin Mary (1854), and the details of the Syllabus of Errors (1864). Called to Rome for the Vatican Council, he casts his vote in 1870 the right way: in favour of the doctrine of Papal Infallibility, the definition of which has been much influenced by Paul Cullen, created the first Irish cardinal in 1866.

No Sale

"It's certainly a very inferior place."

"I'll dance at my own funeral rather than stay here."

The last vessel in the long list of transportation ships, the *Hougoumon*, lands in Western Australia. This is the only Australian colony that still accepts prisoners and, now, even in this labour-short jurisdiction, the practice is ceasing.

"A miserable place."

"A nation of humbugs."

On the *Hougoumon* are sixty-two "Fenian" prisoners, more formally, members of the Irish Republican Brotherhood. They were the largest segment of a collection of 105 Fenians who had been convicted between the autumn of 1865 and the spring of 1867, when an ill-planned and well-advertised Irish revolution had been attempted. Seventeen of the transportees had been in military units in the United Kingdom army.

> "The population of Western Australia may be divided into two classes – those actually in prison and those who more richly deserve to be ..."

The Irish political prisoners who arrive in 1868, like the men of 1848, are snobs, even if of a lower social class than their '48 predecessors. They look down on the Australian colonies and their citizens, whether free, emancipist, convict. Their own purity of motive makes them superior to these colonials and their own future lies in the USA or, at worst, back in Ireland, they reckon.

"Land of thick-skulls and narrow-minded bigots."

"The refuse ground of Old England."

The first to escape was the hard-driving John Boyle O'Reilly, a former Hussar, fine athlete, florid writer, the sort of person who would be wildly successful in Australia. On his fourth escape attempt, in 1869 he boarded an American whaler, and, by way of St. Helena, Liverpool, and Philadelphia, settled in Boston as editor of the influential Irish newspaper, the *Pilot*. Others followed, but escape was hardly necessary, as the London government was intent on getting the Fenians off the public-sympathy list as quickly as possible. Besides, a lot of Australians objected to having anyone but ordinary decent criminals on their pitch. Forty-five Fenian prisoners had been pardoned by the end of 1869. Of these only seven decided to remain in Australia.

"Land of boils, from its head to foot."

"Ants, flies, and pseudo-democrats."

By the early 1870s, a generous, if haphazard policy of pardoning everyone possible left only seven prisoners, former Irish military men with desertion or mutiny on their charge sheets, and one of these escaped. The final six were liberated in a daring venture planned in large part by John Boyle O'Reilly. By 1876 the Fenians' footprints were blown away, transient marks in the sand.

No more than a dozen of the Fenian convicts spent a significant amount of time as free men in Australia. They left as quickly as their pardons came through. But their disdain for Australia and Australians was clearly remembered. This condescension merged in public memory with the same attitude evinced by the Young Irelanders. Thus, when, later in the century, Australians of Irish background look for symbols of nationality, they ignore the men of 1868 and of 1848.

Their forebears are declared to be the rebels of 1798, a different heritage entirely.

CLONTARF PARK, SYDNEY, NSW. 12 MARCH 1868

A Family Matter?

The Australian colonies would have been a slightly better place for Irish Catholics had Henry J. O'Farrell not bellowed "I am a Fenian – God save Ireland!" just after he shot Prince Albert, the Duke of Edinburgh, in the back. The prince was saved by his thick braces. Albert, to his credit, argued for clemency for O'Farrell on the grounds that the man was insane, which he certainly was. Nevertheless, O'Farrell was hanged on 21 April, a remarkably quick carriage of justice. Part of his delusion had been that he was a Fenian: he was not.

Try telling that to the keener Protestants of Australia. Already they were on guard against Fenian disloyalty because of the sixty-two Fenians who had recently arrived in Western Australia, sixty of the sixty-two were Catholics, and though the Irish Catholic population did not take to the Fenians, Protestant orators made great play about Catholicism and disloyalty, using motifs that ran all the way back to the English Reformation. A Protestant Protective Association sprang up in Sydney and ran a rancid anti-Catholic campaign for ten years or so before running out of vitriol.

Unfortunate for the Catholics and beclouding of historical understanding.

Rewind the tape and look at the O'Farrell family and it is clear that the whole business had little to do with English royalty, Irish oppression, or Catholic disloyalty.

Observe two brothers, Peter and Henry O'Farrell, part of a family of eleven children of a prosperous butcher. They were born in Dublin, spent time in Liverpool and then the whole family migrated in 1841 to Melbourne: without requiring governmental assistance. The elder O'Farrell became a minor city official. Peter qualified as a solicitor and Henry attended seminary, studied in Europe and took deacon's orders. But Henry was never priested, as he had a row with Bishop Goold of Melbourne about church doctrine, never a good thing to argue about with an Irish bishop. Frustrated in his religious vocation, Henry drank heavily, became delusional, paranoid and violent.

His brother Peter was for a time much more successful. He did well as a young solicitor, but then he too had problems with Bishop Goold. They arose because he had represented the bishop in a defence against the creditors of St. Patrick's Cathedral, which Goold was financing in complex ways, including not paying the construction bills. The business became very nasty, and Peter O'Farrell ended with both Bishop Goold and most of the prosperous Catholics of Melbourne shunning him. He had to leave Melbourne for several years as it was impossible for him to find clients.

In common: careers blighted, each brother believed, by Bishop (Archbishop 1874) James Alipius Goold.

Fast forward: in August 1882, Peter O'Farrell stalks Archbishop Goold and shoots at him. He misses, but the shock sends the archbishop into a mortal decline.

Peter O'Farrell knew whom he was trying to kill. In contrast, his brother Henry, mad as a march hare, hearing voices, forming imaginary Fenian units, might have been trying to kill the Duke of Edinburgh. Or, equally likely, the family nemesis, Bishop Goold.

ROCKHAMPTON, QUEENSLAND. 1 JUNE 1868

A Head of His Time

> *"Quite a nice specimen of its sort."*
> *"Oh, may I hold it?"*
> *"Careful, it's a bit large."*

Thomas Griffin of County Antrim had a good record in the Royal Irish Constabulary and had won two decorations in the Crimean War.

He easily moved up the ranks of the colonial police services and was magistrate and gold commissioner in Rockhampton. It was demeaning, certainly, for him to be reduced after his death to serving as a mere conversation piece on a banker's mantel.

> *"However did you come to have this?"*
> *"Oh, I daren't tell you, my dear. Quite the treasure though, isn't it?"*
> *"Does hair grow on it after death?"*
> *"I should say so: remember Blessed Oliver Plunkett."*

Griffin, hounded by demands for payment of his heavy gambling debts and by a deserted wife for money, held up a gold and specie shipment and shot the two troopers who were escorting it. He tried to muddy the investigation, as he was nominally in charge, but he spent some of the notes. They were traced to him.

Hanged 1 June 1868, his body was dug up within a week by an unusual set of grave robbers: the local surgeon Dr. O'Callaghan, Thaddeus O'Kane, the town's newspaper editor and the banker, R.H. White. They were curious about such a murderous monster and felt he would be well worth dissecting. Completing this task shortly after dark one night, they passed the rest of the evening at their weekly whist game.

Griffin, they observed, had an unusually large head.

ELEVEN MILE CREEK, NR GRETA,
NORTHERN VICTORIA. 1869

Kick the Cat

The first time Ned Kelly was up on charges was for kicking about a Chinaman. At age fourteen, that was a rite of passage for any Irish back-country lad, something like shooting a kangaroo or getting drunk for the first time. Ned beat the charges, but spent twelve days in the local lock-up while the court waited for a Chinese interpreter to arrive.

"Red" Kelly, Ned's father, had died in 1866 and the family had moved to a compound owned by Ned's grandfather, James Quinn. This was a run of 25,000 acres on desperately spare land: fifty acres were needed to pasture a single bullock. Still, there were sufficient resources in this vast patch to support the extended family that lived on it. They only had to want to work.

That's why one phrase that came up in the trial was revealing: according to the Chinese chicken and pig dealer whom Ned had dusted up, Ned had said "I am a bushranger."

QUEENSLAND. 1869

Trained

The tenth anniversary of the creation by the Queensland government of its Native Mounted Police arrives and everyone is pleased. Created by one of the first executive acts of Governor Bowen after Queensland received responsible government, the force has been remarkably efficient, and it's a pleasure to watch. Only 200-250 men, Aboriginals under white officers, the force saves hundreds, perhaps thousands, of white lives. "The Native Police are the only men who could be of any use" to fight the blacks in heavy bush, writes Edward Quinn, police magistrate of one of the contested districts.

The black police pick up the language of their officers. They call the indigène whom they drive out or hunt down "niggers." Like collaborator units the world over, the Native Police attack, mutilate, kill their own kind with such cruelty and enthusiasm that it scares their white officers. "All they think or talk about," one officer observes, "is the number of niggers they have shot."

It's all the officers can do to keep them from running amok and becoming a terrorist tribe all their own.

Naked, save for an ammunition belt around the waist, a rifle in one hand, a large bush knife in the other, they hunt the wild Aborigines with a ferocity that is born of the deepest self-hatred.

SYDNEY, NSW. 1869

Very Well Trained

Meeting in Synod, the Australian bishops do what Paul Cullen, now (since 1866) Cardinal Archbishop of Dublin, wants. This is not surprising. Twelve Irish bishops are appointed by virtue of Cullen's influence between 1846 and his death in 1878. Cullen is also one of the cardinals in charge of the Sacred Congregation of Propaganda, and that gives him a direct involvement in Australian matters.

Both the Holy Spirit and the will of Cardinal Cullen being present, the bishops proclaim to the Australian colonies a condemnation of "mixed" education. This was a restatement of the decree by Ireland's Synod of Thurles of 1850, condemning Catholic and Protestant children being educated together, unless in a strictly Catholic environment. The bishops demand their own school system, at government expense, and eventually they will win, though it takes long decades. Segregated education, their ideal, will keep their people both Catholic and Irish. So they believe.

NORTHERN VICTORIA. 1870

Intuition

"By-Christ, you scare me lad." Henry Power, experienced bushranger of the Greta country, put out his hand. "We'll shake as we part, now." Ned stared at a fixed point six inches behind Power's brow. "That I'll take with no offence." He shook the offered hand, then turned, mounted, and rode off.

Ned was not quite fifteen and he frightened a man like Power: an Irish felon, who had ranged the region for the previous six years as an escaped convict; famous nationally for robbing anything that moved, from solitary wayfarers to public coaches. He was totally fearless, yet Ned Kelly frightened him. He had taken Ned on as a protégé and there was no denying the lad's abilities.

The trouble was those cold eyes. They usually seemed to be focusing on a target. Henry Power was proud of never having killed a victim or even a policeman and that in over 600 robberies. Power's professionalism and surgical precision did not impress young Ned, though he certainly learned the practical bits. No, he only showed enthusiasm when talking of his own future: dazzling, against-the-odds robberies and the killing of police and all pursuers. At those moments, Power observed, Ned's eyes turned red, like a feral cat's, and they flickered rapidly, as if seeking for something to dismember.

SYDNEY AND MELBOURNE. 1870

St. Patrick's Song

On the fifteenth of June 1870, just three days before the First Vatican Council decreed the doctrine of Papal Infallibility, William Cordner died. The Vatican meeting was oecumenical in the old-fashioned sense; his life ecumenical in the modern. For, trained as a chorister in Armagh's Anglican Cathedral, Cordner had brought St. Patrick's song first to St. Patrick's Roman Catholic Church, Sydney, and then to St. Mary's Cathedral. It was passing strange to have a choral master who was Protestant and a rough former-seaman as well, but for a dozen years he made the Catholic cathedral the fountainhead of choral music in Australia.

A gentle story in an era of increasing Catholic-Protestant harshness, but not unique. In Melbourne, David Lee, also trained as a chorister and as an organist at Armagh Cathedral School (ten years after Cordner's time) was spreading music of the same Irish school. He taught choral music to several Protestant congregations, but his biggest performance was in March 1880, when he inaugurated the great organ at St. Patrick's Roman Catholic Cathedral, Melbourne.

MELBOURNE. 18 SEPTEMBER 1871

Irish Poetic Circles

When, in May 1870, Gerald Supple shot and wounded the sometime editor of the Melbourne *Age*, for having offended in his treatment of Irish matters, it was his duty in honour.

The circle of fate was unkind to Supple, for he only wounded in the elbow Ireland's supposed enemy, and the bullet passed on, killing an unoffending Irishman, Sean Walshe.

Supple was a direct descendant of Edmund Spenser who had conquered a bit of Ireland himself and had made excellent verse. In his youth, Supple became a minor Young Irelander, and he wrote bad verse that tried to undo the conquest.

In Australia, he came up for sentencing while his old editor from the *Nation*, Charles Gavan Duffy, was premier of Victoria. The circle stayed unbroken: Duffy worked hard for a commutation of Supple's death sentence, which the governor granted.

NR. SHEPPARTON, VICTORIA. 1872

Invisible Category

Catherine Treahy has recently married James Morrow, one of the thousands of migrants from the tense districts of Ulster – in his case, County Tyrone.

She spends the nights alone, the first hours of darkness in tears; the next segment in fear and frighted prayer as she listens to the sounds of the bush and imagines terrors, animal and human; finally she sleeps fitfully and awakes to a day of small animal husbandry and a war with a crude hearth and few domestic comforts.

Catherine's life is not unusual. If the Australian colonial census had possessed a category for things-no-one-mentions, it would include a count of the thousands of women who live alone on a piece of land, fulfilling the settlement duties required for legal possession, while their husbands work for cash elsewhere.

Catherine is lucky, for James, a mechanic and inventor, works most of the week in town, and he comes home on Saturday night or, at worst, early Sunday morning. But in the harvesting season he does custom work with a threshing machine and then he is gone for weeks at a stretch.

The arrangement is successful, for the Morrows acquire, first 320 acres and then, with Catherine in charge, an additional 1,000 acres.

All these women: invisible because few of their names are even on the registry of land titles.

MELBOURNE. 1873

Blackbirding

"Right, now. What's the count?"
"Twenty-seven sir."

"Full complement then."

"Aye, sir."

The warship *Alacrity* is detailed to make a futile gesture. It is to return a small number of men and women who have been enslaved: "Kanakas," from a Hawaiian word for man or human.

The Australian colonies never admitted publicly to permitting slavery, yet between 1863 and 1904, nearly 60,000 men, and some women, from the Pacific Islands were enslaved. In theory they were contract workers, and some were returned to their home islands, mostly in the Solomons, New Hebrides, and Gilberts, but no one cared to calculate the mortality. Queensland and the far north of New South Wales was their field of servitude, on cotton, or more often, sugar plantations.

Like all slavery, "blackbirding" operated by seduction (sparkling goods displayed in the holds of ships), abandonment by traditional chiefs (they sold "engagements" of their fittest young men), and sheer brutality: sinking native canoes and fishing the swimmers out of the water and into captivity.

Even in this brutal game, the rules could be broken. The *Alacrity* is sailing with its repatriated Kanakas because Dr. James Patrick Murray had gone two steps too far. He had filled the hold of his blackbirding vessel with men and women from the New Hebrides and Solomons mostly by running down native canoes. When the hold was full, a fight broke out between men of different islands, a common occurrence. Dr. Murray ordered his men to fire into the hold and they did so with withering effect: fifty natives killed and sixteen wounded. All these bodies, dead and living, were thrown overboard and the ship scrubbed down and whitewashed.

What put Dr. Murray two steps beyond acceptable behaviour was the evidence that while himself firing at the natives, he sang the American Civil War song "Marching through Georgia."

MELBOURNE. 1875

XXXX

Privileged Catholics, like privileged Protestants, use the Australian colonies in the same way: as places for second, third … seventh, eighth sons to maintain social and economic positions at a level impossible at home in Ireland. The migrants benefit, but so do the colonies, for these migrants bring with them both financial and intellectual capital.

Nicholas FitzGerald arrives in Melbourne in 1875, the eighth son of a big Catholic brewer. Like many Irish Catholics of his class, he has studied at Trinity College, Dublin (never mind it's nominally Protestant) and then kept his terms in the Inns of Court. One of his brothers is on the way to being accountant-general of the United Kingdom's navy, and another has just started a brewery in Melbourne. Nicholas joins the brewery as joint manager and eventually becomes managing director.

A blessing to the entire world: the Castlemaine brewery.

And Nicholas fully deserves the papal knighthood that he receives from Leo XIII.

MELBOURNE. 1875

Mild at Heart

As chancellor of the University of Melbourne, Redmond Barry presides with a mixture of pomp, verbal rodomontade, wit, and genuine love of learning. Although not always credited with the fact, he was the primary founder of the university and he served as chancellor from its foundation until his own death.

Similarly, he was the founder of the Melbourne Public Library which, long after his death, evolved into the State Library of Victoria. This bit of charity was slightly self-serving as Barry wanted to preserve his own personal library from overuse: for he was so affable a man, and so keen on useful knowledge, that he allowed the general public to use his house and its newspapers, periodicals and books, as a public reading room.

The son of a major-general with a County Cork estate, he had done Trinity College and the Irish bar and become a mild nationalist: a close friend was his fellow Anglican, Isaac Butt, legal defender of the Young Irelanders and later founder of the Irish Home Rule Movement. Making no fortune at the Irish bar, Redmond Barry emigrated in the late 1830s and became a success in Victoria: successful at law, where he did a lot of unpopular cases, especially those involving Aboriginal interests, for which he received no fees.

Successful socially, too, but perhaps a bit too good with women. On his emigration voyage, Redmond Barry had been locked in his cabin by the captain of the ship because he was too-obviously sleeping with a married woman whom he had met on board. And, in Melbourne in the mid 1840s he had a long affair with a woman who bore him four children. He supported the children and he, his lover, and the children often appeared together in public. As a benevolent wildman, Redmond Barry had a free pass: he was accepted socially at the top of Melbourne society.

Barry became the first solicitor-general of the independent Victoria Colony in 1851 and then, a year later, he became one of the three supreme court judges for Victoria. He was given to harsh sentencing, but fair trials. Most of the rebels from the Eureka stockade were tried before him, and there were no charges of unfairness.

Of all the judges in the Australian colonies, he was the one who was least apt to make a circus of a really important criminal trial.

SYDNEY. 1876

Remembering Zion

The square-built man in his mid-thirties said to himself time and time again, "I wish I'd never done it."

James Patrick Garvin of County Limerick agreed to be co-chairman of the Irish patriotic celebrations for the centenary in 1876 of Daniel O'Connell's birth in 1775. Garvin was the founder and owner of three insurance companies and of a steamship line. The celebrations were well within his considerable abilities.

But he was nearly driven mad by the comments that followed the patriotic event. "Fine celebrations. First class. Pity they were a year late."

And, some Irish patriots did not even mention the Liberator.

All they wanted to do with Garvin was reminisce about that historic day, more than fifteen years earlier when Garvin, a superb athlete, had thrown a cricket ball a record distance, 121 yards, one foot.

ADELAIDE, SOUTH AUSTRALIA. 1877

Weight of Office

No justice in it at all: Captain William Wellington Cairns of Cultra, County Down, had soldiered smartly through the labyrinth of empire: postmaster-general of Ceylon, lieutenant-governor of Malacca and then of St. Christopher and then of Honduras and then of Trinidad. Then his health became ropey and for some unexplainable reason the colonial office made him governor of Queensland.

Next, he is appointed governor of South Australia.

He dutifully arrives and after only eight weeks resigns because of insomnia.

His subjects learn of this with envy: whatever can he have found to keep him awake?

BEECHWORTH, VICTORIA. 9 OCTOBER 1878

Second Impressions

Mrs. Edward Kelly and Justice Sir (since 1877) Redmond Barry encounter each other in the bare and small courtroom in Beechworth. They know each other, having previously met in court, so their encounter has a tired quality, as if each has heaved a sigh and said, Oh, naught's to be done.

Mrs. Kelly has seen a hundred Redmond Barrys. He is only the polished household-god version of what most of her "respectable" Irish neighbours wish to be. His amiability with the locals when he is not deliberating, and his contrasting solemnity while on the bench, involve just the squire-like characteristics that lace-curtain jump-ups wish to emulate. He's like the plump priest of a fat parish somewhere in County Meath. Oh, she knows him all right, and there's no changing. Beneath his evenhandedness, she knows, is the same righteousness as that of her respectable neighbours who have tried to her run off her little farm at Eleven Mile Creek because she is the centre of a criminal network.

Justice Barry sees a tough woman, shebeen owner and sly-grog dealer. He honours her request to be called Mrs. Kelly, and to be regarded as a widow. Fair enough: the Californian horse-thief with whom she has lived for four years has suddenly disappeared, leaving her with the two children he had sired and a third very obviously on the way. Barry knows this sort of Irish mother: hard as nails, keening her own fate like a banshee, and producing childer that, if they are male, spend their entire lives trying to please her and feeling guilty as a tree full of mortal sins for not being able to do so.

Mrs. Kelly is in court, along with her son-in-law, for aiding an attempted murder on Constable Alexander Fitzpatrick. It's a serious charge, but Barry, a shrewd judge, senses it has a tinge of alum around the edges. Constable Fitzpatrick is a green trooper and his story, of having been shot in the wrist, smacks of a face-saving tale. He certainly had been drinking in Mrs. Kelly's house (and not having tea and scones as suggested in a fanciful twist that serves both the constable's and the good widow's interests), when he had something of a run-in with Mrs. Kelly, her two alleged accomplices and her son, Dan Kelly, who has as yet not been apprehended. The weird part of the story is that the constable also names Ned Kelly as participating in the brawl and, in fact, shooting several times. Ned was nowhere near.

In their minds' eyes, both Mrs. Kelly and Redmond Barry see the missing lads, Ned and Dan. Each lad has a warrant out for him for horse stealing (at which they are very good), each has spent prison time already (at which they also were quite good, nearly model prisoners when they wanted to be) and now, each faces this floating attempted-murder warrant. The lads, in their twenties, could be any pair of stockmen, trail riders, drovers in the hard country that runs from northern Victoria all the way up to Queensland. They wear plaid shirts, moleskin trousers with tightly pegged strapped bottoms so that they don't ride up while the men are in the saddle. Thin, rake-faced, they sport cabbage tree hats, set back at a cocky angle. And their faces: their rule is to wear no expression that would give a hint to an outsider what their emotions might be. A hint of a smile is permitted, however, when the spurs on their California boots are slashed along the flanks of a horse and it bolts into a furious gallop. They each carry a stubby pipe and a rope of tobacco and a rifle and a revolver. Only in their firearms are the Kelly boys oversupplied.

The jury finds Mrs. Kelly, her son-in-law, and her neighbour guilty of abetting an attempted murder, but Justice Barry puts off sentencing them. He needs time to find an equilibrium. Of course the jury had no alternative but to find them guilty, for both a constable and a surgeon had testified to a bullet wound. Cooked evidence, Barry reckons, but only in that the young constable was beaten with a shovel, rather than shot; the habitués of Mrs. Kelly's shebeen would indeed have killed him if he hadn't gotten out of there when he did.

Finally, Redmond Barry decides on a sentence that is so short for abetting an attempted murder of a police officer that it makes the constabulary observers blanch: Mrs. Kelly gets three years and the two men six years each.

That's as close as Justice Barry could come to impeaching the official witnesses. He's canny, though; no one ever said he wasn't. In passing sentence, he blows and bellows about Ned Kelly, who of course isn't there to inhale this cloud of judicial smoke. Barry says that if he were here, why Ned Kelly would be sentenced to twenty-one years.

That's the kind of thing the police like to hear.

LIVERPOOL AND SYDNEY, NSW. 1878

The Resurrection of the Body

The gravediggers use a silver-plated shovel. This at the insistence of Dean Dwyer, eminent ecclesiastic and grandson of Michael Dwyer, guerilla leader of 1798. The body of the Dean's grandfather is disinterred from the small burying ground in Liverpool and is reburied reverently in the Devonshire Street Cemetery in Sydney. Now Michael Dwyer rests beside his wife Mary, who died in 1860, and one of his daughters. A respectable railing and headstone mark the family plot.

STRINGYBARK CREEK, VICTORIA. 2 OCTOBER 1878

Repetition

Dear God, it's old.

What is now the "Kelly gang," Ned and Dan Kelly, Joseph Byrne and Stephen Hart (all Irish) are pursued by Sergeant Michael Kennedy and

Constables Michael Scanlon, Thomas Lonigan, and Thomas McIntyre (three out of the four are Irish).

Then, when the police gang rests and reconnoitres, the Kelly gang pursues them. The involuted pattern is like the snakes in the Book of Kells.

At 5:00 in the afternoon, the Kellys jump Lonigan and McIntyre who are resting at camp, while Scanlon and Kennedy are scouting. Lonigan is shot through the head, and McIntyre is taken captive. He is given a cup of tea and the Kellys wait for the other two lawmen to return. When they do so, McIntyre mouths the words Ned gives him: surrender, surrender, surrender. Scanlon starts to unsling his rifle and Ned shoots him dead. Sergeant Kennedy takes a bullet in the arm and is captured. McIntyre, in all the confusion, jumps awkwardly onto Kennedy's horse and, sprawled sideways, makes his escape.

Seated on the ground, his back against a tree, Kennedy pleads for his life. Dan Kelly wants him shot straightaway and keeps pushing the muzzle of his rifle against Kennedy's chest. Finally, either Ned or Dan shoots the sergeant: no one knows. What is clear is that Ned requires all four members of the gang to shoot into Kennedy's body, joining each of them to the act.

Dear God, it's an old story: Irishmen killing each other, all over His world.

"KELLY COUNTRY," VICTORIA AND NEW SOUTH WALES. JANUARY 1879-JUNE 1880

Problem Solving

Sir Hercules Robinson was one of the empire's better problem solvers. His family estates in the Irish midlands had been bankrupted by the Irish Famine, but he had been excellent at arranging famine relief and Dublin Castle and, later, London, repaid him. He sorted out in the early 1850s the archaic, chaotic, and often-violent snarl that Irish fairs and markets created; and having done that well, was rewarded with the presidency of Montserrat. This burgeoned into the governorship-in-chief of all the Leeward Islands, and then success as governor of Ceylon and next, in 1872, the governorship of New South Wales.

The fat, bald little man might not have looked like much, but he had a brain.

So, in March 1879, as he is about to take his next post, the governorship of New Zealand, he solves a family problem and helps preserve Australian social order at the same time.

Sir Hercules's young nephew, Standish O'Connor, finds himself in a spot of bother because of soft-minded clergy. An Anglican bishop has reported to the colonial secretary that Sub-Inspector O'Connor and his section of the Native Police have rounded up and massacred twenty-eight Aboriginal males. Naturally, O'Connor's superiors support him, but he needs to be kept out of sight for a while. Thus, exiting-Governor Robinson has his nephew, six black trackers, and a sub-officer detailed to search out the Kelly gang. If they have success, fine, but for heaven's sake, stay low and avoid moral crusaders.

To his chagrin, Standish O'Connor is treated as a contact-leper by the regular police. They have no time for someone who uses black boys to chase white men. Yet, for the next fifteen months, it is these black trackers who prey on Ned Kelly's mind more than any other danger, save informers. The Native Police and Sub-Inspector O'Connor, accustomed to hunting natives in Queensland, work smoothly together, communicating by hand-signals, silently working a copse like beaters on a grouse shoot.

Ned has his lads put away their horses and move about on foot. With the proceeds of two stylish robberies in hand – Euroa in Victoria and Jerilderie in New South Wales, where the gang had taken the whole town captive – the four bandits can afford to go to ground.

The Kelly gang has another problem: three informers, of which they know of only one. One is a drover who moves about the countryside buying and selling stock and removing diseased beasts. He is unknown to them, as is the second one, Pat Quinn, an uncle of the Kellys. The third informer, however, tips his hand: Aaron Sherritt, boyhood chum of Joe Byrne, son of a Royal Irish Constabulary officer, husband of Joe's sister.

That problem, however, is solved on 27 June 1880, when Joe Byrne and Dan Kelly knock on Sherritt's front door: he answers and they blow his brains into the roof.

MELBOURNE. 20 JANUARY 1880

Public Policy: A Control Case

Being the son of the rector of Rathfriland, County Down, had its advantages for Andrew Scott. He knew how to act in proper circles, so that upon his arrival in Melbourne in April 1868, at age twenty-six, he was quickly appointed stipendiary lay reader in the Anglican Church of the Holy Trinity. Scott moved on to serve as lay reader to a parish near Ballarat and there he made friends with a local bank clerk. Scott used this friendship to ease himself into his first robbery: in disguise, he held up his friend's bank and left a note signed with the Irish catchword "Captain Moonlite." His spelling was intentionally inaccurate and thus a century ahead of its time.

A few bad cheques and an escape from Ballarat lock-up later, Scott found himself before Justice Sir Redmond Barry who gave him eleven years of hard labour: ten for the bank robbery and one for escaping gaol.

After seven years, Andrew Scott was released and became, as many prisoners do, a strong advocate of prison reform. Had he and some former prison mates not attacked a sheep station he might have been all right, but they took two children hostage. In the ensuing gun battle with police, a trooper was killed.

That is why Andrew George Scott's feet do not touch the ground on 20 January 1880. Executing police killers is a matter of public policy, and Scott's hanging sends a message into the scrag country of northern Victoria.

MELBOURNE GAOL. 11 NOVEMBER 1880

Pre-Writing History

The last person to deal officially with Ned Kelly was an Irishman, for how could it be any other way? Ned's whole life was fought within an Irish world. The man was Henry Glenny, an enthusiastic Wesleyan Methodist and temperance promoter from Newry, County Down. Well-known as Victoria's most successful insurance salesman, he had papered northern Victoria with the policies of the National Mutual Life Association. As a justice of the

*peace (rather than in his capacity as the Ballarat secretary of both the Society
for the Prevention of Cruelty to Animals, and of the Prisoners' Aid Society),
he examined Ned's body and signed the gaol register certifying that Mr.
Kelly had been hanged by the neck until dead.*

Ned Kelly won, if one takes the long view, which Ned tried to do.
He would not have been pleased, of course, that his head was removed and passed to a phrenologist. That, however, would not have
surprised him: famous criminals were often beheaded for bogus-sci-
ence or as keepsakes. Ned's head served as a police paperweight for a
time and then gathered dust on a shelf and finally disappeared.

*The second-last person to have significant official dealing with Ned Kelly
was also Irish. Justice Sir Redmond Barry who, after the jury pronounced
Kelly guilty of the murder of Constable Lonigan, pronounced the death sentence. Kelly's trial was correct procedurally and, given public policy of the
time, the sentence was just: Kelly could have been had for other murders, but
one was quite enough. Redmond Barry was himself under a death sentence,
as his health was imperfect. He died twelve days after Kelly's execution. He
was loved and celebrated as an Irishman who had come to Melbourne in
1839 when it was a small backwater, and he had invested his life in building
it into a major city.*

Nevertheless, Ned won. Petitions for his reprieve from execution,
containing 32,000 signatures, were presented to the governor and executive council of Victoria. To no effect: but they show that already,
even before his death and before his history was rewritten as legend,
he was carrying a large public with him. He was game, the lone man
against the long odds, the cheeky lad in a society still close enough to
its convict roots to admire someone who gave the short stick to authority.

*The police sergeants, inspectors, sub-inspectors who commanded the de-
struction of the Kelly gang at Glenrowan at the end of June 1880 were
mostly Irish. How could it have been any other way? Senior Constable Kelly,
Sergeant Sadleir, Sub-Inspector O'Connor, Sergeant Steele (an RIC veteran). Most of the men under them were first- or second-generation Irish.
This was an intra-tribal matter.*

Ned Kelly won the war for his name because he gave up on winning the war for his life. His permitting his gang to be surrounded in
a small Victorian town was unnecessary: they actually waited for a
police train to arrive, planning to ambush it in some berserker *Götter-
dammerung*, and when the train driver was warned, the Kelly gang
did not disappear into the bush, but took the town over and drank

heavily and prepared to die. Suicidal? Only God can know, but it is hard to explain why Dan Kelly and Steve Hart were provisioned with poison which they swigged down in liquor bottles as, wounded, they faced the bullets and fire bombs of the police; what killed them first, bullets or toxins, is beyond examination. Only Joe Byrne died unambiguously of gun shots.

Most obviously suicidal was the gang's dumbfounding creation of suits of body armour, weighing nearly an hundred weight, pounded from the metal of mouldboards of plows – the cast-iron section that cuts the earth and turns the furrows. This armour was not merely mediaeval in concept, but in practice: for wearing these devices precluded flight, and traveling light and flying fast was what a bush outlaw gang had to do to survive. And they had only one helmet between them, severely limiting the value of their armour against bullets. Ned wore the helmet, and he walked out into the open, guns blazing.

By any normal standard he was a ridiculous sight: a big talcum tin on legs. That, of course was his trouble: while bullets bounced off his torso and helmet, Sergeant Steele simply shot Ned in the legs and he became a big land tortoise that had turned upside down.

Ned Kelly won: really? Yes, because he wrote one of the most brilliant pieces of Irish nationalist propaganda ever. Forget comparing Kelly to his American fellow-sociopath Billy the Kid, another Irish intelligence, but far inferior to Kelly. Instead, Kelly deserves to be mentioned in the same breath as the greatest of all Irish propaganda-masters, John Mitchel. He is that good. John Mitchel seduced the hundreds of Irish historians who followed him into reading Ireland's greatest natural catastrophe, the Famine, as an English conspiracy – a brilliant reinvention of history. Ned Kelly did something equally amazing: he *pre*-invented history, his own.

This Ned achieves in early 1879 in the town of Jerilderie, New South Wales. The entire town is being held captive: the two local policemen are locked inside their own barracks, sixty citizens are kept in one of the local hotels, and the Kelly gang gets ready to empty the local branch of the Bank of New South Wales. Ned has brought with him a bundle of papers. He has written an 8,000 word declaration that he wants the local printer to set in type. Alas, the printer is out of town. So Ned gives this "Jerilderie letter" to a bank clerk and only years after Ned's execution does it become known to historians. Thereafter, they are in his thrall. A rolling white-hot blend of vituperation, self-justification, theodicy, and paranoid hallucination, the Jerilderie letter has the same sort of power found in the Book of Enoch, or the Apocalypse of Saint John. Pure hatred, so pure that it becomes apocalyptic art.

Ned believes: Irish convicts throughout Australian history have been virtuous, the victims of English oppression. *"More was transported to Van Diemen's Land to pine their young lives away in starvation and misery among tyrants worse than the promised hell itself. All of true blood, bone and beauty, not murdered on their own soil, or had fled to America nor other countries to bloom again another day were doomed to Port McQuarier, Toweringabbie, Norfolk Island or Emu Plains ..."*

Ned believes: the police are *"big, ugly, fat necked, wombat-headed big-bellied, magpie-legged, narrow hipped, splay-footed sons of Irish bailiffs or English landlords ..."*

Yes, the Irish were the largest national group in the Victoria and New South Wales police and half of them, roughly, were Catholics. Ned believes: the Catholic policeman *"... is a traitor to his country, ancestors and religion, as they were all Catholics before the Saxons and Cranmore [Cranmer] yoke held sway."*

If so, then why did Mrs. Kelly, Ned's mother, use the Victoria police in a family feud? – when her brother-in-law had tried to seduce her forcibly and had been stopped by a bottle of gin shattered on his head. He had then tried to burn down her house and she and her children were lucky to escape alive. At that time, 1872, the judge, Redmond Barry, protected Mrs. Kelly and her children by sentencing her brother-in-law to death, though this was later commuted. And, further, if the police were such an evil bunch, why did Ned's uncle, Patrick Quinn, who hated the lawless gang, voluntarily provide information to them?

Ned believes: the entire legal system *"is a Saxon yoke ..."*

And, if so, why was the legal system that pinched on Ned and, allegedly, on all Irish people, run in Victoria mostly by Irishmen? They were 40 percent of the lawyers in the 1850s and after; and four of the five ranking justices were Irish.

Ned Kelly leaves hints of a half-formed idea for a no-go zone that will exclude the forces of law and order. Later romantics can see this as some inchoate, instinctive Irish republic to be formed by the resentful, barely-above-subsistence Irish small farmers of Kelly country. Certainly the "Greta Mob," of three dozen bush larrikins would have supported Kelly. And if police records and later memoirs are accurate, probably ten dozen local farmers were on his side. And if their extended families are included, maybe 1,000 persons would have been actually willing to aid him and maybe to go to war for Ned. Maybe. No one mentions that for each follower of Kelly there were several who remembered him as a thief, and a bully, fearsomely violent. Kelly's republic would have been the arena for a nice little civil war.

Still Ned wins and it's because he was able to pre-write his own history, and to project into a wider world the tawdry events of a local tribal war. What was shabby on site – the drunken gunmen herding the citizens of Glenrowan into a hotel to use them as shields, becomes, when projected onto the clouds of Ireland's freedom struggle, a tactical move of unimpeachable purity. And the entire, long suicidal trek that ran from Jerilderie to the gallows is converted from the doings of three drunks led by a madman into a holy pilgrimage along the path of martyrdom.

Ned won big.

ST. MARY'S ANGLICAN CHURCH, BALMAIN, NSW. 1882

Complexity

Irish Protestant bigots, like their Catholic counterparts, are much more complex than they appear on the surface, and they too have historical roots that the dust of their day-to-day actions obscure.

In late 1882, the Rev. Mervyn Archdall assumes the rectorship of St. Mary's, Balmain, a lead church in a very evangelical diocese. He has a horror of anything that smacks of Rome, especially Ritualism within the Anglican church. "First it comes purring gently and with feline step, and asks only 'toleration.'" But then, he warns, "once tolerated it soon threatens until it can safely show and use its claws." The Rev. Mr. Archdall became one of the leaders of the Australian Protestant Defence Association.

An opportunistic demagogue? No. His father had been a priest in the Church of Ireland and Archdall's parents had been run out of Ulster by Catholic violence.

A simple hater? No. The Rev. Mr. Archdall was one of the leaders of the Australian protests against the Russian pogroms against the Jews. He was fluent in Hebrew and deeply read in French, German and Dutch theological writings.

And here is the long skein: his County Fermanagh ancestors, while fighting a constant colonial war against Catholics, included one Mervyn Archdall, Anglican rector, authority on Irish history, author of *Monasticon Hibernicum* (1786). And a collateral descendant of the same name (albeit variant spelling) became minister for agriculture and commerce in the government of Northern Ireland, pressed hard against Catholic civil rights, while zealously preserving ancient Catholic historical sites.

The Archdalls, like everybody Irish, are part of a long, often invisible chain, of which no individual member knows the full length and duration.

MELBOURNE. 1883

Evangelists

The brothers John and William Redmond make the first of their several missionary tours of Australia and New Zealand. They are the apostles of Charles Stewart Parnell, unswervingly loyal to the man and to his principle of Home Rule for Ireland.

The Redmonds' tour begins in Adelaide, swings east, plays Sydney and ends with a convention of the Irish National League in Melbourne. They raise about £15,000 for Parnell's cause.

The missionaries are so tactful, so careful not to adopt Fenian or revolutionary postures that their opponents are reduced to attacking them as being extremists in the guise of moderates. The Redmonds attract mostly, but not solely, Irish Catholics (Henry Higgins, rising young Protestant lawyer, for example, risks his career by appearing on a platform with them). The Redmonds point out that all Ireland is asking for is what the Australian colonies have had since the 1850s when New South Wales, Victoria, and Queensland obtained responsible government.

Great and winning tact, and never more so than when the Redmonds, who were the genteel products of Clongowes Wood and (in John's case) of Trinity College, Dublin, had to visit the homes of local Irish leaders. They take tea in dozens of wooden boxes of which their owners are very proud. Homes that, if two storeys, form almost perfect cubes. Everywhere they are expected to admire the view from the veranda. Families that are substantial enough to contribute a few hundred pounds to the Home Rule cause must be cultivated, and that means spending long hours in drawing rooms that are decorated on the principle of the-gaudier-the-better: marble mantels, gilt mirrors, chairs that are covered in cretonne in colours and patterns that could be used for railway safety signals. And carpets designed for hotels, random patterns intended to absorb spills and expectorations.

The Redmonds say a prayer of thanks every time they encounter a middle class supporter whose house does not contain a piano or, worse yet, a daughter who knows partially most of the songs of Thomas Moore.

BERRY, NSW. 1884

Royal Progress

She is destined to be known as the White Queen of the Aborigines, but she starts as a governess. Daisy May O'Dwyer of a Church of Ireland family of ancient lineage, is twenty-one years old. Her Tipperary accent has been gentled by tutors, expensive schools, and finishing in Switzerland. Education has not gentled her fondness for riding hard to the hounds and asserting strong political opinions (she is a devotee of Charles Stewart Parnell). Daisy's father, whom she adores, drinks brandy as if it were water and tosses money at horses with the sole effect of making them run slower. His wife (whose family, the Hunts, has money), keeps O'Dwyer père from financial embarrassment, at the price of having the O'Dwyer children renamed O'Dwyer-Hunts, which sounds like something one calls a pack of beagles.

Daisy is saved from having to marry any one of the regiment of chinless wonders of the Anglo-Irish gentry who are collectively sliding into bathetic insolvency, by tuberculosis. Bishop George Henry Stanton, Anglican prelate of North Queensland, and an old family friend, offers to see her set up in a healthy environment. So, briefly, Daisy will become a governess in Berry, New South Wales.

She adores her voyage to Australia, for the residual effect of the world-shaking Krakatoa eruptions leaves a series of sunsets that old seahands compared to nothing on earth, save the aurora borealis. And the ship mounts the rogue waves that are circling the earth, the legacy of the massive tidal waves created by Krakatoa, like a decent hunter taking a hedge.

Australia will suit Daisy.

SYDNEY, NSW. 1886

No Surprise

Sir Patrick Jennings, of Newry, County Down, a simple man with a large paunch and a bigger heart, becomes the first practising Catholic premier of New South Wales. He's a solid Gladstonian in imperial politics and that counts with the electorate. Almost totally irrelevant is his pride that his family, which once held title to Ballymurphy (later part of Belfast), gave it up in the seventeenth century rather than change from the Old Faith. Fine. It neither wins nor loses him much in the way of votes.

And Victoria has already had a Catholic premier, Sir Charles Gavan Duffy.

Jennings's elevation in New South Wales is no big surprise, for this isn't America: the Australians are becoming accustomed to Irish Catholics being elected leaders of government.

ADELAIDE, SOUTH AUSTRALIA. 1888

More Songs from Armagh Cathedral

When her husband, the organist and vicar-choral of the Church of Ireland Cathedral in Armagh died, Mary Walsh Lee was past fifty and, with seven adult children, could expect a reasonable retirement. Instead, she made for South Australia where one of her adult sons was ill.

He died and to keep busy, Mary Lee took up the ladies' secretary-ship of the Social Purity Society, not quite as lifeless a body as its name implied. Its key purpose was to raise the age of consent to sixteen, something close to a revolution in outback Australia.

Mary caught the reform bug and she and some of her Social Purity veterans founded the South Australians Women's Suffrage League in 1888.

In 1894 South Australia became the first of the Australian colonies to give women the right to vote on the same terms as men. And they could stand for parliament.

Way ahead of the rest of the English-speaking world.

MOYODE CASTLE, CO. GALWAY. 1890

The Old Ways

Although he is high sheriff of County Galway and master of the Galway Blazers, De Burgh FitzPatrick Persse is only passing through. He is serving a stint as head of the Galway Persses, but his heart is in Queensland. There he has opened for pastoral farming vast tracts of land, some of which had not even been seen previously by a white man, much less conquered. He's now a Queenslander, and soon he returns.

The young Irish poet with the bow-tie never meets this man, but envies the authentic feudalism of the Persse family. De Burgh FitzPatrick Persse has married his own cousin, Mary Persse because, realistically, where else but in the family is he to find the right sort of woman? He is himself the youngest of sixteen children and through each of his parents he is a cousin of Isabella Augusta Persse, wife of the former governor of Ceylon. In the next decade, she teaches the young poet quite a bit.

LONDON. 1892

Don't Bait Lions

The two instinctively dislike each other: the young poet and the almost-ancient founder of *The Nation*. Both are in London, William Butler Yeats to further his career and Charles Gavan Duffy, to close his. Yeats would prefer to be in Dublin and Duffy in Nice, where he has retired, but sacrifices must be made: but not to each other

The Irish Literary society has grown out of the Southwark Literary Society with Yeats as the animating figure and Fenianism as its covert ideology. Sir Charles is put in as titular head and he teaches the young poet a lesson: in later life Yeats will cut the throats of his rivals with all the deftness of Machiavelli, but Gavan Duffy is too old a cat to be fucked by a kitten. He has, after all, been premier of a large, political snakepit of a colony.

A Library of Ireland is proposed, Yeats advances himself as an editor and pushes for studies of patriotic martyrs, such as Patrick Sarsfield and Wolfe Tone and, of course, something by himself, an essay on nationalism, perhaps. Sir Charles cuts Yeats off with the ease of a chess master playing a teenager in a public park: he gains control of the Library contracts by dealing directly with potential publishing houses.

Yeats is reduced to writing sour reviews of the Library as its volumes appear.

KALGOORLIE, WESTERN AUSTRALIA. 1893

Timing

Nobody will begrudge Paddy Hannan his good fortune. Quiet-spoken, a moderate drinker, solid, fifty years old, thirty-one of it spent prospecting. He and two mates, Tom Flanagan and Dan O'Shea work furtively on a new find. When strangers ride by, they pretend they're just camping here for a while.

They've discovered the richest goldfield in Australian history.

Timing: Paddy had been born at Quin, County Clare, on the eve of the Famine and somehow his parents had pulled him through and provided him with an elementary education. His timing now makes up for everything, for his find helps to pull Australia through the century's worst depression.

No one begrudges Paddy his £150 annual pension from the people of Western Australia.

BROKEN HILL, NSW. 1899

Remittances

It is beside the point that Patrick McMahon Glynn, later one of the founders of the Australian Federation, arrived in Melbourne as a young attorney just in time to attend the sentencing of Ned Kelly.

And it is equally irrelevant that his grandmother saw the labourers erecting the gibbet upon which Robert Emmet was hanged.

Those were unusual events. Patrick Glynn is more significant for his being usual – for doing something hundreds of thousands of Irish emigrants did during the nineteenth and twentieth centuries: they sent money home, in varying amount and at odd frequencies, but they sent enough to improve the lives of literally millions of Irish stay-behinds. "Remittance" was the term and if these were frequently taken for granted at home that does not mean that the gifts did not involve sacrifice and a good deal of vexation on the part of the philanthropists.

Patrick Glynn not only sends the money (many migrants just use telegraph money orders, efficient, but voiceless), but he complains, loudly.

He sends money home to Gort, County Galway, and as he does so he points out that *on this side of the world my poor relations are legion. [They] are numerous, respectable, and eternally hard up. Such small matters as a few pounds are too inconsiderable to ever call for an acknowledgment. If I send a fiver to one quarter, I am sure to receive an application within a week for another from somewhere else.*

As for the people in Ireland, *Both [brother] Eugene and myself have written home to say we will, if drunkenness has made the old home intolerable, give my mother £100 a year, but neither he nor I can at present see our way to help pay [our in-laws] the O'Donnell's debts ...*

Patrick Glynn had the grumpy honesty to admit what few Irish migrants would: that having to send money to impecunious relatives, whether in Ireland or someplace in the Irish diaspora, was an imposition and if the migrants did so, they deserved to be thanked, indeed lavished with praise. That so many migrants fulfilled family obligations is beyond admirable, for there was nothing, save their own sense of right and of shame, to compel them to do so. Unlike virtually every other migrant group from Europe and the

British Isles, the Irish returned home in very very small numbers. So men and women like Patrick Glynn were not investing in their own future, or buying an insurance policy permitting possible return.

It grated, but they did their duty.

SYDNEY. 1894

Enthusiasm

No privileged immigrant could ever have been more enthusiastic about her new land than Daisy O'Dwyer-Hunt. She loved everything about it, from the bizarre animals (oh, wouldn't it be fun to pet a crocodile!) to the clever Irish and cockney peasants who took flocks into the Queensland bush and, my, didn't the darlings just make a go of it in the most wonderful way? And, yes, I myself plan to have some of those grazing leaseholds that the government of Queensland offers and wouldn't it be jolly fun to be a milk maid in New South Wales, and that's what I'll do. Oh, and I really need a husband of the real Australian sort, a strong quiet man who in the still of the night will tell me tales of driving cattle overland and of fabulous adventures.

Daisy still rides a horse side-saddle and that should have been an obvious sign. She charms, seduces, inveigles wild men with ease. Some memoirs say she married in Queensland the legendary Breaker Morant and then left him. It is certain that she married Jack Bates (whether bigamously or not is unclear). Bates was a breaker of wild horses, overland drover, indigenous Australian, and despite his being a Roman Catholic, they were married by an Anglican vicar: in their riding clothes.

Within days of the wedding, he leaves on a six-month cattle drive. Daisy cools. When at home, Jack is by turns withdrawn and violently drunk. The Bates have one child in 1886 and after that they cease sexual intimacy.

In 1894, Daisy Bates boards a ship for England where she has arranged to work on the *Review of Reviews* and intends to learn to write.

She leaves for five years and apparently gives hardly a thought to her husband or son.

She's very enthusiastic about her new career.

SYDNEY AND MELBOURNE. 1898

The Webbs We Weave

One can scarcely hold it against Beatrice Potter Webb that her father filled the family home with the likes of T.H. Huxley, Francis Galton, Cardinal Manning, and Herbert Spencer, and consequently the world was forever falling short of her own early experience. She and her husband Sidney were formidable: Harold Laski was in awe of Kingsley Martin's actually asking during a dinner party to use the lavatory in the Webb's house.

Australia could not be expected to come up to their standards during their 1898 tour of inspection. *Sydney, in spite of its exquisite harbour and lovely Botanical gardens, is a crude chaotic place. It is seemingly inhabited by a lower-middle class population suddenly enriched: aggressive in manners and blatant in dress ... In this city there is neither homeliness nor splendour: only bad taste and cold indifference.*

As for city officials, *The Mayoress, attired in a long silk gown, turned out to be the quintessence of vulgarity: not only a total absence of "H's" or grammar, but in ostentation and snobbishness.*

Premier Reid was particularly generous with time and attention to the Webbs. *His figure is indeed a caricature, and the features of his face are not more refined than his figure; and his clothes are dirty and ill-fitting.*

Alfred Deakin: *He is a tall and slight man with long black beard and a plentiful crop of hair growing low, on a somewhat narrow forehead – insignificant in features and manner – more like an American professor than a lawyer or a statesman.*

They had dinner with Henry Higgins, who had attended the same school as George Bernard Shaw. *He is a bald-headed, small-eyed man of medium height; with a cultivated mind and a pleasant manner.* Doubtlessly the result of association with Shaw.

Francis Mason, a farmer and incorrigible fixer from County Fermanagh, earned Beatrice's enmity. *"He was a vulgar individual who had tried on three different occasions to entice Sidney to have a drink."*

SYDNEY. 1898

A Necessary Hero

The 1798 Memorial Committee had a hard time overcoming the objections of Archbishop Patrick Francis Moran (Cardinal, 1885) to Michael Dwyer's being raised yet again from his grave. For Moran, Dwyer smacked too much of violence and was too attractive to the working-class Irish. Faced with enormous popular pressure, however, Moran permitted not only Dwyer but his wife to be exhumed.

They lay in state in St Mary's Cathedral, Sydney, while thousands passed by. The subsequent reburial procession completely jammed College Street with a crowd whose size had been seen previously only upon Royal visits.

Dwyer was necessary to Irish Catholic Australia, for neither the Young Irelanders nor the Fenians were embraceable, since they had themselves rejected Australia. Michael Dwyer, the guerilla leader of 1798 who was never captured, and who surrendered after five years of fighting, had agreed to be transported to New South Wales as a free citizen, not as a felon. He lived a full life in his new home and without the snobberies towards Australia of the later patriotic "martyrs."

Dwyer and his wife were re-buried, this time at Waverly Cemetery, Bronte, Sydney. They are provided with a monument worthy of Gaelic nobility.

EARNEST ACCOMMODATION.
NEW ZEALAND
AND OUTER POLYNESIA
1845–1900

Marriage Lines

If one does not count the formal visit in February of the new governor of New Zealand, George Grey (and few in Wellington did), then the marriage of Colonel Wakefield's daughter to Edward William Stafford was the social event of the year. Emily Wakefield was the product of William Wakefield's abduction of the daughter of Sir John Sidney in 1826. Emily's mother had died a year later and the child had been brought to adulthood in the perilous care of her father.

The colonel believed he had been a good father, for Emily was marrying into the Irish gentry, the Staffords. County Louth landowners of considerable wealth, they had made a family career of helping to misgovern Ireland and a profitable business it had been. Edward Stafford, a younger son and thus perpetually at loose ends, had been unable to make it through Trinity College, Dublin, and then had retired to the family estate where mostly he rode, fished, and drank, with considerable skill. He had emigrated to Nelson in the company of some distant relatives in 1843 and, after the unfortunate death of Captain Arthur Wakefield in the Wairua massacre, he had come to the fore as one of the leaders of Nelson.

A rising man, obviously, and a comfort to a solicitous father.

Emily deserved all the protection Stafford could provide, for her father was always at the edge of disaster. He fought a duel in 1847 against Dr. Isaac Featherston, the editor of the local newspaper and a leading landholder himself. After Featherston missed with his shot, Colonel Wakefield gallantly shot into the air, and said that he really could not kill a man who had seven daughters.

A bit more than a year later, pater Wakefield died of his fierce temper and consequent apoplexy.

And Edward Stafford later became premier of New Zealand.

Steeped in the Faith

Dr. John Johnson, New Zealand's first surgeon-general, was a precise observer and a respectable person, at a time when most Pakeha were not. He visited Rotorua.

"We crossed the Utuhina stream by a very rickety bridge formed of an old cannon and soon reached the ancient stockade which surrounds the pa, now neglected and falling into decay ... we took up our abode in a well built and commodious whare, belonging to Hohepa, one of the Christian teachers, who always accommodates respectable Pakeha.

"We arose at daybreak, and on going out found the whole pa enveloped in vapour, which was rising from the numerous ngawha, and we could hear the voices and the splashing, though we could not see the persons ... who were enjoying the luxury of a bath in the common bathing place ...

"Here were a party of the seniors of the pa, seated in the water, quietly enjoying their morning pipe – and there, a family, from grand-father to grand-child, and mothers with infants at the breast enjoying this agreeable luxury; but the strangest scene of all was a row of young men sitting up to their necks in water, in front of whom was squatted a man who was asking questions, which were answered by the posse in full chorus.

"I found on enquiry, that these were a set of young novitiates aspiring to an entrance into the Christian field, who were repeating the ten commandments to their teacher."

NORTH ISLAND, MID-1847

Captive Audiences

Actors, unlike ethnographers, usually pay attention to pieces of business that reveal character unintentionally and, frequently, accurately. W. Tyrone Power – named for his affine, the early nineteenth-century Irish comedian Tyrone Power who had died in a shipwreck in 1841 while returning to Ireland from the United States – has the family touch in that regard. (It's one that runs through the second Tyrone Power and through the great director Tyrone Guthrie as well.) When he visits New Zealand as a tourist, he watches what counts, and how it compares with home: such as the business with the pigs. The Maori, it seems, handle the beasts differently than do the Irish.

"One rarely or never witnesses those disgraceful exhibitions of obstinate contention between man and beast, so common in English and

Irish fairs and markets," Power observes. "If a Maori porker objects to go into a canoe, he is not forthwith kicked, and punched, and seized by the legs and tossed on his back ... but he is coaxed, patted and nudged, and to every grunt of the porker the Maori appears to grunt again in responsive sympathy, till a perfectly good understanding is established."

What charms Power most is the frequent sight of a large pig seated like a doge in a gondola. "Once in the canoe, the Maori pig appears to be quite aware of the ticklish nature of the craft, being rarely seen to indulge in any refractory movement that may end in his getting a cold-bath; and I have frequently seen a fat porker, squatted on his hunkers in a small canoe, and apparently as well acquainted with the necessity of maintaining its equilibrium as the man who was paddling it."

Just business.

WAIMATE, NORTH ISLAND. FEBRUARY 1848

Dignity

"If your discussion is a serious one, permit your opponent to surrender with honour." That was one of the maxims that Richard Whately drilled into his pupil, and subsequent friend, George Grey.

Now as an experienced colonial administrator, transferred from South Australia to New Zealand, Grey adds a tandem maxim, one of his own devise: "Always rename your losses as drawn battles and your drawn battles as victories."

In a mission house at Waimate North, he is preparing to practise both of those precepts. With 1,300 imperial troops he had apparently cleaned up the trouble in the far north, especially with Hone Heke's hapu of the Nga Puhi.

Apparently. In fact, once he had isolated Hone, Grey showed little inclination to charge into the bush and fight on his opponents' turf; nor would he accept the shrewd, but distasteful advice, that burning the crop land of Hone's supporters would solve the problem. Instead, he let Hone sit. Both men wanted peace, both needed honour.

Hone finally arrived to parley. Of course he kept Grey waiting. The chief was accompanied by his own lieutenants, as was Grey.

Before entering the mission house, Hone paused briefly and looked pointedly at the flag pole.

Grey admired that.

Hone, who understood symbolic language as well as anyone who ever had lived, gave the colonial governor as a gift his own greenstone mere.

A superbly ambiguous gesture: Grey could present it to the Pakeha as a symbol of victory; Hone could tell his supporters that it was a gift in whose acceptance by Grey reaffirmed that the government would honour its commitment under the Treaty of Waitangi.

Dignity preserved all around.

THE NORTH SHORE OF AUCKLAND HARBOUR.
17 JUNE 1848

A Reasonable Assumption

They took the prisoner down to the water's edge. There he was put in a rowing boat manned by prison guards and taken to the north shore of the harbour. He was escorted to the spot where he had murdered a naval lieutenant, his wife, and daughter for the money they kept in their house. He had slashed and mangled the bodies so they formed a Pakeha's nightmare: a seeming harbinger of a native rising. For months, Auckland was on alert.

Joseph Burns, born of Irish parents in Liverpool, England was hanged on almost the exact spot where he had committed the atrocities. A large group of Maori and Pakeha took in the spectacle, the first European in New Zealand to be judicially executed.

WELLINGTON, NELSON, AUCKLAND.
MARCH-DECEMBER 1848

Oedipal Wrecks

Oh, dear Lord, one just wouldn't credit it. The papers and periodicals full of stories. The dangerous life on the fringes of Empire, and, dear me, everyone born male a hard man or a born hero or a criminal lunatick straight from the womb. If so, then, sweet Lord, tell me why I spent half my life renting rooms, sometimes whole suites, even entire houses, to the softest mother's boys in the world. Good men, but given to crying over mother's miniature portrait when they are alone. You should see their letters home.

Nelson. May 1st 1848.
My dearest mother, we wish so often that we could have some of you sitting by our little cosy fire side to comfort you. It is of course foolish to think of such a thing, but you do know how happy we should be if we could take you in to live with us …

Sweet lad and he goes on and on. Hard to credit that he has just been made civil and military secretary to Governor Grey or that he has 2,000 sheep, sixty head of cattle, six mares, some colts. But then, he is doing none of the farming himself: the Hon. Constantine Dillon, fourth son of an Irish viscount, officer, former aide-de camp to the Lord Lieutenant of Ireland, and later aide to the governor general of Canada, Lord Durham. Lovely boy, plump little wife, six children, tragic death in 1853.

And what a serious little worrier that Thomas Arnold laddie is – so sensitive.

Dear Mother,
… you will easily understand what has brought this premature old age on my spirit is the sad fate of love which had inwoven itself into every fibre of my existence …

He was, he told me with a handkerchief to his face, referring to the rejection of his offer of marriage by Miss Henrietta Whately.

… Then too, I live over again the happy days and hours passed at home or in the society of loved friends, and though the tears flow, the heart is comforted and strengthened.

Oh, Lord. And this is what he wrote to mother when he saw for the first time, Stewart Island.

It had a singular charm … which has for so long had a subjective existence in one's imagination, that when actually seen its features seem already homish and familiar, and the peculiar feeling comes across one of having seen it before.

Oh, how I wish to have seen his description of first seeing an iceberg. It would melt a mother's heart, so I think.

Thomas Arnold Jr., son of the Empire's own pure schoolmaster, convert to Roman Catholicism, colonizer in Tasmania, teacher under John Henry Newman in Birmingham Oratory, reconvert to Protestantism, re-reconvert to Catholicism, professor of English at Newman's Catholic University in Dublin, father of the novelist Mrs Humphry Ward, grandfather of Julian Huxley and of Aldous Huxley, grandfather-in-law of G.M. Trevelyan.

A nice man, sweet, but when he came to visit me and Captain Dougherty at Cutter's Bay, I wish he would have stopped after he had told his mother that I was *a very agreeable, well informed woman*. I don't like the part about our family, *of four pretty little girls*. A sweet man, yet he somehow left a person feeling as if one had been holding a piece of candy and now there was a lot of sticky lint in one's palm, and not sure how it came to be there.

HOWICK, NEAR AUCKLAND. NOVEMBER, 1849

Shared Accommodations

Fights break out frequently in the little frame houses. Howick is unattractive enough without the constant aggravation: roads that are mud in one season and dust in another, chickens forever escaping their wattle enclosures, tiny gardens that yield false hope and little else. But it's the bickering that drives the locals spare: petty arguments swarm, like flies that will never go away.

Patrick Fitzpatrick and his wife Ann are able to watch the Howick furore with more tolerance than most, since they have a house all to themselves. Patrick, from Galmoy, County Kilkenny, managed to make it through seventeen years of his twenty-one year enlistment, soldiering through lice, filth, cholera, and perpetual diarrhea in India. Then they invalided him out in England, made him a "Defencible" – always shortened to "Fencible" – the term for broken men with a few years left, who are kept on part-pay and given light garrison duty. He marries a woman he has known long since: she is the daughter of the bailiff who lived next cottage to his own. Bailiff, but good Catholic.

Should tear the things down, Paddy declares. Bad promises, bad houses, bad company. That's the way the government runs this bloody colony.

Paddy and Ann and two children had taken a free passage to New Zealand in 1847. The bargain seemed a good one: in return for doing twelve days a year soldiering (more in emergencies, of course), and standing church parade on Sunday, Paddy will be a colour sergeant in a Fencible unit in New Zealand. He and his family are to receive free passage half way around the world and when they arrive, will have a free cottage and an acre of land.

Some cost-free voyage: the vessel was cramped as a slave ship and, though Ann delivers one new baby safely, one of their other children dies. And some cottage. It takes two years before the government finishes building the rudimentary structures. And here Paddy can only shake his head in wonderment: all the private soldiers (thank God he is a sergeant) are given half of a double cottage. These are two tiny structures joined together, but with no middle wall to provide privacy. An invisible boundary line runs through the middle of the big double-sided chimney that stands smack in the centre of this miscreation. Bairns run from one house to another, cooking smells, urination, sexual congress, everything runs together and every family either fights with its cohabitants or freezes into glacial incivility.

Good Christ, Paddy observes, if the government doesn't keep its promises to its soldiers, what's it doing to the rest of the country? And if army-disciplined soldiers cannot live in the same house, how in God's name are we to live in a land with complete strangers?

MARAETAI, NORTH ISLAND. FEBRUARY, 1850

Tyndale's Disappointment

Though not a prepossessing man, Robert Maunsell possessed considerable mana, and not just because he was a man of the cloth. He was willing to march, apparently fearlessly, into the middle of disputes between hostile tribes and to mediate their differences. He was rewarded by one very old chief with a parrot (apparently taken quite young in its life from a sailor): it spoke only Maori. Maunsell, ever the linguistic scholar, realized that this bird was a memory bank of language as spoken by the old people and thus a reservoir of Maori before it was corrupted by English intrusions. He intended to study the bird: listen to it carefully.

His wife Susan was delighted with the bird. One day when Robert was away from the station, she purchased another parrot from a passing swagger, a former merchant navy man down on his luck.

When several days later Robert returned home, he discovered the two parrots conversing with each other in a creole of archaic Maori and filthy English.

WELLINGTON, NOVEMBER 1850

Seduction

Edward Gibbon Wakefield loathed the Irish in general and the masses in particular. Still, some of the upper-class were useful to him. They had good English connections; many of them often had a bit of money, although always less than it appeared; and, most importantly, because of the shape of Ireland's economy, they were much more willing to think about schemes of emigration than were their fellows in Scotland or England. But they needed guidance, seduction, or they became gentry revolutionaries like William Smith O'Brien and the band of silk-cravat brigands of 1848.

John Robert Godley was one of Wakefield's conquests. Not a pretty one: Godley, the eldest son of a large landowner in counties Meath and Leitrim, was ill-formed. His head looked as if his upper cheek bones had been squeezed in a carpenter's vice, so that he had an amazingly large forehead and then an indentation, and below that a slight widening for his jaw, the sum total resembling a goober pea as grown in the American South. Throughout his life he suffered from a laryngeal complaint, and he never learned to carry on a normal conversation: he either declaimed or was silent. The one truly fine thing about the Anglo-Irish gentry, Wakefield occasionally reflected, is that they made no concession whatsoever to human weakness, including their own hereditary incapacities. Thus, young Godley was made to ride, attend school, shoot, do all the things a gentleman does, and anyone who could captain the Harrow School XI had a bit of the right stuff.

Still, Godley had almost gone astray and become a democratic reformer, or worse, like his brother-in-law Smith O'Brien, a revolutionary. And that's the trouble with the Irish, even the gentry, Wakefield often thought: they're all related to each other and can pick up the spores of bad ideas like contagion from a coughing crowd. Or bad jokes. During his courting of Godley, Wakefield had to hear twenty times if he heard it once, the family pun. It was about Godley's mother's brother, Robert Daly, an influential evangelical, who was briefly the dean of St. Patrick's Dublin, and then bishop of Cashel. A worthy man of the sort who worried about the peasantry in Ireland and about the natives in foreign lands. The family joke actually was Archbishop Whately's, who once opened an episcopal synod by asking "why is the Church of Ireland so poor?" "Because," Whately answered, "it has only one bob daily!" Every time he was told this, Wakefield had to slap his thigh and pretend great merriment.

John Godley took a second in classics at Christ Church, Oxford, was called to the English and Irish bars, travelled about the continent and in 1842 made a tour of North America. In rejection, rather than imitation, of Dickens' *American Notes* of 1842, Godley brought out in 1844 *Letters from America* published by John Murray. Its cod-fish solemnity is easily conveyed by William Ewart Gladstone, then a rising young Tory, having judged it to be the best account of America yet written by an Englishman. So much for Dickens and so much for Godley's being Irish.

Godley retired to his family estates in Leitrim, served as head on the county grand jury, which controlled local government, and was elected high sheriff. And he worried.

That is the point when he became potentially useful to Edward Gibbon Wakefield. Godley had toured Ireland when he was just out of university and he knew the country sat on a knife's edge of near starvation. Now, as the Famine broke, he thought in terms of a revised and generous poor law, a national program of railway building and a state plan for assisted migration. In 1847, he was secretary for a brief time of the Young Ireland party, but while William Smith O'Brien went towards the left, Godley turned towards the right. Godley put forward an extraordinary scheme, in 1847, one that almost was bought by the government, of using Upper Canada as a massive palliative for the Irish famine. It was a scheme of rural settlement (Godley had seen too many immigrants linger in urban

American slums) and most importantly, it would be ecumenical:
Catholic clergy would be part of the scheme, as they had been in Lord
Baltimore's Newfoundland. Every Catholic priest, like every Protestant minister, would be endowed by the government. The whole
thing was too big of course (up to one million persons were to be
given fare to Canada and land); most Protestants would not accept
endowing Catholic clergy, and the Catholic church was too suspicious of the government to accept anything for their people.

Grab this man! And Wakefield at this moment needed help. He had
had a stroke in 1846 and was off-again, on-again. Taking the waters at
Malvern in late 1847, Wakefield met and courted Godley. The
younger man was depressed by the Irish disaster, disheartened at his
own ability to achieve anything, was suffering from his chronic throat
complaint and showed the early symptoms of tuberculosis. Wakefield, magus that he was, transferred some of his own energy, enormous even now, into Godley, and at the same time converted him to
the latest version of the Wakefield gospel. Godley reaches out his
hand, touches the Master's garment and is healed, converted, seduced in the same moment.

From dwelling on the hideous problems of the Irish peasantry,
Godley turns to producing a colony for the younger sons of the pam-
pered. He becomes an official of the Canterbury Association, which is
formed, at Wakefield's direction, to set up an Established Church
settlement on the South Island. On the association's foundation pro-
spectus were listed two archbishops, eleven present or future peers,
eight present or future bishops and a whole gaggle of baronets,
deans, and the like. Fourteen were alumni of Christ Church, Oxford.
Godley gave his old college's name to the capital of the new settlement. It was all very gentlemanly, very Wakefieldian, in that social
control was to be very strict. A colony for people brought up with decent china.

And it was very close to being a giant bubble, since the association
did not actually own the land it proposed to settle.

Godley, who had married in 1846, went out with his wife and
infant son in late 1849, an advance missionary for the Canterbury
Pilgrims.

He discovered that all the available funds had already been spent
by the other advance-agent. So, the family journeyed on to Wellington, there to wait and to consider if Godley had not been dishonourably seduced and perhaps abandoned.

PORT LYTTLETON, SOUTH ISLAND.
16 DECEMBER 1850

Surf

"Godley, je suis ici." The man bounding through the surf was the first off the four boats that formed the First Fleet, as it were. "I am the first Canterbury Pilgrim." He was not under-dressed for the occasion.

James Edward FitzGerald embraced Godley, much to the older man's embarrassment. Still, Godley knew that he was FitzGerald's hero, so he tried to give him a hearty thump on the back, while controlling the distaste on his countenance. He liked FitzGerald, certainly, but they were different sorts: Godley was Silas Marner with leeches applied; FitzGerald was Don Quixote on amphetamines.

Strange that, for they were so close in origin. FitzGerald, like Godley, had poor health that was overcome by a strong spine: in his case, frightful eyesight and a dicky heart. Like Godley, FitzGerald had done a walking tour of Ireland and seen its rabid discontents. Like Godley, he had, for a time, taken up the cause of the Irish poor: in his case, he hatched a scheme for creating a New Ireland on Vancouver Island in British North America. He was even better born than was Godley – he traced his line directly to the eleventh earl of Kildare and believed himself to be the rightful heir to the peerage. This was somewhat hard to reconcile with his having been employed through most of the 1840s as a junior assistant keeper in the antiquities department of the British Museum.

"How fares our kinsman?" FitzGerald asked later, referring to his cousin (and Godley's brother-in-law), William Smith O'Brien.

"Still supporting democracy, apparently," Godley replied dryly. "Van Diemen's Land does not seem very promising soil, one must admit."

Governor George Grey, who distrusted the Canterbury colonists, but who knew that policemen are necessary and that energetic law enforcement was the only sort, quickly appointed FitzGerald as sub-inspector of police.

Mrs. Godley, who had as keen an eye for local detail as had Jane Austen, observed that FitzGerald "grew more wonderful than ever in dress and appearance. His hair is all brushed and shaved away from his face, except a very long mustache." And, "on hot days he used to wear the most frightful long brown Holland blouse, left very open, with a belt and turndown collars, and on wet or cold days he sallied forth in a celebrated green plush shooting jacket."

When, in 1852 the constitution of New Zealand was revised – no more "New Munster," "New Leinster," "New Ulster" – FitzGerald was elected the first superintendent (meaning pro-premier) of his South Island colony. Gibbon Wakefield, who always had disliked the pyrotechnic FitzGerald, was very displeased to learn of this.

FitzGerald farmed badly, painted watercolours well, wrote poetry doggedly, refused the governorships of both British Columbia and of Queensland, condemned the government's grabbing of Maori lands, and on St. Patrick's Day, 1863, initiated the South Island's first daily newspaper: in all, a better record than most of the descendants of the Kildare earldom.

TASMANIA, AUSTRALIA. JANUARY 1851

Second Thoughts

William Smith O'Brien, the most chivalrous of the Irish patriots of 1848, considers his future.

He writes to his brother-in-law in New Zealand, John Robert Godley, offering to serve under him in that portion of the Empire.

Refused, he thereafter takes no interest in politics except, in later life, to denounce Fenianism.

LYTTLETON, NEW ZEALAND. DECEMBER 1851

Things That Really Count

Charlotte Godley – Mrs. Godley, if you please – writes in her commonplace book. The book is her friend, for she is even more quiet than her husband, and she talks to no one unless absolutely forced to do so.

She recalls the arguments her family had presented against her migrating to New Zealand with her husband and feels it is now safe to record them.

The most telling argument put forward by her sisters, the one that almost convinced her to stay behind, was that the New Zealand voyage would spoil her hands.

SOUTH ISLAND, NEW ZEALAND. 2 OCTOBER 1852

Corrective Bargaining

Just before the name "New Munster" disappears from the geography of the South Pacific, an Irishman initiates the first police strike in New Zealand history.

Arthur Edward McDonagh, of vaguely gentry origins in Ireland and a sometime officer in the Fifth Fusiliers, was one of the thousands of former soldiers who took advantage of special passages to the Antipodes. Like many of them, he became a policeman. Because he was an officer and a gentleman, he was appointed as a ranking officer and a magistrate as well. Unhappily, wherever he was stationed, money went missing. McDonagh was good at policing, just weak at financial stewardship. Gambling.

Finally, he hit a low: he diddled his men's pay packets and his thirteen-man force went on strike.

Knowing that the inevitable investigation would find wholesale embezzlement on his part, McDonagh took the honourable way out. On 26 October, he ended the strike by blowing his brains out.

LYTTLETON. 22 DECEMBER 1852

Just Recompense

Tired of doing all the heavy lifting for the Canterbury settlement, John Robert Godley embarks with his family for England.

Not long back, he receives an unexpected offer from the chancellor of the exchequer, William Ewart Gladstone.

Godley is offered the commissionership of income tax for Ireland.

He accepts.

Decline of the Pod People

Evolution is always terribly cruel, and one of its characteristics is that it recognizes not this cruelty: only losers and winners, for a while, and then the winners become losers.

The Pod People were hard served, weren't they? Perfectly adapted to mesmerize, romanticize, publicize in the soft social climes of Great Britain, they could not adapt to the difficult regimen of colonial life, the harsh rubbing that occurs on the fringes of any empire, where there is competition, not automatic hierarchy.

Consider the first generation of the New Zealand Wakefields:

Colonel William Wakefield, exited the world, his massive head congested with apoplexy, Wellington, 1848.

Captain Arthur Wakefield, killed by the fiercest of South Island Maori groups, in an unnecessary dust-up caused by sloppy work conducted, in part, by his brother William. Wairau, 1843.

Felix Wakefield, the most successful of the lot: an 1830s migrant to Tasmania where he was superintendent of public works, then a colonial theorist back in England, and in 1851 a farmer near Christchurch. Returned to England and in the Crimean war was a lieutenant-colonel and built the railway from Balaclava to Sebastopol. Died, New Zealand 1875.

Daniel Wakefield, inexplicably migrated to New Zealand, under the pseudonym of "Bowler," leaving his family behind. Lived anonymously in New Plymouth until learning of his brother Arthur's death in 1843. Moved to Wellington and was a small-time lawyer and then, on family grounds, made attorney-general for New Munster. Resigned from this position after a fight with Sir George Grey. Impoverished, he moved into the home of his eldest brother in Wellington, along with a seven year-old daughter, born well after his having left England. Died 1858.

Edward Gibbon Wakefield, who stepped confidently onto the New Zealand shore 2 February 1853. Expected to be the prince regent of the Canterbury colony and of Wellington. Wasn't. Humbled by Sir George Grey and distrusted by most of the colonists, took to virtual seclusion, 1857. Attended by a German manservant and entertained by his young niece, at Tinakori Road, Wellington. Retreated to his room, his huge head an echo chamber. Noise of any sort pained him intensely. Buried beside William and Daniel, 1862.

And, hear: the second generation is like unto it:

Edward Jerningham Wakefield, b. 1820, sole son of Edward Gibbon. Closely attached to his father's causes. Returned to Canterbury, 1850. Minor political successes. Great disappointment to father, who saw him as dissolute and thrill-seeking. Alcoholic. Married 1863, to a twenty-three-year-old. Died insolvent, drunk, disgraced, leaving two daughters, 1879.

Emily Charlotte Wakefield Stafford, b. 1827, daughter of William. Most successful of her generation. Married at age nineteen, Edward Stafford, who became long-serving premier of New Zealand. Died, childless, 1857.

Oliver Wakefield, b. 1844 in Tasmania, son of Felix. Educated in London, rose to chief secretaryship of New Zealand department of mines. Killed in Dunedin, 1884, by a tram.

Edward Wakefield, b. 1845, Tasmania, son of Felix. Educated in London. Given political plum, private secretaryship to the premier (widower of his cousin, Emily Charlotte) and secretary to the New Zealand cabinet, 1866. Later journalistic and political career aborted through his chronic incivility and inconstancy. Last three-and-a-half decades of life spent in Europe and England. Blind, in a London almshouse, died 1924.

WELLINGTON, NEW ZEALAND. JANUARY 1854

Prevailing Westerlies

Note the pattern. Sir George Grey (knighted in 1848), having set up institutions of representative government, leaves New Zealand. He will be back, but for the moment he is following one of the invisible patterns of empire. Ireland-to the Antipodes-to Africa or to North America. He is becoming governor of the Cape Colony in southern Africa. There he will deal with roughly the same issues he has handled already in New Zealand: native-settler relations and the creation of partial self-government for the colonizers.

Important men, middling settlers, the pattern was shared. John Patrick Fitzgerald, a doctor from Carrickmacross, County Monaghan, migrated early to New Zealand, becoming the physician of the Wakefield infirmary in 1840, while Wellington was still called Port Nicholson. He married a fellow Catholic, the daughter of a Dublin solicitor, and became the lay leader of Wellington's Catholic community. His Catholicism and his then-eccentric methods – he favoured decent ventilation, the use of anesthetics, and kept his hospital open to Maori – made him a target of the Wellington establishment as it in-filled with British newcomers. Sick of fighting off the begrudgers, Fitzgerald accepted in 1856 an appointment in King William's Town, in the eastern part of the Cape Colony. He became superintendent of Grey's Hospital, built and named with characteristic modesty, by Sir George Grey. There he served for thirty-two years before returning home: to England.

WELLINGTON. 21 JULY 1856

Judge Not

The "Royal Tigers" – the 65th Regiment of Foot, based in the North Riding of Yorkshire – disembark. They are here to help with the "Maori-troubles," whatever that may mean: they really don't care. They are soldiers and it's soldiering they're here for, never mind the details. Their officers have tried to keep them in parade-shape, but as they walk down the gangways, it's clear they do not have land legs. Everything is messy and to pier-side onlookers, a bit comical. Good value, watching the unloading, the hoisting off of tons of baggage and the disembarking of the wives and families of the soldiers: that's always last, and the watchers always find the family-followers the most interesting part of the business.

The *Lancashire Witch*. Near the front of her unloading is a private, Martin Day, from near Castlebar, County Mayo. He has grown up Catholic, immersed in stories of the local battles in 1798, illiterate, and unsure of his age. In his late teens or early twenties he went to Liverpool and enlisted. Now, still in his early twenties, he is a thin, hard-boned soldier, small by the standards of Irish soldiery, 5'6" only.

Near the end of the disembarkation, a daughter of the regiment walks down, holding her mother's hand. Her father, another Royal Tiger, has already gone ashore. The girl, Mary Ann Garvey, is nicely kitted out: white frilled pantalettes, a maroon cashmere jumper and lace-up boots. She is very composed and she surveys her new world as a dauphinesse opening a particularly interesting present. She is three years old.

Move ahead thirty years. Mr. and Mrs. Day – Martin and Mary Ann – are living a life that, were it described in the English papers, would read like an emigration tract. They own forty acres of sea-front land on Pakihi Bay (known locally as Day's Bay) on Waiheke Island. They live in a house built with their own timber and are abundantly self-sufficient. The children – the Days are on their way to having ten – keep the family's flock of milk goats. The boys spear flounder near the shore, collect oysters and mussels, and exchange snapper and other fish for bread and butter from passing fishermen. Wild honey is collected and an ancient style of home brew – honey mead – is fermented. Cattle and sheep are kept in an onshore paddock and on an off-shore island, to which they are taken by boat. The evenings pass with Mary Ann reading to the family or playing the accordion, a skill she picked up during her school days. A perfect picture, and not one produced by throwing a rose light upon this tiny stage: it's real.

So, judge not, ask not, how the marriage came about. Do not consider how it came about that, on 15 October 1867, a Catholic ex-soldier in his mid-thirties, has married, in a Protestant service, a bride allegedly of fifteen years of age. Do not, especially do not reflect on the courtship that formally began two years earlier, when Martin Day was mustered out of the service and settled on Waiheke Island where Mary Ann and her parents had settled after her father had finished his enlistment in the Royal Tigers. And, in the name of all that our society holds decent, do not contemplate the possibility that Martin Day moved to Waiheke to continue a relationship that had begun well before he and Mary Ann's father left their regiment.

No, nor judge not, ask not, how the sudden death of Martin – appendicitis – in 1890 affected Mary Ann. Her family pulled around her and the farm continued to prosper. She kept busy, but always now had her eyes on a distant horizon. Evenings she no longer read or played music, but when the weather was good, fished off the rocks below the house. One evening in 1895, a warm summer evening, quiet, the kind of evening lovers treasure, she went down to the rocks and never returned.

Judge not: for there are more ways to happiness than the law allows.

DRUMBALLYRONY, NR. DOWNPATRICK, CO. DOWN. 1859

The Virtues of an
Ulster Presbyterian Childhood

Later, he remembered:

I went to see my old schoolhouse. It still stands just as it was. All the nightmare of that miserable time came back to me.

The Rev. Rutherford Waddell, M.A., D.D., Minister of St. Andrew's church, Dunedin, recreates the hell of being nine years old in an Ulster school, and that in 1859, the year of the Ulster Revival, of God's river in spate:

Mine was a country school consisting of one room and one all-supreme dominie. He was a man of hot, hasty, ungovernable temper. He had only one arm. His face was like a harvest moon when the setting sun fired it with its beams.

The Irish national school system gave one of colonialism's few blessings to Ireland: a state system of literacy-formation four decades before similar systems developed in England or Scotland. Unhappily, what had been intended as a way of bringing Protestants and Catholics together became the dust of a thousand tiny sectarians.

His chief instrument of punishment was a ruler about two feet long and a couple of inches broad ... When he was in a rage, which was frequently, he was not careful where he would strike. Yet I never knew a parent to lodge a complaint against his cruelty.

And this was how the son of the manse – his father the local Presbyterian clergyman who also was the patron of the school – was treated. No softness in Ulster. Waddell, leaving school at age fourteen, was apprenticed by his father to a Banbridge draper, and worked twelve-hour days for wages that would buy him nought but the scrag ends of stale loaves.

Are the scriptures right? Are the sins of the father visited upon the son, even to the fourth generation? A good test, for Rutherford Waddell, at age twenty, decided to follow his father into the Presbyterian ministry. After a Queen's, Belfast, first degree, and a licence in theology from the Presbyterian College, Belfast, he married and emigrated to the South Island of New Zealand.

Well, are the scriptures right? Thank God, not always. Waddell became the leading Presbyterian cleric of his time, forty years in the same pulpit in the Scottish Presbyterian city of Dunedin. His Sunday school was the plinth of his ministry and with children he was gentle as a mother cat with a kitten; with youths inventive (a cricket club for young Presbyterians was nothing if not a new idea); with women, mildly radical: he convinced his congregation to appoint the first Presbyterian deaconess in New Zealand, a first step towards female ordination.

The star in his crown, the final evidence that abused children need not become abusive adults, was this: in 1889 the Rev. Mr. Waddell was elected the first president of the Tailoresses Union of New Zealand, a symbolic honour that he held for three months to show solidarity and then passed it on. This seemingly eccentric encomium was for his having led the campaign against sweated labour in the clothing industry. He remembered his own days in the draper's shop in Banbridge, and he saw women in New Zealand sewing from 8:30 a.m. to 11:00 p.m and he knew it was wrong. And unchristian: *The working classes do not go to church because the capitalists pray for them on Sunday and prey on them during the other six days of the week.* A Royal Commission followed, and then anti-sweating laws, the start of New Zealand's social welfare system.

DUNEDIN, SOUTH ISLAND. 1860

Methodist Madness

Visitors laugh. The missionary continues. Locals smirk. The missionary carries on. Authorities give minimal support. He works on.

His mission station is a slab shanty, slightly more than three hundred square feet. Around it is a small and muddy yard and then palisades of sawn timber.

Here Henry Monson runs the best gaol in all New Zealand. Monson and his son had owned a successful building firm in London until the crash of 1847. Then, the combination of the Irish Famine and the effect of the sudden introduction of Free Trade put a temporary halt to most construction work and he went bankrupt. A very devout Methodist, he knew this was part of God's plan and he strained hard to find out His will. He and his sons took passage to Otago province, rare English Methodists among all the Presbyterians.

God has a niche for Monson and he fills it humbly, but assiduously. For the past ten years, he has been the gaoler. Not young – he is sixty-seven now – he keeps his prisoners in line without the use of any force whatsoever. And he has some of the hardest of convicts to keep from skipping: sailors, rugged men, not used to confinement on land, and above twenty of them in the tiny gaol at peak times. They are there for short sentences, a few days to three months, and then they will take passage to some other land. Not easy men. Yet there have been no escapes.

A curious visitor reads the words scratched on a shingle, "Her Majesty's Gaol," and knocks. A face peers through a grating and then the door is opened. By an inmate. "The Old Man is out," the visitor is told. "He's gone for a pint, but he'll return."

The healthy prisoners do eight hours of work on the roads under police guard each day. The weak and halt, unable to engage in public works, are allowed exercise for two hours. When the yard is muddy or the gaol too crowded, Monson permits them to exercise outside the walls.

Monson is not a creeping-Jesus. He reads the Bible to the men some nights, but more often he plays the fiddle, or teaches reading and writing. He conducts a constant battle with the authorities for more money so that the damp, unsanitary gaol can be made minimally decent. A curious, deep bond develops between gaoler and prisoners. He never uses solitary confinement or corporal punishment, both standard in other gaols and prisons. The bond is simply that it would not be decent to rat out the Old Man: we won't embarrass him or do anything to cost him his post.

Occasionally, he lets some of the men out for a bit of a spree. He admonishes them to be in by 8:00 p.m or they will be locked out. He says this with a straight face and they hear it with a smile and they return on time for they understand that it is not wooden palings or iron grates that keep them in line, but the invisible bars of moral suasion.

PUTUKI, NR. WANGANUI, NORTH ISLAND. 1861

Reading the Cards

He is no ordinary tohunga. In early middle age, Te Kere Ngatai-e-rua carries the wisdom of an octogenarian. This is not communicated by any bodily trick, for he moves like a man of twenty; nor by ageing. His moko is spare and he has no creases on his face, which wears the colour of a hickory nut. Te Kere is an ascetic man: he would have been at home in an Anchorite community in a desert land. He eats alone, draws water from his own well, and fasts frequently. He is on the road to becoming a prophet.

And therefore he can read the cards. He knows without consulting Pakeha newsprint where the game is going. Gifted linguistically and in calculation, he is fascinated, however, by the government census of 1858: 56,049 Maori, 59,413 Pakeha.

If the tide is to be stemmed, it must be soon.

As a youth Te Kere had spent time on a whaling boat and learned some white man's games. Now he tells his people:

Don't sell – be wise
In what you do.
Turn up your cards:
It might be a full house.

THE NORTH ISLAND OF NEW ZEALAND, 1861–72

"The New Zealand Wars": Stump the Experts

An enthusiast for the settlement of New Zealand told an early Victorian audience that New Zealand provided a unique opportunity for "Progress without the price, paradise without the serpent, and Britain without the Irish."

Not terribly astute an expert: New Zealand could not have been settled without the Irish as the shock troops of empire.

The wars for the North Island, 1861–72, are now called by experts, a "civil war." An amazing piece of Stalinism, that. The older name, "the Maori Wars" was more accurate, for despite all the inter-tribal complications among the Maori, the wars were an attack by one race upon another. Hear an imperial victory song:

> *Sing a song of sixpence*
> *A tale about the war.*
> *Four and twenty niggers,*
> *Cope up in a Pa.*
> *When the Pa was opened,*
> *Not a nigger there was seen!*
> *Is not that a jolly tale*
> *To tell before the Queen?*

The Irish. Of course they were on all sides of the multi-sided conflict – they always are – but overwhelmingly they were fighting to destroy the social and economic structure of the Maori people. Experts say that roughly 40 percent of the imperial troops (the real professionals, 12,000 of them in service in 1864), were Irish Catholics. Toss in the Irish Protestants and all the Irish, Catholic and Protestants, in the local defence forces and it's clear that probably 10,000 Irishmen were engaged at one time or another over a decade in a race war.

And not just as foot-soldiers. Sir George Grey returned from sorting out the Kaffirs (his word) in South Africa late in 1861 and when the war went too slowly, took over command. When the London government dismissed him in early 1868 for being too keen on the whole business, he was replaced as governor of New Zealand by another Irishman, Sir George Bowen, whose previous imperial credits included the eirenic post of president of the University of Corfu and the much harder school, the inaugural governorship of Queensland, Australia. And both Grey and Bowen worked inharmoniously with the Irish-born, Irish-living head of the elected branch of government: premier Edward Stafford who, at the age of forty-three (in 1862) had just ridden his own horse to victory in the Canterbury Cup and who refused to resume the dullness of political leadership until 1865. Oh, this was a very Irish war.

And an embarrassing one. The imperial forces did not win, though they claimed victory, and the Maori forces did not lose, though they were careful not to claim anything save survival.

THE SOUTH ISLAND. 1861–72

Sand Crabs

They materialize like sand crabs. Out of the blue ocean they are tossed up in waves; they scuttle hurriedly towards some predetermined destination, and then the beach is empty until the next wave of these digging beings arrives. They are prodigious workers and move quickly. Each one is independent of the other, but they have a herd instinct, and move from place to place in concert, as if hearing a vibration in the earth that is resonant only to their own kind.

The gold miners and their outriders, the searchers for greenstone and other semi-precious stones.

Gold exercises the same domination over events and has the same episodic quality in the South Island that the anti-Maori wars have in the North: 1861 major discoveries in Otago at Gabriel's Gully; 1862 on the Clutha River; 1862 at Arrow; 1863 the Taieri; 1864 Hokitika, Greymouth, and lesser, more difficult alluvial finds into the 1870s.

The governments of the day keep solid control. They offer rewards for finds, £1,000 to £2,000 for big discoveries, and this means that everything goes public quickly. Then the authorities move swiftly, and, compared either to California or to Australia, the gold rush is fairly orderly. Claim registry is efficient. Mining licences are only £1, so there's little of the anti-government feeling that ran rancid during the Australian rush.

Many of the diggers were veterans of California in 1849 and thereafter; or of New South Wales or Victoria after 1851, and sometimes of both American and Australian rushes.

The experienced digger was easily identified. He traveled in moleskin trousers, high American boots – "Nugget Boot" was the prestigious U.S. brand – a flannel shirt, a broad-brimmed, high-domed hat that could, in a pinch, carry water. The ones who had been in California often wore a Spanish-American waist sash, and kept a crimson one for social occasions. But whether experienced or not, these highly mobile sand crabs had one thing in common: they were not the poor of the earth. Broke often, but not the real paupers. The rural poor of Ireland or the urban proles of Britain could not afford the expensive travel gold mining demanded, especially long trans-oceanic voyages. Most miners could be considered artisan class, but there was a surprising proportion of middle and upper-class miners who took to this lottery as their gamble on life's wheel.

And behind the miners came some of the smartest prospectors: those who set up hotels, post offices, brothels, supply shops, assay services, anything the miners might need and would pay for in cash. Perhaps 50,000 of these sand crabs scuttled about the South Island during this decade. Mostly male – 85 percent. A quarter to a third were Irish. Irish miners were best known for moving swiftly and burrowing into a new field almost the day after it was discovered.

The castings left by these sand crabs washed away quickly in history's tide. There remain empty mines and a few historical plaques.

In this valley and across the Mont D'or watershed the pioneer prospectors – John Donnelly, James Liddle, Michael Donoghue, John Redman, Jones, Craig, and their parties – discovered gold in 1864–65, so founding the town of Ross.

Small memorials: the sand crabs got what they wanted and could let the glory be taken care of by later generations.

NEW ZEALAND. 1861–68

Toffs At Work

Gentlemen, English, Irish, Scottish, adaptable, at loose ends. The Gold Rush and the anti-Maori wars were great fun for them and they did not embarrass themselves. They drank, dug, whored, fought, shot, just as well as their colleagues from the working classes. And because they had an attitude of oh-isn't-this-a-lark, they often did better. Besides, they always had a ticket out of deep trouble: if necessary, they could speak, in the proper way, with the chappies in charge.

Hence the lark of Charles Money, who left England in 1861 by first class passage and nothing smaller than a £5 note in his waistcoat pocket. He joined up in Canterbury with people of the right sort: an Anglo-Irishman (a Fitzgerald, actually), of powerful build and strong local connections (no points here for identifying which Fitzgerald family it was); another young man who was to become a life fellow of

Trinity College, Cambridge, and a third the son of an Anglican archdeacon just out of Christchurch grammar school. They staked their own claim – Fitzgerald was the leader in this business – built a sluiceway, worked twelve hour days and made a little money and a lifetime of dinner-party stories.

Money a bit later moved north and joined the Wanganui Yeomanry Cavalry – good wheeze that – under Captain (later Colonel) Thomas Macdonell Jr., and did a bit of native hunting, what. They were merged for a time with the 18th Royal Irish, and the last thing one would want to say is that such gentlemen adventurers were discriminatorily racialist. Quite the opposite, they were very even-handed, as this bit of Money's memoir indicates:

Our little farrier-major, Duff, with customary Irish impetuosity, was as usual one of the first in place, and I caught sight of him firing off all the barrels of his revolver in reckless style round the corner of a "wharry" door into the inside, which was crammed with niggers. The next minute I was potting an old villain with a head like an oakum mop in dry weather, and he had just dropped when I heard someone shout "Duff's down!" I instantly ran towards the spot where I had seen him last ... with the help of the troop sergeant-major of the Wellington Defence Force, I carried him off to the doctor, and left him to his care, though it was but too evident that all was over with him.

Can't say fairer than that, can one?

PENRHYN ISLAND, THE COOK ISLANDS. 1862

Economic Reality

Penrhyn is the northernmost of the Cook Islands. Also called "Tongareva" or "Mangarongaro," it was so pitifully poor in the mid-nineteenth century that its people were constantly on the verge of starvation, both physical and spiritual: the islanders went through periods of malnutrition and, collectively, they could not even support a palm-thatched church.

No one was adverse to the decision, in 1862, of a band of about 130 men to take work contracted for three years on plantations in Tahiti.

It might have been a decent idea, but the islanders were terribly abused. The lucky ones returned after three years. Forty-five of them were kept on for an extra two years before being dumped on one of the remotest of the Society Islands, having first been robbed at gun point.

The French were as nothing compared to the Peruvians who unashamedly admitted to maintaining a slave economy. Thirty or more vessels formed a full-time slave-capturing fleet, and it hunted through Polynesia like a pack of killer whales. The isolated northern Cook Islands were good hunting grounds – Penrhyn, Pukapuka, Rakahanga – but the killer pack also ranged close to the central islands, grabbing victims from Atiu and Mangaia. Their methods ranged from signing-up gullible islanders to labour "contracts," to drugging them with mixtures of brandy and opium. Men, women, children, all were profitably deposited in the holds of the Peruvian vessels: unique boats, with iron grillwork and heavy locks where normally simple wooden hatchways were located.

Under international pressure, Peru abolished slavery in 1863 and its government ordered that the whole spectrum of Poly- and Micronesian slaves be sent out into the Pacific, a process that was as cruel as had been their enslavement. Men, women, and children were dumped on islands they had never seen, among peoples whose language they had never heard. Of the 743 Cook islanders who had been taken slave by the Peruvians, not more than fifteen found their way home.

Penrhyn Island, having lost four-fifths of its native population to slavers, then had a group of Gilbert islanders marooned on them, so that a Micronesian language and culture suddenly swamped a Polynesian island.

In Rarotonga, which was developing into the de facto capital of the Cook Islands, the elders began to speak of the need to be protected by a big friend, one who had big war canoes, like Britain.

ARROW, SOUTH ISLAND. NOVEMBER 1862

Good Day

Riding towards Arrow, Sergeant-Major Bracken of the mounted police reviewed in his mind every maxim he knew about policing. A veteran of the Victoria, Australia goldfields, he knew enough to know that nothing was predictable. The only formula that seemed universally applicable was: if possible, let the people do the police work.

He was heading into a pack of "Tipps," meaning men from Ireland's most troubled county, Tipperary, and their fellow Irishmen who took on that label as part of a terror campaign. The Tipps were going about jumping some of the richest claims in the new field. Most miners did not carry guns, nor did most of the Tipps. It was a matter of shovels-to-skulls, and of a dozen Tipps stomping on one or two miners before the victims hied off, leaving their claims to be pillaged.

As Bracken, a County Monaghan man, rode towards the crowd, he thought of all the derogatory words from his childhood that applied to the Tipps: gulphins … gypes … gumphs …

"G'Day lads," he said without dismounting. "I've been sent to enforce order, and by God I will." He placed his revolver on his saddle and spun the chamber, as if inspecting it to be sure it was fully loaded. "So, I have a proposal …" He said the only way to end claim disputes without bloodshed was to appoint two disinterested miners to assess each case. He rattled off a set of rules quickly and the majority of the miners called out their approval. The Tipperary men were too stunned to do anything but look on, and they lost their fearsomeness the minute the community agreed to police itself.

One policeman. Fifteen hundred men. Good order.

DUNEDIN, SOUTH ISLAND. FEBRUARY 1863

Alluvial Deposits

A pain. Pleasant, though. Going to the bank. Since becoming a full scale wholesale grocer five months earlier, Robert Wilson had to pay money into the Bank of New Zealand virtually every second working day. Though he had the body of a hardened labourer – brought about by carrying two-hundredweight sacks of wheat as a twenty-year-old storeman in Victoria – he was a merchant adventurer. He knew that it was easier, and usually more profitable, to find miners than to find gold.

Wilson had emigrated to Australia at age twenty with his parents, who were small flax farmers in Omagh, County Tyrone, Protestants in a region of continual Catholic re-assertiveness. Once in Australia, they had bid Robert to make his own way, and he had walked to Geelong where he became a labourer, and then a storeman and then a drayman and then a very successful drayman for he worked out a system of delivering water to miners during a six months' drought. In those six months he cleared about £2,000. So, he arrived in Dunedin in 1861 well capitalized. The gold strike on the Clutha by the Irish-American Christopher Reilly and his partner Horatio Hartley, in August 1862, was all that Wilson needed. He and his reps travelled the gold fields in bullock carts, providing everything from bars of soap to tea and white sugar.

He never saw much romance in the gold business, just ledgers. His only recorded remark of note is that he wished he had done less business and made larger profits.

MOUNT IDA GOLDFIELD, SOUTH ISLAND.
25 SEPTEMBER 1863

All's Ill That Ends Ill

Sergeant John Garvey, an Irish career soldier, was named a Chevalier of the Legion d'Honneur for his heroism in the Charge of the Light Brigade. He expected a reasonable career in New Zealand's colonial police force. Late in September 1863 he was sent by his sergeant, another Irishman, Thomas Ryan, into a heavy blizzard to check on the dispersed Mount Ida diggings. Even when the extent of the snowstorm became clear, Ryan did not send anyone to help Garvey.

After Garvey's body is found, the Mount Ida miners turn on Sergeant Ryan, whom they despise as much as they had revered Garvey. They surround Ryan and almost kick him to death.

He is saved by Robert Bremner, who works for the Dunedin merchant prince Robert Wilson. Bremner takes a number of boots aimed at the policeman and finally drags Ryan into his store. After that Ryan escapes and soon gets a transfer to a safer district.

Strange intersection: Garvey, the war hero dies while doing his duty in New Zealand. Ryan continues a career that at one point includes his riding into a gold town, revolvers at the ready, before staggering into the tent that serves as the local brothel. Miners, who expect more than fornication from their police, cut the tent open, interrupting his exercise. He starts shooting and is beaten up. Somehow, half drunk, half deluded, he managed to become Canterbury's first detective and then to be fired by half a dozen different police forces before dying in the Sunnyside Lunatic Asylum in Dunedin, broken down from drink and chronic lung disease.

Robert Bremner, who at Mount Ida selflessly had taken part of the stomping intended for Ryan, married in 1870 Elizabeth Wilson, the Omagh-born sister of his boss Robert Wilson. Bremner, a husband, decent man, improvident businessman, was reduced to writing to his nephew, the son of the now-late magnate Robert Wilson, asking for help in taking care of his own son. This plea was a promise he had made to his late wife, and it ground hard upon Bremner's dignity: "And now I feel that I have done my duty in this, to me, a very disagreeable work."

MOUNT IDA, SOUTH ISLAND. LATE 1863

Comic's Relief

"Och, he's only a poor fool, an amhadhan. Give him a shilling now, and god bless the fellow."

At Mount Ida, and later fields, Roach played being a shingle short with no compunction and almost no limit to his behaviour. He was the community's licensed fool, and a profitable living it could be. In Mount Ida he was know as "Mear's Irishman," in Mear's The Wonder of the World Drapery. There he played flunkey to everyone with an excessive courtesy that was well past parody. Since Mear, a fellow Irishman, always gave his customers a luck-penny, and since that luck-penny invariably was a shot of gin, Roach's chief activity was to bow and scrape the customers in and out of the emporium (thus picking up a shilling or two from miners in luck), and to be sure that the gin supply did not run short.

Fool or not, he became the orderly of the police and inspectors' camp, an unofficial but accurate title, and there he brushed boots, kept uniforms clean and always both bowed to and saluted the officials: there he picked up frequent tips. Soon he was orderly for everything – officially the court orderly and unofficially the quartermaster who bought provisions for the prisoners. He never toned down his act and he sometimes took prisoners from the gaol to the wholesale grocery. Then he would have them wheel the supplies back to the gaol, while he did some high business along the way.

Roach kept his money in a coffee tin, the same way that miners kept their findings: buried in the ground. Except Roach, who turned all his little bits of profit into sovereigns, had to get himself a second tin, and then a third.

NEW ZEALAND. 1862–1962

The Power of Prayer

Prayer. Preaching. Prophecy.

When faced by a more powerful imperium, the underdogs react in many ways: sometimes by embracing the victor's values so strongly that they surround the imperialist from within; other times by complete withdrawal into a ghetto; and at still others by creating a new mix, a culture that blends the invaders' tools with the traditional tribal instruments to create a new entity, the cultural equivalent of a pa, a defensive structure for a besieged people.

Several distinctive Maori religions arise, as well as some very curiously ornamented forms of Christianity. Here are five: Hau-hau, the Ringatu church, the Kaingarata religion, Te Wairua Tapu, and the Ratana movement. Outré as they may at first appear, you have seen them before, at least in process if not in detail: for they are the result of the same processes that produced from ancient Judahism the new religion, Christianity; that turned Christianity from a Jewish form into a Greek religion; later syncretized this religion with Roman imperial organization; and in the Celtic lands came to terms with Pagan culture by adopting many of the pre-Christian practices. Nothing new here at all.

Hau-hau. The raw ancestor of several Maori indigenous Judaisms and Christianities (most lean towards the former) has been called by observers, "a sort of Maori Fenianism," thus showing an extraordinary impercipience on both matters. Founded as the result of a set of visions in 1862 by Te Ua Haumene, a Wesleyan-educated Taranaki leader, wherein the Angel Gabriel announced that the Last Days of the Book of Revelation were at hand. Te Ua was no theologian, but he churned Christianity, turning Jesus into a prophet, and the Maori into the Chosen People. Traditional Maori practices, such as divination around a pole that had out-stretched sections, like arms, fit well with the new prophetic system. The real problem came when this neo-Christianity hit political reality. Some of the Hau-hau (the word has many meanings, most relating to spirit and to insight) took to believing they were bullet proof. Also, some continued to follow the Maori tradition of head hunting and, probably, cannibalism, customs that when practised upon Europeans led to trouble. In particular, the ritual killing in March 1865 of an Anglican missionary brought swift government revenge. Te Ua was taken prisoner and after a period of house arrest in Auckland, became a campaigner for peace. The religion faded, its threads being picked up most clearly in the two faiths described next.

The Ringatu church is the monument to Te Kooti Arikirangi Te Turuki, one of New Zealand's best military tacticians and most charismatic prophets. A top student at Whakato Anglican mission, he immersed himself as a youth in the Jewish and Christian scriptures. As a young man, he was opposed to the Hau-hau movement in its military form and fought on the government side. However, the sole thanks he received was to be decried as a spy (which he was not) and as a trouble-maker (which he certainly was) and sent as a prisoner to Chatham Island. There, he had visions and acquired magical powers. In early 1867, he led a brilliant escape.

The characteristic raising of the hand in homage to God at Ringatu services began the moment Te Kooti and his party of escapers reached land: they thanked God and replaced, by Te-Kooti's decree, kneeling with the hand-raised salute. Te Kooti fought the government for a half dozen years, and then declared himself a pacifist. From 1873 onwards, he articulated a set of visions that read in their complexities, heat, and ambiguity like those of the Minor Prophets in the Old Testament; a vision of Seven Seals, clearly re-interpretations of Revelation, also was articulated, and a myth of Te Kooti's Diamond – an indigenous version of the Holy Grail – spread. Te Kooti died in 1893, but his burial site was a secret, not unlike that of the man upon whom he modelled his ministry.

The Kaingarata religion was a South Island mixture of diluted Hauhauism, and the story of the Exodus, stirred thoroughly by the expansion into south Marlborough and northern Canterbury of white settlement, and all this with a prophetic garnishing by Hipa Te Maiharoa. He represented a tribe that had lost its land in a tribal war in the 1820s, so when the land was sold by the Maori conquerors to the Pakeha, a double-dispossession occurred. The key characteristics of the Kaingarata faith was its pacifism and its belief in a New Jerusalem. They had experienced an exile from land they loved; they called themselves Israelites and after Te Maiharoa died, one of his disciples was said to walk on water.

Te Wairua Tapu. In the Ureware, the hardest, least invaded portion of the North Island, Rua Kanan Hepetipa took a last stand. He founded a New Jerusalem at Maungapohatu, a millennial dream enacted in the real world. Rua had learned his Christian scriptures well while part of a sheep-shearing gang that worked on the east coast near the turn of the nineteenth century. He appreciated the tactical lesson of the New Testament, namely that a prophet, to overthrow a preceding one, needst only declare that the predecessor was a forerunner. Thus, Rua declared that Te Kooti had been his own forerunner, as John-the Baptizer had been that of Yeshua of Nazareth. Rua claimed to have seen the diamond, the Holy Grail of Te Kooti, and declared himself to be the Messiah. In 1907 he built an architecturally stunning round church at Maungapohatu, the hub of a Utopian community. The model for the church was the Islamic masterpiece, the Dome of the Rock in Jerusalem.

The Ratana Movement. In the twentieth century, the influenza pandemic was as disastrous to the Maori population as was smallpox and tuberculosis in the nineteenth. On 8 November 1918, Tahupotiki Wiremu Ratan, a Protestant Christian, saw a strange cloud rise from the Tasman Sea and cruise directly to his house. "Fear Not, I am the Holy Ghost," it told him, and added he had been chosen as the speaker – the hinge between God and Man for the Maori people. And so he was. A serious Christian – he did not approve of traditional Maori beliefs – he pressed for a purified Christianity, involving faith-healing and, equally importantly, political power for his people. Twice, after his death, the Ratana bloc held the balance of electoral power and they kept Labour in government.

Religion and power: no, nothing new here at all.

NORFOLK ISLAND. 1863

The Pale People Retreat

Perhaps it was the cold. Or the ambiguity of having fifty acres for each family: too much space.

After two years, two families return to Pitcairn. As they leave Norfolk Island, the folk on shore sing a hymn, and it is echoed by those departing on the small boat.

Perhaps it is the worldliness of Norfolk Island, for some whalers have been permitted to use it as a base.

Five years farther on, a second party leaves: in October 1868, Mr. Christian, his wife and nine children, and a number of their extended family, including an old widow whose husband had been on the *Bounty*. As they left, they sang a song that had been composed in the Pitcairners' antique English, especially for this departure.

> *Again dissevered is the tide*
> *Brethren and sisters part.*
> *The mournful separation nigh*
> *Pervades with grief each heart.*

"MESOPOTAMIA," NR. THE RANGITATA RIVER, CANTERBURY, SOUTH ISLAND. MARCH 1864

Sterling's Character

He named the holding of tussock and gravel "Mesopotamia," rather than Nowhere. A close decision, for the latter would have brought him ill-fortune, the former, a place in the Golden Crescent. That is how important names are.

Now, Samuel Butler, who traced his origins back to the Anglo-Norman conquerors of large chunks of Ireland – the Butlers, earls of Ormonde – was setting his life in order. Having farmed and painted water colours and written long letters and short poems, he was selling up and returning to England. Unlike most settlers, he could not remember working very hard.

Butler had started with £4,400 in capital and after five years in New Zealand it had turned into £8,000. He honestly did not know how that occurred and for the rest of his life marvelled that he had not, in fact, lost every penny.

GATE PA, NR. TAURANGA, NORTH ISLAND.
29 APRIL 1864

Chivalry

What is that crazy woman doing?

I was in the firing trench when I heard the wounded officer lying in our lines calling for water. There were other wounded soldiers distressed for want of water.

Gate Pa is an incredibly boastful piece of business, built so close to the port of Tauranga that it cannot be ignored. It is a glove slapped in the face of one Regency dandy by another: come, let us duel.

When I heard these cries I could not resist them. The sight of the foe with their life-blood flowing from them seemed to elate some of our warriors, but I felt a great pity for them.

Tauranga, being a port, makes it easy for the imperial forces to bring up heavy ordnance: an Armstrong gun that lobs 110-pound shells, and seventeen field mortars and assorted cannons. They paste the Pa for two days.

… and I remembered also a rule that had been made amongst us that if any person asked for any service to be performed, the request must not be refused …

The speaker has many names – Heni Pore, Jane Foley, Heni Te Kiri, Jane Russell, Jane Kelly – but under all of them she is a history of an entire world, wrapped in a carapace of adamantine courage.

So I rose up from the trench, slung my gun, and was about to run back to the cooking-place where we kept our water when my brother asked me where I was going. I told him that I heard the dying men crying for water and could not disobey the call …

Heni is the daughter of an Irish sea captain, William Thomas Kelly, and Maraea, who as a child had been captured by the Nga Puhi in intra-tribal warfare. Heni was well educated at the Anglican mission at Paihia and then at a Wesleyan secondary school. Gunfire came early to her life: as a young girl she saw Hone Heke's burning of Kororeka and the response from off-shore naval guns.

I had to go about ten yards to the rear of the trench, and as our fence was almost demolished I was in view of the troops. I found that a small tin in which I had some water had been capsized, but that there was still the iron nail-can full. It was so heavy that I had to spill about half of it before I could conveniently carry it to the soldiers ...

Married at age fourteen or fifteen, to Te Kiri Karamu, a gum-digger, Heni has five children in quick succession. When the Maori King movement emerges – an attempt to unite tribes in a single entity, a fighting of Pakeha fire with fire – she joins. She is the only woman at Gate Pa, in a company of 230 male warriors. She digs tunnels and trenches with the men and knows how to shoot accurately.

... I carried it in my arms to where the Colonel was lying. I did not know then that he was a Colonel, but I could tell by his uniform that he was a senior officer. He was the nearest of the soldiers to me. I went down by his side, took his head on my knees and said "Here's water" in English ...

The imperial forces overrun the pa. After the bombardment it should be easy, and besides, we have 1,800 men. Time a lesson was taught ...

... I poured some of the water in one hand which I held close to his lips so that he could drink. He said "God Bless You," and drank again from my hand ...

It takes only ten minutes for the lesson to be learned. The soldiers encounter a vermicularium too complex to fathom, impossible to capture. The Pakeha army runs from Gate Pa in complete confusion. A hundred dead, dying, and wounded are left behind.

... I went to the three other soldiers and gave them water one by one in the same way. Then, placing the nail can so that it would not spill, I ran back to the trench.

The warriors are too smart to play the same game twice. They collect the rifles and ammunition the imperial forces have left behind and, under cover of night, they are gone.

Heni fights on for a time, and then, having been born of an Irishman, in 1869 she marries another one, Denis Foley, who is in charge of the government's military canteen at Maketu. They run a hotel for a bit and then farm at Kati-Kati, soon to become the only Irish plantation in New Zealand, and have six children. Denis, alcoholic and perhaps schizophrenic, attacks her in 1870 with a billhook and does significant wounding; he was acting under the impression that she was bewitching him. Despite this, and despite his being certified insane, she bears him six children.

Heni – Jane – later becomes a leader of the Women's Christian Temperance Union.

And her image is found in a stained glass window in Lichfield Cathedral, a tribute by the Empire to a chivalrous opponent.

TARANAKI, NORTH ISLAND. 1865–67

Household Pakeha

Whether they were slaves or domestic servants is a close call: in theory most Maori had given up keeping slaves under the dual pressure of Christian missions and English law. Still, when they acquired a deserter, it was a matter of each chief's judgement whether he had acquired a piece of property or a useful consultant on military affairs.

More than any other national group, Irish Catholic soldiers deserted to the enemy, but there is no need for raised eyebrows: there were more Irish than any other group in the forces. Mostly, the deserters led lives of hard work, little dignity, and less future. Some – such as Jack Hennessy of the 57th Regiment of foot – deserted, served with the Maori and managed to re-desert: in Hennessy's case he even escaped the regimental charge of desertion.

Others – take Humphrey Murphy, also of the 57th – deserted and failed to prosper. Murphy was the slave of two chiefs, a food carrier and a general piece of white offal. A fool, he talked to another deserter of killing his Maori master and stealing money to make up for wages he believed were due. He died in his sleep, a mere crashing through his cranium.

Another – Charles Kane of the 18th Royal Irish Regiment – after deserting he took a bullet from the imperial guns and later tried to re-desert to the Pakeha. His Maori owners caught him. Terrified, Kane promised never to try to escape and then immediately skipped the pa with a watch, a revolver and some stolen clothing. Re-captured, he was given a meal and left alone in his tiny whare. One warrior crept up and tried to take off his head with a billhook. He missed, only gashing Kane's nose. Kane leaped up to defend himself and an old warrior who had been keeping watch from outside, dropped Kane with a single blow from an ax. Then the deserter's body was hacked to shreds and thrown into an abandoned potato pit.

CHRISTCHURCH, SOUTH ISLAND. AUGUST 1866

Mixed Marriage

"Meet your future husband."

Ellen Moran blushed deeply. She was just off the boat and had been lucky to find a good job as a housemaid for a substantial merchant.

"Well, come now, lass, you must say something to Mr. Marsh or he will be offended!"

Ellen half-curtsied and tried to think of the right colonial words. In Nenagh, Tipperary, her family had been good at slathering layers of ironic courtesy on their betters, but here that would be taken as rude sarcasm. And her employer meant well. "Thank you, sir, "she finally managed, and then, straightening, "he seems very tall, sir."

Her employer laughed, but George Marsh did not. He looked her in the eye and smiled and Ellen, not long used to being an inside servant, did not cast her gaze deferentially downward. "Your employer is chaffing you," Marsh interjected," but he means no harm."

Two years later, Ellen Moran and George Marsh were married in the Catholic pro-cathedral in Christchurch. Marsh did not convert. The couple had eight children and they were all raised Catholic.

Just before she was widowed, Ellen witnessed her husband's turning to the True Faith.

HOKITIKA. SOUTH ISLAND, NZ. 1866

And This All Men Call Progress

A great historian has pointed out that all the colonial capitals – San Francisco, Melbourne, Sydney, and Dunedin – owe their prominence to the discovery of gold. Why even Hokitika would have been only an anagram in the back of the *Atlantic Monthly*, were it not for gold's discovery.

The seal of Hokitika's elevation beyond urbi to metropole was the building in 1866 of a roller-skating rink and of a wax works. The wax museum had Lord John Russell, the Pope, some Maori murderers and the murderer of the Finnigan family. The rink had fewer local heroes, but still did quite well.

RANGIORA, CANTERBURY. DECEMBER 1866

Fair Effort

The lady – and make no mistake, she is a lady – who wins the grand prize for her Merinos at the Northern Agricultural and Pastoral Show accepts the riband with the good grace of someone who has the advantage of knowing that she deserves victory. A strikingly handsome woman in her mid-forties, she makes a short acceptance speech that would have fit, in vocabulary and style, the Royal Dublin Society's agricultural show. Sarah Russell O'Connell is Anglo-Irish to the core.

As a child in County Cork, her father, a half-pay army officer, had taken her to see the former estates of Sir Walter Raleigh and of the earl of Cork, and, like a Sandhurst instructor, had lectured on the dangers of bad logistics and on the discipline of labour. Mind you, he might have done better to manage his own finances with more detail, for with his wife and thirteen children he had to migrate to Australia, where Sarah met Major Edward O'Connell.

Mrs. O'Connell – one wants to add an honorific prefix to her name – is now a widow and manages a 25,000 acre pastoral run and one of the province's largest dairy herds. The refined ladies who are the backbone of Canterbury's pseudo-gentry society find Mrs O'Connell admirable, but very Irish.

Irish here means competent, adaptable, and a touch too ruddy-cheeked to be a lady: in the English sense.

NEW PLYMOUTH, NORTH ISLAND. 1867

Smoking Kills

Perhaps he is another of Sir Walter Raleigh's victims; perhaps not.

Sergeant Karira, one of the nation's most experienced and effective native policemen, takes to his deathbed. He is worn out with years of straddling two worlds. Now he believes that a ngarara has settled in his throat. It is a devil, shaped like a reptile.

Probably Karira has throat cancer. His own explanation for the devil that is strangling him is less medical: he is, he says, dying because he violated tapu by smoking a pipe while burying the bones of his ancestors.

NEVIS. SOUTH ISLAND. 1867

Dowry

William Barry, English-born son of an Irish veterinarian, was one of the best hustlers, grandest liars, and sharpest small-time money-spinners in the country. He had few inhibitions, but every now and then his own cheek scared him.

He worries now, because of what he has just done. A young Pakeha woman has come up to him and asked if he, an auctioneer among his other trades, will sell her. "I don't know how it will go, but I'll try." This is during the middle of a goods auction, and Barry has a halter put on the woman and she is paraded around the sale ring. Most of the crowd are diggers, some of them with gold money to spend. The bidding ascends swiftly and eventually a miner named Newton wins her at £175. He makes a £5 cash deposit and leads off his prize, still in a calf halter.

Barry worries that he has conducted a slave auction and that he will be in deep trouble. Actually, he has participated in a practice that was accepted custom in rural England in the eighteenth century: a husband's auctioning off of a wife as an agreed form of divorce; or a young woman-of-no-means raising her own dowry. A queer old custom, but neither insane nor immoral.

NEW ZEALAND. 1867

Scorecard

Precise numbers aren't important, though you can have them if you wish.

What counts: in 1858 the numbers of Maori and Pakeha were effectively even.

In 1867 another census is taken: Maori population stable, Pakeha not quite quadrupled.

Who's winning?

RAROTONGA, THE COOK ISLANDS. 1867

Brown Apostles in Old Age

Old men see far, both ahead and behind. Brown apostles see no far-ther or more clearly than white missionaries, but they see different things, for their perspectives have been formed by concentrating on different points on the horizon.

In his last year of life Papehia, apostolic conqueror of Rarotonga, still serves the same church at Arorangi that he had been assigned in 1839 and there he had spent his years as curate to a white minister. Before that he had been for a few years on the out-island of Atiu, in full charge of a small world. Now in his declining months, he is so stooped and gnarled that he can only get about on all fours.

Papehia's confidant is Maretua, one of the few individuals who shares enough of his life's experiences to permit easy conversation in the short breaths old age allots. Maretua, since his return from Man-gaia in the mid 1840s, has been on missions to Manihiki and Rakah-anga, far in the northern sector of the Cook Islands, and now he is serving the church community at Ngatangiia, where he is called "the senior native pastor." Maretua always wears an English-style jacket and keeps one hand out of sight.

What do the two men see as they look back? "Jehovah's presence. Good and gentle changes," Papehia summarizes. To Maretua's sur-prise he adds, "Of course the Papaa missionaries always see the wrong thing."

"Always?"

"Yes. They see Jehovah's presence and, because they want to see only great changes, they miss the little matters that only move gently down the beach."

"And a good thing, those little matters."

"Indeed, my friend, indeed."

The little matters were concealed by the presence of Jesus-Tangeroa, the new god, Jehovah: no more wars, for the new god's Son gives no credit for despatching enemies, no matter how heroically it is done. And no more ritual killing, not even when a new ariki is created; Jesus has done one sacrifice for everyone, and throughout the islands there are still people who thank the Jesus-god for keeping them alive.

Yet little matters count. Papehia and Maretua are keenly aware that most of their flock view the churches simply as a marae for the new god. The Christian heaven is easier to enter than the warriors-afterlife under the old beliefs, but it is not much different. It's a good place. Granted, the old priests were put out of business, but now the tohunga, mixtures of medicine men and faith healers, lay spells, give potions, and keep alive many of the old myths. The stories, as long as they do not blaspheme Jehovah or his Son, are accepted by the Christians. The old pantheon of Cook Island gods has been destroyed, the people now have dozens of devils, demons, dominions, powers, angels, archangels, all called to their attention by the scriptures. These figures, many of them given specific names in the Bible, cloak the continued presence of the deities from the old pantheon.

Did the heathen priests bless new boats and men who went out on long sailing ships? Now the brown teacher or the white missionary wades into the water and says a prayer, long and loud, for safety and success. And did the heathen chiefs spend long evenings having their genealogies recounted and their ties to the old gods articulated? Fine, now they spend long hours listening to the genealogical portions of the Hebrew scriptures. The missionaries may think that the ariki are taking in God's word and maybe they are: but for the purpose of improving their own genealogies. The Cook Islanders work out that they are the descendants of Shem and this ties them all the way back to the day of Creation, the point that all true aristocrats see as their dawning day.

The Old Testament shows priests near the top of the social scale and a graded hierarchy throughout society. This was also the way it was in Polynesia before the new religion came and it remains.

"Does your arm still hurt you, Maretua?" Papehia asks.

"No, it is just a small cross to bear." Papehia has asked because he knows it is an odd source of pleasure to his friend. Maretua had three fingers severed in 1841 when trying to fire a salute to a whaling ship that was departing Mangaia. Thereafter, he wore an English jacket and kept the hand in his pocket. Later, when he was ministering on Manihiki a man asked him why he always kept his hand out of sight. "If I show you the hand, you will die," Maretua replied. The man persisted and eventually Maretua relented and showed his disfigured hand. The pesterer went about the village and told everyone what he had seen. The next morning he was dead.

Maretua was happy that his god had the same power to punish those who defamed holy men as had the old gods.

When eventually Papehia and Maretua left to be forever in the presence of Jesus and all the saints and apostles, they were given lavish encomia by the Papaa missionaries, long details of the treasure they had stored in heaven.

Their congregations were equally interested in their earthly legacies. When he died in 1867 Papehia left large blocs of land at Arorangi (though nothing like the thirty chunks of land he and his partner Tiberio had grabbed before the white missionaries had arrived in 1827, and which they had been forced to return). Papehia's most talented son was educated in England and took charge of the church at Arorangi. And his grandson, trained in the islands, became pastor of Aitutaki and then came back to serve Arorangi. There the dynasty ended, for Papehia's grandson had no children. Still, a title of Papehia-rangatiri (meaning, roughly, sub-chief) continues to the present day.

And Maretua, dying in 1880 at about age seventy-two, spent his last seven years in failing health but undiminished mana. Each week he was carried to his church on a couch by his deacons. There, his congregation leaned forward, straining to hear every breath of advice he offered.

His son became a missionary, married the daughter of the high chief of Takitumu, a district on the south side of Rarotonga. This couple had no children, but adopted a boy who was the offspring of a French father and a Rarotongan mother. This lad they named Maretua.

Civil war, of the old sort, almost broke out when this latter-day Maretua in the 1890s took the title of ariki. Only when the second Maretua died childless did peace fully return.

HOKITIKA, SOUTH ISLAND. MARCH 1868

The West's Awake

Hokitika cemetery was not a large space, even given the optimism of the town fathers. Still, it had a proper set of wooden pickets around it and an iron gate.

Father William Larkin, Maynooth-trained and Australian-experienced, led a procession to the cemetery. He and John Manning, one of the co-founders (along with Father Larkin) of *The New Zealand Celt*, had organized a symbolic protest, the first clear expression of radical Irish nationalism in New Zealand's history. They marched with empty coffin and Celtic cross in a funeral procession. When they found the gates of the cemetery locked, they broke down some pickets and went inside for a burial service that was half-eulogy, half-political rally. They were protesting the execution in England of the "Manchester Martyrs, "members of the Irish Republican Brotherhood, who had killed an unarmed policeman while trying to free some Fenian prisoners.

The men executed were called William O'Meara Allen, William O'Brien, and Michael Larkin. Locally it was believed that Father Larkin was the brother of the executed murderer Michael Larkin, but he never said.

AUCKLAND. 20 OCTOBER 1868

Chinese Puzzle

The Most Rev. George Augustus Selwyn left for Auckland harbour in a carriage pulled by enthusiastic young supporters. The Anglican metropolitan of New Zealand was returning to England to serve as Bishop of Lichfield and in his honour Auckland celebrated a public holiday.

Unintentionally, Selwyn had provided a key to one of the most rasping of Irish puzzles: how to get rid of the Anglican state church without killing the kernel of religion that resided within the corrupt Erastian husk. At Eton, Selwyn had become a lifelong friend of

William Ewart Gladstone, who in later life carried Ireland's pains with him the way a monk wears a scapular: close to his heart and omnipresent. Gladstone had become convinced by the mid 1860s that the Protestant state church in Ireland had to be cut off from its preferential status. But as a devout Christian he wanted the Church of Ireland to continue as a religious body, dependent only upon the devotion of its adherents. The Chinese puzzle was how to effect this.

Selwyn provided the answer and by example. In 1859, he had expanded the Upper Canadian precedent of electing bishops into a full religious constitution that maintained catholicity and episcopacy, but also provided rights for the clergy and the laity. It worked.

When, in 1871, the Church of Ireland ceased to be a state church, it assumed, by virtue of Gladstone's legislation, the organizational contours that George Selwyn had first laid down in the Antipodes.

HOKITIKA. SOUTH ISLAND. 1869

Nature's Dowry

Ellen Walsh, from Paulstown, County Kilkenny, understood the bounty of nature, and especially so because she was born in the famine year of 1847. She understood that being a female was a cruel fate, that in Ireland a woman without a male protector was submarginal, a parasite at best. But that in the Empire, women were precious and nature's bounty followed from being female.

At least if one knew where to go and what to sell.

The goldfields of any country were a good place for even the most lubricious bint, and for a good girl, they were a great place: the higher the fruit on the tree, the higher the bidder.

Ellen, her sister and brother moved first through Australia – no joy there – and then to Westland, the western locus of the New Zealand gold rush and the place where there were more Irish and more Catholics than anyplace. Hokitika, with gas-lighted dance halls and unlighted hotel rooms was perfect for the Walsh sisters, who wore virtue on their sleeves and scented handkerchiefs on their bodices.

Ellen won big. A Swiss-Italian Catholic hotelier who owned the "Helvetia" fell in love with her and soon she was the "hostess" of the

hotel and the hotelier's wife. She had children and practised an ancient form of birth control: extended lactation. Her second born, a son
named Siverino, was breastfed until he was so old that he could pick
up a stool and bring it over to her to sit on while he was at the teat.

Ah, fortune. The Swiss-Italian husband died when Ellen was only
twenty-six and she spent the rest of her days buying and running hotels, marrying an illiterate named Dennis Maher and wearing shamrock earings and brooch, and an ornamental harp on a chain, all made
from Westland gold. She gave conspicuously to Mother Mary Joseph
Aubert and the Sisters of Compassion and, in her later days, was
know to slip a fiver to a drunk, saying "Have a drink on me, Mick."

LONDON. 1870

"Meet and Right, So to Do"

The Meade family, Irish Catholic sometimes, Irish Protestant at others, winds through Empire history from the seventeenth century
onwards. In some places their name becomes a talisman and is taken
on by their indentured servants and by their former slaves. When in
1870 a book by Herbert Meade, late lieutenant in the Royal Navy is
published in London, it deals with Empire and does so with an expert
eye: *A Ride through the Disturbed Districts of New Zealand; together with
some account of the South Sea Islands.*

A fine piece of travel literature, but posthumous. In his dying, the
Hon. Herbert Meade (hon. because he was the fourth son of the Earl
of Clanwilliam) tells us everything about his manner of living. He
was only twenty-seven when he met his end, a victim of enthusiasm:
for, as a keen naval officer, Meade loved gunnery. And, having independent means, he rented a workshop in Portsmouth, where he was
stationed after his return from the Pacific, and there he and an assistant developed a new form of torpedo.

Unfortunately for Meade, one afternoon in mid-July 1868, the device exploded.

Meade, with his insides hanging out, refused medical attention.
He knew it was a waste of time. Instead, he dedicated his last
moments to being certain that his wife, who was pregnant, would
receive his private fortune. And, he asserts that his torpedo gun was

a great invention. His last words are, "Tell my friends it was nothing connected with my gun."

AUCKLAND. DECEMBER 1870; PORT CHALMERS, OTAGO. FEBRUARY 1871

Two Irishmen

Two Irishmen get off their boats; the wrong one gets back on.

Both are newly appointed bishops.

Both have recently attended the first Vatican council.

Both are clients of Paul Cardinal Cullen, archbishop of Dublin and, save for the Pope, the most influential person in the Catholic church. Cullen's vision of serving Christ involves putting Irish clergy into every possible benefice and bishopric in the English-speaking world.

The first cleric off the ship is Thomas Croke, recently appointed bishop of Auckland. The Right Rev. Dr. Croke was a shambolic administrator, but a fine spokesman for the faith. Tall, a former athlete, he was the offspring of a mixed marriage, and not of the tenant-trash variety; his mother was the real item, Anglo-Irish horse-Protestant, disowned for marrying a Catholic. Croke knew how to talk to others than his own flock and how to put a soft face on Catholic demands in a Protestant world. "When it is announced that he will preach at Vespers, the church cannot contain the numbers that flock in," a sister of Mercy writes home to Ireland. "Jews and Protestants of all denominations come to hear him."

Croke departs New Zealand in early 1874 to become archbishop of Cashel. He becomes a nationalist saint: following Parnell despite the displeasure of his superiors. He was the first patron of the Gaelic Athletic Association, a body he treated as if it were a holy order. In turn, the association, when it builds its equivalent of a cathedral in Dublin, names it after him: Croke Park.

The second cleric is Patrick Moran (not to be confused with his unrelated namesake, Cardinal Patrick Francis Moran). He has recently been bishop of the Eastern Cape, centred in Grahamstown, South Africa. There he had overlapped with Sir George Grey with whom he is once more geographically united. This to Grey's amusement and Moran's irritation. As bishop of Dunedin, he was a confident and competent administrator. To non-Catholics he was distrustful at best, offensive mostly, and aggressive to a fault. Within the church he identified "Irish" and "Catholic" as synonyms, a position that went down hard in a country whose Catholicism came from France and had been nurtured by English clergy more than Irish.

By the time of his death in 1895, Moran had won. The New Zealand church was controlled by the Irish, run by Irish precedents, and saw Dublin as its metropole. And the church was alienated from the larger society, attempting to build its own Irish ghetto.

PORT CHALMERS. 18 FEBRUARY 1871

The Genteel Touch

Better than secular priests (who were always angling for promotion), better than the Christian Brothers (trustworthy thugs whom he planned to use as shock troops) were the nuns of the better orders. Especially the Dominicans. So thought Patrick Moran, new bishop of Dunedin. The nuns raised the standard of Catholic womanhood and that, the bishop knew from his colonial experience in Africa, was invaluable.

Mother Mary Gabriel, prioress of a community of Irish Dominicans, led her flight of nine Dominican sisters off the vessel that she shared with Bishop Moran, various minor clergy, and a hold full of migrants. Whereas the emigrants, who had been packed together like herrings in a barrel, tumbled forth as if by explosion, Mother Mary and her nuns disembarked like butterflies, hardly touching the gangplank in their exodus.

The Dominicans were everything the bishops of the post-Famine church in Ireland prized: upper middle-class, refined, well-educated, chaste, devout. In New Zealand, they founded schools and worked among the daughters of the Irish migrants with the same devotion, and with no more distaste than they would have done for black Africans.

Occasionally, Mother Mary had to discipline her nuns, as they sometimes acquired vulgar customs from their students. Indeed, she once was forced to inform her confessor that when one of her senior pupils had sneezed, she herself had instinctively uttered the old pishrogue, "God bless the baby!"

Her confessor had assigned as penance that she contemplate daily the Mandylion of Edessa and the Veronica. Mother Mary found this penance both condign and suitably refiné.

ROTUMAH, C.400 MILES NORTH OF FIJI. 1871

Faiths of Our Fathers, Living Still

Night falls on the preparations for civil war. Armies light their separate fires and prepare for the morrow's contest. The Catholic soldiers take the Sacrament and are given a special blessing by their priests. The Protestants sing hymns and penitential songs. Witnesses later compare the scene to the eve of the battle of Naseby, when Oliver Cromwell met and defeated the Royalists.

Rotumah. Three hundred miles from the nearest land. The pinpoint in the Pacific Ocean where geographers traditionally see Micronesia, Melanesia, and Polynesia touching each other. Culturally rich, a society with complex inlays from each of the main Pacific cultures, an ornate and wondrous creation, as complex as the surface of a Louis XIV credenza, but lighter, freer.

Rotumah. Three thousand inhabitants, perhaps. Sixteen square miles of effusively fertile land, an almost-vulgar effulgence in an ocean of harsh coral and volcanic islands.

As the darkness thins, and the pre-dawn light becomes marked, men who have been sitting all night on their haunches, shake out their limbs and look to their weapons. There are few workable guns on either side, although some fallible rifles are to hand, more for psychological effect than military purposes. This civil war will be fought with the weapons of Rotumah's fathers.

But it will be fought to defend the faith of the fathers of a distant world. In the late 1840s, the Marists brought Roman Catholic Christianity to the island. They found that Wesleyan Methodist preachers, Samoans, Tongans, and Fijians, had arrived two years earlier. Bitter rivalry ensued, with a third party, the "heathen" wishing bad cess to both sides. Matters came to a head when the question arose of whether or not taxes should be paid to the major chief of the island, who was heathen and proud of it. The Catholic priest counselled following Jesus' advice, to render unto Caesar what is Caesar's. The Wesleyans, however, repeated St. Paul's advice and refused to render any homage to the worshippers of idols.

Not surprisingly, the high chief's party agreed with the Catholics, and thus the sides were drawn: Catholics and heathen against keen Protestants.

As at Naseby, the Protestants won. And, as in the English civil war, the victors burned the chapels of the vanquished. Coming upon the priests' vestments, the Wesleyans tore them to shreds. The monstrance with its communion vessels was broken open and later used as a target for the few guns that were in shooting order. Clubbed down, speared, their homes burned, the Catholics were forced to one small sector of the island and there they were permitted to live in near starvation.

A great Protestant revival followed and, though it slackened, the revival came alive again after the Protestants won Rotumah's second civil war in 1878.

Yes, the Rotumians were fighting old tribal battles. Not those of their own tribe, granted.

KAWAU ISLAND, NR. AUCKLAND. 1872

Noah's Ark

Wallabies. Emus. Zebras. Antelope. Ostriches. And much more. The richness flummoxes Sir George Bowen, governor of New Zealand. He is on a courtesy call to his predecessor Sir George Grey who, after being dismissed as governor, had run for the parliament in England and then, defeated, returned to New Zealand to be Noah. Grey's ambition was to have at least a dozen species of animal on his island from each of the places in the Empire he had governed.

Bowen, the son of an Anglican rector from County Donegal, has been on the same world-circling voyage of administration as Grey, so he recognizes most of the species. He tries to be composed as he and Grey walk the island. They chat about mutual friends, and they agree that if Home Rule were to come to their mutual homeland, it would be a fine precedent for New Zealand.

They spend an hour feeding rabbits to one of Grey's large constrictors and Bowen wonders if there is any lesson in this exhibition.

BLUFF HARBOUR, SOUTH ISLAND. 28 APRIL 1874

The Rantle-Tree

Why the run of New Zealand society was mildly anti-Catholic is not a matter for explanation: Protestants did not like Catholics and that's a law of gravity.

Irish Catholics, especially the women, made good pioneers – that is to say, they did as well as anyone else in a New World where adaptability and shrewdness were the most valuable of all skills. Annie Corkery (*née* Reddy) could have told you that. She stepped off the *Carrick Castle* at Bluff, straight from Cobh Harbour, and immediately found a job.

Annie married little more than a year after arriving. Denis, her husband, was twenty-three years old, from Mitchelstown, County Cork, and Annie twenty-one. Denis did heavy railway work, until fifteen years and seven children later, the family had enough money to set up a bush farm at Te Wae Wae.

That Annie and Denis and thousands of other Irish Catholics settled and prospered in New Zealand was in large part owing to Julius Vogel, London-born, Jewish, who, as a Dunedin newspaper proprietor, had fought the prejudice of Dunedin's inbred Scots against Gold Rush migrants: and then, as prime minister of New Zealand in the 1870s, had initiated a massive emigrate-to-New Zealand campaign. Assisted by government funds, Annie and Denis jumped half way around the world. By the mid-1880s, the Irish (both Catholic and Protestant) were almost one-fifth of the Pakeha population.

Annie had brought with her a rantle-tree from her home in Kilkenny. It was a harsh piece of ironwork, forged by a local blacksmith, but it held any cooking pot weighing under a hundredweight. When Annie and Denis expanded their bush farm into a successful dairy, the rantle-tree became part of the machinery, swinging heavy loads from one spot to another.

Like the rantle-tree, Annie and Denis became part of the machinery of their new country. Annie had nine children, one of whom was killed in action in Belgium in 1917.

YAP, THE CAROLINE ISLANDS, MICRONESIA. 1875

Floating Capital

This is the first time he has had trouble with ambition. No trouble at all motivating himself as a young jack to leave Ireland during the starvation. None at all to turn him into a blockade-runner for the Confederacy. No trouble in becoming a smalltime sea captain in post-war Savannah, always looking for the big payload. He had no trouble at all raising sufficient ire to kill an insubordinate seaman. And, just cleared of that act's being a murder, he killed easily another of his subordinates who was drunk, angry, and who could not swim very well: after being battered unconscious. No, ambition of all sorts comes easy to David O'Keefe, and no time easier than when, having cleared off from the USA, he is shipwrecked in late 1871 at Yap.

It's there ambition becomes his problem. Not his own ambition, for it still flames greedily. The difficulty is the Yapese. Virtually alone among the Micronesian islands, the Yap people are beyond all but the most trifling seductions of modern merchant trade. They maintain a reputation for spiritualism and sorcery that makes them invulnerable to other tribes; no one attacks people who have such strong medicine. In fact, leaders of other islands send them tribute, unbidden. It's enough to make the tall, red-haired O'Keefe drink himself unconscious: how does he make this people ambitious, and thus malleable?

Finally, he cracks the problem. The Yapese, for all their preference for traditional clothes and foods, for all their finding modern manufactured goods unattractive, love money. Not just any money, their own money.

And what fine money it is!

The currency comes from the island of Palau, 300 miles distant, where the coinage is taken from limestone quarries. The smallest piece of change consists of a disc weighing at least a ton, six feet across. And that's just the kleingeld. These huge discs have value proportionate to the risk and loss of life in quarrying them and transporting them by sea to the home island.

Limited they are as a means of exchange – since no one else in the world wants them – but they do serve as a storehouse-of-value for the Yapese.

O'Keefe, serpent in Eden, offers the Yap chiefs a bit of ambition: he will take the risk of freighting the heavy money from Palau to Yap, if they will provide him with a given amount of copra for each coin.

They agree.

Within three years, the entire adult male population of Yap, once the Tibet of Micronesia, is involved either in producing copra or quarrying limestone discs, using stone tools. Many of the young men are contracted by their chief to work gangs for six month terms.

David O'Keefe has solved the ambition problem. By 1880 Yap is the commercial centre of the Caroline Islands.

CROMWELL. SOUTH ISLAND. 1876

Clerical Judgement

"Dear Lord! Even Cromwell wouldn't have done this in Cromwell."

The nightmare happened all too often. Bishop Moran of Dunedin, even more than the other Catholic prelates, believed in good Catholic schools as the means of uplifting his flock. Political and social power followed from education and so did decorous Catholic behaviour. In the outlying parishes, where teaching brothers and nuns were not available, it all hinged on each parish priest's finding good school masters and mistresses.

"The man has made off with £50. No, more, it's nearly £60!"

Father Kehoe, parish priest of Cromwell, had appointed a sharp, seemingly well-educated man of thirty to run Cromwell's Catholic primary school: Robert Butler, who at the time went under the name of C.I. Donnelly. He was a good schoolmaster and he also conducted a more advanced night school where, for a fee, he taught French, Latin, algebra and Euclidean geometry.

"When I taxed him about it, the wretch tried to blame the theft on his star pupil."

The schoolmaster knew his subjects well because he had spent most of the previous fifteen years in various Australian prisons, for larceny, burglary, and armed robbery. He had used his prison time learning any subject he could find a book on.

Father Kehoe was devastated. In reporting the matter to Bishop Moran, he came close to tears.

Neither Father Kehoe nor his bishop forgot the incident, but each found it a consolation to learn that before finally being apprehended, Robert Butler has taught for a time in a Protestant school.

AUCKLAND. 1877

Chains

What looks to the jaundiced eyes of early social enumerators as a simple matter of subtraction and addition was not. Irish migration was mostly a matter of chains, almost all of them invisible. Few of the Irish migrated any place without at least some information sent back home by earlier migrants to guide them. Before the Famine and from the early 1850s onwards (leaving out, then, only the panicked outrush of the Famine migration), virtually every migrant had a cousin, a brother, a sister, or at least someone from the old home parish who had gone ahead and could be contacted for advice and perhaps for aid. Sometimes the old hands took advantage of the new, but at least learning the ropes was made easier.

Sometimes – the Brosnahans of Timaru are a good example – an entire family network was transferred from Ireland to a new world. In their case, over a fifteen year period, from 1860–1874, a kin network from County Kerry moved to Kerrytown in south Canterbury. Even the old folks were brought over, thus sealing the abandonment of the old country as permanent.

Other times – for example the Corkerys of the parish of Clondrochid, near Macroom, in west Cork – the chains remained anchored at each end and were multiplied into a worldwide network. Corkerys spread throughout Cork, and there are documented chains, built family by family, from County Cork to Southland, New Zealand, Upper Canada, New York State and Missouri.

But it's not all sweetness and familial warmth. Take the Kellehers, the other major family group in Clondrochid, West Cork. Between 1859 and 1875 three brothers went to the USA from Clondrochid. The first of them serves in the Union Army in the American Civil War. Another brother joins him in Lawrence, Massachusetts after the war, and the third arrives in 1875. A nice family scene, except that the first two brothers are devoted Irish nationalists, and the last one to arrive has spent twelve years in the United Kingdom army, having taken the shilling from the recruiting sergeant at Macroom. There is no family reunion. The two nationalists refuse to speak to the imperialist. Frozen out, he, his wife, and infant son migrate to New Zealand in 1877.

Tellingly, each branch of the now-split family responds the same way: suppression and denial. One son of the nationalist Irish-Americans is told of the existence of his imperial uncle only when he has reached twenty-one years of age. And in New Zealand, the knowledge that there were Americans of close family is suppressed for an entire generation and resurfaces only when an American soldier, a Kelleher of a younger generation, appears in New Zealand on leave during World War II.

KATIKATI, NORTH ISLAND, 1878

Ulster's Wee Colony

After the battle of Gate Pa in 1864, the Maori withdrew to the interior, leaving the government with a notional victory and a stunned military. The government's response to its humiliation was to declare the Katikati and Tauranga blocs confiscated. Whether or not this action was carried out with full legalities is still a matter of negotiation.

In the short-run, however, there was a lot of virtually empty land and the need to fill it, before the tribes re-settled.

That is why the *Lady Jocelyn* eased out of Belfast Harbour in May 1878. It carried 378 immigrants, know as "Stewart's No. 2 party," and they were part of one of the largest land-scams in New Zealand's history. Not that these people, earnest, middle class Ulster farmers, merchants and clerics, were directly involved in the swindle, or even its major beneficiaries.

George Vesey Stewart, an Irish Protestant of gentry pretences, was the younger son of one of the thousands of plantation families that had settled in the tough borders of Ulster, in their case Ballygawley, County Tyrone. In the post-Famine years, the Catholics pushed back at them, and it was all these families could do to keep their lands, much less expand them. So, all over the Ulster borderlands there were families like the Stewarts who were running out of room for their children.

Stewart's genius was to realize that these Ulster Protestants constituted a market for a very simple product: agricultural land. With striking prescience and the ability of a snake oil salesman, in 1873 he convinced the New Zealand authorities to give him 10,000 acres of land for nothing, provided he filled them with good Ulster Protestants. This was the Katikati region, and Stewart returned to Ulster to become a one-man evangelist, salesman, emigration agent, and development officer for his scheme. He got the Orange Order behind him, so that the enterprise had an aspect of the Great Crusades: redeem the land. In 1875 his first settler-party arrived, 258 individuals, including 34 family groups, and Stewart sold them land in twenty or forty acre blocs. These were middle class settlers, so they required no government aid and they paid for the land without demur. A brilliant exhibit: Stewart sells government land and pockets all the proceeds.

Things will be a little tougher for No. 2 party, for Sir Julius Vogel, the doyen of New Zealand emigration schemes, recognizes what a honey pot Stewart has his paw in. So, this second time, Stewart acquires another 10,000 acres near his previous bloc, but now he has to pay £1 per acre (half of it upfront, half later). Still, it's a profitable enterprise, for land goes between £2 and £4 per acre, and Stewart's chief expenses are an endless rain of pamphlets endorsing his scheme with which he floods Ulster. In the end, Stewart makes roughly 250 percent on his money and organizes a No. 3 and No. 4 party.

Out of all this, New Zealand acquires a weird mixture: hardworking Protestant middle tenants; foppish sons of Irish failing gentry who are sent out as "cadets" to learn farming under Stewart's tutelage; a handful of decent clergy, and a generation or two later, David Gallaher, the captain of the All Blacks in their legendary 1905 tour of Great Britain, and John Mulgan, the foredoomed writer.

Of course, Vesey Stewart had dreams of gentry glory for himself. He built a large house and there played the squire, holding tea dances and presiding over a tiny world where women still wore white gloves. Things turned from risible to ridiculous, however: he lost most of his money in a railway scheme. His grandiose renaming of Uretara, at the southern section of his township as "Waterford," had to be rescinded when it was found that most telegrams directed there were sent to Ireland. And in later years he married his housekeeper, shuffled about in carpet slippers, tried odd promotions, such as

selling specially-imported seeds to his colonists, and gradually became an old man with a straw hat on his head and tufts of hair
sprouting from his ears.

TIMARU, SOUTH ISLAND. BOXING DAY 1879

Something Missing

Smell the air. Something's missing. To a worldly observer, New
Zealand in some way is like the mountains to someone who is used to
breathing salt-sea air. What's missing is the acrid tang of heavy sectarianism. Granted, Protestant and Catholic school kids throw rocks at
each other, but these are baby-wars, and the children would be pitch-
ing rocks at the other school in any case. Team games work that way.

The first parade of the Orange Order is held in 1877. In the South
Island, an Orange parade on Boxing Day 1879 results in a spontaneous response from a bunch of young Catholic labourers who kick the
Prods around quite handily. And in Timaru, in South Canterbury
which has a strong Catholic population, many from tight County
Kerry families, marchers in an Orange procession, are forced to take
off their regalia and to abandon their walk. Convictions were few in
Timaru, mostly because the Orangemen did not show up in court,
possibly because of fear of retribution.

These instances stand out, for something happens to Irish persons
in New Zealand. Protestants continue a low-level snobbery. And
Catholics continue to feel aggrieved, but mostly it is in a vague Faith-
of-Our-Fathers sort of way, part of the genetic code of their culture.

The grandchildren of the nineteenth-century Irish immigrants look
at Ireland and are puzzled by its incivility.

VITA LEVU ISLAND, FIJI. 1881

Totally Bad

The chances of the Australian-Irish barrister, James de Courcey
Ireland's being known as the wildest, most totally kickass, lock-up-

the-women white man on Fiji took a downward turn the day of his duel with the offensive Teutonic settler Wecker.

Mind you, Ireland's form sheet was good. He had exited Australia after being imprisoned and fined for riding his horse at full speed through a crowd of 4,000 citizens who were gathering to celebrate the opening of the new Melbourne town hall. This prior to his horse-whipping a policeman who tried to arrest him. That sort of pettifogging cuts the heart out of James Ireland's faith in Australia as a place where freedom of the spirit prevailed. So too does losing a court case a week after being released from gaol: his legal defence of a man who had punched his wife to death. The jury could not accept Ireland's argument that this was perfectly reasonable behaviour.

Fiji offered more freedom, a chance to recapture a world of strong moralities. That was why Ireland now is a small trader and bigtime member of the local Irish community. He presides occasionally over a kangaroo court that settles disputes among white settlers and features a makeshift boxing ring where debtors and lenders settle their differences.

Obviously, Ireland cannot accept an insult to Queen Victoria (whom he venerates, not entirely accurately, as the Virgin Queene) by a Knothead, a German.

Wecker and Ireland meet on the sands of the northeastern side of Vita Levu. "Blue water will run soon with red blood," Ireland declares and tells his second to load his pistol.

The two duellists march off twelve paces. Neither of them notices that the two seconds are standing dangerously close to the line of fire.

Turning precisely on the count of "twelve," the representatives of two contesting empires fire. The duellists' shirts turn crimson, but neither falls. The seconds, sensible men, have substituted red-currant jelly for lead.

CHARLESTON, NELSON PROVINCE, SOUTH ISLAND.
MARCH 1884

Mourning Has Broken

The *Charleston Herald* chronicled a community that had been formed in 1866 with Timothy Linahan's finding gold: a late strike and the town matured quickly. Police, newspaper, a full line of stores appeared. St. Patrick's day in Charleston, as in all the west coast gold fields, was a holiday for everyone, the Irish sharing it and celebrating in a secular fashion, quite unlike the pious day of holy obligation honoured in the homeland. In Charleston, a feature of the day was an undeclared, but vigorously contested, dress contest among the matrons, young wives, prostitutes and bar girls.

Tides ebb. In 1884 the *Herald* mournfully reported that for the first time the town had failed to celebrate St. Patrick's Day. This, it said, was a clear indication of how dead the place had become.

AUCKLAND. NOVEMBER 1885

Balance of Power

"Just look at the woman," John Ballance whispered to an aide as a party of foreign dignitaries approached. "She's as broad as a three-ox team." Ballance's County Antrim-burr made it sound as if someone had braided three oxen so that they were tame, and his secretary was slightly puzzled. Undeniably, the woman was amazing, good threehundredweight wrapped in a floral print. "Thank goodness she moves slowly," the secretary replied with heartfelt sincerity.

"Welcome to three," Ballance pronounced when the diplomatic party was within earshot. "I should say," he corrected himself, "Welcome to thee." That form of address, inherited from his Quaker mother, often came out when Ballance was under pressure. He knew that the visiting Polynesians were devout Christians, and he reserved the intimate form of address for spiritual matters. Oh, now I've offended her, he thought. "You are most welcome," he corrected himself yet again and this time the mountain in the floral print smiled solemnly.

Actually, Queen Makea of Rarotonga was an attractive woman, once one became accustomed to her size. Coal black eyes and equally black hair set off a face that was unlined. Despite being in her mid-forties, she still had all her teeth and she spoke English with a slow staccato beat and in a low, husky register. Makea was Queen of Rarotonga by virtue of being the senior ariki. It was a courtesy title, and all the main ariki now called themselves "king" or "queen," in imitation of the Europeans. Four of the ariki now were women, something that never would have occurred before contact with Europeans: if a Queen was good enough for the United Kingdom and all its domains, it was good enough for Rarotonga.

Queen Makea and her fellow aristocrats on Rarotonga and on the neighbouring islands have two problems and they need help. The first of these is that while the mixture of aristocracy and theocracy, of traditional hierarchical social control and missionary-prescribed morality, work well among the islanders, there are too many foreigners coming among us. "There are strangers in the lands," is the biblical phrase she uses to describe the matter to Ballance, who, as minister for Native Affairs, is the most responsive person in the New Zealand government to her concerns. Neither European traders, nor immigrants from other Polynesian islands respect the laws. The police are overworked. The once-balanced system is breaking down.

"And, Mr Ballance, there are the French!" This was Makea's most immediate concern.

"Yes, the French." A small voice came from a man who had been obscured by Makea and her diplomatic party, consisting of two ladies-in-waiting and three male outriders, plus this old man: her husband, Rangi Makea Vakatini who was the hereditary chief of Atiu, Mauke, and Mitiaro, and styled himself "king" of those isles.

He was about half the size of Queen Makea and had the apprehensive look of a man who had lived his entire life under an overhanging cliff.

Briefly, Ballance pictured the arachnidal form that the regal mating of these two might take and shuddered. He was not surprised when he later learned that they had no progeny.

The native leaders of Rarotonga were no fools and they understood, however incompletely, that the balance of the entire world was becoming unsettled and that they could be hurt, badly. France had declared a protectorate over Tahiti and the Society Islands in 1842, and the United Kingdom had annexed Fiji in 1874, moving the capital from Levuka to Suva, and using it as command-central for the entire South Pacific. "Do our British friends care?" Makea asked. "Do they care that the French might invade us?"

Ballance, by nature a dangerously honest man, almost told her the truth: not really, they really do not care. Instead he waffled and talked about how much the New Zealand government cared, which was a lot: annexation of various Polynesian islands indeed had been an intermittent dream of many New Zealand politicians. So Ballance, who shared the dream, sent Queen Makea on a week-long tour of the choicer sights of the North Island, a royal progress marred only by one of her male aide's proposing to a Maori beauty he fancied, a bit of romance that, by conservative count and LMS missionaries notwithstanding, would have given him wife number five.

John Ballance provided Makea with a written promise that the "islands" (he was not sure how many there were, actually), would come under "the protection of the British Crown" at any time the ariki requested it. And New Zealand would provide a protective alliance based on economic reciprocity and on the islands' right of internal self-government.

Whether this cheque had anything to back it up would only be discerned if the islanders some day tried voluntarily to enrol in the British empire.

MARTINBOROUGH, NORTH ISLAND. 1886

Traffic Patterns

No question, John Martin was a man of vision. The son of a County Londonderry clergyman, he had arrived at Port Nicholson in 1841 and, starting with a pick and shovel, had worked his way into a large and largely-honest fortune. Having paid cash for a 33,000-acre estate in 1879, he set about developing it. The depression of the early 1880s set him back a bit, but not his dreaming.

For Martin sets forth the town of Martinborough with the eye of a true patriot. A town square is laid out and then Martin has all the streets leading to the square arranged in the most patriotic fashion possible: they duplicate the several crosses that at varied angles intersect each other on the Union Jack.

Even in the days of horse-drawn transport, getting from one side of the town to the other was an adventure.

RAROTONGA, THE COOK ISLANDS. 27 SEPTEMBER 1888

Protection Racket

"Can't hear a word the chappie's saying," complained one of the two old India hands who had settled on Rarotonga.

"Frightful din, all that stick-banging by the nig-nogs."

"Drums, actually. They're hollow."

"Still, the chappie should speak up. He's Irish, isn't he?"

"Don't see why that should keep him from speaking louder. Known some frightfully loud Paddies in my day."

"... and therefore," intoned Captain Edmund Bourke, "I pronounce these islands ..." his words were obscured by a twenty-one musket salute that his lieutenant had mistimed. Having said his piece to his own satisfaction, Bourke turned on his heel and marched back to his waiting six-oared dinghy. He left the admiring populace happily entertained, but mystified.

Bourke had made a complete mess of annexing the Cook Islands. When, in July 1888, a petition from the ariki of several of the islands had finally arrived in London, the colonial office took it seriously, a big change in outlook. Now the London authorities were convinced that the French really intended to invade the "Hervey Islands."

That the potential invasion was now taken seriously was largely the result of the unremitting pressure and publicity generated by the Roman Catholic bishop of Tahiti, who had a following among the clergy in France. He promised a rich harvest of souls and the re-conversion of thousands of Polynesia's Protestants. Even this might not have moved the London authorities to budge, but France, Germany, and the United Kingdom now were involved in a scramble to grab as much of Africa as possible, and their mutual rivalries spilled over into the South Pacific. And, besides, some French engineer had come up with the idea of cutting a canal across Panama and, in the unlikely event of that succeeding, well, all those Pacific islands would be a lot closer to Europe.

So, in over-haste, Edmund Bourke, captain of the *Hyacinth*, was despatched from Hawaii to deal with the matter. This was unfair to him as he had no experience whatsoever in diplomacy or geo-power politics. And to this day, no one knows exactly what he did.

Apparently, instead of declaring a protectorate over the islands, he declared them annexed. The Colonial Office went along with the annexation for a couple years, then backed away and said only a protectorate was involved. And how many islands? It was not clear, as Bourke visited only six of them, but eventually, London decided that all fifteen were included and that they were no longer the "Hervey Islands," but the "Cook Islands."

Bourke sailed away quite pleased with himself. He especially liked that part where, on several separate islands, he had been permitted to plant a Union Flag and say "I take this land in the name of the Queen of England," a phrase he had adopted from the novels of navy life he secretly read.

CHRISTCHURCH. 1889

Dreams Come True

It's dangerous enough when anyone's dreams come true: for a Kiwi the worst wish that can be granted is to make it big in the Old Country.

In 1889 William Pember Reeves, editor of the *Canterbury Times*, throws his weight behind the Liberal politician – the Irishman, John Ballance – and virtually guarantees his becoming prime minister a year or two later. And, in 1898, Reeves writes the best history of New Zealand to be published between the country's European settlement and, say, 1950: an enviable achievement.

Alas, he makes it big in London, first as an agent for the New Zealand government and then as a social expert. Reeves has the misfortune to be ensnared in the web of superior righteousness of Sidney and Beatrice Webb, and he becomes so close with them that he is sometimes permitted to say a word or two. He is treated as a near-equal by George Bernard Shaw and the two have contests praising how witty the other one is: Reeves always wins. In 1908 the Webbs fix up his appointment to the directorship of the London School of Economics, a glorified Sunday School that Reeves manages with notoriously bad temper. In the same year, his daughter runs off to Paris with H.G. Wells and returns pregnant. Wells, already married, uses this affair as fodder for yet-another of his novels and Reeves spends the remainder of his life denouncing Wells. That's life in the bigtime.

WELLINGTON. JANUARY 1891

Political Castles

Men of Irish background in the nineteenth and early twentieth centuries become chief ministers or prime ministers of New Zealand with the same ease with which they become presidents of the United States of America: James E. FitzGerald (first minister, 1854), Edward Stafford (prime minister, 1856), Sir George Grey (1877), John Ballance (1891), Joseph Ward (Melbourne-born, son of Cork City emigrants, 1901 and 1928) and William Ferguson Massey (1912). They fit the times, spikey personalities, bluntly spoken, often to-a-fault. Mostly Protestant, but Ward's being Catholic did not prove much of an impediment.

John Ballance formed the country's first Liberal government (1891–93) and he took as a negative template much of his Irish inheritance. Having seen the Belfast riots of the 1850s, he abhorred sectarianism and, in fact, gave up Christianity: he moved from his father's evangelical Anglicanism to being a leading advocate of Free Thought. Raised as a standard Empire loyalist, in New Zealand he refused to accept being drafted into the Wanganui militia, since he opposed state compulsion. He favoured Home Rule for Ireland and as prime minister he argued for votes-for-women with an equal mixture of Ulster outspokenness and canniness.

That is: he declared his belief in the absolute equality of the sexes and in women's right to vote.

But only after the *next* election.

PORT HILLS, CANTERBURY, SOUTH ISLAND. 1892

Draught Animals

"Mother, I am home." One of the Carney daughters reports dutifully.

"So you are dear. Now give me a hand with the rendering. And mind you don't let that lye splash." She was making soap, a job requiring considerable strength and vats of pork-fat and lye and potash, caustics that could burn or blind. Mary Carney had come to New Zealand from County Cork in 1871 in the company of a heavy-drinking brother whom she was expected to look after. He eventually went awry and she went upcountry in Canterbury. She worked on the "Mesopotamia" station, once owned by Samuel Butler, and for the first years she did so for food and lodgings, no wages.

Brutally hard labour, human beings as draught animals. No one could blame Mary if she becomes as hard as the callouses on her hands. She marries a bullock driver who is away from home for weeks at a time. Mary has five children and raises them in a two-room sod house. Finally, the family is able to move to its own small farm, bush bought for sixpence an acre.

Because the family needs a bull, one of the daughters at age thirteen is sent to work for a better-off neighbour. She pays off the price of the bull at a notional salary of one shilling a week. Gone from home for four years, she does the same sort of manual labour her mother always has done.

She's home now, the family's debt paid. She is not at all surprised when her mother immediately puts her to work.

WESTPORT, SOUTH ISLAND. 1896

The Old Rules

Mary Campbell of Cronadun, County Donegal, falls in love with a stranger. A foreigner. A Protestant. Julius Schadick is a trained engineer who had designed the water works at Westport.

The couple marries and has a happy life. Its basis is a covenant that was common in the rural parts of Ireland: in the case of a mixed marriage the boys follow the father's faith, the girls follow the mother's. It's not a universal practice, but one that frequently is the key to defusing an explosive social situation.

The Schadicks have four girls and a boy. The girls go on to become the mothers of good Catholic families and the boy qualifies as an engineer and in 1942 receives an OBE for his services to the community.

Slightly more than a decade later this sort of thing becomes impossible. From 1908 onwards, the church permits mixed marriages only if the non-Catholic partner signs an agreement turning the religious education over to the Catholic parent: this is the *Ne Temere* decree, one of the most religiously divisive promulgations of the twentieth century.

RAROTONGA, THE COOK ISLANDS. 1898

Colonial Oppression

The bald dome of Frederick J. Moss's head is blotched from a skin disease that his physician cannot diagnose, but probably it is nerves. Serving as resident commissioner in the Cook Islands has driven Moss farther than his central nervous system can bear. He will be gone soon, for he is drafting his letter of resignation.

His time in Raro has been one long bout of colonial oppression.

For instance, only after his arrival did Moss learn that he in large part owed his appointment as resident commissioner to Queen Makea, who had firmly told the Colonial Office that the Cook Islands needed "a new man," someone the islanders did not as yet have any prejudices against. What she meant was that she refused to be ruled by a "known man," the commissioner of the Western Pacific. The British holder of that position lived in Fiji and Makea believed he was dominated by Fijians. She was having none of that: she wanted a nobody.

And, though Moss understood that the London government was skin-cheap, he had not realized what that would mean in practice. London refused to put a farthing into the administration of this tiny part of the empire, and all the expenses were borne by New Zealand. But to whom did he report? The London-appointed governor of New Zealand or the elected parliament of New Zealand? In any case, given that he had virtually no budget beyond his own office-and-travel expenses, it would have helped mightily if the local business-man whom Moss appointed as the government auditor had not been an Englishman who, in a wide career, had stolen $20,000 from the Wells Fargo Company while employed as one of its cashiers in San Francisco. This man had adopted the proleptic alias "Charles Wells Banks," without arousing the suspicion of his employer. Later, skipping America, he had prudentially married one of Queen Makea's daughters. It would have been courteous, Moss frequently reflected, if Queen Makea, who knew of the man's past, had told me of it before I appointed him. And, indeed, it would be even more of a courtesy if she did not continue to block his extradition.

In his idealistic way, Mr. Moss appointed only two Europeans in his administration (the auditor and the post-and-customs commissioner). All the other jobs went to islanders, that is to the family of the ariki or their major clients. And, dear, dear me, Moss reflected, someone really should have given me to understand that the three paramount ariki on Rarotonga were so intensely jealous of each other that island social life resembled backstage at La Scala. Queen Makea, Queen Pa and Queen Tinomana, all very large females, each a diva.

Frederick Joseph Moss spends an entire day writing his letter of resignation. He finds temporary solace in a small case of treasures that he has used as an analgesic during his oppressive years on the islands. A book of venery, richly illustrated, is his prize: he has often found solace in mezzotint illustrations of medieval knights at the chase, hunting a noble stag.

Moss, poor sod, should have been the perfect appointment. He had been around, in the best sense. Born on St. Helena to English parents, he was educated at the East India Company School on the island and then had worked as an apprentice in his uncle's business in Port Elizabeth, South Africa. He'd done well in what was known in his time as "the Seventh Kaffir War," one of a series of nasty border wars with the Xhosa, who had less appreciation of the advantages of being under London's rule than did the Pacific Islanders. Having married an Irish woman (a Carew) he'd migrated to New Zealand, been a businessman, a newspaper proprietor, a member of parliament and had made the right Irish-Imperial ties: the freemasonry of Irishmen who wished to see the British Empire expanded was especially strong in the Antipodes, and he became, first, a follower of Sir George Grey and then of John Ballance, each of whom was keen on New Zealand's having a little solar system in the South Pacific. Good bloodlines; wrong race track.

Still avoiding writing his resignation, Moss re-reads yet-again, a letter from Robert Louis Stevenson: Stevenson had retired to Samoa, and despite being in ill-health, he kept himself well-informed on Polynesian happenings. Thus the now-worn letter that Moss treasured, because Stevenson said, "You are that very rare curiosity, a man in the right place."

Indeed, Moss had compiled an admirable record, but very few admired it. He had somehow cajoled the ariki into sitting in a bicameral legislature that gave outsiders a tiny look-in on power and influence. He had led this legislature to repeal some of the sillier missionary laws. Mostly, he was proud of having been a fervent and effective proponent of education. He had found a world where virtually everyone over age ten could read, but in which they only read the Bible and many of them had memorized big chunks of it, especially the bloodier portions of the Old Testament. His Public Schools Act promised £60 towards each teacher's salary, but the London Missionary Society was less than delighted, for Moss permitted Seventh Day Adventists to open a school and, worse yet, in 1895 a French Roman Catholic order, composed mostly of Irish nuns, established the first of several Catholic schools. The full horror of having Sisters Marie Hearn and Cecelia O'Donnell competing for souls, made the LMS froth. So, too, did Moss's directive that all primary schools must teach some English and his plan to set up a secular secondary school.

Moss momentarily smiled. He recalled that several Samoan chiefs had come to observe the Cook Islands' legislature in action, as a model of representative government and of beneficent colonial relationships.

And the Tahitians had come too … oh … Moss's head starts to itch and he grips his desk to keep from tearing at the torment. Raiatea, the base for the missionaries, both brown and white, who converted the Cook Islands, sent its ariki, Queen Vaine of Avera, to observe. Moss hated himself for behaving correctly: since France had formally annexed Raiatea in 1888 he had not received her with the dignity she deserved as the representative of a proud people. That, though, would not have changed the future of the Raiateans – the government in Paris, being much less mawkish than was Mr. Moss, sent 700 French soldiers, mostly Marines, to punish the Raiateans for showing insufficient enthusiasm for their inclusion in French Polynesia. Seventeen natives were killed and 150 of the leading families were exiled to the Marquesas.

Frederick Joseph Moss finally writes his letter of resignation, but he misses the main point of his experience. He knows that he is being forced to resign because he has mishandled a judicial reform measure that would have involved the island's supreme court gaining jurisdiction over Europeans, a plan he had explained insufficiently clearly to the Cook Islanders and much too clearly to the Europeans.

Moss does not perceive that he has done less damage and more good by being a failed imperialist than if he had been one of his champions of medieval venery, charging heroically through the forests, sticking his lance into every living form that fled from such mad progress.

MOURN THE WILD COLONIAL BOYS? 1845–1900

Venture Capitalist

The well-furnished office at 12 Pall Mall East, London, was a long way from Joseph Charles Byrne's start in life as the son of a small-time Dublin cattle drover. Byrne operated out of London and Liverpool and his natural marks were middle-level farmers and Wesleyan artisans. The farmers came because they needed more land, as farmers always do, and the Wesleyans because William Shaw, the Irish-born Wesleyan minister of Grahamstown in the eastern Cape, had interested a band of English Wesleyans in the opportunities that lay in Natal. There the artisans that were the backbone of urban Wesleyanism could learn market gardening, and live a better, more Christian life.

J.C. Byrne's office was filled with leather furniture and decorated with charcoal drawings of Zulu, none of them in the war-posture that the settlers were later to encounter. He was a big man, given to double-breasted Paisley waistcoats. He made a great point of being meticulous with money. He never took a penny without providing a written receipt in return.

Byrne provided passage to Natal for £10 per adult passenger, which was good value, considering that it was a three months' sail and provisions were included. And once there, twenty acres were provided each emigrant, courtesy of the Colonial Office. Bigger tracts were available at low rates. This was a good time to be cadging government largesse: the repeal of the Navigation Acts left the Yankees in control of the emigration trade to North America and, in southern Africa, blocking Afrikaner settlement on the Natal coast was a nice strategic move.

When a farmer would sit across from Byrne and sign on for a voyage, the Irish cattle-drover's instinct would come to the fore and he could sense what the man was worth. If the farmer had the air of a substantial citizen, Byrne would say, "Terribly important that you know this now: no banks. No banks out there. Soon will be, of course. Not now though."

"Dear, oh."

"Wouldn't want to keep your funds in a trunk now would you? Could fall overboard, heh-heh."

"Yes, what do you ..."

"I can serve as a bank of deposit for you. Simply leave your surplus funds with me – I shall provide you with a receipt of course – and you can later draw them in your new home. Be all very safe. Convenient too, I should add."

Byrne had an agent in Natal, John Moreland, who was honest but unable to keep up with the demands for landing the twenty ships that arrived in 1849–51 placed upon him. Never mind surveying and parcelling out all the twenty-acre plots. Worse, he never really understood Byrne's method of financing. He was given expense money for his Natal office and salary, but what was he supposed to do about all those table-banging Yorkshire farmers who demanded the money they had banked with Byrne in London or Liverpool?

Moreland should not have been surprised when he received a solicitor's letter announcing that Joseph Charles Byrne, Esq., had gone bankrupt and that all claims should be sent to his London receivers.

POINT BARROW, ALASKA. 14 OCTOBER 1852

A Gentleman's Gifts

Rochfort Maguire is taking part in the British Empire's nautical sporting event of the mid-nineteenth century: he is searching for Sir John Franklin, who had departed England in 1845 and has not been heard from since. Franklin of course was searching for the same Holy Grail that had mesmerized explorers since soon after the days of Marco Polo: a route – the adventurers now called it the Northwest Passage – across the western hemisphere, to Asia.

Finding Franklin becomes an end in itself and three Royal Navy expeditions are set in simultaneous search. Amateurs also join the chase, including the schooner *Nancy Dawson* of the Royal Thames Yacht Club, whose owner brings her north from Hong Kong. Good hunting, what?

Maguire has taken over command of a glorified supply ship, the *Plover*, from another Irishman, T.E.L. Moore, whose chief achievement in the hunt for Franklin had been to teach those Inuit leaders he encountered a new word, *tunuk*, which they infer means a substance new to them, alcohol. They learn the word in Moore's signature sentence, "Well, it's time for our tonic."

Rochfort Maguire has the gentleman's gift of knowing how to order people around. The younger son of minor County Westmeath gentry, he had entered the Royal Navy College, Portsmouth, in 1829 and since then had been moderately successful. He concluded that his present post, dealing with the Kakligmiut tribe that dominated the icefield in which *Plover* was overwintered, and dealing with Irish tenants was not all that different.

Fairness and a bit of force when necessary, that was the recipe. Worked well when several aggressive Inuit made off with one of *Plover's* sails. Maguire, accompanied by one of his ship's brass three-pound guns mounted on a sledge, talked to their leader.

That explains why, in mid-October, seven Kakligmiuti are approaching Maguire and with considerable fear. They bring him a device that looks like a Persian rug sewn by an asylum of mental patients. Very strange patterns indeed. Still, the needlework and the arrangement of the cloth is a tribute to the women of the Kakligmiut, for the men had taken *Plover's* sail and had cut it into small sails for their umiaks. Putting them back together was heroic. As a ship's sail, the device was useless, but Maguire considers himself a success, as he has established respect from the Kakligmiut without violence.

When an incident arises among his own tribe two months later, his tone of voice – Irish gentry-loud – proves equally effective. Several of his men came down with gonorrhea which they had picked up from Inuit women who, earlier, had slept with visiting sailors and thus had become carriers. At Maguire's orders the men stopped screwing the natives, but several of them wondered if Captain Maguire really understood what the Empire was all about.

WESTMINSTER. 1854

Big Step

For a state that was said to have an empire, the United Kingdom was mightily casual about it.

The Colonial Office, a minor sub-branch of the War Office, ran the empire, to the extent it ran anything, from a house located at the end of Downing Street. There officials wrote, read and rewrote letters to other officials around the world and mostly let them get on with doing whatever it was they did out there.

Only in 1854 are colonial matters judged important enough to become a separate governmental department with a secretary of state in charge.

BANNU, INDIA. 1855

Lord, Suffer Thy Servants

A jirga of minor chiefs approaches John Nicholson, now deputy commissioner of half the Punjab. They are made brave by their numbers and one of them shows his contempt for the British by hawking phlegm on the ground before Nicholson.

"Orderly. Make that man lick his own spittle."

Nicholson's orderly springs forward, grabs the chief by the back of the neck and forces him to the ground.

Nicholson stands immobile, daring any of the chiefs to draw a dagger. None does. The offender is literally kicked out of Nicholson's compound and the others become noticeably politer.

"Reducing." Fine Victorian word. John Nicholson receives great credit for reducing a large swath of the Punjab from lawlessness to good order. By English definition of course: meaning that burglary, murder and highway robbery were virtually stopped.

It helped, having one's own disciples although, as Our Lord discovered, being shadowed constantly by a band of crackpots can be vexing. They rarely get the big picture.

The founder of the sect of the *Nikalsainies* was a Hindu named Gosain, who believed in avatars and reincarnation and perceived Nicholson as a corporeal representation of the Brahmanic godhead. He was ecumenical, however, for the the sect came to include Sikhs and Muslims. The sect grew to a dozen full-time devotes and several thousand other Indians who put Nicholson on their list of gods.

When he entered a town or village he was greeted with awe that went way beyond that paid to soldiery. So vexing, to be always tripping over these fakirs, and Nicholson's fierce temper led him to kick them whenever possible. Or give them a slash of his riding crop. This made his disciples more loyal, for only a deity would treat his followers with such heaven-sent disdain. The faithful wore any wound he gave them with as much pride as a British officer would wear a medal for valour. Unspoken contests arose to win his scourge.

Wherever he went, Nicholson sought out brooks or rivers. The sound of water running drowned out the voices that he heard so frequently, voices that were less-and-less biblical in phrase: they were becoming his voice and, maybe, he sometimes thought, he was a god.

Nicholson built a platform over a stream in Bannu, and there, in his own ashram, he would spend days at a time. There he had peace. His disciples followed him and sat under bushes and observed their god. On one occasion, they made noise enough to disturb the master. He descended, and they cast themselves at his feet. All of them he beat furiously till blood seeped through their robes. And then he made them promise to stop believing he was a god. Nicholson told them to worship a fellow officer.

They promised.

And were outside Nicholson's own bungalow when he returned in a week's time.

WESTMINSTER. 1855

We Shall Never See Their Like

"We can thank their Lordships that we shall see nabobs no more."

On this and upon the Irish question, Sir Charles Trevelyan, an old India hand, and his brother-in-law Thomas Babington Macauley, historian and former secretary of the supreme council of India in the days of the East India Company, agreed. Strange, how Indian experience bred a love of efficiency. Certainly Trevelyan would have been less rigorous in his application of Famine Relief in Ireland had he not been through Indian food scarcities and seen how indiscriminate spreading of available foodstuffs merely increased starvation.

"Not as quickly as we wish, my friend. The nabobs will linger, but at least we shall supplant them with truly efficient – dare I say professional – civil servants."

Under Sir Charles's supervision, entry into the elite rulership of British India – the Indian Civil Service – was changed from patronage to merit, or so he believed. Previously, a cadet was nominated to

Haileybury College, the EIC's training school, by someone of stand-ing and after passing rudimentary examinations and an interview, was trained for a time and sent out. Really well connected young men became direct cadets and went to India without any of that rigmarole.

"We shan't have any more John Nicholsons, thanks be."

"Correct. No more wild Indians." Macauley and Trevelyan permit-ted themselves a smirk.

Competitive entry, based on really difficult examinations in history, philosophy, and politics, was meant to bring gentlemen-professionals into the service. And it did. The trouble was that the young men who were expected to do best in these written exercises – Balliol sorts – did not. The graduates of Irish universities and of the sub-fusc University of London did. In the old Haileybury days, the Irish had been about 5 percent of the intake of top-class rulers. Now, men from Trinity, the Queen's colleges and, oh dear, Newman's Catholic place, jumped over the Right Sort. In 1857, Irish recruits were one-third of the Indian Civil Service intake, and one-quarter in the first full decade of the system.

So, in 1865, the system is re-rigged, with the specific intention of limiting the intake of the Irish, who show such an excessive enthusiasm for furthering their own position in life by supporting the Crown. So terribly middle-class that. Even then, several hundred Irishmen enter the top echelon of the ICS between 1865 and the Great War, about one-quarter of them Roman Catholic.

"BRITISH KAFFRARIA," THE EASTERN CAPE, SOUTHERN AFRICA. 1857

Field Control

At times, Whitehall loved Sir George Grey. When he wished to, he understood money: in 1844, while governor of South Australia, he had refused to sanction an expenditure of 8d for the sharpening of pencils by the government's office boy.

Because he understood money, he could be insanely difficult to control at those moments when he was insubordinate, as he had been when governor of New Zealand and now was as governor of the

Cape Colony. He foresaw the need for federating all the southern African colonies and as a step on that road he was pushing the eastern frontier into Ciskei, which he called British Kaffraria. Sir George was successfully selling lots in the rudimentary provincial capital of King William's Town for the ridiculous price of £52 a town lot, which worked out to £406 an acre. With that kind of income he could ignore the Colonial Office's orders to go slow.

Of course, he required settlers and here he accepted the Colonial Office's suggestion that he take as frontiersmen several cadres of the German Foreign Legion, who, now that the Crimean War was over, were at loose ends. The Germans made good settlers, didn't they? – why just look at Pennsylvania in the former American colonies – and they would come with wives and families.

Not entirely true.

The facts are that whilst 2,300 soldiers of the German Legion have landed in this colony, Sir George wrote to the home authorities, *with a very unusually large proportion of officers and gentlemen cadets, only 330 females have accompanied them.*

Grey had been around enough to know what this would mean. *The results of this will be disastrous to the whole community: it has created considerable alarm in the minds of the native population; great immorality will result from it. They will roam over the whole country in search of females and will probably be frequently murdered by the native population, whilst as a military force, they will be quite useless for the defence of the colony.*

How to keep these potential-Huns as a useful and disciplined group on the new eastern frontier? The answer is the same one that echoes in similar circumstances all over the empire: import women to civilize the men and, in practice, that means Irish women.

A cadre of 163 Irish pauper girls – not a large enough number, but a start – is despatched to the eastern Cape. Their average age is twenty-two and they are marriageable. They settle permanently, but most of them do not marry German mercenaries, but regular British Isles settlers.

Grey keeps the randy Germans under arms, drilling and military discipline being the only way to control them and, just as well he did: when the Indian Mutiny breaks out, he gains credit with the Colonial Office by sending immediately 1,700 men to defend the Jewel, one corps of which is made up of very horny Germans, much to the ultimate discomfort of the Indian female population.

DELHI, INDIA. 1857

Endgames

Rishti. Among the mutineers in the Indian army in 1857, that was the word for the soldiers they most feared. Meaning the Irish. They were distinguished from the *Angrese* who were less often bloodswilling mad. If the imperial army had any luck in the set of gameboard in 1857, it was that although roughly one-third of the regular troops in the Indian army were Irish, the units around Madras, Bengal, and Bombay were nearly half Irish.

And then there was John Nicholson, now a brigadier-general in command of the unit that the re-conquest of India depends upon, the Punjab Moveable Column. His disciples, whom he still regards with irritation, especially when he trips over one of their prostrate forms, believe that he is bulletproof and now he has moments when he too believes he is. He no longer is aware of hearing voices, but instead, hears with surprise words, orders, decisions, proceeding from his own mouth. They come forth independently of any conscious mental activity on his part. He follows these orders faithfully. Sometimes he is surprised to hear himself utter an order and then pronounce *It is My Will.* He considers: perhaps my followers are right and the divinity in me is being made manifest.

Nicholson appears as an apparition at the fords of Ravi, where sepoy mutineers are encamped on their way to Delhi. He has marched his men forty-four miles in a single day in dust and heat that are beyond cruel. They endure this because he wills them to. And, exhausted though they are, he gives them no rest but, immediately upon sighting the enemy, attacks. Nicholson himself is the first into the mutineers' camp and he disables the rebels' field piece himself by literally cutting in two with his cavalry sword an artilleryman who was putting his firestick into the cannon's ignition-hole.

Re-taking Delhi is the key to ending the mutiny and Nicholson arrives at Delhi in mid August. Though raked with rifle fire, he leads a party that captures thirteen field guns and most of the equipment of a sepoy unit that was manoeuvring to catch the imperial forces' unguarded flank. The sepoys are good soldiers, well trained, but the legend of Nicholson's immunity from bullets means that many of them won't fire at him and that others are unsteady. Firing at an avatar is not good business.

On the fourteenth of September, General Nicholson commands the main party storming Delhi and does so in the only way he knows: he is in the lead of nearly 1,000 men and he is unprotected. So sure is he of his victory that he has obtained permission to personally command the pursuit column that will hunt down the mutineers after their defeat. This time, his divinity runs short and he takes a bullet in the chest. He dies on the twentieth, the day the imperial army finally takes Delhi.

The death of Nicholson was understandably hard on his disciples, for they either had to rethink their belief that true gods are bulletproof or conclude that Nicholson had not been a true divinity. Either way, for some of them the light had gone out of the world. Upon hearing the news of Nicholson's mortality, one of his leading disciples immediately cuts his own throat, and then another does so. A third converts to Christianity, since Nicholson was, to untrained eyes, a Christian. One particularly faithful follower digs his own grave before putting himself forever to sleep in it.

The others drifted away, but the impact of the Irish divinity lingered. A dozen years after the mutiny, an English administrator in the border regions was told by a chief that "our women at night wake trembling and saying they hear the tramp of Nikalsain's warhorse."

In 1885, the *Cyclopaedia of India* compiled by Edward Balfour, sometime surgeon-general of India, solemnly and tactfully summarized John Nicholson's career. *He had more influence with his subordinates than perhaps any native of the British Isles in the east has ever had.*

LIVERPOOL. OCTOBER 1857

Swings and Roundabouts

On Monday, the eleventh of October, the African explorer Dr. Livingstone arrived in Liverpool. Always ready to address a crowd, the next day he filled the Cotton Salesroom and accepted graciously the Quality's resolution that he should continue to do in Africa whatever he was doing. Liverpool had always been keen on the Dark Continent.

Wednesday the twenty-seventh of October was designated by Royal Proclamation to be a day of national fasting and humiliation: the Indian Mutiny.

And, on the tenth of March, 1858, Dr. Livingstone again passes through Liverpool, this time to board the *Pearl*, carrying with him documents that appoint him as Her Majesty's consul in south-eastern Africa; thus he is enabled to continue the adventures whose popularity in character is equalled only by their otiose nature.

THE EASTERN CAPE, SOUTHERN AFRICA. 1857

Reflections in a Blood-Red Eye

Sir George Grey never lost his belief, acquired as a young officer in Ireland in the 1830s, that the only effective relief for the poor of the British Isles was for new lands of settlement to be opened to them. But, from late 1857 onward, as he administers the Cape Colony and, once again, New Zealand, he cannot forget the red tide.

The red tide occurred during his attempt at moving the eastern Cape frontier further out, thus allowing more settlement.

As an old man in the 1890s, living in a London hotel room near his club, Grey still cannot understand it; at nights for decades the tide has been the source of all his nightmares.

Dozens of explanations for the red tide exist, past and present, none of them satisfactory.

For in 1857, the Xhosa are feeling the effects of believing the prophecies of Nonggawose, a girl, young, scarcely with breasts or hips: if the Xhosa will kill all their cattle and destroy their own crops, the Europeans will disappear. The Xhosa gods will see to that.

The blood of hundreds of thousands of livestock drips into the ground. The smell of rotting animal corpses floats for 200 miles and hyenas travel from as far as the Great Karoo to feast. Vultures find so much to feed on that rather than circle in the sky they hop awkwardly from corpse to corpse, sampling, like bon vivants at a degustation.

Totally inexplicable: although Grey can produce and parse explanations as well as anyone in the empire. No, the little prophetess was not a particularly charismatic person. Yes, the killing filled a need. Yes, the Xhosa were being pinched between the British and, indirectly, the Zulu, and yes, there had been a tuberculosis epidemic in the preceding years. Yes, of course, sacrifice of animals was something that the missionaries had told their few converts about, but the Christian story was all about the abolition of the need for the blood sacrifice of animals.

Grey remembered most vividly the vermillion colour of the killing grounds, but he also could not forget the smell, the mixture of char-brown earth where grain and pasture had been burned. And the stench of animal flesh, rotting in puddles of congealed blood.

This red tide was profoundly unsettling to Sir George, because he was one of the few colonial governors of the Victorian era who believed any group he dealt with – Maori, Australian Aboriginals, Africans – was capable of being as civilized and possessed as much intelligence as did the white man: admittedly a paternalistic view, but rare in its non-racist character. The Xhosa's acting in such a delusional fashion, destroying their own livelihood, destroying their own lives, benumbed him.

Seventy thousand of the 105,000 Xhosa in the immediate frontier district of the east Cape starved themselves to death while the red tide washed away their daily bread. Grahamstown, Fort Beaufort, and King William's Town were haunted by walking skeletons.

Sir George was himself haunted by the visceral reaction he had let rule his response to this mass of millenarian suicides: he had ordered arrested fourteen of the headmen and had them executed on the grounds that they had encouraged the Xhosa self-destruction. This was as mad as was the Xhosa behaviour: did not the diminution of the Xhosa population make easier his expansion of white settlement along the eastern frontier? Why would he punish those responsible? Later, he can only explain to himself that he had gone mad with grief, besieged by the recognition that perhaps he was wrong, that all peoples were not as one and could not be ruled under the same flag and by the same rules.

In his last days Sir George Grey took to being the only vegetarian at his London club. It was an eccentricity the staff permitted the old gentleman. He always insisted that they seat him at a table where his back was to the daily roast joint, soaking in its own juice.

LONDON AND THE CANADIAN ARCTIC. 1857–59

Orientation

Few individuals have the force of Jane Lady Franklin, the widow of the happy wanderer in the Canadian arctic. Her husband had been dead for nearly a decade and Lord Palmerston, the prime minster, finally said "no" to any more public money being spent on finding his remains. She promptly launched a national appeal and acquired enough donations (including U.S. government support) and offers of *pro bono* seatime from experienced mariners to permit her to send her specially-purchased private steam-yacht on mission. Palmerston, a political realist, gave in and provided more U.K. help.

Two hundred tons and nicely refitted, the *Fox* was captained by an experienced arctic hand, Leopold McClintock of Dundalk, a pudgy, easy-going redhead who did not make mistakes in haste. He knew the far north well enough to understand that fighting against it was sure disaster. He took with him a knowledgeable crew. For his purposes the most important of these was Dr. David Walker, a physician from County Down who had Royal Navy experience and was known for his forensic skills. McClintock knew that they weren't going to find any survivors. He needed someone who could interview skeletons.

McClintock and his men spent more than a year sledging over vast barren ice fields, sometimes interviewing Inuit, and, finally, finding the face-down skeleton of a white man who had fallen and frozen in place. Others turned up, and a cairn and some notes were found, proving beyond all doubt Franklin's death. All these items made tragic sense.

Captain McClintock wrote a best-selling chronicle of the search and in later life was an advisor to Scott of the Antarctic.

Dr. David Walker, having met some American officers attached by the U.S. Navy to the *Fox*, decided that North America deserved a look and he spent twenty years as a U.S. cavalry doctor before retiring to Ireland.

McClintock talked constantly of the Franklin search and Walker talked about it almost never; yet they shared the same niggling question, the one part of the puzzle that never fit: why was the master-sledge, the most substantial of those framed by Franklin's crew as a means of escape, why, in the name of all that is holy, was it, when discovered, pointing north?

WESTMINSTER. 1858

A Bit of Realism

Two big changes, each at least half a century overdue.

The United Kingdom's government directly takes over running India. The nabobs of the East India Company no longer have half a continent to mulct. India is the only colony to have its own secretary of state.

And chaplains with the armed forces are finally awarded commissions. These are appointed in numbers directly proportional to the religious composition of the forces. Catholic chaplains are particularly praised as having been notably heroic in staying with the men, encouraging and comforting them, from the 1790s, through the Napoleonic Wars, the Crimea, the Indian mutiny.

One of the chief functions of the army chaplains was *keeping the Other Ranks under surveillance.*

THE VATICAN. 1860

Cut to the Chaste

Yet another Irish Brigade fights in Europe. This one is outfitted in grey tunics and grey forage caps, rather than in green, like Napoleon's Irish Legion, or in scarlet, like the original Jacobite Irish Brigade. Were the location not wrong, they could at a distance have been taken for soldiers of the Confederate states. They are kneeling to receive a fulsome blessing in St. Peter's from Pio Nono – Pius IX. When they arise it is clear they are not from the Confederacy: they wear bright red trousers.

His Holiness, easily the most unpopular man in Italy, was still piqued that he had been turned out of the Vatican in 1848 and only restored by an appeal to the armies of Catholic countries, particularly the French. Now, in 1860, he was determined to maintain the Holy See as a temporal state as well as a religious one. The Italian people, on the other hand, wanted most of his land secularized.

The pope sent out another call for help to the Catholic countries. The heads of state ignored him, but three companies of volunteers were put together from Belgian, German, French, and a few Italian keeners. The Irish, well on the post-Famine road to becoming the most Catholic country in Christendom, send an entire brigade of 300 men. Solid men, with names such as: Shiel, Kirwin, McCony, Blakeney, Carey, and the inevitable Captain Lawless. They were funded by a special offering taken up in Catholic parish churches in Ireland. Those same churches had already sent thousands of pounds to the Vatican to support Italian priests who were alleged to have been put out of their benefices by the evil secularists.

So important are the Irish faithful to Rome's present and future defence – both spiritual and temporal – that the chamberlain to Pio Nono personally greets the Irish Brigade when it arrives and takes them immediately into the papal presence.

They fight well, along with their continental comrades against the evil encroachments of the modern state, Garibaldi and his attendants. The Irish engage the Italian alliance's army of 20,000 and when enough of the papal army has died, the Irish Brigade surrenders with honour. Its members dissolve into non-history, some of them returning to their trades and professions at home, others becoming mercenaries in a Europe that was fast reshaping itself and needed men who could fight as if they believed.

DUBLIN. 1863

Excrescence?

"Excrescences" was the term that Paul Cullen, archbishop of Dublin used to his domestic chaplain whenever he referred to the Protestant cathedrals in Dublin, Christ Church and St. Patrick's. Their existence in alien hands – "They are Ours," Cullen frequently said – vexed him so much that whenever possible he travelled through Dublin on a course that made it unnecessary for him to view either of the heretical edifices.

That guaranteed he would not see any indication of an event that would have turned him to rage: members, past and present, of the 18th Royal Irish making their way into St. Patrick's. This was the anniversary of the end of the Second Burmese War in which, ten years earlier, the regiment had taken heavy casualties.

The imperial authorities may have been cavalier and incompetent in the way they assembled their eastern empire, but no one could deny that they built brilliant monuments once a conflict was over.

The soldiers do not enter St. Patrick's in formal fashion, for their commanding officer understands that for Irish Catholics to be forced to enter a Dublin cathedral of the Church of Ireland would be the cause of newspaper articles and certainly would make recruiting harder: the army as a threat to the faith and all that. He is no fool.

The men enter, some in mufti, and each pays tribute in his own way to St. Patrick's memorial to the Royal Irish at the taking of Rangoon. It's the most marvelously accurate piece of sculpture. There, on the steps of Great Pagoda, lies a fallen trooper amidst the advancing figures of his comrades. The monument is a stunning mix of triumph and loss, and the men who stand there silently know that this is what soldiering means.

The regiment's Catholic chaplain – now, like all army chaplains, officially an officer of the imperial army – enters by a side door. This was against canonical rules, going into a Protestant church, but the priest, who had been with many of the men when they died, reasoned that there are orders and there are reasons; and, sometimes, compassion is more important than canon law.

THE VATICAN. 1870

Divine Equation

Pio Nono has finally come to understand that he is part of a divine equation: for every temporal power the papacy loses, it shall be granted an increase in spiritual force: provided he acts responsibly as Christ's vicar on earth.

Thus, in 1864 His Holiness compensates for his being deprived by the nascent Italian state of almost all of his worldly realms by issuing the Syllabus of Errors, condemning most "liberal" and "modern" errors of thought and practice. A useful gauge of this syllabus was that the pope considered John Henry Newman to be a dangerous liberal.

And, thus, Pius IX's understanding of the divine equation led to his forcing through the curia his doctrine of Papal Infallibility.

And here, he used the Irish well. Instead of the Irish Brigade of soldiers (which besides being ultimately ineffective, were, the pope said, given too much to wine and to depredations on virtuous Italian women), he used the Irish prelates: especially Paul Cullen, who drafted the English version of the new dogma.

After winning affirmation of his spiritual Infallibility, Pius IX had the unfortunate experience of being attacked in the physical world (he still controlled Rome) by King Victor Emmanuel. The French, having the newly-unified German state to worry about, withdrew their protection and the pope had to face the Italians on his own. Wisely, almost serenely, he ordered his troops to engage in only symbolic resistance. Having gained the ultimate palm of victory, Infallibility, he could leave the tawdry temporal world behind.

Secretly, he has his chamberlain search for a buyer for the Vatican's sole remaining battle frigate.

KIMBERLY, SOUTHERN AFRICA AND ARMAGH CITY, IRELAND. 1867–84

A Nation of Shopkeepers?

Although John Robert O'Reilly, second generation Irish from Grahamstown, won immortality in 1867 by his discovery at Du Toit's Pan (soon to be renamed Kimberley) of the diamond that changed southern African history, he and the Irishmen who followed him were only part of the story, although certainly the loudest part. First came the diamond miners and then, with the discovery of gold in the Witswatersrand uplands, the gold miners. This ended forever the chance of the Afrikaners remaining a quiet landlocked tribe. The U.K. annexed the inland portions of southern Africa with scarcely a moral qualm.

Miners, though, come and go, and the Irish people who came and lasted were urban merchants. Robert H. Henderson is a good example. A smart county Armagh lad, the third of thirteen children, he knows he has no future in Ireland, bright though he is in school and sharp though he is as a shop assistant. So, age eighteen, he leaves Armagh. At that time a number of smart young Ulster people, both Protestant and Catholic, are leaving for southern Africa and he joins them. He is typical of a class of shrewd young people who emigrate with a solid functional education, swift computational skills, and become small and then larger businessmen in southern Africa. The breakdown religiously in this, as in the mining population, seems to be about 60:40 Protestant: Catholic, but that is of slight relevance. The skills are what counts and these Irish people form a business class in Johannesburg, Durban, and Cape Town, and in country towns.

They represent the lower middle class in Ireland that is rising from the ashes of the Famine. They are lucky. And very good at shaving the silver off a shilling.

Not bad people. How could young Mr. Henderson have turned bad, when the final emigration gift he was given by his minister was *The Young Man's Guide Through Life to Immortality*?

IRELAND. 1875–1900

Scrambling Africans

The last quarter of the nineteenth century witnesses the biggest cut-up of territory in human history: the scramble for Africa. The entire continent is grabbed by European powers in a series of moves that resembles a game of draughts played with guns. The United Kingdom does the best, acquiring almost five million square miles of land and the most strategically important spots.

At all levels of colonial administration, the Irish do well. The most telling indication is that *below* the officers' rank between 1875 and 1900 there were never fewer than 25,000 Irishmen in the U.K. army and at times as many as 40,000.

These are the representatives of Ireland's male working class. They are about 80 percent Catholic, 20 percent Protestant, roughly the proportions they bear in the home population. They sign up not because they are intent on gouging indigenous people (though that is their chief task) but because they see the opportunity for a little adventure and a great improvement in their prospects in life: a steady job, land overseas if they want it at the end of a short-service enlistment or, if they take long-service, a nice pension so that they can retire anywhere the Union Jack flies.

LIVERPOOL. 1875

A Missionary to the End

Among the fabulous virtues of Henry Morton Stanley (originally John Rowlands) was the ability to find things and the predisposition, when he had done so, to send them home. He was particularly generous in returning to the British Isles with stories and advice garnered in Africa. In his books he called it *darkest Africa* and began a fashion that shows no sign of dying.

In Liverpool, where he has emigrated to take a clerk's job, Charles Henry Stokes reads a letter Stanley has sent to the London *Daily Telegraph* describing the wonderful harvest of dark souls that is awaiting those would dare-to-be missionaries in Africa. Stokes, a well-educated product of Portora Royal School, Enniskillen, was Anglo-Irish on the way down: his father's death had left him without the means of supporting a middle class life. And one grants him genuine religious feeling: he enrolls as a lay evangelist for the Church Missionary Society and prepares himself to be among the first Protestant missionaries in Uganda.

Arriving at Entebbe in February 1879, it takes him less than a year to discover that the European Catholics (the "White Fathers") are doing a better job than ever he could and that he really lacks the talent for selling intangibles, such as God and virtue.

But he can sell anything else. He becomes an astute trader and, perhaps in English eyes, a traitor, for he does business with the Germans in east Africa.

His white wife dies. He accepts a new one from Chief Mitiginya of Usongo, Uganda, and later a second one from King Mwanga. It would be foolish, Stokes tells himself, to offend any powerful ruler and, besides, his experience as a trader has taught him that in the bush it's always best to pack a spare.

The missionary in Stokes is not completely extinguished, for he was a most ethical trader, setting his own rules in a world where there were none: he never beats his natives; he sells guns and ammunition sparingly and only under duress; he won't touch the ivory trade; when he can, he buys slaves from the Islamic traders and frees them.

Yet, nothing keeps him from retailing to the Germans his immense influence with the natives of the interior of eastern Africa. Thus, in the late 1880s a cadre of German colonial administrators arise who speak Swahili with an Irish accent. Stokes's explanation is that his mediating between Muslim, German and native factions prevented tribal warfare of epic proportions.

Fatally, in the 1890s Stokes decides to begin trading with the peoples of what becomes known as the Belgian Congo. It's a tricky business, for the Belgians, unlike the Germans, don't want outsiders in their hellish African kingdom. With little sense of this – Stokes has a blithe faith that all Europeans are pretty decent chaps at heart – he meets a Belgian captain and submits peaceably to what he believes is a pro-forma arrest-and-release. Instead, he is marched to a provincial centre and hanged for assisting rebels against the Congo Free State, something he certainly did not do.

And thus he joined the ranks of Irishmen who, for better or worse, were stretched. *That night, when the moon was high, Stokes was taken out and hung. I saw him. His eyes were covered; they stood him on two boxes, the rope was put around his neck, and the boxes were taken away and so he died.* Thus an eyewitness.

Months later, in London, his will was read. He had made it in the Congo before his last trading journey. He left £20,000 and to everyone's surprise, three-quarters of it was to go to the Church Missionary Society *for the promotion of God's glory in Eastern and Central Africa.*

IALANDLWANAGA, ZULULAND. 22 JANUARY 1879

More Dominoes Fall

When Sergeant Timothy Anthony Byrne decided to fetch a canteen of water for one of his troops who was moaning piteously in his last moments, he raised himself, slab-like, and clearly outlined against the horizon. He immediately became a casualty himself, his last good Intention being an intention only, but still a credit to his immortal soul.

A mixed army of U.K. regulars and local troops is engaged in its first real fight with Zulu, and the colonists are losing badly. The British and the settlers are accustomed to fighting with Xhosa, who are fairly immobile. They traditionally fight behind big ox-hide shields, five feet by three feet in size, and either throw assegai or, in close combat, use light stabbing sticks. Given their relative immobility, the Xhosa are easy blacks to pot. So the Brits have become overconfident.

Now they deal with Zulu, a war culture that produces an army of 20,000 men, and they are frighteningly mobile. The warriors manoeuvre in double columns, carrying only assegai and short stabbing spears. They attack quickly, and with the cry of "Tah!", "Tah!" they employ the stabbing spear in hand-to-hand combat with terrifying efficiency. They are proficient with throwing-spears as well, and have some firearms, but hand-to-hand is their forte. The U.K.'s defeat by

King Cetywayo is comprehensive. The Zulu general sprang a trap so that the foreigners were surrounded. Few survived and fewer remembered clearly the details of their defeat.

Zululand was a domino that had to fall. Situated between Natal and the Transvaal, it had to go, according to imperialist theory, once the annexation of the Transvaal was decreed in 1877. Thus would a clear corridor of control on the east of the gold fields be created.

The empire regroups and puts nearly 15,000 soldiers in the field and in July, at Ulundi, they defeat an equal number of Zulu. The imperial troops prepare carefully and win bloodily, and, Cetywayo captured, a peace treaty is signed.

The dominoes that fell were not merely blocks of territory. They were human beings, black and white.

CONGO-UGANDA BORDER REGION. 13 AUGUST 1887

Where He Leads Me, I Will Follow

"Mammy, what are those two men doing with each other?"

"Never you mind. They are Protestants."

"But, mammy, that's a statue to a hero."

"If that's what heroes do, then it's time we had a revolution. Or two."

The statue that later caused such embarrassment to decent Dublin Christians was a life-size memorial to Surgeon Major T.H. Parke. It stood outside the Natural History Museum in Dublin and showed him in full African kit, leaning on a rifle. That was all very well: people could look upon it without having impure thoughts. The trouble was the plinth, where a bronze plaque showed, with unfortunate ambiguity, what his heroic act had been.

"*Jesus Christ, Parke, that hurts like the very devil.*"

"*You've taken a Washenzi arrow near your heart.*"

"*Damned blackmen. Never fight fair, unlike …*"

"*Poisoned, sir.*"

"*The blacks?*"

"*No, the arrow, and it's broken off inside.*"

The arrow is inside the breast of William Stairs, a Nova Scotian of an Ulster family that had done well in Philadelphia, Grenada and Halifax. A graduate of the Royal Military College, Kingston, he had heard the call of Henry Stanley, the P.T. Barnum of African exploration, and had been the first recruit selected for a Big Adventure from among nearly 4,000 applicants for a crusade to find and save the last loyal lieutenant of General Gordon of Khartoum. That this man, Emin Pasha, was quite happy living in the bush and was displeased eventually to be found and dragged out of the jungle, was an irrelevance. Stanley found things and brought them back: no back-talk.

Stanley could sell anything to a white audience (hadn't he served on both sides of the American civil war and gotten away with it?) and the donations he arranges for this expedition include buckets of money from King Leopold II of Belgium and a Maxim gun from that article's inventor. This was not intended to be a humanitarian venture.

Thomas Parke, at age twenty-nine, applies because he is bored being a garrison doctor in the army. If he joins Stanley's expedition, he assumes, correctly, that his medical talents will be applied only to the Europeans in the party.

"There's only one thing for this, Stairs."

"Try not to die while you're doing it, chappie."

What the unfortunate bronze plaque on Parke's monument eventually depicts is two men, one prostrate on the ground, the other sucking at his breast. The elbow of the heroic surgeon, who is risking death by winkling out fragments of the poison-tipped arrow with his tongue, rests on his patient's lower abdomen in such a way that Stairs seems to possess a giant erection, which would have been a considerable achievement under the circumstances.

"Filthy beasts! Don't let me ever catch you casting your eye on that bag full of mortal sins, you hear me!"

MATABELELAND, SOUTHERN AFRICA. 1888

Double, Double, Double-Firsts

Deep trouble. One of Cecil Rhodes' representatives to King Lobengula has a profusion of scarlet foam seeping from the side of his mouth. The bodyguards of the king seize him, punch his solar plexus so that he vomits out the fluid, and then they strip him naked and bring him before Lobengula. The king is furious, for James Rochfort

Maguire has been brushing his teeth with water from a sacred pool and using tinted toothpaste to do so. Clearly, Maguire has offended the spirits.

It is a monument to Maguire's ability to talk fast that he escapes with a fine and the loss of his dental hygiene gear.

This James Rochfort Maguire – born in 1855, the same year that one of his affines, Rochfort Maguire, was messing about on the west coast of North America, allegedly looking for Sir John Franklin or, at least, the Northwest passage – is a dazzler. The son of a County Limerick Anglican rector, he obtained a double-first at Oxford (mathematics and jurisprudence), and a fellowship at All Souls. A lovely, witty, seductive young man, he easily made the acquaintance and then the friendship of the most useful people: Baron Ferdinand Rothschild, for example, and Cecil Rhodes.

And Charles Stewart Parnell. Maguire serves as the link through which the arch-imperialist Rhodes donates over £10,000 to Parnell's anti-imperialist party, a massive sum in that era. Maguire, in his mid-thirties sits for North Donegal under Parnell's patronage and then, after the leader's death, for West Clare.

He completes yet another double-first when, in 1895, he leaves politics and marries Julia Peel, daughter of Arthur Wellesley; and then in 1906 becomes vice president of the late Cecil Rhodes' British South Africa Company.

Maguire is made president of the firm in 1923 and also serves as chair of the Rhodesian Railways and in his entire life everything is easy and profitable and the only tight moment he had was that single incident with the toothpaste and the sacred pond.

LONDON. 1890

Another Big Wind

The Big Wind of 1839 had wrecked hundreds of thousands of Irish dwellings. And the Big Wind that had swept through the War Office in 1840 was fear. A military enumeration revealed that over 37 percent of the soldiers in the British Army were Irish, much the largest group. The officers, mostly Anglo-Irish, might be trustworthy, but the Irish soldiery had to be feared. Could they become an Irish army of liberation?

Ah, the Famine. Just as it solved the Irish Catholic church's problem of too many poverty-stricken parishioners, so it assuaged the British generals' worries. The great reduction in young people living in Ireland that followed the Famine – heavy emigration and a precipitous drop in the birth rate – left fewer Irish lads for the recruiters. By the early 1890s, 14 percent of the British army is Irish, and even if one counts every possible second-generation Irish recruit from Britain, the proportion is only 18 percent, a much less worrisome number.

Thus, the War Office's worries had, like the wind, gone away.

ZAMBEZI RIVER, SOUTHERN AFRICA. 9 JUNE 1892

To Katanga and Part-Way Back

The shining cut-glass quality of the early generations of successful Belfast merchants – the generation of Mary Anne McCracken and her father who contributed to chapels of faiths other than their own, formed subscription libraries, argued sensibly in debating clubs – is totally lost by the generation of William Stairs: he of a Belfast family that has become wealthy in the USA, the West Indies and Nova Scotia and he now marches on Africa.

After serving on Henry Morton Stanley's African expedition of 1887–89, Stairs, though a British military officer, signed on with King Leopold II of the Belgians to reconnoitre Katanga, long known as a repository of gold and copper. Leopold wanted formally to assert control over the province as part of his royal fiefdom, the Congo Free State. William Stairs had learned nothing from his escape from near death by a poisoned arrow, only that he despised the natives more than ever. His own men steal his tobacco, secret the best produce for themselves, and drift away whenever the going becomes difficult; and those are his allies. *Have we whites the right to divide among ourselves this vast continent and to throw out the local chiefs and impose our own ideas? To that there can be only one answer, yes!* So Captain Stairs reflected at the start of his own expedition. *What value would it have in the hands of the blacks who, in their natural state, are crueller to each other than the worst Arabs or whites?*

Excepting, perhaps, Belgians, or men such as Captain Stairs himself.

At first he tries to buy slaves as porters from the Islamic traders, but the local Sultan prohibits this, for he see what Stairs and the Belgians are doing. Stairs found that *the prohibition had proven to be tiresome and time-consuming*. Still, he makes the trek from Zanzibar into Katanga. When his men become sick, five to ten percent of his bearers at a time, he blames it on their smoking hemp. That's also the reason, he says, that their skin opens up so easily when they encounter abrasions. Or are lashed. He does not want to send the sick ones home, for he has paid each of them $US20 in advance and he would lose that sum on every one of the disabled. Still, he has the decency in the early stages of his journey to bury those who die of exhaustion and thirst. Later they just drop and the vultures arrive.

In his rare spare moments, he writes verse.

When, less rarely, he goes spare, he amputates hands or feet of deserters or thieves. It is a practice he has learned from the Belgians and he approves of the way they discipline natives.

Inside Katanga, Stairs encounters several Plymouth Brethren missionaries, but they refuse to tell him what they know of the local king, Msiri. Nevertheless, Stairs's expedition outraces that of Cecil Rhodes and therefore Katanga comes under Belgium's rather than England's rule.

Captain Stairs, listing badly to port, turns towards the Zambesi, which he knows will lead him to the Indian Ocean.

On the way, he pays respects to the grave of Mary Livingstone, the sainted wife of the sometime missionary and notable African explorer.

Soon after that, the diseases of Africa kill Captain Stairs. He puts his parchment-thin skin under a muslin curtain and dies. Malaria is the formal diagnosis but, ultimately, brutality was its own reward.

When it was proposed that a plaque to Stairs be placed in the garrison church in Halifax, Nova Scotia, the then-commander, the duke of Connaught, who lacked almost everything but class, vetoed the proposal.

He could not forget that Stairs had died serving a foreign king.

Nor, that among Captain William Stairs's final effects was a tin kerosene can in which Stairs was keeping the head of King Msiri as a gift for someone special.

"RHODESIA." SEPTEMBER 1892

The Fingers of His Hand

Living a life of taking credit for many things that he had not done, and denying many of those that he had, Cecil Rhodes was an ideal competitor in the Great Game that was the division of Africa.

He was like a magician whose hand one sees but whose fingers are only perceived when he commits intentional acts of misdirection.

In September 1890 he sends a Pioneer Corps into the territory north of Bechuanaland, which he calls Rhodesia. It is a corps of 800 armed whites under the Wexford-born Colonel Edward Pennefather, who chooses the site of the capital, Salisbury.

Other invasions are less direct, but serve Rhodes' purpose: those of missionaries, of gold-hunters, of ivory and trophy hunters.

Rhodes engages the Moodie family, now a network that spans the southern tip of Africa, from Cape Town to Natal, in a lattice of large farms and high governmental posts. George Benjamin Dunbar Moodie, grand-nephew of John Weddeburn Dunbar Moodie who shivered his life away in Upper Canada, leads a party north that in its heroics, if not its number of participants, rivals the Great Trek of the Afrikaners earlier in the century. Dunbar Moodie (as he usually was known) did not need the money: he was already colonial secretary of Natal and manager of a gold-mining company. He needed the drug that southern Africa promised those whose identity was that of white settlers – as distinct from resource miners, financial capitalists and the like. That drug was land. Addiction to the acquisition of land, of spaces that could not ever be truly possessed or even fully farmed, only possessed temporarily; addiction to saying this is mine, this is our family's land, and now get off it; an addiction that like the tie to heavy opiates can never be broken, only temporarily assuaged or stayed. This addiction of the crowded tenant farmers and declassé landlords of the Old World, the lust that makes them the ravagers of New Worlds. This addiction Dunbar Moodie could not shake.

Moodie puts together a nine-month trek that yields a phalanx of British Isles and Dutch settlers in Gazaland, and serves as a palisade between Rhodesia and the Portuguese colony in east Africa. That is why Rhodes approves and promises the Moodie party of thirty families (nine of them Moodies of various sorts) vast amounts of land: 3,000 acres for each immigrant, 6,000 for the leading Moodies and 24,000 for Dunbar Moodie and his family, all of which they eventually receive.

Nine months of travel in ox-waggons, loss of several children by wild animals, dehydration, short-rations, an epic journey. Both Dunbar and his uncle, the foreman of the march, lose their wives along the way.

They say all this is worth it and Cecil Rhodes does not object when they name their new family fiefdom "Melsetter," after the Moodie family's original estate in the Orkney islands, the source of their land addiction.

KILMACHDAUGH, "RHODESIA." 1892–94

Useful? Idiots

The Eyre brothers of Eyerscourt, County Galway, Arthur and Herbert, were a good example of the human limits that Cecil Rhodes faced. They had the intelligence quotient of meat.

Still, they were stout lads, sons of an Indian army colonel, and they enlisted in his Pioneer Corps and put in for a land grant. They were rewarded with nearly 19,000 acres in the Lomagundi region in 1892 where they built a pole-and-daga homestead, with a thatched roof, and lived like bachelor brothers inevitably do; no maidens, so the place became a midden.

The brothers are better at shooting things than they are at growing them, a common characteristic of early Rhodesian settlers, and they kill in 1892–94 three of the last white rhino in the region. The trophies are sold to the Natural History Museum in Dublin, to the czarist government, and to Cecil Rhodes, who gives his to the Cape Town Museum.

Arthur then goes prospecting and he discovers, pegs, and names the "Eldorado," which, in the early twentieth century became one of the richest gold mines in the world. Arthur, however, never bothered developing his mine and sold it before its worth was understood.

Herbert, at home farming, was killed by his farm staff during the Mashona rising of 1896.

And Arthur, having lost his brother, decides to marry in 1897 a Miss Tyler Stewart, the beauty of Fort Salisbury.

Even that he cannot get right: he dies of blackwater fever shortly before the wedding.

JESUS COLLEGE, CAMBRIDGE. MARCH 1895

Travels Without My Mother (1)

It came as a disagreeable surprise to Ewart Grogan, godson of William Ewart Gladstone, that his mother died before luncheon, while washing her hands. That he was not there at the time made the event no less painful. His father, sire of twenty-one offspring by two successive wives, had already passed on and the young man was suddenly without guidance.

He took to obsessive playing of the banjo and mandolin, which his mother had mistakenly taught him, and then to practical jokes. The flock of sheep packed into his tutor's rooms had ended his university career. The poor don had to sell his collection of Persian carpets at a ridiculously low price.

Fortuitously, young Grogan caught a newspaper advertisement placed by Cecil Rhodes for volunteers to fight in the interior of southern Africa, and despite his having no experience, his vast self-confidence led him to become one of Rhodes' scouts and eventually one of the inner circle that travelled with that great man, like a pillar of cloud by day and a fire by night.

He and the other scouts would sit by a camp fire at night and listen to Rhodes expound his dream of an African empire that ran, by road, train, telegraph, and territorial acquisition, from the Cape to Cairo, the length of Africa. Ewart Grogan took Cecil Rhodes as his model, a man of immense vision who, nevertheless, was a true democrat. To Rhodes, Grogan believes, *all men black or white, Kaiser or scullion, be they men, were one.*

On those dark nights, circling the shaman of imperial Africa, Rhodes' scouts entered an unworldly realm, where *the spell of greatness was in the air.*

BEIRA, PORTUGUESE EAST AFRICA. JANUARY 1898

Travels Without My Mother (2)

Because he had already in previous years travelled from the Cape to Beira, Ewart Grogan thought it fair, and no one ever disagreed, that he could start the second leg of his Cape-to-Cairo journey in what is now Mozambique. As a child, Grogan had devoured every Rider Haggard book he could lay his hands on. *King Solomon's Mines* was his favourite. Grogan knew definitively what a ripping adventure had to be and to be the first to traverse the Dark Continent from south to north was spot on.

After learning how to shoot game proficiently from Dan Mahony, the best hunter in Portuguese East Africa, he and Harry Sharp, a portly but able outdoorsman, took themselves northward.

Grogan refused to travel without sufficient supplies of Worchestershire sauce, pajamas and boot-trees.

And, remarkably, his party reached the Upper Nile and eventually the Mediterranean.

Grogan immediately wrote the requisite book (whatever happened to secret explorers?) and became a national hero.

The great-grandson of Cornelius Grogan, whose head had been put on public display after his support of the 1798 Rising, was commissioned a captain in the 4th Royal Munster Fusiliers.

SURPRISE HILL, SOUTHERN AFRICA. DECEMBER 1899

Brothers

The Second Anglo-Afrikaner War. Or Boer War, if you prefer.

As the Afrikaner forces fall back before the imperial advance, one fighter begs for mercy. "Don't pink me, I'm an Irishman."

"So am I, cunt," replies the trooper as he thrusts his bayonet into the supplicant's entrails.

SOUTHERN AFRICA. 1899–1902

Conundrum

At most 500 men fought in two Irish brigades for the Transvaal Republic or the Orange Free State or in Natal against the United Kingdom's invasion. Thirty-one died. Sixty others were wounded.

Probably 10,000 Irishmen (nobody is sure of the precise number) served in the U.K. army that fought and conquered the Afrikaners. Specifically Irish units included the Irish Fusiliers, the Connaught Rangers, the Dublin Fusiliers, the Inniskillings, the Irish Regiment and the 5th Royal Irish Lancers; they were only a portion of the Irish recruits, however. The Irish were more than one-third of the total army.

Who was on the right side? The U.K. army was engaged in a naked grab of the mineral-rich interior of southern Africa, and was doing so against the will of the white "owners" of that land. Two independent settler polities were snuffed out as political entities.

So, Viva the Irish volunteers in support of the Afrikaners!

Except that the volunteers were supporting a society that had come into existence in the 1830s as a protest against the empire's softness on the treatment of kaffirs (their word). If slavery was no longer possible, keeping the descendants of Ham in servitude still was a moral duty. The Bible said so. The Transvaal's president, Paul Kruger, not only believed this to be true, but believed the world to be flat. He was not joking.

The imperial army invents the concentration camp and starves 26,000 Afrikaners, mostly women and children, to death, or so close to it that they die of the first disease that lodges in their emaciated frames.

The Irish brigades care only about whites. As far as the Irish volunteers are concerned, the Afrikaners are right about the kaffirs. Still, the blacks do have their uses. John MacBride, second-in-command, but the real leader of one of the two Irish brigades, escaped with most of his men into Mozambique in September 1900. MacBride left behind, without any provision for support, a Cape Malay woman with his bastard child. He goes off to marry Maud Gonne in Paris in 1903 and neglects to mention this matter to her.

MAFEKING, SOUTHERN AFRICA. 17 MARCH 1900

St. Patrick's Day in the Morning

The 153rd day of the siege of Mafeking is special for the surrounded imperial troops only because of the calendar. The Irish lads are not allowed to celebrate very much. Two Irish brothers, Tom and William Hayes, serve as surgeons and keep diaries. *We cannot afford to wet the shamrock very freely, but hope to make up for it later on.*

The Cape Boys shot a Boer today in the Brickfields.

The former were playing concertina, jigging and singing and shouting to the Boers to send over some of their vrouws, as they wanted dancing partners.

One of the Boers looked over the fort wall and was immediately shot dead by our riflemen.

Ruse of war.

SOUTHAMPTON. 26 NOVEMBER 1900

Great Names

The Liverpool Irish, as the unit was usually known, was welcomed home by its new commanding colonel. A volunteer company, in existence since 1860, the Liverpool Irish were taken into the regular army as a self-contained unit in the Boer War, an unusual honour. They were well trained and this was remarkable because as volunteers they had been required to buy their own green uniforms (modelled on those of the Irish Rifles) and pay an annual subscription. This the post-Famine Irish of Liverpool had been doing of their own free will for forty years.

They become the 1st battalion of the Royal Irish Regiment and fight with distinction, at one time garrisoning the South African town of Belfast under heavy fire. Most of them are rotated home on the *Avondale* and are welcomed by a regimental band which plays them to the train that eventually returns them to Liverpool and a massive parade and civic reception.

The unit always had been mixed Catholic and Protestant, and successfully so. Most of the officers were Protestant, but the senior chaplain, Father (subsequently Monsignor) James Nugent, was Catholic as were most of the rank-and-file.

Even individuals were ecumenical. The new commander, Lt-Colonel Myles Emmet Byrne, was a descendant of Myles Byrne, leading rebel of '98, Irish brigadier and memorialist of the Wild Geese in France; and also a distant connection of Robert Emmet.

Lt-Colonel Byrne in civilian life was a director of a large firm of jewelers and an impeccable imperial patriot.

DUBLIN. 1899–1902

Other Views

In contrast to the Liverpool Irish and to those of London and Glasgow, most of the people in Dublin were mildly-to-strongly pro-Afrikaner. One street song celebrated the most obdurate Protestant in the world, "Oom" Paul Kruger, president of the Transvaal Republic and hard-shell flat-earther.

Later, a memorial arch was built to those men of the Dublin Fusiliers who died in service in South Africa. Immediately it was given the popular epithet, Traitor's Gate.

LAND OF THE
TERMINALLY VICTORIAN.
UPPER CANADA
1845–1900

A New and Burning Evangelicalism

Adolphus Egerton Ryerson was his full name, but he insisted on being called Egerton Ryerson, under the mistaken conviction that this was much more matey than Adolphus. The son of loyalists persecuted by the Americans, he has always had faith in the British constitution and, since age eighteen, in Methodism. Remarkably handsome and articulate as a youth, Ryerson had been, first, the boy-wonder of several Methodist circuits, then a trusted negotiator on behalf of the faith with British Methodists and, finally, he became generally known as the Methodist Pope.

Now, full of years – he is forty-three but conducts himself with the gravitas of Moses on Mount Nebo – he has added a new faith – namely, in education. And with zeal: universal education of the common people will be the salvation of Upper Canada. Right now he is drafting a letter to be sent to educationalists overseas. He has lost none of the intensity of his circuit-preaching youth, but his hair is now greying a bit and is refusing to sit still. This, and the electric blink of his eyes give him the air of a prophet or a madman.

Ryerson writes, *The Board of Education for Upper Canada ... having heard of the excellent system of elementary schools which the Commissioners of National Education have introduced into Ireland ... desire ...*

Ryerson is being candid. Having accepted his own appointment as superintendent of education for the province in 1844, he had done so with the stunned alacrity of St. Paul on the Damascus Road. It was God's will. And like Paul, he was blind after the revelation – what was he to do to realize his new responsibility? – especially considering that the province already had near 2,500 elementary schools in a higgly-piggley mess, each township's schooling different from its neighbour's. Like Saint Paul (at the moment that actually is how he thinks of himself), Ryerson has allowed himself to be led around by his well-wishers: in this case, "educationalists" in the USA, Germany, Scotland, England.

His defining revelation came in Dublin. There he sat across the table from the Commissioners of National Education and talked to people who ran the best common school system in the British Isles and, indeed, the empire: Daniel Murray, Catholic archbishop of Dublin; James Carlisle, a leading Presbyterian minister; and, crucially, Richard Whately, Protestant archbishop of Dublin and an energetic proponent of anything that would improve the everyday life of the common people. He was an educational zealot and he and his wife had written portions of some of the Irish schoolbooks. And, very useful to Upper Canada, Ryerson had immediately recognized, was the fact that the head civil servant in the Irish educational system, Alexander Macdonell, though Protestant, was a relative of Bishop Macdonell, the Scots-born Roman Catholic prelate of central Canada.

Ryerson buys the Irish package – central administrative system, teacher-training, standard textbooks – but in his public pronouncements preaches sermons on educational principles and then pretends to derive the Irish-patterned actions from those great clouds of vapour. Here, in his private office he can be direct. ... *desire ... to profit by the successful labours of the Commissioners of National education in Ireland and to introduce a similar system of schools, as far as the circumstances of Upper Canada will enable us to do so, and especially the Dublin system of Normal School instruction and ...* He wants to duplicate Dublin's Marlborough Street teacher training college and the various "model schools" scattered around the countryside where Irish pupil-teachers received their rudimentary training. He proceeds with New World directness. He asks the Irish commissioners to send him their best man. They comply. When Thomas Robertson, a graduate of Trinity College, Dublin and formerly head-inspector of Irish national schools, arrives in Upper Canada in November 1847, a training college is set up.

While he's at it, Ryerson imports from Ireland George Hodgson, a graduate of the Dublin normal school who had worked under Alexander Macdonell in the central administration. He introduces to Upper Canada school inspection and other ways of controlling the vagaries of local school boards, just as in Ireland.

... and ... the series of school books which have been published under the sanction of the Irish educational board. There was the pivot of the enterprise. The Irish books were the best in the world (they were the most-used texts in English elementary schools at that time) and, crucially they were not, not, not American.

Whenever Ryerson thought of the indoctrination in incivility, disloyalty and, dear, he almost used the name of the Deity, in damnable republicanism, that ... that was occurring because so many school boards bought the cheapest books they could and of course these came from the Cheapside republic to the south ... oh, he had to engage in a silent prayer for personal peace. And for victory. Yes, the Irish series of school texts would give him victory over the Americans. The Irish commissioners sold their books to Ryerson's Upper Canadian board at a special price and from 1 January 1847 all foreign (meaning, all Yankee) books were to be gradually excluded from the schools. Ryerson required their replacement by the Irish books and by 1859 the purge was complete and U.S. material completely excluded. So, from the late 1840s most children growing up in Upper Canada (and, from 1859, *every* child) were taught to read, write, and, crucially, what it meant to be Canadian, by a curriculum that was defined in Dublin.

Of course it was "West British," meaning that it taught a vague sort of British Isles culture and a loyalty to the Crown, avoiding specific political and religious issues as if they were leprosy spots.

Realize, though, that the tens of thousands of migrants who continue to pour into Upper Canada from 1845 into the 1870s are mostly young adult men and women and that they are not illiterate. They have had elementary schooling in Ireland in the very same textbooks that now define the official culture of Upper Canada. When they have children of their own who enter the common schools of Upper Canada, they find that the children bring home texts that are familiar: not the frightening rules of some unknown world.

The comfort, and the advantages, the Irish system of education as it operated in Upper Canada gave to Famine and post-Famine migrants was unintentional. Yet, it is not inaccurate to see Egerton Ryerson, his eyes always fixed on some distant horizon, as a prophet.

BELLEVILLE, UPPER CANADA. 1847

Empathy

Tragedy, like religion, makes good people better and bad people worse.

As news of the first potato failure of 1846 passed through the Upper Canadian papers, thoughtful men and women realized that in the next emigration-season Ireland's problem would become, in part, North America's. In the summer of 1847, thousands of dishevelled and often diseased migrants (the quarantine was far from perfect) made their way to Prescott, Brockville, Kingston, Belleville, Toronto. The migrants were like an army in defeat: at each stage many of their number could carry on no further and in each town the decent people set up fever hospitals and emigrant-aid societies. Every town on the St. Lawrence sea-highway eventually had a communal burial ground, where not just the Irish, but local citizens who had helped them, were interred.

Among Upper Canadians, some helped, others fled. Some faced reality, others looked the other way.

For the Moodies, the Great Famine coincided with their (meaning Susanna's) breakthrough into modest literary celebrity, and they forever after looked upon 1847 as a good year for the right sort of people.

John W.D. Moodie was ever less of a force and certainly not much of a sheriff. His left wrist, wounded in Holland in 1814, now incapacitated his entire arm, and he now had a bad leg and could not walk without a cane. It was all he could do to keep his constables at their duties. Yet, he was still the durable old soldier and he knew tactics. "All this emigration from Ireland is bound to excite interest at Home about what it is like to settle in Canada." He pulled out the two proposals for a book on settling in Canada that his publisher, Richard Bentley, had turned down in the 1830s. "Now might be the time, you know." He reckoned that he was no longer capable of writing much. "You could do this book, Susanna. I would set you up with Bentley. Or, anyroad, we could draw up a programme and each write a bit. I'll help you. My South Africa book is a decent pattern-plate, if I do say so."

"John, I think we should do it in little pieces. Just like in Papa's carriage factory. If we do it right, the pieces will come together."

And, she could have added, we can sell the same bits of rope two or three times.

The Moodies were in an unusually good position in 1847. John Lovell needed more and more material for his *Literary Garland* and an aesthete named Joseph Wilson bankrolled the Moodies in planting their own literary flower, the *Victoria Magazine*, a periodical "for the people" of Canada. In fact it served the tastes of lawyers, doctors, wealthy widows and retired military officers. It was comprised of tasteful material, most of it put together by the Moodies themselves, the majority of it previously published.

There was, though, new material both for Lovell and for Wilson, and it all burst forth because of Grosse Île. The Irish suffering of several forms of fever in 1847 put Susanna evocatively in mind of her own migration to Canada during the cholera epidemic of 1832. There the contact ended: Susanna stayed indoors during the summer of 1847 and shunned strangers and refused to go near the Belleville waterfront. When John, as sheriff, was scheduled to inspect the social regulation of the fever hospitals, she told him not to touch anyone and to stay as far away from the migrants as possible.

Enclosed in her carapace of self-involvement, Susanna, with some help from her husband, produced in 1847 eleven sketches and essays that were later published in *Roughing it in the Bush; or, Life in Canada* (1852). For her, 1847 was the year of miracles.

The Irish were the key. The staggering and feverish wretches she was told of by her husband became archetypes of her own passage through Grosse Île. The Moodies' ship had not been quarantined, but they had been taken as sightseers to look at those that were. For Mrs. Moodie, the shock was the beauty of the island compared with the brutal nature of the immigrants. *I had heard and read much of savages, and have since seen, during my long residence in the bush, somewhat uncivilised life; but the Indian is one of Nature's gentleman – he never says or does a rude or vulgar thing. The vicious, uneducated barbarians who form the surplus of over-populous European countries are behind the wild man in delicacy of feeling or natural courtesy. The people who covered the island [Grosse Île] appeared perfectly destitute of shame, or even of a sense of common decency.*

This observation, retrospected by Susanna to the year 1832, also represented Susanna's feelings about the immigrants as they passed through Grosse Île in 1847. And, most telling, was her demon figure. *Here we encounter a boat, just landing a fresh cargo of lively savages from the Emerald Island. One fellow, of gigantic proportions, whose long tattered great-coat just reached below the middle of his bare red legs, and like charity, hid the defects of his other garments, or perhaps concealed his want of them, leaped upon the rocks and flourishing aloft his shillelagh, bounded and capered like a wild goat from his native mountains. "Whurrah! my boys!" he cried. "Shure we'll all be jontlemen!"*

There was Susanna's horror, held tight in memory for twenty-five years: the New World being peopled by the savages of the Old, and the worst of them, the Irish, having the cheek to conceive of someday being gentlemen. No wonder she never gave alms for the sick and starving Irish.

If she did no good, she did well. John Moodie's earlier work provided entrée to his publisher, Richard Bentley. Once the Moodies had cobbled together her pieces with three of John's, they sent them to a friend in London, John Bruce, who acted as their agent. He made some alterations. Susanna did not mind: that was how she had always worked. Bruce sold the book to Richard Bentley and it was before the public, as *Roughing it in the Bush* in early 1852.

Her treatment of the Irish migrants brought Susanna to the notice of the *Observer* of London. The English newspapers of the time were notable for their prejudice against the Irish, so one had to go fairly far to offend them. Thus the *Observer*'s comment indicated that something especially noisome emanated from *Roughing It* ... "She describes the Irish emigrants in terms which a reflective writer would scarcely apply to a pack of hounds – as 'filthy beings sullying the purity of the air and water [of Grosse Île]' ..." To her they are "vicious, uneducated barbarians ..." And more. Susanna's only sympathetic Irish characters are two Irish servants of whom she makes great sport, and this despite these servants keeping the Moodies alive – by saving them from their British gentry incompetence.

The *Observer*'s review was reprinted in the Montreal *Pilot* – that hurts her feelings.

As for her contempt for the Irish, she had yet to reveal even the half of it. Starve on, savages, starve on.

LONDON, ENGLAND, AND UPPER CANADA
["CANADA WEST"]. 1850

Continuing ... Continuing

Only when the Great Famine is nearly over do the London authorities decide it is time to get their emigration-counting system in order. During the Famine they lost track of how many Irish people left and from what ports.

Ireland's emptying continues throughout Victoria's reign. Now, however, British North America is the third choice: the USA first, then England, then the Canadas.

Curiously, the big shift to the USA means that collective character of the Irish who come to central Canada changes little. Most still come from the economically advanced eastern half of Ireland; two-thirds are Protestants; overwhelmingly both Catholics and Protestants make their way to rural areas and become farmers or small town merchants. A census of 1871 shows that once the dust settled, the Catholic Irish did as well as the Protestant Irish in the rural economy. All this contrasts with the USA, where the Famine and post-Famine migrants are mostly from the far south and west of Ireland, are largely Catholic and, if not overwhelmingly urban, are more city-bound than most other ethnic groups.

Upper Canada, the most Irish jurisdiction in the empire, stays pretty much the way it was.

BELLEVILLE, UPPER CANADA. 1850

Brotherhood

"No, you cannot marry him," says the lady with the large mole and several bristles sprouting from it.

"Yes, I can," replies her daughter, bristling, verbally.

"The boy ..."

"He's not a boy, mother, he is ..."

"A gambler, I know it from good sources."

"Who, the people who threw you out of the church that you and Daddy belonged to?" The daughter coughs.

"And, there, you see, you are already acquiring one of the diseases that is, to his people, *common*, you have ..."

"No, mother, I do not have consumption. And, dear mother, what do you mean by 'his people?'"

"The people who do not pay their debts."

"Unlike you and father?"

"Never you mind, young lady. Your father is here, supporting the Empire and being sheriff in Lord-knows-what dangerous circumstances and your boy's father, why ... why.."

"He is in London, actually mother."

"After having left large debts behind."

"They're being paid, mother. And, after all, he was clerk of the legislative council and he saved this province in battle twice. As I recall."

"We all do, dear. He never stopped reminding us."

"And, darling mother, I have a letter from Aunt Jane who reports, quite fully, actually, that she has met Colonel FitzGibbon and finds him a fine example ..."

"Of what, I wonder?"

"Of Upper Canadian gentility."

"Mercy! No wonder she never writes me, why, the last time ..."

"When was the last time your sister Jane wrote to you?"

"Impertinent question! And as for your 'beau'– may I use that horrible Yankee word? – he is, nevertheless, totally and unredeemably ..."

"Irish?"

"Not the word I would have chosen. *Subitaneous*, actually, dear. Not a born gentleman."

Thus Susanna Moodie dealt with the difficult matter of her daughter Agnes's requesting permission to marry Charles FitzGibbon, son of Colonel James FitzGibbon, hero of the Canadas. Mother and daughter argued for days, but when the flour was all done being sifted, young FitzGibbon had only one flaw: he was Irish and when the Stricklands on the other side of the ocean learned that her daughter had married a Paddy, even a Protestant one and even one whose father ... oh dear, Susanna could not bear the thought.

She deflected her social disappointment: as in the instance of the Jew-Editor, Susanna dipped into a well of hatred within herself. From this contretemps with her daughter arises Mrs. Moodie's second-most racialist piece: nothing to rival her Jew Editor items but close. In a fury of loathing for the Irish, Susanna pens a story that she controls no more than she did her vilipending of "Benjamin Levi," the Jew-Editor in "Richard Redpath." Entitled "Michael Macbride" this "sketch" (Mrs. Moodie's term for everything she wrote, save poetry and personal letters) is a virtual compendium of every Protestant canard and derogatory rumour about Irish Catholics that floated through Victorian English society. The victim of the sketch (there is no hero), Michael Macbride, is an Irish Catholic youth who has been cheated and physically abused by his uncle, who lives near Peterborough. The lad is abused until he is near the point of death. He finds his way to a neighbour's house, and begs food. By long-reach coincidence, his mother arrives from the Old Country. She is motherly and deeply concerned but is "ignorant and beside herself." She does not wish the Bible to be read to the dying youth, though he begs for God's Word. "Och! what do yu mane by disturbing him in his dying moments wid yer thrash?" The lad dies in a Victorian deathbed handkerchief-wringer and there the sketch should stop. Susanna has bile left, however, and instead tacks on the mother's tale of how her own brother, Michael's uncle, had brought the boy to Canada because the lad was to receive a £300 inheritance when he came of age. The uncle, coveting the money for himself, brought the lad up to be a Catholic priest, which young Michael did not want to be. In fact, he wanted to marry a Protestant girl and to turn Protestant himself. In Mrs. Moodie's sketch, the evil uncle imprisons the beloved girl until she dies during a severe winter and, of course, Michael Macbride himself eventually dies tragically. This is a good Irish Catholic family according to Susanna Moodie, and she'd like her English readers to know about it. She publishes it first in a periodical and then she includes "Michael Macbride" in the material she is baling together as *Roughing it in the Bush*. Indeed, so warm is her heart behind this screed that she sends it separately to Richard Bentley, asking that it be included in the manuscript that she and John Moodie already have sent him.

For once, her practice of selling everything twice saves Susannah from some embarrassment, at least for a moment. "Michael Macbride" appears in the *Literary Garland* of Montreal early in 1851 and she has a nasty shock. Her anti-Catholic, anti-Irish reading of the world was not accepted passively. *The lady is evidently ignorant of all the genuine characteristics of that fine people ... She draws them, it is plain, from the exaggerated account of those who love them not, and the consequence is that they come from her hands distorted and unnatural.* That is from a Montreal Catholic paper, but there is a good deal more elsewhere, and thoughtful readers are beginning to recognize her other hatreds as well, not least her disdain for Upper Canadians.

Wisdom prevails briefly. She hastily writes to her London publisher and has "Michael Macbride" removed from *Roughing it ...*

Then wisdom is undone: when Bentley wants to bring out a second anthology of Canadian sketches by herself and her husband, Susanna goes to her compost heap and digs out "Michael Macbride." The publisher blanches: slagging the Irish is an English hobby, but now, in the wake of the Famine, a bit more delicacy is desired.

Susanna overrides him by passionately stating exactly the argument she is to use to justify her anti-Jewish attack. *It was strictly true*, she writes and underlines the phrase in her letter. Her "Michael Macbride" reappears in *Life in the Clearings versus the Bush* (1853).

Susanna Moodie can never understand why Upper Canadians do not have much time for her writing. The farther away her readers are from her in place (England, for example), the more they seem to accept her writings.

As is the case with many producers of hate literature, Susanna believes in both the accuracy of her specific observations and in their being representative of larger truths. Susanna sees herself as an honest bystander when, in reality, she is the first casualty of her own toxic imaginings.

TORONTO. 1853

And Still Continuing

To help to fill his paper during a slow summer, George Brown, editor of the Toronto *Globe* invented the first Canadian opinion poll. He assigned a reporter whom he especially disliked, a man known as Lazy Ike Cashman, to go by road coach to Brockville and back and to ask ten adult persons in each town along the way what was the most despicable creature in Upper Canada. Brown, an ardent reformer and deep anti-Catholic, assumed that Cashman would bring him back the name of an arch-conservative or, better, that of a Catholic bishop.

Lazy Ike Cashman phrased his question exactly as his superior had told him, with the result that he returned and wrote a remarkably evocative column entitled The Despicable Creature: Why Upper Canadians hate the Black Fly. Cashman was particularly vivid in his expounding the facility of Canadian black flies, which, although they do not sting, actually gnaw on their victims. Clouds of these creatures, he said, had been known to make a man's head resemble a pumpkin covered with hickory-nut sized swellings. This was a sight, Cashman said, except for the victim, whose eyes usually were swollen shut. Madness frequently ensued.

George Brown fired Cashman, then rehired him, and made him his chief fishing and agricultural correspondent.

TORONTO. 1854

Loving Steward of Thy Bounty

The young shopkeeper loved the profit-and (almost never)-loss aspect of his trade; 300 per centum mark-up on needles, more on thimbles, big margins on little things. And cutting down the price of his suppliers was a joy. He looked forward to the day when he could buy in such large quantities that he, rather than the market, could set the price.

Timothy Eaton of Ballymena had spent his apprenticeship as a merchant hawking small goods in the sectarian-jagged region west of the Bann, and this in the aftermath of the Famine. If he could make a living there, he could any place. Upper Canada is his destination, 1854.

The only thing Eaton dislikes about shopkeeping is the custom, almost universal in the British Isles and the Canadas, of making most sales on shop-provided credit and, therefore, having to maintain a separate price for each item, depending upon how risky each customer was. A man can't build a really big business if he has to assay every customer personally and set every price individually.

Eaton's big leap-of-faith came in 1869 when he opened a Yonge Street, Toronto, store: a large cash-only, all-items-fixed-price store. And if not satisfied, just return the item. He hadn't invented these ideas, but he bet his stake on them and won. He became the biggest private retailer in the country.

Shockingly decent to his staff (they had jobs for life and Saturday afternoons off), he gave large sums to the Methodist church and, for Protestants from Ulster, was the nineteenth century's equivalent of the social safety net.

All right: so he had the curtains on his store windows closed on Sundays.

BELLEVILLE. 1856

Never in My Life

"Never in my life have I seen anything so disgraceful."

"No, dearest."

"To have a Jew elected to parliament! That tribe will asking to be royalty next thing one knows."

"I doubt that, Susanna."

"You take this all too lightly."

Sheriff Moodie did not bother much these days about the danger of Jewish infiltration of the Decent Classes, or even the Catholic or atheist dangers. His leg throbbed terribly and he just wished the laudanum would kick in. "You did your best, dear. No one can say you didn't."

Susanna had learned that George Benjamin was preparing for a by-election in North Hasting in 1856 and she would stop the little Jew if she could. Her *Matrimonial Speculations*, including "Richard Redpath," which was her depiction of most things wrong with Jews and everything wrong with George Benjamin had appeared in London in October 1854. However, the American publisher refused to take the work, the only one of her volumes he ever refused. And no other American publisher stepped forward: anti-Jewish polemics were a minority taste and not a sound publishing investment.

"No one can say you didn' do your best, old darling." The laudanum had finally reached the sheriff's brain.

"Mr Moodie," Susanna corrected him sharply. "You must not slur your words. What if one of the local folk heard you?" This was unlikely, as ever since the Famine Irish epidemic, Susanna had kept the house tightly curtained and only allowed a door or window to be opened on the warmest summer days.

"North Hastings! I cannot get over this, John. So close. We are almost represented by an Israelite."

Since no American publisher would take her book and Bentley in London owned British Empire rights to it, Susanna was reduced to badgering her friends in the wholesale book trade to import quantities of the volume, most of which she bought herself. "Thank God for our lovely Mr. Lovell. He was ever so helpful." John Lovell could afford to be. Having closed the money-losing *Literary Garland*, he now was minting money: he had the exclusive contract to print the Irish National Readers for use in Upper Canadian schools.

"Pithy ... pity it di' nae work," added the sheriff, who returned to his Orkney roots when reminded of them by opiates. Susanna had sent copies to important figures and had made certain the book was advertised in the Toronto and Kingston papers and that they were available, as the advertisement said "Wherever Fine Literature is Retailed."

In spite of this, George Benjamin not only became the first Jew to win election to the Canadian parliament, he did so by a three-to-one margin. This he achieved by the seemingly miraculous achievement of winning most of the Orange and most of the Green vote. He did so by promising the Orange that he would fight to the death against annexation of the Canadas by the United States and, simultaneously, coming out four-square for the governments's funding of Catholic schools.

"None of these demented Canadians can say that I did not warn them."

"Nae..ya' certly worn them."

THE CANADAS. 1857

Coins of the Realm

The 22nd of January 1857 is so brutally cold that all around the Great Lakes trains stop: their boilers cannot be kept up to heat. Near Stratford, a woman sits beside her husband in their ox-drawn sleigh as they travel towards North Easthope. They are veterans of a dozen harsh winters and know how to protect themselves from the cold.

When the sleigh arrives at their destination, the husband lifts from the sled his wife, who had been silent for the last few miles. She is frozen dead and he is surprised.

In the summer of 1857, the Canadian Mint begins cranking out a strange set of coins. Five, ten, twenty-cent pieces. Not shillings and pence. Canada is breaking away from the mother country on this fundamental issue: where one's money goes, one's heart follows.

The force behind this decision is Francis Hincks, son of a County Cork Presbyterian minister, educated at Inst in Belfast, at various times head of two successive banks, newspaper owner, railway promoter, co-premier, Canadian enthusiast and, perhaps, bigtime stock swindler. As a man of business, he knew one thing: "If we want the Yanks' money, we'll have to make things simple." This becomes the unstated premise of all subsequent Canadian monetary policy.

The specie are minted, new bills are printed and a year later are in circulation. Francis Hincks is away from Canada and doesn't immediately have to face another nasty winter: London, strangely, rewards him for his Canadian nationalism by giving him a two-year appointment as governor of Barbados and the Windward Islands.

LONDON, UPPER CANADA ["CANADA WEST"].
8 JULY 1857

Democratic Impulse

With few exceptions, the Anglican clergy who meet in synod wear modest surplices. Even compared to most Presbyterian clergy, their plumage is undemonstrative. Technically, they are members of "the United Church of England and Ireland," but even they just call it the Church of England. That is not simple convenience: it suits their purposes.

They are electing a bishop for the new diocese of Huron. Election? This is the first time that a bishop will be elected any place in the British Empire. No politicians, no Crown involvement. All but the very few High Churchmen go along with this. "If we are not to be a State Church, then we ought not to suffer state interference."

Not a big event, really, except that as the Roman Catholics are marching strongly in the authoritarian direction – Ultramontanism is leading inexorably to the new doctrine of Papal Infallibility – the Anglicans are becoming more democratic.

Yet, this small event becomes a precedent for electing Irish bishops in the homeland, after the State Church is disestablished in 1871.

And so it should, for the business confirms what has been the case since the wave of Irish immigration of the 1830s: the "Church of England," despite its label, is really the Church of Ireland's largest overseas branch. Trinity College, Dublin has provided it with more clerics than has any other institution. The man elected bishop of Huron, Dr. Benjamin Cronyn, is from TCD and Irish-trained clergy are the biggest segment of his clergy. When one adds second-generation Irish, it's clear that the majority of Anglican clergy in Upper Canada are Irish. They establish a low-church tradition – little in the way of flash, fire, or incense – and create seminaries that maintain the low-church tradition, long after its practitioners even know from whence it came.

Notice: the Irish don't mind being called "English," as in Church of England, so long as they can quietly run things.

TORONTO. 1858

One Step at a Time

There's a name for the disease that Egerton Ryerson acquires, but one is not allowed to use it unless one has a licence. It's like being a Free-mason: certain words can only be used among the initiated.

The disease is simple enough. Ryerson is convinced that he has two wooden legs; lathe-turned pieces of maple that begin below the knees. He can walk on them without difficulty, but he knows they are wooden because he cannot feel any pain in them. Yet, he can plainly see that each is being gnawed at by industrious dogs, one a common pug, the other an aristocratic Afghan hound. He knows they are there because not only are the curs visible, but they make it hard for him to move about as freely and as quickly as he wishes.

These phantasmagoric hounds first came to the superintendent of education for Upper Canada in a dream, but they now are with him during his waking hours. He has spent enough of his Methodist med-itations parsing the books of Daniel and of Revelation to understand that he is seeing a physical manifestation of spiritual evil. Demons. His faith is great so he knows that he will overcome; but he is embar-rassed to be walking around with two hounds on his shins.

One, the elegant Afghan, is the Right Rev. Armand Francis Marie, comte de Charbonnel, an ultramontanist, appointed Catholic bishop of Toronto in 1850. He is disdainful of the state, brilliant in polemic, and has only one guiding principle: his church is the only acceptable moral voice in all matters. Ryerson's other tormentor, D'Arcy McGee, has a face like a pugdog that has recently run into a sledgehammer, is often drunk, and nevertheless is unerringly eloquent. A rebel of 1848 (and for a time co-editor with Gavan Duffy of the *Nation*), he has had a mercu-rial career as an anti-clerical American-Irish patriot until 1852, when, in his own Damascus experience, he decides the church is the font of wis-dom, that the American-Irish are wasting their lives in a racist society that keeps them in ghettos, and that they must escape the USA in order to share the full bounty of the New World. By 1857 he is in Canada and in December 1858 is elected an MP for one of the Montreal ridings.

Egerton Ryerson has done wonders for education since he took over, nearly doubling the number of elementary schools and bringing the Upper Canadian schools up to Irish national school standards of curriculum and administration.

Poor man, he has read too much theology. When he had examined the Irish system, he had been converted to its theory – that Catholic and Protestant children should be educated together – rather than to its reality: they weren't very often being schooled together and would be less and less so as time went on. His own goal is to be sure that the state elementary schools of Upper Canada are non-denominational, religiously integrated, and that they will produce social peace.

Bishop Charbonnel is a close follower of Cardinal Paul Cullen and an admirer of the Synod of Thurles which had condemned "mixed education." He rallies his flock against the mixed system, "a regular school of pyrrhonism, of indifferentism, of infidelity, and consequently of all vices and crimes." McGee for his part is less direct, but once he has settled into Canadian politics, he formulates the covenant that will eventually dictate a final school settlement: if the Protestants want their own school system in Quebec to be preserved, they have to give the Catholics their own separate system in Upper Canada.

Each passing month, Ryerson moves more slowly, his demons nearly immobilizing him. He knows, as do they, that he has an Achilles heel: before the passage of the 1846 Common Schools Act, an obscure act of 1842 granted Catholic and Native-Canadian parents the right in each township to demand separate schools. Ryerson did not have this earlier act repealed for it would have been contentious, but instead tried to ignore it in all his later work. But as thousands of Irish Catholics poured into Upper Canada in the 1840s and 50s, they increasingly meet the numerical minimum requirements for separate schools in their communities and demand their own institutions.

Some days, Egerton Ryerson foresees that the demon-beasts will win. He looks down and sees them planted four-square, and his own body now weak, as of a palsy, is unable to move.

OTTAWA. 24 MAY 1861

Newtonian Physics

Like so many Irish families, the McKinneys (or McKinstrys as they sometimes spelled it) of Sentry Hill, County Antrim, cast their children like dice around the world: New Zealand, Canada, Australia, South Africa. Some paid off, some did not and others just spun back home.

William Fee McKinney arrived in Canada in early 1860 with the strong back of a young farmer and the letters of one Anglican and two Presbyterian clergymen to introduce him. He easily found work near Ottawa: tillage, harvesting hay, ploughing. He saw the foundation stone of the new parliament being formally laid in Ottawa on 1 September 1860.

Mosquitos, black flies, followed by a bitter winter he found painful: the full Upper Canadian experience.

On Queen Victoria's birthday, 24 May 1861, he watched the national holiday being celebrated on parliament hill. When the soldiers in charge accidentally sent a two hundredweight stone into the crowd, he decided life would be safer back home at Sentry Hill.

BELLEVILLE. 1861

Vengeance Is Mine, Saith the Lord

Up Lord, and help me, O my God, for thou smitest all mine enemies upon the cheek: thou hast broken the teeth of the ungodly.

When he entered his sixties, George Benjamin had taken up daily reading of the Scriptures. Although his biblical Hebrew is still serviceable, he prefers the Book of Common Prayer. If his problems are in the world of English speakers, that's where he wants his God to be. And the Psalms are often appropriate.

O take not away my soul with the sinners, nor my life with the blood-thirsty; In whose hands is wickedness, and their right hand is full of bribes.

Benjamin is planning to retire from parliament at the next election, but before then he has one mission to achieve: to level things with the Moodie family. He has nothing special against the now-bumbling sheriff, especially since the man has experienced a serious stroke and has lost his left side, but the Hebrew scriptures teach that guilt often is a family affair.

Their right hand is full of bribes. Benjamin obtains solid proof that in 1856, John Moodie, instead of appointing a deputy sheriff on merit, had sold the post for £300. He presses the case and Moodie resigns in humiliation in January 1863. Because he does so, a court lets him away with the finding that he had taken the bribe inadvertently and so Moodie avoids prison time.

It is a good thing to give thanks unto the Lord and to sing praises unto thy Name. His task of seeing Sheriff Moodie brought to justice, George Benjamin leaves public life.

He makes his final peace with his Maker. *Sing unto the Lord a new song, and his praise from the end of the earth, ye that go down to the sea and all that is therein: the isles, and the inhabitants thereof.* Still, to the very end, George Benjamin cuts things close: he was paralyzed in his lower limbs in December 1863 and he survives only until the next September.

On 8 January 1864, he and his wife Isabella are baptized by the rector of St. Thomas's Anglican Church, Belleville.

BELLEVILLE. 1863

Flayed Alive

From the minute her husband John resigned his shrievalty in disgrace, Susanna Moodie's descent was rapid: socially and personally. Her pretense of being Suffolk gentry, the protective cloth that, thin though it was, had kept her from the black-fly reality of Upper Canada, was in tatters and every day the rents in the cloth became more visible. Her sisters in England had several times expressed their embarrassment at her Canadian writings, for they indicated how far she had slipped socially by emigrating. Now, they would hear of her husband's judicial humiliation. She hated what was happening to her and from the well of toxic prejudices that her English semi-gentry status had given her, she stirred her long-held hatreds.

"Mulatto"

"Quadroon"

"Mustee"

"Mustiphini"

"Quintoon"

"Octoroon."

She knew all these words and their precise meaning from her days working for Thomas Pringle and from transcribing the lives of former slaves. Susanna never used the word "nigger," even though it was in common usage at the time, but when she wished to refer to a certain person whom she despised, she said "that Quadroon," with a hiss that left no chance of the word being merely descriptive.

As the Moodies slipped further below the salt, race hatred became one of Susanna's analgesics. This was unusual in Upper Canada for, since Lieutenant-Governor Simcoe's proclamation of 1793, slaves had been gradually emancipated and not replaced. Granted, Upper Canada was the last stop on the Underground Railroad, but that produced mostly pro-black opinion in the short run, because after 1850 the U.S. Fugitive Slave Act led to attempts to kidnap former slaves who were in Canada.

The Moodies were unusual, however. From the late 1850s, they had boarded as genteel paying guests two Quadroon girls, Elizabeth and Julia Russell. Their father had passed through Belleville and he and the Moodies had played at being English gentry. He was, he said, a colonial administrator in the West Indies and it was "so difficult, terribly difficult, don't you know, to have one's daughters grow to be women in a tropical climate. So, oh what does one say? so unBritish." The Moodies fell in with this and offered for a fee to board the girls and to help them, in their early womanhood, to become "proper English ladies."

This was a mutual confidence trick. Russell indeed was a minor administrator in the West Indies, but he was merely one of the cadet branches of the once-powerful Russells of Nevis, whose members had drifted around the Caribbean and, in his case, done a fair deal of administering that was not official. He really did not wish to be saddled in Jamaica with two daughters who obviously were not white English roses. And, in that world anyone who could do arithmetic would rightly infer that the girls' mother had been a Mulatto, and, where was she, by the way? For their part, in reality, the Moodies could offer as cultural advantages only a piano, conversation with Susanna, and the complete, if short, run of the *Victoria Magazine*. Still the Hon. Thomas Russell was impressed with Susanna's habit, initiated in response to the Irish Famine, of keeping the house as closed as possible. Only indirect sunlight suffused through the drapery. "Admirable," the colonial administrator judged.

The girls, in their late teens, were beautiful, finely proportioned, and worldly beyond their years: they knew what they were marketing. When J.A. Dunbar Moodie returned to Belleville, at age twenty-eight, from the sluices and bordellos of the Nevada and California gold-fields, he had his pick of the girls, just as if he'd been in a San Francisco whorehouse. After sampling, he chose Elizabeth – "Eliza" – and they married in 1862 and had two children quickly. They lived near the senior Moodies and everything seemed balanced.

Until, that is, the Jew-Editor brought down Sheriff Moodie and left Susanna and the stroke-ridden John Moodie with scarcely £200 in the bank (they thought in terms of sterling still, not those terrible decimal dollars) and their house.

At that moment, the Moodies left the shirttail-gentry. They made a peasants' bargain with Dunbar and "his Quadroon" as they called her. They would give title to their fine stone house to the young couple if, in return, the young people would share the house with them and promise to take care of them in the old peoples' declining years. This was the same bargain that was being made hundreds of times daily among the Irish and lowland Scottish peasantry. Sometimes it worked. But the peasants understood something the declassé Moodies did not: to work well, this arrangement had to allow the new woman to be the boss of the house. This was transition of power, not its sharing. Susanna, by turns frail and then fiercely crabbit, won't have it. The women fight, say terrible things, and at one point slap each other. Susanna uses the slurs of race that she knows so well.

Three years later, when she has cooled off and is writing to the Moodies' English publisher, Richard Bentley, she describes *my son's West Indian wife. A selfish, cold hearted, arrogant Quadroon, a woman of little intellect, and who despises it in others*. That written to someone she is trying to impress with her gentility and high-born liberality.

Susanna overplays her hand. Dunbar and Eliza simply sell the house from under the older Moodies and move off to a farm in Delaware, leaving a half-hearted invitation for the old folks to join them in the United States. The old people rent a small cottage and Susanna, who hasn't been doing any real writing since 1851, and then only under John's supervision, is reduced to painting pictures of flowers, an art she had learned as a girl. She sells them to friends who buy them out of pity.

Susanna has plenty of time to curry her dislikes, distastes, and hatreds. For Upper Canadians: *The Canadians will never forgive me for disclosing the secrets of that rural prison-house, the Bush. I have no doubt they consider our present distress is just punishment for telling the truth*. For America: *I never did like the idea of turning Yankee in my old age ...* For the Irish, in this case because her daughter Agnes's husband, Charles FitzGibbon, whom Susanna had never liked, possessed the bad taste to die. *To add to our many sorrows, my dear daughter Agnes has* [in February 1865] *lost her husband and been left with six small children, the youngest only two years and a half old, without any means to support them. Her*

husband had the place of Clerk of the Surrogate court, which brought him an
income of four hundred a year, but [was] an improvident Irishman who al-
ways lived beyond his means.

Most of all, her hatred swirled around the two mixed-race Russell women. Eliza had stolen her best son and had forced Susanna out of her genteel stone house and into a workman's cottage. And, to add the final insult, her alcoholic son Donald, having sampled the charms and abilities of the other sister, Julia, skulked off to the USA and, in Brooklyn, New York, married her in February 1866.

"Quadroon!" It was enough to kill a suffering mother.

TORONTO. 1864

Tattered Soles

Almost everyone Ogle Gowan dealt with knew of his disgrace, but it was not the class of matter one talked about openly and, besides, he could still sting like a viper. Ogle spent his days moving slowly about central Toronto. He was the city's inspector of licences, a soft job that required him to be in and out of spirit groceries and taverns two or three hours a day and provided plenty of opportunity for taking back-handers. Better to keep Gowan sweet, than be closed down.

Ogle Gowan had moved to Toronto after the death of his wife in the early 1850s and had played at local politics and had been an MP for North Leeds, his old Orange hinterland, from 1859 to 1861. Then he had retired from elective politics because of a vice that, in his time, had no name.

Now, for a dozen years, he walks, ever more slowly, around the taverns and groceries in the morning, and then calls in on city hall. After that he proceeds to Orange headquarters. There he is an es-teemed elder statesmen – the Founding Father he loves to be called – and then he ambles homeward. He returns to his rented house – called grandiloquently "Nebo Lodge," after his father's estate in Wexford, "Mount Nebo," itself a reference to Moses' viewing place over the Promised Land. There are no promises left for Gowan to see. He lives alone and, as has been the case since his wife's death, he has bouts of blackness. A visionary with no visions: a man in prison.

At intervals he has his good moments. He pumps himself up to his former strut in 1867 when he represents the Canadian Orange Order at Belfast in the formation of the Imperial Grand Council of the Order. He brings with him representatives of the Mohawk lodges and parades them as if he had captured them himself. (The Mohawk are natural Orangemen, being both loyal to the Crown and Protestant. They are in fact the most trustworthy of adherents; 100 years later, when most of the white lodges have folded, the Mohawk will continue to be staunch.) Then Gowan returns to Toronto and to personal darkness.

Ogle Gowan's sin, it turns out, was not much of a crime in Toronto of the high Victorian age. In late-spring, 1860, when he should have been attending parliament (then being held in Quebec City), he stayed at home, mired in melancholy. He was trying to write a history of Orangeism, but was making no progress. He sat in his garden, catching the sunshine and taking a lift from the radiant energy. He was a sorry sight: as a concession to advancing age, his once-ginger hair was now dyed black, badly, and he was in an old smoking jacket and carpet slippers. One afternoon a young girl entered the garden and said "Please Sir, may I see the Lodge Goat?" This was a locally-famous item, a full-sized stuffed buck goat given to Gowan as a token of respect, apparently, by a rural lodge.

Soon Ogle is involved with this girl and then with one of her friends. They are age twelve and, in a matter of weeks, one of them has an obvious sexually transmitted disease and Ogle is for the chop. "Criminal assault" is the closest to child molestation that the Toronto Police Court has to write on its charge sheet. On such matters, this court acts like a grand jury: it decides if a criminal case should be brought in a higher court.

Gowan's only good luck is that the premier, John A. Macdonald, is also serving as attorney general. He is a fellow-Orangeman and he owes Gowan at least one big favour. Although Macdonald cannot influence the evidence given in a local police court trial, he can appoint an Official Observer to report on whether or not the incident runs beyond the remit of the local court and should be tried as a major criminal code incident in a higher court. Macdonald appoints a lawyer who was a longtime bagman for Gowan. Thus, even before the police court hearing, the premier has quietly guaranteed – *almost* guaranteed – that Gowan will not be tried for a major crime.

Nevertheless, molesting two girls – good Irish Protestant girls at that – was still a dangerous charge, and there were two witnesses, and this met the Victorian standard of evidence. So one of Ogle's outriders arranged for one of the girls and her family to go fishing on the day of the trial. This was suborning a witness and it cannot have been inexpensive. With only one wee girl left, and she being cross-examined aggressively, even brutally, by Gowan himself, the case broke down.

At the end of the trial, the magistrate, instead of deliberating on his own, called the Crown Observer into his chamber. Soon thereafter, the magistrate announced that it was clear that no jury would convict on the evidence provided and therefore the case had to be dismissed.

The police magistrate came as close to holding his nose as he could while maintaining dignity: he did not declare Gowan innocent, merely not convictable.

Everyone present knew what that meant.

Ogle Gowan in the late 1860s and early 70s continues on his daily rounds. In the summer months he wears his carpet slippers all day long and he shuffles. Finally, in 1874 his licence inspectorship is cancelled. He dies in 1876 and his funeral is attended by so many Orangemen with their medals clanking that it sounded as if they were working in a foundry that made little tin gods.

BRITISH NORTH AMERICA. 1866

Just Tell Me What Was in Their Heads

Have you ever noticed that they're not there when you need them? Just when there is some massive aberration in human behaviour, something that requires real knowledge of cross-cranial temporal lobe transfer, your phrenologist is on vacation. Always. Never fails.

Where were they all, at some kind of convention in Baltimore or Philadelphia? when the Fenians invaded British North America? Leaves the rest of us non-scientists in the lurch, eh? Would have taken the noble missionary of the science, Johann Caspar Spurzheim, and a dozen assistants, to explain such events: attacks on New Brunswick, Upper Canada, and Quebec in 1866, some desultory shooting in Quebec again in 1870 and in the Northwest in 1871.

Whatever was in the Fenians' minds? Did they really think they would "free" the Canadas by, in the actual event, defeating one militia unit and otherwise occupying Canadian territory that, in total, was the size of a county, for all of forty-eight hours?

A team of good phrenologists would have felt the Fenians' heads carefully, and made casts of the most startling examples. Certainly most of them must have exhibited highly developed, if oddly shaped organs of moral sentiment (they were, certainly, Irish patriots). Their organs of domestic affection, on the other hand, probably were underdeveloped, as most of them had long been away from home, fighting on one side or the other of the American civil war and obtaining useful practice in killing people. It would be in the lobes of pre-cognition that the phrenological scientists would have helped us most: were the lobes working at all? One suspects they were clotted with amphibole, reification, hypostatization, provincialism, sectarianism, antinomianism, and needed a good cleaning.

Otherwise all of the Fenian leaders – they were not unintelligent men, by and large – would have foreseen clearly the obvious fact that attacking New Brunswick would turn the Maritimes into supporters of the much-mooted Canadian Confederation. Canadian national unity, or even partial unity, was the opposite of what the liberators of Canada wanted, if they thought about it. Ah, you say, maybe the "off" switch, the hypothalamic precipice identified in advanced phrenological diagrams, was in the wrong position and they could not think. That makes sense, for why would they want to bring out anti-Irish Catholic prejudices in the Canadian population? – especially as there were fewer Fenians in the Canadas capable of leading the oppressed Catholics than there were locomotives on the Grand Trunk Railroad. And the Catholic clergy condemned the Fenians as if they were a pork chop on a Friday. Hard to miss that.

Perhaps if our absent phrenologists had taken a cast of each Fenian soldier who invaded Canada and had also, in an heroic study, compared them with the head-casts of 10,000 randomly-chosen white Americans they would have discovered that the Fenians actually were not so very different from the average Yankee: that in both groups the organ of arrogance was hyper-developed, to the dysfunction of all other faculties. Certainly that would explain the prevalent illusion, apparent as early as 1812, that Canadians wished to be freed from being what they were and, like amphibians, crawl back to their primordial pool, to become once again colonists of America.

George Combe: where the hell are you?

OTTAWA. 7 APRIL 1868

The Constitution of the Irish Free State (1)

When D'Arcy McGee lay bleeding outside his boarding house in the small hours of the morning, he was a victim of the truth: he had not been economical in its use. In Canada and, recently, back in Wexford, he had said all-too-memorably that the Fenian invasions of Canada – that already attempted and those that were being planned – were a treason to Irish interests.

The new Dominion of Canada that McGee had so ceaselessly campaigned for, was a fact in mid-1867, and had expanded to run from sea to sea by 1871. McGee's death occurred in the morning shadows of Canada's new neo-gothic parliament building.

When speaking or writing to Irish nationalists, McGee spoke often in a code. He referred to Daniel O'Connell's repeal movement and to the Irish constitution of 1782. To any savvy Irish nationalist, the new Canadian Confederation was recognizable in its main outlines as the Irish constitution of 1782: self-government, a Crown representative with limited powers, and judicial appeals on intractable legal matters to Westminster. With one major difference: Catholic rights in religion, voting, property–owning have always been guaranteed to be the same as those of everyone else. There is no penal past.

Why, McGee asked often, do the Catholic bishops and clergy support the new Canadian federation so strongly? Because it guarantees them something that they cannot obtain any place else in the English-speaking world. During the 1860s, the church had won an expansion of the right to separate schools, which meant that in Upper Canada (where the Catholics were in a minority) they would have a state-provided system of Catholic education. Crucially, the negotiations for Canadian federation produced constitutional guarantees for the continuation of separate schools. The bishops and McGee could only see the present, of course, but it was to take a century and more of strenuous effort to obtain the same rights in Australia and in New Zealand, and they are never gained in the United States. At the Confederation conferences, it was McGee who had introduced the call for constitutional guarantees for the educational rights of religious minorities.

D'Arcy McGee's last political office was as minister for agriculture, immigration, and statistics, not a glamourous post and he left the work to his officials. Still, from the numbers, tables, and tabulations that his department drew up, he was aware of a pattern that the 1871 census, the first of the new Dominion, would confirm: that despite hideous pockets of sectarianism, despite cases of direct discrimination, the Irish Catholic immigrants to central Canada and their children had, by the time of Confederation, won: as a group, they had the same wealth and occupational profile as everyone else. They were mostly rural and mostly bourgeois.

Canada worked for them. *Therefore ... we are loyal to the Queen in Canada. Were it otherwise, we would be otherwise.*

Telling such home truths was enough to get a man killed.

BELLEVILLE, ONTARIO
[FORMERLY "UPPER CANADA"]. 1869

Postlude

John W.D. Moodie's last years were not happy, but he was game to the end. To help with family finance, though his left side was crippled by his stroke and his old war injuries, he recycled some of his South African anecdotes and his war stories into *Scenes and Adventurers of a Soldier and Settler* (1866). The Canadian material was notably thin, despite his having in his trunk a vivid description of the 1837–38 Rebellion that Susanna only discovered after his death. Upper Canada had drained the life out of the man and that leeching of the spirit had begun early. In a doleful introduction to the book he defines his first big mistake in life – "*viz*, in going to Canada instead of return to South Africa." Of course, he won't blame Susanna, or anyone, for he is still an officer and a gentleman. "But I suppose, the love of adventure, so powerful an impulse with Scotchmen generally, and more particularly with Orkneymen, was too strong for me." Moodie gamely sells his book to friends, by subscription, and to small shops.

Susanna keeps his life as orderly as possible through, as always, the employment of a servant. "Margaret," she writes to a friend in late 1868, "is a good and faithful woman though *Irish* and a *Catholic*." She is trustworthy despite her background, Susanna believes, and a true friend.

John dies of a massive stroke late in October 1869 and is buried in the graveyard of St. Thomas's Anglican Church in Belleville.

There the problem lay – for he lies in the same consecrated ground as his nemesis and Susanna's arch-enemy, the Jew Editor, George Benjamin. This sits like a chancre on the soul of Widow Moodie: when the Resurrection of the Body occurs there are some people one simply does not wish immediately to encounter.

Susanna spends the rest of her life as a house-guest of long-suffering relatives, the most enduring being her youngest son Robert. She was unable to write without John's now-absent direction, but then, it had always been the case that she could only colour in other people's outlines. Susanna died in Toronto, in 1885, and in accordance with her wishes, was interred in a new burying ground in Belleville, near the Bay of Quinte. John Moodie's body was dug up and re-buried with her, a long way from the remains of the hated Jew Editor. Thus, in death, the Moodies were able to enforce a social distance from the undesirable that they had been unable to achieve in life.

TORONTO. 1871

The Constitution of the Irish Free State (2)

The most ethically-conscious politician in late nineteenth-century Canada, Edward Blake, was always quitting. Not in pique, ever, but because, like some protean, but slightly incompetent yogi, he had wrapped himself in some moral conundrum from which he could not extricate himself. He experienced frequent headaches, severe depression, anxiety-driven sieges of workworkwork and religious doubts.

He carried a heavy load. His parents, the cousins, William Hume Blake and Catherine Honoria Hume, had been among the *jeunesse dorée* who had chartered their own emigration ship in 1832. The father of his eventual wife was also on that ship: Benjamin Cronyn, the first bishop to be elected by clergy in the Empire. Sickly, educated at home until early youth by an epically Victorian mother, Blake was so conscience-oppressed that he made William Ewart Gladstone seem to be a free spirit.

In a very dirty age in Canadian politics, this large, fat-faced Sunday School boy became the second premier of Ontario (typically, he quit after a year), founded an Ontario Liberal party dynasty that lasted from 1871–1905, sat in the federal parliament for more than two decades and did not become prime minister of Canada only because, at a nodal moment, his conscience would not let him take the leadership of his Liberal party.

Like many of the genteel Irish migrants and their descendants, Edward Blake is a liberal and a strong Canadian nationalist – within the Empire of course: for descendants of the Anglo-Irish gentry understand what the Irish Constitution of 1782 was and that they had done very well under it, thank you, and they will do well under its counterpart in the New World. And, instinctively, the old gentry look down upon the Protestant rabble, who, with their Orange Order, wed themselves to conservatism. Carriage-trade liberals. Blake, of course, reaches his nationalism at a conscious level through reasoning, based on Christian principles and upon the bombastic logics taught at the Canadian bar.

His speeches are impossible to read today without growing weary; yet, in an oratorical age, he convincingly defended the new Canadian Confederation against Westminster's backsliding: he beat the colonial office in arguments about the powers of the Canadian supreme court and on limiting the governor-general's authority. And, being Blake, every second year he took a rest cure for one of his nervous breakdowns.

Out of a totally empty sky, in June 1892 he is invited by the Irish nationalist party to stand for a safe seat in Longford South. He says yes and a month later is an Irish nationalist MP. The Irish party needs him, his gravitas, his bison-like straight-ahead walk, his high rhetoric, his commitment (shared vaguely by almost all Canadian liberals) to Irish Home Rule within the Empire. Blake stands with Michael Davitt alongside John Dillon (son of the young Irelander, John Blake Dillon) in an Irish party badly split after the fall of Parnell in 1891. Blake gives a good deal of his own money to help the Irish party, makes long rolling speeches for Irish Home Rule, Australian federation and self-government (the analogy to Canada in both cases is drawn by Blake at impressive lengths) and, annually, begs to be allowed to retire as his head is hurting him and he craves sea air and he simply needs to compose his thoughts and he never has had time to read Catullus in the original and …

Finally, in 1907 a serious stroke gives him licence to retire permanently from politics. Blake's total integrity, his immensely boring Upper Canadian seriousness, served Irish nationalism well and helped to make possible the re-uniting of the Irish national party under John Redmond. In turn, the Irish party was educated in Canadian nationalism. *The case of Canada is that which offers the completest resemblance of the symptoms which prevail in Ireland, and, therefore, the completest argument for applying the same cure.* So, John Redmond, 1907.

THE ADVENT OF THE BELATED IRISH. THE USA 1845–1898

The Ever-Expanding Republic

Agreed. Yes, James Buchanan was certainly the laziest president that the United States ever had and probably the most indolent secretary of state. But he was no idiot; he observed well and while acting as James K. Polk's secretary of state, he watched Polk transform himself from a vigorous 49-year-old, the youngest U.S. president to that date, into a man in his fifties who had the bent posture and grey face of an overworked seventy-year-old.

Though James K. Polk refused to endorse the Presbyterian creed of his mother, wife and many of his own extended family, he lived it – unconsciously, yet on a grand scale. Work, work, work. His presidential diaries show that he thought he was doing the merely quotidian, but really, he was the nib on the pen that translated the predestinationism of old-kirk Ulster-Presbyterianism, into the political slogan that still rings through the American halls of power. *Manifest Destiny*: a phrase invented by John O. Sullivan of *The United States Magazine and Democratic Review*. Nothing sells in the United States, then or now, like a secular idea that has been pre-sold as a religious one.

Manifest Destiny was taken by President Polk to mean that the United States possessed a presumptive and predestined right to expand. He used it to cover retroactively the "re-annexation of Texas," yet another war with Mexico and the seizure of Mexican lands west of Texas running all the way to California. Manifest Destiny was tied to Polk's heavy promotion of the California Gold Rush, and his subsequently bluffing the United Kingdom into settling the northern border between the USA and British North America.

If Polk did not keep all he captured (the U.S. army took Mexico City but, really, who wanted it?), nevertheless his furrow-browed imperialism was astoundingly successful. He added half-a-million square miles to the territory of the United States.

Internationally, this is the counterpoint of the Russian Czar of the time, Nicholas I, pushing his empire into Hungary. In the Czar's case, a quick local onslaught, carried out by professional soldiers, was necessary to settle the native inhabitants. The native Americans, on the other hand, were dealt with in a miscellaneous fashion, usually by the relentless tramping forward of white settlers. Only occasionally was it necessary for the U.S. federal and state governments to engage in pogroms large enough in scale to leave a smudge on the historical record.

Manifest Destiny, the divine right to take whatever it wanted, became an unwritten, and seemingly permanent, clause in the United States constitution. It is a wonderfully circular and self-protecting concept, for those that hold it must also hold that the State is predestined to do right in extra-territorial matters, and since Manifest Destiny is morally right, then it is also inevitable: predestined. Thus did the ligaments and cartilage of the eighteenth-century Ulster Presbyterian mind become the marrow and spine of American geopolitics.

James K. Polk barely lived three months beyond his presidency. He had no serious disease; he had worked himself to death. *He was the most laborious man I have ever known*, commented James Buchanan shortly after Polk's demise. *In a brief period of four years he had assumed the appearance of an old man.*

That, manifestly, was a portion of his predestiny.

CALIFORNIA. 1846

More Room

The iron in Kit Carson's soul prevented his having any sense of irony. So he did not see any amusement in his having been part of both the conquest and the re-conquest of California, first as a member of the U.S. navy and then of the army. Nor was he amused that he was creating more room in America for the Papish hordes whom he despised.

The naval part of taking California was easy enough. The United States formally annexed California on 7 July 1846 and sent Commodore Robert F. Stockton, a Princeton graduate and more of a comedian than a commander, to raise the flag and shoot all the right objectors. Stockton enlisted John Frémont's elite army exploration corps as The Navy Battalion of Mounted Men and sent them down the coast to San Diego by ship. Kit Carson, who had never been at sea, was ill the entire voyage and thereafter never got on anything larger than a river raft.

No battle occurs and Kit is sent to Washington, D.C. as a messenger, a trip of four months if he is lucky.

Half way, he encounters an old friend.

"What are you doing here?" It is Tom Fitzpatrick and he is guiding the Western Army under General Stephen Watts Kearny who is on his way to California. On his way Kearny is declaring the American empire over everything in his path, which includes New Mexico and parts of Arizona. Kearny is more a lawyer than a general at heart. In New Mexico he issues Kearny's Code of Laws, a canon that prevails until 1886 when legislation finally replaces it.

Kearny detaches Kit from his original mission: Tom Fitzpatrick can take the despatches to Washington. Kit is now back in the army, he is told, and he will guide the dragoons to California. The Mexicans have risen, he learns from later messengers from California, and have taken back all of California save San Diego and San Francisco and the Monterey region. It is only a setback: they are efficiently suppressed by Kearny and Stockton's forces.

As was so often the case, the people whom the Americans now liberate do not fully understand the privilege that is being conferred upon them.

Like Kit, the conquered never seemed to get the joke.

NEW YORK CITY. JUNE 1847

Lord, Lettest Now Thy Servant

> We welcome not a monarch
>   with a Crown upon his brow.
> Before no haughty sceptre,
>   As suppliants we bow.

President James Polk, though a prodigious man-of-work, had needed a break from life in the not-quite-White-House, and had decided that a swing through the northern cities would be sufficient reason to travel: he wished to shore-up support for his war on Mexico.

No gorgeous throne, no princely pomp,
  In this fair land we see;
We boast a true Republic here:
  The home of Liberty.

The president, although devoted to his wife Sarah, needed to escape from the compound that she commanded: no dancing, no card-playing and no alcohol provided at functions in the presidential home. Weekly formal dinners were thus reduced to solemn interchanges on improving topics: mere politics was banned. And she did not much approve of humour. Not that Polk was much fun, but he was capable of telling jokes in stump speeches and of enjoying public adulation.

Hark, one united burst of joy
  By heart and tongue is work.
One chorus rends the listening air,
  Hurrah for James K. Polk!

Hurrah, indeed, thought Polk, who was beginning to miss his wife. He had just listened, with some difficulty, to a dozen verses recited in his honour by a young female resident of the Ninth Street Asylum for the Blind. Polk's difficulty was not with the girl's extremely loud voice and odd diction, but he wondered how, if she had really written this poesy herself, was she was able to fill the middle verses with so many visual images? Better not to ask.

Next, the president was taken to Tammany Hall where there were so many baroque patriotic objects arranged amidst the pack of portly, perspiring, cigar-smoking bosses, bagmen, and office holders that the politicos seemed to be in some kind of forest. Where, Polk wondered, did the Tammany mob find thirteen banners with authentic pre-revolutionary iconography, and how did they acquire so many flag stands with huge gold-leafed eagles atop each one, wings outspread, as if attempting to take the flagstaff and its banner to heaven? And couldn't they have stopped at three cheers? Six was a bit much before the presidential speech and then three more after. Very well disciplined, however, Polk had to admit.

Near midnight, when the toasts were done and a German band was thumping out polkas and marches, President Polk finally escaped.

The next day, Sunday, he heard the church bells and said a prayer of thanks that a day of peace was declared. He was a regular church-goer when in Washington because Sarah would have put a bayonet through his back if he had not marched purposively towards God's House.

Now, of his own choice, this Sunday, the 27th of June, he attends three separate church services: morning, afternoon, and evening. By nightfall, he is at peace and ready to depart New York.

NR. MEXICO CITY. 13 SEPTEMBER 1847

Costs

Manifest Destiny is not without cost: although it does produce one of the first non-sectarian, multi-cultural political movements in the American Southwest.

That is why thirty men, mostly immigrants, are standing on a massive scaffold near Mexico City. They are Americans, indeed, former American soldiers. They are labelled as being Irish because they belong to the San Patricio Battalion and are led by an Irish officer. In fact, only 40 percent of the unit of 200 men is Irish. And the Irish, mostly immigrants, are split evenly between Catholics and Protestants. What they all have in common, those who are about to die and also those who have been pardoned, is a hatred of serving in the U.S. army in the invasion of Mexico. They have deserted and become a foreign legion. Why? Their motives are unknowable, but range from vicious treatment by their U.S. sergeants to individual personality fractures to idealistic refusals to see a weaker people bullied by a stronger one. Whatever the reasons, they have served under Major John Riley, of County Galway, who had deserted first from the U.K. army in Canada and then from the U.S. army in Mexico. He designed their battle flag: emerald green with a harp and shamrock emblazoned.

The U.S. colonel in charge of the hangings has a nice sense of the moment. He likes the fact that these deserters were themselves captured by a band of Mexican deserters attached to the U.S. army. Before today he has already hanged sixteen San Patricios, and today he decides to coordinate the thirty hangings with the American attack on a nearby Mexican military college. With his spyglass, he can see the hilltop citadel being assaulted two miles away and when a U.S. flag is there raised in victory, he finally gives the signal to drop the prisoners. He watches to be sure that their necks are properly broken, then goes back to admiring the Stars and Stripes.

CHILLICOTHE, OHIO. 1849

Line Dancing

American Presbyterianism is now in its Mahogany Age, so weddings are not much fun: respectability is everything. And nothing could be more respectable than the marriage of Joseph Ruggles Wilson and Janet Woodrow. It is conducted in the Presbyterian manse in Chillicothe by the bride's father, the Rev. Thomas Woodrow.

The two sets of parents of this couple had themselves been married in a Presbyterian manse: the Woodrows in Carlisle, England, and the Wilsons in Philadelphia, not long after their ship had arrived from Londonderry, Ireland. These Wilsons were from Strabane (the bridegroom) and Belfast (the bride). They were married by the Rev. George C. Polk, orthodox Irish Presbyterian cleric.

The bridegroom at the 1849 manse wedding was ordained a Presbyterian minister a month after the union was celebrated.

The son of that union, Thomas Woodrow Wilson, later dropped the "Thomas" because its sonority was not, he judged, sufficiently respectable.

Woodrow Wilson married the daughter of a Presbyterian minister in a ceremony conducted in her father's manse.

Straight-line Presbyterian respectability of the highest sort. Woodrow Wilson became president of the Athens of American Presbyterianism, Princeton University; governor of New Jersey (before that became an indictable offence); and the twenty-eighth president of the United States.

"WHEATLAND," LANCASTER COUNTY, PENNSYLVANIA, AND WASHINGTON, D.C. 1850–68

Wrong Man, Wrong Time, Wrong Place

My firm conviction is that in four years from this time the union will not be in existence as it now exists. There will be two Republics ... There will be no civil

war. I sincerely hope that I am wrong, but such are my deliberate opinions.
Thus, James Buchanan wrote to a close friend in 1850 at the time when
Buchanan was conducting his quiet campaign for the Democratic nomi-
nation for the 1852 (or, if he failed) 1856 election. In the style of the time,
he stayed at home and had minions shuttle back and forth to the major
power brokers, talking principles at the top of their voices and patronage
in whispered tones. Buchanan was the last man to believe that he could
himself save the Union. He closed his letter with a weary *Nous verrons*.

The tired man in his sixties failed to gain the Democrats' nomina-
tion in 1852, but did so four years later and in March 1857 became the
fifteenth president of the USA and the third American-Irish one,
though that meant little to him. In fact, it's hard to tell what did matter. His inaugural speech, 4 March 1857, was hardly into its second
paragraph when Buchanan declared himself to be a lame duck president: *Having determined not to become a candidate for re-election, I shall
have no motive to influence my conduct in administering the Government
except the desire ably and faithfully to serve my country and to live in the
grateful memory of my countrymen.* He then vaguely indicated his disapproval of slavery and, simultaneously, his approval of the supreme
court's forthcoming Dred Scott decision (which he had helped to craft
and which was leaked to him): slave owners who moved into any of
the new U.S. territories could keep their human property. And he
burbled a bit about the perplexing Kansas-Nebraska matter, unaware
that a tiny civil war was taking place in that wild world.

The New York Stock Exchange having collapsed, the ensuing Panic
of 1857 brought the following comment in Buchanan's first Annual
Message to Congress late in 1857. *Our thanks are due to Almighty God
for the numerous benefits which He has bestowed upon this people, and our
united prayers ought to ascend to Him that He would continue to bless our
great Republic in time to come as He has blessed it in time past.* No new
federal projects would be initiated to make work, although a few
loans might be in order, Buchanan suggested. Economic depression
worried him less than the Kansas situation which he now noticed was
getting out of hand. To deal with that problem he used sympathetic-
magic. He did nothing, but instead had Brigham Young fired as governor of the Utah Territory and sent in the U.S. army to kill a few
Mormon rebels. There, that would show Kansas what he could do.

Yet, after John Brown raided Harper's Ferry in October 1859, President Buchanan told congress that *without the authority of Congress, the
President cannot fire a hostile gun in any case except to repel the attacks of
an enemy.* That was as close to a licence to conduct limited military

activities, as anyone could give the southern states. Oh yes, Buchanan added, as he had mentioned in his previous message to Congress, he would be pleased if he could be given permission to buy Cuba.

The Republican Abraham Lincoln was elected over the Democrat Stephen Douglas in November 1860, but James Buchanan was still in office when, in mid-November 1860, South Carolina made explicit its threat to leave the Union of American states. Three weeks later, in early December, Buchanan told Congress that no state had the right to secede, but at the same time he asked: *has the Constitution delegated to Congress the power to coerce a State which is attempting to withdraw or has actually withdrawn ...? After much serious reflection I have arrived at the conclusion that no such power has been delegated to Congress or to any other department of the Federal government.* He ended by suggesting mildly that the whole matter could be cleared up by a set of constitutional amendments that guaranteed the rights to slaves in those states in which slavery now, or later, would exist; that new territories could enter the Union either Free or Slave; and that fugitive-slave laws be declared binding throughout the nation. Buchanan did not, as Abraham Lincoln caustically noted in his own inaugural address in March 1861, bulk up the national army.

Thus, Buchanan, the soft-handed fixer, paved the way for the North American continent's biggest war between white people.

He retired to Wheatland and wrote a defence of his presidential administration. In this task he was considerably aided by a newfound appreciation of strict old-line Presbyterianism, with its emphasis upon predestination. He was admitted to that faith near the end of the Civil War, just before his apologia was published.

It was all very convenient, for his new-found religious faith provided a copper-bottomed theological justification for everything he had done: The Lord God in heaven knows, he told his editor, I could not have done a thing differently.

THE USA, 1851ff

Communication (1)

Irish women. Girls really, many of them.
　　Amazingly forgiving. Amazingly saving.

Hundreds of thousands of emigrant Catholic women become domestics. At first, in Irish boarding houses, hotels, taverns. Later, many find better posts in Yankee houses and businesses. Some enter the needle trades. They save and in a decade are buying small shops and boarding houses.

Not yet, though. First, they take care of family business. They fund tens of thousands of pre-paid transAtlantic tickets and often bring over to America their entire band of sisters and brothers. Men sometimes do the same, but it is the women who make the Atlantic fordable.

Forgiving? Extraordinarily so: farm women in Irish society had no chance of inheriting anything of real value, save in unusual cases such as widowhood in a family that had no male members. Young women were lucky to receive a dowry, and that was in the good times. Yet, these women send remittances home to Ireland regularly. They do so when they are single; when they are married, they do their best to put their hands on their husband's weekly pay packet before it disappears with him into a tavern. And they scrape pennies, hide them, and send money orders and cash remittances to the old people at home: to support the survival of the very social arrangements that were so parsimonious with them. Generation after generation. The amount is well over $1 million-a-year by 1870 and it continues, approaching $3 million on the eve of the Irish revolution.

This is no casual pattern. The tiny farms of the west and southwest of Ireland, thin scabs of ill-drained soil upon an impervious bedrock, survive only because generations of women leave for America, but nevertheless continue to pay a moral mortgage that they can neither understand nor deny.

THE USA. 1851ff

Communication (2)

Lord, in their desperate, baffled, stumm quality they break your heart.

Early in the 1850s, newspapers throughout the United States fill column after column with real news. They have done it before, but now the form blooms. Black orchids: thousands of advertisements for missing brothers, sisters, parents, cousins. INFORMATION

WANTED the columns say. They don't say Information Wanted by Broken Families. They should.

INFORMATION WANTED. James Craddock, native of parish Kilurse, Co. Galway. When last heard from was in Perrytown, Mercer County, Pa. Any information respecting him will be thankfully received by his brother, Myles Craddock, Bath Maine.

INFORMATION WANTED. Michael Tobin, from Miltown, Malbay, Co Cork, who lived in Quebec in October 1847. When last heard of was in Savannah Ga. Any information respecting him will be thankfully received by his sister Hannah Tobin, care of Rev. Wm. McDonald, Manchester N.H.

Hundreds of thousands of these part-told stories and no idea of how they turned out.

Notice, though, that most of the missing are men.

And do not assume that their going missing always was accidental. Losing themselves in America, rejecting the pain of their past, was neither unusual nor a stupid way of coping.

NEW YORK CITY. 1851

Communications (3)

Honest women: sort of. The Irish whores of the Five Points knew themselves for what they were and would have carved the liver out of anyone who thought of them as Sex Workers, or any nineteenth-century equivalent.

Mind you, they worked hard and gave value for money.

A competitive trade, what with all the fresh young talent coming off the boats. Five-a-penny the whores were. Or, to be more accurate, and if you were ambitious, two-for-a-dollar.

Like their more respectable sisters, many of them were great savers.

When their pimps or husbands (overlapping categories) asked them in surprise where they'd found the money to buy a new shift or a piece of knockdown furniture for the tenement, they would answer with the phrase used by generations of dissimilating Irish rural women.

Ah, I just bought it off the egg-money.

NEW YORK CITY. 1853

Leading the Blind

When S. Grover Cleveland joined the staff of the famous New York Institution for the Blind, the memory of the visit by President Polk in June 1847 still was a treasured one. Each year since that visit, the top girl student recited at the school's Open Day the ode to Polk that had been delivered on that occasion.

Cleveland – known as Big Steve to his friends – was sixteen years of age and ready for college, but the death of his clergyman father put any chances of further education to rest. He was fortunate that his older brother was the principal of the male section which, on the female side boasted blind Fanny Crosby, one of the nineteenth century's most popular hymn writers. Big Steve taught part-time and was the institution's book-keeper and bursar.

He and his brother loathed the place and they left the next year: bad food, low pay, little social life, and all those depressing blind children who were taught that their lot in life was not a lot. S. Grover Cleveland learned as much from the blind as they did from him. He was given an older "mixed" class – both boys and girls – to teach and he discovered that he liked to touch things. Nothing improper, but he especially liked to introduce an unknown object into the classroom, and then have a blind girl guide his hands as he closed his eyes and pretended to be sightless. Thus, like her, he fed the sensation from his fingertips to his brain, uncensored by the prying eyes that his Presbyterian clerical father had told him must be ever-vigilant against temptation.

EAST OF THE MISSISSIPPI. 1854–55

Prosaic

Jeremiah O'Donovan, the McGonagall of Irish poets in the United States, spends 1854–55 travelling from. town to town, flogging to Irish Catholic immigrants his History of Ireland in Epic Verse. The lyric masterpiece only covers the period up to 1690, so he has a lot of time to fill.

O'Donovan keeps copious notes on all the Irish people he meets and before departing from each town or city posts a parcel of scratchings to his home address. He plans a big travel book and also a verse version of his meetings with the American-Irish. Most encounters are with an angel (if female) or a saint (if male).

Thus he meets a young female ferry-keeper. He tells her that he is an eminent surgeon on his way to perform an errand of mercy in the most desperate case of his professional career. She, angel that she is, refuses his proffered payment of the ferry fee. His innate gallantry and glorious prose style produce a chivalrous response. *This negative only augmented my generosity, and as my resolution is always, and in all case inflexible, I then insisted on her taking what I offered. Now, my dear reader, came the critical moment. After a little voluntary pause, I took her tenderly by the hand, and reverently bowed, bent, scraped, sobbed, sighed, sorrowed and said nothing, and at last, with considerable difficulty and reluctance, I took my departure.*

Curiously, O'Donovan's marvelously orotund observations about America are full of Irish shoe and boot-makers. Literally. He became matey with the shoemen of Cincinnati and they gave him the gnomic key to addressing their brotherhood all across the USA. In return, he *acknowledged the superiority of their intellectual attainments* over other trades.

He sells a lot of epic verse to men who keep tacks in their mouth.

Still, O'Donovan never forgets that all Irish people – and he means the real Irish, not the Protestant drippings of the oppressors – *are a missionary race, scattered all over the globe for [the purpose of] spreading the unerring doctrine of the primitive church among heathens and infidels, and that it is for that very purpose that they are so numerously preserved by Divine Providence.*

Having written those words, he moves on to Baltimore, where he is very, very sick.

CASTLE GARDEN, NEW YORK CITY. 1855

Protection

Not solely the Irish: the abuse of all immigrants into America is so vicious that it has to be stopped if the USA is to attract the human material it needs to conquer the inlands of central North America, while simultaneously undergoing the birth agonies of its own industrial revolution. New York City is the most abusive landing place, the first place that must be reformed. How can immigrant jobbers be permitted onto immigrant vessels before any government officials? There they sell bogus railway and canal tickets, trade flash money for foreign coins, direct in-comers to venal boarding houses and to labour contractors who would be dismissed as slave overseers for being too harsh.

So bad is the scene in New York harbour that in 1855 the Commissioners of Immigration create a protective enclave for newcomers: the wharf at Castle Garden. It becomes the Gateway to the New World.

Now sailing ships drop anchor in the North River and the passengers are brought to the Castle Garden wharf by steam launch. Ocean-going steam vessels are brought all the way to the wharf by pilot vessels. The entire enclave is fenced and closely guarded. Outside the fence, touts and con artists mill and shout their wares. Inside: calm. Each migrant is registered. The commissioners run a labour register, a railway and canal ticket office, and a money exchange. This model is soon adopted at other ports.

For the first time, the USA is controlling immigration.

NEW YORK CITY. 1856

Leader in the Promised Land

From the beginning of language, scared men and women have sat around fires and told lies to each other. Analgesic lies: the seed of the deepest literature, the sort that temporarily puts a universe in order and gives hope. Even false hope is better than none; even a chimerical god is better than a lightless sky; even a fantasy hero is more comforting than considering the enhulling enemies.

So in the Five Points and Bowery of south Manhattan Island even the hardest men and women in the world, while professing to fear no one, make a shrine of a language. It is a little pile of myth that they create to protect themselves.

The Bowery Boys (sometimes: the Bowery Boyoos), almost entirely Irish Catholic, established well before the Famine, are constantly at war with a dozen or more other gangs, some Irish, others native-American: the Dead Rabbits, the O'Connell Guards, the True Blue Americans, and on and on. Most of the gangs are organized around volunteer fire companies, but are funded by prostitution, gambling, all forms of thieving, and protection rackets that terrorize recent immigrants. They are good at what they do, and the better established gangs tie into the new Tammany political network.

When the men and women (some of them more frightening than the men) of the Bowery gang sit in a saloon in the darkest hours of night, shortly before dawn, they smoke cigars, drink neat whiskey, and create their tribal god. His figure slowly forms in the expanding wreaths of their cigar smoke. He is an admixture of Cuchulainn, Hercules, and Moses. Named "Mose," he is the mythic warrior, skilled strategist, and forever-protector of the Bowery toughs.

He died in 1848, but lives. Mose: eight feet tall, massively strong, hands like an iron stamping-press, boots with copper soles as big as the lid of a firkin barrel, armed always with a butcher's cleaver, able to pull an oak tree from the ground, capable of carrying a full barrel of whiskey under each arm and, most importantly, of dealing incapacity and death to anyone who touches disrespectfully the Bowery Boys' turf.

With Mose there, briefly corporeal in the moment just before darkness is broken by the first splinters of dawn, how could anyone be afraid?

BLACKHEATH, ENGLAND. 1857

Pond Scum? or Penicillin?

The algae that, by 1960, cover two-thirds of the Protestant minds in America, have a very precise origin. Yes, there is the matter of ambient conditions and confluences and synergies, but when all is said and done the genetic line runs directly from Ireland and leads to Billy Graham and all his imitators. The starting point is precise, the modes of holy contagion well-defined. Remember the Rev. Mr. Darby?

The moment of creation is when John Nelson Darby, Anglican priest and avocational ascetic, came down from the Wicklow mountains in 1827, broken in body, unstable in mind, incandescent in belief. He creates a tiny religion in Dublin whose chief characteristic is that it is everything that the Church of Ireland is not. His Brethren are not ordained, not salaried, not corrupt, not accepting of dogma. They are committed to a literal reading of the Bible, and what a reading it is.

These people expand in England into the Plymouth Brethren and of course fight with each other. In 1849 the Darbyites (who are the Exclusive Brethren, and should be called the Extremely Exclusive Brethren) split from the others.

But the Brethren's circle is not broken, for the Rev. William Kelly – an Ulster Anglican priest, turned freelance Bible expositor – still respects Darby's beliefs even if the great man will no longer break bread with him. The Rev. Mr Kelly begins in 1857 to edit the Bible Treasury, a task that he sticks with until his death fifty years later. And, simultaneously, he edits in thirty-four volumes the ravenings of Darby, making the incoherent at least seem intentional.

1857: The Bible Treasury first arrives in America and quickly becomes the inexpensive source of good, clear Christian ideas, the very thing that pastors need when preparing sermons for their Baptist, Church of Christ, rural and small town Presbyterian congregations. The mind of John Nelson Darby, mediated by William Kelly's biblical commentary, will control the thinking of a lot of everyday people. Just wait.

BOSTON, MASSACHUSETTS. 1858

Let's Reflect on This

The last thing the keepers of the Irish memory have ever considered is learning anything from the modern Jews. In the case of America's Irish Catholic royalty, that is a pity. The dominant Jewish practice for the last 2,000 years has been (with exceptions of course), to trace property ownership and naming practices (David Ben Yosef, etc.) through the male line. But the really big question – are you Jewish? – has been decided by the female line: is your mother Jewish? If not, you're not, according to the purists.

We would understand a lot more about the Kennedys, and about hundreds of thousands of Irish families, if that had been the Irish mode of memory.

Take the case of the Founding Father of President Kennedy's clan. That creature is Patrick Kennedy (the Wexford cooper) who migrated during the Famine; the next link is his son Patrick Joseph Kennedy, who made the first family money and became a smooth Boston political broker; and then the hubristically ambitious Joseph P. Kennedy, who became very rich, was the U.S. ambassador to England and who drove his children mercilessly towards the summit of American political achievement. That's a nice progression and makes sense on the surface: successive generations of males rising by standing on each others' shoulders.

Except: here (as in the hundreds of thousands of anonymous cases of Irish families that do not rise so high), it does not work. Both the cultural continuity and the shaping of children depended in this case, as in so many others, on an Irish woman about whom we know little – but without whose strength as Founding Mother, none of the later male genealogy makes sense.

Here it is the nearly anonymous Bridget Murphy – how much closer to anonymous can one get in nineteenth-century Irish Catholic America than to be named Bridget Murphy? – who married the cooper Patrick Kennedy and bore him three daughters and then, in January 1858, a son, Patrick Joseph. Less than a year later, father Patrick died of cholera and Bridget became the sole support of a family, surrounded by the infestations, moral and physical, of an East Boston slum. This is the point where the story might end, with the family crumbling, the mother losing control of the children and of herself, and the whole lot drifting into generation-after-generation of poor education, bad jobs, crime: the poverty trap.

Yet notice, twenty years later, in 1878, this single mother has produced a strapping son, who has been well schooled through, roughly, grade eight, in Catholic schools, knows how to work (he starts as a stevedore) and certainly knows how to make money – and how to save it. By age twenty he is working in a saloon and he is doing what his mother has taught him: save, save. And be alert, keep the customers happy and your mouth shut. Bridget Murphy has somehow kept things together, and, crucially, everyone's pride intact. She has been a hair dresser at Boston's Jordan Marsh store and there she learned what acceptable appearance was when dealing with the Quality and how one works one's way into their approval and thus their pocket books.

And notice again, in 1898, her son is partner in three saloons, one of them very lucrative and almost up-market, and he owns several large pieces of real estate. Here Patrick Joseph Kennedy was not behaving like your average Irish stevedore, but like a group we know something about: Irish women who have no men – widows and permanent spinsters – and who have a tiny bit of money in hand. They are the world's greatest savers; and they invest in property. No speculations, no gold-futures, no Czarist bonds: in property, boarding houses first, and tenements, and, if things go well, hostelries. Patrick Joseph Kennedy, you see, acts the way he has been taught by an Irish mother who taught him save, save, save, invest, invest, invest, but always in real things, places where people live, eat, or drink.

It is the farthest thing from an insult to suggest that Patrick Joseph's acquiring of investments, and, indeed, his quiet style as he grew to be one of Boston's major Democratic political operators, was female. As a politico: listening and being cunning, rather than adopting lead-the-army male bravado. Irish Catholics in trouble came to Patrick Joseph for advice and aid the way a child comes to a mother. He took care of them and they remembered.

JFK's becoming president of the United States makes no sense without the Founding Mother. She kept the line Irish; she maintained the family's decency in its worst hours; she did her job and, like her counterparts all over Irish-Catholic America, quietly disappeared from the story.

NEAR NEWBLISS, COUNTY MONAGHAN.
THE 1850S AND 60S

Geology

Martha Moorehead, daughter of an Anglo-Irish landlord, and Hannah Kirk, daughter of a Presbyterian strong farming family, grew up at the same time and within ten miles of each other in the small lake-district that was formed in County Monaghan by retreating glaciers. Yet they never met: less surprising than it may seem, for they were of a different caste in religion and social level; and Monaghan itself multiplies physical distances, with roads twisting around drumlins and half-circling the scores of small lakes and marshes, before meandering on their unmarked way to next-to-nowhere.

Martha marries Tyrone Power (Mark II), son of the drowned comedian. He is a senior officer in the U.K. army, whose commission his famous father had wangled through Lord Melbourne, a fan of overacting and farce, as anyone who has studied his dealings with the young Victoria realizes. They meet when Power is detailed to oversee relief works during the Famine and he eventually returns, having fought in the Crimea, to marry her. She brings an estate, Annagh-ma-kerrig, of the middling sort: an austere ten-bedroom house that overlooks a private lake. It is hers free and clear, which makes her the economic lever of the family, and she does not let her now half-pay husband forget it.

Martha keeps in touch with the children of Tyrone Power (Mark I), who are her own children's cousins. One of the offspring of the famous comedian, the third son, Harold Power, becomes an actor, emigrates to America, where he marries and has a son: Tyrone Power (Mark III) who, by virtue of his stunning handsomeness and relentless womanizing, becomes, from the late 1930s through the late 'fifties, one of America's best known film actors.

Hannah Kirk also participated in a theatrical tradition, although she would have been insulted to have been told so. She had emigrated to Scotland and married a young clergyman who turned into one of the Kirk of Scotland's most famous preachers: Dr. Thomas Guthrie, a white-maned prophet. One of his sons became a medical doctor and took a practice in the north of Ireland, where he met the young woman who was the only offspring of Tyrone Power of Annagh-ma-kerrig. From this union is born Tyrone Guthrie, a distant cousin, and, eventually a good friend, of Tyrone Power. Guthrie, raised in Ireland until public school, becomes one of England's most successful and front-edge stage directors in the 1930s and 40s and an evangelist of the gospel of regional theatre in Canada and the USA in the 1950s and 60s.

The two Tyrones, Irish-born or Irish-spawned, remnants of the retreating Protestant planters in Counties Monaghan and Cavan: yet, like those artful and confusing hills left by the retreating glaciers, special, nearly unique.

TUCKALEECHEE COVE, TENNESSEE. 1859

John Mitchel's Perfect Revenge

For a time, John Mitchel did well in the North. His "Jail Journal" ran serially in 1854 in New York, and sold very well when the pieces were collected as a book. The portions denigrating Charles Gavan Duffy and William Smith O'Brien were taken as gospel by his American readers. And they did not have much trouble with his attitude towards his fellow-felons in Van Diemen's Land – "What to do with all our robbers, burglars and forgers? Why, hang them, hang them!" – those were the opinions of a forthright fellow, best sort of patriot.

The North, though, rubbed Mitchel the wrong way and in April 1855 he bought 130 acres in Tuckaleechee Cove in the mountain country of east Tennessee. It was a perpetually poor area (few of his neighbours could afford even a single slave), and why he settled there is a mystery. But living there (interrupted by various Irish-American patriotic missions) allowed Mitchel to get even with most of the world he hated, which was most of the world. And, as a fortuitous by-product, he was permitted time to write what is easily the greatest Irish novel of the nineteenth century, and the most effective piece of Irish hate-literature ever. Full stop.

In Tennessee, Mitchel wrote for a small weekly paper that had been founded in late 1857, the *Southern Citizen*. In its pages in 1858 he wrote a series of public letters explaining the history of the Young Ireland movement and, almost as a secondary topic, the course and meaning of the Great Famine. Mitchel's letters were a private revenge, on William Smith O'Brien and Charles Gavan Duffy in particular, but fundamentally, on any Irish patriot who was not John Mitchel: compelling reading if one were personally committed to Irish nationalist politics, but not of much interest to anyone else. Where Mitchel switched from encaustic miniaturist to broad-brush master propagandist was when he dealt with the Starvation.

John Mitchel invented the Great Famine.

In this sense: before Mitchel, no writer, no seanacaí, no priest, no patriot, had been able to force the Starvation into a pattern. Mitchel did this in a brilliant artistic triumph, one that is killing people to this day. For Mitchel transformed Ireland's greatest tragedy into a conspiracy and did this in a mode anybody who reads English can understand, and identify with. His formulation, like all master-propaganda, is a big, believable lie. "The Almighty indeed sent the potato blight, but the English created the Famine." Thus, the immense bad fortune of the Irish people is transformed into a political engine, one fired by the pure anthracite of hate, an engine that will draw the Irish national cause forward. Mitchel collects and reshapes his newspaper columns into a book, *The Last Conquest of Ireland (perhaps)*, and it is published in Dublin in 1860 and in London and New York the next year.

John Mitchel would have been satisfied with the effect of his work. Nothing written about the Famine since then has escaped its magnetic field, whether one is repelled by it or attracted. More than a century later, Cecil Woodham-Smith followed Mitchel's line and produced *The Great Hunger*, which some authorities cite as the single best-selling non-fiction book in the English language. Certainly it is the biggest-seller dealing with Ireland: ever. In 1996, to the horror of most historians of Ireland, Mitchel again revenged himself: the New York State department of education required a unit on the Irish Famine as "genocide" to be taught in all New York state schools before high school graduation.

Mitchel had taken an event that was beyond indignation and turned it into a source of burning, highly personalized, anti-Protestant, anti-British hatred.

For two years, 1860–62, he was in Paris, but then returned to America because his principles called him. Not only did he believe in states' rights (as did William Smith O'Brien) but he actively advocated slavery for the blacks. Mitchel's skills as a propaganda master were now well-known and Jefferson Davies enlisted him as editor of the *Enquirer*, the Confederacy's main propaganda sheet. He was as brilliant in attacking the Union states of America as he had been in attacking the Union of Great Britain and Ireland. And equally sincere: he tried to enlist in the ambulance brigade and two of his sons died for the Confederacy and a third lost an arm.

Just before he began to write the letters that became *The Last Conquest of Ireland (perhaps)*, John Mitchel had written a personal letter to a Tipperary priest who was shocked at his advocating slavery. "All my behaviour from November 1845 seems to myself to be consistent, to be of one piece." Indeed it was: for at the same time he was telling another correspondent, "I consider negro slavery to be the best state of existence for the negro."

John Mitchel indeed was consistent all of his adult life: his heart pumped the constant vitriol of hate, and his eyes, always and ever, saw only in black and white.

THE UNITED STATES. 1861–65

Heroic and Baffling

"They did what you told them to do." High praise from a field officer at the end of the Civil War for Irish Catholic immigrants in the service of the Confederacy. *The other boys just did what they liked.*

The bravery of the new Catholic American-Irish on both sides of America's great bloodletting is too well documented to need arguing. They were praised all around. That helped to naturalize them in post-war society, but their split allegiance puzzled many. An Irish visitor guyed this puzzlement a bit, but he had the problem right. The native American will tell you, he said, that *North of the Potomac, Paddy shouted that the Union must be preserved, and Secession put down at all cost. South of the Potomac, Paddy declared himself the upholder of State Rights and free whipping of the Nigger. In both cases, he was equally ignorant; he knew nothing whatever about the Constitution, and he was wholly unaware what State Rights meant. The nearest thing he had to a reasonable motive was his uniform hatred of the Nigger; but that didn't prevent him from, on the whole, backing the North rather more than the South.*

Later studies show that Irish-Catholic immigrants fought in the Civil War in nearly the same proportion as did Americans as a whole and that they distributed themselves on the two sides in the same proportions as did Americans as a group. The same was true of American-Irish Protestants, though they were more apt to be second, third, and fourth generation. The reason more Irish of both sorts fought for the North was that the North had more of everything – industrial strength, population, munitions, and the Irish were simply part of that "more."

At home in Ireland, the Southern cause was overwhelmingly favoured, both by nationalists and anti-nationalists. The anti-nationalists, most living in Ulster, objected to what the Union blockade did to their textile industry. And the nationalists saw the North's snuffing out of the independence of the South as a parallel to Britain's having done the same thing to Ireland. Few echoes of Daniel O'Connell's brave anti-slavery speeches were to be heard.

A litmus item: of the "Martyrs of 1848" who make their way from Australian exile to the U.S., only Thomas Francis Meagher becomes passionately and unambiguously committed to the North in general and the cause of anti-slavery in particular, and then only as a result of a conversion in his beliefs in April 1861. Most of the other heroes drift off into ambiguity. Others, as in the case of Richard O'Gorman and John Mitchel, actively support the slave states as being morally right.

Such a baffling contrast. At the disastrous first battle of Bull Run, Thomas Francis Meagher fought heroically, and back in the Irish section of New York, he made the most forgiving of toasts. *Now that you have testified your loving admiration for the brave Irish soldiers of the Union, I call upon you to give three cheers for the two sons of John Mitchel, who are fighting as bravely on the other side.*

Mitchel learns of the toast and, from Paris, writes venomously, suggesting that Meagher's Irish battalion should be fighting British red-coats, not the decent protectors of Southern freedom. They, who faced the Confederate General Beauregard's *artillery and rifles until Bull Run ran red, will not be likely to shrink on the day (when will it dawn, that white day?) that they will have the comparatively light task of whipping their weight in redcoats.*

BULL RUN, VIRGINIA. 1861

Between the Lines

Contemporary observation: *Perhaps the men of the Irish Brigade [the 69th New York infantry, augmented by the 63rd, 88th, and the Second New York artillery battalion] lived on better terms with the rebels than any others. Often times, when the rebel pickets were bitterly firing on our men, they would cease as soon as the Brigade relieved the others, and a most friendly feeling would soon spring up, and a regular barter of coffee, sugar, whiskey and tobacco take place! An officer on our side would hold up a paper, as a signal that he wanted an exchange. This would be answered on the other side. They would meet between the lines, enquire about mutual friends; would perhaps learn that some cousin or dear friend was on the other side, and send for him. The canteen would be emptied, old times and friends discussed, as the little party seated themselves under shelter of some clump of trees between the lines.*

Early wartime civility: not long to last.

Crackers for Christ

They all were believers in the South, states' rights, and slavery. No doubts there.

Cyrus Ingerson Scofield, a weedy nineteen-year-old who has to lie about his age, enlists in the Tennessee infantry in May 1861. This is an unusual step as he had been raised on a Michigan farm. But he had lived in his late teens with his sister in Lebanon, Tennessee and come to believe in the Southern cause.

Scofield, who lives until 1921, performs in the early twentieth century the most radical rewrite of the Jewish and Christian scriptures since the Reformation. When he does so he centralizes in his system of interpretation the views of John Nelson Darby. As the Scofield Bible becomes the favourite version of American fundamentalists and, later, evangelicals, he helps mightily to win the mind of American Protestantism to Darby's outré County Wicklow Christianity.

Branson Radish Riley moves his family from Green County, Indiana, back to his home turf of Kentucky shortly after the Civil War starts. He hails from an Irish family that turned from Catholic to Protestant so long ago that the event is lost to mind. A strong proponent of slavery, he nevertheless does not serve in the military, but raises children and tobacco on a small cash farm. His one regret in life is that he has not been able to fulfill his lifelong ambition: to be a preacher.

His son, *William Bell Riley*, born in lower Indiana just before the move back to Kentucky, will fulfill that ambition for Branson Riley. W.B. Riley, who lives until 1947, becomes one of the two strongest figures in the American fundamentalist movement, an unswerving promoter of John Nelson Darby's literalist and apocalyptic reading of the Bible, and the organizational godfather of the twentieth century's most influential preacher, the Rev. Dr. Billy Graham.

Like the Rileys, the family of *Benjamin Coffey* has been American Protestant so long they cannot remember when they were Irish Catholics. Ben, in his twenties, joins the Ninth Carolina Regiment and is part of Pickett's Charge at Gettysburg. There he falls with a shrapnel wound that eventually requires his left leg to be amputated. And, while writhing in pain on the ground, a bullet takes out his right eye.

A remarkably resilient man, Ben Coffey lives until 1916. He is the material of folklore but, sadly, he never meets on this earth his grandson, Billy Graham.

The Worst Job in the World (1)

Earlier in history there had been worse jobs in the world than being appointed Abraham Lincoln's military governor of Tennessee, but none at present. In the English-speaking world, the only similar job historically was to be the monarch of England, Ireland, and Scotland during the War of the Three Kingdoms, and that resulted in the unfortunate incumbent, Charles I, having his head turned into a bowling ball. Tennessee was fractioned into pro- and anti-slave forces and (what was not the same thing) into pro- and anti-secession factions. The Union forces, ostensibly united, were themselves split by byzantine intrigues, not least among the military officers themselves. Everyone had guns. At any given moment, there were half-a-dozen sides in play and the permutations of alliances shifted as swiftly as the patterns on a child's kaleidoscope.

Andrew Johnson was the right choice. He had the hard eyes and pockmarked face that said he meant business: he had never had the disadvantage of being handsome and long ago had decided that being forceful was quite enough. He carried almost no cultural baggage. Johnson had not spent a day at school in his life. He was vaguely aware that his father's parents had come from County Antrim in the late 1750s and that his mother, Mary McDonough, was American-Irish and also his stepfather (Andrew's father died when the lad was four), Turner Daughtey; so too Andrew's eventual wife, Eliza McCardle. Of course they were all Protestant here in America, albeit of no particular sort: finding a Roman Catholic in rural Tennessee was harder than discovering gold nuggets. The deity Andrew Johnson most worshipped was the late Andrew Jackson.

As a brigadier-general, Andrew Johnson mixed the occasional show-execution of spies and mutineers with a courtliness to wealthy slave-owners, so long as they stayed on the sidelines. He allowed himself to be spat on by the Confederate belles of Tennessee (that was their favourite form of political expression) and merely bowed to them and passed on. As a slave owner himself, Johnson was the right man for Lincoln to place in charge of raising 50,000 black troops. No northerner could speak their language.

By saving Tennessee for the Union, Johnson did as much as any general who fought on the conventional military front. The only senator from a secessionist state to stay with the Union, his work in Tennessee made him a national hero. Lincoln, needing a southerner, nominated him as his vice-presidential candidate, and on the 4th of March, 1865, Johnson took the oath of office, vertical, but otherwise dead drunk. That was the beginning of the end of his career.

FAIR OAKS, VIRGINIA. 1 JULY 1862

Pep Talk

Boys, I stake my stars on you.
General Edwin ("Bull") Sumner points to the stars on his epaulettes. He is encouraging the men of the Irish Brigade before battle.
If you run away now, I'll tear these off …
He thunks his epaulettes so hard that it sounds like someone is chopping wood, and then adds less resonantly, *… and run with you.*

NR. HARPER'S FERRY, VIRGINIA. 14 SEPTEMBER 1862

The Curing of Souls

Father William Corby, chaplain to the Irish Brigade, was a regular priest, but far from a monastic. He marched with the men for three years. His detailed memoirs, which with priestly discretion he long kept to himself, were only published in the 1890s, shortly before his death. They are guilelessly revealing.

Near Harper's Ferry, after a Union victory, men and horses, dead and dying, distributed themselves upon the landscape. *I dismounted occasionally, and when I found men still living, did what I could for them.*

If Catholics, I heard their confession, and, if Protestants, baptized them as individual cases required.

Fr. Corby later prepares the Irish Brigade for the Battle of Gettysburg. He permits an outside observer to detail his actions. *The Brigade stood in column of regiments, closed in mass. As a large majority of its members were Catholics, the chaplain of the Brigade, the Rev. William Corby, proposed to give a general absolution to all the men before going into the fight ... Father Corby stood on a large rock in front of the Brigade. Addressing the men, he explained what he was about to do, saying that each one could receive the benefit of the absolution by making a sincere Act of Contrition and firmly resolving to embrace the first opportunity of confessing his sins, urging them to do their duty, and reminding them of the high and sacred nature of their trust as soldiers and the noble object for which they fought ...*

As he closed his address, every man, Catholic and non-Catholic, fell on his knees with his head bowed. Then, stretching forth his right hand towards the Brigade, Father Corby pronounced the words of absolution.

More than one-third of the men are killed in the next two days.

Father Corby serves with the Brigade until September 1864. He becomes president of Notre Dame University.

NEW YORK CITY. 13-17 JULY 1863

The Dark Passions of the Heart

Not long after he escaped from Australia and made American shores as an Irish nationalist hero, Thomas Meagher writes to his comrade of '48, Charles Gavan Duffy. In New York City, he has found *more bigotry and intolerance in this country, amongst our countrymen, than ever I was sensible of in Ireland.* He means race-bigotry

He is right, but that in the middle nineteenth century Irish Catholic immigrants have the worst relations of any ethic or religious group with African-Americans hardly needs explaining. America sets the two groups battling for scraps and inevitably they maul each other. The Irish especially hate Free Coloureds, for they directly compete, man against man, for jobs. They are the ones the Irish go for when they race riot – as on the New Orleans docks and in Brooklyn and in

Memphis – and the Free Coloureds are the ones who have no protectors. Before 1865, in slave states, one did not mess with blacks who were the property of powerful owners.

The Draft Riot, of 1863 in New York, is misnamed.

It was America's worst race riot, and, though it had flank issues, race was at the heart.

President Lincoln's formal Emancipation Proclamation of January 1863 set the stage. It had been expected ever since his preliminary proclamation of September 1861, but now it inflamed two groups: the African slaves, whose hope it is, and the Irish Catholic immigrants of the post-Famine years, who dread it: more than ever, they will have to fight with the newly freed blacks for the lowest jobs.

Then, in March 1863, a Draft Law is passed, to become effective in July. Any Irish immigrant with a brain can read the probable future effects of the law. He will be drafted to fight for a cause that he does not believe in and, if he is lucky enough to return in one piece, he will find that he has lost his place on the docks, in the cart line or in the arduous sector of the building trade, to the very black-skinned people whose Emancipation from slavery he has opposed. The Draft Law is not just a recipe for riot, but for civil war within the North itself.

The first ballots for Union service are drawn in New York just a week after the Battle of Gettysburg. Saturday, 11 July is the first draw and everything is quiet. This will go well, the Union authorities believe, wrongly: a week-end is a long time in Irish history. On Monday, Manhattan starts to burn. First, Irish collaborators with the draft system are destroyed – Col. H.F. O'Brien is kicked to death and Col. Robert Nugent, an officer of the Irish Brigade who is chief organizer of the draft, is torched out of his house. Then, the Irish turn to general sack, arson, murder. It takes 2,300 police (who lose nearly 300 men), 1,000 Volunteer Specials (mostly young men of property), and, eventually, a reserve platoon of the Irish Brigade to quell 70,000 rioters. Serious rioters: between 1,200 and 1,500 white insurrectionists are killed by police and army; over 1,000 of these are Irish Catholics.

That is the white death count.

Nobody knows the cost to non-whites, the real losers, but certainly more than all the whites combined.

The fundamentally racial nature of the New York Draft Riot is obscured later by a strange piece of special pleading: that the Draft Law was unfair and, therefore, inflammatory, because it allowed men who

had $300 in pocket to buy their way out of the draft – a social-class is-
sue, in other words, not racial. Unfair, certainly, but it had little to do
with the immigrant Irish who could not have bought themselves out
in the usual case if the amount had been only $50.

The riot pivoted on the real issue: Irish men would be taken away
and their livings would be stolen by black labourers.

The behaviour of Irish Catholic family women makes this clear. Their
incredibly violent actions make sense when one does what they did:
read or listen to the Draft Law carefully. Suddenly it becomes obvious to
them that the act is aimed at grabbing married men! The only large un-
tapped pool of bodies the Union has left. Married men! In the Five
Points, Bowery, the fourth, sixth, fourteenth wards, these Irish Catholic
immigrant women, who are holding together families, fighting for a
touch of respectability, pinching pennies to open savings accounts at the
Emigrant Savings Bank, struggling to keep their children alive and, if
lucky, in elementary schools, these women understand that the Draft
Law is nothing less than an attack on Irish Catholic families.

Getting rid of former slaves is both displaced aggression and economically rational. Lucky are the blacks who are merely lynched.
Cruelly unlucky are those whom the Irish women get hold of. Their
eyes are gouged out. Tongues cut, or, worse, bitten off by family
women in full howl. So many are castrated by the vengeful Valkyries
that one saloon empties its pale-blue bottle of pickled eggs and fills it
with testicles that the women have severed from the Africans. When
flying squads of Irish women find an African choking on a lynch-
rope, their favourite recreation is to douse him in petroleum distillate
and watch him flip about as the pain overcomes his increasing suffocation. These actions and hundreds more odious comprise the racial
jacquarie that no one wants to remember.

Friends, their actions say, you simply do not fuck with the Irish
Catholic family. Learn that.

ROME. 1864

Home Rule

Bishop Patrick Lynch of Charleston is not happy in Rome. The native
of Clones, County Monaghan, had been a protégé of Paul Cullen at

the Irish College in Rome and he expected that he would have the ear of the Pope, almost by right. Instead, His Holiness stalls.

Lynch is the Confederacy's envoy to the Vatican and has been charged by Jefferson Davis with gaining political recognition for the South. As is the case with all the Catholic bishops in the South, he favours the Confederacy, but with perhaps excessive enthusiasm: when Fort Sumter fell, he had a Te Deum sung in Charleston's cathedral. Bishop Lynch owns nearly a hundred African slaves, and sees the case of the Confederacy as being the same as the case for Ireland running its own affairs. He write pamphlets in favour of household slavery, for which he finds in ancient Rome a noble example.

When Pius IX finally sees him, it is only as an individual bishop, not as a diplomatic envoy. His Holiness refuses diplomatic recognition to the Confederacy and Bishop Lynch returns home at war's end only by virtue of a presidential pardon.

APPOMATTOX, VIRGINIA. 9 APRIL 1865

The Long View

Having spent significant portions of the Civil War stone cold sober, Ulysses Grant remembers with clarity many moments and matters about the war, including the surrender negotiations with General Lee.

These instants of sober recall aid him considerably when, twenty years later, he sits down at his summer home in Long Branch, New Jersey, to assay the war in his memoirs. He remembers thousands of unrelated incidents, but they do not add up to much. In the long perspective, the only thing he can see that the Civil War accomplished was in the side battles and civic matters that received little publicity at the time – the breaking of the Plains Indians; the defeat of the Sioux in Minnesota; the mining rushes into the Colorado and Nevada territories; the fractioning of huge tracts of land into further pieces of the U.S. empire: Arizona, Idaho, Montana. The Homestead Act of 1862 conquered more land than did the Union Army, he reckons.

It is probable that the Indians would have had control of these lands for a century yet but for the war. We must conclude, therefore, that wars are not always evils unmixed with some good.

WASHINGTON, D.C. 15 APRIL 1865

The Worst Job in the World (2)

Unlike his vice-presidential swearing-in, when Andrew Johnson took the presidential oath of office he was steady on his feet. His seriousness was underscored by the threatening glower that he unconsciously projected when he was determined to do something right, whether convincing a political opponent or punching him in the face. Johnson had one great advantage over most U.S. presidents in that when younger he had mastered an honest trade – tailoring: almost all the others were trained as lawyers, professional killers (that is, as military men) or were rentiers. Knowing intimately how a suit of clothes is built out of disparate pieces is not a bad background for repairing the rips and tatterings of the fabric that covers the body politic.

But Andrew Johnson was the wrong tailor. His previous stature as a hero in the North had come from his being a southerner who was willing to be tough on the Confederacy. Soon, the war over and the Restoration begun – Johnson hated the word Reconstruction and seldom used it – he was suddenly a southerner who was too soft on the South. Forgiveness, amity, reconciliation may have been attractive goals in the former secessionist states, but those states and their leaders had little power and whatever relieved pressure on them made the northern hard-liners distrust Johnson. Hadn't he been a slave owner and hadn't he held back on Emancipation? And it didn't require an abacus to calculate that if the secessionist states quickly received their rights back, the Democratic Party would soon be back in power in most states and, probably, federally.

Andrew Johnson had been thrown into the one job in the world worse than being military governor of Tennessee. Jesus Christ on a winged white stallion could not have put America back together without engendering seething hatred.

Johnson enters into a political war with the legislature. He vetoes the Civil Rights Bill of 1866 and becomes the first president to have a veto overridden. He talks softly, arguing that to hold power over the former rebels by terror and by devastation is repugnant to humanity. In Congress, he is referred to as "the late lamented Andrew Johnson," as close to a political, and perhaps a personal, death threat as one can utter in that chamber.

Johnson's response to Congress indeed is politically fatal. He does what presidential protocol of the time prohibits: he interferes directly and publicly in the congressional election campaign, making a train swing from Washington to St. Louis, by way of New York, Ohio, Michigan, Kentucky, and points in between. At each stop he begins by saying he won't make a speech and then he does, a dumb, rancorous, Tennessee stump speech that does not play well in most of the northern cities.

Meetings turn raucous; he is heckled and yells back and loses his self-control and says things about individual congressmen that are defamatory at minimum. He gets little right, and the New York *Tribune* summarizes his visit to St. Louis under this headline. *The President's Trip ... He Denies He is Judas Iscariot.*

The rest is rubble. The new Congress, heavily anti-Johnson, draws up articles of impeachment and he becomes the only U.S. president to be sent to the senate for trial. Conviction fails, but Johnson is now politically as dead as his enemies had predicted.

Andrew Johnson, the president of the Union, had gone to trial for his post-war exertions, while the president of the Confederacy, Jefferson Davis, was never tried for his wartime actions.

With a grim smile upon his face, on the fourth of July 1868, Andrew Johnson grants a full pardon to all Confederates, save those on treason or felony charges. Then, on Christmas Day, he extends the pardon to all former secessionists with no exceptions.

WASHINGTON, D.C. JUNE 1866

Tennessee Fenians

The secretary to President Andrew Johnson opens a letter from Tennessee and puts it into the Death Threats file. The folder is bulging. This one is different from most. It is in the conditional – a refreshing change, the secretary feels. He has read too many in the imperative mood. The threat comes from Tennessee, and that is no surprise: Johnson's time as military governor of Tennessee had produced thousands of enemies and, more recently, scores of death threats. This one is very unusual because it is signed, if that is the proper term, by "Fenian."

The secretary reflects for a moment and removes the letter from the file. He decides to pass it on to the Secret Service for investigation. Disgruntled Fenians in New York, Massachusetts, or Pennsylvania are common enough to be ignored. But in Tennessee?

Perhaps it is the legacy of Andrew Jackson (a prodigious hater of the English) but, uniquely, the Fenian movement in Tennessee is ecumenical, embracing Catholic immigrants and old-line Protestant frontier families who agree with Andrew Jackson's now-hallowed view that eventually Canada had to be liberated from British rule.

In Nashville, the Fenians are an above-ground civic club as well as a secret revolutionary society. They establish an orphanage, publicly subscribing to the purpose the profits from their St. Patrick's day celebration and from a fair that they held in the McKendree Methodist Church: over $8,000.

John O'Neill, a former colonel in the Union army who settled in Nashville, became in 1868 the "Head Center" for the Brotherhood in the United States and led the second attack on Canada, that of 1870. It was a remarkably flaccid affair, easily overcome by the locals.

That was largely because most potential invaders of Canada realized that there was so much more of the USA left to conquer, and that was an easier and more remunerative task.

THE USA. 1866

A Grip on the Future

Much more swiftly than their east-coast grandchildren choose to remember, the post-Famine Irish Catholics spread out all over America: farms, small towns, canal sites, lumber camps, mining towns, big cities. They were not for long simply an east coast people.

Wherever they went, they had one collective advantage. They were the first group (ethnic, religious, call them what you will) who had experienced a brand-new social phenomenon: urban life in the era of the American industrial revolution. *Many migrating onward from New York, Massachusetts, or Pennsylvania, were familiar with the routines and disciplines of urban life and came with skills learned in years of residence in those states.* Thus, Malcolm Campbell, a prescient Australian observer of American life. The Catholic Irish were not hicks. They could work in the countryside and then market their wares or themselves in cities, knowing full well the rules of urban life. Other, older groups were better off financially, but none had this collective flexibility, the knowledge of how to make it anywhere. Ultimately, a century after the civil war, American-Irish Catholics will be the second most successful group in American society, exceeded only by the Jews.

But here: the cost of this apprenticeship in urban American economics – the cost was horrifically high. Multiply by a factor of several thousands the report of the New York Metropolitan Board of Health, describing widespread Irish Catholic living conditions in 1866. *The first and at all times the most prolific cause of disease was found to be the insalubrious condition of most of the tenement houses in the cities of New York and Brooklyn. These houses are generally built without any reference to the health or comfort of the occupant, but simply with a view to economy and profit to the owner. The provision for ventilation and light is very insufficient, and the arrangement of water-closets or privies could hardly be worse if actually intended to produce diseases ... The basements were often entirely below ground, the ceiling being a foot or two below the level of the street ... The cellars, when unoccupied, were frequently flooded to the depth of several inches with stagnant water and were made the receptacles of garbage and refuse matter of every description ... In many cases, the cellars were constantly occupied, and sometimes used as lodging-houses, where there was no ventilation save by the entrance and in which the occupants were entirely dependent upon artificial light by day as well as by night. Such was the character of a vast number of the tenement houses in the lower parts of the city of New York and along its eastern and western borders. Disease, especially in the form of fevers of a typhoid character, was constantly present in these dwellings and every now and then became in more than one of them epidemic. It was found that in one of these twenty cases of typhus had occurred during the previous year.*

FORT BENTON, MONTANA TERRITORY. 1867

The Last Flash

The best-known and most-loved of the Irish Catholic immigrants who fought for the Union, slides into the muddy waters of the Missouri River and disappears.

Thomas Francis Meagher always was an Irish gentleman. That was clear on St. Patrick's Day, 1863, when, as Brevet-General of the New York 69th, he had led the way in making the Irish patron saint's day a holiday for the entire army of the Potomac. That day he had appeared in his own special uniform: white buckskin breeches, high black riding boots, a white, frilled stock under a swallowtail riding coat, and a beaver top hat. This was the riding-to-the-hounds rig of an Irish country gentleman and his Irish troops recognized it immediately. Meagher wore it by right: the son of a prosperous Waterford merchant in the Newfoundland trade, he had spent six years boarding with the Jesuits at Clongowes Wood and four more years of Jesuit polishing at Stonyhurst College in England. There he perfected his English public school accent. A widower married to the daughter of a wealthy New York businessman, he was a New World gentleman whom the immigrant Irish would follow, through hell if necessary.

He was not blamed by his idolizers for being relieved of his command in February 1865, for every man has a little weakness and, anyway, who would not stay drunk as a way of making the war pass more quickly?

Meagher was rewarded in the summer of 1865 with the secretaryship and acting-governorship of Montana. There he waged a personal war against the Blackfoot nation, largely successfully, and another personal war against the bottle, very unsuccessfully. Increasingly he believed himself surrounded by assassins, vigilantes, and Freemasons, and perhaps he was.

All that is certain is that on the evening of 1 July 1867 Thomas Francis Meagher disappeared from a paddle steamer into the dark Missouri waters.

His last flash was a brief glint reflected from a medal he wore around his neck for good luck: given to him by the Jesuits at Stonyhurst for Improved Deportment.

NEW YORK CITY. 1867

True Blue and Bruised

Easy to forget: all immigrants are scared, unless they are complete fools. The Irish Protestants who continue to make up at least 10 percent of Irish migration to the USA, do not all have a smooth ride: especially not those working-class migrants from the north of Ireland who settle amidst the massive Catholic populations of New York and Philadelphia.

Thus, in 1867, the Orange Order comes above ground in New York and, three years later, the Loyal Orange Institution of the United States is founded, with two score lodges. The Irish Protestant immigrants want protection.

If only they could have dropped their parading tradition. They march in New York City in 1870 to celebrate King William's victory at the Battle of the Boyne. Irish Catholics attack them and nine people die, split between Orangemen and Catholics. The next year, the police, the New York State militia, and the Catholics all are better prepared, and the Orangemen more prudential. Seeing the build-up of a large and well-armed Catholic mob, only 161 Orangemen actually go out to parade, protected by 800 police and 2,200 militiamen. Two soldiers are killed and thirty-one rioters.

Orangeism never catches on in the USA, for it increases, rather than reduces, the vulnerability of its adherents.

NEW YORK CITY. 1868

Spiritual Reconstruction

A group of well-dressed men, serious but brimming with suppressed energy, convene several times in substantial Manhattan homes. Most are clergymen in prosperous pulpits. They understand something important: that the USA has entered a period of great confusion and that the entire nation, not merely the South, needs reconstruction. Indeed, for the first generation their work and that of their heirs is in the broad band of industrializing cities, running from New York through Chicago, and splaying to Minneapolis to the north and St. Louis to the south. Their cure for the confusion is the Bible, especially the study of biblical prophecy. Their methods are very different from those of the old frontier revivals. For their followers they introduce intense courses of private Bible study, serious summer conferences where biblical prophecy is parsed like philologists working over Greek grammar and, above all, they point to something they call the Dispensations of the Almighty.

George C. Needham, in his late twenties, was the youngest of this cadre. He had just arrived from Ireland where he had been a preacher for the Plymouth Brethren, Darbyite faction. Needham, and others who had Brethren background, pushed the Bible-conference idea: meetings for pastors and serious laymen and women that would last one or two weeks and mix intense daily study with a nightly star-preaching performance.

The Brethren knew where this idea came from: the initial conference, to which all the American Bible-prophecy conferences harkened, occurred in the early 1830s at the huge estate in County Wicklow of the young widow Theodosia Wingfield, Lady Power-scourt. Thirty-five clergy, fifteen laymen and, crucially, twenty women, spent long hours considering the meaning of "days" in Bible prophecy. The next year, they worried about "Should we expect a personal Antichrist?" and related issues. These first two conferences were mostly composed of Anglicans, but by the third, in late 1833, John Nelson Darby was the dominant force; Lady Power-scourt left the Anglican faith, and most of the prophetic adepts became Plymouth Brethren.

This Brethren method of spiritual reconstruction is taken up by American pastors, few of whom are Brethren themselves, but men open to the Brethren influence. They embrace a series of Biblical prophecy conferences beginning in 1875 and running until 1901. Held most often just across the border at Niagara-on-the-Lake, Ontario (hence the generic name, "Niagara Conferences") these were nothing less than the creation of an alternative version of American Protestantism; and all done with the Plymouth Brethren as stealth ideologues, willing to let Baptists and Presbyterians and Congregationalists and even some Anglican leaders assimilate and preach the Darbyite gospel.

Whatever else it was, the Darbyite theology – *Dispensationalism* – had nothing of Catholic rationalism about it. None of that looking at nature and learning about God from his creation. Its tenets were simple, perfect for a world of rapid change and confusing flux. *Rightly dividing the word of truth* (2 Timothy 2:15) was the inscription on the Dispensationalist foundation stone and it meant, first, read the Bible literally and jettison all church dogmas. Second, when you read the Bible literally you will find that God divided Time into seven segments ("Dispensations").

Now it's the last two Dispensations that are gripping, for, unlike the first five, they have yet to happen. If one reads Daniel and Revelation and some of the off-key bits of Paul's epistles and of the Gospels, you, you dear, searching Christian reader, will discover that in the last two Dispensations the *Secret Rapture of the church will occur* – that is, all true believers will be spirited up to heaven, leaving a lot of traffic confusion and uneaten dinners behind; this Rapture will in some way be related to the *Second Coming to Earth of Jesus*. There's terrific room for argument here and Dispensationalists fight over chronology. But, sometime in the whole process an *anti-Christ will arise*, there will be a *world-shattering battle at Armageddon* north of Jerusalem, and Jesus will rule for 1,000 years (*the Millennium*) and after that, those of us who have got all this right will reside with him in heaven and watch the rest of you being most deservedly tortured throughout eternity.

If you, reader, are a Roman Catholic, you need to know this stuff. Mention it any time some Protestant tells you that Catholics are a credulous and superstitious bunch. All comes from Ireland, too.

NR. FORT LARNED, NEBRASKA. 1868

Listed Species

Kiowa
Zuni
Snake

The man William Cody was guiding was certainly no dude, but he acted like one. He was always dropping behind on his horse and Cody, on mule, had to pull up and wait. The man had a notebook and he kept taking it out and checking something he wanted to remember and then he would say something aloud, like a school child trying to remember his times-tables.

Creek
Cherokee
Iroquois

Cody, who had taken a year off from hunting and guiding in order to run a hotel, was happy to have this queer fellow along, for the work certainly beat chucking out drunks and keeping whores from fighting with each other. In fact, this was the first week on his new job and Cody was happy.

Navaho
Arapaho
Klamath

Cody had got the job through William Hickok, an old friend (and later, briefly, an employee in his Wild West Show, where Wild Bill Hickok proved too wild to mix safely with urban America). Cody was chosen as an Indian Scout, a job he coveted. It meant spending days on his own and then reporting where the various tribes were. Somebody else would then decide whether they should be avoided or whether they could be attacked with a reasonable probability of victory. Cody didn't much care either way. For him sniffing-out the game was his pleasure.

Not, however, the Boy General whom he was guiding and who, damn him, why couldn't he keep his mount to a decent pace? Cody, riding spread-legged on a mule without a proper saddle, left him so far behind that he had to circle back every hour or so and let George Armstrong Custer catch up.

What Custer was doing, he explained to Cody at one of the unnecessary rest stops that he insisted on taking, was committing to memory the names of all the tribes from which he had killed at least one member. And he was keeping a separate list of those he had yet to blood.

Moduc

Mohave

"Mormon," suggested Cody who had religious convictions.

"Doesn't count," Custer ruled.

They reached Fort Larned, and despite its being late in the evening Custer, the twenty-nine year old Civil War hero and military genius, was given a meal that rated as a banquet.

Mid-morning the next day, Cody encountered Custer in the fort's main square.

Cody saluted and laconically asked "Sioux?"

"Yes indeed," said Custer. "So easy to forget."

MISSOURI AND WEST. 1869

The Great War

In the Great War on the Native Americans, running from the end of the Civil War to roughly 1890, Irishmen were stand-outs. At first they were former soldiers from the Union and Confederate sides who were addicted to military life. Later, the horse soldiers were recruits too young to have fought in the Civil War, and who desperately want to make up for what they had missed. Basically, this Great War's task was to clear of Native American resistance the old Louisiana Purchase and the territories taken in the 1840s from Mexico. Useful work, a quick way to become creditable American citizens, and good adventure to boot.

In 1869, Philip Henry Sheridan is appointed general of the U.S. forces in the west, with headquarters in Missouri. President Ulysses Grant thinks highly of him, as does the General-Commanding of the U.S. army, William Tecumseh Sherman: during the Civil War Sheridan had laid waste to the Shenendoah with ruthlessness and efficiency that augured well for his future as an Indian fighter. That Sheridan is a man with a future is confirmed when he is seconded to observe the Franco-Prussian War of 1870–71. He learns a lot from the Prussians, and applies the lessons on his return to the American west.

Among his gifts is one for language, the abrading tongue of his County Cavan parents, middling Protestants forced out in 1830 by Catholic intimidation. Born in America in 1831, Sheridan never admits to being Irish, not consciously.

He enters American mythology on two fronts. When negotiating with a Comanche leader, he listens to the man describe himself as "a good Indian."

Sheridan replies immediately. *The only good Indian is a dead Indian.*

And Sheridan is selected for rapid promotion and special assignment by George Armstrong Custer of the 7th Cavalry. As he wrote to Custer, *I will back you with my whole authority.*

MINNESOTA. 1870

Daft Defamations (1)

Every ethnic group gets unfairly slagged and its people figure out a way to deal with it: that's the history of America. Some of the stereotypes turn out to be right: nobody's perfect. What is bizarre about the Irish Catholics in the USA is that they self-generate a whole historical literature that casts themselves in an unflattering light, and unfairly so.

This strange and self-hating literature has one basic tenet: that the Irish Catholics who arrive from 1846 onwards are either too thick or too emotionally insecure to make it on the American frontier. Not that the majority might have *chosen* not to deal with rural and small town life, but that they just could not handle it.

Possibly. From 1846 through the mid-1850s the Irish immigrants pile up in the port cities. Evidence of their inability to farm or become small traders on the westward-moving border of America? Possibly. Or, possibly, port cities are where people get off ships, and it takes a while for poor people to save enough to move elsewhere. Just an idea.

The U.S. government census in 1870 enquires for the first time both where people are born and, if they are American-born, were either of their parents foreign-born? Useful. The enumeration reveals that 44.5 percent of the Irish immigrants to the U.S. live in cities (defined as places with 25,000 or more people; not necessarily big cities). So, the majority of Irish immigrants (including those just off the boat) are not living in cities but in small towns and in the countryside. These people are not starving; they are not incapable of adapting to either one of America's rapidly changing frontiers: that of the industrial revolution or that of the westward farming flow. A fair reading of the occupational census suggests that about 30 percent of Irish-immigrants (never mind the better-established second and third generation) are in the rural economy: farmers, ferriers, drovers, hired men and women.

On the Great Middle Border – the Old Northwest, with Iowa and Minnesota as its western limits – Irish Catholic immigrants and their children farm successfully. These Irish farmers do not arrive all at once: they begin in the early 1850s. *In the spring of 1853 John Mitchell came down [to Illinois] from Minnesota to buy cattle ... By this time all the homesteads in Illinois had been taken up and it was expensive to buy land.* The Irish Catholics who choose Minnesota are aided by the Tyrone-born Irishman James Shield, who had been a federal land commissioner and he points them to the richest land in the state, the southeast corner, where the meanderings of the Minnesota and Mississippi Rivers over millennia had deposited deep layers of fertile top soil.

Minnesota: the toughest place for a comparison of immigrant farming groups: all those industrious Germans and rurally-experienced Scandinavians. The results: the Irish Catholics have a higher percentage of people in farming than does the state of Minnesota as a whole. And long-term studies show that they did as well or better than the average.

Same thing happened in Iowa and Wisconsin.

And in pockets, sometimes just individual farms, all over the USA.

The Irish Catholic immigrants were not an immoveable bolus in the gut of urban America: despite what the descendants of the Famine and immediate post-Famine immigrants want to believe. In fact, if we take into account those immigrants' economic starting point – they came down the gangplank desperately poor, most of them, and certainly not carrying the tool kits and caches of small implements the northern Europeans brought – then, by 1870, the Irish Catholic immigrant community has moved more quickly, geographically, socially, and economically, than any other ethnic group of significant size. These people were not perfect: merely amazing.

VIRGINIA CITY, NEVADA. 1873

Digging with Both Feet

To watch them together, as they pored over geological maps and tailings reports, one would have thought that they were having a taciturnity contest: the Dublin Catholic and the Belfast Protestant. No, they both were professionals and not given to wasting words, in boast, threat, plan, or predation. John Mackay was born in Dublin and brought to the U.S. when he was nine and James Fair arrived with his parents at age twelve. Both were acclimated Americans in the sense that getting a job of work done was more important than the old World separations: they needed each other.

Like many of the smartest and most ambitious Irish immigrants, they each had hit California early, Fair in 1849, Mackay in 1851. They both had stayed in mining, done their time underground, the equivalent of a Ph.D. in mining geology, and had crossed over the mountains into Nevada in the early 1860s as the Comstock silver lode drew prospectors inland. Smart men. As mining turned industrial and required joint stock companies, mile-long underground tunnels, and large sluicing mills, they had learned, adapted, and slowly built up equity positions in the mines that they worked. They were ready for the big winner.

In the later 1860s, they had the same idea: that the Comstock lode was not as mined-out as it appeared. Quietly, like Freemasons on a bender (they both actually were Masons, as were their later junior partners), they bought up defunct mines. Fair was the better geologist, Mackay the sharper money man. With expensive, big-dollar technology they reckoned the old mines would yield silver or gold, the way the Rock spewed water when Moses struck it. They were right. Following a tiny vein of silver for a quarter mile underground, borrowing every penny they could, they hit the Big Bonanza. The vein spread out and eventually became a 300 foot wide seam of silver. There are rivers that aren't that wide!

Mackay, who had a double share (40 percent) in the company became one of the richest men in the USA and one of the wealthiest private citizens in the world. He stayed a quiet man, albeit with an ambitious Yankee socialite wife who insisted on homes in London and Paris and soirées that left him speechless, more than ever.

In contrast, Fair learned to speak in public and bought himself a seat in the United States senate.

SANTIAGO DE CUBA. 4 NOVEMBER 1873

Practising for The Bay of Pigs

Owning Cuba was a bad idea whose time had not yet come. So reflected General (self-breveted) George Washington Ryan, as he spat out his cigar.

It did not fly far, as Ryan was on his knees in front of a firing squad. At least the Cubans had provided him with a Corona Grande, a mark of respect. And no blindfold. Hard to smoke a Grande wearing one.

Ryan, who had been born William Ryan either in Ireland or in Toronto (his story varied), looked over at his three Cuban comrades. They were still puffing like chimneys.

He watched for a while. Since they were all kneeling before a white-washed prison wall, there was not much else to catch his attention, save a large spider that was trying to build a web from one of the gables to an outshot twelve feet away. Impossible job, and as he observed the spider, Ryan reflected on what an idiot Robert the Bruce had been. Try, try again? Don't try at all, dolt.

General Ryan and his three Cuban colleagues had led one of the early American attempts to liberate Cuba, which is to say, incorporate it into the U.S. empire, and had done so on a boat originally named *The Virgin*. Might as well call it the Faerie Queen for all the hope we had, Ryan realized.

Hard to liberate people who don't want to be, he concluded, just before the firing squad's bullets slammed into his back.

PORTLAND, MAINE. 1875

Anomalies

Modestly quadroon. Nice straight hair. Disciplined nose. That's what every parishioner said about all three men.

Their father, Michael Healy, had migrated from County Roscommon to Georgia as soon as the Napoleonic War was over and got what he had come for: a cotton farm of 1,500 acres, fifty slaves and some very tasty black women. Healy fathered a dozen children (nine survived) by his favourite mulatto slave, and heaven knows how many others. The children of this favoured relationship were given expensive educations in the North and the gifted ones prepared for the church.

James Augustine Healy, trained in Canada and France, became the first African-American bishop. He was installed in the diocese of Portland in 1875. His younger brother Patrick Francis Healy had already become the first African-American to earn a doctorate and, in the previous year, 1874, was named president of Georgetown University.

A third brother, Alexander, became rector of a parish in Boston.

Two sisters became nuns in Quebec.

Anomalies in their day.

The Catholic church in the USA has few resources to spend attracting American blacks. It has literally millions of Irish and German immigrants to take care of first. And it has little interest in American blacks, whatever their shade. Until World War II, the church spends more money on foreign missions than it does on outreach to African-Americans.

They notice. And they remember that the Abolitionists had been almost universally Protestants, while the Catholic bishops in the South were all pro-slavery.

African-Americans become Protestants, often with dashes of creativity that keep the Holy Spirit lively. And as a badge they adopt Protestant names: like, fine example, Martin Luther King.

ROME. 1875

In the Image of the Almighty

The most influential person in the Catholic Church in America between, roughly, 1862 and 1962 never set foot in America and died in

1878. Cardinal Paul Cullen, archbishop of Dublin. He formed the church in post-Famine Ireland in the shape of an ecclesiastical army running from laity through the Vatican. And then clergy trained in Ireland poured into the USA. Crucially, they founded seminaries run by Cullen's rules: strict obedience to superiors, sound theological training, and no compromise with the secular state or Protestant authorities. Thus, second-generation Irish seminarians were trained in the U.S. the same way priests were trained in Ireland. Pockets of resistance from midwestern German Catholics held out for a generation, but Paul Cullen won.

The cincture on Cullen's capture of the American church comes in 1875. At his behest, in 1874, Rome had sent a questionnaire to the American bishops asking them about the public school system: was it safe for Catholic children, and could the American church afford to withdraw its children from the dominant American society? Based on this, in 1875 Rome issues a formal Instruction that says that public education, even if religiously neutral, was not satisfactory. This, in fact, is a restatement of the ruling of Ireland's Synod of Thurles of 1850 where Cullen had led the Irish church to condemn "mixed" education with Protestants and to demand schools run by priests, staffed by Catholic teachers and, in the usual case, attended only by Catholic pupils. In 1884 at a Plenary Council in Baltimore, the American bishops give their clergy two years to set up a parochial school system that will segregate the Catholic children from the Protestant mainstream.

Whether good or bad is moot: historically, the Catholic Church's having the confidence and the financial ability to attempt to withdraw its children from American society says one thing about the Irish Catholic populace: they had grown sufficiently strong economically and confident of their place in America that they could afford to make this effort. A long way from 1846.

THE BIG HORN VALLEY, DAKOTA TERRITORY.
26 JUNE 1876

Deserving Survivors

They both lay wounded and valueless. They had survived the previous day's battle, but were still unable to move. They had done their best. They nearly lost their lives helping to carry out the policy that General Sherman had suggested to General Grant after a Sioux defeat of the U.S. Cavalry in 1867. *We must act with vindictive earnestness against the Sioux, even to their extermination. Men women and children. Nothing less will reach the root cause.*

Now, the two hemorrhaging survivors lay amidst human corpses that were mutilated in ways that spoke of sadism as well as warfare: noses and ears cut off, some with genitals missing, scalps severed, fingers removed, feet amputated. They had not survived a battle among gentry.

One survivor was George Armstrong Custer's dog, a beast he had always claimed was a present from Queen Victoria. Variously remembered as a greyhound and as a large bulldog, he was in fact a Borzoi. The beast has taken a musket ball that entered his anus, and travelled all the way through his body and passed out his right shoulder. Somehow, the animal recovered, and a week after the Battle of Little Big Horn, dragged itself into Fort Lincoln. He served the rest of his short life as a regimental pet, sleeping in the sun and dreaming of the days when running behind the man with the long curling hair had been all the happiness the world need offer.

The other Seventh Cavalry survivor, Commanche, the horse of the now forever-sleeping Major Myles Keogh, was a large brown gelding, mostly thoroughbred, with a touch of Indian pony in his blood. His master was a minor Irish legend. Myles Keogh had served with the Irish Legion that had volunteered to protect the Pope in 1860. They failed, for the Italians easily overwhelmed them, but Keogh received a medal, the Cross of the Order of St. Gregory, from Pius IX. Keogh had then migrated to America, served with distinction as a Union officer, had become a U.S. citizen, and had become Custer's chief aide in the campaign to cleanse the Northern plains of the indigenous inhabitants.

Commanche had spent a lot of time trotting in rhythm to Irish tunes, for Keogh, with Custer's approval, had kept morale up by turning the Seventh Cavalry into an ersatz-Irish regiment. He introduced as the regimental march the tune "Gerryowen," which was an Irish quickstep and drinking song and one that had been popular when Keogh's own father, an Irishman in the U.K. army, had been stationed near Limerick. Custer liked the march so much that he personally put $50 towards buying instruments so that the Seventh had a rudimentary band.

Major Keogh's body was found, stripped naked, but not mutilated, trapped beneath the body of Commanche. They had been felled by a single bullet which had gone through Keogh and into the horse. Keogh kept firing until killed, all the time clutching Commanche's reins in one hand. Though Keogh was stripped naked, the victors left him with a single item, the Papal medal, which for good luck he had worn on a chain inside his shirt. The dead man's hand, still clutching the reins, kept the Sioux from taking Commanche. They let Major Keogh ride to the next world on his own mount.

Commanche, taken on a sling to Fort Lincoln by the white soldiers who discovered the scene, spent the rest of his life as a military mascot. He was the subject of numerous newspaper stories and of special interest in Ireland, where he was celebrated as a distant Irish patriot. Commanche died in 1891.

The rapid March of Civilization in the American west is clearly indicated by there being a public university in existence in Kansas in 1891. It acquired Commanche and had him stuffed. Only for the World's Exposition do they allow him to travel. He is taken to be exhibited alongside dozens of specimens of exotic species that the infant university displayed to show the strength of its scientific collections.

One of the other specimens on display at the Exposition comes to visit Commanche: Buffalo Bill Cody.

Unblinking, he and Commanche stare at each other and then Cody, a bighearted man, whistles to Commanche a full rendition of "Gerry-owen."

CHICAGO, ILLINOIS. 1877

The Very Man

Thin and weathered as a piece of old leather, John Nelson Darby made his last trip across industrial America. Darby had briefly visited the U.S. and Canada in 1862 and after the Civil War he spent as much time as a missionary in the States as he could. In fact, in the sixteen-year period 1862–77, inclusive, he was in the USA almost seven full years. There he worked quietly. He taught local groups of Plymouth Brethren and gave private "Bible readings" to influential laymen and clergy of the main Protestant denominations.

Bible-readings. Strange term. The Darbyite way of studying the scriptures was to take a single verse or a short passage and then to worry it for hours, sometimes days. These "readings" took the form of a re-writing of the scripture under the guise of interpreting it. A typical meditation or sermon would consist of a set of loosely connected texts that were supposed to illuminate the original verse. Possibly that happened, but, given that the core of the Bible is a set of narratives, rearranging them totally changes their meaning. Not that the Darbyites considered that was what they were doing; they were unlocking Truth.

In Chicago, Darby meets for the final time Dwight L. Moody, the evangelist who in the nineteenth century was as influential as Billy Graham in the twentieth. They have never liked each other: two lions, one cage. But Moody is deeply impressed with the Bible-reading technique of the Plymouth Brethren – he once heard one of them expound John 3:16 for five straight nights – and he accepts the Darbyites' view that big events, the completion of the Sixth Dispensation and the Seventh and final Dispensation are on the way.

Darby visits St Louis where one of his chief followers is still a Presbyterian, but also a Dispensationalist: James Hall Brookes, pastor of the Walnut Street Presbyterian Church. In that church two years later, Cyrus Ingerson Scofield, now an alcoholic former lawyer, gets religion and becomes eventually the most influential Dispensationalist scholar on the planet.

In 1882, John Nelson Darby approaches death. He has come a long way from his days as a hunger-crazed mendicant curate in the Wicklow hills, but he is deeply melancholic. Despite having pointed steadfastly to the truth, he has to accept the same disappointment that every Dispensationalist meets at life's end: he dies before Jesus Christ returns to earth.

SAN FRANCISCO, CALIFORNIA. 1878

Daft Defamations (2)

Wonderful how a visit to San Francisco can open one's eyes. One notices, for example, *a public fact, that fifty Irish Catholic millionaires, with their myriads of rich employees, are, through their wives as well as themselves, constantly at the feet of the Jesuits, who here, more than any other place, really swim in a golden sea.*

So observes Charles Chiniguy (born Charles-Paschal-Telesphore), sometime curé of one of Quebec's most prestigious parishes, Notre Dame de Beauport, former Catholic temperance campaigner, late entrant to the Oblates of Mary Immaculate, special missionary to the *Canadiens* in the Chicago area, dissident against Irish Catholic control of the American church and, finally, an excommunicated rebel who takes with him from the Catholic church 2,000 of his *Canadien* followers from the parish in St. Anne, Illinois. God, he hates the Irish. *The Roman Catholic priests, with the most admirable ability, have massed their Irish legions into the great cities of the United States and the Americans must be very blind indeed, if they do not see that the day is very near when the Jesuits will rule their cities, from the magnificent White House of Washington, to the humblest civil or military departments of this vast Republic.*

The Rev. Mr. Chiniguy marries, spends some time in the religious wilderness and then leads his congregation to join the Presbyterian Church. He is kicked out in two years, but readmitted to the cloth because he certainly can keep an audience of anti-Catholics spellbound. His best performance is his re-enactment of what goes on in the confessional between a priest and a vulnerable young lady. He plays it throughout the northeast of the United States and across Ontario and parts of Quebec.

The reason that Chiniguy visits San Francisco is that his incessant anti-Catholic preaching has given him a continual cough. He spits blood often, and his doctors tell him that a trip across the Pacific Ocean, and a long spell in Australia and New Zealand will do him a world of good.

Chiniguy is loopey as a rabid fox but, as he surveys the Romish snake pit that is his San Francisco, he has one thing right: some day there will be an Irish Catholic in *the magnificent White House of Washington.*

WASHINGTON, D.C. 1881

Keeping Up Appearances

The best thing that can be said about the presidency of Chester A. Arthur is that, though he had not expected the job, he nevertheless always looked presidential.

After President James A. Garfield had been shot just weeks into his term of office, Arthur stayed quietly in the background, and, as Garfield lingered on, showed little appetite for power. When Garfield finally died in mid-September 1881, Arthur assumed the presidency in a private ceremony.

He waited a decent interval – three months – and then gave his first state dinner: a fourteen course affair for former president and Mrs. Grant. Thirty-four guests, a full bouquet of roses at each lady's plate, gilt-edged place cards, eight wines, and the U.S. Marine Corps band playing selections from European operas. That was his start, and he was soon giving twenty-one course meals frequently.

In public he did the one thing he could do well: wear quality clothes with authority. Six feet, two inches tall, strongly built but not fat, sporting impressive side whiskers, he acted with the studied seriousness and decorum of an actor playing a serious and decorous president. He had at least 100 tailor-made suits and sporting jackets and a full range of formal evening wear.

Other than that, he did not like the job and put in at most thirty to thirty-five hours a week of actual work.

Still, a very smooth gentleman and that is something for a man whose father was from The Draens, fornenst Cullybackey, County Antrim: Cullybackey is so close to the-back-of-beyond that if one leaves it in any direction one is heading towards civilization. Chester A. Arthur in his way was a triumph of the American system.

NEW YORK CITY. 1881

Daft Defamations (3)

The Englishman Edward Freeman had studied the history and society of the United States and now was visiting to confirm his opinions.

This would be a grand land if only every Irishman would kill a Negro and be hanged for it.

Good sentence structure, as one would expect from the Regius Professor of Modern History, Oxford University.

NEW YORK STATE. 1884

Vital Fluids

Say Grover! Move over:
Give Maria some room!

Tammany Hall did not mind dirty elections, and the presidential campaign of 1884 was as dirty as any in U.S. history. What it did mind was getting the mucky end of the stick. The Democrats had not had a presidential victory since the Civil War and it was now or, probably, never. Their man, Grover Cleveland (he had dropped the "Stephen" and even the "S" from his name), was a big problem for his Tammany backers.

The Widow Halpin got two helpings,
Whenever Cleveland was home.

The street-doggerel was nation-wide, but it hurt most among the Catholic American-Irish who, whatever their own personal lives, were moving collectively into their lace-curtain phase, building churches, and listening to priests from the old country who demanded high moral standards. And during the 1884 campaign the Republicans had discovered that in 1874 Grover Cleveland had, while sheriff of Erie County, New York (encompassing Buffalo), been named as the father of an illegitimate child. The woman involved was a lady, a respectable thirty-one year-old widow who was well-educated, spoke French, was stunningly beautiful and moved in the best social circles. She had been shared by several of the men in Cleveland's own circle, mostly lawyers, and when pregnant really had no idea who the father was. Cleveland – he was still Big Steve then – was the only bachelor of the group, so she decided that he was the responsible party. Acting both honourably and prudently, the same thing for an aspiring politician, Cleveland had bought her silence by paying for the adoption of the infant boy through the Protestant Orphan Asylum and arranging for adoption by a family in western New York. Cleveland never cast eyes on the child, but he met the Widow Halpin soon after the birth and gave her enough money to start a women's apparel shop in Niagara Falls. None of this was what Tammany wanted to talk about to men whose wives listened intently to political gossip and badgered them on how to vote. And, if that was the case in New York State, it held more for the conservative outlying pockets of Irish Catholic America where Tammany was frequently looked to for a lead in political matters.

Blaine, Blaine! He has no stain,
For he is one of us!

Worse yet, the Republican candidate, James Gillespie Blaine, was a supporter of the Irish Land League and other Irish nationalist causes. Moreover, though Blaine (like his father) was Protestant, his mother and sisters were Irish Catholics and one sister was the mother superior of a midwestern convent. In contrast, Cleveland was descended on his father's side from a long list of Protestant clerics running back to the eighteenth century. And, though he was partially Irish, there was the wince-producing fact that his maternal grandfather, a Neal, had left Ireland after jumping Faiths.

Tammany and the Democrats were on to another loser. Except that, miraculously, Blaine found a political banana peel. In the last week of the campaign he met with a group of high-influence Protestant cler-gymen, and he nodded drowsily as one of them, a septuagenarian, croaked out that *We are Republicans, and don't propose to leave our party and identify ourselves with the party whose antecedents have been Rum, Romanism, and Rebellion.*

Rum, Romanism, and Rebellion!
Rum, Romanism, and Rebellion!

What a gift to the Democrats! Blaine let the phrase slip by without negative comment, and next day every paper in every big northern city bannered this Republican insult to the patriotism and public propriety of a huge bloc of voters.

Might as well call all the Irish Catholics traitors and drunks and be done with it. Suddenly the election was close enough to steal.

Cheers for Maria. Cheers for the kid!
We voted for Cleveland and glad we did!

Cleveland, with skilful vote theft by Tammany Hall, won New York City by a little more than 1,000 votes and New York State by 23,000, well within the capability of dead men voting. And New York was the margin of presidential victory. The U.S. tradition of filling the presidency by theft, like that of emptying it through assassination, was becoming entrenched.

WASHINGTON, D.C. 1885

Try Not to Look

Oh, Lord, let me breathe!

Those were the words of the Widow Halpin in the days when she had to put up with the weighty attentions of Sheriff Big Stevie Cleveland and his friends. If only for aesthetic reasons, the sex life of most U.S. presidents does not bear contemplation – save perhaps that of the Don Juan of the presidency, John Kennedy – and Grover Cleveland's was particularly unattractive. There was of course that matter of Mrs. Halpin. She had been passed around, but the two who shared her most were Big Steve and his law partner (Cleveland kept a practice while being sheriff of the Buffalo area), Oscar Folsom. Which neatly explains why the name on the resulting bastard's birth certificate, as set down by the Widow Halpin, was Oscar Folsom Cleveland.

Then there was that touching-thing that Cleveland had possessed, and had possessed him, since his days teaching at the New York Institution for the Blind. He just loved smooth objects. A particular favourite was Frances, the daughter of Oscar Folsom, born in 1865. Cleveland was always around the Folsom house. He provided her baby pram as a christening gift and as she grew, he held her, bounced her on his knee, and, as she grew, played games with her. To her, he was Uncle Cleve. My God, he loved that beautiful child.

Then, in 1875, Oscar Folsom died and S. Grover Cleveland (he was beginning his name change), found himself named guardian of the ten-year-old child and executor of the estate left to her mother. Frances was his legal ward. This delighted him and, though he feigned surprise, he always had known the contents of his law partner's last will and testament and, indeed, Cleveland had suggested that very clause. Now, he could spend hours alone with Frances, and if she still sat on his knee and if Uncle Cleve felt the smoothness of her limbs and explored the smoothness of her vulva, that was nothing he could stop or that she would. *Oh, Lord, give me breath!* she would cry and flush suddenly with an intense pleasure. And then the two of them would play jacks or hopscotch.

The intimacy continued, but was reduced when, in 1882 Grover Cleveland (his newest name) became governor of New York State and Frances Folsom went off to college. Even so, the Widow Folsom, Cleveland, and Frances spent holidays together. The governor of New York formally asked Mrs. Folsom for permission to court her daughter and soon the young woman's room at Wells College was filled with flowers from the state house, Albany, and with tiny gifts, including a puppy. At his presidential inauguration in March 1885 Cleveland insisted that the widow Folsom and her daughter stand at his side. Word began to go round that the president was to marry a Folsom. But which one, the widow or, could it possibly be her daughter: Mrs or Miss?

The president, age 48, waits until his ward, just turned 21, has graduated from college and then, in the summer of 1885, they become secretly engaged.

Grover Cleveland was lucky to live when and where he did. Were he in Victorian England, he would have been tried in Chancery for seducing his own ward. And had he lived in the USA in the second half of the twentieth century he would have had enough paedophilia, child abuse, and statutory rape charges in his closet to keep him locked up for thirty years, if found out.

And he was incredibly lucky in his unusual marriage. It worked. Frances Folsom Cleveland was not only the youngest First Lady ever, but charming, well-educated, a fashion setter, and much the most beautiful mistress the White House ever had: even the later Mrs Kennedy did not rival her. And she loved her husband. A miracle: he had become grossly overweight, with a walrus mustache that was all-too-consonant with his huge body and the rolls of neck-fat that protruded just like those of the walruses at the Washington zoo. Resolutely inactive, Cleveland could barely walk a single circuit of the White House lawn without becoming winded.

The United States Marine band, conducted by John Philip Sousa, played for the June 1886 White House Wedding. There was no dancing, however, as the president could not waltz for thirty seconds without becoming flushed and perspiring heavily.

Somehow between 1891 and 1903 the diminutive bride and the massively corpulent husband managed to produce five children. The unison cry, *Oh, Lord, let me breathe!* was heard by the servants who tried not to imagine the configuration of the two bodies.

Sadly, the first child of this union, Ruth, who was the nation's child sweetheart, died at age eleven in early 1903.

In a fittingly saccharine memorial to her parents' strange but wonderful marriage, she is still remembered daily: go out and buy a Baby Ruth candy bar.

GRAND RAPIDS, MICHIGAN. 1888

The Long Road to Irish Unity

The Great War on the Native Americans is almost over and Lieut. John Filmore Blake is bored. He has served thirteen years in the Sixth Cavalry and has ended on a high note. Given command of a company of Navahoes in 1888, he helped General Nelson Miles pursue Geronimo, chief of the Chiricahua Apache, into Mexico and finally apprehended the last legendary warrior of the American southwest. For Blake, from that moment onwards everything in America seems humdrum.

Blake marries and tries for a while to be a businessman, but starched collars and neckties choke him. In late 1894 he deserts his wife and takes off for Southern Africa, where the Transvaal Republic seems to him a noble creation. When the United Kingdom comes to war with the Afrikaner republics, he creates his own commando unit of 200 men, about fifty of whom are American-Irish and the rest a mixed bunch, mostly from Ireland.

Blake's second-in-command in his fight against British imperialism is Major John MacBride, fated to be a martyr of 1916.

They hate each other.

Later, John Blake writes a 160,000-word memoir of his experience in the Second Anglo-Afrikaner War, 1899–1902.

He mentions MacBride only once.

HATTIESBURG, MISSISSIPPI. 8 JULY 1889

Throwback?

Bare-knuckle prize fighting was banned in all thirty-eight states when John L. Sullivan fought Jake Kilrain for the world championship of a sport that would immediately cease to exist. (The next world championship was held with gloves, since reformers preferred the fighters' receiving long-term brain injury to having douches of blood sprayed impolitely all over the ringsiders.)

Both fighters were American-Irish, but Sullivan was a throwback to the legendary Mose of the Bowery Boys: a war chief with violent pathology in his soul and a need for alcohol and women that would have done credit to the Huns. At age thirty, he was brought back from alcoholic delirium and physical breakdown by a $10,000 purse and a very tough Irish trainer.

The American-Irish love Sullivan, but no longer need him. They are making it on their own, mostly honestly, and the deepest pits of immigrant violence are largely memories and those that still exist are shrinking, destined to be crowded out by lace curtains and the Catholic temperance movement.

John L. Sullivan indeed is a throwback.

But for late nineteenth-century America, he is the first wave of the future: the celebrity sportsman who makes more money from his side businesses than from his sport.

Sullivan defeats Kilrain in 75 rounds. He fights only one more time, with gloves, and is clobbered by Jim Corbett. But as a vaudeville act, temperance lecturer (yes), and speaker at lodge banquets, he picks up nearly a million dollars in side money over his career. He spends one half of it on women and whiskey and he wastes the rest.

OMAHA, NEBRASKA. 31 AUGUST 1898

Cloudwatcher

"Keep your heads up," he had told the youngsters among the Indian Scouts who followed him. "You watch the ground, sure, but you'll see Indian signs mostly on the horizon. And especially in the clouds."

Solid advice if you are intent on killing as many savages as possible, but Colonel William F. Cody had always watched clouds as portents and as memories. The Indian-signs were secondary. His father had taught him to read clouds.

Now, at Colonel Cody Day at the Trans-Mississippi Exposition, he played the part of Buffalo Bill before 24,000 spectators. He had to do four shows to keep his fans happy and at age fifty-two that was a lot of work, considering the shooting and riding he did, along with the mock battles. Thank goodness for his longtime manager John Burke and for Mr. and Mrs. Frank Butler: Mrs. Butler, as Annie Oakley, opened each show and took some of the pressure off Buffalo Bill.

Between shows, Colonel Cody repairs to his special tent. It is patrolled by two guards and nobody gets near him. The tent is made with a drop-flap near the top and Cody opens this, reclines on a large divan that he brings from town to town on his tours, and slowly blows trails of smoke from a long cheroot. The smoke contrails upwards and leads, like a winding hill trail, to the clouds. Bill Cody rests between performances by reading in the clouds the shape of his own past.

Shapes: the Chicago World's Fair of 1893 where he had been the biggest single attraction and had taught America what the West had been about. The London season played at Earl's Court, the good Queen Victoria attending not once, but twice. Sitting Bull his employee. At least for a few months. The problem with the chief was that, unlike Buffalo Bill, he was not a cloud watcher: he insisted on the rights to the royalties on all photographs taken of him and he kept his eyes on the pennies, not the horizon.

Like all good cloud watchers, Colonel Cody was patient and knew that if he waited the clouds would form shapes that other people, even those with the most literal vision, could see. That's what he had done when, in the 1870s, he had started to take rich dudes out shooting. Russian royalty. English nobility. The sort of people who liked to kill things and talk about it. Cody offered them shooting and, more importantly, his own reputation. That had been built by real actions, but equally by the dime novelist Ned Buntline. Bill Cody learned how to sell clouds.

Sometimes as he watches the clouds, he sees the annals of his own real life and he flinches: he had been a crack Indian Scout for General Sheridan, and a killer. That was one of the moments when the clouds took the shape of gargoyles, and he did not like to remember his multiple butcheries. He took to saying, when asked how many Indians he had killed, "I never killed any, 'cept to save my own life." Mostly, though, he was proud of his skill in having used his reading of cirrus, cumulous, nimbus, to hunt down renegades. The pleasure was in the cloud-reading, not the combat. And, on those moments when a tiny dust devil swept across the Omaha show grounds and skittered over his tent, it put him in mind of the dust of the great buffalo herds, kicking up clouds as they moved. And that glorious day, when he had bested Bill Comstock in a buffalo-shooting contest, 69 to 46. Bill Cody had used his .50 calibre rifle, affectionately named Lucretia Borgia. Good moments: potting Mormons in his teens and, earlier, at age eleven, becoming well-known in the Nebraska territory for shooting near Fort Kearny his first Indian. Cody could read the newspaper report of that exploit as if the print were in front of his face.

Occasionally, in the clouds, Buffalo Bill sees his surrogate father, Kit Carson. The twelve-year-old Cody had encountered him in 1858 and Carson's amazing ability with Bowie knife and firearms, combined with his quietness and small size, made him an idol – but an approachable one. At Fort Laramie, young Will Cody hung around Carson like a disciple. In later life, Cody's only son, fated to die young, was christened Kit Carson Cody.

And, in fleeting clouds, Cody catches glimpses of his real father, Isaac Cody, of a formerly Catholic family that had been in the Americas since the mid-eighteenth century, and who remembered not their religion, but their mythology. And particularly the legend, shared by hundreds of thousands of Irish people, that they were directly descended from Milesian royalty who, in myth, were Gaels from Spain who had first conquered Ireland. Isaac Cody taught young Will that clouds were portents as well as monuments. He practised what he prescribed. His people, the Irish people, why, hadn't they driven out the barbarians sometime in Time's ancient mists? And are we not doing the same here? Isaac Cody saw his own destiny as being limited by the confines of Scott County, Iowa, near the Mississippi River, and in the mid-1850s moved to Kansas, near Leavenworth, a land of great opportunity, but also a guerilla-combat zone between pro- and anti-slavery forces. War to the knife. Practice for the Civil War.

It was a knife, long and thin like a cirrus cloud, that turned Will Cody into an orphan at age eleven in 1857. His father was killed for being anti-slavery and he was, but not in any clear, blue-sky sort of way. *I was one of the pioneers of the state of Iowa*, he told a public meeting. *I voted it should be a **white** state, that Negroes whether free or slave should never be allowed to locate within its limits*. That, in the Middle Border, passed for red-hot abolitionism and led to his death.

Cloud watchers, the best of them, know that nothing is ever permanent, that signs are always transient; and that immortality on bas-reliefs on terra firma is merely a matter of reading the clouds and pointing out to one's followers that what they want to see is what you are showing them.

Colonel Cody rises from his divan. Refreshed, he is ready to create America yet one more time.

AN IRISH HISTORY OF CIVILIZATION

Book Four

America's Century

THE ROAD HOME.
IRELAND
1900–1923

Second Sundays

No. 2 Belvedere Place, just off Mountjoy Square, is an imposing four-storey Georgian row house suitable to a Member of Parliament. It is home to David Sheehy, MP and, more importantly, to his wife Bessie. She is immensely shrewd and she has turned the house into a casino. Not the usual sort of gambling den, but the place where she places her wagers on who will run Ireland when it gains Home Rule and has its own parliament and full suite of governmental posts in Dublin. With not a trace of embarrassment at her own hubris, she is selecting the ruling class for Catholic Ireland.

Every second Sunday she holds an evening salon. The guests are the age of her own sons and daughters, but she is not holding a marriage mart. (Three of her four daughters obtain university degrees, a rarity in that era.) She invites the brightest young men and a few women from the Jesuit College of the Royal University – the heir to John Henry Newman's Catholic University: it had proved too much for the Irish bishops to run and in 1883 the Jesuits had taken over and now was on its way to becoming, in 1908, University College, Dublin, part of the National University of Ireland. Mrs. Sheehy's calculation is that the quickest, brightest, most charming Catholics of this generation in Dublin will be just the right age to manage Ireland in a decade or two.

Chief among her young lions-to-be is Tom Kettle. Darkly handsome, clad in expensively tailored suits, he is the most obvious future-winner in Bessie Sheehy's stable. He already had been auditor of the "L and H," the Literary and History Society, meaning that he is the best debater and sharpest on-his-feet thinker among a passle of very nimble verbal kittens. He's on his way to being Ireland's youngest MP.

More compelling, with squeaky voice, weird northern accent, and a straggly red beard that is more ambition than achievement, is Francis Skeffington. He argues brilliantly for views that are feminist, pacifist, socialist and occasionally vegetarian, at a time when those were heroic concepts. He has the passionate charmlessness of the pure northern-Catholic, which is to say, he argues everything with the dead seriousness of an Ulster Presbyterian, combined with the dogged determination of the forever-victimized Ulster Papist. Bessie Sheehy believes in horses-for-courses and can visualize him as the minister for culture and education in a Catholic state that would, regrettably, include Ulster Protestants who would require to be spoken to sharply.

Mrs. Sheehy's pet project is a lad who always arrives late and always immediately approaches the high-backed chair in the corner of the drawing room where she presides, like a vicereine at a durbar. James Joyce, much less secure than he ever lets on, sits at Mrs. Sheehy's feet and lets himself be petted because he needs mothering. He's a bit over his depth in this crowd. They're from wealthier families, and he's not as brittley clever as they are: he's headed for a pass degree and he fails in his bid to become auditor of the L and H. In these days, in fact, he's seeking comfort in the college's Sodality of the Blessed Virgin Mary, which he had joined when at Belvedere College. He's not a cynical member, no matter what he later claims.

Despite his appearing to be a second-class runner, Mrs. Sheehy sees a glint of something special in Jimmy. This says a lot for her, since she could scarcely bring herself to look at his grimy shirt collars and long, dirty fingernails. Joyce impresses Bessie Sheehy mostly because of his spine. She admires (though disagrees) with a stance he had taken the previous spring, in opposition to most of the bright-young-things in her salon. Most of them, including her own sons, Tom Kettle and Francis Skeffington had signed a letter protesting against William Butler Yeats's play *The Countess Cathleen*. They did so on the grounds that the play, set in the time of the Great Famine, showed a female selling her own soul to save the peasantry. Strictly speaking, this was heresy, and it gave the Catholic *jeunesse dorée* a chance to kick a Protestant in his sins.

Jimmy Joyce – Dirty Jimmy, Jimmy the Hatter, his friends called him – refuses to sign, and they cannot move him.

Bessie Sheehy has no idea where young Mr. Joyce will fit into her haute-Catholic universe, but she has no doubt that he will become a fixed star.

DUBLIN. NOVEMBER 1901

Days of the Devilment

Of Bessie Sheehy's young lions, the pride most proud consisted of Skeffington and Joyce. They agreed on little save their respect for each other and, that aside, each found almost everybody and everything wrong. For them, a great game was bedevilling the Jesuit authorities without being turfed. Their best moment came in 1901 when the faculty censor of the college literary magazine, *St. Stephen's*, rejected an article by each. Skeffington's was a denunciation of the college for not admitting women to equal status with men. Joyce's was a free-swinging attack on the parochial nature of the Irish theatrical revival under Yeats and company and a call for Continental standards and an escape from the trolls who were controlling the Irish cultural revival. Balked by the censor, in November each threw in a few pounds and 85 copies of *Two Essays* were printed.

A bit of devilment, but more.

In 1904, Francis Skeffington, having been appointed as the first lay registrar of the college, a plum post guaranteeing an income for life, resigned. He would not moderate his views on female equality to suit the Jesuit fathers.

And, in 1905, James Joyce quit Ireland, pretty much for good, rather than accept suffocation.

DUBLIN. NOVEMBER 1902

Battle of the Network Stars

Near the entrance to the National Library occurred the most mythologized intersection in Irish literary history since Grainne's head met the rock.

Neither genius remembered accurately anything the other said. And each several times re-invented his own words.

Yeats and Joyce were awkward acquaintances not only because of their age difference – seventeen years – but because they repaired to a Harcourt Street café and ordered chocolate and sticky buns, an aesthetic mistake. The treacly icing on the buns made little crumbs of bran stick to the fingers. Yeats kept wiping his hands with his pocket handkerchief, as if he had recently been in a particularly nasty public lavatory. Joyce let the crumbs and icing accumulate and looked longingly at them. He had not had breakfast and if he were alone he would have licked his fingers.

While moving their lips in discussion of serious matters, each lets his mind wander:

  – *How can anyone have such long and filthy fingernails?*
  – *Christ, I wouldn't even want to be hanged in such a silly-looking tie.*
They agree to keep in touch.

DUBLIN. CHRISTMAS DAY, 1903

Ghosts (1)

In middle age Gabriel and Gretta Conroy spend Christmas Day remembering. They do not go out and they do not call on friends. Their only servant, a country girl who finds them aloof and enigmatic, has the holidays off: that perk is one of the only reasons she stays on with them when there are so many better positions available. The Conroys treat themselves to a coal fire and watch the patterns of light as the afternoon draws in on them. They remember the good times, at least that's what they call them now, when the Misses Morkan held their annual Christmas dance. Gretta and Gabriel censor their reminiscences. They are careful to avoid the bright talk and snow-traced pain of the 1892 party, when Gabriel learned for the first time that he was not the only light his wife's eyes had seen. They let that ghost lie.

Arthur Griffith spends Christmas Day 1903 alone, writing carefully. He has a natural simplicity of style that contrasts with the false-Latinate prose that is typical of the men and women in the nationalist movement. He considers them to be his betters and it would be above-his-station to imitate their florid style. Griffith is a printer by trade, a nationalist by vocation. A broad-shouldered figure, he always looks as if he is about to punch someone – and hard: his Achilles tendons were deformed at birth and he has to walk with his weight on his toes. In actual fact, Arthur Griffith is the nicest revolutionary in the world. Everyone agrees.

Griffith is completing a series of articles he will publish in his paper, the *United Irishman*, and later repackage as a pamphlet. This proposal for Irish independence, published in 1904 under the surprising title *The Resurrection of Hungary*, is the product of a genuinely gentle disposition. Following what Griffith sees, rather generously, as the Hungarian pattern, he wants the Irish nationalist MPs to abandon London and come home and set up an Irish parliament that rests on its moral power, not on force. Irish people will buy Irish goods. And the relationship with Great Britain will be that the two nations will share a monarch, but nought else. This is the Catholic version of the beloved ghost of the old Ascendancy: a return to the constitution of 1782.

Much of the uncanny persuasiveness of *The Resurrection* lies in Griffith's own character. It shines through the prose and, in the tiny world of nationalist Dublin, everyone knows Griffith and grants his sincerity. When, in 1905, Griffith proposes that his nonviolent, self-creation policy be adopted by the vaguely organized Irish National Council, he succeeds. A friend, Maire Butler, has told him to give it an Irish name and that helps. The policy, now labelled *Sinn Fein*, is endorsed and then migrates swiftly to being the name of a newspaper edited by Griffith and the name of an organization dedicated to bringing back a past that never was. In English, Sinn Fein later comes to mean Just-Us, but in Arthur Griffith's mind it meant justice, gently arrived at.

LIMERICK CITY. MID-JANUARY 1904

Not Yet Bloomsday

"You heard whast the priest said, so you did!" The stumpy man in the duncher digs his mate in the ribs."So let's get on the job, lad!" The two men are the vanguard of three dozen men and a few ragamuffin followers. Their job, divinely inspired, is to break the windows of the Jew-shops.

"Dagocide! That's what the good Redemptorist said they do. They do Dagocide!"

Windows shatter and a torch is thrown into the shop. The men move on.

"Killers of our Lord!"

"Rag-sheenies and cheats!"

"Ireland for the Irish!"

"Noses on them like fish-heuks."

"An' bloated bellies, like a poisoned pup, so!"

The Limerick Pogrom of 1904 simmers on and off for several weeks. Jewish merchants, scrap dealers, small traders, are attacked in the street, their carts upset, houses stoned, their children harassed. Some beatings occur, but no killings. The pogrom fits the style of the times, but by the standards of serious pogroms, such as that going on in Russia at the same moment, the Limerick effort was small-time: in part because it was hard to find sufficient Jews to persecute.

The mixture of Redemptorist enthusiasm and nationalist purity was an embarrassment to some Irish nationalists: the one-armed prophet Michael Davitt did not forget the virtue of Zion, nor did his tongue cling to the roof of his mouth. He denounced the pogroms as a barbarous malignity that disgraced Ireland. Most nationalists outside of Limerick watched in neutral bemusement and took the event to be one of those local habits, such as virtually every Catholic adult male's belonging to a sodality, that made Limerick a curious place.

Years later, James Joyce predicated his time-catch of 1904 on the assumption that, outside of Limerick City, one could be both Jewish and Irish, of a sort.

DUBLIN. OCTOBER, 1905

God Save Ireland, Cry the Heroes

Cardinal Cullen was right! Let the students have an ounce of freedom and they will produce a pound of trouble. How could blessed Newman be so wrong?

Seeing an old-fashioned Jesuit in the act of crying is a terrible thing to behold and while Fr. William Delaney, the president of the Jesuit College, Dublin, wept, his second-in-command edged his way out the door. The president had every right to tears, mind you, for weren't the Jesuits underwriting with their own unpaid toil the education of the most promising youths of Catholic Ireland, and in fall-down mansions at 85 and 86 St. Stephen's Green that had for dignity only a good address? With Trinity College within sight on a bad day, opulent and self-contained and full of heresy, Fr. Delaney's post was uncomfortable enough. Trinity granted its own degrees, but the Jesuits' students had to sit for the examining body, the "Royal University," as if they were, were, ... natives or something. Father Delaney has been pressing hard for a governmental charter and some funds for actually teaching his flock. He is nearly seventy years of age and mortally tired.

His students have been Irish patriots, rioting in support of grants to the Catholic university, just the sort of action that would put the garnering of new grants at risk. The Earlsfort Terrace home of the Royal University had been invaded by a band of the Jesuit College's brightest sparks during the ceremony conferring degrees.

Just as the audience was to rise to sing God Save the King, down from the top of the Royal's massive pipe organ abseiled the coxswain of the Catholic university's heavyweight crew, Francis Cruise O'Brien. His mates followed him and O'Brien yelled loudly that they would not permit the imperial anthem to be sung. As the authorities moved in on them, they marched out of the hall loudly singing God Save Ireland.

Father Delaney puts his head in his hands and weeps.

FORKHILL, COUNTY ARMAGH. 15 MAY 1906

Real Revolutions

"Dear People. We must go outside and divide." Father McCartney, the parish priest, was chairing a meeting to decide if the tenants of the Forkhill Estate would become owners of the land they rented. He had called the meeting to be held at the Maphoner national school, and now he realized it was too small: the tenants were packed tighter than sheep at the Newry market. "Outside. Now!" He had the loudest voice in the parish and no one ever misheard a word Fr. McCartney said.

Outside, he directed those in favour of coming under the Wyndham Estates Act of 1903 to line up beside the school pump. Those opposed to stand by the school's boundary baulk.

The decision was unanimous: acceptance. And within a year, men and women who had never been anything but tenants owned their own farmlands.

Across Ireland similar meetings took place, irregularly, without pattern, like a wet hay rick burning, but with undeniable results. The dull, unsung land acts of 1903 and of 1909, the culmination of a skein of land legislation begun in 1870 by successive Liberal governments, turned over the ownership of Irish farmland in an economic revolution more radical than anything in Europe before Bolshevik collectivization – and longer lasting and more successful. With a wisdom so rare as to be random, the United Kingdom's government gave a bonus to any landlord who would sell out his estate to his tenants, and provided a mortgage for the tenants at a rate so low that the tenants' buying their own farmland was cheaper than renting it. And back-rents were wiped from the books. By 1920, *before* the Irish political revolution (and, in the north, counter-revolution) was effected, eleven million acres either had passed to their farmer-occupiers or were in the process of being transferred. That is to say, most of the farmland of the nation.

"My people," Father McCartney pronounced. "This is a great day. We have spied out the Promised Land. And it is ours."

EAST TYRONE. JULY 1906

Rising Star

In the hills of east Tyrone, Tom Kettle, clean-shaven, handsome, articulate, is the nationalist candidate in an important by-election. Kettle is the first of Bessie Sheehy's guild of young lions to break out of the urban Catholic elite at the Jesuit College, Dublin, and make an impression on the outside world. He is helped by the old Second Sundays gang: Frank Sheehy-Skeffington (now, with a hyphenated name as he has married Hanna Sheehy), and the Sheehy boys, Eugene and Richard. And Mary Sheehy, whom Kettle is courting.

The heavy fighting, however, is carried by grizzled local nationalists and the charming young solicitor, Kettle. It's a cockpit area, split dead evenly between unionists and nationalists, meaning between Protestants and Catholics. "You've a terrible road ahead of you," one of the veteran nationalists tells Kettle.

"Is it full of hills?" he asks innocently.

"No, it's full of Protestants."

Kettle's charm and good looks seduce just enough Protestant voters (well, the man does have a very Protestant look to him) to allow him to squeak in by eighteen votes.

Ireland's youngest MP continues to court Mary Sheehy and in September 1909 they are married in the pro-cathedral, Dublin.

Bessie Sheehy purrs with satisfaction.

THE VATICAN. 2 AUGUST 1907

Modern Marriage (1)

Pope Pius X issues his *Ne Temere* decree. The Catholic bishops celebrate. It's the cordial for which they long have thirsted. To Protestant clergy and lay leaders it tastes like wormwood and confirms everything they believe about the imperial nature of the Romans.

Ne Temere erases the Dutch Precedent, the mid-eighteenth-century escape clause that recognized as valid in Catholic canon law Catholic-Protestant marriages, even if they were conducted by a Protestant minister. (This for countries where Catholics were under penal laws.) With penal days long past, the bishops wanted the full Tridentine treatment for Ireland and they got it.

Henceforth, no mixed-marriage would be valid under Catholic canon law (even if valid in civil law) unless a Catholic priest presided and the non-Catholic partner signed a legal form that was imperious in tone and humbling in detail. The non-Catholic affirmed that he or she would not interfere with the religion of the Catholic partner; the Catholic partner affirmed that he or she would endeavour in every way to bring the non-Catholic to the True Faith. They both swore and signed that all children of the marriage would be baptized Catholic and educated in Catholic schools. And they both swore that they would not engage in any parallel marriage ceremony – either civil or Protestant. The only marital bond was the Church's.

Then, and only then, the mixed-religion couple could be married in a side-chapel and without a nuptial mass.

The *Ne Temere* pledge reads like some jog-trot insurance document or commercial bill-of-sale and would be easy to ignore. Error: it is in fact one of the most inflammatory pieces of prose in twentieth-century

Irish history. Protestants are not keen on mixed marriages any more than are their Catholic counterparts. But what they hear, accurately, is that any marriage that includes a Protestant is necessarily second-rate. And, crucially, they understand that the children of any mixed marriage will be "grabbed" – that is the most common term – by the Roman Catholics.

Their politicians are worried that Home Rule will be Rome Rule.

Their pastors and the parents of children of marriageable age are more worried that Home Rules will be Rome's Rules.

PARIS. 1908

Modern Marriage (2)

Even before *Ne Temere* was issued, Maud Gonne had decided that its principles were the embodiment of wisdom. She was in love, wildly, with "Major" John MacBride. On the surface the union was unlikely. MacBride was the son of Catholic small shopkeepers from Mayo and he was the perfect bogman: big, red-haired, hard-drinking, ultra-patriotic and totally unreflective. But Gonne, though she might play at being the astral lady for W.B. Yeats, liked a bit of the rough. So when MacBride became a hero in the small Irish Brigade that fought in South Africa, a campaign she zealously approved, their stars crossed. (Mind you, exactly why Irish patriotism should involve fighting on the side of the Afrikaners, who still saw slavery as a practice of their Golden Age, is beyond rational explanation.)

In 1902, Miss Gonne agreed to join the One True Faith and, after she took instruction from French nuns, she was received as a Catholic. In 1903 she and MacBride married. They had more in common than at first appears. Gonne had already borne two illegitimate children, one boy (dead), and a girl, Iseult. And MacBride, while liberating the Afrikaners from English influence, had sired at least one coloured child and probably others.

They lived in Paris, London and Dublin, but by 1905 Gonne was spending most of her time in Paris with her eleven year-old daughter Iseult, her seventeen-year-old half-sister, Eileen Wilson, and with the fruits of the MacBride-Gonne marriage, Seaghan (later modernized to Sean). And MacBride for the most part lived in Dublin. A French divorce suit followed. Gonne charged MacBride with many offences, only one of which was undoubtedly true: he was a violent and constant drunk. ("I have spent my life looking down barrels," was his standard line to the Irish police, and the well-known response was, "Yes, indeed: porter barrels.")

But for the rest of her charges, who can know? Did MacBride seduce the seventeen-year-old Eileen Wilson? Did he sexually abuse the eleven-year-old Iseult? Did he forcefully penetrate his wife's several orifices without her consent? Did he ...? oh, one could go on and on and Maud did. No one can tell, because truth is the first victim of a nasty divorce.

The French courts grant Maud a judicial separation and custody of the boy, but MacBride has visiting rights, an indication that the court did not believe all of Maud's charges. She fights on and in 1908 is refused a French divorce, although MacBride's visiting rights are reduced to once a week. Gonne stays in Paris and raises young Seaghan as a French speaker, as a means of limiting communication with his father.

A modern marriage? failed? Not by the standards of the church, or of Maud Gonne.

When John MacBride was executed as one of the Irish martyrs of the 1916 Easter Rising, Maud Gonne wrote "As for my husband, he has entered Eternity by the great door of sacrifice which Christ opened and has therefore atoned for all ..." He had become a saint, "so that praying for him, I can also ask for his prayers ..."

Thereafter, she took to wearing widow's weeds permanently. In black regalia, very tall and now very thin, she becomes the ceaseless voice of the raven, pronouncing doom upon all who fail to hew to the pure and narrow line of Irish republicanism.

ST. PATRICK'S COLLEGE, MAYNOOTH. 22 JUNE 1909

Terribly Thin-Skinned

From the turn of the century onward, the most effective advocate of the Irish language revival was the Rev. Dr. M.P. O'Hickey, chair of Irish at St. Patrick's College, Maynooth. Without him, in hundreds of small towns throughout rural Ireland there would not have been any Gaelic League branch, because the local parish priest would not approve the Protestant-tinged gentility of Dr. Hyde's League. But when Fr. O'Hickey came around, all brusque enthusiasm and 100 percent trustworthy Catholic, they threw in with him and became local sponsors. The Dublin intelligentsia took the credit, but O'Hickey did the hard pulling.

Why then, is he standing before the trustees of Maynooth Seminary, defending himself against dismissal?

Because, unlike the down-country parish clergy, they prefer the gentlemanly conduct of Dr. Hyde with his "advocacy of compulsory Irish, but in language worthy of a gentleman."

Having won in 1908 what they had long wanted – a confederation of Catholic universities paid for by the state – the bishops had come under strong pressure to be sure that the new National University of Ireland would require knowledge of the Irish language for admission and as part of the university curriculum. Most of their constituents – the Catholic middle-class – agreed.

But Fr. O'Hickey pushed the case too hard. He not only argued for compulsory Irish but he dared to make a joke. And in a pamphlet where the lawyers and professionals of Ireland could savour it. It was not much of a joke, really, and was only a response to the Catholic episcopal standing committee (who doubled as senators on the governing body of the new university) saying that they opposed Irish because it might lead some Catholic students to enrol in Trinity College, Dublin, which had no such requirement. Regarding the bishops' committee, Father O'Hickey had written that of these five persons, one was staunch, but "as for the others, I shall say nothing further than to recommend them to your earnest prayers."

Not much of a joke. But the five ecclesiastical officers, headed in this case by the president of Maynooth, Monsignor Daniel Mannix, who was on his way to becoming an Irish hero in Australia for his allegedly dead-true nationalism, demand O'Hickey's head. The full bench of trustees comply and he is dismissed, in mid-July, on the grounds of insubordination. His bishop offers him a mission – not even a parish – in Waterford.

The bishops' authority is preserved. So it is safe, in June 1910, for the senate of the National University of Ireland to decide that, beginning three years thence, Irish shall be required for university entrance.

LONDON. FEBRUARY 1910

Dreamtime and the Cobra

The time foretold by St. Malachy has come again. That's what they say up the Sperrins. Shorter-viewed nationalists remember 1885, when, as now in 1910, they held the balance of power in the Westminster house of commons. A deal is struck: the Irish nationalists will help the liberal party spancel the house of lords and, in return, Home Rule for Ireland will follow.

Do not celebrate too soon.

Sir Edward Carson, Dublin's hardest lawyer, is elected leader of the Irish unionists in mid-February. He has only twenty-one seats in a parliament of 670 members.

Do not enter dreamtime. Remember that Sir Edward already had shown that he not only possessed a quicker wit than did Oscar Wilde, but that he had considerably greater powers of concentration.

BELFAST. 1911–12

A Practical Revolutionary

There could scarcely be a tougher time or place to be a labour organizer, so James Connolly discovers. For a time, he has been successful in organizing the Belfast dockers, stokers, and seamen and garnered for them significant wage increases. But there his victories end. Since June 1911, he has been working as James Larkin's northern delegate for the Irish Transport and General Worker's Union and he has big hopes.

Because of the sectarian split in the Belfast working class, union organizing is especially difficult. It's made much rougher by the indirect rivalry (among the Protestant working class) provided by the grass-roots Unionist campaign that is rising in response to the threat of Home Rule for Ireland. In September at least 50,000 Unionists of varying stripes and colours (Orangemen, Royal Black preceptory and everyday sympathizers) march to Craigavon House and are there addressed in a near-treasonous call to unity by Sir Edward Carson. That's a hard act to cover.

To make matters worse, Connolly's next assignment is to organize female linen workers. Getting women to form a union and then to act militantly was extraordinary difficult – they did not even have the vote, much less a sense of collective female economic identity.

Connolly's moment of possibility occurs in 1912, when several Belfast linen manufacturers, clearly working in collusion, post regulations forbidding their mill and factory girls from singing, laughing, or talking on the job! These women are hardly Bolsheviks; for the most part they like their work and the economic freedom it gives them. But not talk to one's friends? even if some of them were of the wrong sort? or share a laugh and a song?

Connolly works hard on these indignities, and though he brings a few mill girls out on strike, he's unable to gain for them any real improvement. Yet in failing, and admitting that he failed, James Connolly reveals something about himself that is important historically. Usually, Connolly is listed as being among the only three persons in the physical-force branch of Irish republicanism who were able to think clearly and write forcefully in ideological terms (Theobald Wolfe Tone and James Fintan Lalor being the other two), and his martyrdom in 1916 is seen as a debilitating loss for Irish political suppleness.

The loss was even greater, for Connolly was a gloriously practical man. Once it's clear that he cannot successfully unionize the textile women, he gives them the best advice they could hear:

I've advised them not to go back in ones and twos, but to gather outside the mills and to go in in a body.

To go in singing.

If, when at work one girl laughs and is reproved, they are all to begin laughing.

If one girl sings and is checked, they are all to sing.

And if a girl is dismissed for breaking the rules they are all to walk out with her.

That's not the advice of a brittle ideologue, but of someone who not only understands workers, but likes and respects them and, dear God, what a difference he would have made to the new Ireland.

BELFAST. FEBRUARY 1912

Mirrors (1)

Bold as brass, unpredictable as the weather, Winston Churchill comes to Belfast. He is in one of his liberal arabesques and will speak along-side John Redmond at a Home Rule rally.

This Churchill has all the volatility and most of the mannerisms of Lord Randolph Churchill, who twenty-six years earlier had rallied the Ulster unionists against the first Home Rule bill.

The Ulster Hall, where Lord Randolph had held his pyrotechnic display, has been booked by the unionists, in a nifty move in the local Catholic-Protestant chess game. Therefore the rally has to take place in Celtic Park, home of the Catholic football club of the Lower Falls.

Seven thousand cheering nationalists hear Winston Churchill praise the British Empire and the place that a self-governing Irish par-liament will have within it.

Unlike his father, he believes the Green Card is the one to play. For the moment.

BELFAST; ISLANDMAGEE; BALMORAL.
FEBRUARY-APRIL 1912

Speed Tests

Exactly along the line that Patrick the Briton had been rowed at the start of his captivity as a slave, is an invisible avenue in the water: the pathway where the ocean liners and freighters that are fashioned in the Belfast shipyards are tested. Markers placed on Islandmagee, thirty-foot high pylons, painted black and white, give speed ratings over a ten-mile test run. One of these is placed on the Gobbins Cliffs, where, allegedly in 1642, the local Protestants sent their Catholic neighbours spiralling downwards to a rocky death. The final one is just at the tip of Islandmagee, at precisely the point where Patrick would have first seen the harbour towards which he was being taken to begin his Irish captivity. There the *Titanic* undergoes its final speed test with no difficulties whatsoever.

The vessel is perfect.

In April, at Balmoral on the outskirts of Belfast, Andrew Bonar Law, the leader of the Conservative party in the commons, speaks to nearly 100,000 Ulster unionists. A Canadian, born of Ulster-Scots parents, he understands their mythology and emotions to perfection. "Once again you hold the pass for the Empire." As in Londonderry in 1689, "you are a besieged city. The government by the Parliament Act [the Home Rule bill] have erected a boom against you, a boom to cut you off from the help of the British people. You will burst that boom!"

The speech is perfect.

By sunset on 15 April, the perfect vessel, the best Belfast has ever crafted, is resting on the floor of the Atlantic Ocean, a monument to the folly of excess, even when perfectly achieved.

DUBLIN. AUGUST 1912

The Rat Pack

James Joyce's final visit to Dublin needn't have been. If only Bessie Sheehy's new-Catholic intelligentsia had been a bit more generous, especially Tom Kettle.

Still, Joyce should have seen it coming: most of his old friends choosing to keep the church happy, whatever the cost in friendship and art. He'd seen the test case, the *Playboy* riots of 1907, when Richard Sheehy and Francis Cruise O'Brien and most of Bessie Sheehy's pack had fought to have Synge's play banned: on the public grounds that it was obscene, describing as it did a woman's undergarment as a "shift"; and in private because the work carried a latent message that the new Gaelic-learning, Dublin-Catholic elite knew was true but dared never openly admit, that they and their ideas had nothing to do with Irish life as it was lived by the overwhelming mass of the people.

So Joyce should have known that when he called upon Tom Kettle – my best friend in Ireland, he told Nora Barnacle – to help him get around the havering of his publisher, George Roberts of Maunsel Publishers, and put *Dubliners* in print, he was asking for blood from a stone.

Kettle was on a long downhill slide. He was drinking heavily, was frequently depressed and had given up his seat in the house of commons just at the moment when the Liberals were passing Home Rule. Instead of stepping further into the corridors of power, he became

Professor of National Economics at the newly-formed University College, Dublin, the state-financed reincarnation of the old Jesuit College. Tom Kettle knew nothing of economics as a discipline and refused to learn. Instead of lecturing, on clear days he took his students out onto Stephen's Green and talked about whatever entered his head.

The publishers, Maunsel, were also the publishers to University College, Dublin. George Roberts of Maunsel's was particularly offended, and his business sense alerted, by Joyce's "An Encounter," concerning a pederast.

Joyce asked Kettle's help, and considering that Kettle had been instrumental in Maunsel's obtaining the printing contract for University College, this was shrewd on the surface.

Yet, "I'll slate that book," Kettle declared, meaning that he would savage it if it were published.

Joyce reminded Kettle that they had both been present when the pederast had made his move and that the story was hardly a figment of imagination.

"Yes, we have all met him."

Truth is not its own justification?

"'An Encounter' is beyond anything in outspokenness that I have ever read."

So, he would not help?

"Maunsel will incur libel suits."

And the church will take away its contracts?

No reply.

Joyce abandons Dublin forever, his book unpublished, his luggage carried up the gangplank by a platoon of invisible Dubliners, creatures more substantial than those he leaves behind.

CASTLEDAWSON, CO. LONDONDERRY; BELFAST.
JUNE-JULY 1912

Mirrors (2)

Just a Sunday School excursion. A group of youngsters and their chaperones on a healthy outing fall victim to bad planning. They are in Castledawson on the same day the Ancient Order of Hibernians is holding a parade. The Hibernians kick the kids and beat up the Sunday School teachers.

Three days later, the Protestant shipyard workers of Belfast take revenge. They expel the Catholics from the yards and beat up as many as they can catch.

DUBLIN. SEPTEMBER-DECEMBER 1912

Heroes

Much more concentrated, more carefully planned, more tactically shrewd than anything the old landlords had done in the countryside was the attack of 1912 on the Dublin working class. Beginning as a strike by tram workers, it turned into, first, a lock-out and then into a full assault by capital upon labour. Big capital, small capital, the church, the police all worked to break the Irish Transport and General Workers Union and, ultimately, the spirit of the newly-forming urban working class.

Lots of blood. But as in so many wars, big and small, the noncombatants, mostly women and children, paid as much as did the men with their crow-bars and bricks, fighting the goon squads and police. Big capital calculated that starving the children was the way to break the men, for children's tears and women's courage are harder for a man to carry than is fear of a hobnailed boot.

The Home Rule elite – Bessie Sheehy's rat pack – was either on the side of capital (the elder statesman, David Sheehy, MP, denounced James Larkin as an anarchist) or in a mushy middle-of-the-road position. (Tom Kettle, Eugene Sheehy, Osborn Bergin tried to form a peace committee, but it was scuttled when Kettle, the chairman, showed up for the first meeting vaporously drunk, a bunch of carnations in one hand and a bag of oysters in the other.)

Only Frank and Hanna Sheehy-Skeffington were unambiguously with the workers. (No surprise, really: years earlier, in a litmus event, Frank had been the only one of Bessie Sheehy's core pack to refuse to approve howling Synge's *Playboy* from the boards, even though he did not himself like the play.)

Frank was now an agnostic, which was just as well, as at this moment the church was decidedly unchristian. Learning that children were becoming cadaverous with malnutrition, English trade unions offered to pay for their fare to England and to feed and house them.

The Catholic bishops and clergy respond with alarm and position priests, supported by armed thugs, at the gangways of the ships. There mothers who try to place their children on board have their names taken, and they are quickly reported to their own local clergy who visit them with a message of the eternal torment such behaviour will bring them. And their children.

The church's surface reason is that though rickets and scurvy might disappear if these youngsters ate a few decent English meals, their eternal souls would starve. The danger of the children's being exposed to Protestantism is too great. Beneath the surface the situation is simpler: at this moment, capital and church are one, for they share a common nightmare: the emergence of an independent working class that will not lie down.

Hanna and Frank, being pacifists, fight with straight backs and ingenuity only. They try to convoy mothers and children through the intimidating lines of priests and thugs; sometimes they disguise the evacuees in middle-class gear; they work out stowaway routes. And, most importantly, they serve as honest witnesses, attempting to shame the clergy in their quayside inquisition.

ULSTER. 28 SEPTEMBER 1912

Distaff Power

Being convinced in our consciences that Home Rule would be disastrous to the material well-being of Ulster as well as the whole of Ireland, subversive of our civil and religious freedom, destructive of our citizenship, and perilous to the Unity of the Empire, We, whose names are underwritten ...

This pledge, harking back to the seventeenth-century Scottish covenanters and, ultimately, to the covenant sworn by the Children of Israel, is signed on a single day by nearly one-half million Ulster citizens. All of the north closed down for the day. Belfast was virtually silent as groups of men and, separately, women walked, four, eight, twelve abreast to pledge to fight to the utmost against being taken out of the Wholly non-Roman Empire.

... do hereby pledge ourselves in solemn Covenant throughout this our time of threatened calamity to stand by one another in defending for ourselves and our children our cherished position of equal citizenship in the United Kingdom.

The intimidating efficiency of this Covenant Day is obvious. If these people can put this display together in a twelve-hour period, what could they do when armed and given time to prepare for warfare on their own ground?

... and in using all means which may be found necessary to defeat the present conspiracy to set up a Home Rule parliament in Ireland.

The shrewder observers note something less obvious. Unlike the various forms of the nationalist movement, which have only a few ornamental or contumacious females, the Ulster unionists have consciously marshalled their womenfolk. A special form is signed by women and nearly half the signatures on the Covenant are those of adult females.

This changes the strategic balance dramatically. The London authorities can see that, in contrast to the southern nationalists, the northern unionists are a solid block, a huge weld of families. This is not some movement of the privileged classes or an all-male bit of chest-thumping. It is much harder to handle: brothers, sisters, wives and husbands are not to be split from each other. This is a politician's and a military tactician's nightmare: to force something on these people will require the conquest of an entire population, barony by parish by townland by family.

In sure confidence that God will defend the right we hereto subscribe our names.

THE ROTUNDA, DUBLIN. 25 NOVEMBER 1913

Mirrors (3)

Eoin MacNeill, a County Antrim Catholic, presides over the first public meeting of the Irish Volunteers. Formed in imitation of the adamantine Ulster Volunteer Force, it is run from the back room by the Irish Republican Brotherhood. MacNeill, a naive professor of Irish and medieval history at University College, Dublin, has no idea that he is a marionette dancing on a set of strings.

This meeting is the last time that Fr. Eugene Sheehy and Edmund – now Eamon – de Valera set eyes on each other.

Or not.

Father Sheehy is in the front row of this recruiting session. He listens intently as the manifesto of the Irish Volunteer Force is read. Implicitly, the Land League priest is giving his blessing to the force. Recruits are called for.

De Valera is among the men in the second row and soon he will enlist.

Neither Fr. Sheehy nor de Valera attempts to catch each other's eye. No sign of recognition passes between them.

Both are patriots. Each knows more about their shared past than either thinks expedient to acknowledge.

DUBLIN. 29 NOVEMBER 1913

Who Fears to Speak (1)

James Connolly writes in the *Irish Worker*:
We are told that the English people contributed their help to our enslavement. It is true. It is also true that the Irish people duly contributed soldiers to crush every democratic movement of the English people from the deportation of Irish soldiers to serve the cause of political despotism under Charles I to the days of Featherstone under Asquith. Slaves themselves, the English helped to enslave others; slaves themselves, the Irish people helped to enslave others. There is no room for recrimination.

THE CURRAGH, COUNTY KILDARE. MARCH 1914

A White Linen Flag

When the commanding officer of the Third Cavalry Brigade at the U.K. army's central barracks announces that he and the overwhelming majority of his officers would prefer dismissal from the military rather than march on the Ulster Protestants, they are acting in an instinctively chivalric way. White men don't attack each other's homes.

It's mutiny, but their masters in London do the calculations. The arithmetic is simple. A provisional government has been announced by Sir Edward Carson to come into effect if a Home Rule act becomes operative. Roughly half-a-million adult Protestants in Ulster have signed a pledge to fight Home Rule by any means necessary. Add in youths and, realistically, one has about a million people to coerce. And they are remarkably well organized. The Ulster Volunteer Force, though still only a shot-gun and small-bore army, is better disciplined than is, say, the militia in England.

The Westminster politicians listen to the generals read out their sums: there are a million thoroughly enraged Protestants and the army cannot be counted on to deal with them.

Ulster is a colony of fire-ants.

LARNE, HOWTH. 1914

Mirrors (4)

Motorcars.

Heavily clouded night.

Near the spot where St. Patrick first touched Ireland.

Twenty-four and twenty-five April, a hulk, the *Clydevalley*, lands 40,000 modern rifles and three-and-a-half million rounds of ammunition purchased in Hamburg.

All telephone and telegraph wires cut.

Through the black night, watchers on the hills behind Maghermorne and Gleno see something they have never previously witnessed: a caravan of motor vehicles with headlamps, moving slowly to Larne harbour and then, vehicle-by-vehicle, moving away. The closest thing to this that Ireland has previously seen occurred in the 1840s, when thousands of pitch torches lit the way to Daniel O'Connell's monster-meetings. Extreme politics with a liturgical solemnity. A candlelight vigil for a disunited Ireland.

By morning the Ulster Volunteer Force has the weapons secure in a thousand hiding places.

Later, in mid-July, at Howth, County Dublin, the Irish Volunteers imitate the UVF, although in a socially upscale manner. They employ a 51' yacht, the *Asgard*, that had been built in 1905 by a Norwegian designer to the specifications of Erskine Childers, an English novelist and political journalist with Irish nationalist sympathies. Like the unionists, the nationalists buy guns in Hamburg. In their case, the purchasing agent is the goateed poet and former Ceylon tea-planter Darrell Figgis. The crew of the boat includes Mary Spring-Rice, daughter of a family of titled landlords – the Monteagles of Brandon, who have been on the liberal wing of Irish politics since the 1830s and are known as progressive Protestants.

The Irish Volunteers' cargo is a tithe of that of the UVF's, and it is almost apprehended before it is dispersed. Almost.

By mid-summer 1914 there are thousands of weapons in Ireland and more on the way.

SOUTH DOWN. 14 JUNE 1914

The South Down Militia are the Terror of the Land

Roger Hall, commander of the Second Battalion of the South Down regiment of the UVF, finds it necessary to remind his men of the standards demanded in his unit.

Ulster Volunteers are not to mix themselves up in riots or street fights unless to protect themselves or other Protestants ...

Volunteers have already been advised to provide themselves with batons or thick sticks ...

Indiscriminate revolver firing is strictly forbidden.

Commander Hall wonders if he is being too strict.

WOODENBRIDGE, COUNTY WICKLOW. SEPTEMBER 1914

All for the Empire?

Civil war in Ulster is averted by the Wartoendallwars.

John Redmond, destined to be the last of the Parnellite political line, calls on the members of the Irish Volunteer Force to enlist. The battle is to save civilization, he says.

Meanwhile, Tom Kettle, who had been buying arms on the Continent for the Volunteers, moves on to Belgium as a war correspondent. There he chronicles German atrocities and comes to identify strongly with the Allies. He returns home, joins the Ninth Dublin Fusiliers as a lieutenant, and stumps the countryside, signing up young men to save the Empire.

The war will be short, everyone knows, so it's important to get in on it. The Catholic elite – the sort of men and women produced by Bessie Sheehy's salon – know that they will only have a country to run if Home Rule becomes real; and that requires a British victory and some gratitude in London's heart to the good decent loyal Irish of the south.

By Christmas 1914, three full divisions are made up of Irish enlistees. One of these, the Thirty-Sixth Division, was the Ulster Volunteer Force in new garb. The other two Irish divisions were mixed, but mostly Catholic. Men enlisted because they believed in the cause and, as always, because a good fight was the quickest route out of the boredom of squint-windowed rural Ireland.

Bit of a party, really.

LONDON. FEBRUARY 1915

Fascism Has Yet to be Invented

The young male secretary – no, make that the former-secretary – to the Great I Am, reads with pleasure the essay he has just had published. It's in *New Age*, just the sort of location that will catch the peripheral vision, of the Eye-'em.

Having spent three soggy rural summers at virtually no pay, listening constantly to the enswirled cosmic secrets of the universe, ancient Ireland, and those newly-created by I-Am, it's time to leave Mr. Yeats's employ.

The essay, "The Non-Existence of Ireland" rips at the mysticism and romanticism of the Irish Renaissance like a pit bull with a rabbit, and it makes even less ultimate difference.

You can't dismember a spectre.
Ezra Pound goes in search of more substantial beliefs.

DUBLIN. CHRISTMAS DAY 1915

Ghosts (2)

Patrick H. Pearse spends Christmas Day at St. Enda's College, completing an essay that would have driven Ezra Pound around the bend, had that been necessary. *Here be ghosts that I have raised this Christmastide, ghosts of dead men that have bequeathed a trust to us living men.* Pearse traces the Irish independence movement back to the first "Separatists," the Celts who fought the Anglo-Norman invasion of the twelfth century. He brings the genealogy down to the present generation, each incorporeal forebear carrying with him an unpaid promissory note. *There is only one way to appease a ghost. You must do the thing it asks you. The ghosts of a nation sometimes ask very big things; and they must be appeased, whatever the cost.*

Pearse is a member of the supreme council of the Irish Republican Brotherhood which in the New Year decides to launch a Rising at the earliest opportunity. Pearse, who has infiltrated the Irish Volunteers as their director of organization, will be in charge of seeing that real bodies turn out and earn the respect of the wraiths with whom he has constant communion.

DUBLIN. EASTER WEEK, 1916

One Domino

The ultimate victory of the 1916 Rising was founded on heroism and bathed in odd luck and adventitious farce: all great victories are like that before the official custodians take the brass polish to them and make everything shiny.

Seizure of the General Post Office, Dublin, the IRB's battle headquarters, was fortuituosly easy. Just ten minutes before its being seized, Arthur Norway, the chief administrator of the GPO, was called away to Dublin Castle to discuss security measures. He left behind a cadre of guards, each with a weapon. Only a weapon: none of the men had been issued ammunition.

Mrs. Norway, the postal superintendent's wife, maintained her own record of Easter Week and she rightly noted that the Dublin populace was instinctively and often violently against the patriots. Still, they were not enthusiastic about the forces of civil order. Mrs. Norway observed an elderly shawlee: after looting a Grafton Street store and finding a fine pair of boots, the old dear had had them stolen while she was doing some additional pillaging. Outraged, the shawlee cornered a member of the Royal Irish Constabulary and demanded to know why the police weren't doing a better job protecting private property.

As the Rising wears on, the rebels become exhausted, none more so than Eamon de Valera, commandant of one of the outer posts. On a scouting expedition, de Valera, overtaken with weariness, slides into a carriage at Westland Row railway station and is instantly asleep. He awakes and is convinced that he has died and is in heaven, as he rightly deserves.

He has been asleep in the royal coach which was kept at Westland Row for ceremonial visits. The cherubs and angels with whom he awoke were ceiling and wall decorations, meant to accompany British royalty.

DUBLIN. APRIL 1916

Pacifists Also Bleed

If the Roman legionnaires could have made room for another ravening prophet around the Jerusalem Temple, Frank Sheehy-Skeffington would have fit right in. Of course a full red beard, Donegal-tweed plus-fours and sturdy walking brogues would have made him stand out among the Zealots, Sicarri and quondam Zadokites, but his intensity of belief would have gained him space in the court of the Gentiles where you did not have to be a believer in the one True God, just a believer in something. Lord, how well Frank had preached: against enlistment in the British army; against violence as a means of achieving independence; for votes for women; for a universe run by a deity who had the good sense not to exist.

Like the Roman legionnaires had done with the ranters who irritated them most, Frank was taken into custody by British troops, more on general principles than for his having done anything in particular.

Like a few others in a similar situation – John-the-Baptizer comes to mind – Frank ran out of luck before he ran out of breath. Detained in Portobello Barracks, he was transformed from a captive nuisance to a vulnerable hostage by Captain J.C. Bowen-Colthurst, a watch commander whose own stem was overwound. Trundled about as a hostage, Frank protested the shooting of a young prisoner.

"Say your prayers," Bowen-Colthurst told Skeffington in reply, "I'll say mine."

The captain read his Bible for a while, said a prayer, and Frank did neither. The captain had Francis Sheehey-Skeffington shot: 26 April 1916.

Captain Bowen-Colthurst was judged by military authorities to have been at least half-mad and he was sent to a lunatic asylum and then released from service on half-pay.

He settled in British Columbia and had a successful career as a bank manager.

DUBLIN. 12 MAY 1916

Christian Socialism

When the rebels of 1916 surrender, it is unconditional. They had nothing they could have bargained, only their own blood, and it would flow whether they surrendered or not.

James Connolly, severely wounded in the leg, is treated as a special case. He has to be kept alive if he is to be executed.

A peculiar socialist, he believes in God some time and prayer any time. Following his court martial, one of the firing squad asks him if he would say a prayer for the men who will be shooting him.

"I will. And I will say a prayer for every good man in the world who is doing his duty."

DUBLIN. 29 APRIL 1916

The Resurrection of the Body and the Life of the World to Come

Eamon de Valera was next in line to be executed: Connolly, then de Valera.

His wife on the near side of the Atlantic and his mother on the other, scramble wildly to find proof that he is a citizen of the USA and thus, in their view, bulletproof. The New York State birth certificate of "George de Valero" is found and they try to play that card. Obligingly, the New York State Commissioner of Health provides a "corrected" certificate for *Edmund* de Valero. That correction is dated 30 June 1916, much too late to be of any immediate help.

Eamon de Valera, as he now is, though sentenced to death, does not follow Connolly. He is reprieved because Prime Minister Asquith recognizes that English public opinion is turning strongly against the martyring of the rebels, and in wartime the public is an army that cannot be lost. When asked who was to come up for the firing squad after James Connolly, the Crown prosecutor says, "De Valera," and makes a mess of the name.

"Is he someone important?"

"No, he is a school master. Taken at Boland's Mills."

A good place to stop the train of martyrs.

But de Valera does not merely ecape death. He has the life confirmed that had first been handed to him by Father Eugene Sheehy, all those years ago, upon his entering the Bruree National School. He now has an official American birth certificate, signed and engrossed, confirming his identity and, crucially in Catholic Ireland of his time, making him unassailably legitimate.

Eamon de Valera no longer needs to look over his shoulder.

DUBLIN QUAYS. 14 JULY 1916

The Tailor and His Shroud

Promoted captain in the U.K. army, Tom Kettle sails to join an active duty unit. He has demanded the assignment. No more recruiting.

Kettle, now never fully sober, alternately cries and rages as he leaves Ireland forever. His heart is full-drawn riven, but his head knows exactly what it is doing. Tom Kettle is searching for a shroud.

As idealistic as any of the martrys of 1916, Kettle alternates between fury at the men of 1916 – they have prevented Ireland from taking its place among the free nations who will win the Great War, he believes – and the wrench that convulses him whenever he thinks of his lost friends: Patrick Pearse with whom he had become especially close; Thomas MacDonagh, a colleague at University College, Dublin and, especially, the honest-man-with-a-lamp, the irreplacable Francis Sheehy-Skeffington. Kettle, in dress uniform, had given character testimony for Eoin MacNeill, and it may have helped: though sentenced to death, MacNeill was moved to the reprieve-list. A small comfort.

The torsion of grieving for lost friends and for, as he believes, the loss of Ireland's future freedom, wrenches Kettle's body so that he no longer walks straight. He develops a sideways twitch in his neck as if directing anyone with whom he speaks to look away.

He fashions his shroud on the Somme. Leading his men against the Prussian Guards, he walks full-upright, forward, forward, forward, and finally, blessedly, downward into moist earth that fits him like a glove.

THE SOMME, FRANCE. 1 JULY-3 NOVEMBER 1916

Who Fears to Speak (2)

The bloodiest battle of the bloodiest war begins on the original anniversary of the Battle of the Boyne. In the centre of the U.K. line is the Ulster Volunteer Force, known officially as "The 36th (Ulster) Division." At 07:30 they move towards the heavily fortified German trenches. No running, no fuss, just ploughmen called upon to turn a furrow, they move straight on. Some wear Orange ribbons and a few officers have Orange sashes.

In two days, they lose nearly 6,000 men. Then they settle into an "offensive" that along the entire western front gains a few hundred yards in more than four months of intense combat.

Drowning in mud is among the worst ways to die. Years later, French farmers were still coming across the corpses of UVF men who had fallen into a shell crater and, unable to get out, had become part of the subsoil of a land they had not learned to love.

The Irish Republican Brotherhood and its outriders refuse to speak of the Somme, for its meaning is all too clear. Indeed, from mid-1916 until the end of the Irish War of Independence, they avoid talk of Ulster in anything but the vaguest way. "It'll all come right, once we're free."

No, it won't and the better tacticians among them know it. Does anyone with an ounce of sense think that the survivors of the Great War, disciplined, hardened, with four years of experience in bayonet gut-killing, will, on their own soil, run from a bunch of wideboys in raincoats with revolvers in their pockets?

The several successive partionings of Ireland now were encreased in steel.

DUBLIN. 12 JUNE 1917

Bold Tactics

The commander-in-chief of the Crown forces in Ireland, Sir Bryan Mahon, has a difficult tactical decision. Two days earlier, a Sunday afternoon rally in Beresford Place, Dublin, had run amok. Held in support of those prisoners of the Rising who still were in gaol, it had the usual speakers: the incandescently hate-filled candle-maker Cathal Brugha and the valetudinarian, weepy Count Plunkett, father of Joseph Mary Plunkett, a martyr of 1916. The afternoon should have passed with a lot of noise but little else, save that Inspector John Mills of the Dublin Metropolitan Police waded into the crowd and tried to arrest the speakers. Many of the crowd carried hurleys, ostensibly because they were coming from or going to a match, but really because they were used as a substitute in Volunteer drilling for guns. Inspector Mills was beaten severely and eventually died from his injuries.

Sir Bryan makes his tactical decision. He issues a proclamation forbidding throughout Ireland the bearing of hurling sticks in public, a fiat about as enforceable as banning walking sticks from the English countryside.

Commanding Heights

Being tall helped and so did being alive. As the ranking Irish Volunteer commander from 1916 not to be executed, Eamon de Valera was the commandant of the Volunteers in the successive gaols he was sent to. His men did not find him loveable, but they admired his manner, the magisterial dismissal of reality. He gave the warders the distinct impression that he and his men were here by choice and would conduct themselves by their own superior rules, stricter than the prison regimen. The Long Hoor, his men called him, with a mixture of affection and admiration.

His ambition was clear enough: to head the movement that achieved Irish independence.

Arthur Griffith, too gentle and too aware of being a printer, not a professor, as de Valera claimed to be, was the first to fall. The nationalist movement needed a front, a pan-national hording behind which everything from the Gaelic League to the Cumann na mBan to the Gaelic Athletic Association could operate: all to be run covertly of course by members of the Irish Revolutionary Brotherhood. Griffith's Sinn Fein was the perfect vehicle, and in 1917 he is told that his idealistic dual-monarchy, peace-by-self-sustenance organization is to be taken over as the national front. For the country's good.

De Valera and Griffith meet a few days before the Sinn Fein's annual Ard Fheis for 1917 and Griffith is read his lines. You will nominate me for president of Sinn Fein, Dev tells Griffith, and if you don't, I have enough votes to be elected anyway, and you will be discarded. Nominate me for president and I shall permit you to be vice president.

"In Eamon de Valera, we have a soldier and a statesman," Arthur Griffith declared in nominating him for president of Sinn Fein and implicitly surrendering control of the organization he had created.

Two days later, in a closed meeting of the Irish Volunteers, de Valera is elected president of the Volunteers' executive. He takes to calling himself president of the Irish Republic, a position that is not actually created until fifteen months later. Prolepsis in the cause of freedom was no vice, he believed.

Of course Sinn Fein and the Irish Volunteers were actually controlled by the IRB, which de Valera refused to join. His refusal was phrased on religious grounds – the church condemned secret oath-bound societies – but de Valera also wanted to keep his own power base independent of the IRB. That is why the skepticism of a seemingly good-natured, unpolished country boy on the IRB senior staff was noteworthy. As Director of Operations, Michael Collins was the central IRB man and, whatever his surface amiability, he had the mind of a chess master and the jugular instincts of a tiger. Like any jungle cat, he could wait his time. When he referred to Eamon de Valera as the Long Hoor it was with neither affection nor admiration.

DUBLIN. 1918

Recessional

Blessedly for Bessie Sheehy she died in January 1918, so she did not have to see her dreams turn into nightmares. As she grew older, she increasingly came to resemble the late Queen Victoria and to admit to a sympathy with her: as a mother of a brood that did not quite live up to expectations. She had planned for the Sheehys and the Kettles and even James Joyce to form a virtual senate for Home-Rule Ireland. She was spared seeing thick-handed culchees, slouching corner-boys, craw-thumping former altar boys, and jumped-up national school teachers replacing Home Rule with a war of independence. Oh how she loathed the Catholic lower middle class, and below! Better a Protestant adulterer as Ireland's champion than those louts.

The coup de grace to Irish Home Rule was provided, unintentionally of course, by the London government. Needing further to flood the Western Front with blood, they introduced conscription in Ireland in April 1918; this, though Irish voluntary enlistments were still strong. They simply needed more blood. This governmental move was the one action that would put the Catholic bishops alongside Sinn Fein.

The bishops denounced conscription as an oppressive and inhumane law which the Irish people had the right to resist by all means consonant with the laws of God. They advised more fervent attention to weekly religious duties and a national novena in honour of Our Lady of Lourdes. Not exactly civil disobedience, but Sinn Fein uses this as a sling-shot – the swirling centrifugal sort young David had employed to kill Goliath. Sinn Fein harnesses the national outrage at conscription and the moral approval of the Catholic bishops, and runs its own candidates in the general election of December 1918.

They virtually wipe out the old Irish nationalist party, the party of Parnell and Redmond. The old party wins six seats, Sinn Fein 73. Outside of Ulster, which remains unionist, Sinn Fein rules. Although this vote was an anti-conscription victory, not an endorsement of the Republic, Sinn Fein cannily claims it as such. Thus they have gone from being an obscure political sect to the vox populi.

An old man, in his seventies, who felt and appeared even older than his years, David Sheehy lost his seat. A one-time IRB stalwart, he had bet on the wrong horse. More than three decades of service to the national party had left him broken and broke.

David Sheehy became a vanished-dream walking. He came as close as a human can be to an incorporeal presence. He lived off the kindness of his daughters and took to attending mass six times daily, once for each of his children. When he died in 1932, obituary writers had to search the newspaper files to find out who he had been and why.

DUBLIN AND SOLOHEADBEG, CO. TIPPERARY.
21 JANUARY 1919

Nicely Timed

Two by two they came up the stairs ... That's the start of a Tipperary folksong in homage to the republicans Sean Treacy and Dan Breen. Right now, it's just in the making.

The men coming two-by-two up the stairs are not those of the song. Dail Eireann is meeting for the first time and in public. It is composed of men (and of Countess Markievicz, the first woman to be elected to parliament in the U.K.), all of whom have the right to sit in Westminster, but who choose to stay home and form a government of Ireland. A declaration of independence is read, an autochthonous government created, and a president of the government of Ireland is chosen: because Eamon de Valera is back in gaol, Cathal Brugha serves as a stand-in until April when de Valera escapes Lincoln Gaol and then assumes the presidency.

Two-by-two ... a pair of Royal Irish Constabulary men accompany a load of explosives towards Soloheadbeg quarry. They, and the work party that carries the goods, are suddenly surrounded by eight gun-men. The attackers are nervous, for this is their first big operation, and there is a momentary stand-off as the RIC men shoulder their rifles and prepare to protect the explosives. In quick response, and at almost the precise moment that Dail Eireann is being called into session, Breen and Treacy shoot the pair of policemen. Thus, the Anglo-Irish War be-gins on the same day that the Irish provisional government is created.

Later, when Treacy and Breen have carried out a string of success-ful guerilla actions, their honour-song evolves, like those of ancient Celtic war-chiefs.

Two by two,
They came in pairs;
And were shot
By Sean Treacy and Dan Breen

WESTMINSTER. 1920

Sure Thing

While the Anglo-Irish war winds on, following the labyrinthian ways of Dublin's back alleys and the countryside's self-circling maze of un-mappable boreens, the course of events in the United Kingdom par-liament is straight and hard as a Royal Marine buggering a street boy. David Lloyd George sees to that.

Using the passage of the Government of Ireland Act, 1920, as cover, he redefines the constitution of the United Kingdom so that its descrip-tion on paper will eventually coincide with the reality on the ground. There is no rush, for nothing is changing in the field, just small-bore atrocities, minor irritations to a world benumbed by the recent Great War. Lloyd George takes nearly a full year to enact a measure that par-titions Ireland and pretends to give Home Rule, separately, to both the northern one-quarter of the country and to the southern three-quarters. Neither portion wants it, but the Ulster Protestants will accept it, for partition and devolved government keep them part of the United Kingdom. Two days before Christmas the measure receives Royal As-sent and the earth begins to open along Ireland's tectonic fault line.

The overwhelming majority of republican fighters are from the south and most of them have never been to outer-Ulster, let alone the

Protestant northeast. They keep avoiding the issue and telling themselves the same old lie. "It'll all come right, once we're free."

IRELAND. 11 JULY 1921

A United Ireland?

The truce in the Anglo-Irish war, signed two days earlier, comes into effect. Peace has not broken out. Instead, British politicians have realized that they can win the war but dare not; and Irish guerillas know that, though unbeaten, they are near the end of their resources.

From the truce onwards, it's increasingly clear that Ireland has been broken into four. The north and the south are already separate, and in Northern Ireland (now a legal entity), the Protestants and Catholics are forever at daggers drawn.

The south (the twenty-six counties, call it what you will) is actually a worse problem, because its bisection is not yet done. Like a piece of marble being slowly truncated by a stonecutter's wheel, the incisions grow daily deeper. The only question is when the break-open point will be reached: Eamon de Valera vs. Michael Collins; the Irish Republican Army against Dail Eireann, whose authority it has never fully granted; members of the IRB against those outside the secret guild; old-line home rulers, trying for a come-back, against the seemingly triumphant gunmen; and everywhere, the reins of control are tangled.

One reality prevails and one question looms. The reality is that the Irish republic, pure, spiritual, untrammeled, unbesmirched by contact with perfidious Albion and its Crown, must be abandoned. That is made inevitable when Eamon de Valera, as president of Dail Eireann enters into a long correspondence with David Lloyd George about the conditions for arranging a permanent end to Irish-British violence. De Valera is masterful and spins Lloyd George like a top. Yet there's no mistaking that, as Lloyd George makes clear, and Dev implicitly accepts in starting the correspondence, it was all about one thing: what kind of a Dominion southern Ireland will be.

The Irish republic died the minute de Valera replied to Lloyd George's opening sally: for if Ireland truly was a republic, there was no need to negotiate a relationship, however special, under the wing of the mother hen next door.

And thus the question, coming closer each day: when, gradually, the Irish nationalists in the south, the Irish Republican Army, the IRB, realize that they have won the substance, but not the ornaments, of full freedom, will they say, "enough, let us rest." Or will they fight on? – and, inevitably, not against the old enemy, but against each other.

LONDON. 5 DECEMBER 1921

The Constitution of the Irish Free State

Number 10, Downing Street. At two o'clock in the afternoon David Lloyd George, who has just chaired a cabinet meeting and then had his lunch, takes a nap. He is to meet an Irish peace delegation and he is confident that he has them on the ropes. He does not need to rehearse his lines, just catch some sleep, for it will be a tiring session: the Irish can talk almost as long as he can.

Described by one of his legitimate offspring as a great Bible-thumping pagan, the U.K.'s prime minister has enjoyed a lifetime of successful seduction of women through a mixture of charm, bullying, and tactical manoeuvring, and he has almost completed the seduction of the Irish delegates. As in the case of his women, he's not interested in whether or not they are happy, but only in being satisfied himself.

The negotiations for an Anglo-Irish peace treaty have been going on for almost two months. The Irish negotiating team is tired, having been back and forth to Dublin on unreliable ferries and having spent long nights trying, unsuccessfully, to hammer out a unified Irish position. They represent the physical force wing of Irish nationalism which, in 1918, had completely supplanted the parliamentary niceties of John Redmond's home rule party. Yet, bunched though they are at one end of the nationalist spectrum, the cabinet of the self-declared Irish government-in-waiting cannot decide what to do about David Lloyd George's latest tactical move.

Brilliantly, Lloyd George has sent them sprawling. In the early bargaining, when Britain offered dominion status, the Irish responded by saying that the Brits really did not mean it. Back and forth that went. Then, when the Irish delegates were home in Dublin in mid-

November, Lloyd George sent them an unsettling offer. They could place in the Anglo-Irish treaty *any phrase they liked which would ensure that the position of the Crown in Ireland should be no more in practice than it was in Canada or in any other Dominion.*

Bastard: Lloyd George has tupped enough of the typing pool to know that pulling a victim forward, and then suddenly letting go, results in her own resistance putting her flat on her back.

And, bloody Canada again: just when the physical-force nationalists thought they had escaped from the old home-rule party's building on Canadian precedents, the march of the Irish nation is once again being defined by Canadian rules.

Lloyd George wakes from his nap refreshed. He has dreamed of the Welsh mountains and of mountainous Welsh milkmaids and he knows he is in good form. Today is the end game. He is joined by Winston Churchill, who would be very pleased to have a war with the Irish, by the Earl of Birkenhead, the hard-driving lord chancellor, and by Austen Chamberlain, leader of the conservative party: a tight, tough little gang.

The Irish final-talks team is: Arthur Griffith, the founder of Sinn Fein and chairman of the Irish delegates; Michael Collins, who, as the mastermind behind the Irish guerilla war had been responsible for the killing of more British soldiers in the previous three years than anyone not actually on the British general staff; and Robert Barton, included as an economics expert and token Ascendancy representative. A tough bunch too, but dog-tired and now confused.

They have been unable to get the Dublin cabinet, headed by Eamon deValera, to tell them if they should sign the draft treaty or not. It gives up the Irish republic but, then, that had already been done by deValera in the truce negotiations: implicitly by his bargaining with Lloyd George about dominion status and quite explicitly, when he had told Lloyd George that "Saorstat Eireann," which the Irish called themselves in their treaty drafts, meant "Free State." *Peace or war, gentlemen?* Will the three Irish delegates sign a treaty that: provides for a virtually powerless governor-general (whom the Irish can choose), an oath of allegiance by members of the Irish parliament to the King as head of the British Commonwealth of Nations (not the "British Empire," but still a sour pill to swallow), appeals in a few special legal cases to the law committee of the U.K. privy council and provisions that, in effect, Ireland could not join an enemy if Britain went to war. It's the Canadian model, but without the buffer of thousands of miles of the north Atlantic between the parties.

We can debate no longer gentlemen. Lloyd George, late in the evening, restates the British ultimatum. *The Irish delegates must settle now. Now. They must sign or else quit.* He paused long. Complete silence reigned. *Then both sides would be free to resume whatever warfare they could wage against each other.*

Continued silence. Michael Collins stares into a distant horizon. There he can see the figure of Eamon de Valera, perched like a vulture on a fence post, knowing that whatever way events turn, he will have carrion for his maw. De Valera, in composing the original negotiating team, was sending Collins to surrender the republic and then will blame him for doing so. Collins understood fully.

The Irish promise to give their answer in the morning. Griffith will sign, Barton is a cipher, and the whole issue falls on Michael Collins. He has already done his sums: he knows the details of Irish military strength better than anyone and he is a realist. The Irish Republican Army was almost out of strength when the truce was signed and it would be thoroughly defeated by a serious British attack. The British navy could flatten most important cities with complete impunity. And Collins performs a second calculation: that most of the hard men, the gunmen, will follow him and accept the substance of Irish freedom; and that the overwhelming majority of the civilian population will embrace it enthusiastically.

Oh for the sake of Christ, he says in the cab that is taking him, Griffith and Barton back to their lodging. *Take the Canadian deal and then take it to the people.* Barton and Griffith are startled at his vehemence. *Better to win a war against our own begrudgers than lose one to the Big Bastards.*

The realism of a damned visionary.

They sign.

When, in mid-August 1922, David Lloyd George learns that Michael Collins has been killed in the Irish civil war, he is momentarily saddened. His own coalition government is coming apart. To prepare himself for the sordid scramble that will follow its crumbling, he has been sitting alone, practising, like an old card sharp, the skill that had served him so well in his five months negotiating the Treaty of Versailles and later in dealing with the Irish: he practises writing simultaneously on three sides of a piece of paper.

DUBLIN. 14 DECEMBER 1921-7 JANAURY 1922

The Prime Directive

Directing a morality play? Directing history? The director's prime rule, the one that counts more than any other, is this: control the curtain. When you decide to ring down the curtain determines what any story means: leave it up too long and victory can become defeat, tragedy turn into farce, comedy into bathos, and the epic into the indecipherable.

Drop the curtain at the point when the truce in the Anglo-Irish War is declared and one can do it with a drum roll and several choruses of The Soldiers Song. A victory (always providing one doesn't miss Ulster too much, which most southern nationalists did not).

But leave the curtain aloft too long – until, say, the end of 1923 – and the story becomes a tragedy, the sacrifice of lives from 1916 onwards a prologue to fratricidal conflict much nastier than anything between the IRA and the Black and Tans.

On 14 December, 1921 Eoin MacNeill opened the "second Dail," the session that would accept or reject the Anglo-Irish treaty. MacNeill was at ease, for the debate was being held in the council chamber of University College, Dublin, Earlsfort Terrace. (The Mansion House, Dublin, the preferred venue, was already booked for a Christmas show.) The members of the Dail comprised one of the most democratically representative assemblies of revolutionaries ever seen. They had been elected under United Kingdom franchise laws that provided the virtually universal suffrage for men (lunatics and criminals excepted), votes for women over age thirty, equal-sized electoral districts, and the right of women to sit in parliament. Of course, only Sinn Feiners sat in the second Dail but, undeniably, this assembly was run by the rules of British parliamentary procedure, not of the French revolutionary directorate.

Still, it was a good thing words could not kill. Countess Markievicz's suggesting that Michael Collins well might intend to wed Princess Mary was gentle compared to many insults that passed as the quality met.

At first Eamon de Valera, as president of Dail Eireann, acted presidential. He engaged, however, in a trick that he later employed hundreds of times in the 1930s and 40s. Because he had only Gaelic League Irish at a modest level, he could not carry on a complicated argument in that language. So he began his opening, supposedly peace-making, speech by explaining, in Irish, that he did not have enough Irish to fully discuss matters and then switched to English and said that since most delegates did not have enough Irish, he would continue in English. That, caught in miniature, was de Valera's method of double-think, and it never failed to enrage his opponents.

For reasons ultimately unknowable, de Valera opposed the treaty. He had on his side dissident IRA and IRB members, and all the women in the Dail. These, plus his tactical advantage in being president of the Dail, gave him a strong position. But it was essentially a defensive position: he could control procedure and stall unwanted portions of debate. His necessity, however, was to attack: attack the treaty, attack those who favoured it: Michael Collins, the majority of the IRB, most of the IRA, plus the old soft-line nationalists who were headed by Arthur Griffith. He had to attack because the treaty already was on the ground and he had to blast it away, as if destroying an enemy's fortress.

De Valera lost the battle by being too cute. He commanded that the Dail meet in secret session for a time (previously the debates had been public). In that secret session he distributed his own alternative to the Anglo-Irish Treaty. He called it Document No. 2, and it was a disaster. It was not a republican document, or anything close to it. Instead, de Valera's theological construct of "external association" with the British Commonwealth was proposed. Go back to war for this? Most Dail members either ridiculed Document No. 2 or stared at it with stupefaction. When it became clear to de Valera that his alternative to the treaty was going nowhere, he demanded that everyone turn back in their copies. It was to be a state secret he said.

Interrupted only for Christmas, the slide towards fratricide continued. When a vote finally was taken, the pro-treaty side was victorious, but only by a count of 64 to 57. De Valera resigned as president of the Dail and was replaced by Arthur Griffith, as nice an irony as one can find in revolutionary politics. And Michael Collins was chosen as chairman of the provisional government, the legal body to which the U.K. government transferred control of southern Irish affairs.

By the first of February, the pro-treaty forces were running the most important departments of state and Britain was swiftly handing over the others.

Withdrawing from the Dail, Eamon de Valera became titular leader of an alienated sect of True Republicans.

He and his colleagues declared the new government of the Irish Free State to be illegal.

Legacy

Seven hundred and fifty years of English imperialism left some contradictory habits.

Both sides of the split on the treaty knew it would have to be submitted to the people. That was one habit that English representative government had taught all save the wildest gunmen. Election required.

Equally, 750 years or so of subverting governments had produced countervailing habits. Thus, in late February 1922, at a special Ard Fheis of Sinn Fein, Michael Collins and Eamon de Valera, hating each other to the bone, agree that no elections will be held for at least three months.

They hope to work things out so that the people of Ireland only have to vote with invisibly pre-marked ballots, ones that have a big "X" where, if God is good, Dev and Mick agree that it should be placed.

Dream Factory

Though he was a large man and often shambled along looking like a bag of old laundry, Michael Collins was surprisingly quick with his feet and hands – and he had a nimble mind that kept thousands of details in order and, crucially, separate from each other. Rarely were two people told exactly the same story by Collins, but he was not a compulsive liar; rather an instinctive intelligence officer.

After the nationalist split on the treaty, Collins sets himself to manufacturing a dream, a cloud by day and a pillar of fire by night, that would lead all his people to the Promised Land, a united Ireland where no British shadows would ever fall. Collins is so dextrous with his magician's hands, so consumed with the detailed weaving of the threads of stories he tells to the hundreds of men and women he has to deal with, that he starts to believe in the dream-tapestry he is weaving.

Having wriggled through many a cellar window in his guerrilla days, Collins first finds a sally-port. It's dead simple, he decides: the constitution of the new Irish Free State has yet to be drawn up, much less approved both by the Irish electorate and the United Kingdom parliament. Only one of God's greatest optimists could have seen this onerous process as a point of hope, but Collins does. In late January he appoints a constitutional drafting commitee and tells them: go to it, boys. They're an uneven lot: running from first-rate legal minds such as Hugh Kennedy (who in later life is chief justice of the supreme court of the Irish Free State); a trustworthy Quaker philanthropist, James Douglas; James MacNeil, a former imperial civil servant in British India and, more importantly, the brother of Eoin MacNeill; a couple of ciphers, and two space cadets: Alfred O'Rahilly, a physicist from University College, Dublin, who had a passionate attachment to the constitution of Switzerland and to the Catholic church; and Darrell Figgis, poet, drama critic, always wearing a Tyrolean hat he had picked up before the Great War when he was buying guns on the Continent for the Irish Volunteers. Not a team you'd start for the Ranfurly Shield. Michael Collins, as head of the provisional government, tells them to draft a constititon that is made-in-Ireland. They can ignore everything that's in the Anglo-Irish treaty, for that is already on paper, he says. In effect, he tells them that he wants no reference in the new Irish constitution to the oath of allegiance, to the governor general, to judicial appeals to the U.K. privy council and no reference to being part of the Empire. Away they go to draft the impossible dream.

Next, he sells the dream of a made-in-Ireland constitution to Eamon de Valera. He's already made the initial pitch in late February, and in early March the Ard Fheis of Sinn Fein agrees to keep its own counsel until the draft constitution is published and placed before the electorate.

And, then, pulling an elephant out of his crumpled hat, Michael Collins convinces the British that he needs the Westminster parliament to pass their ratification of the Anglo-Irish treaty right away, in order to strengthen his hand against republican extremists. They do so at the end of March and give him four months to come up with an acceptable constitution: acceptable to the U.K. cabinet and acceptable to the majority of the southern Irish electorate.

If he were on the stage, you'd be nudging your neighbour and saying, god-this-guy-is-good. Collins is doing his magic-and-juggling act at a time of maximum distraction. In the countryside, local pro- and anti-treaty leaders from the War of Independence are turning themselves into warlords. A map of the countryside begins to resemble a map of ancient Ireland in, say, the sixth century, with myriad local rí heading their own tuatha and jealously guarding their borders.

Never mind that in early March Collins' constitutional drafting committee gives him three conflicting drafts of constitutions; and pay no mind that in mid-April, extreme dissidents seize the Four Courts in Dublin. Michael Collins dances and juggles and blows smoke and spins plates on bamboo sticks and, oh land of miracles, completes the final binding of Eamon de Valera.

They make their final deal. The Pact it is called in public, but it's really a secret treaty, a covenant to keep the dream of an independent Ireland alive. Reached in mid-May, the Collins-de Valera pact confirms elections for 16 June and promises to rig them. The electoral results will duplicate the present pro- and anti-treaty split in the Dail and the cabinet seats will be split five-four between the two groups.

The Brits can tell that something is going on, but can't get at the details: Collins' hands are quicker than their eyes. Here is what the below-table deal was: both de Valera and Collins would stand behind the radical constitution Collins now was cobbling together and thus the extreme (meaning habitually violent) republicans would be isolated and could be dealt with; de Valera would get a seat in the cabinet through a weird provision in the new constitution that would allow someone to have a cabinet seat and yet not bear collective cabinet responsibility; a mini-war on Northern Ireland would be started at the earliest opportunity, but first, the re-united Irish warriors would face down the British and, although stuck with the Anglo-Irish Treaty, would have an almost-republican constitution. Collins and Dev spent three full days locked together in a room in University College, Dublin, and there must not have been much more oxygen left than when Harry Houdini did one of his underwater escape tricks.

Yet, here's the trouble with dreaming and with sleight of hand: the first keeps your eyes on too distant a horizon and the second concentrates it on matters too close to hand. The middle-ground is easily forgotten and that's what Michael Collins, virtuoso though he was, did: he forgot the Brits, the cruel reality that stood between his own little magic show and the ultimate goal of complete independence.

They shit. Winston Churchill, as secretary of state for the colonies, had special responsibility for southern Ireland and he would not have minded levelling an Irish port or two. Called to account for the Pact, the Irish soon found themselves being grilled on the new constitution. For two weeks they were shoved back at point after point, until the constitution fit within the framework of the Anglo-Irish treaty: an oath of allegiance; a position within the Empire; judicial appeals to the privy council; a governor general, and limits on their conduct of foreign affairs. It was immensely humiliating, but the British were serious. A sea embargo or even the bombarding of coastal targets was on the cards.

Dream making was over. From the fifteenth of June, when the Irish delegates in London agreed to British demands on the constitution of the Irish Free State, civil war in Ireland was unavoidable.

IRELAND.14-16 JUNE 1922

Smiler With a Knife

As a magician, Michael Collins was so good that one completely forgot that the same hands, the same prestidigitator's smile that charmed an audience while he seduced them with mirrors and dreams, could instantly become the hands of a lethal bar-fighter. He could break a pint glass on a table-edge and have the shards cutting a man's jugular vein even while telling him a wee joke. My-God-the-man-was-good.

Eamon de Valera, with the pecksniffian air of someone who had spent too much of his life cultivating the company of Maynooth professors and Blackrock priests, patronized Collins: no corner-boy could truly represent the Irish people; it was a higher calling.

Dev paid: for he never respected Collins's genius.

As late as the sixth of June, even as the British were putting their threats to Collins and his constitutional drafting crew, Collins and de Valera joined in asking the electorate to respect their Pact in the approaching election. Collins gave Dev no hint of what was really happening in London. Collins covered himself beautifully: if the Irish could hold their ground, then he had de Valera and most of the anti-treaties with him; if the Irish retreated before the British on the constitution issue, he could always twist the glass into Dev's jugular.

The latter. On the fourteenth of June, just two days before the supposedly-rigged election, Michael Collins returned home to Cork. He and his delegation had already surrendered to Churchill and Lloyd George, but he kept his magician's smile in place. He told his constituents that in two days they would be voting. *I am not hampered now by being on a platform where there are Coalitionists*, he said, referring to de Valera's anti-treatyites. *I can make a straight appeal to you – the citizens of Cork, to vote for the candidates you think best ...* He gave his magician's wink. *You understand fully what you have to do, and I depend on you to do it.*

He had repudiated the Pact and done so at the very last instant. Most newspapers did not catch the full story until the next day, and de Valera's people were completely blind-sided.

With a master's eye for detail, Collins had the new constitution printed in the newspapers on election morning, 16 July. So, now, the general election of 1922 was a referendum both on the Anglo-Irish Treaty and on the constitution of the Irish Free State as framed under that treaty.

A big win for the Yes side: 58 pro-treaty, 36 anti-treaty, and 34 from other parties (labour, farmers, etc.) who supported the treaty and the constitution. Or so the new government could claim.

The subsequent Irish civil war was not about the Anglo-Irish Treaty (or it would have begun in January 1922), but about the real marrow of government, the constitution, and that is why it started in the summer of 1922.

Eamon de Valera, late in July, formed his own government-in-internal-exile. He had little, if any, control over the hate-soaked gunmen in the alleys, the hills and valleys, but he attended to his spiritual duties and his Special Intention was that he be forgiven for dreaming every night of the death of Michael Collins.

DUBLIN. 16 JUNE-22 AUGUST, 1922

The Real Score

When, after World War II, the English empire begins to disintegrate, southern Irish politicians and their overseas outriders proudly point to Ireland as the world leader: the country that set the pattern, the first successful breakaway from the British Empire. True enough, if one allows that the job was not completed until 1949 and forgets Ulster, but still, it was a pattern that African and Asian nations admired and to some degree imitated.

Most also imitate, though they did not wish to, the full Irish pattern.

It's the modern revolutionary paradigm: a successful revolution is followed by a split, a civil war, and as much blood is spilled by former comrades fighting each other as was lost fighting the old enemy. In southern Ireland, at most 5,000 men and women fought actively in the War of Independence; indeed, most estimates would put the number at 3-4000. In the Irish civil war, the Free State army alone has more soldiers than that actively involved. Civil war indeed.

The cost in terms of leaders was especially high. Arthur Griffith, the wise man of the moderate side and still president of Dail Eireann, simply wore out. He became uncharacteristically querulous, and as old friends killed each other, his spirit ebbed. In late July he suffered an attack of tonsilitis. That passed, but he really did not wish to speak much anymore. Taken to a nursing hospital, he died on 12 August 1922. His doctor, Oliver St. John Gogarty, was on duty in the hospital at the time and hearing that Griffith had suffered a sudden cerebral haemorrhage, he immediately opened a vein in Griffith's arm. No blood flowed.

Michael Collins, minister of finance and head of the provisional government of Ireland and commander-in-chief of the Irish Free State army, was caught in a crossfire at Beal na mBlath, County Cork and had the back of his head blown off. Blood flowed.

Eamon de Valera, who was in the vicinity, but not involved in the assassination, had a brief nervous breakdown. As his handler hurried him back to a safe house in Dublin, he kept saying, "I told them not to do it."

SOUTHERN IRELAND, 28 SEPTEMBER-8 DECEMBER 1922

Cleaning House

Between the moments when the Dail gave military courts the power to try anyone and to execute the death penalty – 28 September –

and when the Catholic bishops condemned the republican rebels as acting without moral sanction and against the law of God – 10 October – the anti-treaty forces lost the war. If God and the Irish people were against them, they could have the hills full of Thompson guns: they'd still lose.

The provisional government (after 6 December, it's officially the government of the Irish Free State) cleans house. It does things the British government never would have dared to do, and rightly so: unlike the foreigners, both sides in a civil war know exactly who is who; exactly who's done what and where; and, with the church excommunicating republicans, even the Almighty concurred. Most lives on both sides were lost in tiny, crossroads battles, but the ones that counted were the executions conducted by the Free State government.

A more effective form of communication is hard to imagine.

Over the course of six months the Free State executed seventy-seven republicans whom they had captured. These were not the judi-cial-manqué proceedings conducted by the British in 1916, but tacti-cal executions, conducted at specific times as reprisals for republican actions in the field. So the prisoners were not really there as malefac-tors, but primarily as hostages. Everyone understood: tribal hostage-taking was an ancient Irish practice.

The showpiece, the event that told the republicans that they would lose, that the Free State had more resolve and was more ruthless than the rebels, occurred on 8 December 1922.

When the constitution of the Irish Free State had officially come into being on 6 December, the republicans announced that they would shoot any member of the Dail, any judge, any journalist who supported it. The next day they killed one member of the Dail and se-riously wounded the deputy chairman of the legislature.

In reply, on 8 December, forget the nicety of trials: four republicans were stood up before a firing squad and inefficiently shot: two of them had to plead for a bullet in the head to finish the job.

Rory O'Connor, one of the four victims in these reprisal execu-tions, had been the best man at the wedding of Kevin O'Higgins, minister for home affairs, the man responsible for public security. O'Higgins' own father was shot by the republicans in reply, but nothing stopped the younger O'Higgins or his colleagues. You kill: one of your mates dies, that is the Free State policy. In late April 1923, Eamon de Valera and Frank Aiken (nominally in charge of military matters) declare that their operations are done, and a month later they formally surrender.

Short swords produce long memories.

IRELAND. 1922–25

The Glitter

Michael Collins had possessed a romantic streak and not just in the carnal sense. He loved old stories and he liked to think of the ancient glory of New Grange, when it had been covered with opalescent rocks, giving it a glitter worthy of a true kingdom. Mother-of-pearl, opals, stones of any sort that glittered and yielded complex patterns fascinated him.

Erskine Childers was given a pearl-handled .22 caliber automatic pistol, a lady's gun, by Collins. Childers, hero of the Howth gun-running, had chosen the anti-treaty side and he was more disliked than anyone by most of the pro-treaty people. Partly it was his plummy English accent – "I will not reply to any Englishman in this Dail," Arthur Griffth had once railed at him. In part it was because he was understood to be the ghost-writer of Eamon de Valera's specious Document No. 2. In part because he was Protestant. And in part because he had a big-mouthed Boston-American wife who hated the English as if she had been at the Boston Tea Party herself and could not keep quiet about it.

Captured with the tiny automatic pistol that the late Michael Collins had given him, Erskine Childers was technically liable to the death penalty. Of course that was unthinkable among civilized men and, anyway, a writ of *habeas corpus* had been filed.

Forget those inhibitions, Childers was executed almost immediately after his capture. He was shot at dawn 23 November 1922.

Michael Collins had given another nice little lady's pistol to Mrs. Darrell Figgis. This was occasioned by the eccentric Mr. Figgis – who wanted to be called "The Figgis," and who looked like a face attached to a pointed beard, rather than vice versa – being grabbed on the street outside his home early in 1922 by some anti-treaty toughs and having his beard hacked off. Since Figgis was involved in drafting the new Irish Free State's constitution, a bit of protection was warranted.

Collins provided the minimum by giving Milly, Figgis's wife, a pistol for her protection. It had a pearl handle that was cross-hatched by an engraver for a solid grip. It shone beautifully.

After Collins's death, Darrell Figgis became the majordomo in charge of setting up Ireland's national radio service. An imbroglio developed with an English consortium that, it turned out, had given Figgis election money.

Her husband's career and her own social position ruined by this revelation, Mrs. Figgis committed suicide with the glittery gun Michael Collins had given her.

Lots of bodies are buried at New Grange, they say.

EVER FARTHER.

AUSTRALIA AND POLYNESIA

1900–1969

The Era of High Chichi

In the South Pacific, as much as in the fountainheads of European civilization, it was a great time for silly ceremonies. In Polynesia, European governments provided their subjects with a round of state
ceremonies, celebrating each group of islands having recently been
taken over by a European power. The richest set of official ceremonies
came on the Samoan Islands. There the locals, most of them serious
Protestant Christians, had been fighting a multi-sided tribal war,
while the United Kingdom, the United States, and Germany played
for place, each wanting control. The U.K., though well-placed with its
Pacific base in Fiji, lost out by virtue of being militarily committed to
the Second Anglo-Boer War. So, in 1899, Germany and the U.S. split
the place, Germany obtaining western Samoa, the U.S., eastern. Each
island capital received visits from warships and was bombarded by
long speeches, but the German visitation was much more satisfactory
than the American: they brought along a brass band and the Samoans
found they could sing the words of a number of hymns they'd
learned from the LMS missionaries, to German marching music.

As consolation for losing any chance of controlling Samoa, the
Americans and the Germans gave to the English the rights to the
Tongan Islands, some of the Solomons, and Nieue. (The latter was
known at the time as "the Savage Islands" because its inhabitants
had given Captain Cook a serious fright).

The Tongans too had their circus: after they signed a "treaty of
friendship and protection" in 1900, they became a "British Protected
State" though, given London's reluctance to spend money except in
ceremonies, they were protected by a very leaky umbrella indeed.

7 October 1900: the governor of New Zealand, Lord Ranfurly,
welcomes the Cook Islands and Nieue to their official annexation.
He steps ashore at Avarua in virtually the same formal garb that
had been worn in Captain Cook's time. White knee breeches, long
silk stockings, black pumps, a cutaway jacket jingling with medals
and a cockaded hat that could have come from a museum. After the
usual twenty-one gun salute, he reads a proclamation and makes a
speech. The speech is short, and quickly translated into Cook
Island-Maori. It puzzles the assembled chiefs as it congratulates

them on voting in favour of annexation, something they might or might not have done, as no tally of the various petitions that had circulated on the matter had ever been announced. Still, they guessed they must have done so, or there would not have been a warship in their harbour.

The more alert of them wondered who was annexing them, and did it matter? In fact, although they were being taken into the British Empire, the annexation was by New Zealand.

Thus do small fish swallow smaller ones.

THE COOK ISLANDS. 1898–1909

Thoughts of the Great Gudgeon

He thought of himself as the paramount chief of the islands: Colonel Walter Gudgeon, the man-on-the-ground who had taken over from the soppy Frederick J. Moss. Gudgeon had bullied and gulled the ariki into accepting annexation and then served as resident commissioner of the islands. The son of a London upholsterer, Gudgeon had made his mark in the anti-Maori wars of the nineteenth century.

In his early sixties, he is unusually tall, still muscular, and he has the ramrod carriage of a man who has been commissioner of police for all of New Zealand. His voice is very loud, his thoughts very dark.

Damned Moss made a great mistake. Started constitutional government – and then had a woman chief of government. It will take me five years of careful manipulation to overcome all this.

Gudgeon had the arrogance of the self-educated, and was proud of his wide reading: he named the two sons of his second marriage Herman and Melville.

He wrote three books which, curiously, he published in his father's name.

If the inhabitants of these islands were Anglo-Saxon or Germans, then we could safely leave them to bring about production of the highest scale.

In New Zealand, Gudgeon has gone from being commissioner of police to serving as a Native Land Court judge. His Maori was excellent, for he had served in mixed companies during the New Zealand Wars, and he became a collector of Maori history and legends. In 1892, he was one of the founders of the Polynesian Society, and he wrote articles for their learned journal, all the while keeping a vituperative private counsel.

The Polynesians are lazy, sensual, and thievish. Therefore the situation here is serious. We may have to force them to help themselves.

Gudgeon was not only chief justice of the High Court of the Cook Islands, but also judge of the Land Titles court. He favoured permitting long-leases of native land to Europeans and hoped for a settler society.

The Cook Islanders are a dying race ...

As controller of the islands' medical resources, he did little, save establish an atoll for lepers. For:

Your Polynesian: he has a capacity for dying under the smallest provocation.

Dying or not, the Polynesians were granted his chiefly passage. Gudgeon had a carriage specially constructed, one of vice-regal proportions, that could only be used on a few miles of passable road near his capital. Even more regal was his ceremonial visit to the island of Atiu, where the canoe that took him from his own ship was carried in relays by fifty men to the top of a cliff.

The Polynesian is unreliable, but afraid of me when I am here.

Gudgeon killed most of the schemes for native education that his predecessor Moss had initiated, put a native boarding school out of action, and strangled a scholarship scheme to send talented youths to New Zealand for secondary schooling.

I have never known nor heard of a people more wanting in moral stamina than these islanders. They do not understand the necessity for self-denial

or self-restraint and therefore to educate such people above the level of is-
land culture would be little short of criminal.

To his own certainty, Gudgeon had enemies. His own body, for example. When, as an embodiment of all that the Empire stood for, he was to
be made a Companion of the Order of St. Michael and St. George in
1901, his body rebelled: he came out covered in boils and could not attend the investiture in person. And the native islanders who had
worked for his predecessor Moss, why, even if not savages, they were
untrustworthy; yes, they all must be replaced and by Europeans; and
then the Europeans, they turn out not to be trustworthy; and Gudgeon
tries to import his own relatives, people he can trust to keep his eye on
the den of thieves. Then, to Gudgeon's horror, his nephew, a Ralph
Gosset, whom he had set to keeping an eye on the Customs Service, is
found to have been siphoning funds. And on and on.
  More. Gudgeon, who had begun life as a Roman Catholic, and
who hated all religions equally, but feared Catholicism totally, becomes convinced that a Roman Catholic conspiracy is directed
against him.

It is the irreconcilable Romanists. They have never forgiven me for leaving them.

He lives in constant fear that New Zealand's Irish Catholic politicians
will bring him down. It is all directed, he knows, from the highest levels of the Vatican.

AUSTRALIA. 1901

Dissonance

Australian Federation comes into effect 1 January 1901.
  The Union of Great Britain and Ireland had become effective 1
January 1801.
  Each was an attempt to make a problem go away by subsuming
smaller units into a single large one.
  For Australia it succeeds; for Ireland it fails.
  Tons of reasons, but a lot of ideas work better the farther they are
from London.

A Strange Duck

Although the Webbs had rather liked him, or at least found him toler-
able, Henry Higgins was perceived as a wayward radical and a dam-
nably solemn one at that.

Elected as one of Victoria's ten delegates to the Australian Commonwealth Constitutional Convention, he had refused to buy
the U.S. model, then had successfully inserted a clause in the Federation's constitution prohibiting the establishment of any religion or
interference with the free exercise of faith – and then he was one of
only two convention delegates to vote against the final measure.

On top of that, he'd opposed Australia's sending soldiers to the
Anglo-Boer War in 1899, for the war was "unnecessary and unjust."
Not the kind of thing to say in jingoistic times.

Maybe it was his peculiar brand of Irish Protestantism – Wesleyan
schooling in Dublin – that made him so dolefully honest.

Higgins represented a working class area of North Melbourne, was a
pioneering advocate of social-democratic legislation, and so irritated
the Labor party that they got him out of the road the only way they decently could: they made him a justice of the High Court of Australia.

Amnesia and Exclusion;
Retention and Inclusion

The multi-volume *Cyclopedia of New Zealand* is launched on a tide of
colonial self-satisfaction. Page after page brims with photographs of
worthy men clanking with army medals, pumiced and preening in
evening dress or, at minimum, in waistcoats and jackets, looking
thoughtfully into the distance. Each photograph is surrounded by
several paragraphs of detail on the man's career and a minimal
amount of personal information.

It's very interesting material, but more revealing is what is left out:
for this is an exercise in white man's amnesia.

Patrick Joseph Felix Valentine O'Neill O'Carroll provides an excellent example. The *Cyclopedia* shows him in full military dress uniform, a sword at his hand, medals on his chest, a Bismarckian beard and a fearsome mustache. Accurately, he is said to have been born in Castlepollan, County Westmeath, to have studied at the Catholic University, Dublin, and to have qualified at the Royal College of Physicians, Dublin. Early in his career he was medical officer in charge of *The Queen of the South* as it brought 440 Lancashire poor to Australia. After qualifying to practise in Melbourne, he came to New Zealand as a militia surgeon. During the 1860s he served with more than the requisite enthusiasm in the anti-Maori Wars and was present at the legendary battle of the Gate Pa. In the mid 1860s he was transferred to New Plymouth, Taranaki, and while serving as surgeon to the armed constabulary he built up a lucrative practice. He received the New Zealand medal, the Imperial Empire long service medal and the Victoria decoration.

True enough, but exclusionary and amnesiac, a Pakeha memory and, seemingly, a picture of a founding father of Pakeha dominance.

Except ... except that a parallel memory, one that is inclusive and retentive, holds the Maori half of his legacy. As a particularly skilled surgeon and devout Catholic, he was revered for his healing powers by many of the Taranaki people, especially the Ngati Tama, Ngati Maru, and Te Atiawa. Dr. O'Carroll married a Catholic woman (née Carrington) and they had thirteen children. The youngest lad, the Doctor's special treasure, married a Maori woman and they had a dozen children, all of whom enter the church and state records as O'Carrolls. The pattern in Taranaki continues down four generations, with names like Kathleen, Anthony, Colleen, Achushla, Dermot, Michael and Valentine being preserved along with traditional Maori names.

Not only does the *Cyclopedia of New Zealand*, as representative of Pakeha memory, close off the possibility of access to this information, it precludes our learning the valuable and healing irony: that one of the great-great grandsons of Patrick Joseph Felix Valentine O'Neill O'Carroll, in the twenty-first century is a chief negotiator for Te Atiawa in the North Island's template land settlement, and he remembers his heritage, both sides.

WESTERN AUSTRALIA. 1903

A Matter of Taste

I am busy at the lambing now ... Ear Marking, castrating, and tail cutting are all jobs I am now expert at.

A man of twenty-nine years of age is writing to his brother who, like their father, is a solicitor in Cookstown, County Tyrone.

I suppose you know a good hand can cut and tail about 1,000 ram lambs a day, keeping two men very busy catching for him. One slash cuts off the end of the purse; the testicles are then squeezed out with thumb and finger, dragged out with the teeth with one back jerk of the head, another slash at the ear, then the tail and 'next please.'

This is a grammatical, polite and thoroughly middle-class communication. Australia and Ireland at the time were largely rural countries and everyday agricultural operations – such as the castration of ram lambs – were talked about matter-of-factly: the post-Victorian prudishness of the twentieth-century urban world had yet to enforce euphemisms and silences about such things.

CRONADUN HOTEL, NR WESTPORT, SOUTH ISLAND,
NEW ZEALAND. 1904

Poes

Two generations of a large extended family, the Gallaghers, moved from Cronadun, County Donegal, to Westland. It was natural that when they set up a hotel on the Westport-Reefton road, it was the "Cronadun Hotel." It contained a pub and a store and a post office was attached. Kate Gallagher and Michael O'Malley, a blacksmith, married in 1901 and took over the family hotel in 1904. They were good at the business and it was a nice small Irish success story.

Kate, their daughter, loved the place. Unselfconsciously and uncomplainingly, she remembered something that every Irish women in "domestic service" must have dealt with, but which is scrubbed from polite rememberings: the necessity of dealing daily with containers of human waste.

"There were poes in every room ... We used to have a kerosene tin with a handle on, and you emptied the poes into it and rinsed them,

wiped them out, and they all went back under the beds ... You used
to get this kerosene tin and take it all the way down the paddock out
to the loo and empty it, a kerosene tin of pee."

Museum Conditions

"Form a line; move closer," the photographer tells the Mangahians.
His accent is improving. He has been to see the Cook islanders at the
Christchurch Exhibition of 1906–07 several times. He still has a touch
of a Taranaki accent, but he has always been good at languages and
the Mangahians are delighted to find someone of substance who
takes them seriously. So they don't complain when Peter Henry Buck
puts them through a whole series of arrangements. He doesn't make
them do anything "savage" or undignified.

Buck's meeting the Mangahians is as pivotal a moment of cultural
contact as were many of the early European-Polynesian meetings, but
this one is infinitely more complicated and its effects are subterranean,
becoming clear only decades later. The Mangahians were one of the
sets of Cook islanders that were rotated though the Christchurch Exhibition. They lived in a "model village" of their own construction and
showed off their handicrafts, sang hymns, and danced. They were not
treated as a freak show but, still, being stared at all day is a disorienting
experience. Buck was a great solace, for he explained that they were
sharing knowledge. And he prayed with them, to the same god.

As impressive as any young man in all New Zealand: twice national
long-jump champion; captain of the University of Otago First XV; brilliant medical student, M.B. and Ch.B. in 1904 and now enrolled in an
M.D. course by research thesis. A serious man, despite his great charm;
already married to an Ulster Protestant woman, and holding a responsible post as a medical officer to the Maori in the North Island.

"Now, let me into the next picture." Buck has one of the islanders
work the picture-machine and he memorializes himself in sombre
black suit among the islanders who lounge about in European casual
garb, looking like a very mixed cricket team.

And, Buck realizes, he wants into this picture very very much.
Peter Henry Buck, talented yes, charming immensely, and extremely complicated. His father was an Irish Protestant from

County Galway: the family were minor horse-Protestants on the way down. Peter Buck's great-grandfather had been a Fellow of Trinity College, Dublin, and pluralist incumbent of three Ulster parishes. His grandfather had been a civil engineer and Peter Buck's father had left Ireland and had been a digger in the Australian and New Zealand goldfields, then a policeman and finally a successful farmer. Da loved words, poetry, language. Peter Buck's mother came from the Ngati Mutunga, and Peter grew up with fluent Maori. And from both sides, a mantle of responsibility.

That's why his telling the Cook islanders that he will see them again, in their real homes, is less a courtesy than the assumption of a responsibility.

In 1907, Peter Buck joins the Polynesian Society and begins to consider seriously the origins of the peoples of the South Pacific.

KIRWEE, CANTERBURY, SOUTH ISLAND,
NEW ZEALAND. 1908

The Really Old Commonwealth

Curious. So William Frizell, a second-generation Canterbury farmer, noticed: the name, the trees, the irrigation pattern. Frizell came of a gleggy County Tyrone family and now was setting up his own farm, "Wharepuna," in the dry soil portion of Canterbury. The local hamlet was usually called Brett's Corner, and that was strictly correct: the plural would have been bragging.

The trees were the strangest part. The 1,000 acre estate of the late James Brett had plantings in a pattern, but what was it? Frizell found out only three years later after he had married the daughter of the local baker-grocer, and found his way into the backrooms of the migrant mind. The "Kirwee" estate had been named by James Brett, a County Wexford career soldier, for a fort that he had captured in British India. His irrigation system, desperately needed on the porous land, was not European, but was modelled on Indian systems.

And those trees, now mature and somehow glowering. Old Colonel Brett had planted them in exactly the pattern that his troops had assumed in his capture of Kirwee, on a distant continent that the map showed, like New Zealand, in bright red.

AUCKLAND, NEW ZEALAND. AUGUST, 1908

The Shadow of the Future

The Queen's representative in New Zealand, his excellency Sir William Lee, fifth Baron Plunket, grinds his teeth so violently that he breaks a molar. Instantly he is ashamed.

Lord Plunket: his father an archbishop of Dublin, his mother a Guinness, his wife a daughter of the Marquis of Dufferin and Ava, the distinguished under-secretary for India and governor-general of Canada. As a diplomat, Lord Plunket thought he knew how to control his emotions and had done so in a long career in the diplomatic service and as private secretary to successive lords lieutenant of Ireland.

He, and his molar, snapped when the American fleet fired off a salute so extensive in Auckland harbour as to be a virtual attack. President Theodore Roosevelt, a natural bully and a bully nationalist, had sent the U.S. Atlantic fleet into the Pacific as a show of force on the increasingly tense Pacific Rim. New Zealand's government had welcomed the implied protection and produced a handsome souvenir book welcoming the friendly invasion.

Lord Plunket might have fumed silently, without dental damage, had it not been for his proximity to the mighty American battleship the *U.S.S. Missouri* when it fired off its twelve-inch guns in such quick succession that the sound waves broke windows.

The New Zealand government's souvenir book noted that the *Missouri* was protected by an armour-belt eleven inches thick: made of Krupp steel.

BLACKBALL TOWNSHIP, SOUTH ISLAND, 1908;
WAIHI, NORTH ISLAND, NEW ZEALAND. 1912

The International Workers of the World

Wobblies. The I.W.W. As coal-mining replaced gold-and precious-stone searching in parts of Westland, the conditions for industrial unionism arose: highly capitalized ventures, operating at predictable profit margins, and requiring large numbers of dependable

workers – workers who were not individual entrepreneurs looking for the big nugget, but wage slaves.

Organizers pour in. John O'Loughlin, Robert Semple, Patrick
Hickey, Paddy Webb, Michael Joseph Savage. Most are of Irish
Catholic background, and most have had experience in organizing
miners in Australia. Tough men. They fight little grievances (pushing for a half-hour, rather than a fifteen-minute daily tucker-break),
deeply oppose the system of governmentally arbitrated wages, and
look for the day of the One Big Union and the apocalyptic General
Strike. They win an eleven week strike against the Blackball Coal
Company in 1908, and use it as the platform to preach the coming
industrial Millennium.

When, in 1912, the Wobblies try to repeat their success at an industrial gold mine at Waihi in the Coromandel, they run into two harder
Irishmen and their thugs.

William Ferguson Massey was built like a massive tree stump. He
came of small Protestant farmers in Ulster (a ten acre holding at
Limavady) and had been a ploughman in New Zealand before becoming a farmer and then a politician. He quoted the Old Testament as if it
were an instruction manual. He has renamed his conservative party
the Reform Party and in 1911 he becomes prime minister, defeating the
Liberals who wore the mantle of the late John Ballance. To Ferguson,
industrial-unionists are something out of the Book of Daniel.

Ferguson's terrible-swift-sword is an Irish Catholic policeman who
is even more opposed to the proletariat putting their heads above the
hedge: John Cullen. First trained by the Royal Irish Constabulary in
1869, he re-trained in New Zealand in 1876 as the first graduate of the
academy of the newly-unified New Zealand Constabulary. Massey
named him the national police commissioner in April 1912, and his
first big task was to break the Waihi strike. In this type of project, he
showed considerable gifts.

Cullen's civilian strikebreakers were organized by Irish thugs –
James Delany the chief – and Irish policemen – Sergeant Cowan and
Detective Cooney. Cullen brought in trainloads of scabs, and a running series of gang fights ensued. The police forced the strikers to
run a gantlet composed of a mob of strikebreakers. Cullen himself
thumped strikers and finally the police broke into the miners' one
place of safety, the union hall.

That only one striker was killed was instanced by the government
papers as a triumph of moderation.

MELBOURNE, AUSTRALIA. 17 MARCH 1909

Googlies All Round

The holder of the governor-generalship of Australia was expected to be reserved and non-political. The new office, created at Federation in 1901, carried vice-regal prestige and the expectation of pomp without substance.

At Melbourne's St. Patrick's Day celebrations, Lord Dudley, who had previously been lord lieutenant of Ireland, bowled a googly. He had been appointed governor-general of Australia by a Tory government and they were fundamentally and unalterably against anything resembling Home Rule for Ireland. So, when Dudley made the statement from the platform that "Ireland should be governed by the Irish," his audience danced.

Nor, a year later, can one see the seams of a pitch made to the minister of defence by a delegation made up of leading Irish Catholic MPs and representatives of the Hibernian Australian Catholic Benefit Society, the Celtic Club, the Shamrock Club and the Catholic Young Men's Society – for an Irish-Australian regiment to be entered among the serried rows of imperial forces.

AVARUA, RAROTONGA, THE COOK ISLANDS. 1909

Hearing Footsteps

Col. Walter E. Gudgeon, CMG, resident commissioner of the Cook Islands indeed was correct: the Catholics were after him. The Roman Catholics. The *Irish* Roman Catholics. He'd known all along they took their orders from Rome, but now he understood more, oh yes, so much more. The actual instructions were passed through the Irish College in Rome and then to the Drumcondra palace of the archbishop of Dublin, and then to the Irish Catholics in the New Zealand government. That's why Joseph Ward, prime minster of New Zealand since 1906, and the son of hard Catholics, strong Catholics, immigrant Catholics, was intent on breaking him.

Indeed, Ward was – on the grounds that Gudgeon was, if not stark raving mad, close to it. His administrative fiats had passed from being merely arbitrary to positively draconian: sentencing youths to six months hard labour for stealing a pair of shoes.

Gudgeon's keeping the lepers on a prison island without provisions was more than hygienic, it was virtually eugenic. And as a diplomat Gudgeon was remarkably offensive. After a recent goodwill visit by Gudgeon to the island of Pukapuka, the locals had pulled down the Union Flag and set up their own court and legislative system. The man was a menace.

"The government has found it necessary to retire you from the Public Service," the New Zealand prime minister wrote in May 1909. With unnecessary tact he added that it was because Gudgeon, 68, had "reached the age at which retirements are being made."

Gudgeon knew the real reasons. "You do not know Catholics," he told a friend. "If I were to return to that faith, all New Zealand could not remove me from here."

"Really?"

"Until I wanted to go," he added modestly.

More persecution followed. A few months later it fell to James Carroll, the new minister for Native Affairs, to set Gudgeon's retirement pension. "I am done for," Gudgeon declared. "That man forced a decent Christian woman to turn Papist at marriage. That solely to have more Romanist souls in heaven, he thinks. He'll stop at nothing."

Carroll, reviewing years of Gudgeon's rule over the Cook Islands, awards him only three months' salary as a retirement sum and makes sure that Gudgeon receives no official decorations for his service.

The Romanists, the vicious Irish Romanists won, Gudgeon knew, and knew with certainty to his dying day. He was scarcely comforted by having his retiring gratuity, on appeal, increased to a full year's salary, nor was he consoled by the post he held for a time at the start of World War I: censor of telegraphic messages.

MAYNOOTH SEMINARY, CO. KILDARE. 1912

Tall Men Talking

In one sense, they met on an elevated plain: Daniel Patrick Mannix and Eamon de Valera were among the tallest Irishmen of their generation to obtain eminence. Other than that, the interview was intensely uncomfortable: Mannix was president of the Royal College of St. Patrick, Maynooth, the premier seminary for Irish Catholic priests. Its theological section had been created a Pontifical University in 1886 and, since

1910 its arts and sciences section had been a recognized college of the National University of Ireland. Although Mannix and de Valera had been to the same Christian Brothers school, they had not overlapped: Mannix was the elder by eighteen years.

De Valera needs a job, badly. The two men conduct the employment interview without admitting that this transaction is occurring. They walk slowly several times around Maynooth's central quadrangle. De Valera imitates Mannix's posture, hands clasped behind his back, perambulating very slowly, bobbing forward now and then to indicate assent to something the cleric says. The two resemble a pair of large herons feeding in shallow water.

De Valera is a mathematician of modest attainments. Later worshippers at his shrine are to claim that he was one of only three persons in the world to understand Einstein's General Theory when it was first published, but actually he had advanced calculus and little more. This does not bother the Rev. Dr. Mannix, for he needs someone to teach mathematics and mathematical physics at a first-degree level for the examinations of the National University.

Mannix's worry is de Valera's nationalism. The president of Maynooth had fired in 1909 the professor of Irish for being too nationalistic and had rid Maynooth of a half-dozen priests who were doing post-graduate studies and who had sided with the professor.

In 1911, Mannix had welcomed the King and Queen of the United Kingdom to the seminary which had been created with London's money in 1795 and still held a Royal warrant.

So de Valera has to work very hard to convince Mannix that he will accept authority, will not teach Irish nationalism in the classroom and will keep his extra-curricular political activities in quiet and respectable channels.

De Valera succeeds and he receives a letter naming him to a part-time lectureship. Mannix already has a new mission: he has been notified that he will be enthroned as bishop of Melbourne.

GISBORNE, NEW ZEALAND. FEBRUARY 1912

Laughter and Good Intentions

Whatever anyone said about Sir James Carroll, they had to admit he was great fun to be around. That's right, *Sir* James. He'd received his big gong, KCMG in 1911, officially for service to the Maori, but mostly because he'd been such good company. He hadn't done much in his long political career, and that which he did wasn't much good (witness his enthusiastic support for the To-hunga Suppression Act of 1907), but, he made you glad to be around him.

He loved it when somebody confused him with Dr. Patrick O'Carroll and he would beamingly prescribe something for the pe-titioner's complaint and go off to tell his friends. Like Doctor Patrick O'Carroll, Sir James Carroll was solidly Catholic, had fought staunchly on the anti-Maori side in the New Zealand Wars, was proud of his Irish ancestry, and, like Dr. O'Carroll, was to be-come the fountainhead of a small Maori dynasty (in Sir James's case by being the foster father of more than thirty children). But Sir James was ahead of the good doctor. Whereas the doctor was pure Pakeha, Sir James was the son of an Irish whaler-cum-coastal trader, and of the chieftainess Tapuke. He had grown up with Maori as his first language.

You wouldn't know that now, however. His English was perfect, and as he leaned against the gunwales of a Cook Islands-bound ship in Gisborne harbour and told jokes to his friends, he did English re-gional accents almost perfectly. Was Sir James, as minister in charge of the Cook Islands, finally intending to visit them? Not on his life. He's never been near the islands and in this case he lingered on board the vessel just long enough to have his picture taken and then left for his racing stables. They were his chief love, and Sir James was one of the leading figures of New Zealand's turf world. No race meeting was truly first-level unless he turned up.

Sir James had always intended to do more in politics than he actually did, but he was seraphically proud of what he called his "young colts," a collection of Maori university graduates of whom he became the mentor and patron. "The Young Maori Party," though they later turned on Carroll, would have been vulnerable without his early protection.

Peter Buck gives respect to Carroll. In 1909, while Buck was prac-tising medicine and completing his M.D. thesis, he was told by Carroll, "Hone Heke is gone. We mourn, but you must stand in his place." So Peter Buck took the northern Maori seat in parliament and somehow still completed his post-graduate degree. Then, in mid 1912, as Dr. Buck, he briefly succeeded Sir James as minister of Native Affairs in a very short-lived liberal government.

Same position, different man: Buck had actually been to the Cook Islands. In fact, he spent the parliamentary recess of 1910 as acting medical officer on Rarotonga, and in 1912–13 he passed through the Cooks on his way to being acting medical officer on Nieue. The fascination with the Cook islanders that began for him at the Christchurch Exhibition of 1906–07 has incubated. He wants to know more, about them, about all Polynesians, if possible.

He won't be a politician.

NULLARBOR PLAIN, WESTERN AUSTRALIA. 1912

Strong Opinions

Daisy Bates keeps her second husband's surname, but that is all that she takes from the marriage. She refers to him as her "late husband," although he is alive and is raising their son. Journalists take her literally, however. Daisy returned to Australia from England in 1899 and lived with Jack for a bit more than two years. She spent most of her time with the indigenous people who lived around their home.

Then, in 1902, Daisy just leaves. She is appointed a researcher into the cultures of the Aborigines by the Western Australian government and she probably learns more about them than does any other ethnographer. In part, this is because she has no theories whatsoever and no academic position to protect. She just watches and listens. Daisy calculates that the indigenous people will disappear (they are down to 31,000 in her day) the same way observers in New Zealand calculate that the Maori will become extinct within a generation.

She defines herself as a combination welfare officer and the recorder of a civilization she knows no white persons and few black will ever see again. She becomes an honorary male and the totem keeper of several clans. She is regarded as the Woman from the Dream Time.

Daisy's opinions are nothing if not strong. She disapproves of any "half-breeds." She tries to keep "her" people, the remnant of the Mirning Tribe, isolated at her camp at Eucla, as desolate a place as exists on the continent. She also believes that the Roman Catholic church is the cause of most of the world's troubles and the Australian Labor Party the source of most of her adopted country's difficulties.

She writes feverishly: newspaper articles, learned papers and eventually a book. Early in 1914, she is invited by the British Association for the Advancement of Science to a peregrinating conference that meets, serially, in Adelaide, Melbourne and Sydney. It is be an all-star intellectual circus: Malinowski, Bateson, Radcliffe-Brown, all in attendance.

Daisy crosses the 250 miles of the Nullarbor Plain in a cart pulled by camels and attends the Adelaide and Melbourne sessions. She is especially keen to encounter the young wonder A.R. Radcliffe-Brown, newly appointed Professor of Anthropology at the University of Cape Town: she has discovered some of her own writings in his.

At one of the Melbourne sessions, Radcliffe-Brown gives a paper on the Myths of the Western Australian Aborigines, and Daisy is asked to comment on it. She rises, every inch the Anglo-Irish lady: "Professor Radcliffe-Brown has given my notes so nicely there is no occasion to add to them."

The profession never forgives honesty.

Daisy spends the next thirty years living in sun-blistered spots near waterholes where Aborigines congregate. She fights constantly for welfare funds for "her" natives and is visited three times by Royals and receives a CBE. She watches without judgement practices other Europeans condemn: child-marriages and, in extreme circumstances, infanticide and cannibalism. She tries to change her people not at all.

Maybe she was crazy.

WELLINGTON, NEW ZEALAND. 1913

Governmental Efficiency

Patrick J. Kelleher, son of the Irishman who had been frozen out of Lawrence, Massachusetts by his brothers for the sin of having served in the United Kingdom army, was perfect for the New Zealand civil service under William Ferguson Massey. In 1912, the strongly conservative, efficiency-oriented Massey reworked the public service and this was Patrick Kelleher's big break. He was thirty-six, a devout Catholic, and a dab hand with numbers. One of his favourite tricks was to have someone write down a square composed of eight numbers as fast as possible, and he would have the sum ready by the time the last pencil stroke was made. In later eras his love of horse racing would have been considered a vice, but New Zealand in the early twentieth century was horse-mad, and Massey himself was a good judge of horse flesh. Kelleher was raised from being a bookkeeper in the Department of

Industries to being chief of clerks for the Department of Internal Affairs, which ran the civil service and everything else important.

A fun-loving Catholic Irishman, an enjoyable boss: forget those music-hall stereotypes. In charge of a school or a business, an office or a shop, such a man was apt to be more severe, more rule-bound, less forgiving than any gone-soft old-money Prod, just ask anyone who served under one. Kelleher's first innovation as chief clerk in Internal Affairs was to keep an attendance book on his own desk and there everyone signed in. At 9:05 a.m. sharp he ruled a line and put his initials under it. Anyone late was punished. The same procedure was used to be sure that no one made it out before 1:00 p.m. for dinner-break. And never, on Saturday's half-day, did anyone get away before noon.

In 1917, Kelleher and his immediate boss, a devout Presbyterian by the name of Hislop, received a request from the charwomen who scrubbed the government building to be permitted to work late on Friday night, so that they would have Saturday morning to be home with their families. Kelleher and Hislop fought a rear-guard action for five years: the artificial light would not be good enough for a first-class job, they said; there would be too many officials still around, tracking things and making a mess, and on and on.

Hygiene, Kelleher frequently noted, was something no government could take for granted.

THE GALLIPOLI PENINSULA. 25 APRIL 1915

Coming of Age

A collective spiritual Bar-Mitzvah would save an ocean of human pain. Instead, most collectivities come of age with a bris: lots of pain, blood spilled, and manhood reduced.

For Australia, the hideous usage of Aussie and Kiwi men by the imperial generals in an invasion of Turkey is seen and celebrated as the moment when the country came of age.

All the Anzac troops were volunteers and Irish Catholics were represented in numbers just slightly less than their proportion of the population.

Conscription for overseas service twice was put to a referendum during the Great War and twice defeated, with Irish Catholics tipping the scales on the negative side. Was this the coming-of-age of the Irish

Catholics: confident enough to refuse to be coerced into joining the imperial war effort, yet loyal enough to do so voluntarily?

MAUNGAPOHATU, UREWARE, NORTH ISLAND, NEW ZEALAND. 2 APRIL 1916

Not the Easter Rising

Pharoahs have always had a hard time countenancing cheeky Israelites. It is Sunday morning, the fourth Sunday in Lent. Prime Minister Massey, now the head of a national wartime coalition, has decided to suppress the rural messianic movement of Rua Kanana Hepetipa. The New Jerusalem is several days from any convenient point for the police, but John Cullen – "Massey's Cossack" in popular reference – is keen to get at the brown bastards. Rua is said to be hindering recruitment among Maori for the European War and that is enough to have him seized. Besides, anybody who claims to be the Messiah is a danger to civil order.

Five days' march through incredibly dense bush finally brings Cullen and his men to Maungapohatu. Rua sees them and is distantly courteous. He shows one of them, Constable Cummings, a Bible and says "Jesus Christ and I are the Holy Ghosts." He adds ambiguously, "And that's the finish for you." Later, he shows some of the police around his circularly-shaped house-cum-temple and shakes hands with Constable Doyle, with whom he chats for a time. Commissioner Cullen breaks up this uneasy, but non-violent, scene by riding up with three men of a special detail, all wearing dark riding breeches, puttees, white shirts with stand-up linen collars and flaming red ties. An unusual uniform, and threatening. Rua turns to run and is grabbed by a sub-inspector and several police. Constable Neill seizes Rua by the throat, while Sergeant O'Hara handcuffs Rua's son, Whatu. When Rua refuses to march away, Cullen shoves a stick into his crotch and frog-marches him. Then some shooting starts. No one ever establishes from whence: but two Maori are killed (one of them another son of Rua) and three others wounded, one being shot in the back.

Rua's trial was the longest in duration that yet had been held in New Zealand, and despite running ankle-deep in police perjury, it produced only a twelve month hard-labour sentence, to be followed by eight months in a reformatory. Even then, eight of the twelve members of the jury signed a protest to the judge saying that the sentencing was too harsh and was based on a misunderstanding of their verdict.

Massey nominated Cullen for the first King's Police Medal to be awarded a New Zealander and found him appropriate re-employment for the remainder of the war: overseeing the forced labour of enemy aliens.

DARLINGHURST GAOL, NSW, AUSTRALIA. 1918

One-Celled Life Form

The entire network of the Irish Republican Brotherhood in Australia poses for its picture: in a single cell in prison.

Irish-Australians had followed the pattern of the homeland in their reaction to the 1916 Rising: at first they were outraged, seeing it as treason to the cause of Home Rule. And then, as the United Kingdom army made martyrs, they were equally outraged at the British. Yet, the physical distance from Dublin was so great, the time spent in Australia so long (often three generations), that the fervour quickly ebbed. Archbishop Mannix, who had changed from being a Castle Catholic to an advanced (albeit nonviolent) patriot, seemingly upon crossing the equator, tried to keep up the fervour. His flock loved him, for he was a marvellous showman, but largely ignored his message.

The seven men in Darlinghurst Gaol are all the IRB could recruit. They are not silly or weak or uninformed. Just very unusual among Irish-Australians.

When, in 1922, the Irish Free State breaks into civil war, Irish-Australians turn away in sadness. They might share the homeland's dreams, but they refuse to participate in its nightmare.

CODFORD, WILTSHIRE, ENGLAND. 1918

A Great War

Dr. Peter Buck did not have a merely good war. He had helped recruit the Maori contingent for the war and, in 1915, had gone with them as a medical officer: through the Middle East and then Gallipoli. Mentioned in despatches and a DSO. When the Maori troops were turned into a pioneer battalion – building trenches and redoubts was no come-down, for the Maori had taught the British army everything it knew about trench warfare, and still had some tricks to spare – Buck applied for combat duty. He served as second in command, was promoted major, and became a minor legend.

Now, working in Codford Hospital in England at war's end, he seeks out the leading British anthropologists of the time. He wishes to do serious ethnography and several of them are quite happy to have a scientifically-trained Polynesian on their side. So Buck borrows from them the semi-scientific equipment of the time, the calipers and macrometers and all the paraphernalia used to classify different racial groups.

On the ship back to New Zealand, Dr. Buck measures the heads, bodies, classifies the contours and body-types of all the Maori troops. It is a very rigorous study, and when published in the *Journal of the Polynesian Society* in 1922–23, it sets a standard to be emulated.

CHRISTCHURCH, NEW ZEALAND. 1918

Trust

It's a slow time of year, and a young Christchurch solicitor spends a lot of time looking out the window. One of the matters that he wonders about is Irish Catholics. Are they really different from the rest of us? Are they different from their Irish countrymen who are Protestant? Below the surface, not just in politics.

He can't find much. Keep everything equal and the Prods and Micks have the same sized families (birth control is still condemned in Protestant churches), do the same jobs and get on with making a living about as well.

Then he discovers wills. Testamentary documents. He goes through the court records and one bizarre lump emerges, something he cannot explain. Unlike everyone else who is wealthy enough to need to make a will, Irish Catholics don't usually appoint either their wives or members of their immediate families as executors.

Is that because they are too cold and distant within their families to engender trust? Or are they so close to each other that they know better?

Over-Hearing

Next to the Jews, the Irish and their diaspora were the twentieth century's most self-overhearing people. They constantly modified what they themselves did by listening to what they said about themselves.

Understanding this, Patrick O'Farrell, the twentieth-century's most percipient observer of Irish migrants in New Zealand and Australia, nailed a sixpenny spike through a worldwide stereotype:

Those emigrants who cared most about what happened back in Ireland ought to have been, according to the nationalist canon, those from the Gaelic Catholic majority. Yet the fact was that these had often cut or had severed for them, all connection with Ireland, leaving neither family nor property. They had no longer any stake in that country, many not even the connection of correspondence or even public news. Those with family remaining in Ireland, with direct interest in property and land there, and with strong links via frequent correspondence, tended to be the Ulster Protestants, the Anglo-Irish and more affluent Catholics, particularly those in the professions, lawyers, doctors, priests. It was they who remained most vitally interested in, and informed about Ireland's day to day affairs.

He's right of course, and it's only the momentary enthusiasms of the crowds for the Manchester Martyrs, or Home Rule, or de Valera's visits, that obscure the deeper, continuing links of the educated and the propertied.

Observe in that context the McKee family of Garvagh and Portstewart, Presbyterians living on a social faultline with the Catholic areas of County Londonderry. In 1864, one young man leaves for New Zealand and within twenty years, five of his seven brothers and sisters are pulled along in a migration chain. One New Zealand member of the clan watches the Irish news carefully, and when, in 1920, Ulster is on the verge of civil war, he returns and brings back to New Zealand from Ulster, four of the eleven children from the family of the one remaining brother (who stubbornly refuses to consider leaving and keeps his wife and remaining brood at home).

The brother's wife, however, wants out of troubled Ulster and for three years she saves, takes in boarders, scratches away at ha'pennies, and finally in 1923, at age 48 packs for herself and her remaining seven children and is ready to sail. Her husband does nothing, and only when it is clear that she and the children are going to the Antipodes, with, or without him, does he grudgingly agree to come along.

This Mrs. McKee is a remarkably shrewd woman: judging correctly that the voyage will not be an antiseptic cruise, she keeps all the family's old clothes for the journey, and when they have done their job, they are thrown overboard.

The family disembarks in their new and safer world in fresh linens.

MELBOURNE, SYDNEY, AND STRATHFIELD (NSW),
AUSTRALIA. 1921–22

Joycean Moments

At age seventy-one, Michael Kelly, Archbishop of Sydney, looks back on a successful career. It has another nineteen years to run, but he is taking no chances. He desires his people to know what is foremost on his mind and so he tells them. "On the day I took my seat on the throne of this cathedral, I said that whoever asks me to sanction a mixed marriage puts a dagger in my heart."

The Rev. William Canavan, priest in charge of Strathfield, New South Wales, is preaching a special mission to the men in his charge. He explains to this congregation that November is the month consecrated to the Holy souls and thus is a month of special prayer for the souls in purgatory.

"Few even of the holiest Christians escape the suffering and cleansing fires of purgatory, for nothing defiled can enter heaven. *Purgatory is a place of suffering and penance.* There souls are cleansed and saved – yet so as by fire. *Purgatory is a place of atonement.* There we must pay the strict price of the smallest sin and least stain. We shall certainly be punished. And, men, I say to you, thou shalt not go out from thence until thou pay the last farthing."

Daniel Mannix, archbishop (since 1917) of Melbourne is asked to join other members of the Australian Catholic hierarchy in a letter of condolence to Michael Collins, chairman of the Provisional Government of Ireland and commander-in-chief of the armed forces of the Irish Free State.

The occasion is the death, through a brain haemorrhage, of the founder of Sinn Fein, the man who had replaced Eamon de Valera as president of Dail Eireann, Arthur Griffith.

Mannix, who has no time for the softness of Michael Collins and of those who had signed the Anglo-Irish peace treaty, refuses.

LONDON, ENGLAND. 1924

Disillusionment

"I have now lost faith in the measurement of heads or skulls, at least in Polynesia." It hurt a scientific anthropologist to admit that, and it took some courage.

"When I started out on my travels over and around the Pacific I had unquestioning faith in the head-form as the ultimate test of race." J. MacMillan Brown still believes that size and shape of the head might be true indicators of race elsewhere – "longheadedness" and "short-headedness" he calls his main categories – but he has discovered that in Polynesia a person's head-shape is a matter of fashion and choice, and no more an indication of a biological characteristic than a Japanese gentleman's wearing a tabi rather than a pair of western socks.

On one of the out-islands of Hawai'i he had discovered the custom of head-moulding. The authorities of the Bishop Museum, the centre-point for Hawai'ian, and much Polynesian ethnography, had never heard of the custom, so it was considered either legendary or at most vestigial. Still, when Brown goes to the Cook Islands, he is on the alert and there he notices the extraordinary character of the heads of the people, both children and adults. To Brown's eyes, they all have "flat-backed, dome-topped, sloping-browed round heads."

He makes inquiries and, on several of the Cooks, he is told that soon after a child is born, his mother and sisters begin to massage the sides and back of the head and to push the brow upwards. Working before the cranial bones are full set, they are literally making living sculptures.

J. MacMillan Brown is a racialist in the old meaning of the term: he believes in the "science of race," but at least he is a scientist. He admits that a good bit of what seems to be laid down by the hand of nature is actually the result of the hands of mothers.

PAGO, PAGO, AMERICAN SAMOA. AUGUST 1925

Traveling Light

She is perfect for the job. The coltish twenty-three year old who disembarks at the American naval base carries no baggage, at least none that she is aware of.

Like Peter Buck, she is partly Irish Protestant by heritage, and she is fascinated by the Polynesian world, but there the resemblance ends. Unlike the generation of anthropologists who believed that physical things, such as race and physiology matter, she is the new sort. She does not have to cart calipers and pigment charts. She doesn't believe in any of it. Culture is what counts.

Even here, she is lucky, for she has a lightness of experience.

She has never witnessed serious physical violence.

She knows almost no history of the place she will study.

She has no knowledge of the Samoan language before she arrives for her few months' visit.

She has no knowledge of the missionary impact on the Samoans, or acquaintance with the extensive archival records of that encounter. Indeed, she is purblind to all religious influences, whatever their source.

She is blissfully unaware of the Polynesian pleasure in misleading white interlopers, as when, in all the major island groups, the natives mistaught the local language to the missionaries: for the sheer joy of seeing them make fools of themselves.

And, unlike Peter Buck, she is not bound by the medical doctor's oath – above all, to do no harm.

She is an upper middle-class American and, though she frets about the effect of the humidity on her hair, she is confident that this Polynesian world is definitely her oyster.

AITUTAKI, THE COOK ISLANDS. 1926

Full-Time

See the Henrys if you really want to get something on Aitutaki. They're the fixers. Keep them sweet or road blocks will suddenly appear. Geoffrey Henry, long-time head teacher of the Araura school, scoutmaster of the island, strong voice in the church choir. Keep him sweet; and now one needs to keep his son in play as well. The lad, Albert Royle Henry, has received a secondary education in New Zealand and will soon be Aitutaki's chief teacher and fixer. Ultimately, decades ahead, he will become premier of the self-governing Cook Islands, will be knighted and will be turfed from office for nepotism and corruption beyond the forgiveness of the notably-generous islanders. A coming man, real ability.

Peter Buck has made the crossroads decision of his lifetime. He has give up public health work and has become a full-time anthropologist. He wants to know his own people, the Polynesians. His good fortune is that a lecture Buck gave in Melbourne, "The Coming of the Maori," had in its audience the director of the Bishop Museum, Honolulu. After meeting Buck, the director offered him a five-year fellowship, a chance to do serious field work throughout the South Pacific.

His work on Aitutaki is Buck's first professional study; and he is conducting an inventory of the material culture of the island, with especial attention to items that are vanishing from the culture. He is a good draughtsman and he records in loving detail a culture in rapid transition. The study appears in 1927.

Buck's success in obtaining access to many of the treasures of the islanders rests on his shrewd understanding of the Henrys, and what they stand for: they are the mediators of flux. The schoolmasters bring in the new knowledge, and at the same time teach respect for the old. At a time when the hereditary chiefs no longer had real power, they still had to be shown deference. And though the missionaries were no longer legislators for the island, the Aitutakians were intensely religious. All one had to do was look at the name Albert Royle Henry to realize the continuing reverence for the missionary legacy: the Rev. Henry Royle had been the first Papaa missionary on Aitutaki, and this transposition of his name was one sign of his veneration.

Peter Buck is able to speak in Aitutakian Maori to the elders who control many of the most interesting materials. Some of them have heard of him, from the Christchurch Exhibition twenty years earlier. Gravity and charm: Buck possesses both. Crucially, whenever the Henrys take him to meet someone who has a particularly significant object, Buck always has a short, but ostentatious, conversation with his schoolmaster guide: he has it in English and he makes the master look good.

AMERICAN SAMOA. 1926

Size

The teen-age girls giggle. They cannot believe that the person they are to deal with is a full representative of her people. Each of the girls, aged fourteen to twenty, towers over the tiny little creature. She is five feet, 2 and 1/2 inches tall and weighs ninety-eight pounds. One of them says that they hope she stays out of the wind, or they will lose her completely.

The Pa'plagi lady, the anthropologist, brings them great hilarity, but they are careful not to show it to her face. They are the children of a society of hierarchy and of fear of their elders, and especially of parental violence, and this little lady must be important – otherwise why would she be staying with the American military man, the dispensary pharmacist? And why would she be given a special talking-room at the back of the American government building? No, they won't disgrace their parents.

It is hard, though, for the little lady (is she a missionary, maybe, of a new sort?) asks such silly questions, and writes down anything they say in reply. There are twenty-five of them, these girls, and they often meet with each other to compare sillinesses. Still, there's something in this for them, the wiser girls say. The tiny lady does not speak very much Samoan – less, actually, than we speak English – so this is a good time to practise English and learn the words for a lot of important things. So they trade vocabularies with her. Soon they know English words such as "virgin," and "menstruation," and "consent," and they look forward to the next time a white missionary comes around so that they can impress him with these important terms.

Of the nine months she spent in the Samoan Islands, the tiny anthropologist devotes only a little more than four months to interviewing these, her informants, on the nature of adolescence in Samoa. The remainder of the time has been employed in learning a bit of the language and in travelling. To those who later are so small minded as to suggest that she should have conducted a study that took longer and delved deeper, the tiny lady replies that in the field of ethnography, size does not count.

Diagnosis

One way or another, Dr. Peter Buck had seen a lot of disease, death, and their aftermath. Gallipoli. The Western Front. And as Director of Maori Hygiene in the early 1920s, he had dealt with the after-shocks of the massive 1918 influenza epidemic, which in New Zealand had fallen most heavily on the Maori.

Now, in 1926, he visits Samoa (Western Samoa is back in British hands, Germans expelled). Technically, he comes as an anthropologist, but he recognizes the same symptoms of post-epidemic trauma that he had seen while serving as a public health doctor. Samoa in 1926 is experiencing black plague syndrome.

That is: in November, 1918, a ship from Auckland landed passengers without quarantining them. Some were suffering from influenza and within five weeks 20 percent of the population of the island of Upolo was dead, an amazingly swift and terrifying rate of mortality. Influenza spread throughout the Western Samoan Islands and the best estimates are that within four months 22 percent of the islands' population had been wiped out. Of course this was part of a world-wide pandemic, but the speed and mortality of the flu epidemic in Western Samoa was greater than that recorded any other place in the world. American Samoa was largely saved, for officials acted quickly and put up a quarantine wall.

To find a parallel to Western Samoa, one has to go back to the Black Plague of the 1340s. As a medical historian – and as an experienced public health doctor – Peter Buck recognized that Samoa was in the diminishing, but still painful, throes of a pattern that was well documented in medieval England: a fanatical chasing after religious explanations by some, denial of the existing god by others, personal guilt for having survived, false gaiety, gaping holes in the social hierarchy, desperate attempts to shore up the social pyramid; violent arguments about social status, inheritance, property, debts and dues.

The Western Samoan Islands in 1926 are in a very shaky state, far from healed. Anyone could see that. This matter, though, is not that gee-whiz-Polynesia-is-amazing story that his benefactors at the Bishop Museum want to hear about; so Peter Buck writes a nice unemotional scientific piece for the museum about Western Samoan material culture.

HAMILTON, SOUTH ISLAND, NEW ZEALAND. 1927

Return on Investment

Near Hamilton, the police find the body of a swagman. It is covered with a blanket and he is flat on his back, as if being asleep and lying in state were a single activity. His worldly possessions consist of one shilling, one-and-a-half pence, a watch chain and an enamel mug and, of course, his blanket.

Dominic Nolan was one of the thousands of men and women from Great Britain and Ireland who came to New Zealand after World War I. An economic depression began in the British Isles almost as soon as the war ended, and taking part of the excess labour supply off the hands of the Mother Country was something the Dominion was happy to do: it needed more workers, the homeland did not. Until 1927, roughly, the new workers were welcome, but as New Zealand eased into its own depression, they were less needed, and life for many of them became hard indeed.

A proud man, Dominic Nolan had come from Ireland, not as an assisted former soldier, but on his own hook. *I paid my passage in full, my passport will show that.* At forty years of age he could not stand the hard life. Swagging from one short-term job to another had broken him. The new life was not all that he expected, but he died not bitter, just disappointed. *Dear New Zealanders: blame not the poor immigrants in this country who have been shipped over here in the last few years, allured by the dazzling advertisements in England, glowing pictures depicting scenes of the Dominions abroad, displaying acres and acres under tillage.* Nolan was referring to the 50,000 or so men and women who had been drawn to New Zealand between 1920 and 1927 by a heavy propaganda campaign. He had not done well, nor had many others.

At his inquest, his letter was read. He concluded by welcoming death and then added, as a final bit of collective responsibility, these words: *English and Irish papers please copy.*

MELBOURNE, AUSTRALIA. 1928

The Old School Lie

Justice Henry Higgins reads a letter from George Bernard Shaw. Higgins reveres Shaw, both as a progressive socialist thinker and as a dramatist. The letter from Shaw arrives in November 1928 and Higgins dies the next January.

In the winter of his life, Henry Higgins wants to know a simple little thing, a matter that has niggled at him for years: did George Bernard Shaw use his name in "Pygmalion"? It's not a nasty question, just something that would help an old man put his life in order.

Shaw replies from the Hotel Beau-Site, Cap D'Antibes, France. The playwright can scarcely deny that he, like Justice Higgins, had attended the Wesleyan Connexional School, St. Stephen's Green, Dublin, but it was something he would have preferred not to remember: the school was decidedly unfashionable and, at the time Shaw attended it, his alcoholic father was a wholesale grain merchant and all the Wesleyan schooling did for Shaw was prepare him to clerk in a land agency on Molesworth Street. "Wesley College," as Shaw calls it, "has sometimes claimed my interest as an old alumnus; but I have not a good word to say for it. It could not even teach Latin; and it never seriously tried to teach anything else. A more futile boy-poison could not be imagined."

Shaw separated himself from Higgins: "I was a day boy; what a boarder's life was like I shudder to conjecture."

But about Henry Higgins? Of course Shaw may have gone through life bumping into tens of people named Henry Higgins, but younger schoolboys do remember the names of their seniors, sometimes in retrospective terror, sometimes in awe. Shaw denies any such possibility. "I don't remember you. In 1865, when you left, I was only nine years old. If we were really at the old Wesleyan Connexional School ... together, it can have been for a short overlap only."

Up to that point the lie is believable, but Shaw, the artist, never could resist one broad brush stroke too many. "There was a boy who came and went in my time whose name may have been Higgins, though I am not quite sure of it, but he was weak-minded, or rather infantile, and used to stand up and sing during roll call when the fellows around him told him that Dr. Crook expected him to do it. He stayed a very short time and should never have been sent there. A most good natured creature, who may have turned out well after all."

Then, the pure and purely unnecessary Shavian knife: "Your dates exclude the possibility of identifying you with him."

NEW YORK, NEW YORK. 1928

A Jewel

In August, William Morrow, a new publisher, brings out the most influential American novel of the 1920s. It is a perfect jewel, Margaret Mead's *Coming of Age in Samoa*. An entire world is created and so lucidly described that the reader wants to walk into the book and live in the Samoa of Mead's imagining. Shrewdly, this Utopia is packaged with some improving advice, as the subtitle suggests: *A Psychological Study of Primitive Youth for Western Civilization*. Jazz Age America is delighted to learn that "ease" – moral, sexual, physical, and social – can be obtained, and in fact it's even good for children. The advice: we should start acting like my Samoans.

Only a young American of the 1920s could have known so instinctively and accurately what the chattering classes wanted to hear. And her moment is perfect: fourteen months later and few would have been listening. But now she tells them that the Jazz Age credo is right: you *can* be anybody you like; your choice, you decide. Nature is a false limit, social hierarchy an illusion, religion an unnecessary spancel.

If, later, her capture and use of Samoan culture is seen as an especially pure and early case of American cultural imperialism, who is to say it's not all for the best? For students of humanity, in any case, it was nice to be shown how ethnography should be done.

GREYMOUTH, SOUTH ISLAND, NEW ZEALAND. 1929

Family Cries

The telegram from Trieste that the nun of the Sisters of Mercy receives is opened with an ivory-handled penknife by the mother superior. She reads it and then hands it to Sister Gertrude who reads it, then folds it neatly, places it back in the envelope and gives it back to her superior. It is the only interruption in her day of holy service.

The telegram was from her brother, seeking to find out if she were in good health and offering to pay for a trip to Europe or Ireland if she needed rest. It is the act of a concerned brother, and also the act of a desperately lonely man.

She does not reply.

When she left Ireland for New Zealand in 1909, Sister Gertrude Mary Joyce took with her the surplice that her brother Jimmy had worn as an altar boy.

She never returned to Ireland and never read anything Jimmy published.

MANGAIA, THE COOK ISLANDS. 1929–30

Impervious to the Light

Dr. Peter Buck finally tastes his dream, and it is rancid. For well over two decades he has dreamed of conducting serious field work on Mangaia. Now he can. The Bishop Museum pays his way, and the Old Boy network created by Sir James Carroll does the rest: Sir Apirana Ngata, once one of the Young Maori Party and a close friend of Buck's, is New Zealand's minister of Native Affairs and is also responsible for the governing of the Cook Islands. He places the government of Mangaia at his friend's disposal. In fact, he makes Buck the government, for the resident agent on the island was on leave and Buck is placed in charge of government services on the island. He already has great mana on the island, where he is universally referred to by his Maori name, Te Rangi Hiroa, rather than by his Irish name. Now he is chief magistrate, the postmaster, the chief of police, the president of the Mangaia Island Council, and head of anything else that needs an official presence. All these duties, in fact, take him an hour or two a day and in return, Sir Apirana permits him to use the police as his research assistants. They do the tiresome work of body and head measurements that are still part of ethnography, albeit now mostly placed in the appendices at the back of research monographs. Buck has the freedom to compel the chiefs to help him make visitations in their districts, and when he wants a site of an old marea cleared, he orders a band of prisoners out of the island's gaol to do it. With his mana, Buck has immediate access to even the most venerable elders on the island and he makes them his informants.

Why does something so perfect, so long dreamed of, now taste like ashes? It is the sorcery of the tiny American. She has made certain thoughts tapu.

When he had heard of her study, Peter Buck had immediately ordered it from his bookseller and the English edition, published by Jonathan Cape, arrives while he is still setting up in Mangaia. It is deeply troubling.

Not because the fieldwork is almost entirely inaccurate and misrepresentational. Although it is. Buck had spent time on American Samoa in 1927, including the Manu'a Islands where the American lady had worked. He knew that, though they did not suffer from the post-epidemic trauma of the Western Samoans, the peoples of both parts of the island were one: a single dialect served them all and a single social order. Observing the rigid intricacies of hierarchy and rank ceremonies at work in American Samoa, Buck had written to Apira Ngata that the complexities were like something out of *Burke's Peerage*. Buck knew that Margaret Mead's Samoans were rank conscious, obsessed with religion, given to frequent violence, and prudish about most aspects of sexual relations. It wasn't a great place to come of age.

The non-existence of the Eden of Miss Mead does not surprise Buck. When younger, he had himself converted Rarotanga into a second-line paradise. In 1910, when he had served as a temporary medical officer on that island, he had written to Apirana Ngata (all their adult lives they corresponded frequently) that the people of Raro "are a happy crowd and much better off than we are." He added, "They have plenty of tucker and every adult female has a sewing machine and every male has a bicycle and an umbrella."

Young ethnographers were permitted to play Rousseau; they would learn better eventually, and, in any case, Peter Buck has always believed in the scientific method and the ideal that good data and good thinking drive out bad.

What is killing Peter Buck's happiness on Mangaia is the possibility that the American anthropologist is not merely wrong, but that, somehow, this Pakeha sorceress has discovered something that the medically-trained Dr. Peter Buck has been taught to believe impossible: that bad ideas, bad science, can be stronger than good.

And, especially now the possibility torments him for, in his middle age, he is observing the march of merchant capitalism through Polynesia, and Mangaia is a painful example. He hates Mead's description of the soft life and easy attitudes of her Polynesians, for they are poetic versions of the bigotries that he encounters everyday among whites on the Cook Islands.

Such as, "*The lazy Polynesian.*" The phrase infuriates him. "The dictum that the Polynesian is disinclined and even has an aversion towards manual labour has been promulgated by alien people who do less themselves than the very laziest among those they unjustly criticize," he writes to Sir Apirana, and advises: "I would strongly urge you to send a publicity man over next fruit season to take moving pictures of the fruit industry in the various islands. It would be an eye opener to the white public."

Peter Buck, despite being a professional anthropologist, is still in his heart a medical doctor: he believes that a right diagnosis can lead to a proper prescription and thence to healing. To hell with the idea of Polynesian Edens, for often they are hell. "It is popularly supposed in temperate climates that oranges and bananas simply grow without any assistance from man. They fall ripe into receptacles whilst the native basks in the sun."

He is furious, because as a medical doctor he recognizes the physical cost of horticultural work, conducted in dangerous conditions. In the eyes of Peter Buck, the myth of Polynesian Eden is a licence to commercial exploitation, a modern equivalent of the myth of the happy slave promulgated a century earlier.

Peter Buck, who wishes to exorcise this evil, this Eden myth, finds that the American sorceress is stronger than he. Every night as he shuts *Coming of Age in Samoa*, he returns to the Acknowledgements, for that is where she has laid the tapu that he dares not break."For a co-operation which greatly facilitated the progress of my work in the Pacific, I am indebted to Dr. Herbert E. Gregory, director of the B.P. Bishop Museum and to Dr. E.C.S. Handy and Miss Stella Jones of the Bishop Museum." The museum is Peter Buck's foster family, Dr. Gregory his foster father. He cannot turn on Miss Mead and reveal the truth.

CANBERRA, A.C.T., AUSTRALIA. 1929–49

The Establishment

With scarcely a break, second-generation Irishmen controlled the prime ministership of Australia from the Crash of 1929 to the beginning of the Korean War: James Scullen (Labor, 1929–32); Joseph Lyons (United Australia Party, 1932–39), John Curtin (Labor, 1941–45), and Ben Chifley (Labor, 1945–49).

Intending to break the Irish Catholics away from Labor, Robert Menzies, Liberal, in 1963 agreed to permit state funding of Catholic schools. This was the one item that had kept the now-middle class Irish bonded tightly to the Labor Party and Menzies was right: from then on, Irish-Catholic bloc voting became a thing of the past.

With no distinct grievances remaining, the Irish Catholics join fully the Irish Protestants as a Charter Group: whites who control the state and the economy complain about immigrants, oppose Aboriginal "privileges" and live some of the most comfortable lives on earth.

It's a long way from Botany Bay.

THE BERNICE P. BISHOP MUSEUM,
HONOLULU, HAWAI'I. 1930

Book Launch

Bulletins number 75 and 76 of the Bishop Museum are published. These are actually books, despite the modest term "bulletin" used to describe the museum's series of ethnographic monographs.

No. 76 is Margaret Mead's *Social Organization of Manu'a*, a restatement in more general term of the "easeful" society of the Samoan people, based upon her nine months visit to Polynesia in 1925–26.

No. 75 is Peter Buck's *Samoan Material Culture*, based on work he had done on the Manu'a islands in 1927, and also work he and two research colleagues had done elsewhere in both American and Western Samoa.

The invisible line that is drawn between the two studies is the recognition of a tapu. Buck, by limiting himself to material culture, does not have to dishonour the Bishop Museum, which he would do if he crossed into social anthropology: for, as his letters to friends show, he knows that the people the American lady studied were highly religious, very hierarchical and have a history of serious violence. Maybe he can be fully truthful, and truly scientific, when dealing with another Polynesian society. Not Samoa.

"RONAN" COUNTRY, NORTHERN TERRITORIES, AUSTRALIA. 1931

Rural Reality

Father and son, Jim and Tom Ronan, second- and third-generation Irish Catholics from Galway, lived as classic bushmen in a vast area on the Northern Territory-Western Australia border. In his later life, Tom writes books about the backcountry life. These are mostly accurate and not sentimental.

The part he does not talk about much is the end of the lives of the stockmen, drovers, bushmen, men who have had full lives: full, but nomadic.

There is little for them. They die sickly in a hut. Or, often, like Matt Wilson, partner and best friend of Jim Ronan, the old bushmen of the northwest blow their brains out.

At the other end of the country, in 1936 the last Tasmanian Tiger dies.

AUCKLAND, NEW ZEALAND. 1931

Redeployment

Patrick J. Kelleher has done very well at the Department of Internal Affairs. His rise has continued and on 1 July 1931 he becomes undersecretary of the department. This means he is the single most powerful civil servant in the New Zealand government and he draws a salary of £950 per annum. He has fought to the top of the tree.

Which makes his sudden resignation nine months later more than merely puzzling. Kelleher's great strength has been numbers; he is proud of being able to add eight columns of multiple-figure numbers simultaneously. So, he is seemingly the perfect man to oversee the "totaliser," the pari-mutual betting system that Internal Affairs licensed at racetracks. And he has supervised the system of state-licensed gambling, quaintly named "art club lotteries," that sports and civic clubs use to raise funds.

But something is very wrong. He resigns abruptly, leaves his wife in Wellington and moves into the Commercial Travellers' Club in Auckland where he becomes a full-time bookmaker, an illegal, but not very risky profession. He's a good one, never making an error, never skipping a pay-out, but a bookie none-the-less. He spends his remaining years – he dies in 1950 – making book, either from the Travellers' Club or from his retirement home in Helen's Bay. Eventually his wife rejoins him.

What ended such a stellar career, and just at the beginning of an obviously-deepening Depression no one ever learns: his family, however, is told that he quit his civil service post to make room for deserving younger men; the family does its duty and believes him.

YALE UNIVERSITY, NEW HAVEN, CONNECTICUT.
DECEMBER 1933

Endgame

He discovers a serpent in his mouth and he cannot kill it.

Bad ideas can be stronger than good, he acknowledges, broken.

He breaks faith with Pakeha science, because he has been broken by Pakeha sorcery.

But he does so in an act so private that it does not come to light until long after his death.

As a visiting professor at Yale, Dr. Peter Buck finishes the teaching term, and sits down to complete the study he has dreamed of for so long: a full-blown ethnography of Mangahian society from before the times of European contact until the near-present. Its publication is already arranged. It is to be published as a research monograph by the Bishop Museum.

The Bernice P. Bishop Museum of Honolulu, Hawai'i.

The typescript of the Mangaia manuscript is over 700 pages. It will be his monument. The long sweep of Mangahian society, seen whole. A Polynesian culture from its mythic beginnings, and its complex material achievements; and the monograph faces squarely the island's febrile post-contact history. A real ethnography, not a children's story.

Yet, Buck, with surgical precision, deletes from the completed typescript a sheaf of sixty-four pages. These are the pages on which he has written thoughts that he believes are unthinkable. This fear of the unthinkable is primitive, irrational, he knows that, but he still recognizes that he cannot express these thoughts and stay a Polynesian. They will render him culturally stateless.

No, he had not contemplated turning on Margaret Mead, for the tapu that protected her still held, and would hold for the rest of his life.

Yet, Buck had danced around the edges of that fearsome monition. He had taken his ethnography of Mangaia and its culture into the missionary era and down to the annexation of the island by New Zealand. He had described early religious wars, especially a heated Christian-Pagan battle of 1828 and, more importantly, in terms of island memory, dealt with the Years of the Great Maretu, the brown missionary whose influence still was the invisible hand on Mangaia in the late 1920s.

Now, he rips out everything to do with events after 1822.

Keeping his pride intact, he explains to Sir Apirana Ngata that he is doing this to protect the material from being too heavily edited by the Bishop Museum people, and that is in part true. But read what he deletes, look at the ideas he transformed out of existence and one understands more. Peter Buck has described a post-contact Polynesian world in which both before and after Europeans arrive, religion is central. It is a world of strict limitations on social behaviour and it provides sharp penalties for those who do not keep their proper place. *The Mangahians exchanged one set of taboos for another, and in the process lost an amount of their individuality, self respect and pride of race. To make up for an inferiority association with the past they carried their zeal to excess in the new culture and became tyrants in the cause of the new religion. The new religion dominated the thoughts and activities of the people to a greater extent than the old religions ever had in days gone by.* When he was writing those words, Buck had sweated like a dock labourer, and now he had tears and suddenly, a terrible chill. His conclusion, the end product of a lifetime of hard labour was this: *Religion thus occupied much more of the waking time of the people than it did in pre-missionary days and than it did in European communities.*

This he cuts cleanly, completely, as if taking out a cancer.

Hence, his final monograph does not question the existence of Polynesia as latent paradise. It does not introduce religion for that clearly is a tapu idea (otherwise, Buck infers, Miss Mead would have given it more than one paragraph, and that only in an appendix in her study), and thus he stays far away from suggesting that there are sharp limits, many of them sacralized, on almost every action in a South Pacific island society.

The serpent temporarily rewards Dr. Peter Buck. Soon Buck succeeds his intellectual foster-father, Dr. Gregory, as director of the Bishop Museum, a post he fills with distinction. Hawai'i suits him perfectly, a Polynesian locale and an American stage. He never again does any serious fieldwork, but his *Vikings of the Sunrise* (1938), a light and charming mix of travelogue, Polynesian mythology, migration theory, and anecdotes, is an international best-seller: not in the Margaret Mead league, but close. Anyone who does Polynesian ethnography pays him a courtesy visit and asks for his blessing. Half in jest, half in earnest, he is called by his fellow anthropologists "the Great Chief of Polynesia." And in 1946, the Pakeha king, George VI of the United Kingdom, knights him.

Sir Peter dies of cancer in 1951, without an enemy in the world, save the serpent that, in 1933, seized his tongue.

AUCKLAND, NEW ZEALAND. MARCH 1940

St. Patrick's Bounty

The largest funeral procession in New Zealand's history honoured Michael Joseph Savage. Easily the most popular of all the nation's premiers, from the mid-1930s onwards he had been virtually beatified: in Catholic homes his picture frequently was on the wall with the lithographs of the Sacred Heart of Jesus and that of the Pope. A former extreme radical – he had been an organizer of the Waihi strike so harshly crushed by Massey and Cullen – he had mellowed and turned into a pragmatic leader of the New Zealand Labor Party.

His proleptic sainthood had a nice symmetry about it: he had been born in Downpatrick, Ireland, not far from St. Patrick's burial place, and his own burial service was conducted in St. Patrick's Cathedral, Auckland.

The only sticky part of the story is that for almost his entire adult life Savage was an arch-rationalist and an opponent of ancient mummery.

Cancer taught him wisdom, however, and in his last months he reassumed the faith of his fathers.

PANGURU, NORTH ISLAND, NEW ZEALAND. 1944

Belated Recognition

Outside a marae, Father Wiremu Te Awhitu poses awkwardly with a group of young school girls. He is unique, something that the Irish-controlled church in New Zealand has prevented until now: he is the first Maori to be entrusted with a priestly vocation.

The various Protestant denominations have had Maori clergy for over a century, and Father Wiremu knows that the contrast is humiliating to him and to his people. He likes it, though, when the girls call him "father."

CAIRO, EGYPT. 25 APRIL 1945

Summation

Even without a war, the weight would have been too much. On his mother's side, his lineage went back to Richard Matthews, one of the first missionaries in the Bay of Islands, who had arrived on Darwin's *HMS Beagle* in 1835. Two worlds there. And a third world on his father's side, a son of Katikati and all the torsion that a Righteous People in Exile exerted on their own.

John Alan Edward Mulgan, the brightest student of his year at Auckland University College, a clear first in English, then Oxford, then an editor at the Clarendon Press, poet, novelist, lieutenant-colonel, hero. Glittering.

Suicide, by morphine overdose.

RAROTONGA, THE COOK ISLANDS. 1969

Missionary Morality

The apostle Paul wins. The Cook Islands since 1965 have had complete self-government. It is a secular state. Albert Royle Henry is premier and he is not so much a crooked politician as prodigal in his definition of governmental resources and feudal in the way he spreads them around.

But no one questions his morality on matters that really count. He, like most Cook islanders, averts his eyes from the Papaa who now bask topless, or naked, on the beaches and who walk about mostly unclothed, even on the Sabbath. And some of them grow marijuana.

Henry brings in legislation to allow the government to deport anyone who is not an islander. That takes care of the nakedness problem and considerably cuts down on occasions for islanders to lust in their hearts.

STILL THE CAVALIERS RIDE

1900–1969

Big Brandies

"Think about Robert O'Hara Burke, gentlemen." Admiral Francis McClintock (ret.) was doing his duty as an advisor to the national arctic expedition. "Remember that he insisted on leading, rather than riding his camels. Clear across Africa, no, beg pardon, Australia." McClintock summoned the club steward to bring himself and his two guests another round of large brandies. "You see, pride got in the way of progress." The admiral settled back and gave his imitation of Plato. "Would you not say he would have been better riding than walking? And alive?"

Robert Scott and his chief junior officer, Ernest Shackleton, listened with respect. McClintock, having found the remains of the lost Franklin expedition nearly half-a-century earlier, had reigned ever since as Britain's expert on arctic exploration, so he presumably knew a good deal about antarctic exploring as well. At least he knew sledges. "Need sledges, my lads." His listeners nodded agreement. "And why pull them yourself, eh?" Scott almost interrupted to say that sounded unsportsmanlike; a gentleman-explorer pulled his own load.

Instead, Shackleton jumped in. "Have horses pull them, right? Fine idea." Shackleton, true to his Anglo-Irish roots, thought that anything with a horse in it was bound to be all right.

"Actually, no," said the admiral.

"Oh?"

"You see, my friends, horses are a bit heavy and break the snow crust. And not very good on ice."

"We could have special ponies," Shackleton volunteered.

"Perhaps. Yes, possible." These young buckos were not catching McClintock's drift. "But lads, be sensible and look at the Norwegians. They use dogs and ..."

"Dogs!" Scott could not contain his contempt.

... and the dogs pull the sleds like the blue blazes on top of the snow's crust and men follow behind ..."

"Walking, carrying their own weight, not riding?" Scott was still chivalric, but willing to argue this halachah with himself.

"In a manner of speaking. They run on *shees*. Special boards attached to their boots and they glide along. Thus the men don't break the crust either."

"Sounds difficult to us, Sir, board-walking on ice." Scott rose to end the interview. "We will, however, give dogs a try." Both he and Shackleton turned quickly so the old admiral would not see them pulling a face.

In fact, they did take dogs along onto Antarctica on *Discovery* in Robert Scott's 1901–04 expedition, the farthest south anyone yet ventured. They brought no skis.

Ernest Shackleton was put in charge of the dogs and he gave them his best effort, but they just hunkered down on the ice pack and whined. Unfortunately, no one had explained to Shackleton what every Norwegian peasant knew: that dogs, if they are to be able to pull anything, need to do so at a trot. That's just the way their bone-and-muscle structure is configured. They can't walk and exert much force, especially not huskies.

And, since neither Scott nor Shackleton nor anyone in their crew had taken up old Admiral McClintock's hint about strapping funny boards to their feet and going along quickly, no one could keep up with the dogs if they were permitted to trot, which they desperately wanted to do. And, of course the idea of the men hitching a ride on the sledge pulled by the dogs simply was not cricket.

Thus, bridled back to a walk, the dogs went nowhere and the men went nowhere and the experiment failed and the United Kingdom's Antarctic explorers concluded that on their next trips they either needed really good horses or that they should pull their loads themselves. The old admiral had been right about one matter, though. Sledges were good things.

"Amusing old fellow, wasn't he?"

LONDON. 1901–1910

Stop Me If You've Heard This One Before

Confident that the U.K. government will bring the Afrikaners into line, Major-General Sir John Ardagh, director of military intelligence at the war office, decides that it is time to start planning for a stable southern Africa once the conflict is over. He had studied political economy briefly at Trinity College, Dublin in an era when the Whatelian notions of emigration were still in vogue: a stable economy and a stable society were the basis of any colony of settlement. He took advice as well from his wife, Susan, countess of Malmsbury, and they agreed.

Namely: the new southern Africa would be infinitely better off if it had more white servant women. Replace as many of those black-boys as possible. Not good to have them in the house. After a few years in service, the women would marry white artisans and produce stout little imperialists.

Ardagh draws up a scheme and Sir Alfred Milner, governor of the Transvaal where white women are most in demand as servants, agrees to foot the bill. Other parties join in, and between the end of the Boer War and 1912, nearly 4,000 female domestic servants are sent to the various parts of southern Africa. The largest number come from London and the second largest from Ireland.

About 30 percent of them marry in that time period, and that's natural enough. Later studies show that when in service they frequently have sexual relations with black-boys who work in the same establishment, and that is natural enough too, but not exactly on General Ardagh's program.

Most of the women eventually end up either married or running their own boarding houses or small hotels, where they employ non-white servants, who are much better value for money.

LONDON. JANUARY 1904

Nightsweats

Human hands heaped in piles, indication of sound discipline.

Penises, kept to show that rebels had been caught and thus the 2½ pence each killing earned was to be paid.

Wives kept in leg-irons, hostages for the forced labour of their husbands.

Rhinoceros- hide whips, cured and tanned into a spiral so that they deeply cut the backs and buttocks to which they were applied.

Ghost towns, entire villages emptied by kidnappers.

Collections by senior officers of African heads.

Officials of a European royal enterprise that operates as a slave economy.

Priests of the Church, liberally paid by Leopold II of Belgium to keep the natives in order.

These things Roger Casement had either seen for himself or had documented thoroughly.

That is why he sleeps as little as possible and works as hard as he can while awake; he does not want these things to come before his eyes without his wearing the heavy welder's goggles of moral outrage that protect him from being permanently damaged. Casement has been twenty years in the Congo, a dozen of those years as a British consul. In 1903, he was sent to report fully on Leopold II's private preserve, an area roughly the size of the eastern half of the USA. Although Leopold had cannily abolished slavery (he used this, in fact, as a reason for taking the vast area under his wing), it was effectively a slave economy: rubber, and secondarily ivory. No one works under the conditions of Leopold's world without being shackled or mutilated or having a family member taken as hostage.

Roger Casement has the twin abilities often seen in the offspring of mixed marriages in Ulster – the ones who do not levant to the New World but stay in Ireland. He grows up with a canny, calculatingly-pleasing disposition on the surface, and a rock-hard sense beneath the surface of what he wants and a determination to have it. Persona and anima are miles apart. As an adult, Casement has a voice that purrs but, equally, a tigerish streak and once he grabs on to something he will not let go.

That he was now being asked to write a report on the most hellish region of all European-tyrannized Africa was in large part a result of the bad luck in 1895 of Charles Stokes: the Irish missionary-turned-trader in British Uganda and German East Africa who had been summarily executed by an officer of King Leopold's Congo Free State, for trespass. London and European newspapers went mad, and, as one German editorial put it, if the Belgians could so easily execute white men, there was no telling what they might do to blacks.

Pressure built, the Americans sent out their own journalists and by early in the new century, the Congo was where you went to find a real story more blood-curdling than any you had imagined. Casement, preparing his report for the Foreign Office, backs each of his conclusions, each opinion, with facts that make his superiors queasy. Do we really need to say hands and penises were severed? Wouldn't it be better, Casement, to ease off a bit on the Church? Vatican relations and all that, you know. And Leopold's father was our late Victoria's favourite "uncle."

Roger Casement whirls like a dervish, yet maintains a perfect poise that leaves him as the undisturbed centre of the cyclone he is creating. He works day and night, refuses to change any of his pointed prose. When the Foreign Office becomes cautiously diplomatic, he leaks sections of his work to the newspapers.

Seven years later, Casement has a knighthood, the U.K. has a bit of the top end of King Leopold's former domain, the French portions of the eastern middle, the Germans some of the western middle, and the government of Belgium has taken the Congo out of royal hands, and is running it as a state colony. They promise reforms: considering their starting point, anything they did would qualify.

DUBLIN. 6 JULY 1907

A Bit Missing

The state jewels of Ireland, worth £10,000 in the currency of the time, were last seen on 11 June 1907 and discovered missing on 6 July. The theft was brilliant and has never been solved. The prime weight of suspicion – then and now – hangs on Frank Shackleton.

This was distracting, and no help in fund-raising for Ernest Shackleton who was simultaneously planning and raising money for a walk to the south pole. Yes: walk. He would take ponies with him, and tons and tons of fodder for them, and he and his men and his ponies would walk to the pole.

That, he calculated, was the easy part of the job: taking his begging bowl to private donors, to the Royal Geographical Society and to His Majesty was the real hard sledging, and having his brother constantly pointed to as the chief suspect in the crime-of-the-new-century made it all the harder. Still, he succeeded, mostly through a charm that his archrival and former superior, Robert Scott, conspicuously lacked. Shackleton played the Anglo-Irishman to the hilt, although this was a bit strained as, although born in Kilkea, County Kildare, he had lived in England since age ten and had attended Dulwich College, London. Being Anglo-Irish allowed him to pass off his brother as an eccentric appendage, amusing and not really dangerous if fed regularly.

Shackleton sailed on 7 August 1907, with immense ceremony, including a pre-voyage formal inspection by King Edward VII, as good a protection from hovering creditors as one could find. Along the way, Shackleton acquired $5,000 from the Australian government. In New Zealand, the jumping-off point of almost all Antarctic expeditions, he acquired some pre-owned dogs: leftovers from previous expeditions from various nations, healthy, but ill-tempered. Since , amazingly, he and his men had not yet bothered to learn either about dog-driving or about ski-running, he kept the dogs tied in huts on the Antarctic ice where they consumed valuable protein and did nothing.

Instead, by dint of sheer will power and lack of common sense, Shackleton, with his men either carrying their own loads or tugging at ponies that were supposed to be carrying loads, walked to just under 100 miles of the south pole. This is a magnificent, if lunatic achievement, like completing a full marathon with a shotput tied to one's testicles.

Yet, compared with his rival Scott, Shackleton was a model of prudence, for Shackleton was neither suicidal nor willing to kill his own men. Scott, in January 1912, becomes the second man to reach the pole (he is beaten by Roald Amundsen, a Norwegian), and Scott loses his entire party on the way back and his own life as well. That, though, was the future.

Ernest Shackleton returns a national hero in 1909 and is knighted.

His homecoming is slightly unsettled by his discovery that his brother Frank, who had been living in Park Lane, London, has just moved to a huge house at 29 Palace Court. It is lavishly furnished, and Frank is driving about in new motorcar costing nearly £1,000.

THE UNION OF SOUTH AFRICA. 31 MAY 1910

Truly Enlightened

For the next fifty years, Westminster parliamentarians, and political writers and historians, pat the U.K. parliament on the back. Enlightened bunch those MPs. Instead of inflicting revenge on the defeated

Afrikaners, the Westminster solution is to call a constitutional convention in southern Africa and then guide it on a trek towards Enlightenment values: a unified South Africa (the old Cape Colony, Natal, Transvaal Republic and Orange Free State) with a democratic government (few non-whites voting and no women); English and Afrikaans each to be an official language of government and, of course, a wise proconsul would be sent out from London to keep the whole business on the rails.

The British applaud their own generosity even more when they compare the apparent docility of the Afrikaners with those revolutionary Irish troublemakers. Glad we handled Pretoria better than Dublin, what? And when, in the 1930s and 40s, the costs of the vindictiveness of the Treaty of Versailles become apparent in the shape of another World War, why, the way we let those Dutch chappies up after we'd beaten them hollow just shows that good old British generosity is the best way all around, correct, eh?

Maybe.

Generosity has both a giver and a recipient.

Generosity to whom?

A legacy called the Natal Formula is left on the statute books and is broadened to cover the entire Union in 1913. It prohibits immigration by any person who is unable to read and write in a European language to the satisfaction of an immigration officer. In practical terms, nobody from India need apply. (So useful is the Natal Formula that Australia employs it against Asians with great effectiveness, thus protecting White Australia.) The same South African immigration act limits the rights of movement of Indian immigrants and leads to Gandhi's first great humanitarian campaign.

Westminster, entranced with the success of white democracy in the Union of South Africa, does not flinch when the 1913 Land Act sets up native reserves and prohibits nonwhites from buying land outside of the reserves; or when the 1923 Native Law amendment act requires removal from urban areas of all "surplus" nonwhites; or at the 1926 Colour Bar, keeping nonwhites out of the skilled jobs in mining and other major industries.

There is no profit in going on and balefully observing another dozen race laws. They all are there well before the Afrikaners finally win a parliamentary majority after World War II.

The apartheid state already was in place, in everything but name, long before that date. The foundation stone of the practice of apartheid (if not the theory) was the enlightened, forgiving action of the peoples of the British Isles, acting through their elected representatives.

IRELAND. 1910–60

The Missionary Revolution

Anno Domini 1910: Holy Mother Church stoops to conquer. An Irish province of the Society of African Missions is formed. The Maynooth Mission to China is created in 1917. The Sisters of St. Columba in 1922, of the Holy Rosary, 1924. The Medical Missionaries of Mary, 1937. And hundreds of Irish-trained priests enter foreign missionary orders such as the French Oblates or take missionary parishes in distant lands.

Why this new-found concern for the red and yellow and black of this world?

Simple occupational overcrowding. The first fifty or sixty years of the post-famine Devotional Revolution required every available Irish priest either to raise the standard of devotion of the home country or to re-Catholicize the Irish immigrant settlers in America, Canada, Australia, New Zealand. Now, in the early twentieth century, there is one priest in Ireland to each 879 Catholics. Although the country can absorb more priests (by 1960 there is one priest to each 558 Catholics), many priests are underemployed, spending long years in minor curacies before receiving any real responsibility. And the nuns are equally wasted. And bored. The old white colonies are beginning to turn out their own clergy, so just dropping into the charge of a parish, or becoming principal of an elementary school in, say, San Francisco, is no longer an easy option.

Thus, the romance of doing hard evangelism, or nursing, or teaching elementary literacy to Africans beats the thought of spending every day until one is fifty years of age or more as a dogsbody-curate in deepest Cavan.

These Irish missionary priests, brothers, nuns, of the twentieth century are the religious equivalent of the explorers and traders of the nineteenth: though they would prefer not to entertain the comparison.

They teach shame and discipline, introduce new gods, destroy old cultures, provide tools for dealing with the advancing Europeans and, simultaneously, seduce the indigène into following European ways.

BUENOS AIRES. 16 OCTOBER 1914

Across the Continent

With the soothing counselling of Roald Amundsen, Sir Ernest Shackleton has finally overcome his phobia of putting long boards on his feet. Thus he will not sink up to his thighs in loose snow, or buckle his knees on crimped ice-packs. Dogs are another issue entirely, but through intensive self-examination, Shackleton has accepted that dogs, not little horses, are the workers of the Antarctic. And now Shackleton will wear fur, rather than treated canvas gear, and will even let the fur come close to his face.

Sir Ernest is on his way to cross the Antarctic continent, starting on one side and, by way of the south pole, coming out the other. This will be called the Imperial Transantarctic Expedition and it is very hard to see its utility. As Winston Churchill, recently made first lord of the admiralty, commented, *These polar expeditions are becoming an industry.* Mind you, it is not Shackleton's fault that a European war is starting just when he is embarking on his journey, for he no more planned that conflict than he did his own wee trip.

His ship is, with unnecessary historical resonance, named *Endurance*.

On this skite, Churchill permits Shackleton to take only one commissioned military officer, the Anglo-Irish Thomas Hans Orde-Lees, a Royal Marine.

He is a collateral descendant of Thomas Orde (later Lord Bolton), who had been chief secretary for Ireland 1784–87, and to Shackleton's great benefit, he knows a lot more about ships' engines than his ancestor knew about colonial government.

THE GREAT WAR. 1914–18

Remember This!

Remember this. "Over twenty-three Irishmen died on average for every day during the four-and-a-half years the war lasted." Thus Patrick J. Casey, the most accurate accountant of this rolling tragedy.

Remember this. Every Irish soldier, officer and man, was a volunteer. Unlike the British, they were not conscripted. They chose to fight.

Remember this. More than 150,000 Irish-born men enlisted, making this the single largest voluntary activity that males 18-35 in Irish society engaged in. Why? Loyalty to the Crown (especially, but not solely, in the case of Ulster Protestants); belief in the rightness of the cause (popular among Catholic intellectuals after the German attack on Belgium); mostly, though, the usual reasons young men go to war: a mixture of lust for adventure with shame among their chums if they turn it down. But note especially the recruiting speeches of leading nationalist politicians such as John Redmond and John Dillon. They preach loyalty to Home Rule for Ireland and to the British Empire and its war effort. They don't use these words, but they mean: we Irish built up this goddamn empire and when the war is won we intend to profit by it.

Remember this. 35,000 Irish died in the war, according to the best figures by Mr. Casey. Of these, roughly 11,000 were from today's Northern Ireland, 19,000 from today's Republic, and the rest Irish-born but living outside of Ireland. If you put those figures county-by-county alongside the census of population, the result is the sectarian paradox of World War I: Protestants were proportionately more apt to enlist and to die. Yet, most Irishmen to volunteer for service in the United Kingdom army were Catholics and so too were most of those who gave their lives.

And remember Mr. Casey's summation of what the Catholic soldiers, the bulk of the army, experienced after their ordeal: **"those who survived were on their return viewed coldly by a changed and indifferent society."**

WEST CLARE. 1915

A Simple Case Study (1)

The Irish Brigades in the Boer War had possessed three leaders.

One of these, Sean MacBride, is an IRB man and planning an Irish insurrection.

The second, John Blake, an Indian fighter, born in Polk County, Missouri, had returned to America and become a professional Irish patriot in New York City. He was found dead in a gas-filled flat. Suicide was denied.

The third, Arthur Lynch, is prospering. An Irish-Australian who carries good luck with him the way other men carry pocket change, he had been the only one of the three to face British justice. Tried before three judges in the court of the lord chief justice, and facing Edward Carson as attorney-general, he had been sentenced to be hanged. This was commuted to life imprisonment and then he was released on a ticket-of-leave. Reconciliation with South Africa was in the air and he let it waft him to Paris. Receiving a full pardon in 1907, he qualifies as a medical doctor in 1908 and then becomes nationalist MP for West Clare in 1909.

Arthur Lynch understood John Redmond's reason for recruiting and now he is on the stump in his constituency, urging the lads to sign up and defend Everything Good.

Lynch, indeed, becomes a colonel in the army he had once fought.

Post-war Ireland, though, is not to his taste: too many young political enthusiasts with guns: pups, and not at all respectful to former officers in the imperial army, even if they had once been legendary rebels against the empire.

So, Arthur Lynch sets up a genteel medical practice just off Hampstead Heath, and lives into the mid-1930s, treating the haute bourgeoisie and going for long walks on the heath with his brace of pedigree spaniels.

THE WESTERN FRONT. 1915

A Simple Case Study (2)

Irishmen died in higher proportions than did English or Scots. And predominantly Irish units – the Royal Irish Rifles, the Royal Inniskillen Fusiliers, and on and on – generally took higher casualties than did predominantly British units. Perhaps the Irish corps were sacrificed callously; equally likely, being composed of volunteers, they were better fighting units and were put where it mattered.

From Day One of the war, Irish units had a cachet as being where you went if you were a serious soldier – or you were seriously motivated and could not find a berth elsewhere. All the Irish units contained men who, though unable to pass the standard physical, gained entry by dodgy means so that they could have a bash at the Huns.

The only son of Rudyard Kipling had the same rotten eyesight that plagued his father. Through his father's string-pulling he was commissioned in a real fighting unit, the Irish Guards. This was soon after war was declared and in 1915 he was shot in no-man's land almost immediately upon reaching the front.

For four years his father refused to believe his son had died. He spent several years writing a meticulously detailed two-volume history of the Irish Guards in the Great War, an act of homage few noticed, even veterans of the Guards.

THE FALKLAND ISLANDS. JUNE 1916

Leaps of Faith

A sign of just how badly the world was turning for the imperial authorities was that when Sir Ernest Shackleton and his men reached the Falklands, it was telegraphed and printed in every newspaper as a great triumph. Never mind that the expedition had been one of the colossal screw-ups of empire history. Everyone had shown immense courage and here was the key: although Shackleton had been forced under paralyzingly arduous circumstances to leave his crew on Elephant Island, he had navigated to South Georgia and then returned and saved every last member of the expedition. OFFICER DOES NOT DESERT HIS MEN, the newspapers said. Despite oceans of official propaganda, so deep and so knowledgeable was the distrust of the officer class by the British public, that an officer who stayed with his troops all the way was instantly a hero.

Not that there was a place for Sir Ernest in the Great War machine that was grinding nowhere.

Royal Marine officer Orde-Lees, however, found his place. All through the Antarctic, he, though raised Church of Ireland, was reading and meditating upon Roman Catholic devotional literature. He silently converted himself to Catholicism and was received into the church upon his return to London.

There, in spiritual triumphalism and in an effort to demonstrate the virtues of the parachute, upon which Orde-Lees also had meditated while in the Antarctic, he made from Tower Bridge a parachute jump, safely: the lowest such jump then recorded.

LONDON. 1916

The Heart of Darkness

Josef Teodor Konrad Korzeniowski was the last man you would want to accompany you on a tiger hunt. Better to be alone with a pointed stick than have him by your side, for he knew how to look in all directions except straight ahead.

He had shared a hut with Roger Casement in 1890 in the unimaginable hell of the Belgian Congo. *I can assure you that he is a limpid personality,* he later writes to a friend. *There is a touch of the conquistador in him too; for I've seen him start off into an unspeakable wilderness, swinging a cork-handled stick for all weapons, with two bulldogs ... at his heels, and a Loanda boy carrying a bundle for all company.* Casement, indeed, had been a remarkable adventurer but, in fact, was just the opposite of a conquistador: he was one of the few true anti-imperialists among white Europeans and he was in the Congo to investigate and then undermine the slavery imposed by Belgium. He saw piles of hands that were severed from the limbs of under-producing native labourers; he documented the depopulation of massive portions of the Congo by European taskmasters and he found enough evidence of sadism and homicide to fill a Newgate calendar. *A few months afterwards it so happened that I saw him come out again, a little leaner, a little browner, with his stick, dogs, and Loanda boy, and quietly serene as though he had been for a stroll in the park.* How could one not admire this tall, dark-haired Ulsterman, agnostic child of a mixed marriage, who was himself so loyal to his ideals? *He could tell you things! Things I've tried to forget; things I never did know. He has had as many years of Africa as I had months – almost.*

Joseph Conrad entertained Casement several times at his English home. Although Conrad had refused to join the anti-Belgian monarchy movement as far as the Congo was concerned, he was happy to see Casement receive a knighthood in 1911. He enjoyed dropping into conversation his Old Days with Sir Roger.

Casement, loyal to his anti-imperialist principles, became a dangerous acquaintance: he worked to thwart the British military recruiting campaign in Ireland, and then actively worked in Germany, finally infiltrating from Germany into Ireland, near Tralee. He was captured three days before the Easter Rising. For Conrad, whose middle-European youth had taught him that the only desirable nationality was the one that was victorious, any association with Sir Roger now became a potential taint.

Conrad vehemently refuses to sign a petition asking for clemency for Casement on the treason charge that inevitably follows his capture. Now he remembers meeting Casement in the Congo and *utterly disliking the man*. Instead of a conquistador, Conrad now remembers a *tragic personality,* one that had of greatness *not a trace. Only vanity.*

On the third of August, the day of Roger Casement's execution (he is no longer Sir Roger, having been disfellowshiped), Joseph Conrad has a profitable luncheon at the Garrick Club. He and his agent discuss turning his novel *Victory* into a stage play.

PUNJAB, INDIA. 1 NOVEMBER 1920

Slipping the Lead

The trouble with kick-ass fighting units is that they sometimes kick the wrong thing. The Connaught Rangers, known as the Devil's Own, had been since 1793 one of the hard regiments in an imperial army that often possessed a lot of soft units. After service on the Western Front and in Egypt in the Big Show, they now were in India. They were a rangy bunch: old toughs who had marched through the World War and a gingering of young recruits who had not yet picked up full discipline. The Indian summer was unusually hot and dusty and the natives swarmed around like a pack of flies. These soldiers were not in a mood for much soldiering.

This in some part explains why Private James Daly, originally of Mullingar, is writing to his mother. *I take this opportunity to let you know the dreadful news that I am to be shot on Tuesday Morning, 2nd November.* He is being helped to compose the letter by the regiment's Catholic chaplain, Father Benjamin Baker, a kindly English Franciscan from London. *But what harm; it is all for Ireland.* Private Daly will have the dubious honour of being the last soldier in the British army to be publicly executed. Thereafter, lives of the disobedient and untrustworthy are terminated, but discreetly, either by private executions or silent assassinations.

The Connaught Rangers' mutiny of 1920 was not because of command's lack of understanding of Irish soldiers. The regiment's commanding officer, Lt.-Col. H.R.G. Deacon, was Irish and had served with the unit since the 1890s. If anything, he was too pally with his men. The divisional general, R.E.D. Dyer, was also Irish. He had sent a force, including some of the Rangers, from Jullundur to Amritsar, the Sikhs' sacred capital, in early April to quell opposition to civil coercion acts. He ordered the crowd fired upon, and with literally 10,000 targets, it was hard to miss every time: 379 natives were killed and 1,200 wounded. Although Dyer was reprimanded for "an error in judgement," the Connaught Rangers had no difficulties with him: or with his Irish superior Sir Michael O'Dwyer, the lieutenant governor of the Punjab, who publicly approved the general's actions and placed the entire Punjab under martial law.

No, it was an Irish matter. In late June, nearly 400 Connaught Rangers, stationed at two separate barracks, simply downed tools. Technically it was mutiny, for they refused to take orders, flew the Irish tricolour and sang of freedom for Ireland. They did not, however, use their weapons in any way against authority. In another line of work, this would have been an industrial action, nothing more, and not fatal.

And had not two protesters been blown up trying to enter the powder magazine (suggesting that perhaps things would soon turn ugly), it might all have passed with dishonourable discharges and no public trials. Once the magazine blew something had to be done and sixty-two men were arrested and convicted of mutiny. Of these, fourteen were sentenced to death.

Realistically, though, only one execution was required, just to encourage the others to behave better, and James Daly drew the short straw. *I wish to the Lord that I had not started on this trouble at all. I would have been better off. But it is done now and I have to suffer.*

Despite his regrets, he dies heroically. Private Daly rips the blindfold from his eyes and stamps on it. When the head of the firing squad, whose members are positioned beyond sandbags for steadiness, tells him to sit down in the execution chair he at first refuses. Only after Father Baker asks him to make it easier on the lads who are doing their duty does he agree to give them a nice solid target.

First, though, James Daly quickly takes off his Connaught Rangers tunic and singlet. Bare to the waist, he tells the firing party, *You might think I'm afraid to die. I'm not ... There is one thing you will never be able to say, unless you tell lies – that you ever put a bullet through Daly's shirt.*

Basic Physics

Nothing complex. Just basic Newtonian physics: centripetal versus centrifugal force.

That explains the behaviour of 99 percent of the Irish settlers in southern Africa, from the Cape to Victoria Falls.

They join instinctively with other whites – English, Scottish, Afrikaners – against the common enemy, the ever-dangerous native populations. Centripetal force brings about the Union of South Africa in 1910 and Irish settlers are thoroughly behind it.

Except, the farther any issue is located from the centre – Pretoria or Cape Town – the more apt some of them are to fly off on their own nationalist course. Centrifugal force. If most Irish people, both Catholic and Protestant in southern Africa favoured Gladstone's Home Rule program, that was understandable, but it had no effect on matters in Africa.

Until 1922. In that year Southern Rhodesia rejects by referendum joining the Union of South Africa and instead becomes a Crown colony with a Responsible Government of its own. Home Rule for Rhodesia.

Charles Patrick J. Coghlan, the father of Responsible Government for Southern Rhodesia, was a perfect embodiment of the countervailing forces that affected most Irish. Born in 1863 in King William's Town, then the capital of British Kaffiraria, he was raised on stories of the Eighth Kaffir War, which had broken out on Christmas Day, 1850 and had run for three years. That was the event that brought his father, a Famine-era enlistee in the U.K. army, to Africa. Coghlan heard tales of native atrocities as his cradle stories, as well as histories of Ireland and its problems. So, understandably, after a Jesuit education at St. Aidans, Grahamstown, and qualifying as a lawyer, he was as strongly anti-native as any other Eastern Cape veteran, while equally vocal in supporting Home Rule for Ireland.

When he settles in Rhodesia, he cannot for the longest time decide if he distrusts the blacks more than he does the authorities in Pretoria (the seat of government of the Union of South Africa) and in Cape Town (where the legislature meets.)

Finally, in 1919, Coghlan takes the presidency of the Responsible Government Association, explaining that what he, as the son of an Irishman wanted, was Home Rule for Rhodesia. The more he thinks about it, the more he distrusts the Afrikaners with their own form of nationalism that certainly does not include a comfortable space for his own people; and he cannot abide the Anglos at the Cape. *Those at the cape are so infernally superior to all matters emanating from the other side of the Cape Flats that no doubt they are supremely indifferent to the views of a small set of – shall we call them – anthropoids inhabiting a region on the South side of a river called the Zambesi.* That's us: anthropoids.

Coghlan wins the October 1922 referendum and landlocked Southern Rhodesia begins travelling the twisting path that finally results in its trying to withdraw from the whole world, following its Unilateral Declaration of Independence in 1965.

NEW YORK CITY. 1924

Informed Opinion

Well-known for getting as close to his British targets as possible – "There are no bad shots at ten yards' range," he counselled his younger com-rades – Sean T. O'Ceallaigh actually had been more of a diplomat during the Irish War of Independence than a gunman. He had been the republi-can movement's envoy to France and had tried unsuccessfully to have Ireland admitted to the Versailles peace conference. Now, a follower of the losing side in the Irish Civil War, he is in France, raising money for de Valera's dissidents and gaining as many allies as he can. Speaking to the Friends of Freedom of India, he suggests that *largely by the work of Irish brains and Irish brawn and muscle* the people of British India *have been beaten into subjection and have been long oppressed.*

It's a big debt. *Until Ireland has taken some very definite steps to win back her good name and relieve herself of the odium that attaches to the race by reason of scandalous work done for England's benefit in India … we Irish have every reason to hang our heads in shame when the name of India is mentioned.*

O'Ceallaigh (or, O'Kelly as he later re-changed his name), was a founding member of Fianna Fail and served as president of Ireland from 1945–59, a period in which he watched India with interest.

RED HALL, BALLYCARRY, CO ANTRIM. 1926

Obstacle

Over the years, several of the guests who stay at Red Hall have bro-ken toes, and one fractured a kneecap. Each time, it occurs in the drawing room, during the middle of the night, when they are silently padding down to the pantry to catch an extra bite of bread and beer for a nightcap. Red Hall did not run to electric lights.

It was the damned sledge. Yes, it was heroic, but why in heaven's name did an Arctic transport device have to be in the middle of the darkened room?

The location of this monument (it would be unkind to call it a mere conversation piece or even a decorating eccentricity) was just opposite the spot where the gun cabinet had stood, the one liberated by James Orr and the rebels of Ballycarry in 1798. The cabinet was gone and now Red Hall was in the hands of Commodore McClintock, the son of Admiral Francis Leopold McClintock, who had won the nineteenth century's most famous and demanding yachting contest: the race to find the relics of Sir John Franklin who had a gift for Arctic exploring and wrong turns. Then-Captain McClintock, of Dundalk, had found the remains of the Arctic expedition in 1859, and he had made a career out of his good fortune: a book in 1859 that went into six later editions, lecture tours, and, finally, a full-admiral's rank in 1884, granted just the day before he retired.

Never keen on female company, the heroic McClintock had married only at age fifty; his eldest son eventually rose to commodore's rank and bought Red Hall. The son did not really understand why Franklin had been one of the previous century's most romanticized English explorers (Livingstone was the other), but he understood that his father's own sledge required preservation. And a place of respect.

He told his guests that they should take a lesson from the Roman Catholics and consider their sprains, broken toes, and barked shins as stigmata, signs of grace.

INDIA. 1925–29

Siren Songs

Despite his having admired the pacifistic Our-Selves alone economic policy of early Sinn Fein, Mahatma Gandhi now has real troubles with southern Ireland. The achievement of virtual independence of the Irish Free State from colonial rule through the use of violence was exactly the opposite of his own principles so, in the 1920s, he had to repudiate any identification of Ireland with India.

Even for Gandhi, that was hard to sell, for terrorism clearly had brought results in Ireland. So, especially in volatile Bengal, Gandhi had to battle daily this Irish blight.

Among the most seductive of Irish political works was the first really successful guerrilla-memoir, Dan Breen's *My Fight for Irish Freedom*, published in 1924 and sold under-the-counter in India in 1925. It's a lovely, chatty bit of bragging, with good barroom stories, but read half-way round the world it became a manual for insurrection. Hard for the ascetic Gandhi to counteract: for Breen made revolution seem so much fun.

Less adolescent, and therefore even more dangerous, was the resonance of the self-sacrifice of Terence MacSwiney, Lord Mayor of Cork. His starving himself to death in Brixton Prison, London, in 1920 was close enough to the self-discipline which the Mahatma himself espoused that he could not convincingly renounce it. Thus, when the violent Indian nationalist Jatindranath Das was imprisoned in Lahore Gaol in 1929, he intentionally modelled himself on MacSwiney.

After Das's death through starvation, the mayor of Calcutta sent a letter to MacSwiney's widow. *Terence MacSwiney showed the way to Ireland's freedom. Jain Das has followed him.*

The First Whenwies

The word is common at garden parties in South Africa and in drawing rooms in Ireland. Two words actually: "when we ..." and later it is taken up by other groups; but first it is used habitually by the Irish.

"When we were in Natal, our houseboys were all so difficult."
"When we were home in Ireland on furlough, my father's favourite hunter died."
"When we tried to find a nanny, all we could find were those terrible Boer women. Quite unsuitable. Almost prefer a coloured."

The Irish who came to South Africa after the dust of the Anglo-Boer War had settled were different from any other group in the Irish diaspora – and they were predictors of a future configuration of Irish society so far beyond the horizon that they were treated as freaks, not as portents. That is: the migrants to South Africa were the most skilled, most highly educated of the Irish diaspora and were actually the model for what later becomes an Irish techno-administrative class. It is one that has nothing to do with religion or the old tribalisms, and its members are devoid of anything save vague cultural nationalism as far as Ireland is concerned.

Engineers, civil servants, geologists, financiers, lawyers, merchants, doctors, venture capitalists and, at minimum, skilled artisans. They are men loyal to their professions. Trained in Ireland, they have jumped at the chance of being in the managerial class of a world where all the heavy, ugly work is done by dark-skinned peoples.

These Irishmen have a higher skill profile than any group in South Africa, including the English and far exceeding the Scots.

The women who accompany them are also unique in the Irish diaspora. This is the only place where the majority of migrant women are not employed after they arrive. They do not seek employment. Most of them are wives or sisters of the Irish men who make up this techno-class. They run the house and that's quite enough, thank you, with all the management of staff that is necessary.

They are a fluid crowd, moving from South Africa to other places in the empire where big mines, venture capitalists, experienced civil servants are required. Often they return to Ireland after spending twenty or thirty years in places with exotic names. They buy houses and acres that they could never have afforded had they not become part of this new class. All around Ireland are middling estates, thirty to one hundred acres, with Georgian houses and well-kept gardens, and men and women, ageing gracefully in tweeds and tattersalls and pretending they have inherited their position.

They give it all away, however, in every conversation. *"When we were holidaying at Knysna ..."*

THE CANADIAN NORTH. 1925–69

The Heyday of Christian Education

The Manitou died.

It's not their fault, they later argue: we were only subcontractors for federal and provincial governmental policies. Anglicans, Catholics, Presbyterians, Methodists. We were just following orders.

The orders, framed in early 1879 as the famous Report on Indian Education by Nicholas Flood Davin, one of the self-made Irishmen of the New World: born Catholic in Ireland, he invented a Protestant upbringing, possessed a plasticity with truth and became a successful lawyer, journalist and politician. Named in 1879 as a one-man national investigatory commission on Indian schools, he studies those of the U.S. and Canada and recommends "industrial schools." This was his code word for segregated Indian boarding schools, the basis of a policy of "aggressive civilisation." *It was the duty of the Government to afford the Indians all reasonable aid in their preparation for citizenship by educating them in the industry and in the arts of civilisation.* Since Davin believed the Canadian First Nations to be a vanishing race, he really was saying that the government should help them and their culture to disappear as efficiently as possible.

Herding together aboriginal children, taking them far away from their parents, allowing them to return once a year, that became the preferred method of civilizing them. Missionary groups, first Protestant and then with increasing enthusiasm in the twentieth century, Catholics, entered the field. Irish brothers and priests joined French orders (especially the Oblates of Mary Immaculate) and ran schools of their own. It was such a great opportunity, to bring in bundles of souls, all wrapped in neat sheaves by the school system and paid for by the governmental authorities. So little investment required for so much salvation.

Of course, there were nay-sayers. As early as 1918, Duncan Campbell Scott, the superintendent of Indian affairs, told the prime minister that the cheap buildings the missionaries used were *undoubtedly chargeable with a very high death rate among the pupils.* Nothing changed. Tuberculosis and a range of white diseases hit a population of young people who had never encountered them before and had no resistance.

Key to the whole process was the separation of children from their parents and thus from their indigenous, pre-Christian culture. The young were taught to despise their parents' beliefs. As a Jesuit missionary explained, approvingly, the residential school system was intended to produce in the aboriginal child *a horror of Savages and their filth.* In other words, of their parents, their elders, their culture.

Yes, the missionaries were following orders but not just following them. The Christian missionaries believed in what they were doing and went beyond mere time-serving. They were enthusiasts.

Their victims only begin to protest in the later 1960s.

Nothing that happened in Canada was unique; only because of the costive nature of successive Canadian governments, records were better kept, and thus public discussion eventually was quicker and louder to be heard than elsewhere.

What Christianity in general, and the Irish in particular, helped to do here was part of worldwide cultural genocide by good, decent, well-intentioned Christians.

There is no balance sheet one can with fairness draw up. The missionaries are gentler than the more brutal imperial exploiters, yet they too have their harsh edges. In the locales where they run isolated native residential schools, the Irish priests are notably sadistic, even beyond the boundaries that tough orders such as the Christian Brothers in Ireland permit themselves. In such places, the sexual abuse of children, especially young boys, is endemic. The governmental records indicate that the Protestant groups are less given to sexual abuse, probably because they frequently send out married couples, but culturally the result is the same.

The Manitou died. Perhaps that was a price worth paying for an introduction to the modern world. Perhaps.

GALWAY CITY. NOVEMBER 1936

Holy War

"Faith of Our Fathers," the battle anthem of Irish Catholicism rings out across Galway harbour.

By train, omnibus, horse cart, hundreds of men have made their way to Galway for a rally before they depart on Ireland's last holy war. They are General O'Duffy's men. Many of them have fought before, in the U.K. army or the IRA or in both, and they are very devout men. They have been moved by the stories that emanated from Spain. Tales of a communist revolution, priests killed and of churches desecrated – "Jew boys swinging a censer," is an oft-repeated phrase that enrages them. So they join O'Duffy's Irish Brigade.

Nobody ever accused Eoin O'Duffy of being anything other than a good Catholic, and the Irish bishops had selected him to organize the most important liturgical event of the half-century, the 1932 World Eucharistic Congress in Dublin. O'Duffy is now bringing 700 men to Spain to fight on the side of Generalissimo Franco. This is the idea of some Spanish officials, but it has been put into O'Duffy's head directly by the archbishop of Armagh, Cardinal MacRory. That for a man of O'Duffy's loyalty was as good as an order. *General Franco was holding the trenches, not only for Spain, but for Christianity,* O'Duffy declares. So, now O'Duffy is loading a converted cattle ship, the *Dun Aengus* with as many volunteer troops as it will safely hold and is off to help save Christendom.

The Irish bishops are strongly pro-Franco. Collections are made on parish steps in support of the Irish Brigade in their support of the Spanish fascists.

The southern Irish government, now headed by Eamon de Valera, makes its only significant break with the will of the Catholic bishops in the first fifty years of independence: de Valera forces through the Dail in February 1937 the Spanish Civil War (Non-Intervention) Act.

Not that Dev has anything against protecting Christianity against radicals of all sorts: if anything, Dev is to the right of O'Duffy politically.

Politics: that's the point. Eoin O'Duffy had been an intimate of Michael Collins in the bad old days: deputy chief of the IRA's general headquarters at the time of the Truce and, as a ranking IRB man, an especially effective opponent of de Valera in the wrangling that led up to the Irish Civil War. Then O'Duffy had gone on to become the first commissioner of the new Irish police force, the Garda Siochana, and head of the Irish army. When de Valera came into power he dumped O'Duffy In turn, O'Duffy put together an anti-de Valera political front and then, finding that too tame, began an Irish fascist movement, the Blue Shirts. Fascism in the Irish Free State had a general appeal, but only moderate success, since it was hard to see which of the two major parties was the less right wing. Redundant, really.

O'Duffy's force fights indifferently in Spain. Generalissimo Franco dislikes O'Duffy personally and the Irish Brigade is very picky against whom it will fight: not Basques, for example, since they too are good Catholics.

Meanwhile, a counter-movement, made up of fewer than 200 Irish volunteers, forms the "James Connolly Column of the International Lincoln Brigade." Anti-fascists, sympathetic to communism, anti-clerical, and, as much as O'Duffy's men, Irish patriots. They arrive in January 1937 and, unlike their counterparts, are mostly inexperienced in military matters. They are thrown without training into the Jarama Valley on the road between Madrid and Valencia. Many of the Irish are given brand-new rifles, still packed in grease and their first, and only, combat preparation is to clear the grease off, fire a couple of rounds into the hills and then move into the combat zone.

The commander of the Connolly Column was Charles Donnelly, twenty-two years old, though he claimed to be twenty-six. He is a secret poet. Killed in battle, his body could not be recovered for ten days. When it was retrieved, the wail of a battlefield poem silenced its readers

> ... *Battering the roads, armoured columns*
> *Break walls of stone or bone without receipt.*
> *Jawbones find new ways with meat, loins,*
> *raking and blind, new ways with women.*

LONDONDERRY. ST. PATRICK'S DAY, 1938

Imperial Moment

On the eve of St. Patrick's Day, the *Derry Journal* runs an opinion piece that summarizes Ireland's view of empire; its own.

Throughout the world the **Irish Colonies** *will fittingly venerate the Saint and at countless gatherings around the festive board will toast anew the undying sentiment of* **Irish Catholic nationhood***.*

In the Irish capital itself, An Taoiseach, Mr. de Valera will attend **Mass in State***, with the members of the Government, and at night will address by radio the* **far-flung Gaelic race***.*

BERLIN. 1940

Was His an Echo?

Dying as he did on 28 January 1939, William Butler Yeats once again showed impeccable pace and timing. Had he lived much longer, the entanglements of his fascist period, the later 1930s, would have become, like the filaments that held down Gulliver in Lilliput, both obvious and incapacitating. As it was, his fascism was not quite tied to Nazism and critics could read his magnificent late poems without having to face squarely all those nasty associations with Hitler and, oh dear, his views on those Jews.

From the early 1920s onward, Yeats had been followed by a worshipful, possibly-rabid, lapdog, Francis Stuart. The son of an Ulster Protestant emigrant to Queensland, Australia, Stuart had returned to Ireland after his father was declared a lunatic, leaving his mother free to marry her first cousin, a rich Texan who paid for a fine English education for young Francis.

A classic diaspora-returnee, Francis took to the Irish revolution as if the script were written for him. He chose a fine, forever-on-stage part: at age eighteen, he married Iseult MacBride (age 25), the daughter of Yeats's inamorata and widow of the 1916 martyr Sean MacBride, Maud Gonne. That placed him continually onstage, but always in the repertoire company of Yeats and Maude Gonne, as distracting a pair of thespians as God ever put on this earth.

Where Stuart is so puzzling is that soon after Yeats dies, he accepts an invitation to give readings of his several novels in Germany and then, just weeks before the war starts, accepts a university lectureship in Berlin. He knows what is going on in Germany, but it doesn't bother him; in fact, he has some IRA contacts and he shares their romantic idea of helping free Ireland from its illegitimate government (real republicans still did not recognize the government of southern Ireland as legitimate): with the help of the Nazis, of course.

Early in 1940, Stuart is asked to make some English-language broadcasts for the Nazis that might help build support in southern Ireland for Germany. He agrees, subject only to the caveat that he does not have to write anti-Semitic material.

Since Ireland was a neutral nation, Francis Stuart never paid any direct price for his collaboration with the Nazis. His broadcasts had as little impact on Irish opinion as did Yeats's final fascist essays. In Stuart's case it was in part because there weren't enough receivers to receive the message clearly: in the west, only one radiogram per thirty-two adults, and that was if their owners could get their hands on fresh batteries.

War Games

"I see you're playing off a four handicap, Flight Lieutenant."

"Yes sir. I've lost ten strokes since we were captured."

"And you, Sergeant?"

"Off a six, sir."

"Good lads. Keep at it."

"Will you be playing today, sir?"

"No, I've promised the commandant to have luncheon at the officers' mess. We shall, I imagine, spend the afternoon discussing politics and Glenmorangie."

"Important topic, that, sir."

These and a dozen or so other Canadians were interned at the Curragh. This lot had bombed Frankfurt and, by virtue of a strong tail wind and loose navigation, had overshot their English landing strip by almost a country: out of fuel, they landed in County Clare, just short of the Atlantic. As RAF fliers, the Canadians were housed with the English internees, next to the camp for the Germans. For the Canadians it was VIP treatment all the way, as their Irish captors didn't much like the English and couldn't speak German, and it was nice to have polite foreign visitors drop in.

Like gentlemen prisoners in the tower of London in the eighteenth century, the Canadian internees were permitted to go wherever they pleased in the neighbourhood, provided they signed a parole form that said they would not escape. The camp commandant, strict in his own way, insisted that they not wear their RAF uniforms outside the camp, save on the golf course.

"God, you'd think this was the middle ages. King Arthur's rules apply."

"Rules are rules, old son." The major cleared his throat. "You weren't thinking of breaking parole and running north were you?"

"I want to get stuck back in, sir."

"Don't ... Just don't. All that will happen is that the RAF will send back here anyone who escapes north after breaking parole. It's part of the rules of war they've worked out with de Valera's people. As long as we don't embarrass them by just popping back into the fray, they'll let the English recruit factory workers in the twenty-six counties. And the odd soldier as well."

"But, sir, isn't the RAF deadly short of pilots and crew?"

"Tis. But you have to view the big picture, right lad?"

"One other question, sir. Why is the barbed wire fence around our camp so thin?"

The major laughed and walked away. "Work that out for yourself," he called over his shoulder.

The answer of course was that the Irish wanted the internees in the English camp to escape without breaking their parole. In that case, the RAF would accept their escape to Northern Ireland as valid and have them back in airplanes in the blink of an eye.

That, then, was each man's moral problem. The promise of being a dead hero didn't sit so well with many of them. Several internees were dating local girls and two of the Canadians were taking instruction in the Catholic faith so that they could convert and marry.

Eventually, in 1943, half a dozen of the Canadians wrote proper thank-you notes to their hosts, tunnelled out, rather than cut the wire, and walked to County Armagh. They were keen on doing their duty and, besides, they were deadly sick of the nightly arguments about how many sacraments there were and what, exactly, is Transubstantiation?

HANOVER, GERMANY. 1943

Dead Centre

On the few occasions when two southern Irish RAF men were on the same bomber, they argued about what every Irish person of the time argued: neutrality, and its designer, Eamon de Valera.

Approaching Hanover, as their pass over the target begins, a bombardier concludes his political discussion with the copilot.

Just as he is releasing the first of the bombs a further thought occurs to him. "One thing you can say about Dev," he radios to the cockpit. "He kept us out of this fucking war."

NORTH AFRICA. MAY 1943

Press Conference

Lieutenant-General Bernard Law Montgomery of New Park House, overlooking Lough Foyle, would have made a good bishop. Like his father, who had served as bishop of Tasmania, he was on very close terms with the Almighty.

More than any ranking officer in the United Kingdom military in World War II, Montgomery crafted himself as an icon. He understood how votive images worked and saw no reason why he should not be one himself. During the long desert campaign in which he defeated the legendary Rommel and then the entire German North African army, he perfected his public posture. He visited each unit and, with photographers present, made a habit of standing on the rear seat of his Jeep and circling the men around him, rather as if he were gathering disciples. In this period he tried several kinds of headgear and finally settled on the black beret of the Royal Tank Regiment.

In May 1943, having cleaned up North Africa, General Montgomery gives a press conference. He begins with a prepared statement.

"As God once said, and I think, rightly ..."

NORMANDY AND CAIRO. JUNE-NOVEMBER 1944

No Respecter of Persons

In the first few days of the Normandy invasion, the Liverpool Irish take heavy casualties as they are among the first on the beach. Among the dead are scores of men whose fathers had fought in the battalion in World War I, or in the Boer War. And several whose great-grandparents had settled in Liverpool during the Famine.

In Cairo, in November, Walter Edward Guinness (Lord Moyne), close friend of Winston Churchill, is the ranking British representative in the Middle East, with the title of minister of state. He is desperately trying to reconcile the need to settle thousands of European Jews with the rights of the indigenous Palestinians. He is making progress but he is in a difficult situation because the Lehi group (sometimes called the Stern Gang), the head of which is Yitzhak Shamir, future prime minister of Israel, has a startlingly unacceptable strategy: to strike an alliance with Hitler and run a war of liberation against the British who are nominally in control of the Middle East. On 11 November 1944, Guinness and his driver are gunned down in Cairo by two Lehi hitmen. Only then do mainline Zionists start cooperating against the terrorists with the U.K. forces; it's too late.

BELFAST. 1946

A Hero's Reward

Only one person from Northern Ireland was awarded the Victoria Cross in World War II, Michael Magennis from the Falls Road.

The Protestants in charge of Belfast Corporation do him scant honour, not even granting him the freedom-of-the-city. His own people, the Catholics of the Falls, turn their backs on him. He can't get a decent job and the windows of his mother's house are frequently broken.

Michael Magennis emigrates to England and there, in a Yorkshire mining community, again finds comrades.

DELHI, INDIA. 1947

Solid Sense

When the United Kingdom was doing its runner from India (Westminster used other terms, of course), a few individuals stood out as uncharacteristically sensible and indeed honourable.

"Paddy" Massey, a lieutenant-colonel, was an excellent pig-sticker, a six-handicap polo player and rode steeple-chase with a monocle.

He looked a complete fake, so perfectly was he the genuine article.

Born at Cavillahow, County Tipperary, he had been taken to England when his widowed mother re-married, and he had learned to ride in Hyde Park. Harrow. Sandhurst. The Bengal Lancers and finally the Viceroy's Own Bodyguard.

At a time when the fierce sectarian passions of Indian society were spilling into the Indian Army, he ran the viceroy's courier service, keeping his Lordship apprised of up-country developments.

Massey's vehicles always made it through: because into each Jeep he put a Hindu and a Muslim and made them each responsible for the safety of the other.

UNION [REPUBLIC, 1961] OF SOUTH AFRICA. 1946–69

On the Pig's Back

For young working- and artisan-class Irish men and women, the end of World War II released stored energy, like that kept overly-long in a piece of spring steel. The several Commonwealth countries that had immigration schemes were a series of Promised Lands. Their schemes ran from 1946–69, depending on the country, and South Africa was especially attractive to knowing, adaptable men and women from Northern Ireland and the eastern half of Eire.

These people are much different from the techno-class, the mining experts and financial arrangers who dominated the previous generation of Irish migrants. These young people have no illusions about gentility. They want a life where there is no food rationing and they can have their own house and later, a swimming pool, and blacks and coloureds to do all the crummy jobs. They expect to become middle level managers (rather like overseers in the Caribbean slave economy generations earlier) and to drink well and live easy.

The Irish, north and south, average about 400 men and women as permanent migrants each year for the twenty-five years after the war's end, but they come in two bulges: just after World War II, and in 1961 and after, when the now-Republic of South Africa, having withdrawn from the Commonwealth, needs to bulk up the number of whites in its populace.

These are not naïfs. From at least 1950 onwards, the migrants know full well what apartheid is and they are not repulsed by it: quite the opposite. It's what makes South Africa so attractive: the promise of life on the pig's back.

The best illustration of how willing these young women and men are to buy into the South Africa system is that, by 1969, nearly one-third of them use Afrikaans as their first language.

DUBLIN. 23 FEBRUARY 1949

Make the World Go Away

The only member of Dail Eireann to speak with a French accent announces that southern Ireland is refusing the invitation to join the world. The accent is not an affectation: his mother had spoken to him in French so that he could not communicate easily with his violent, wife-beating, child-molesting father, even if he visited Paris, or so Maud Gonne said. Sean MacBride was the legitimate son of the 1916 martyr of the same name, and of Maud Gonne. Once his father was dead, he was raised mostly in Ireland, by a mixture of republican priests and by his forever-black-clad mother. Neither influence helped his colour sense and he dressed like a mortician's assistant on a duty call.

Yet, this Sean MacBride had something, a cold fury, that made other men follow him, at least for a time. In the mid-1930s he had briefly been chief-of-staff of the "New IRA" (that is, those hard men who still refused to recognize the government of the Irish Free State). Then he quit, qualified as a barrister and, having made a small fortune, became in the later 1940s the founder of his own political party, Clann na Poblachta. When a coalition government toppled Fianna Fail and Eamon de Valera in 1948, his share of the spoils was the ministership for external affairs. Given the fragile character of the coalition, he pretty much does what he wants internationally.

Which explains his frenetic round of diplomatic letters and visits to European and North America capitals after he has decided that Ireland will continue to renounce its geography. Ireland will not be part of western Europe or of the new American empire. Ireland will not, emphatically not, join NATO.

Why? Because as he explains over and over and over again, the island of Ireland is still divided. Brandishing the Sore Thumb this is called and a whole division of external affairs is given over to a propaganda campaign. Spies are sent to the north to obtain intelligence. The persons thus sent enjoy the train trip to Belfast and the chat with the locals and return and tell MacBride stories of the dangers they have gone through and of Northern Ireland's oppression of Our People.

In charge of the propaganda exercise was the now-rising star of the foreign service, Conor Cruise O'Brien.

The curious thing about the literally millions of pamphlets, books, post-cards distributed worldwide in the Sore Thumb War is that they never used the P-word: Protestant. The Six Counties were either full of British Forces of Occupation or of misguided Unionists. But nary a Prod.

MONTSERRAT. 1951

Poll Book

A nice little tool: the Montserrat electoral register. This year, 1951, is the first for which universal adult suffrage prevails in local elections. Previously a property qualification was in place.

So every adult name on the island is registered.

If read obliquely, the poll book is more than a register of voters. It is also a list of the names that the black people were given upon emancipation. Previously a favoured few slaves had surnames, but most only had a first name. The emancipation process and subsequent breaking up of plantation lands required two names, "christian" name and surname. Most former slaves took on the surname of their former master.

Hence, the poll book of 1951 acts like a census of slave ownership on Emancipation Day, 1834.

As confirmation that the Irish had held on to their slaves to the very end: nine out of ten of the most common black names on Montserrat are Irish.

KENYA. 1960

A Man of Principle

Lieutenant-Colonel Ewart Scott Grogan – Cape to Cairo Grogan – has assembled and now is disassembling a massive personal empire in eastern Africa. He has also set the East-African Record for Adulterous Affairs (European division).

Now a heart attack slows him considerably. His minder, a very keen Catholic lady, brings a priest to hear his confession.

Grogan, who had always embraced with devout indifference the Church of England, is upset and sends the priest away with a crisp ticking off. He is not offended by the man's trying to make a sale, it's the business he's in, isn't it? What annoys Grogan is that the pest so badly wanted to hear what Grogan describes with commendable accuracy as eighty-five years of interesting sins.

ST. STEPHEN'S GREEN, DUBLIN. JANUARY 1960

A Grateful Nation Remembers

Dublin Corporation's bin men are the first to notice the lump in the pond, and they call the civic guards who laugh and call the public works department and they bring along some cables and a lorry with a winch on the back.

Everyone involved finds it a bit humourous, but the remarks they cast are of the uncomfortable sort. Not until the sixties are well and truly over will the Irish Republic begin to deal with the Great War, for several hundred times more Irish men and women had participated in that conflict, and on the side of Great Britain, than had been part of the Irish War of Independence. It's a topic best avoided or shelved. That's what happens to the bust of Tom Kettle that is dredged from the pond in Stephen's Green. It goes into the Works storage shed where no one has to look Kettle in the eye.

Wonderful, that an inanimate object can have an animated history. Tom Kettle, the bright political hope of a generation of rising Catholics – James Joyce's generation – had effectively committed suicide (though, of course, no one used the word, for suicide remained a mortal sin) leading his troops on the Somme. Funds for a bust to be placed on St. Stephen's Green were raised in 1917, but the likeness was not completed until 1927. By then, a change in national management meant that a war memorial that had been approved by Dublin Castle had to go before the new Irish commissioners of public works. They insisted on censoring the inscription and did not withdraw their objections until 1937, when the image finally was permitted public display.

In 1960, as part of a hiccoughing upsurge in IRA activity in the far south (mostly consisting of slogan-painting and the cutting down of telephone poles), Dublin was briefly cleansed of the confusing image of a man who gave his life for Ireland, but did not do so in the officially approved fashion.

ELISABETHVILLE, THE CONGO. 16 SEPTEMBER 1961

Once Again the Cursed Congo

The special representative of the secretary-general of the United Nations, Conor Cruise O'Brien, tries to hitch a ride with his boss. O'Brien has been effectively in charge of the UN's first real peace-keeping mission and it has turned into a mess. After the Belgians had simply cut-and-run in mid-1960, the newly independent Congo became the scene of tribal warfare, using modern weapons, a phenomenon not then familiar to the members of the world's press, who approached the conflict as if it were a matter of spear-throwing natives. With the covert encouragement and aid of Belgium, France and the United Kingdom, the mineral-rich Katanga province had broken away from the new state, thus setting up a regional war. Two UN military operations had failed to break the Katangese, in part because those European powers (especially the U.K. with its corridor to Katanga in northern Rhodesia) wanted to see the rebellion succeed.

On 16 September, O'Brien is not quite sure that he still is the secretary-general's representative. Dag Hammarskjold has flown to Leopoldville and it is clear that O'Brien is to be the scapegoat for the way things are going. Which is why, when O'Brien hears that the enigmatic Swede will be flying to Ndola in Rhodesia to meet the Congolese strongman Moise Tshombe, he wants to hitch along and find out where everything stands.

Hammarskjold refuses O'Brien's request on the morning of 17 September. For reasons of security, the secretary-general waits until nightfall, then boards his plane.

It crashes.

The plane came into Ndola on a perfect flight path, but eight miles short. Pilot error.

Two months later, Conor Cruise O'Brien is brought home in disgrace. U Thant, the new secretary-general of the UN, expects him to fall on his sword: to take the blame for everything gone wrong in the Congo.

O'Brien, following the example of Roger Casement when bureaucrats tried to bottle up his findings on the Congo, uses the press. He calls a conference, reveals big cysts of putrescent material embarrassing to the Great Powers and then he ends his career as a diplomat with a flourish: he writes a book, *To Katanga and Back: A UN Case History.*

Like Casement, O'Brien wins. But whereas Casement received a knighthood, O'Brien receives his P45 and must immediately start sending out resumés.

THE VATICAN. DECEMBER 1965

Lateral Movement

The Second Vatican Council concludes its three-year run. Decrees on a wide range of issues are promulgated, including a Mission Decree. Paragraph seven reads:

*Therefore, though God in many ways known to himself can lead those culpably ignorant of the Gospel to that faith without which it is impossible to please him (Hebrews 11:6), yet a necessity lies upon the Church (cf. 1 Corinthians 9:16), and at the same time a sacred duty, to preach the Gospel. **Hence, missionary activity today as always retains its power and necessity.***

MONTSERRAT. SEPTEMBER 1966

The Imperial War Museum

The lady sits with one of her lovers and receives guests. She is enthroned on a high-backed terrace chair. Its broad arms and arched rattan back allow her to sit regally and the chair's placement upon a flat piece of ground, just before the hill slopes off, permits her to look down upon those who seek an audience.

This is one of the world's greatest imperialists and America's most compelling novelist of the twentieth century: at work.

The little village over which she is temporarily queen has been built by the Osborne family, a proud band of black Montserratians who had possessed a family-name longer than had most of their fellow islanders: they looked back to having been the property of the island's second governor, the murderous Irish Protestant Roger Osborne, sometime owner of the Waterwork Plantation. Now the

Osbornes own one-half of the island's profitable businesses and are creating on a pristine hillside a colony for rich whites. Comprised of a dozen hexagonal cottages, overlooking the seaside and hills of western Montserrat, this village is ideal for anyone who wishes to visit an exotic locale without coming too close to the locals.

Members of the extended Osborne clan bring their most presentable friends to meet the queen-lady. The Osbornes have political ambitions, and the road to the chief ministership of Montserrat runs through the village of Respectability. The present chief minister of Montserrat, W.H. Bramble, and the local poet and university-college tutor Howard Fergus are brought up to make conversation and everything is very pleasant. When talk lags, the visitors refer to the recent seismic motions in the island's volcanic field and ask the queen-lady if she has felt any tremors. She looks at her lover and smiles slightly.

To the secret discomfort of the Osborne family, the great lady is most animated when she meets members of the Mead (or Meade) clan, for they are the Osbornes' chief rivals for future political power.

"Brother, sister!" she exclaims and embraces one Mead after another. A reserved and mannerly people, the several Meads respond to her politely. They, like the Osbornes, are aware of their own unusually long heritage on the island: going back to a Protestant Irish attorney who served Governor William Stapleton in the late seventeenth century. One of the descendants of that Irish attorney in mid-eighteenth century owned the iconic Waterwork Plantation, another source of pride. The Meads are accustomed to shaking hands politely with the governor of Montserrat – the only remaining white official – at his annual New Year's levée, but being hugged by a short white lady of whom they have never heard makes them uncomfortable.

Margaret Mead is engaged in field work – the anthropological sort, not the kind done by most of the Meads of Montserrat. She tells them loudly that her Irish grandfather, Giles M. Mead, had fought on the side of the Union army in the American civil war. She believes this will put her on sound footing with the black Meads. She is also confident that her own ancestry, going well back into the pre-Famine years in Ireland, will fit with the pride the locals proclaim when tourists are about – that they all have Irish blood and live in the Emerald Isle of the Caribbean and love their Irish heritage. Nobody tells her that these things are all part of a shuffle-and-jive for the outsiders, certainly not the Osbornes who plan on cashing in big with the Boston Irish.

When the lady introduces her lover to visitors, it is simply, "This is my friend, Rhoda Metraux." The natives, unlearned in the arcane customs of anthropologists, take it that Metraux is a friend and also the queen's lady-in-waiting.

Which she is.

Metraux has been waiting to get anything significant done for almost a dozen years now. In 1953 she had assigned herself to the village of Salem in Montserrat and had returned after eleven months with one of the shortest, most baleful field reports ever done in her trade: the Montserratians, she said, were depressed, had little knowledge of their own history and culture and, in effect, couldn't make water run downhill. So depressive was her research that it found public utterance only in the *American Journal of Orthopsychiatry* and in the anthropology section of the *Transactions of the New York Academy of Science.*

She still thinks she was right in her observations, for now, only a dozen years later, nobody on the island remembers her.

Margaret Mead, however, is buoyancy incarnate. She and Rhoda will go back to Salem, she says, and will administer standard projective psychological tests to the locals. Then they will compare the results with the same tests given to the Manus of Papua-New Guinea! She's so excited, for Mead knows that they will discover that the people of Montserrat have a rich inner life and a covert pattern of personal behaviour, and that, really, this dusty and imperfect world the Montserratians pretend to inhabit is actually a world of tropical breezes, secret and joyous couplings, and spiritual richness in the form of pre-modern truth. She'd done that before in Samoa and she feels that she and Rhoda are capable of another act of world-making.

Rhoda and Margaret spend their days driving about the island. They take pictures and tape-record a few interviews, watch the workers work and work at not watching their own watches: anthropology is dreadfully slow.

Each afternoon they sit on the terrace of the Osbornes' wee private village and look up at Salem and reflect on all they have already learned.

Each day they learn more and learn it more quickly, so that each day they are back a little earlier, sitting on the terrace, drinking the rum punch the staff makes oh-so-well.

Slowly, like a mudslide in slow motion, their field work recedes and they watch it disappear into the blue waters of indolence, self, sensuality.

CAPE TOWN, SOUTH AFRICA. 1967

In the Blood

Ten years old, the grandson of the martyr Sean MacBride listens carefully to the adults who are speaking softly. They are in a tin shack in Factreton, where his family had been forced to move in the previous year when District Six, a longtime coloured location with some decent housing, was declared a White Group Area. Under the complex rules of South Arica's apartheid system, the lad is officially "coloured" although he is actually half-black, one-quarter white, one-quarter Malay.

The adults he is respectfully attending are members of Umkonto we Sizwe (the "MK"). It had begun in 1961 as a semi-violent organization – it aimed at damaging property but not people. After the arrest of Nelson Mandela in August 1962 it had been forced deep underground: and now in the townships its adherents are planning to become a real guerrilla army.

Robert MacBride listens and already knows his future: he will someday be an MK commander and will, like his grandfather, stare into many rifle barrels.

ANGUILLA, THE CARIBBEAN. 29 MAY 1967

Not According to Script

From a distance, the Anguillan revolution looked right. Three hundred or so *sans culottes* gathered angrily and eventually rushed the police barracks. They disarmed the constables and sent them back to St. Kitt's, their home base. Then the rebels took down the barracks' flag, symbol of tyranny, and ran up their own emblem.

The Union Jack.

Anguilla, in forced federation with Nevis and St. Kitt's, had been "granted" independence three months earlier. The Brits were in the business of getting out of the colonial business and, understandably, they failed to ask the Anguillans what they wanted – which was to be a colony of the United Kingdom.

Although Westminster could not be greatly bothered by 6,000 blacks on a long sandbar, a two-man parliamentary delegation was sent to the island. They were puzzled by the misguided attitude of the locals and, according to John Updike who was vacationing there at the time, called them "poor dears."

Clearly, quelling this revolution required a pro-consul of Roman proportions. Instead, Westminster sends a third-generation Irishman, Anthony Lee, whose family roots were in County Cork. The task is not considered worth the time of a real foreign office person: Lee is a contract employee, and carries the title Senior British Official which is accurate, for most of the time, he is the only British official. A willowy 6' 4" and soft-spoken to the point of inaudibility, Lee just wants his contract to run as long as possible and quietly. He cannot bring himself to explain clearly to his superiors in London that this particular revolution is not for independence, but for continued colonial status.

For two years the matter slides.

Then, in March 1969, William Whitlock, parliamentary undersecretary for the foreign office, flies to Anguilla to give the revolutionaries a stiff talking-to. He is puzzled to be met at the island's airstrip by a happy crowd singing "God Save the Queen."

Somehow Whitlock, who is being advised by Lee, manages to offend everyone on the island – mostly through bad manners – and he becomes convinced that the 6,000 islanders are well armed. Actually, if one said there were two dozen firearms on the island, it would have been an exaggeration. Anthony Lee has in fact seen four.

So, on 19 March 1969, 300 elite troops – paratroops and Royal Marines – and fifty London Bobbies in full woollen gear, invade Anguilla. They encounter no resistance and, victorious, run up a flag on the island's administration building.

Union Jack.

LONDON. 1969

No English Need ...

The book-launch went well and the early reviews were solid, although not raves. This was for *Master and Commander*, the first of what becomes a series of twenty novels by the twentieth century's most successful celebrant of English empire in general and naval might in particular. Two million copies sold.

Patrick O'Brian declared that he was born into a genteel Catholic family in Galway. Because he was sickly as a child, he was tutored at home, so he said.

Rather: he had been born in London. He was not a Catholic. His mother was English and his father of German background.

Like the royal family.

DUBLIN. 1969

Rubrics

After Eamon de Valera left active politics in 1959 and became the ceremonial president of the Republic of Ireland, a charm and thoughtfulness that had been hidden during his long rule of Fianna Fail and his terms as Taoiseach, came to the fore.

When Conor Cruise O'Brien and his wife Maire MacEntee adopt a baby, the president and Mrs. de Valera invite them to Aras an Uachtaran to mark the occasion. This is both thoughtful of de Valera and his equivalent of a certificate of kashrut. The president was saying that although the O'Briens were not legally married in Ireland (even church-granted annulments were not acceptable, so Conor's divorce held no legal weight), this child was like any other, to be treasured. And infant Patrick's being half-Irish, half-Ghanaian was irrelevant, rare as racial mixing in Ireland was at that time.

The two families had tea and then photographs were taken. After the guests had left, the president sat silently for a time and then asked his wife, "Will the British empire eventually come to find its home in Ireland, do you think?"

By long experience she did not reply.

"We have always led the way and we will welcome anyone," the president declared. "As long as they are as good Christians as we are."

THE LORD HAS MERSEY,
AND LOTS MORE.
ENGLAND
1900–1969

Mercy's voice

The mouth of the Mersey contains two vessels, old square-riggers. These are the way out of a life of violence and indigence for hundreds of children of Irish parents. Not a soft route, though.

The two old boats mirror Liverpool society: one is for Protestant boys, the other for Catholics, which in practice means Irish Catholics. The lads, delinquents and minor criminals, usually have been separated from their parents long before they are put on the boats: either dumped on the street by their elders or taken from them by the workhouse system. Slummy boys they're called.

These are the lucky ones. They spend five years learning to be seaman. Five years of hard discipline and elementary schooling. They later may learn to love the seaman's life, but that is not what this is about. It's about the berth at the end of the term, a job that pays real money.

Honest money.

Tinting the Gene Pool

Mollie McQuire does her part. She marries "Galley" Johnson, a misshapen, but dependable merchant seaman. She bears him seven coffee-coloured children. That is a familiar situation in the Liverpool docks area and if Liverpool in the nineteenth and early twentieth centuries leads England in producing nonwhite members of the Irish diaspora, it's only the cutting edge. Any port will have the same thing happening and the racial mixing then moves inland.

During the seventeenth through mid-nineteenth centuries, the Irish bought, sold, abused, sometimes loved non-white women all over the world. Prominent as slave overseers, they produced battalions of children with Irish names and often little else of Irish culture.

The basic pattern has changed. Slave and early-post slave times involved Irish men taking advantage of black women. Now, as in

Molly McQuire's case, the usual pattern is the opposite: Irish women using black men for their own advantage. Molly, and hundreds like her in the Liverpool docks, are delighted to have a regular income (the shipping companies pay them directly at husbands' orders) and a big chunk of signing-on money each year. And then the men disappear for eight to ten months at a time leaving the women economically secure and living in peace. It's a lot better than having a docker as a husband who says the Rosary each night before slapping the family around, that's what the women say.

Galley Johnson does not mind. He figures he is receiving value-for-money. When Mollie dies after twenty years of a satisfactory marriage, Galley goes out and finds another Irish wife, Maggie McCoy.

But he misinterprets the mental economics of these Irish women. A tacit part of the marriage contract is that the men stay away most of the year.

So when Galley Johnson puts his savings into ownership of a boarding house and announces that he is settling down and will be superintendent of the facility himself, his new wife Maggie leaves him immediately.

LONDON AND LIVERPOOL. 1910

Missing in Action

In London, Brigid Dowling falls in love with an everyday sort of German: it is a working-class-Irish, working-class-German union. They move to Liverpool and live in an Irish settlement. The couple has a son and then the German, who is a half-brother of the future Führer, disappears.

During the late 1930s, "Hitler's English Nephew," William Patrick Hitler, later Hiller, gains momentary fame. He goes on a lecture tour of the USA in March 1939 and settles in New York. He registers for the draft and eventually serves in the U.S. Navy.

He has four sons. They, the Führer's great-nephews, quietly settle in Long Island and become small businessmen and turn out religiously for the annual St. Patrick's Day parade.

LONDON. 1906–16

Finishing School

It is the high quality of the Irish Intermediate Education system that allows Michael Collins to obtain his post as a minor governmental employee in England. He has a responsible job, being a postal clerk, and from his vantage point in Shepherd's Bush Road Collins learns how big organizations work and how central the control of communication is to any activity.

Collins attends the usual Gaelic revival meetings in London, but his real love is for English literature. Given the choice, he'd spend all his free time with Dickens or Conan Doyle or Mrs. Gaskell.

When he returns to Ireland shortly before the 1916 Rising, he lovingly packs his favourite book, the volume he would hold to his heart if there were only one book in all the world: *The Mill on the Floss*.

THE SOUTHWESTERN IRISH COAST. 7 MAY 1920

Repellant Boarderers

Not a minute too soon, a small flotilla of Royal Navy boats, including destroyer-class vessels, intercepted the *Baltic*, carrier of a dangerous cargo.

Supercargo, actually: Daniel Mannix, now archbishop of Melbourne.

Long-distance sea travel has done Dr. Mannix a power of good. The sea air, doubtlessly. He had left Ireland after a career as an energetic flunkey for the Irish bishops and as an opponent of anything but the most genteel nationalism. Now he was trying to return to Ireland and he came as the most radical prelate in the world on Irish matters and as one unwilling to take discipline from anyone, save, maybe, His Holiness. In Australia he had led the anti-conscription campaign during the World War, and later he came out fulsomely for Irish independence.

Trying to return home, he said, to visit his dying mother. This phrase was always pronounced in Irish circles as Visit His Dying Mother. Like a Muslim's journey to Mecca, it was something every good Irish son was supposed to do once in his lifetime though, like the Islamic obligation, it was honoured more in the breach than in the breeks.

The Rev. Dr. Mannix has moved very slowly towards Ireland, apparently confident that his Mammy will not fade too fast. He has preached his way across the United States, the gospel of Irish independence taking precedence over the gospel of Christ, though Mannix has no doubt about Jesus' position on Irish-British relations. He is now headed for Liverpool and a few days' more mission work before passing onward to Ireland.

Frightened that the enthusiastic greeting Archbishop Mannix will receive at dockside in Liverpool will be massive and explosive, the government has the Royal Navy intercept Mannix and take him on board a destroyer. He is not exactly a prisoner, just a guest. He is landed in Cornwall and permitted to go to London by train.

There he accurately described his capture as "the greatest naval victory since the battle of Jutland."

DUBLIN. MAY 1922

Exit Visa

Michael Collins as head of the provisional government of Ireland prepares to meet a delegation of the General Synod of the Church of Ireland.

When their representatives, Archbishop John A.F. Gregg and Sir William Goulding, enter his office he is struck by how small they are. In his youth Protestants were taller.

He knows why they want to talk. During the War of Independence, in the far south, especially west Cork, the burning of Protestant homes, mostly Big Houses, had been common and Collins had winked at it: kept morale up. Now, after the treaty, the burning of major architectural landmarks had spread north, to Tipperary, Leitrim, and the Ulster counties just south of the Partition line. Sir William and Archbishop Gregg tell Collins that since the truce 190 Protestant houses have been torched. Collins silently corrects them: "It's more than 200." He expresses his regret and promises to do everything he can to have the burnings stopped. He knows that in fact he can do little until the septic rupture with de Valera and with the extreme republicans is either healed or cauterized.

Shrewd and informed as Michael Collins is, he is surprised, and slightly embarrassed, at how broken are these, the once-haughty. In very soft tones and with a stammer Archbishop Gregg asks *to be informed if they were permitted to live in Ireland or if it was desired that they should leave the country*. It is a serious enquiry and indicates a victory that Collins neither sought nor will accept. He assures them that they are needed in the new Irish Free State.

From 1919 onwards, Protestants have been streaming out of southern Ireland. Landowners, small farmers, business owners and, after 1921, civil servants and military and police officers. Mostly they go to England. In the weeks just preceding the outbreak of the Civil War, the tension for many of them becomes nearly unbearable and, in late May, a Protestant deputation waits on Winston Churchill, U.K. secretary of state with responsibility for the provisional government of Ireland. *It seems miraculous that up to this time all the Protestants and loyalists have not been massacred*, they tell him in agitated tones. *It is a moral certainty that they will be in the future.*

Overwrought they certainly were. The victory of the pro-Treaty side in the Civil War led to the restoration of order and a suppression of direct attacks on Protestants. In fact, the new government of the Irish Free State worked hard to keep them.

Yet, the Protestant outflow from the twenty-six counties continued and after 1922 it was not an exodus of the hysterical or the agitated, but of sensible, level-headed people who assessed the future for themselves and their children and decided accordingly. By 1926, the number of Protestants in the Irish Free State has dropped by one-third, compared to the pre-war numbers, and in a period when the Catholic population has declined by only 2 percent. Granted, some of these Protestant emigrés were former government administrators, but at least 60,000 were ordinary private citizens. The biggest decreases were in Dublin (the business class having done its sums) and in the border counties – Monaghan, Cavan, and Donegal, where rural Protestants faced continuing intimidation as part of the backsplash from the Partition issue.

Most of those who stay in southern Ireland are able to lead peaceful everyday lives, but they increasingly realize that, in practice, political life and government jobs are closed to Protestants (with rare exceptions) and that the new state will enforce more and more forcefully a set of civil practices that are based on Catholic theology and on a denigration of English-language culture as the Protestants know it. And, in rural areas, there are fewer and fewer marriage partners available for their children, and they shudder when they think of the way the new state promises to enforce as civil law the Roman church's *Ne Temere* decree.

That is why the next wave of Protestant emigration tells so much, for it was composed of those who had stayed in southern Ireland and given the place a chance. Between 1926 and 1946, the Protestant population in the twenty-six counties drops by one-quarter at a time the Catholic population was only slightly decreasing.

Ireland's loss, Albion's gain.

LONDON. JANUARY 1922

Timing

The English-born, McGill-employed professor of Political Economy, Stephen Leacock, was known as the funniest Canadian of his generation, which was not unlike being the best one-legged competitor in an ass-kicking contest.

In 1921–22, he does a Mark Twain-style lecture tour of England and turns his observations of the country into a book.

He refers to the Irish question. *It is settled. A group of Irish delegates and British ministers got together round a table and settled it.*

Henceforth the Irish question passes into history. There may be some odd fighting along the Ulster border, or a little civil war, with perhaps a little revolution every now and then, but as a question the thing is finished.

He had some other rib-tickling things to say too.

Pity he never lectured in Crossmaglen.

ENGLAND. 1930ff

The Liverpool Machine Grinds On

By the end of World War I, the Liverpool machine is showing signs of wear. It will continue operating at heavy load until the late 1940s, but as far as the Irish are concerned, by 1930 it has become obsolete, if still occasionally useful.

For the Irish, the machine in the 1920s and 30s acts like a slowly moving sluice gate. Now it diverts them from the USA to England as their preferred destination. Now they pass quickly through Liverpool and on to the Midlands or, mostly, to London. Of course, Liverpool is just the mechanism. The USA after World War I becomes fussy about the immigrants it receives. Quotas are announced in 1921 and tightened down in 1924 and again in 1929. By 1930, migrants to the USA have to show evidence of skills or sufficient capital to avoid their becoming a charge on the welfare system. England replaces the USA as the primary place of Irish migration, and it remains that way throughout the rest of the century. The Irish are not suddenly turned off America, but they never fill their quota. It is not U.S. restrictions that are the direct problem, but a change of context. England is close and cheap to get to and it allows a worker to go home for the holidays; and it has much better welfare and public medical systems than does the U.S. Going to England seems so much less final and a lot less risky and there are so many places and methods of entry.

Thus "the Irish" in England become that nation's largest ethnic group and, simultaneously, an amazingly complex one.

They are layered. That is, a continued flow of young women and men means that a fresh stratum of Irish immigrants is always present. The new are easily identifiable and, like all young people, often come a cropper. Many stay only a year or two. Those that stay on merge into a larger community that identifies them less and less as being Irish. Intermarriage with English and Scots is frequent (25 percent was one clerical guess for the 1940s and it is reasonable). And then there is the second generation, dispersed widely throughout the country and mostly occupying skilled positions, owning small businesses or becoming, by virtue of the Catholic school system, white collar workers. By the third generation, one cannot bet on someone with an Irish name's being Catholic (it never has been a sure thing, given Irish Protestants' predilection for settling on what they call, when being intentionally irritating, the Mainland). And one can no longer be sure that someone with an Irish name will feel that he or she is Irish. Identity becomes voluntary. After two or three generations, many people of Irish background think of themselves as English, chiefly: if, maybe, English with a dash of bitters.

Nightmares

As is the privilege of all the recently-deceased, Tom Barclay listened to his own funeral, eavesdropped on his friends, and revisited memories of his own life that would fade at exactly the same rate that other people's memories of him would grow pale. Having been waked by almost the entire fellowship of the Leicester Secular Society, Tom was charmed to see himself, as in a Cinematograph, as a ten-year-old, in 1862, awaking each morning and blessing himself before dressing, saying the Our Father, a Hail Mary, and the Apostles' creed before breakfast and reverently listing aloud the Holy Family:

Jesus, Mary, Joseph, O offer my heart and life.
Jesus, Mary, Joseph, assist me in my last agony.
Jesus, Mary, Joseph, may I die in peace in your blessed company.

Tom Barclay had died in perfect peace but only in his own company and that is why he, and hundreds of thousands like him, were the nightmare of the English Catholic church.

Tom had been part of the Devotional Revolution as it swept from post-Famine Ireland through the Irish empire, worldwide. His parents, Irish immigrants, both of whom worked fiendishly long hours in the rag and bone trade, kept Tom and his brother and sisters locked all day inside a series of one- and two-room tenements and there the children learned to read from the thick layers of newspaper that were plastered on the walls, each sheet a forlorn attempt at keeping out cold and disease.

At age eight Tom had his first full-time job, as a rope worker on Taylor Street and, once outside his own home, he read voraciously: *The Glories of Mary,* and of course several versions of the Lives of the Saints and he became a youthful seeker after holiness, and if possible martyrdom and sainthood, a longing many Catholics of his time found admirable, if immodest.

Tom became a nightmare to the church only because he kept on reading. He did not stop at tracts and devotionals, but read anything he could put his hands on and in his twenties was at the Working Men's College and reading everything they could lend to him.

The wraith of Tom Barclay smiles because, skeptical of the church as he had become, he had all those Irish friends, especially from his Gaelic League days: Pierce Beasley (as he was then), Sean O'Cahan, and Professor Henry, now of University College, Galway, all of whom he had studied with in London. Old Tom Barclay, those that remembered him were saying now, what a fine man, and so good with the Irish and not a drop of religion in him. Tom, taking stock of all this, laughs the way wraiths are permitted, from the stomach and never mind good manners, for no one can hear and what's the use of good manners when you're not in the land of the limited? He still believes that he and a mate called Dick Hancock, an Englishman of Jewish origin, were the only two people in Leicester who actually could read an Irish book or newspaper, not just natter in some bog dialect.

International Socialist, English radical, working class "bottle washer" his professed trade, Tom Barclay slips peacefully away demonstrating that in England one could be second-third-fourth generation Irish, proud of it, and drop the church: which institution, it must be said, preferred it the other way round.

LIVERPOOL. 1936

Slow Learner

When he died, it's a wonder he got the message. Patrick Jeremiah Kelly was the last of the old-time Irish politicians in England – the ones who thought the Irish immigrants and their descendants could be organized as an ethnic group and inspired to take over parliamentary seats and fight their own corner under their own steam.

Born in Moy, Co. Tyrone, Kelly had the doggedness of the northern Catholic and that's often as much a handicap as an advantage: it's especially debilitating to slow learners. P.J. migrated to the most-Irish part of the most-Irish city – the dockland of north Liverpool in 1886 when he was seventeen: there being ten other brothers and sisters in the family made his emigration nearly as automatic as is grass going through a goose.

Gregarious by nature, Kelly found the perfect job as an insurance agent for the Royal Liver and that position gave him his original political base. The weekly, fortnightly, or monthly collections of an agent among the poor (annual policies were not even dreamed of), meant that he saw his prudential flock more often than did the parish priest. And he organized his fellow insurance agents into a union. After several unsuccessful attempts, he became a municipal councillor in 1914 under the umbrella of the Liverpool Irish National Party.

And it 1920 it was P.J. Kelly who organized the mass welcome in Liverpool for Archbishop Mannix. It did not come off, but Kelly was in the limelight. That's a blinding place to be, for he could not see the signs.

The signs: that in the parliamentary system there was only one constituency in all of England – T.P. O'Connor's seat in Liverpool – where the majority of Irish voters thought of themselves as Irish first and not primarily as workers or businessmen or Catholics or English or women (important after 1918) or anything. And the simple arithmetic: easily three-fourths of persons of Irish background in England had been born there, not in the Motherland. They could be played to, but they weren't brute votes that one could drove to the polls.

Unless there is a more widespread exertion, the Irish in England will be simply ridiculous, as having vapoured, and talked, and done nothing: so said the secretary of the Home Rule Confederation of Great Britain in 1877 and little changed thereafter. The Irish National League of Great Britain never had more than 40,000 members. The few moments of Irish cohesion did not coincide with the holding of national elections, or with electoral boundaries. By the mid-1920s, anyone with a brain had given up on pure ethnic politics, especially if the issues had to do with the other side of the Irish Sea. Except for More Money for Religious Schools (and that a demand shared with the Anglicans), there was no unifying Irish-Catholic issue in England, many though the petty grievances may have been.

P.J. Kelly was unable to reconcile himself to the big fact of Irish politics in England – that Irish interests, diverse as they were, would be handled mostly by politicians who weren't Irish, and the way to prosecute the Irish cause was to act like any other set of English voters who had an axe to grind. Nothing he tried worked and the Labour Party slowly sawed away his lifeline, giving the Irish working class better local and national representation than an Irish national party could do. Trapped in the heart of Liverpool like a woolly mammoth in a tar pit, Kelly, by the time of his death in December 1936, was well on his way to being fossilized.

MANCHESTER. 1938

Oh God

Intermarriage, always a stomach-knotting problem to both sorts of Irish people in the homeland, becomes a Gordian knot in England: for it's not at all straightforward.

In Ireland, a Protestant named Tomlinson married a Catholic woman and the children were raised Protestant. One of these children married a Catholic girl and they moved to England. Though the father remained Protestant, the children of the marriage were brought up Catholic.

Now, John Tomlinson, one of the offspring of this mixed marriage, is a leader of the laity in a working-class Manchester parish. He is devout, leads the sodality and raises money for Catholic charities like a man possessed.

Two successive generations of mixed marriages. Complicated enough?

No: in later life, John Tomlinson's Protestant father turns Catholic.

And: his Protestant grandfather undergoes a deathbed conversion to what he also has come to believe is the One True Faith.

LIVERPOOL. 1939–45

The Household Cavalry

The Halligans, a multi-generational extended family, lived in a shared house and in another one across the road from it and in a couple of other houses in central Liverpool. Like anyone sensible, they spent the war being scared: Liverpool was a prime target. They had no yard space to dig a bomb shelter, so every time the air raid siren sounded they slid like otters down the coal chute of the house of one of their numerous aunts. That's how the children later remember it: sliding like otters and then being packed like sardines.

In an extended family this size everyone was an aunt or uncle; the term came to mean "relative," but carried no precision.

One aunt's tenement was near the carters' stable, St. Anne Street. One night a lone German bomber got through and, without any siren's sounding, dropped a load of bombs that hit the stables, killing some animals and freeing two-score others that ran wildly around St. Anne's square.

Panic ensued when one of the old dears came out of her home and, surveying the situation, convinced everyone that a German invasion was imminent as they were already dropping horses.

WESTMINSTER AND LEINSTER HOUSE. 1939–45

Silent Alliance

Southern Ireland, though officially neutral during Word War II, worked a silent alliance with England. Between 50,000 and 150,000 men from the Free State served in the U.K. military: the numbers are open to argument because neither government has wished them to be known.

Equally important, certainly more than 100,000 Irish men and women built airfields, worked in munitions factories and served as home front nurses in England, thus freeing an equal number of English persons for the military. Both the enlistees and the migrant workers sharply reduced Irish unemployment at a very difficult time and, obviously, Britain's war effort was helped.

Irish newspapers censored reports of the workers and of the enlistments and Irish post-war summations scuttled direct references to recruiting and to cooperation with the U.K. British official war summaries scarcely mentioned the Irish and that was just fine with the de Valera government. Ireland's official policy of neutrality had to be protected and, besides, it was highly embarrassing to have to admit that England at war had bailed out the Irish economy at peace: not least because de Valera had declared an Economic War on the United Kingdom during the 1930s.

Embarrassment has been the reason for the suppression of a longer-term fact as well. For its first fifty years, the independent Irish government was dependent upon the British state: Britain kept southern Irish unemployment down to politically palatable levels by permitting the short- and long-term employment of Irish workers. And by being the source of billions of pounds sterling in remittances sent back to the Twenty-Six Counties by those same migrants. Between 1939 and 1969, 2.2 billion in the money of the day was sent back to Ireland in the form of postal telegrams and money orders alone, never mind cash and cheque.

Ourselves Alone?

LONDON. 1939

An Equal Distance

Ilkane at says ocht again the Son o Man will be forgien his faut; but him at speaks ill o the Halie Spirit will nane be forgiven. Nesca Robb, who spoke perfect standard English most of the time, often summed up the really important things in her life using the language of her Presbyterian grandmother. She, like tens of thousands of northern Protestant women, joined the war effort; they were sometimes in the military, but mostly in civilian jobs. The only difference between these women and their Catholic sisters was that Protestants were allowed into high-security jobs. (The British establishment never figured out how to decipher the social coding of Catholics from Ireland, so they viewed them all as useful but, equally, as potential fifth-columnists; and some were.) Oh, and one other difference: many, probably most, of the Protestants were not working in England primarily to make money. They believed. The British patriotism of Ulster women was sometimes so fervid as to be frightening. They could accept being slagged off by Catholics in their home province, but for anyone not to believe that the war against Hitler was a war against evil – that was a sin against the Holy Spirit.

Nesca Robb is not unusual in her commitment, only in her abilities. She has been a scholarship student at Oxford and has run a school in Italy. When, in 1938 the Italian anti-Jewish laws come into effect, she is back in England and she works to get Jews to safety, officially as treasurer of the Committee for the Relief of Refugees from Italy, and unofficially as a refugee smuggler. She remembers Zaccariah's words about the Covenant with God. *He swuir til Abraham our forefaither take cleik us out o the haunds o our faes.* She keeps the Covenant and works to save His people from their foes.

The Almighty's people include the British and of course her own Ulster tribe. Nesca joins the Women's Employment Federation which, when taken over by the Ministry of Labour, becomes the central registry for several highly skilled occupations, male and female. She specializes in identifying and recruiting skilled women, everything from confidential secretaries to code-breakers. Half her job is to find mini-boffins, the other half to make sure that women displaced from their usual jobs by the war were not wasted. And always there is refugee work

Hero? Perhaps. But she would have denied it. She had not fought heroically for England, but instead had simply done her duty for her own country, something larger, different, distant. The English, whom she often thinks of as the Sassenach, were to be respected, but not assimilated to her soul. Had she been given to doing needlepoint, she would have worked into a cover for a large puffy pillow her own view of the English which had been articulated for her by an old Ulster friend whom she encountered in England. She inquired of her friend, "how do you like the English people?" and received God's own reply.

"I can't stand them. They're so gushing."

DUBLIN. 1943

Great Distances

Eamon de Valera had spent most of the 1930s in an Economic War with England. Its cause was his self-pride and its result was purer, but poorer, Irishmen and women. Now, on St. Patrick's Day, 1943, as he stands stiffly in the neutral zone between Hitler and the Allies (neutrality being a proof of the independence of the twenty-six counties), he makes his most famous speech. It is on radio, a medium he distrusts as being modern.

[The] Ireland which we dreamed of would be the home of a people who valued material wealth only as a basis of right living of a people who were satisfied with frugal comfort and devoted their leisure to things of the spirit ...

Never mind that during his Economic War hundreds of thousands of Ireland's youth had left, or that the British war effort was now run on fires stoked by men and women who had left his frugal paradise to make a living wage and to put a little bit aside for their own futures.

... a land whose countryside would be bright with cosy homesteads, whose fields and villages would be joyous with sounds of industry, the romping of sturdy children, the contests of athletic youths ...

For most of the hundreds of thousands of economic migrants (not refugees, voluntary migrants), the distance to England is not great. Navvies, nurses, city girls, don't find England all that hard to negotiate. They fit in quickly, much quicker than any other ethnic group that comes to England in significant numbers at the time. With one exception among the Irish.

... the contests of athletic youths, the laughter of comely maidens, whose firesides would be the forums of the wisdom of serene old age.

The one exception was rural Irish girls who had not trained as nurses or teachers, tens of thousands of girls who had left school at age fourteen and never had lived in a town larger than 5,000 souls. These Irish rural girls were laughed at by the other Irish immigrants and shunned by the second generation – "Bridies," "Bridgets," or, sometimes "Harps" they were called by the more sophisticated. Usually the only work outside their own family that these girls previously had done was as farmers' "maids" in Ireland, meaning girls-of-all-work. They'd milk cows in the morning, make breakfast, clean house, make a big noontime dinner, help muck out the byre, scrub floors and make the evening meal. Day after day, usually in contracts of six months at a time.

And then, sick of the muck and the constant bullying, they'd make the big jump to England, terrified, full of contradictory information about the dangers of English life and the wonderful freedom they would have. It's not just in the war years. From the early 1930s through the 1960s, rural Irish girls – de Valera's *comely maidens, whose firesides would be the forums of the wisdom of serene old age* – move in large number to a land that, though only a few shillings away, is as far away as the New World was for Sir Walter Raleigh. Wonderful girls, lively girls, scared girls, girls thick as two planks, make this heroic journey. Often they are lucky – the Irish Catholic Church does a good job of setting up reception centres and hostels for them – but always they have 100 years of social and economic learning to catch up on in a matter of months.

The wonder is not that some return home on a tide of tears, that others lose their virtue and become hard women. No, the wonder is that so many do well, work through a succession of jobs until they find comfort, start an English family, visit the Old People back in Ireland and send them money. And these girls, now grown to mature women, look back on their younger selves and have the grace to laugh and delight in their earlier innocence, and to say without embarrassment, "och, weren't we the lucky wee flidgits."

MANCHESTER, 1946

Leverage

In the same way that the smart Irish figure out within a few years of their arrival (whenever that may have been) that they would never form a political power bloc in England and would often need to have their interests represented by someone outside their group – in the same way, politicians of several stripes figure out how useful the Irish could be to their own careers.

Entente.

One of the best of these alliances developed in Manchester in the 1940s, when Leslie Lever, Labour MP and eventual Lord Mayor of Manchester, declared himself Irish – and he meant Irish Catholic – in politics.

This he did, as a conscientious Jew, by respecting certain Christian niceties. In Manchester, Catholics had a parade to the city centre on the Friday before Whit Sunday and Protestants had one on the Monday after.

Lever walked in only one parade and that on Friday.

He knew his constituency.

ENGLAND. 1948–69

The Lord's Day

If the post-war migrants to England had one saint's day they should have honoured, it was the birthday of Lord Beveridge, architect of the welfare state. The post-war English economic boom, coinciding with the birth of the welfare state, put the Irish migrants on an economic and social escalator that they could not match any place else in the world. That's why four-fifths of Irish overseas migration after World War II was to the place the heretics among them called "the Mainland."

Conversely, the English should have said a *Te Deum* for the Irish: England could never have been rebuilt, nor the Welfare State constructed, without hundreds of thousands of Irish men and women doing the hard graft.

One bunch, the navvies, has been talked about a lot, mostly because they talked about themselves a lot, rarely modestly. In truth, they were important. The army of Irish farm boys, escaping the doldrums of the post-war Republic (which, because of its neutrality in World War II did not receive gift aid from the U.S. after the war and its economy stagnated), worked immensely hard, did the heavy-lifting that Englishmen would not do, sometimes broke their own health, more often broke each other's heads. The reflective ones, such as Donal MacAmhlaigh, recalled, *Britain was a revelation to the work-eager Irish who flocked here during the great postwar boom, and I often wish that Englishmen, who persist in the notion that the Irish dislike them and their country could only have heard the remarks which were commonplace when the Irish workers spoke among themselves* ... How many of the navvies stayed in England no one knows. Some were the equivalent of the old agricultural spalpeens who worked a few months across the water and then came back to the family farm. More stayed longer, a year or more at a time and then returned home for a month's drinking and then back to a place they sometimes said they hated, but that gave them both work and freedom. ... *spoke among themselves. I say among themselves for with a stubborn loyalty the Irish never admitted to an outsider what they were forever saying to each other – that there was nothing "back yonder," that the crowd in Dublin couldn't run a booze-up in a brewery, that Britain was the best bleddy country in the world* ... Many thousands stay on year after year, transforming themselves from lumpen-navvies into skilled builders, tradesmen with tickets, and they marry and have kids who go the English Catholic schools and talk funny, but are great little chisellers all the same. ... *best bleddy country in the world, better even than the States where, for all the blow and big money, a man couldn't afford to fall sick.* Lord Beveridge's welfare state and the realism of the English authorities gave the Irish workers the same medical, unemployment, and even voting rights as possessed by English citizens. Disability pensions, everything. And for the sharp-eyed among them, a system there for the cheating. Irish tradesmen were famous for claiming to be independent contractors and thus avoiding their employer's having to pay their stamps for social insurance schemes: hence, they could take lower pay on construction jobs and were rarely out of work. Navvies went up the ladder to become unlicensed tradesmen, many to be licensed tradesmen, or to be small businessmen who employed a crew of their own (each an "individual contractor" of course), and at the top, the big construction firms were owned by hard, sharp, second, third generation Irish. (No English Need Apply could have been their motto.) Those builders, successful men who employed others, made sure of returning to Ireland each summer, bringing the overdressed wife and the underdisciplined kids. Their airs made the locals cringe and to recall almost with affection the despised Returned Yanks of yesteryear.

Not a modest bunch, the navvies, but necessary.

More self-effacing and more apt to thank the Lord, Beveridge, was an equally important group, the nurses. Without the Irish nurses, universal health care in England would have foundered before it even left the starting gate. Young Irish women had been recruited as nurses, especially for military service, in the nineteenth century, and the tradition continued. During the Second World War, the English pool ran dry so that one-third of the travel permits given to women in Ireland to go to wartime England were for nurses and nurse-trainees. And then came the national health scheme. English recruiters scoured rural Ireland, much like farmers at a hiring fair. The recruiters looked for strong girls of high moral character (they loved quoting Florence Nightingale that moral strength was the most important character of a successful nurse). Physical strength did not hurt, however, and these big farm girls could move a patient just as readily as they could lift a calf.

The Nurses Act of 1943 gave two entries into the profession, "assistant nurse," and full nurse. Neither course of study was for idiots, and though most of the Irish girls had left school at fifteen or sixteen and now, recruited at seventeen or eighteen, they were not given a soft ride. They were entering a profession and one that was fighting hard to rise up the status scale. They entered a regimen where they wore a starched collar all day, and learned basic human sciences, starting with human physiology. They learned the basics of reading pharmaceutical directions and of dispensing techniques. Then ward duties. They had two to three hours of free time a day, two half-days a week and alternate Sundays off: plus one full week's holiday in their first year, two in the second and a month in the third. Matrons were inspecting them all the time; the students slept in cubicles or shared rooms in hospital, and they were always being chivvied about their posture and bearing as a nurse.

They became great nurses and, as far as the Irish community in England was concerned, the natural leaders, though they were much too well trained to say so. A good estimate is that, in the mid 1950s, 10 percent of the Irish-born women working in England were nurses.

They're just the opposite of the navvies, who do best when bending the law. These are women (almost entirely the Irish in the profession are female), who work within a rigid discipline and, when they make decisions on their own, do so according to protocols they have memorized while in training. They don't jump back and forth between England and Ireland whenever they please (though they have more than sufficient funds to travel home for holidays). They are long-stayers. They comprise the largest block of skilled Irish women in England. Nursing is a career, unlike navvying, which is merely a job. And it's a career that rewards working within the rules, unlike being a cowboy builder which rewards playing outside the lines.

The women in starch are the starch in the Irish community and their children and grandchildren the first large band of Irish-English to fit securely, snugly, and often smugly, into the English upper-middle class: accountants, lawyers, pharmacists, stockbrokers, medical doctors, professors, and scarcely a priest or nun among them.

BARROW-IN-FURNESS. 1949

Ambition

Peter Donnelly wants to be a writer, an honest ambition, but harder to explain than, say, a desire for chicken pox. Worse, he lusts after becoming an Irish writer: so make that small pox.

Against all odds, Peter has a contract for his memoirs and he is just composing the painfully honest last paragraph. *The Yellow Rock is the [English language] name of the townland in which I was reared, and my ambition now is to go back there, to live frugally and carry on writing.*

Peter Donnelly, second-generation in England, has no distance on England, only a curiously uncomplaining dissatisfaction. *To my undying regret, I came to be born in Barrow-in-Furness on the 18th of February 1914. ... In a life mercifully free from plaints, I have this complaint, that I was born out of Ireland.* Donnelly's father was an Irish-born steelworker and his mother a school teacher from a strong farming family. Peter spent much of his youth back in Ireland, in south Armagh, between Newry and Newtonhamilton, the heart of Ulster nationalist country. He attended the Christian Brothers in Newry and had a brief try at a religious vocation, and then he was twenty-one and working in England, like half the Irish young folk of his time.

Peter genuinely has no complaints about England that aren't those anyone would have. He does not experience anti-Irish discrimination. He lives well enough, as a steel industry worker, time-keeper, shop steward, secure as one could be on the cusp between working- and lowest-middle class. But always there is a gauze of rose-coloured memories between him and his English real world: his uncle leading the family in the nightly Rosary, the sheaves going into the threshing mill, the summer-smell of just-saved hay, thatch roofs over smoke-blackened rafters, and bacon frying in a deep skillet over a turf fire. He even remembers the B-Specials in south Armagh as brutes, but also as necessary players in the noble theatre that is the Ireland of his mind.

Men and women such as Peter, no matter how successful in England, were never fully successful in their hearts. Will Peter Donnelly return to his imagined home? He is self-reflective enough to know that *I am vain as a peacock, and vanity may still persuade me that it is a better condition for a writer to be rich than to be poor, and distract me with dreams of growing rich and being admired.* But he is not sufficiently self-reflective to recognize that he will probably be neither rich nor poor as an Irish writer, but, rather, merely unsuccessful. So he dreams. *I cannot deny that I want these things, but I want also to write one poem that will make men gasp to read it.*

LONDON. CHRISTMAS DAY, 1950

And Proud of It

Margaret McCarthy is Irish and proud of it. She's second-generation Irish in England and is rare: few of the second or third or fourth generation think aloud on what it's all about, being English and Irish at the same time.

> *Dare to be a Daniel,*
> *Dare to stand alone.*

Margaret is writing her memoirs. As she works through them she keeps hearing the old Methodist hymn, one that has been the basso-continuo of her entire life.

> *Dare to have a purpose firm and*
> *Dare to make it known.*

Margaret is English and proud of it. Her mother was a Catlow and they trace themselves back to thirteenth-century Normans. Eventually the family had become common as church mice in north-eastern Lancashire and twice as poor. The family had become firm, no, fanatical Methodists and when Margaret's mother had married a "loose Catholic" (would they have preferred a staunch one?) they scissored her out of the family network, the way some families cut from a family picture the face of a member who's disgraced the clan. Never mind, Margaret knows she is a Catlow.

> *These things shall be;*

Margaret is working-class and proud of it. Her English grandfather had been a Lancashire cotton worker in the hard days of the American Civil War, her mother a weaver, and her Irish father, though well educated, passed from one short-term job to another. Margaret began her working-life as a "reacher" for threads in a cotton factory.

> *… a loftier race*
> *Than e'er the world hath known shall rise,*

Margaret's salvation and pride in life is politics, deep politics. Certainly not religion: christened Catholic, brought up shirttail Methodist, Margaret watched with fascination as her mother turned atheist and she eventually followed along that path, though the Methodist hymns kept resonating in her heart.

With flame of freedom in their souls
And light of knowledge in their eyes.

Margaret is a socialist and proud of it. The English side of the family had been politically involved going back to the Chartists and the Irish side had a political genealogy that ran from the Land League to Home Rule to early Sinn Fein to the Independent Labour Party. Politics had been the meat and drink of her childhood and, for a strong, very bright working class girl, it was a natural step to join the British Socialist Party and then to migrate to straightline Communism. Margaret during the 20s and 30s works at a series of just-poverty day jobs and spends all her remaining energy in party matters. She visits Russia and is given the Designer Tour, the same one that thousands of British Communists are given, and she, like most of them, comes up inspired: it looks so very good, so incredibly noble.

The only part of her life that embarrasses her is that she left the party later than she should have. She is very coy about the date: after Stalin's major bloodlettings, but exactly when she still does not, in 1950–51, wish to say. She has become a full-time trade union official in the postwar years and is vulnerable to anti-Communist investigations.

Proud. Stiff-necked. English. Irish. Protestant. Catholic. Atheist. There are no sociologists' boxes tight enough to confine the identity of Margaret McCarthy, nor those of other equally complex mid-twentieth century women and men of Irish background and English nationality.

Dare to make it known.

IRELAND AND ENGLAND. 1950–69

Socially Transmitted Diseases

– a Liverpool Divorce
– P.F.I.
– *London Dry Gin*

All common terms in Ireland, especially in the Republic; and in the Irish neighbourhoods of England; all part of the Irish polity's way of flushing impurities from its system.

That is:

– the ending of an unsuccessful marriage by the husband's going to England permanently. Sometimes this was family abandonment, but more often a truce at the end of a family war: the wife kept the children and the Irish house and furnishings and he stayed away. The family and neighbours were told that Da was working in England and everyone pretended that he was sending money and that Mother was taking a job just to buy a few wee extras for the childer.

– Pregnant from Ireland. Standard abbreviation. Irish girls, often not having the slightest concept of how the human body functions sexually, were turfed from their homes to have the child in England. God bless the welfare state. The neighbours were told that the darling girl had fine class work in London. If she gave up the baby or later married, she was allowed to visit her parents in Ireland. How much bigger babies born in England were than those born in Ireland, and how often they were "premature," was an observation made nationwide.

– an abortion. Not yet available free in England, but fairly freely obtainable. If a PFI-girl took this route, she never told her parents. Always she had miscarried.

Priests and bishops denounced the immorality of England and from the pulpit they warned of the dangers to a decent and pure Irish girl's "character" (the term for her sexual purity) of emigrating to England. They thanked Almighty God and all His angels that they lived in a republic where divorce was not just illegal, but unconstitutional and annulments – even those granted by the Vatican itself – were not recognized in law. They uttered praise, both of the Almighty and of themselves, that Ireland had the lowest rate of illegitimate births in the whole world; and that the communication of any information about birth control was illegal and that distributing the Devil's products, those preventers of natural procreation, led to prison sentences for the purveyors; and, most importantly, abortion could never occur legally in their holy isle.

Pacem in Utero?

BALLYSHANNON, EAST DONEGAL. 1963

Laying the Right Foundation

Each year the family, two boys and a girl, along with their mother come home to renew family ties. Some years the father tags along, but not usually, and he never stays long. The head of the family is Hazel, née Corscaden, and her family has been in the area since the seventeenth century. The Corscadens are a very tight family, as are most Donegal Protestants, for they have been under siege for centuries; and since the Free State was created in 1922, they have lived under constant and intense pressure to leave. Hazel is head of her own small unit, and no place more than here on the beach at the Sands Hotel, Rossnewlagh, for the land around here had once belonged to her people. The children play on the beach, throw sand-balls at each other, take turns burying each other, all unaware of the fight their mother is waging. She had been part of the Protestant exodus from Donegal. In the 1920s her father had died and the immediate family had moved to Glasgow where her own mother married a Scottish butcher. But her mother went home to Ballyshannon each summer and so now does Hazel.

This year is emotionally wrenching. Her husband, Leo, is with them on the journey, but he cannot speak. A brilliant law lecturer (originally from Glasgow, he had taught in Edinburgh and now is teaching and practising law in Durham), he has been taken down recently by a stroke and he is silent: it will be three years before he utters a word.

Hazel walks on the beach for long hours. She has an immensely hard task, raising three teen and pre-teen children, comforting a speechless but notably bad-tempered husband, and nothing but his legal residuals to cover expenses. She considers for a time bringing the children back to Donegal to live, but that, she knows, is crazy: there is no future for Protestants.

Mostly she worries about the middle son, Tony. He is doing well in the Chorister's School, Durham, and the headmaster says he is a fine little gentleman and the Head thinks he can find him a place in a good public school. The lad is already very popular and has a good playground sense of politics: he is never on the losing side of a schoolyard maul.

Hazel Blair takes young Tony for a walk along the Donegal strand. She explains to him that the next few years will be difficult financially, but that he must never reduce or modify his ambitions. Before his stroke, Tony's father had talked politics with the lad and told him that he might make an excellent MP, something the father had always wanted for himself. Before his stroke, Leo Blair had made a mark as a klaxon of highly conservative legal and political opinions. That was fine with Hazel: there are no left-radicals in her family.

Hazel Blair holds Tony's hand as they walk along the beach, and he tries to pull away, for he is of the age when being seen like that is embarrassing.

"No, son. Listen." Her voice is strong and he stops and they face each other. This is Big Advice Time: "If you are ever on the rise in England," she tells him, "go as long as you can before telling people that you are Irish." And she adds, gripping him tightly by both wrists, "Never let the bastards know that your people have been Orangemen for 150 years and, by God, will be for another 150."

He looks her in the eye and nods his understanding.

As she hugs him she whispers, "You really like having secrets, don't you son?"

FALL RIVER, MASSACHUSETTS. 1963

Requiem

One of the last of the agricultural spalpeens is dying. Having been turned out by his parents to become a farm labourer at age twelve – the money was needed to pay the priest of Glenties, County Donegal for his building fund, or a curse would be laid on the family. As the eldest of eleven children, the lad had no choice but to turn up at a hiring fair.

Two years of this and he becomes a potato digger in Scotland and follows this and other labouring jobs, including serving as a private in the London Irish during World War I.

Patrick MacGill was a genius of a sort that universal literacy was making unnecessary: a self-taught person – he had six months or so of schooling and the rest was acquired on his own. MacGill became the poet, novelist, chronicler of the disappearing spalpeens, and he was totally untouched by the Celtic Renaissance. While the litterateurs were acquiring mock-peasant Irish, he, who spoke the real thing from youth, was acquiring arthritic hands, a permanent limp, and an intimate knowledge of what actual Irish peasant life was like. He did not recall picturesque pishrogues, but rather the words of his parents, frequently repeated, that a man who did not turn over every penny of his earnings to his parents would never have a day's luck in his life. Scant wonder that he finally cut off communications. They saw him solely as a dray pony and that's how much of the west and northwest of Ireland lived: tiny uneconomic farms, with parents surviving as parasites on the remittances of their children sent from all corners of the earth.

Amazingly, Patrick MacGill wrote, and sold door-to-door, a book, *Gleanings from a Navvy's Scrapbook*: eight thousand copies' worth. Amidst his labouring, he somehow produced more tales, poems, and the epic *Children of the Dead End* (1914) and *The Rat Pit* (1915).

An heroic spirit, forcing the remembrance of people and of conditions that Ireland in the misty Celtic Revival wished to forget.

God's justice to Patrick MacGill is that the hardness of his parents was counterbalanced by the kindness of his own children. Having settled in New England in 1930, he continued to write, but his works did not sell as once they had: *Children of the Dead End* had sold 10,000 copies in the first fortnight of publication. Still he wrote.

Stricken by multiple sclerosis, and hobbled with a wheen of old labouring injuries, he continues to write, through the 1950s and into the sixties. His daughters make their own remittances, voluntarily. They do not let him learn that his books no longer sell; from their own earnings they present him with annual royalty payments and with enspiriting, albeit forged, statements of the sales he deserved.

LONDON. 1964

Learning Irish Law

"The children are mine. It's my house. Everything here is mine. And I *own* the children."

Remembering the words of her husband, spoken two years earlier, Betty McDowell bitterly acknowledges that he had been right. It took a sojourn in England, consulting with Irish-English women's groups, and a trip back to Ireland for her to learn Irish law. Or, more precisely, the law of the Republic of Ireland, for the hateful words had been spoken in County Louth.

How the marriage had gone so wrong Betty never understands, except to say it was doomed from the start. She, a Protestant-turned-atheist from Belfast, had joined the Fourth International, and married another communist, a Catholic-atheist. They considered their registry office marriage a badge of honour and the future unity of the working class the eraser of all Ireland's social problems. The young couple had lived in Dublin and Louth and produced six children.

When the breakup came, Betty learned that Eamon de Valera's constitution of 1937 had enshrined Catholic canon law on the family as the foundation of the Irish state. And, as a Belfast näif, she was horrified to learn that in the twenty-six counties, custody of children in a separation (no divorce, of course), was always given to the father. He could be drunk, abusive, anything short of a serial killer: as long as he put bread on the table, he owned the kids. *One thing I wasn't sure of until I came to England, until I went to Ireland to get custody, was the fact that I had no legal right to my own children.* She learns what thousands of Irish women also had discovered: that to gain custody of children was like an Orthodox Jewish woman's obtaining a divorce. It could only be done with the husband's permission and that was expensive, either in terms of money, begging, self-prostitution, and of all kinds of humiliating things a woman wants to forget. Betty eventually negotiates custody of her six children, but she remains perpetually stunned by the experience. *I mean, here I was with this feeling of them being so completely mine if you like, and yet suddenly to be told by law they were the father's children.*

PRESTON, LANCASHIRE. ASH WEDNESDAY 1966

Acclimatization

On Ash Wednesday night, eight of the twelve young women staying at St. Philomena's Hostel for Catholic Young Ladies engage in projectile vomiting.

The hostel's warden has served them meat. The warden, a devout lay Catholic, would never do anything that would upset her charges, rural Irish girls who were recommended by their parish priest as of good character and were permitted to stay in the hostel for up to a year as they learned about England. She cared for these girls like a mother, and now that the Vatican Council had said eating meat on Fridays and on Ash Wednesday was all right, well, hadn't she found a lovely rack of lamb and made a special meal for the dear things.

They all knew about the new rules, and they tucked into the meal, but then one of them bolted from the refectory to the w.c. and everyone could hear her stomach rejecting the Vatican's ruling. She was from Clare and only three weeks in England. The others tried to ignore her, but a liturgical stomach is a terribly contagious complaint and soon seven others were bolting for the basin. They didn't mean to be rude to the warden, really, but their upbringing would not allow them meat on what always had been a holy day of obligation.

The four who did not take ill were the young women who had been in England longest, nearly a year. They looked smugly at the eight empty places and offered to remove the extra plates for warden. Then they went off to the hostel's small common room for a meeting of a tiny society they called their Book Club. They were studying collectively and intently a pamphlet they had picked up at the department of social services entitled "Methods of Birth Control: the Choice is Yours."

OLD TRAFFORD, MANCHESTER. 27 SEPTEMBER 1969

Not Quite Pur Laine?

They met first at Old Trafford and shared a laugh. They tried to guess if their great-grandfathers had ever met. One of them was the finest striker the old English First Division produced, drunk or sober, and sober probably the world's best: ever. The other was one of the handful of black footballers who were collectively doing in England what Jackie Robinson had done in the USA.

Neither of these men is Irish according to the rules that were then being written by the ideologues who were soon to make The Troubles a modest description of the last one-third of the twentieth century in Northern Ireland. The one lad, from Belfast, was a Prod and they were now declared *pied noir* and told to go back where they had come from a few hundred years previously, mostly England and Scotland. As for the other one, from Bermuda, via slavery, he couldn't be Irish because he was totally *noir*. It was unthinkable in Ireland at this time that someone of Irish heritage could be as black as the infants on the Save The Black Babies box that was passed around each Catholic school at regular intervals.

Sod the begrudgers. Instead, watch George Best who, like a mayfly, skitters across the surface of his own private pond, and turns Manchester United from a good parish side into one of the most-watched teams in the world. And enjoy Clyde Best who, somehow, is an effective striker though he physically resembles Sonny Liston and moves with the ball as if he is on his way to a train wreck. It doesn't hurt that he plays alongside Bobby Moore and Geoff Hurst. He works so hard and is so honestly amused at his own mistakes – he has hoofed so many balls over Upton Park's North and South Banks that the trainer threatens to make him pay a deposit. The fans on West Ham's "Chicken Run," later to be infamous for their racialism, have all the time in the world for Clyde; he's an honest article.

Around the world, local memorialists of the Irish diaspora are beavering away and almost universally they define Irish as Catholic and as white. So that's what the history of the Irish diaspora is: white Catholics living outside of Ireland.

Clyde Best and George Best could have taught them otherwise.

Especially in America where they meet on the pitch one more time. In the North American Soccer League, a brave and doomed attempt to bring religion to the heathen.

OXFORD UNIVERSITY. 1969

Reflection

John Hall, destined to be a pioneer of the "new historical sociology," gravitates at university to the orbit of Christopher Hill, a wise choice. Hall, age twenty, is – like the entire pool of "the Irish" in England – beyond stereotype. His mother is Catholic of Irish background; his father a rabid atheist. The family is upper middle-class.

Hall reflects on his English-Irish background and reaches two conclusions.

"That religion is nonsense, nonsense which becomes less important as modernity takes root."

And:

"British ideas get worse, the more they take culture seriously."

SO FAR, SO FAST, SO SO FAR.
IRELAND
1922–1969

No Accounting

In the warren of small streets that run off York Street it is dangerous for strangers to wander around aimlessly or to ask too many questions. The little man with the mustache and the satchel of file folders and papers was taking his life in his hands as he went door-to-door in Nelson Street, one of the rookeries where everyone knew that he was not one of them.

Without hesitation, he knocks on door after door and is met by large housewives with hands on their hips or by men in their vests and braces, looking as if they are ready to throw a punch. The caller tips his hat, politely asks a question or two and does so with real skill: he does not ask to come into the homes. Instead, he backs far enough away so as not to be threatening and keeps his hands clearly in view.

He gets his answers.

This is the under-secretary of the Northern Ireland branch of the Returned Servicemen's Advisory and Benefits Service. He is trying to tally benefits owed to various veterans of the Great War or their widows and, quite unintentionally, he is performing an audit of one tiny section of the Belfast riots of 1920–22. The riots are over: before his death Michael Collins and the prime minister of Northern Ireland, James Craig, had made a deal: Craig would halt the yobs from throwing Catholics out of their shipyard jobs and burning their houses and Collins would call off the southern boycott of northern goods and produce and stop the sporadic attacks by gunmen on Protestant targets in the north. Neither man was entirely sincere, but the deal held together, just barely.

Nelson Street had been a mixed neighbourhood until January 1922, and then the Catholics were burned out. Twenty-one little one-family houses were torched; twenty-one families disappeared into the Catholic areas of Belfast or went back to live with relatives in the countryside: save for the six that were killed in the rioting.

The little man in the mustache with all the papers to fill out discovers that from these twenty-one Catholic families, sixty-five men had served in the U.K. armed forces or merchant navy during the Great War and ten of these had died in the service.

Usually his job gives him satisfaction, surprising a widow with a pension or providing a grant to a disabled former soldier. But when he has done his work in Nelson Street, he walks away with a taste in his mouth that no amount of spittle can clear.

BELFAST. 7 DECEMBER 1922

And, Please, Which Was
the Irish Revolution?

With the solemnity of bank managers cashing money orders, the members of parliament of Northern Ireland vote formally to withdraw from the Irish Free State. Both houses agree and they do so without a division: unanimity is possible because the Catholics who were elected in the May 1921 elections – six Nationalist and Six Sinn Fein candidates, including both Michael Collins and Eamon de Valera – had refused to take their seats. Thus the practice of Catholic "abstentionism" that was not fully abandoned for decades.

The Westminster government had done everything it could do to lend this inevitably Protestant parliament legitimacy. King George V had opened the parliament in June 1921 in Belfast City Hall.

Not much later, the second Dail Eireann met in the Mansion House Dublin.

Each regional government quite accurately claimed that it represented the democratically-expressed will of its people: but that was not automatically a Good Thing.

While the southern government is sliding into civil war, the northern government consolidates its own position. Sir James Craig (Viscount Craigavon, 1927), heir of a wealthy distilling family, former Belfast stockbroker and longtime chief lieutenant of Edward Carson, becomes prime minister. Carson, a southern Protestant, is willing to sit for one of the Belfast divisions in the Westminster parliament, but he refuses to become prime minister of Northern Ireland. He takes Partition as a sign of failure, not victory. And, besides, he does not really much care in practice for the Ulster Protestants, however well he may argue their case in theory. They are, he says in private, too much like the Hairy-Backs in South Africa, by which he means the Afrikaners.

Craig, the perfect prime minister for the northern Protestants and thus the complete nightmare for the Catholics, spends many of his early months in office shoring up Protestant confidence. He is direct in speech, very serious in public demeanour, and lines up a series of public events all of which have the trappings of State Occasions. How else broadcast that Northern Ireland is a state? Thus, Sir James's series of monument dedications in 1921–22. The best of these from a visual standpoint is the ceremony for the dedication of the highly evocative memorial tablet in Lisburn Cathedral to the Indian God, John Nicholson. That ceremony is attended by ancient veterans of the 1857 mutiny and by Field Marshal Sir Henry Wilson, former chief of the Imperial General Staff. He is on Michael Collins's hit list and is fated to be assassinated in London on 22 June, exactly two months before Collins is himself killed.

If, three years later, we look at the two governments, Dublin's and Belfast's, where was the Revolution?

Under the Dail there are between 21,100 and 21,200 civil servants who had served under the previous United Kingdom government, and only 131 who had been personnel of the revolutionary Dail. The departments and the public servants in day-to-day charge of them stayed the same. The disturbance to their everyday way of conducting business caused by the Irish revolution was only slightly greater than that which occurs when a new party wins a parliamentary election.

Business as usual.

In Northern Ireland, a whole new apparatus comes into being. A few of the civil servants are from the pre-1922 days – notably the head of the education service, the Catholic Napoleon Bonaparte Wyse – but they are few. Departmental policies in Northern Ireland varied (the ministry of education was notably "liberal" in its appointment policies) but for most the words of Sir E.M. Archdale, the minister for agriculture were emblematic. *I have 109 officials, and as far as I know there are four Roman Catholics, three of whom were civil servants turned over to me whom I had to take when we began.*

Unlike the south, in the north the usual business was definitely not business as usual.

THE IRISH FREE STATE. 1922–23

Suffer the Little Children

A shadow falls across the land. It is the silhoutte of the silent giant, Father Timothy Corcoran, S.J. For more than half a century, he has more influence over the daily lives of the youths of southern Ireland than any political figure. Corcoran, a silent, basilisk-like man, never smiles. He is in the D.P. Moran school of great-haters of everything English, including the language. And he is professor of education at Univesity College, Dublin.

That post allows him to be the chief educational policy maker for the new Irish Free State government and he believes that the primary duties of the school system should be the salvation of the soul of each child and the revival of the Irish language. On the souls issue, his colleagues in the parish ministry (who are also the managers of most of the Free State's schools) will take care of things: but he needs governmental force to help him revive the language.

Ah, the Irish language. Key to the soul of the nation. Antidote to the influx of foreign ideas, most of which arrive through the sewer that is the English tongue. Professor Corcoran has a vision of the day, only a generation hence, when Irish will be the first language of the nation and English will be spoken only haltingly and then by the upper middle classes who will have received sound clerical secondary schooling and will have been trained to reject impure ideas from abroad. Mind you, Father Corcoran knows the task is great. Less than one percent of the Irish population are monolingual Irish speakers (Corcoran's ideal state of linguistic grace) and well under one-fifth can speak Irish at all and most of these bilingual speakers prefer English. Yes, Corcoran is right: only state authority will save us.

Under Corcoran's influence (he uses the Gaelic League and the Irish National Teachers' Organisation as levers), the new Free State government introduces a truly radical educational-cultural program. Its first full year is 1922–1923 and it aims at making Ireland an Irish-speaking nation, starting with the infant schools.

It can be done. Father Corcoran says he has himself seen it done.

In the United States of America: there, he says, children at age four or five, immigrants, speaking Italian or German or Yiddish or some horrible east European language, are put into schools that teach them only in English and they learn the language. Destroying the home language of the children this way works, he claims, and unless one destroys the home language, linguistic purity is impossible.

Thus, suddenly every single word of English is banned from the Irish infant schools. This is bewildering for the children, threatening to the parents, and insane-making for the teachers, most of whom are not fluent in Irish and can only fake it and pray that the school inspector is generous.

After two years, as a concession to parents who wish their children to learn to read and write English, the subject is permitted to be taught at the end of the day, but not during regular school hours.

Variations of this program, each slightly milder than its predecessor, continue for decades; Irish, however, remains compulsory
for several hours a day through secondary leaving certificate, and
subjects taught and tested "through the medium" receive extra
credit: such as the bonus given for taking one's physics examinations in Irish. Entry to university requires a high level of Irish language proficiency and it is requisite for any decent government job,
which will, however, be performed almost entirely in English in
most departments.

The language is saved. By the mid 1940s more than one-fifth of
the citizens of southern Ireland can read and write Irish, and the
portion is slowly rising. They know it as their second language,
however, like Latin in seminaries. Only in 1954 is the first evaluation of the Irish language teaching program undertaken, not a day
too soon.

BELFAST. 1923

The Golden Rule

The ministry of education of Northern Ireland operates by the same
binary rule that runs through all northern policy: if the Free State
government is for anything, we are against it.

And the Catholic bishops run on a similar rule: if the government
of Northern Ireland is against something, then we are for it.

So in 1923, when the Catholic schools finally accept that they
will have to deal with the northern government and not Dublin
(which has been paying the teachers but can no longer afford to),
the two sides simultaneously affirm their Golden Rule: the Catholic leaders ask for the Irish language to be part of the daily curriculum and the government says that it can only be taught after
regular school hours.

This exchange is transacted in the rarified strata of policy makers,
church and state, respectively.

On the ground, the issue lies dead until the early 1960s. Hence, the
only word of Irish that two generations of working-class Protestants
can remember hearing is *wankers*.

DUBLIN. 22 MARCH 1923

James Joyce Wept

In the Bentley Place district, the most efficient campaign of sexual control inaugurated in the twentieth century before the Chinese Revolution, springs to life. Men in celluloid collars, working in pairs, go up to strolling women and badger them. Any man who comes near the women is interviewed and those men quickly turn on their heels and scuttle away. The Association of Our Lady of Mercy is beginning its campaign to *crush the head of the serpent* as its leaders say, with unconscious Viennese accuracy.

Dublin has one of the two largest red light districts in Europe and seamen, when discussing matters of semen, agree that it is the best value. From fresh Irish farm girls to gamey old slappers, the place is alive with infectious flesh. It was near Bentley Place that James Joyce caught his first dose of the clap. Some day a large blue plaque will mention that fact and once a year American professors will come around and venerate it as part of their rogation of Joyceland.

> *I know that thou, O Holy spirit, who has come to regenerate the world in Jesus Christ, Has not willed to do so except through Mary. That it is by her, and to whom she please, when she pleases, and in the quantity and manner she please, That all gifts and virtues and graces are administered.*

The Association of Our Lady of Mercy, founded in 1921, changes its name to the more-accurate Legion of Mary in 1925 and becomes the only way in post-revolutionary southern Ireland to combine socially approved activity with thinking about dirty sex. It enrols both men and women, suitably segregated, and applies itself to sharing stories of sexual depravity and driving the whores out of Dublin.

> *I stand before her as her soldier and child*
> *And I so declare my entire dependence on her.*
> *She is the mother of my soul.*
> *Her heart and mine are one.*

The Legion members swear this oath to the Blessed Virgin Mary, and not only rid Dublin of the dread vice, but found chapters in every diocese in Ireland, including rural areas where the chief attraction of the Legion is hearing about the terrible goings-on in Dublin and the need to keep our eyes on our neighbours.

By 1930, the only way for an honest whore to make a living in the Irish Free State is to get married.

She is the mother of my soul.

DUBLIN. 7 JUNE 1925

Chains

"Would you look at that, dear God!"

"Shhh! Quiet now. The man's a saint, so he is, and you don't want to be calling attention."

The two black-shawled matrons – they would be elders in a tribal society – are washing the body of a man who had died suddenly at a spot in nearby Granby Lane. It is that of the Dublin legend, Matt Talbot.

Talbot had been a sometimes-employed workingman with a drink problem until his conversion in 1884, at age twenty-eight. He gave up drinking and cursing and became the urban equivalent of a desert monk.

Each morning Talbot arose at 2:00 a.m and prayed on his knees in his rented room until 4:30. Then at 5:00 he would go to church for mass, sometimes having to kneel outside the chapel until it was opened. He would go to his work at 6:00 a.m. and at noon, instead of lingering over his dinner, would spend most of his time in private prayer. After work, at 5:30 in the afternoon he again visited a chapel to kneel before the Blessed sacrament. He spent the evening in prayer and spiritual reading. Each Sunday he knelt in prayer for at least eight hours, rising only to receive the Host.

No whiskey. No cursing. And, crucially, no sexual thoughts. Matt Talbot especially feared night-thoughts, impurities that could infiltrate his mind when asleep:

> From all ill dreams defend our eyes,
> From nightly fears and fantasies;
> Tread under foot our ghostly foe,
> That no pollution we may know.

That was his prayer against nocturnal emissions. Against impure thoughts while awake he had his daily liturgies and a secret antidote that only is revealed after his death.

"Dear Lord, those must have hurt."

"A sharp razor is what we need."

The corpse-dressers had to deal with the discovery that Talbot had worn chains around his thighs, abdomen and scrotum, to keep himself from sexual sin. These mortifiers of the flesh had been bound so tightly and worn so long that portions of them were embedded in the dead man's flesh.

"Perhaps we should leave them as they are. The other saints will remove them for him at the resurrection."

"Yes, so. A glorious example."

On 7 June 1945, the twentieth anniversary of Matt Talbot's death, the archbishop of Dublin, John Charles McQuaid, inaugurated the canonization process for this most saintly of Dublin's men.

CAVE HILL, BELFAST. DECEMBER 1925

The Devil in Sir James

"Gif ye ar the Son of Ulster, bid yon slouches turn intil God's own solyers."

Sir James did not approve of the unvarnished Ulster Scots tongue, even when spoken by Beelzebub. It cheapened things.

"I rather feel, sir, that is beyond my power." Craig had a problem and the devil knew it. Sir James in November 1921 had set up his own army to keep the Teigs down: the Ulster Special Constabulary, consisting of full-timers (the "A"s), part-timers, serving in their own home areas (the "B"s) and an emergency reserve (the "C"s). The Special Constabulary had done rather too good a job of bashing the Catholics and London had demanded the As be disbanded. They responded by mutinying.

"I shall mak ye Lord of Ulster's glorie. An they shall be the solyer a thy dominion."

"You will? Extraordinary. Indeed, I could use some help."

"Aye, for thy Lord God hae haundit owre tae me the keys tae thy glorie."

"Could you be a bit more specific?"

"I can gie ye an army – an I am amind tae."

"That I already have. Too much of one really."

Sir James adjusted his tie. "In case you haven't noticed, my problem is how to rid myself of most of this lot. It was all a very good way of keeping track of every lunatic who owned a gun in the province, but now they've decided to …"

"Ye needs but gang doun on your knees tae me, an …"

"And?"

"… an I shall gie ye the B-Specials as a bulwark for 'er an 'er. For it is written i the Buik – 'He will gie his angels chairge anent ye, tae fend ye frae hurt an hairm.'"

"Ah, that does quite sound like the B-Specials," admitted Sir James. "And the As and the Cs – they will disappear?"

Beelzebub nodded and pointed to the ground.

Sir James Craig dropped to his knees before the tall man with the coal black eyes: the As accepted disbandment before Christmas, and the Cs stopped all recruitment six weeks later.

Only the Bees remained to pollinate Ulster's groves of hatred.

SA'UL, DOWNPATRICK. 1926ff

The Last

The last Protestant to be able to reach out and touch the '98 Rising has had his ashes scattered among the graves of his own people at Mallusk, County Antrim. He had grown up listening to Carnmoney men whose fathers had been out in '98, and he had not permitted the confusions of the north's troubles to erase their words. Instead, he had spent his own life collecting Ulster history, including 3,000 rare volumes that he willed to the Belfast Public Library.

At Downpatrick, with no clergy officiating, though the Catholic bishop of Down and Connor is present, Francis Joseph Biggar is remembered by his friends. They stand near the granite slab, incised to

St. Padraig, that Biggar had paid to have cut in the Mournes and placed on the grave of Ireland's patron saint.

The imperialism of Armagh had been no matter to Biggar. He knew the truth lay here.

DUBLIN. 11 AUGUST 1927

Democracy Warming (1)

I didn't really take an Oath. My fingers didn't touch the Bible.

The elected representatives of the southern Irish people are still not at home in Leinster House, although they have been meeting there for three years. They were happier assembling in various Dublin Corporation buildings or on the premises of University College, Dublin; meeting in the massive house built in 1744 by the 20th earl of Kildare is not exactly homey, and the building's having been home for over 100 years to the Royal Dublin Society did not make it sit any the more comfortably with the people's representatives. Having to walk past the National Library and National Museum, which extended forebodingly, like the arms of a Christian Brother, on each side of the forecourt entrance to Leinster House, made many TDs uneasy. Many of them often had a ball or two of malt in Molesworth Street before making the daunting walk.

Today promises to be messy, and a test of whether or not the Irish Free State will continue as a democratic polity: hate-filled, civil-war torn, but democratic. Eamon de Valera and his new party Fianna Fail ("the soldiers of Ireland") must decide whether or not they will play the democratic game. Dev, having spent a year in jail as an opponent of the new, independent southern Irish government (a terrorist in later language, but in fact a very mild and theoretical one), was sick of living in the political wilderness: especially because he believed himself the rightful leader of the all-Ireland republic that, inconveniently, did not at present exist. In 1926, therefore, he had come above ground, founded a political party, and won forty-four of Dail's 153 seats, a good start.

The problem is the hated Oath; it declares recognition of the king as head of the Commonwealth.

Dev, in these years, explains his support of the antigovernment side in the Free State's civil war on the basis of the Oath that Michael Collins had brought back from Dublin during the treaty negotiations with the United Kingdom. There was much more to his opposition than that, but he stuck to his public story. Now, to assume their seats in the Dail, de Valera and his followers would have to take the Oath. In so doing, they would be accepting Michael Collins's argument that the treaty with the U.K. was worth working with because eventually it would yield complete Irish freedom. Agreeing with the dead Collins, the man whom de Valera hated more than any human ever, was bitter gall.

The Fianna Fail Deputies hereby give public notice that they propose to regard the declaration as an empty formality …

De Valera does everything he can to avoid signing the Oath. He prepares a court challenge (never launched), and moots a referendum on the Oath which, under the Free State constitution could be called by a petition of 75,000 persons. That is cut short by the assassination of Kevin O'Higgins, the strong man of the Irish government. Dev can no more be seen as part of the O'Higgins assassination (which he was not) than of Collins.

De Valera and his followers enter the Dail chamber. He announces that *I am putting my name here merely as a formality to get the necessary permission to enter among the other Teachtai that were elected by the people of Ireland.* Then he bends to sign his affirmation of the Oath. He sees a Bible nearby and moving as if he has a broomstick lodged in his spine, he takes the Bible and deposits it on a table in the far corner of the chamber. *Remember that I am taking no oath,* he declares upon returning and then signs the Oath.

For the rest of his life he claims, variously, that he did not read the Oath, that he signed it as if it were merely a piece of paper or a conventional letter, and on and on.

Eamon de Valera never learned to wear the shit-eating grin, the false bonhomie by which those who are humbled rob the victorious of the pleasure of seeing them grimace as they drink bitter gall. He alternately sulked and hissed, like an inept cat pulled from a fish pond.

Yet his taking the Oath – oh, he did that, no question there – made final the ending in southern Ireland of the Civil War and the beginning of a true and functioning democracy.

Cultural Implosion

To avoid the mistakes which have led to the deformation of the intelligence, and through the intelligence the literature and institutions of these countries [England, France and Germany], especially in relation to the supernatural order, we must aim to return to the sane education idea of the Middle Ages. So an article printed under the bishops' authority in the *Irish Ecclesiastical Record* in 1923.

The Irish cultural renaissance started as an explosion and ended with the long suuumph of books, newspapers, artists' canvasses being sucked into a vacuum of nonbeing. Medieval theology, nineteenth-century economic orthodoxy, linguistic nationalism and, above all, rejection of sexual intimacy, produced a society as inward-looking as that of Tibet: curious, indeed, given that it exported overseas one-third or so of its children.

Don't blame the Catholic clergy. Or credit them. The laws were made by laymen and women. Good Catholics to be sure, but mostly operating on their own energy, enacting laws their constituents approved of. Censorship of films begins in 1923 and it's no great matter. Films are cut so that a woman goes from looking dreamily at her beau to having six children in four frames. How that occurs is one of the Holy Mysteries in post-independence Ireland and so it should be. Any road, it's difficult to really Get Bad Ideas when the parish priest supervises the weekly evening film for adults shown in parish halls. (And, in County Monaghan a parish priest has no trouble enforcing his own rule in the local commercial cinema: men and women, even the married ones, sit on opposite sides of the aisle.)

Irish Catholic democracy in 1929 enacts its first really important edict for the control of adult culture (the schools were already doing a good job with the childer); the Censorship of Publications Act. Again, there is no church pressure, just lay members of the legislature deciding for themselves what their electors should read. Not most papers from England, for example, for they had dirty stories and, increasingly in the tabloids, pictures of attractive young women, displayed provocatively. And not anything that advocated birth control (including, in 1949, the report of the United Kingdom's Royal Commission on Population).

The literature, the dirty foreign books, were the worst danger, as they appealed to the imagination:

Sherwood Anderson, *Horses and Men*

James T. Farrell, *Studs Lonigan*

Somerset Maugham, *Cakes and Ale*

Sinclair Lewis, *Elmer Gantry*

All banned, and hundreds more that are standards of world literature: this under the 1929 act by powers given to the minister of justice, who took his instructions from a five-member panel of worthy citizens who in turn looked at books marked as dangerous by the customs authorities who, mostly having only primary school educations, in their turn read portions marked out as salacious by men and women who had examined the books and, as part of their duties as citizens, turned them in to be banned.

An amending act of 1946 (which stayed in effect until 1967) allowed for appeals of these decisions, but these were few. Instead, more bannings:

Kingsley Amis, *Lucky Jim*

Ernest Hemingway, *Across the River and into the Trees*

Thomas Mann, *The Confessions of Felix Krull*

And on and on.

It's not our business. If a culture does not want to think about new ideas there is no reason it should have to do so, is there?

DUBLIN. 9 MARCH 1932

Democracy Warming (2)

Eamon de Valera, having won seventy-two seats at the February general election now headed the biggest party and, with the help of Labour and a few independents was able to form a government.

This brings post-1922 southern Ireland to the second fork in the road by which it obtains political democracy. De Valera has already come above ground and renounced violence, though tacitly he has accepted IRA support in the form of intimidation and the occasional assassination. Still, he is wedded to the ballot box. Will the old pro-Treaty party, called Cumann na nGaedheal and, later renamed Fine Gael, accept the decision of the electorate or use their control of the police and the army to effect a coup?

It's a very close run decision but, ultimately, they settle for a large fire in the Phoenix Park in which they burn the most dangerous of their security and counter-intelligence records. And then they hand over the keys.

Eamon de Valera reciprocates. With the army and the police loyal to the civil state, he no longer needs the Irish Republican Army and he slowly moves against it. This is made easier by the Catholic bishops having condemned the IRA in late 1931. So, in mid-1936, Dev has the IRA declared an illegal organization in the twenty-six counties. He interns scores of his former colleagues and sets them to making mail bags in special prison camps. They do not forgive him, but now that he has political power he decides those fanatical supporters of the pure Republic are more trouble than they are worth.

DUBLIN. 22-26 JUNE 1932

Glorious Things of Thee Are Spoken

When Roman Catholics wait for trains in Larne and in Ballymena, they have to dodge rocks and broken bricks thrown by enraged Protestants. The Catholics are pilgrims on their way to Dublin for the Thirty-First International Eucharistic Congress, the world's biggest liturgical celebration. Their train will be attacked on their return, this time in the Portadown-Lurgan area. It is all part of being a pilgrim, however, and in memory will become part of the spiritual glory of which they speak.

The congress was indeed dazzling and for once crowd estimates were low. Easily one million Irish Catholics participated on the final day, a combination mass and procession, with all of Dublin as a single parish. Beginning with High Mass celebrated in the Phoenix Park by Archbishop Curley of Baltimore, the procession streamed into the centre of the city where the final benediction and pontifical blessing was given by the Papal Legate to Ireland.

Long files move out of Europe's largest city park.

First the various brotherhoods, singing: de La Salle Brothers, Marist Brothers, Patrician Brothers, Christian Brothers …

Following them, several boys' choirs march and as they sing, the tens of thousands of spectators along the route take up their song.

Then regular clergy: Franciscans, Carmelites, Augustinians, Dominicans, Jesuits, Redemptorists and members of a dozen more orders, most with hands held as if in prayer and eyes modestly focussed on the ground.

Next the secular clergy. Parish priests who walk with the wide-stanced gait of men who are accustomed to having authority. They do not smile, but look at individual members of the crowd, as if inspecting pupils in their own local national schools.

More music. The Irish Army's No. 1 band moves by, trying with indifferent success to mute its brass sections to a decorous level.

Then a choir of priests and a parcel of monsignori.

By specific instructions, the crowd is silent as the next votive item passes, the statue of Christ the King.

And then the highpoint, the canopy under which the Papal Legate is carried on an open palanquin. He kneels during the entire process, holding up a monstrance in which the Host that had been consecrated at the Phoenix Park is preserved. Everyone bows and blesses themselves as the Host passes them.

The Legate's canopy. To be permitted to be a canopy bearer is the ultimate certification of spiritual respectability in Catholic Ireland. Teams of dark-suited canopy-bearers change off. No women of course. Crucially, the first eight bearers, the ones who take the Legate and the Host from the Phoenix Park towards O'Connell Bridge, include not just the former head of the Free State government, William Cosgrave, under whose administration the congress had been planned, but Eamon de Valera, under whose regime it now is being held.

Then, more than 250 archbishops and bishops from around the world, looking like an army in their reds and purples, and finally, all manner of worthies.

Two hours for this to pass any given point. Very hard on the Papal Legate's knees, not to mention the bladders of the older prelates. The Legate requires two men to lift him to his feet when his litter finally reaches the altar constructed on O'Connell Bridge. The entire mass of people kneels and receives his blessing.

Then they sing Faith of our Fathers and go home rejoicing.

Honestly?

Despite the presence of royalty, compared to the Eucharistic Congress, the opening of the Northern Ireland parliament buildings is a pallid affair. Externally, Stormont Castle is not so much a castle as an Ulster replication of the architecture of the major temples being constructed in the same era by the Church of Jesus Christ of Latter Day Saints. The occasion is dimmed by King George V's refusal to open the building. He had done his duty by opening the first Northern Irish parliament in 1921 and he saw no reason to repeat that tedious experience. So he sends the Prince of Wales, the future Edward VIII, who is too tiny to look regal and too dandyish to be trusted by the Ulster populace. They want a person of royalty who looks like a battleship.

Yet, in its curious combination of naked isolation (it sits as if designed by an American golf-course architect) and in its fortress-like character, Stormont is perfect for the northern government. *A Protestant parliament for a Protestant people*, asserts Lord Craigavon in debate, 21 November 1934, in a moment of complete and completely unnecessary candour.

Smartening Up

The lady-of-a-certain age is most happy in the company of her sherry bottle. Once a classical beauty, she has fallen on hard times. She still looks good from a distance and her conversation is excellent, when she can keep her focus. Up close, the cracks in her heavy facial paint are obvious.

Of late, she has descended to drinking the cooking sherry and in the mornings she tells herself that she must, absolutely must, smarten up or it all will be over.

In the 1930s, Trinity College is still a small college occupying the most valuable piece of real estate in Dublin. Lovely Georgian buildings, yes, but up-close the lack of maintenance is clear: grass grows in the eavestroughing and cracks in the facades are cemented over rather than having proper masonry work done. The place is living on its capital, social, financial, and intellectual.

Sooner or later the old lady will have to accept her own diagnosis and smarten up. That means recognizing that Trinity is now a residual Protestant institution in a Catholic state and a residual monarchist citadel surrounded by an embryonic republic. She is not going to receive larger state grants until she stops getting loaded and toasting the king.

TCD begins to sober up in 1935. The college officially flies the Union Flag for the last time on 22 June, the Silver Jubilee of George V. Then, the flag is carefully folded and, by unspoken consent of the Fellows, is not again flown as the college's national emblem. "God Save the King" still is played at degree-grantings until the Second War and then it fades out, for southern Ireland is a neutral nation and playing the anthem of one of the war's participants is not acceptable. The king's Health is still drunk at formal meals, the students and staff in evening suits pretending to be an aristocracy when in fact they represent the quicker members of Ireland's middle class. But the old girl is pulling herself together. The king is toasted for the last time in 1945.

And, thereafter, as Trinity's finances improve, the old darling puts away forever the cooking sherry.

DUBLIN. 25 OCTOBER 1936

Up the Cause

In front of the old Parliament House a meeting of 100,000 takes place. All right: so it is only 50,000 and you really have to be an historical fanatic not to see it as happening in front of the Bank of Ireland. But so.

They meet in a downpour, and more credit to them for that, and the multitude endorses Generalissimo Franco. The Irish Christian Front, representing the views of the Irish Catholic bishops, is mobilized for Fascism and against the Red Tyranny.

The crowd boos and hisses for a full five minutes when they are reminded that the Presbyterian General Assembly, meeting in Belfast, has recently voiced sympathies with the anti-Fascists, some of whom are, God forgive them, Communists.

Much later, after the end of World War II, the Irish church goes through all manner of gymnastics to explain to the American government why it had instinctively backed Fascism. It's a silly exercise, sure. The Irish church, despite external appearances, was never *really* for National Socialism or its Irish equivalent, and, really, we were just anti-Communist. You understand that, don't you, Senator McCarthy?

DUBLIN. 1936–37

A Catholic Constitution for a Catholic People

Had a blind man, sitting with a tin cup near the steps of the office of the president of the executive council (soon to be renamed the Taoiseach's office), reprised his aural memories for the mid-1930s the most robust would be contrasting sounds: the roar of couriers' motorbikes and the sound of the hard-leather heels of the couriers' knee-high boots as they hurried up or down the stairs delivering or distributing drafts of state documents; and the contrasting whispering as ranking civil servants came and went and the respectful silence as a prelate or a leading ecclesiastic arrived, or the president himself went silently off on a mission, dealing with a detail of business that he mentioned to no one save himself.

Eamon de Valera was creating a true Catholic State and he tried to move with lynx-like discretion. In public, by the end of 1936, he had removed the U.K. monarchy from all internal aspects of southern Irish government: the Oath and the governor-general went, and the Crown was recognized only as a symbol of Ireland's "external association" with the Commonwealth. That was housecleaning.

The real task was to put holiness back into government, a quality lacking since the high middle ages, Mr. de Valera believed. This, more than obtaining a republic, was at the forefront of his consciousness. Had anyone paid any attention to the portent, a telling indication of de Valera's values was that at one of the first caucus meetings of Fianna Fail after it took office in 1932, the meeting agreed that a high priority was the erection of a crucifix in the Dail chamber.

Mr. de Valera is a wise enough politician to understand that the Vatican must approve any new Irish constitution and that its officials will communicate their approval privately, while publicly refusing comment:

to approve publicly would be to court Protestant and secularist comment the world around. Power exercised silently is the Vatican's policy.

The first Irish ecclesiastic de Valera turns to is Fr. Edward Cahill, a Jesuit at Milltown Park. In the autumn of 1936, de Valera asks him to draft a preamble for the new constitution. Fr. Cahill's effort is a bit of a mess, but de Valera is able to rewrite it as follows:

In the Name of the Most Holy Trinity, from Whom is all authority and to Whom, as our final end, all actions both of men and States must be referred,

We, the people of Eire,

Humbly acknowledging all our obligations to our Divine Lord, Jesus Christ, Who sustained our fathers through centuries of trial,

Gratefully remembering their heroic and unremitting struggle to regain the rightful independence of our Nation,

And seeking to promote the common good, with due observance of Prudence, Justice and Charity, so that the dignity and freedom of the individual may be assured, true social order attained, the unity of our country restored, and concord established with other nations,

Do hereby adopt, enact, and give to ourselves this Constitution.

Not exactly Jeffersonian. The name "Eire" is to replace "Saorstat Eirean" and "Irish Free State." De Valera does not translate the new name and thus consciously rejects the opportunity of calling his nation, in English, "the Republic of Ireland."

It is Catholicity he cares about and the family is the heart of the issue. On this he brings in as his chief advisor early in 1937, the Rev. John Charles McQuaid, a Holy Ghost father and president of de Valera's old school, Blackrock College. He leads de Valera through the "social" clauses. Key is article 41:

1.   *1. The State recognises the Family as the natural primary and fundamental unit group of Society, and as a moral institution possessing inalienable and imprescriptible rights, antecedent and superior to all positive law.*

2. The State, therefore, guarantees to protect the Family in its constitution and authority, as the necessary basis of social order and as indispensable to the welfare of the Nation and the State.

De Valera and McQuaid agree that women are the key to maintaining the virtue of the Catholic home:

2.   *1. In particular, the State recognises that by her life within the home, woman gives to the State a support without which the common good cannot be achieved.*

2. The State shall, therefore, endeavour to ensure that mothers shall not be obliged by economic necessity to engage in labour to the neglect of their duties in the home.

These articles replaced the guarantee in the old 1922 constitution of equal rights to all citizens, including women. In practice these new sections are used to legalize the forcing out of teaching and the civil service of women as soon as they marry. Employment in this Catholic family structure is for men; home and raising children for women. Making this a constitutional imperative may seem excessive, but remember: Eamon de Valera had been abandoned by his own mother. He wants women at the hearth, children tugging at their aprons, and none of those factory-working married females like they have in Belfast.

And, both de Valera's fathers – biological and step-father – had abandoned him. He realized that not all illegitimacy could be stamped out ("the spawn of Lucifer," as children of unwed mothers were called at the time), but at least Mr. de Valera could prevent marriages from coming apart once they had been contracted:

41.2 *1. The State pledges itself to guard with special care the institution of Marriage, on which the Family is founded, and to protect it against attack.*

2. No law shall be enacted providing for the grant of a dissolution of marriage.

3. No person whose marriage has been dissolved under the civil law of any other State but is a subsisting valid marriage under the

law for the time being in force within the jurisdiction of the Gov-
ernment and Parliament established by this Constitution shall be
capable of contracting a valid marriage within that jurisdiction
during the lifetime of the other party to the marriage so dissolved.

When John Charles McQuaid had read the draft of this section, he smiled, a rare event. Mr. de Valera on this was purer than the Pope. The officials of His Holiness's court frequently granted papal annulments of marriages, for reasons ranging from non-consummation to lunacy. And, further, under canon law, a person who had been married under a form that was not Roman Catholic was not considered to have had a binding marriage, so if that person divorced, then he or she could re-marry and do so in the Catholic form. Mr. de Valera was having none of that. A marriage wasn't just for Christmas: it was for life.

Where Father McQuaid was most helpful was in dealing with the section on the various churches. No one, least of all the Irish bishops, wanted a Catholic state church (state interference was a great fear of the Irish church, irrationally in a deferentially Catholic society; but in any case the Church had what it most wanted – namely, control over a state-funded educational system). The real problem was that the Papal Nuncio wanted the Catholic church to be mentioned and no others. McQuaid and de Valera, with the agreement of the two main Protestant churches, drafted the following:
Article 44.

1.   *1. The State acknowledges that the homage of public worship is*
         due to Almighty God. It shall hold His Name in reverence, and
         shall respect and honour religion.

         2. The State recognises the special position of the Holy Catholic
         Apostolic and Roman Church as the guardian of the Faith pro-
         fessed by the great majority of the citizens.

         3. The State also recognises the Church of Ireland, the Presby-
         terian Church in Ireland, the Methodist Church in Ireland,
         the Religious Society of Friends in Ireland, as well as the Jew-
         ish Congregations and the other religious denominations ex-
         isting in Ireland at the date of the coming into operation of
         this Constitution.

Then, this drafted, the Irish sent a senior diplomatic official, Joseph Walshe, to Rome and, with McQuaid's coaching, he managed to gain the Vatican's silent approval of the recognition of the existence of non-Catholic denominations.

The final stage, before the draft constitution was published for debate on 1 May 1937, was a translation and here Mr. de Valera was at his most elliptical. It was important to him personally to be able to say that the constitution had been drafted in the Irish language and then translated into English. So, he had his draft translated from English into Irish. Then he had the original versions locked away and his Irish language version was translated back into English.

This explains why occasionally the 1937 constitution takes some strange rhetorical jumps and why a few phrases read as if they are pidgin.

Still, there is no question that the constitution fit southern Ireland like a bespoke glove: a Catholic constitution for a Catholic people.

NORTHERN IRELAND. 1937ff

Grizzly Adams

How does one catch a bear?

Maybe with honey.

Possibly with a well-disguised bear trap.

But never will you catch a bear by unrolling a large coil of barbed wire near its lair while you make as much noise as you possibly can. Bears hate that shit.

Eamon de Valera decides to entrap the Unionist bear of Northern Ireland by such methods.

He declares in his constitution that Dublin has a right to rule Belfast. *The national territory consists of the whole island of Ireland, its islands, and the national territorial sea.* This applies whether the population of Northern Ireland agrees or does not. Democracy has to stop somewhere and in this case the point is just north of Dundalk.

While proclaiming that a Roman Catholic constitution is the just (although for the moment inapplicable) law for the Protestant north, he adds a few frills that, while not strictly religious in nature, are perfectly designed to enrage the northern Protestants (and thus, Dev seems to miss, make life worse for the northern Catholics). Language for instance.

Article 8:

1. *The Irish language as the national language is the first official language.*

2. *The English language is recognised as a second official language.*

That outrages Protestants.

In contrast, Mr. de Valera's prohibition in his constitution of the legal dissolution of marriage by any process whatsoever does not so much vex Northern Prods as make them shake their heads sadly, as if observing the rites of some primitive tribe that disfigures its youths so that they can nevermore be seen to be unfettered. Divorce is no great draw in Northern Ireland (Presbyterians and Anglicans are very strong on stable marriages), but, realistically, marriages fail and hitherto, in practice, divorce has been the preserve of the rich. Women, especially working class women, need protection. So, in 1939, Northern Ireland adopts English precedent and allows women (and a few men) to file for divorce in the case of physical cruelty, lunacy, rape, bestiality, non-consensual sodomy and adultery. In the Twenty-Six counties they suffer in god-given silence.

Surely, the northerners approve of the 1937 Eire constitution's section on education, written by John Charles McQuaid?

Article 42:

1. *The State acknowledges that the primary and natural educator of the child is the Family and guarantees to respect the inalienable right and duty of parents to provide, according to their means, for the religious and moral, intellectual, physical and social education of their children.*

Actually, the northerners are too experienced in Catholic dogmatics. They understand that the article in the 1937 constitution means something in substance other than what it seems to say on the surface. As Dr. McQuaid himself explained in the 1940s,

Parents have a most serious duty to secure a fully Catholic upbringing for their children in all that concerns the instruction of their minds ...

Only the Church is competent to declare what is a fully Catholic upbringing, to the church alone, which He established, our divine Lord, Jesus Christ has given the mission to teach mankind to observe all things whatsoever he has commanded.

No, they're not buying that in Cullybackey.

The 1937 constitution of southern Ireland marks the point where northern Protestants finally and definitively stop thinking of themselves as Irish. Northern Irish, maybe, Ulstermen, perhaps. Irish no.

This is merely the fulcrum in a long process. Up to, say, 1880, most Ulster Protestants saw themselves as Irish, although of a special sort, but no more special than did Kerrymen or Tory Islanders. A subset, not a different species. The Home Rule movement galvanized their fears of being run into a Catholic state. Still, even as late as 1912, Protestant opponents of Home Rule could claim they held that opposition because *we love our country. We love Ireland.* After Partition in 1920, they increasingly identify with their own tiny state and with the U.K. within which it huddles. They listen to Eamon de Valera in his Christmas Day broadcast of 1935 declare that from the time of St. Patrick onwards, Ireland has been a Christian and a Catholic nation and that *She remains a Catholic nation,* and they know that Irish identity has left no room for them. The 1937 constitution confirms in fulsome detail the fears of Rome Rule they always have had. The erosion continues and, in 1969 a social survey reveals that only one-quarter of Irish Protestants consider themselves Irish in any way, and the percentage was projecting downward.

Still, they take their small and ironic pleasures in their ejection from Irishness. Mr. de Valera's constitution is a frequent source of amusement in that it contains a batch of terms for governmental functions and offices that are open to bad puns and worse limericks: taoiseach, oireachtas, tanaiste.

Most northern Protestants continue to refer to the Twenty-Six counties as the Free State, although some, trying to be correct, accept the new term Eire, which, in their conflation becomes the Eerie Free State.

DUBLIN. 16 AUGUST 1938

None Is Too Many

The minister for external affairs has become concerned that a large increase in aliens entering southern Ireland is occurring and that many of them show no signs of leaving.

Eamon de Valera is not only taoiseach (as the head of the government is now called), but has named himself the head of external affairs.

His departmental secretary, the civil servant in charge, is Joseph Walshe, the man whom de Valera had entrusted with bringing the Vatican to accept that his new Irish constitution could mention the existence of Protestant denominations without endangering the special position of the Catholic church. Now Walshe has an important task of judgement: to decide if more aliens, persons with German passports and of Jewish origin, should be granted visas to enter the Twenty-Six Counties.

After evaluation and discussion, he writes to his counterpart in the department of industry and commerce. *The Minister for External Affairs*, he says, referring to Mr. de Valera, *is satisfied that it is more than probable that all such persons, once out of Germany, will be deprived of their German nationality and consequently permanently debarred from returning to Germany.*

Certainly Walshe and Mr. de Valera are right about that. So, as the most Christian state in Europe, indeed, in the world, southern Ireland will provide Christian charity. Surely?

Surely not. *The country granting the visa is accordingly bound to keep them, despite the fact that the validity of the visa or the permit to reside may have been restricted to a very short period. This has already been the experience of a number of countries.*

The minister for external affairs therefore decides that no Jews will be allowed into his country unless there is a guarantee that they will be permitted to return to Germany.

This decision is made three weeks before *Kristallnacht*.

That event does not in any way change Dublin's policy.

One must understand here that neither Mr. de Valera, nor the Irish civil service nor the people of southern Ireland are anti-Semitic. It's just that they don't want any of those alien hook-nosed killers of Christ arriving in the land of saints and scholars, that's all.

The Greatest Place ...

Finnegans Wake (1939), which merely comprehends rural Ireland, is bracketed by two books that understand it. *The Irish Countryman* (1937) by Conrad Arensberg and *Family and Community in Ireland* by Arensberg and Solon Kimball (1940). Read these latter two alongside Joyce's *Dubliners* and one has the rules of Irish Catholic society perfectly laid out for the first two-thirds of the twentieth century.

Kimball and Arensberg are gentle and are genuinely appreciative of life in rural Ireland. They are so tactful that it's easy to miss that their work is aimed at explaining one simple social observation. It is the phrase uttered hundreds of thousands of times by Irish immigrants after they've been in Liverpool or Chicago, or Sydney for a while and can reflect on the worlds they know. They say *Ireland's the greatest place in the world to be an old man and the worst to be a child*. They exaggerate, certainly, but the kernel is there.

Living with and observing the people of County Clare, the ethnographic visitors observe one of the most age-graded cultures in the world, one that rivals medieval Chinese society in the power it gives to elders, especially men. The mechanism is simple enough: land is the primary economic resource and the father controls that piece of land completely. He can play one son against another, can hold on to the land as long as he wishes, and the result is that men in their late thirties and in their forties who have yet to inherit land are still called "boys" and are treated as such. Girls rarely inherit and in most cases they are exported as being surplus to requirements, though Arensberg and Kimball do not use such harsh terms. The occasional girl is kept at home and married to a farmer's son who, at age forty or fifty or sixty finally is given control of his family farm. Usually the marriage is an arranged match.

It's a great place to be an old fella, this rural Ireland. Respect and power increase with age, and if someone is sitting in your preferred seat in the pub when you enter, they're out of it immediately, and dusting it off to be sure it's fit for yourself. Any gradient has a top end and a bottom.

At the bottom are the children. Childhood is looked at as a disease to be cured, not a condition to be indulged. The easiest way to see this is to ask what percent of national income does southern Ireland spend on educating its children and how does that compare to other portions of the British Isles: Scotland (6.5 percent), Northern Ireland (5.4 percent), England and Wales (3.9 percent).

And Eire (3.4 percent).

Why deny yourself for the children when you're just going to send them overseas anyway?

DUBLIN. 27 DECEMBER 1940

Fair Reward

The pro-cathedral in Dublin sees the most elaborate ceremony of the past fifty years: the elevation of John Charles McQuaid to the archbishopric of Dublin. This is one of the first important appointments made by Pius XII, who had assumed the papal throne in 1939 and had a lot on his mind besides Irish ecclesiastical politics.

It was a just appointment. Eire's minister of external affairs made sure of that. Dr. McQuaid had taught Mr. de Valera's sons at Blackrock College and McQuaid had been the chief ghostwriter of the theologically-tricky sections of the 1937 constitution of Eire.

McQuaid becomes to the twentieth century what Paul Cullen was to the nineteenth: the most influential cleric of the era. A native of Cootehill on the border with Northern Ireland, he disliked Protestants as much as Cullen did. He vehemently opposes any laxity on the "mixing" issue.

He gains the unaffectionate respect from his people. He is universally referred to as John Charles – pronounced John Charr-less – or, alternately, as Your Man in Drumcondra, where his palace was located.

Whether or not he eventually became the most powerful person in southern Ireland is an open question: unlike politicians he never had to face the electorate.

BELFAST. 14-16 APRIL, AND 4-5 MAY, 1941

Land of Peace

Southern Ireland, having declared itself officially neutral in September 1940, has every right to expect the war against Hitler to be quiet on its own home front. The accidental bombing of seven sites in the south by the Luftwaffe in January 1941 is taken as an oversight, or at least an overflight, on the Germans' part.

Northern Ireland is another matter. Belfast is a major shipbuilding centre and it has virtually no anti-aircraft defences: the U.K. concentrates its resources on protecting England.

Hence, German reconnaissance planes fly lazily over Belfast on Monday 14 April, determining targets with pinpoint accuracy. The nights of the 15th and 16th, several hundred bombers concentrate on the Haarland and Wolff shipyards and on textile mills. The night sky is bright as German aircraft drop parachute aircraft flares over the city, lighting it up like a shooting gallery. Unlike London and the English industrial towns, there is no place for the population to hide: Belfast is built on slobland and even major buildings sit on hollow piles and have only rudimentary underground spaces. There is no equivalent of the luxury of the London Underground. More than 700 people are killed in the April raids, and as many wounded.

The scene is repeated in early May at a time when a cloudless night and a nearly-full moon make the city resemble a pre-marked battle map: bomb here, and here, and here.

Children are evacuated from Belfast in the thousands, and this is the first sight many of them have of fields and lakes, and the first sight that Ulster's prosperous farmers have of the urban urchin. This moment of mutual perception helps to explain why the Ulster Protestants, so instinctively conservative politically, are among the strongest advocates of the post-war U.K.'s social-democratic welfare state, especially in educational and medical care.

Nevertheless, it takes a generation for the children who are moved from their homes to the countryside to sort out what had happened in their own lives. It's amiable confusion, mostly, like the Pentecostal lad, who learns to sing "Bringing in the Sheaves" on a small farmstead in Fermanagh:

> *Bringing Japanese, bringing Japanese.*
> *We shall come rejoicing, bringing Japanese.*

DUBLIN. 1942

The Trinity Ban

John Charr-less needed to assert his authority. With no experience as a parish priest and most of his career having been that of a schoolmaster, he had been chosen over all the other Irish clergy, including the most wise and wizened bishops, to rule the church's most powerful see.

And rule he will. He chooses the symbolic issue of Trinity College, Dublin, and uses it to show his fellow bishops that he cannot be pushed by them.

Since 1875 Trinity College, Dublin has been condemned by the Catholic hierarchy on the grounds that Catholics and Protestants should not be educated together. In practice, however, each bishop has been allowed to grant his own exceptions. Typically, the parents of a bright student who receives a scholarship to Trinity, visit their parish priest and explain the situation and the priest, after ritual argument, recommends that the diocesan bishop grant an exemption. Thus, another member is added to the rising Catholic middle class on which the church depends for its financial well-being. Trinity, as a result, is about 10 percent Catholic.

McQuaid, though, declares that only under pain of mortal sin will Catholics in his archdiocese attend Trinity. Catholics are to go to Catholic universities. He later elaborates, *Only the Archbishop of Dublin is competent to decide, in accordance with the norms of the instructions of the Holy See, in what circumstance and with what guarantees against the danger of perversion, attendance at that College [TCD] may be tolerated.*

In practice, it is not worth a parent's time asking for permission for a child to experience Trinity's "perversion."

Thus, Trinity collects Catholics from outside the Dublin area, all permitted by their own diocesans to attend, while the urban Catholics are fenced out, under pain of mortal sin, by John Charr-less.

And, thus, John Charr-less has created the only regional mortal sin in Ireland, unless one counts the ban on men and women taking the waters together in the municipal swimming bath in the diocese of Galway.

DUBLIN. 1942–46

Very Great Humanity

As both head of the Eire government and minister of external affairs, Eamon de Valera knew in detail what was happening on the foreign front. He was the original micro-manager and, besides, the southern Irish government was so small that its total civil service was less than the bureau of Indian affairs for the state of Minnesota. Dev knew what was going on.

The man who said that he had only to look into his own heart to know what the Irish people wanted, collected information on the Jews of Hungary. He asked the chargé d'affaires to the Holy See, Thomas Kiernan, what he knew. Of course Kiernan's only source was the Holy See itself, and he relayed to Dublin that *anti-Jewish laws are being applied fortunately with very great humanity.*

Mr. de Valera would never ask for triangulation on a Vatican report: the Hungarian Jews were doing well, which he and the Irish people wanted to hear, particularly as there were reports that a man named Adolf Eichmann and his crew had been rounding up Hungarian Jews. Nothing in that, thank goodness.

This, and similar reports from the Holy See relieved pressure on the southern Irish government stemming from the Irish Medical Association. The Irish doctors were very concerned that the Dublin government would admit Jewish doctors and thus simultaneously reduce their own earnings and raise the level of patient care.

The European war against Nazism was known in southern Ireland as "the Emergency," and it was called that in the same tones a caterer would use if she found that she had run out of tonic water and lemons to go with the gin. During "the Emergency," no more than sixty Jewish refugees from Hitler were permitted into southern Ireland. Total: in this, the exemplar of anti-imperialism.

In late 1945, long after the nature and details of the Nazi death-and-concentration camps are known – if nothing else, by pictures so heart-rending that only a zombie could turn a cold eye – an application is made on behalf of nearly 100 orphan children, refugee survivors of the Belsen-Bergen camp.

The application is refused on the grounds that they might some day in the future seek employment in Ireland.

IRELAND. 1946–69

Roofs

As an inheritance, and a good one, from the pre-Independence days, both halves of Ireland have an excellent public housing program. This harks back to the Irish Labourers Act (U.K.) of 1883. In the south of Ireland after World War II, about one-third of new houses are built by the government and by local authorities and the big majority of private housing starts – nearly 90 percent – receive state grants. Thus, four-fifths of the capital spent on new housing comes from the state and there is no homelessness. Transience, of course, but not homelessness in the modern sense.

Neither in the north. There, as in southern Ireland, the standards of housing are well above the European average in terms of space-per-person. From the end of World War II until the late 1960s, the Northern Ireland government goes on a housing binge, on the same principles as the southern government, but involving more new housing, because the population of the north, unlike that of the south, was not declining.

Here's the tricky part. Catholics in Northern Ireland are granted nearly their fair share (nearly, don't ask for miracles) of new public housing, meaning about one-third. What they are *not* allocated is permission to have the houses just any place they want them. Protestants are provided with houses in any area they wish. Catholics are given houses in carefully delimited areas.

The reason is that the franchise for local government elections (and that's where control of most local governmental jobs sits), depends on the occupancy of a house. No Protestant politician is going to give votes to people who will vote him out of office; politicians aren't total head cases, you know. So Catholic houses are clattered together in compact housing estates that are all within gerrymandered electoral areas. Nice houses, wasted votes.

The long term effect is totally unpredictable but harshly real. When the Troubles begin, the Catholic areas are contiguous with each other and therefore become natural defensive areas. Soon they are No-Go areas for the police and then they are quickly under the control of para-militaries.

All because of one of the most generous post-war housing policies in western Europe.

SOUTHERN IRELAND. 1947–69

No Sex Please, We're Irish

"Will French kissing make me pregnant?" asks a country girl from County Clare. She is writing to the advice column of an Irish women's magazine. *"How can I tell if I have had sexual intercourse?"* another wishes to know. These publications are very careful to stay within the church's moral guidelines. They always conclude their clinical information, opaque though it usually is, with a line or two on the need for chastity and complete sexual abstinence. *Is there any way in which I can perform my wifely duties without having another baby? I am worried it will kill me.* That last query from a mother of eight. The level of questioning about basic sexual matters and about simple issues of hygiene is astonishing in its innocence, even among long-married women.

When the result of the 1946 census of the Twenty-Six Counties appears, it is depressing news to the Official Class. The population has continued its decline: the decline that began in 1846 has continued since then. Politicians and higher civil servants had allowed themselves to become optimistic during the Emergency, for it had been impossible during the war to take the usual five-yearly enumeration (too many men and women had found employment in British war industries) and the previous census had been conducted in 1936. Certainly, since then, we have stopped the trend that makes us unique in the western world: a society that has diminished in numbers with each passing year for a full century.

Hope confounded.

Of course the public reflex is to blame everything on emigration. A "Commission on Emigration and Other Problems" is appointed, but when it finally reports in 1954 it tip-toes around the Other Problems as if they were landmines.

The Other Problems are simply stated, and that indeed is part of the problem. As one anthropologist reported, to his peril, southern Ireland was *one of the most sexually naive of the world's societies **past or present***. And, more than naive, it was one of the most actively *anti*-sexual. All forms of physical intimacy were discouraged once persons had reached age two or three, when they might begin to perform "indecent" acts with each other. Throughout the Twenty-Six Counties, it was the policy of the bishops that in Catholic infant and primary schools, girls and boys should be segregated unless absolutely impossible because of the small size of the school. In the archdiocese of Dublin, John Charles McQuaid did not grant even that exception: co-education – the mixing of boys and girls – in infant and primary schools was a mortal sin. End of discussion.

Do your sums:

1. Southern Ireland has the lowest illegitimacy rate in the world: 2.5 percent compared to 3.1 percent in Northern Ireland (all those promiscuous Prods, doubtless) and 5.1 percent in Scotland. (No comment required.)

2. Alone among the countries in the western world is information on "non-natural contraception" not only illegal, but the ban is tightly enforced. This only begins to change in the mid 1960s.

3. And condoms are illegal as are all other birth-control devices. Some middle-class Catholics make a yearly trip to Belfast to pick up condoms, but it is a risky business and, besides, it is a mortal sin.

4. Therefore, given the extremely low level of non-marital child-bearing, and the difficulty of learning about, much less practising birth control, we conclude, don't we? that southern Ireland has by far the lowest level of non-marital sexual activity ever documented. Unless, of course, the entire population was jacking off like a convoy of orangutans in heat. Oh, forgot, masturbation is a serious sin.

Right, next issue … Oh, there's a question in the back from the gentleman who looks to be a Christian Brother. Speak up sir. You object? I'm sure some of your students have objected too, but what's your point? Ah, I see, you say that Irish Catholic men and women when they marry have large familes. Very large families. Correct you are, Brother, and thank you: the marital fertility rate – that's what demographers call it, sir – is gynormous. It turns out that one out of every five women giving birth in the Twenty-Six counties has already produced five *or more* children. You see, sex within marriage is only for procreation, not recreation. The Rhythm Method of birth control is legal, but not publicized and most married couples do not know about it. Besides, having children is a moral duty. As the Rev. Dr. Cornelius Lucey, bishop of Cork and a real worrier about Other Problems on the government's commission on Emigration and Other Problems, says, *parenthood is usually avoided for selfish and self-indulgent reasons.*

Can it be that the pressure to have all those children to support might just discourage young women and men from marrying, despite the fact that it is the only practical way to engage in physical and emotional intimacy with someone of the opposite sex? (And, same-sex relationships are so far beyond the pale that the Irish church lists them with sheep-shagging on its tabula of Things We Never Even Talk About.)

Indeed, that seems to be the case:

- The average age for new grooms after the Emergency was about thirty-three and about twenty-six for brides.
- Southern Ireland, from 1922 onwards, had the lowest marriage rate in the western world. In the 1950s, for example, nearly half the women aged 15-49 were unmarried and more than six-tenths of the men. No country with trustworthy records came close to equalling that aversion to marriage. Basically, one in four men stays a life-long bachelor and one-in-three women a permanent spinster.

Christ, you'd think there'd be a revolution. Not a bit, you foolish person: probably a Yank, I'd say you are. This extreme sexual asceticism, and deep-dish ignorance is absolutely necessary if the century-long readjustment of Ireland to the post-Famine world is to succeed. It's a nest of syllogisms: *if* we are never to starve again and *if* agriculture is to remain the main source of our nation's income, *then* we must reduce the number of farmers and simultaneously increase the size of farm holdings. That will produce wealth surplus to everyday nutritional needs. *If* that is our goal *then* we must reduce our population. *Because* we are good Catholics we cannot permit artificial birth control, abortion or, dear God, infanticide. *Therefore* we must reduce our population by *sexual abstinence* outside of marriage, by *discouraging* marriages unless the couple has a means of livelihood, usually the family farm, and by *exporting* to foreign lands the excess children of those men and women who do marry.

Those syllogisms are cruel, but they explain why the southern Catholic population is so willing to accept the church's anti-sexual pronouncements; the church's doctrines sanctify social behaviours that are founded in heartless economics. Thus Bishop O'Doherty of Galway in his 1925 Lenten pastoral forbids Catholics to take part in Saturday night dances and a multitude of worried parents heartily agree. And everyone understands what the bench of bishops means when, in the same era, it observes that *it is no small commendation of Irish dances that they cannot be danced for long hours ... Irish dances do not make degenerates.* Or permit much touching, they need not add.

Local priests helped parents keep an eye on the youths, especially the girls. In parish after parish, roadside dance platforms were smashed by the priest and his curate. Sometimes concertinas were commandeered and destroyed. And the Catholic women of Limerick established a Modest Dress and Deportment Crusade wherein they undertook to see that when their daughters went out, there wasn't much to see.

Well, *will French kissing make me pregnant?*

OTTAWA, CANADA. 4 SEPTEMBER 1948

A Final Nudge

The last British-Isles born governor-general of Canada may have been sent by Central Casting rather than by the Cabinet. Lord Alexander of Tunis was so handsome, polished, athletic, and well-connected that the Canadian government would have been crazy to turn him down. He had been the youngest major-general in the pre-War British army, had kept the retreat from Burma from being a complete shambles, and had served as the senior commander in the Mediterranean. And his wife, Lady Margaret, was firmly Ascendancy, being part of the family of the earls of Lucan. She looked like Jane Wyman who also had married an

Irish actor. Perfect keepers of the self-image of English-speaking Canadians, especially Upper Canadians.

The man was also a cloth-head of the sort that, on a much smaller scale, the Moodies of Canada had represented: prejudiced, unable to get along with those below him, and disdainful of foreigners, by which he and his lady wife meant everybody outside the British and Anglo-Irish gentry class. A throwback who, though born in London, hinged his own social identity on family lands, taken from the Catholics, at Newtown, near Limavady, County Derry, in the 1660s. He was immensely proud of having been made a freeman of the city of Londonderry. Not, emphatically, Derry.

This was not the man to host a dinner for the Taoiseach of Eire on behalf of the Canadian government.

Lord Alexander and Lady Margaret laughed at the Irish civic vocabulary. "Sounds a wee shop where they sell scones – Tea Shack, what?" And "Erie. Strange isn't it, pet, to name a country after a lake in Canada?" "Actually, dear, it's Eire." "Oh, you mean it isn't the 'Eerie Free State?'"

"Droll, dahling. We shall have to be most careful."

They weren't at all careful. Throughout the visit of John Aloysius Costello and his wife, the Lord and Lady Alexander made the visitors feel ill-at-ease and out of place. Which they were, but a host, especially a governmental host, is supposed to make uneasiness melt. Costello, though a fine legal mind, was a shy man, and ruled an Irish coalition government through his inherent decency, rather than political or personal strength. His daughter once described him as "the sort of man who spends the evening perched on the edge of his favourite chair, in dreadful discomfort, because his dog is occupying the centre of the seat and he doesn't like to disturb it." It was not merely easy, but such fun, for the governor-general of Canada and his wife to play silly-buggers with these oiks.

Take the matter of table decorations. The custom of Lord and Lady Alexander was to place centrally on the head table of each formal dinner they hosted, an ornamental replica of "Roaring Meg," the most famous of the guns that had reigned death upon the Catholics during the siege of Derry in 1689. A charming eccentricity, the Canadians found it. Not so charming at a vice-regal dinner for the Irish Taoiseach. There's no doubt that Lord Alexander was saying to Mr. Costello: "we won, little man."

Costello could handle that, for it was merely a personal insult. He could not tolerate, however, a sequence of insults to his country. Three days earlier, the Taoiseach had addressed a meeting of the Canadian

Bar Association in Montreal and, though there had been a toast to the King and to the heads of other sovereign states, Eire had been left out. Costello did not want the same thing to happen again at the formal dinner that the Alexanders were hosting. His country was sovereign, no question: during the 1930s, Eamon de Valera had proved Michael Collins to be an accurate prophet, for Dev got rid of the governor general of Ireland, the oath of allegiance and, in 1937, introduced the constitution of "Eire" which was a republic in everything but name.

Now, despite the promises of Canadian diplomats, at the formal dinner only "The King" was proposed. And when Costello protested quietly to the Canadian prime minister, William Lyon Mackenzie King, who took political advice both from his dead mother and his dog, King said the most unintentionally disastrous thing he could: "Surely the Royal Toast covers Eire."

Three days later, John A. Costello announces in a press conference in Ottawa that Eire will become a republic. The least impulsive of men, Costello does this without reference to his cabinet in Dublin.

Some things just have to be done.

DUBLIN. 1948–49

A Sense of Reality

Sean MacBride, who took over from Eamon de Valera as minister for external affairs when the coalition government of 1948 superseded Fianna Fail, knew something about diplomacy, as one would expect from somebody who was eventually to win both the Nobel Peace Prize and its cold-war counterpart the Lenin Peace Prize: not bad for a former head of the IRA. He ascribed his balance in all things to never having lost his wholesome sense of reality by paying excessive attention to the BBC.

MacBride's main focus in office was to hasten the reunification of Ireland. As he explained in August 1949 to the Vatican, *An integral part of the campaign against the reunification of Ireland is an attempt to create and maintain the belief in parts of the six north-eastern counties, that if Ireland were reunited, the Protestant population in the north-east would find themselves dominated by Rome ... This belief is entirely unfounded ...*

Interestingly, when he had taken office in February 1948, MacBride had sent the following telegram on behalf of the government of southern Ireland to His Holiness. *Its members desire to repose at the feet of your Holiness the assurance of our filial loyalty and our devotion to your August Person as well as our firm resolve to be guided in all our work by the teaching of Christ, and to strive for the attainment of a social order for Ireland based on Christian principles.*

Certainly it was no fault of MacBride if Protestant bigots misinterpeted this message as anything other than a mere diplomatic nicety.

DUBLIN. 1948–51

Bilious Attack

John Aloysius Costello's announcement that Eire would soon become the Republic of Ireland surprised his own cabinet members more than it did those of the United Kingdom. The Brits responded by guaranteeing that Northern Ireland would not be forced into the Irish Republic against the will of the majority of its people and, with subtle cruelty, declared that citizens of the Irish republic were not aliens in the U.K. Thus migrants from the Twenty-Six Counties still could vote, take any job offered and receive unemployment, welfare, and medical benefits. Nasty business, British imperialism.

As a new republic, southern Ireland had its first public church-state crisis. The minister for health, Dr. Noel Browne, proposed the creation of a pale version of the British national health service which was being quite widely praised in Vatican circles and was doing nicely in Northern Ireland. The version was pale because the Republic was broke (having backed the wrong horse, or no horse in World War II, it did not receive American gift aid at war's end, only small loans). The Irish bishops had their own views, however, especially John Charles McQuaid.

Noel Browne, who dressed like a spiv and was tainted by being an orphan and educated as a child in England, was not the best man to deal with the bishops. He proposed pre-natal care for all pregnant women, and free health care for children up to age sixteen. Local health authorities were to educate women and children in the matters of hygiene and preventive medicine.

In response, the Irish Medical Association, sensing a loss in income, came out strongly against the idea. They wanted payment on the barrelhead from each patient; or in rural areas, a couple dozen eggs, a cured ham, some hedge-trimming, depending on the seriousness of the illness being treated. On the virtue of such arrangements, the bishops agreed. The bishops denounced the Browne plan as socialistic, taking away as it did the right of the 90 percent of parents who could pay for medical care to do so, merely to help the indigent 10 percent. *It is not sound social policy to impose a State medical service on the whole community on the pretext of relieving the necessitous 10% from the so-called indignity of the means test*, their lordships declared.

And teaching women how pregnancy worked, how to provide for personal hygiene for themselves and their children was, the bishops decided, an invitation to immorality. *Education in regard to motherhood includes instructions in regard to sex relations, chastity, and marriage. The State has no competence to give instructions in such matters. We regard with the gravest apprehension the proposal to give to local medical officers the right to tell Catholic girls and women how they should behave in regard to this sphere of conduct at once so delicate and sacred.*

Their lordships clearly did not wish to interfere with a woman's divine right to yeast infection.

Dr. Browne was summoned to meet a committee of the bishops. He, of course, went to them; Irish bishops did not make house calls.

Archbishop McQuaid made it clear that the whole plan was unacceptable. The next day, McQuaid summoned the prime minister and told him the same thing, although more gently as Mr. Costello was an obedient man.

In the end, Sean MacBride, head of the political party to which Noel Browne belonged, forced Browne to resign from the party and thus dropped him out of cabinet; and the new Republic of Ireland was saved from having a national health system.

NORTHERN IRELAND. 1959–66

Better and Better?

In the late 1950s, the Queen's University of Belfast was still a Protestant bastion, but an increasingly porous one. The round-faced fresher from St. Columb's College, Derry is not at all put off by the tone of the place, though he is canny enough to have purchased a second-hand tweed jacket, well broken in and a little threadbare: his mother had insisted that he take his St. Columb's blazer with him, but he knows that wearing it would be to paint a target on his chest, never a good idea in Belfast.

Other than that, he makes no conscious adjustment, but marches through the English department's lectures and tutorials with the same happy enthusiasm he had shown as a school boy. He is blessed with that rare form of self-confidence that people find endearing rather than irritating. Like thousands of other Catholic students from Northern Ireland who are attending univerity in Ulster or in Great Britain, he is covered by the U.K's grant scheme that makes university education virtually costless. The English department at Queen's is starchy, but it takes Anglo-Irish literature seriously and the youth, as he turns into a man, acquires a sure confidence that writing about things Irish and doing so in the English language is no petty calling.

From the end of World War II until the middle 1960s, things in Northern Ireland seemed to be getting better and better, and not least for the Catholics. The unprecedented period of economic growth that covered most of western Europe benefited Northern Ireland more than any place, save perhaps southern Italy. Jobs multiplied, incomes rose and, crucially, this took place at the same time the U.K.'s expansion of educational, medical, and social security benefits became a full welfare state. The northern Catholics did well: the path to the middle class becoming much broader, and the benefits for the unemployed becoming generous enough to live on, especially since most unemployed were in subsidized housing. Things were getting better and better for the Catholics and shouldn't they therefore be quiet?

The Catholic lad in the tweed jacket graduates from Queen's: of course he takes a brilliant first. Then he teaches for a year in a Catholic grammar school and after that spends three years as a lecturer at St. Joseph's College, preparing bright young men to go into the Catholic schools and preach English, poetry, pride. These institutions, the Catholic secondary schools and the teachers' colleges, have well over nine-tenths of their operating expenses paid by the government and their governors' only real complaint is that they want ten-tenths.

That of course is the problem. The Catholics of Ulster are doing better and better all the time, but they still are not receiving their fair share, so they feel. A revolution-of-rising-expectations is still a revolution.

Meanwhile, in 1966, *Death of a Naturalist* appears and wins the Somerset Maugham Award. The now-poet from Derry lectures at the

Queen's University, Belfast for six pleasant years and then after more prizes and *Wintering Out*, he becomes a full-time poet, one of the few to make a living by that route.

A rare man, he rarely forgets to say thank you.

THE DIAMOND, COUNTY ARMAGH. 1967

Arguably

The first time I saw the Rev. Ian Richard Kyle Paisley was at the Diamond, Armagh, where the battle that was the crystallizing event of the Orange Order had taken place. Mr. Paisley's meeting was Proclaimed, meaning that under Northern Ireland's security regulations it was banned. Mr. Paisley spoke from the back of a flatbed lorry.

Mr. Paisley is widely misunderstood by the outside world, especially Brits and Yanks, and is accurately taped, right down to one-sixty-fourth of an inch, by both Ulster Prods and Micks. Nobody with an IQ higher than their knees takes him literally. But everybody takes him seriously. Approach him any other way and you're in trouble.

You see, he's a consummate pro in this world and, simultaneously an inhabitant of another world, one that's invisible, apocalyptic, and approaching us like a large meteor, and all this swirls around in his head with figures of Protestant martyrs, demons, archangels, the anti-Christ, and, if I am not mistaken, a barely suppressed joy that the end of everything is At Hand.

So, I took a mate to see Mr. Paisley speak. My friend was shaking for he assumed that the congregation assembled around the flatbed would tell in an instant that he was an American-Irish Catholic. It's our squinty eyes, he said, checking the car mirror. But, heroically, he put on his dark glasses and took out the Leica that he had treated himself to after obtaining a Yale Ph.D. in medieval studies.

Good decision. Mr. Paisley took him to be a photographer from the *New York Times*. They were doing a story on him, and he preached his entire sermon to my friend. My mate would go around to the side of the truck and Mr. Paisley would strike a Carsonesque pose. My friend stood out front and Mr. Paisley dropped his voice, looked right into the camera and put on a look that said sincere-yet-firm. The guy was a pro, no question.

Taking pictures blocked out the content of a screed so remarkably anti-Catholic that even B'nai Brith would have condemned it. Later, I told my friend that the nicest thing Mr. Paisley had said was that he did not hate individual Catholics.

Decent that.

But, I should tell you, I added, that he also said he did not hate those who suffered from cancer, either.

Oh Christ, said the Yale-trained medievalist, he stole *our* line didn't he? – You know, the Augustinian concept: hate the sin, but not the sinner.

I suppose so, but much more than Augustine, Mr. Paisley is a pragmatic theologian: all the time he was on the back of the heavy goods vehicle, the driver was inside, his hand on the gear lever and the truck's motor was kept running.

SOUTHERN IRELAND. 1960–69

My Cousin's Marriage

Things won't come apart the way my cousin's marriage did, but come apart they will. His marriage crumbled quickly when his wife found a new baby seat in the back of the family Volvo. At the time, he was applying for a job working with young offenders.

In the 1960s there are no surface hints that by the time the copyright date on films becomes decipherable – "MM" – young men and women will be told about the old Irish sexual-familial code and about the power of the church and they will reckon they are being codded. Nobody could have lived like that, they will say.

They could and did. The sixties are the last decade that the full weight of the Great Famine still presses on Ireland.

Thoughtful people, social scientists and medical doctors, note some troubling national symptoms, but have no idea how to treat the underlying disease. They note that although southern Ireland has a terribly inefficient medical system by European standards, it has proportionally more psychiatric beds than other nations. In 1961, for example, the Republic has 7.3 psychiatric beds per 1,000 of population, compared to 4.6 in England, 4.3 in Scotland, and 4.5 in Northern Ireland. (The USA has 4.3.) Statistical anomaly or accurate self-diagnosis? No one is sure. More digging reveals that in the mid-sixties, one Irish person in seventy, from age twenty-five and above, is in a mental hospital. These are not just geriatric cases, but young, physically able men and women, especially rural workers. And, though cross-national comparisons are dicey, the Republic appears to have one of the world's highest (perhaps the highest) rates of schizophrenia. As they go further, the researchers conclusively discover that those most apt to be hospitalized are those who, as a result of the Great Famine's restructuring of the Irish rural world, are denied sexual expression and its related emotional intimacy. Celibacy. Bachelorhood. Spinsterhood. More than four-fifths of the Republic's large schizophrenic population is unmarried.

This monstrous social cruelty eventually will stop, though try to tell that to anyone in, say, 1966. But, unlike my cousin's marriage, it cannot disappear quickly, because even if the Republic became instantly wealthy, and thus could afford a variety of ways of living, the generation that was deformed in the mid-sixties would still be around, ageing, emotionally injured, in the next millennium.

Yet, if a prediction of the eventual crumbling of the Irish sexual code would have been hard to sell in the 1960s, an even harder pitch to make would have concerned the hideous carcinogenic secret of the Post-Famine Irish church. The "Devotional Revolution" that followed the Famine made the church stronger, more influential, with each passing year. The church reaches its zenith in the 1950s and 60s, with approximately 5,500 priests and 18,000 nuns and males in non-priestly Orders – the Christian Brothers and the like. Say a total of 15-16,000 men and 7-8,000 women given fully to the celibate religious life and to forming the minds of the young and to patrolling the morality of the community.

What no one would have foreseen is that the generation that was five, ten, fifteen years of age in the fifties and sixties would solidly document, at century's end, more than 3,000 cases of sexual abuse by priests and brothers. Almost entirely this was adult male sex perpetrated on young boys.

This number – 3,000 – must represent only a tithe of the actual cases of abuse: by MM death will have taken its toll. And most survivors of sexual abuse did not make formal complaints. They repressed, they suppressed, they suffered.

Can you tell us exactly, dear Lord, when did this predation begin?

STORMONT. 28 APRIL 1969

Messy Slate

The day the Hundred Years War began, no annalist wrote down, "Hundred Years War starts today." Nor, when the northern Troubles began did any journalist file a story, "Troubles Begin: Big Death Toll Expected."

Things had been going in the right direction: towards a stable society that would produce equal rights and privileges for Catholics. The prime ministers of the north and south were taking turns visiting each other and being civil. The U.K. and the Republic had signed a free trade agreement. The Nationalist party of Northern Ireland had become the official opposition at Stormont and was fighting its corner skilfully. And in 1968 the prime minister, Terence O'Neill, had announced a governmental reform plan that would have taken away anti-Catholic discrimination in local government, housing, and would have reduced the tilt of the police force. Perfect it was not, but what a distance from the old Unionist vow of Not An Inch.

So calm, so cool. So easy.

And soon all is chaos. The activist Catholics want the whole civil rights package now and the promise of a united Ireland in their lifetime. The majority of Protestants still won't admit there really is discrimination. Terence O'Neill is caught in the pincers of these two steel-hard opponents. O'Neill is forced out by hard-line Protestants in late April 1969 and that would be as good a date as any to start the annals of this particular Hundred Years' War, though of course unbeknownst to the particpants. This is the moment that journalists start keeping score of the victims. They do so like a wary barman watching an alcoholic run up his slate.

The spasming of Ireland in the summer of 1969 can be chronicled, facilely explained, picked over by political scientists, but the descent into tribal atavism resists understanding. The northern working class, Protestant and Catholic, defy Karl Marx and decide that they have a common enemy and it is each other. They burn each other out in mixed neighbourhoods – the ratio is two Catholic houses torched to one Protestant, just what one would expect from the census – and working class Belfast is resegregated. The British army tries to step between the two sides and gets kicked in both knees for its efforts. The government of the Republic goes momentarily lunatic and sends its army to the border. The opposition in the Dail goes to the north to investigate and talks only to Catholics and does not think that strange. Maverick ministers in the Republic's cabinet steal Dail funds and use them to buy arms. Unwittingly, when they spread some of their money around Belfast, they fund the embryonic Provisional IRA, previously a tiny band of Belfast IRA men who had no time for social class politics and just wanted to get at the Prods, reunite Ireland and, oh yes, overthrow the illegitimate government that rules the Republic.

Yes Lord, and while you're at it, where did the North go so wrong?

THE CREATION OF
THE AMERICAN CENTURY
1898–1969

Opportunity

When Captain William Owen ("Bucky") O'Neill joined the Cuban-bound Rough Riders in 1898 it was the first time he had admitted to having been born in Ireland. Previously, he had declared on military documents that he came from Washington, D.C. or St. Louis or, more recently, Prescott, Arizona. Now, though, he figured Irish birth was becoming a useful attribute for an ambitious future politician.

Bucky had served with Teddy Roosevelt's original Arizona Rough Riders and, besides wanting more action, he reckoned that being part of winning a war with Spain (how could America lose? he asked), would look good on his qualifications.

That is why he uses his political weight (he owns an influential newspaper), to arrange matters so that he is the first man in Arizona to volunteer for federal service against Spain. This he does on 29 April; just to be certain he has his patch of glory, general enrolment is not opened until two days later. Bucky O'Neill plans to return a hero from Cuba, and to run for the U.S. congress on a statehood-for-Arizona ticket.

A good plan, but flawed. Captain O'Neill, commanding A-Troop of the Rough Riders, dies below Kettle Hill. He was walking with studied casualness in the open, refusing to take cover under heavy fire, in an effort to steady his men.

He was talking loudly when a bullet entered his open mouth with fatal effects.

Others do better. Theodore Roosevelt, in brown trousers, blue shirt, and white suspenders crossed over it so that he resembled a Scottish flag, became a legend as he led a group of Rough Riders onto San Juan Heights, his revolver waving over his head like a cheerleader's pom-pom.

Out of the larger war with Spain, the USA acquired Cuba (which it ruled militarily until 1902 and informally thereafter), the Philippines (granted Independence 1946), Puerto Rico and Guam. Spain was paid $20 million.

The Spanish foreign minister who negotiated the October 1898 treaty with the United States was Carlos O'Donnell y Abreau.

DETROIT, MICHIGAN. 1899

Fine Name (1)

Henry Ford, the son of a Famine-immigrant father from Ballinascarry, County Cork, lost his mother early and was dumped by his father onto a decent family from Cork City, Patrick and Margaret O'Hern, Michigan farmers. Young Ford grew up hating manual labour and aware that something was wrong with the world but that it could be fixed.

In 1899, having spent a decade tinkering with internal combustion engines, he forms the Detroit Automobile Company, but that goes nowhere. He needs the big idea to fix things.

This he introduces on a practical scale in 1913: the machine-driven, standardized production line, where people are robots and the products are all essentially the same. (In the case of his first vehicle, the Model T, even the products were identical, down to the paint job.) He introduces to humanity the dehumanization of work: almost as if he had used Karl Marx's writings as a cookbook. As a recognition of his Irish heritage he sets up one of his vehicle plants in Cork.

Yet, what Henry Ford actually cares about most after, roughly 1919, is fictitious: the Protocols of the Learned Elders of Zion and other anti-Jewish hate literature. He is convinced that the Jews and the Communists will take over the world unless he helps to set things right. He secretly donates large amounts to anti-Semitic causes, publicly takes over the weekly *Dearborn Independent* and fills it with hate literature, including the Protocols of the Learned Elders of Zion which are collected into a book in 1920. Subsequently, he supports Adolf Hitler although he later explains (after WWII) that he was not really so keen on the Führer personally, as on what he was doing, a distinction without much difference. Among the things he admires about Nazism is that it takes no nonsense from labour unions: in the late 1930s the Ford Motor Company was repeatedly charged with breaking the Federal Labour Relations Act. Only after a long strike does the old man give in and in 1941 allow unions.

Ah, for a man of Hitler's character, reflects Ford.

The German leader returns the admiration. Henry Ford's picture is hung prominently in Hitler's state office.

THE VATICAN. 1899

Benumbed

The American Catholic bishops are stunned by the letters on "Americanization" they receive from the eighty-nine-year-old Pope Leo XIII. Under the title *Testem Benevolentiae,* they are anything but kindly. Basically, he tells the American bishops, mostly Irish, that they are not doing their job responsibly.

This is a surprise, even given His Holiness's advancing years, for Leo XIII had been a realistic diplomat in his younger days, restoring good relations with Germany and sending an Apostolic Delegate to represent the Vatican in Washington. He opened the Vatican archives to secular historians and encouraged Catholic priests to study the Bible, a departure in practice if not in theory from precedents. So, why, suddenly does he see American Catholicism as a potential plague?

Because it is becoming American. Simple as that. The U.S. doctrine of separation of church and state is a corrosive deterrent to the correct view of the church as the final social and moral arbiter; worse yet is the passion for individual rights and individual responsibilities inherent in the American system: it undercuts the corporate judgement of the church. And the American predilection for free speech is essentially immoral: *the passion for discussing and pouring contempt upon any possible subject, the assumed right to hold whatever opinions one pleases upon any subject and to set them forth in print to the world.* That, His Holiness says, cannot be tolerated.

The American bishops, who as a group have been doing a good job working out a means for their people to be both American and Catholic, justifiably feel betrayed. Has the old saint gone gaga?

Perhaps, but he still may have been right, for he indirectly raised a chain of questions central to all denominations, indeed all religions, in the USA: after a time, won't they all become American?

And – here's the real thorny nettle – if they do deviate from the Ancient Faith, is it not likely that the Americans in their boundless self-assertion, will publicize internationally their local version as being the One True Faith?

Pope Leo XIII: old, but not an old fool.

NEW YORK. NOVEMBER 1900

Another Hero

Because the late Victorians sensibly did not start their new century until 1901 (it's a bit daft to celebrate the arrival of a zero isn't it?), Cape-to-Cairo Grogan was the last item in the line of heroes of the nineteenth century, not one of the first of the twentieth. No matter to him. World famous at age twenty-six – Africa had not yet been replaced by the Antarctic as the site of big boys' adventures – he had recently married a wealthy wife and with leisurely elegance was letting the world interview him.

He learns a few things. The American newspaper publisher William Randolph Hearst invites him to luncheon. They sit at a table twice the normal size, loaded with enough fat, sugar, and cream to fuel a logging party. Hearst frequently asks Grogan to repeat himself, explaining that he is hard of hearing.

Later, Grogan learns that Hearst had a reporter underneath the table, taking shorthand notes.

The meal he later had with Woodrow Wilson, president of Princeton, was considerably more ascetic. The supper consisted of cold meats and an even less vital lecture from Wilson on Grogan's duty to the world.

Later, when told by a friend that Woodrow Wilson would some day be president of the United States, Grogan says "God help America," a phrase that, in later years, was frequently on the pursed lips of Wilson himself.

BUFFALO, NEW YORK. SEPTEMBER 1901

"No One Would Wish to Hurt Me."

Pretty much a miracle that no American-Irish president was assassinated before the twentieth century, given that there were so many of them and so many head-cases with guns. William McKinley was an old darling: when he was shot he looked at the assassin and, with a vengeful crowd approaching, said to his bodyguards, "Don't let them hurt him."

The president died eight days later of gangrene.

MINNEAPOLIS, MINNESOTA. 1902

Moneychangers From the Temple

Only a preacher of rare genius or extreme self-destructiveness would dare to get rid of the wealthy members of his congregation and replace them with hordes of working class and lower white-collar workers. That was the strategy of William Bell Riley who took over the First Baptist Church of Minneapolis in 1897 and within five years cleansed it of the moneychangers. And rich patrons they had been: the Pillsburys and associated families, the heads of the grain and milling trade that centred on the upper Mississippi River. Rich, cultured northern Baptists, who played the same role in Minneapolis that the Rockefellers did in the Baptist communion in Chicago.

Riley, who dressed like a corporation lawyer and argued in full sentences and careful paragraphs, found First Baptist too worldly: he abolished pew rents, cut out church bazaars (tithing was his remedy) and condemned any event, especially church socials, where card playing and dancing took place. The rich left.

And with them went the educational level of the congregation and anyone too modern (Riley's pet word) or liberal (another term of disparagement).

Riley introduces his version of Darbyite pre-Millennialism, and all the elements that are soon to be woven into Fundamentalism and, later, most forms of Evangelicalism in America. He expands his church's membership five-fold and they are loyal: they are just the kind of people who later help him organize the Scopes monkey trial.

And, in 1902, William Bell Riley founds, in his church hall, Northwestern Bible College. Aimed at training laity and church workers for the rural midwest, this is not a seminary: it is the logical culmination of John Nelson Darby's vision of every-believer-a-priest, of intensive and literalistic Bible study, and, most importantly of filling of souls with prophecy about the Rapture of the church, the imminent return of Jesus and the horrors of Armageddon. Thus, the vision of a former Anglican priest from the Wicklow mountains was transmitted by an American-Irish preacher to a swarm of working-class Swedish-Americans.

SAN ANTONIO, TEXAS. 1905

Irish Politics

"The meat course, Mr. President?" Theodore Roosevelt had already eaten an entire prairie chicken and a partridge and his appetite was growing. "Some cracklins from that pig, a bit of steer, and some of that buffalo you somehow found for me. Good of you to do that."

Roosevelt, who was never happier than when he was being one of the boys, was attending the Rough Riders reunion. He was having a great time. Pat Garrett was his special guest. "Tell us again, Mr. Garrett, how you dealt with Billy the Kid."

"Twice, actually. Some of our jails aren't too solid." Pat Garrett was in his mid-fifties, but still a powerful figure, 6'4", slim, with a long drooping mustache in the style favoured by law officers and gunmen. Ever since he had killed Billy the Kid in 1881, and had immediately joined with a ghost writer in writing the Life of Billy the Kid, he had lived off the fame. The book was full of good stories and was remarkably non-judgemental concerning Billy. Garrett's sections of the book (he wrote the last one-third himself) read like a deputy-commissioner's report from somewhere in the Raj, detailing the necessity of shooting a rogue tiger. Garrett, in fact, rather liked Billy and had known him before he became the paranoid sociopath that littered the west with bodies.

"William Bonny was his proper name, Mr. President. Born in New York City in an Irish slum in 1859. His mother moved west, and he was killing by the age of twelve. Used a lot of names, mostly Bonney, Henry McCarty and Kid Antrim, but he favoured Billy."

"Fine steak," said the president, who had the ability to hold eight ounces of meat in his mouth and carry on a conversation at the same time.

"Well, 'twas steak that helped me catch him first time."

"How's that?"

"Late in 1880, my posse trapped him and his gang near Fort Sumner. Only five of them and Billy. We shot two of them and then Billy and I had a nice chat. He was complaining that he was short of breakfast wood. I told him to come out and be sociable, but he wasn't having any of that. Nicely mannered man, though. About four in the afternoon our supply wagon arrived, and we cooked up a lovely supper. Billy and his lads hadn't had anything to eat for a day or so, and finally they decided to come out for a bite to eat. We trussed them up and then fed them real good."

President Roosevelt roared with laughter. Just the kind of thing he would have done himself. "Pity Billy escaped."

"Not from me he didn't! begging your pardon. That was weeks later after he'd been sentenced to hang. Did set me back a bit, mind you."

Teddy Roosevelt had now turned to a chocolate creme cake and was dividing it equitably: half for himself, half for the rest of the men at table. "And tell us about the second capture of the great desperado."

"Oh, it wasn't much, Mr. President. Tracked him. Got off a shot before he did. Killed him. Lots of men could have done that."

President Roosevelt has long been a fan of Patrick Garrett – he had read the book several times. In 1901 he had made the soft-spoken Patrick Garrett collector of customs for El Paso.

In a brief moment alone at the end of the big feed, Garrett asks for a job for his friend Tom Powers, a saloon-keeper. Pat tells the president that Powers is one of the biggest ranchers in Texas. Later, back in Washington, D.C., Roosevelt discovers the truth and fires both Powers and Garrett.

"Pat's stories were probably all twaddle anyway."

DUBLIN CASTLE. JUNE 1908

Nuggets

The senior clerk to the chief secretary for Ireland sorts the mail for Augustine Birrell to read. He smiles as he carefully arranges the pile. The item on top is a gem. He knows Birrell will enjoy it.

According to the postmarks and internal address it came from Alaska and had gone first to the parliament buildings in Westminster and then onwards to Dublin Castle.

Everything is set for the chief secretary's arrival at his office: regularly as clockwork, he appears at 10:00 each morning, nods briefly to senior staff members and closes his office door. This morning he can be heard laughing.

An Irish gold miner, Martin Gately, had apparently found his fortune, as had several of his Irish mates. They wanted to know, in all seriousness, if the British were willing to sell Ireland and if the chief secretary could give them a general idea of what the price might be?

Birrell, for whom Ireland is a load of woe, is tempted to reply.

MONTREUX, SWITZERLAND AND NEW YORK CITY. 1909

The Most Audacious Task Ever

When the self-confident polymath Thomas Jefferson had rewritten the scriptures so as to make them more palatable to what he hoped would be a theist America, he had been relatively modest, at least in comparison to Cyrus Ingerson Scofield. The famous Jefferson Bible had simplified the Christian scriptures, leaving out all the miracles and prophecy and vivid Semitic visions – and made Jesus into a mild ethical philosopher of the Greek sort.

None of that modesty for Scofield, whose religious genealogy goes straight back to the Wicklow hills: John Nelson Darby who converted to Dispensationalism. James Hall Brookes who was the mentor of Cyrus Scofield. And that yields the most ambitious rewriting of the scriptures since the early Christians cannibalized and rewrote the Hebrew "Old Testament." For Scofield rewrites both Old and New Testament and does it so deftly that his version infiltrates all the Protestant denominations and in the case of the Baptists, Disciples of Christ, and most Presbyterians and Methodists, replaces their official theology with John Darby's reading of the scriptures.

Here's how it worked: Scofield, shrewdly, disclaimed all originality. And he resolutely avoided tinkering with the King James text. Instead, he produced a set of study-aids built into his edition of the scriptures: indexes, maps, etc., but most importantly, a column that runs down the centre of each page that either links the passage that one is reading to others that have similar wording, or that hold related meanings. Occasionally, he defines an ambiguous word, and once in a while there is a footnote about which Dispensation the text is referring to at a given point.

It all looks so innocent. What it does, though, is rearrange the whole Bible. Now, when someone parses Jesus' words about the kingdom of God being all around us, the reader is sent to the Book of Daniel and then the concordance sets one onto a cascade of references that end up with the bloodthirsty mess depicted in Revelation and so beloved of Dispensationalists. Every ancient Israelite, from the patriarchs onwards is tied by this reference system into this peculiar Darbyite form of Christian kabbalah.

To totally change the meaning of the King James Version of the Bible is something only an American of the industrial age could have accomplished. Scofield, who had served as pastor of a large Baptist "mission church" in Dallas, was given enough money from (among others) the majority stockholder of the Union Oil Company, to retreat to Switzerland and put his work together. Then, Oxford University Press, one of the owners of the copyright of the King James Bible, published the Scofield Bible in 1909. It was so popular that a revised edition was needed in 1917.

Only the Catholics completely escape this equivalent of the cuckoo in the Christian nest, and that is because they are interdicted from reading the Protestant version of the scriptures and, in any case, in this era are not encouraged to study the Bible. Every Protestant denomination is influenced by it. The Episcopalians and upper-end Presbyterians are least bent, although their clergy often use the Scofield Bible because of its convenience for drawing up sermons. Where the real impact occurs is in the Baptists, Disciples of Christ, strict Methodists and orthodox Presbyterians. There, the Bible that believers carry to weekly Bible studies, to Sunday Sermons, to summer Bible conferences, is the Scofield Bible. And in their colleges and divinity schools the students use it because it makes writing papers and drafting practice-sermons easy; and in the pastor's study of thousands of churches, the Scofield Bible is the one the preacher uses to write his weekly sermon.

Just as the ideas on organization and discipline of the Irishman Paul Cullen dominate the Catholic Church for most of the twentieth century, so the ideas of the Irishman John Nelson Darby are the single most influential matrix of concepts in the American Protestant churches in the same century. Of course there are massive differences: one set of ideas is primarily organizational and formal, the other ideological and independent of formal church structure.

But still, one might ask whether it was accidental that two Irish clergymen, Darby and Cullen, born within fifty miles and three years of each other, both members of the strongly self-assertive pre-Famine Irish middle class, came to rule the lives of so many Americans and so long after their own death.

Either God or the devil is in the precise details.

NR. APPLETON, WISCONSIN. NOVEMBER 1908

Hard, Silent

The inhabitants of "the Irish Settlement" in upper Wisconsin were not much different from the descendants of that great sluice of immediate post-Famine Catholic immigrants who, after a time in east coast cities, moved inland. There most of them settled in small towns or homesteaded and now their children and grandchildren were having the same problems that befell so many rural Americans: making it on a 160-acre farm no longer was a sure thing. Twelve-hour days of heavy labour make subsistence, but not what Americans now think of as a real living.

Joseph R. McCarthy is born into a hardscrabble farming family that is frugal, church-going, and not given to small talk. Just like the Protestants in the neighbouring township: in lands where the soil is thin, there is no such thing as a Protestant Ethic or a Catholic Ethic, just unremittingly hard work.

Joe McCarthy is a typical son of thin soil: he swears he will get an education and get the hell out.

THE UNITED STATES. 1910

The "X"

Agitate your grievances was the advice of The Liberator to the Catholic people of Ireland and it was taken up not just by them but by the Irish Catholics of the USA.

"Always make the poor mouth," the old people advised, and the American-Irish Catholics did so. They burnished their grievances, some centuries old. It was a good strategy, for in fact the Catholic Irish immigrants and their children rose extraordinarily quickly and the last thing anyone wants is to be envied. Once people start envying you, the next step is that they begin wanting what you have. So, complain, complain, complain.

About 1910 – there is no profit in arguing about the precise date – the American-Irish Catholics as a group hit the "X" point in their history. That is, their rise intersects the overall American average in matters of income and education. Now most American-Irish Catholics are second, third, or even fourth generation and they have sussed out the American system. Respectability has become the hallmark of progress and now they rise because the men begin to catch up with the women. The women, who had first brought home middle-class notions of propriety from the families in which they were domestics, had in the next generation often become teachers, nurses, or sales clerks in refined stores. In the urban areas, the men were no longer dominated by day-labourers and the lowest construction hands, but were led by those in skilled trades, fire, police, or solid civil service jobs, and lawyers. The church and the women turn them respectable and the parochial schools give their children the keys to the next stage upwards.

The generation of American-Irish Catholics born between 1900 and 1910 was more apt to attend college, have a professional or at least white collar career, and to make more money than the average American. Correction: average *white* American.

Even recent Irish immigrants did better than the immigrants from other countries. Why? Because, after, roughly, 1860, the Irish immigrants were overwhelmingly literate (Ireland under U.K. rule had one of the most efficient mass school systems in Europe); they were literate in *English*. No learning a hard new tongue for them; and, they understood how collective political organization worked (Daniel O'Connell had taught them that) and how a local clientalist civic democracy operated. Life was rarely easy for an immigrant, but the Irish Catholics arrived knowing the game. So of course they played it well.

But, dear, they could complain. To hear some of the orators on St. Patrick's Day, you'd think Oliver Cromwell had put them all on the boat himself, and that they all were waiting for the first opportunity to go home.

Quite right: *Agitate your grievances.*

THE SMOKY MOUNTAINS, NORTH CAROLINA. 1910–31

Saving Rare Butterflies?

What a decent man, Horace Kephart. He smoked his pipe, listened respectfully to everyone and did not say much. He was a good fisher and hunter, as good as an up-north citified man could be. Always willing to learn. In his shirt pocket he carried a notebook, and people he spent time with soon were comfortable with his suddenly taking it out and asking them to repeat what they had just said. He went to church and he did not mind living alone and he never bothered others with his troubles. The Smoky Mountains don't take easily to strangers, but Mr. Kephart was satisfactory.

Mostly, he collected words and phrases. Some of them, like his list of pigs' ear-marks, suitably illustrated, were unique to rural America. Pigs ran wild in the Smokies, and pigs had to be notched in the ears at about the same time their tusk-teeth were broken off, and then the ear holes would grow into the equivalent of a brand as used in the west on a horse or cow:

> Crop
> Slit
> Thief mark
> Poplar leaf
> Swallow fork

And a dozen more. Nothing important. Just ways practical people in a New World had adapted over several generations to their environment.

Mostly Kephart was concerned with recording the way mountain people talked before the steam-iron of state-defined education cleared out the creases and wrinkles that tied these people directly to an older world, one much closer to the British Isles in the eighteenth century than to the Americas in the twentieth.

Kephart came by his interest honestly and his competence was not accidental. Born in Pennsylvania during the Civil War, he and his family had followed his father, a professor in small colleges, as he moved to the Iowa frontier, then back to Cedar Rapids and then back to Pennsylvania where the father taught, and the son studied at Lebanon Valley College. He picked up decent Latin, Greek, and French, and then did a year of graduate studies at Boston University before working for five years at the Cornell University Library and he sorted out their Petrarch collection in Florence, Italy. No slouch.

Still, the passion of his life involved things like writing out all the words for moonshine and the social and economic derivates from it. And grammatical variants that were being school-forced from standard English. The eggs is fresh: things like that.

Light work, you might think, for a man who at the height of his secular career had been assistant librarian of Yale University. There, to translate a saga from Finnish into English he learned Swedish, because at that time the only texts available for studying Finnish were in Swedish. Next he became head librarian of the St. Louis Mercantile Library. That last job drove him to a nervous breakdown in 1903 and he left his wife and children and moved to Appalachia and after seven years of hunting and fishing in various Appalachian locales, Kephart settled in Bryson City. He spent his summers camping and fishing up the mountains, and the rest of the time collecting words. He made a frugal living by writing hunting and fishing articles for gentlemen's sporting magazines, and he always paid his bills on time. Good neighbour. No trouble to anyone. Never crossed your property without paying respect. Never messed with anyone's wife or daughter. Shared a deer steak when he had good hunt.

When he died in a freak car accident in 1931, Kephart left behind one loving book on folkways, *Our Southern Highlands* (1913), a 400-word list of Western North Carolina terms, published in 1917 and, as a result of his quiet political campaigning, the certainty that a national park would be created in the Smoky Mountains he so loved.

The 400-word list was not complicated, mostly showing vowel patterns that hailed from the Old World and had already changed in most other places in America, but not in rural pockets:

> Ferget
> Jist
> Sarvicable

And elided consonants and vowels:

> Hisself
> Reg-lar
> Scandlous

And a few semi-obsolete words that were still not extinct:

> Varmint
> Bodaciously
> Wheedle

This word list of Kephart's becomes as important in the invention of American history as does Bill Cody's Wild West show, for once the talkies start, his rural Carolina word patterns are used in the wild west movies, the Saturday afternoon mind filler of half of America's urban youth, to define how people in the rural world talked. No script writer of B action films could operate without Kephart and they all had fragments of his word lists and phrases that they employed, often without knowing the source.

Actually, Kephart kept much fuller notes on other items that he never published: 2,000 words and phrases, each noted in context. Kephart was the equivalent of a collector of rare butterflies and he thought that his prize specimens were items of Elizabethan English that had died out in the Old World and were kept alive only in his corner of the New.

A keen collector, but he got his species wrong, even though he undeniably caught some wonderful specimens. That occurred because in his isolation, he could use only the standard Oxford English Dictionary to check his words. He never ran any comparison to living speech in the areas of the Old World that were like his, where English and Lowlands Scots and a bit of Gaelic all rubbed up against each other: the rural areas of the western Scottish-English borders; and the parts of Ulster where the eighteenth-century English of Armagh and Londonderry rolls up against the Lallans of Antrim and Down, with Irish words intermingling. Had he done so, he would have found that the locals of those areas in his own lifetime understood almost every word and phrase he employed, save those specific to American life. Provided they accommodated to the slower American mode of speech:

Brattle
Fadge
Mear
Ranpiked
Snitter.

In fact, what became the certified pattern of mountain-speak in America was not some set of rare Elizabethan linguistic butterflies, but the tough and ubiquitous everyday words of rural men and women, mostly from Ulster, and these terms and patterns hung on in the Old World as well as the New. Hard people: durable words.

WASHINGTON, D.C. AUGUST 1914

Beginning of the Great Depression

President Woodrow Wilson holds the hand of his wife and thinks back to their marriage day, in her father's Presbyterian manse. He is not an emotional man, rarely given to tears, but he squeezes her hand so hard that she gasps.

Wilson himself has had at least two minor cerebral strokes in the past ten years, but each time his spine, his Calvinist character, has allowed him to fight back. He admits to no deficit or damage, though he increasingly has difficulty in keeping his spirits up.

His clearest instruction to family and staff as he comforts his dying wife is "Don't tell Mrs. Wilson about the war in Europe."

HOLLYWOOD, CALIFORNIA. 1915

Fine Name (2)

Sean Aloysius O'Feeney, the youngest of thirteen children of an Irish immigrant family from Cape Elizabeth, Maine is wearing a hooded white sheet, and is following closely behind two men who are bearing a burning cross. They are on their way to burn out some uppity blacks and protect the honour of the American South.

Jack Ford: that's his name now and in a few years he will change it again: to John Ford.

Right now he is doing a bit part in the perversely brilliant *Birth of a Nation*. Within two years he will be directing his own features.

Choose your favourite: *Drums along the Mohawk, Young Mr. Lincoln, The Grapes of Wrath*, or half a dozen other brilliant essays. John Ford was teaching Americans how to see themselves – and occasionally (as in *The Informer* and *The Last Hurrah*), how to view the Irish.

QUEEN'S, NEW YORK. 1916

Irish Revolutionary

Almost all creditable Irish revolutionaries spent some time in prison, but their sentences usually bore no relationship to their significance.

The most influential of all American-Irish revolutionaries spends her time in the Queen's County Penitentiary. For thirty days.

She had coined the term *birth control* and in Brooklyn had set up the first family planning clinic in America. She campaigned for the legalization of contraception. Holy Mother Church went mad, as did the less sophisticated of the Protestant denominations. (The Episcopalians were on the way to a worldwide acceptance of contraception, in 1928, but they were the educated elite.)

Margaret Higgins Sanger serves her jail time in the fashion of the leading twentieth-century Irish rebels: she sets up classes and teaches. She comes of an Irish family of eleven who had migrated to the USA by way of Canada. The family was no less Irish for the mother's being a devoted mass-goer and her father a stubborn atheist.

Of course she's a sinner, everyone agrees on that. She's divorced; she sends dirty ideas through the mail (such as *What Every Woman Should Know*, 1917); she is one of the founders of Planned Parenthood (1942), and worst of all, she refuses to accept the church's doctrine that sexual activity must always be part of procreation.

More than any brigade of revolutionary gunmen even dreamed of, Margaret Sanger changes the lives of Irish people all around the world.

THE USA. 1916-22

The Hardly United Front

Most American-Irish Catholics were mildly in favour of independence for Ireland, or at minimum, Home Rule, but they had lives to lead and church and family to attend to. In contrast, a politicized minority cared more about Ireland's future than about almost anything else and they filled the air with energy and, equally, with rancour.

Even at a distance of decades it's like looking at a dust cloud. Most politically-involved American-Irish nationalists, though usually attached to the Democratic Party, disliked Woodrow Wilson. In the cases of Daniel E. Cohalan, the Grand Sachem of the Tammany Society and of John Devoy, longtime head of the physical-force nationalists, the hatred was personal. The most active of the American-Irish nationalists hoped for a German victory in the World War and did everything they could to keep America out. President Wilson called them disloyal "hyphenates." The Third International Irish Race Convention met in Philadelphia in 1918 and demanded that the right of national self-determination be applied by Wilson to the Irish in any peace negotiations. He refused. Meanwhile, the U.S. was crisscrossed by political activists from Ireland, many of whom were not speaking to each other, and some, such as Eamon de Valera, who were at daggers-drawn with the American leaders such as Devoy and Cohalan. Then, in December 1921, the Anglo-Irish Treaty was signed and the activists got down to really denouncing each other.

PARK ROAD, NORTH CAROLINA. 7 NOVEMBER 1918

King David's Royal Line

Not many women are capable of quoting the entire sixteenth chapter of the Book of Revelation during childbirth, but the mother of the not-yet-emergent Billy Graham could, and did. She found the sanguinary Opening of the Seven Vials of the Wrath of God to be comforting. Whatever pain she was undergoing now was nothing compared to what the unrighteous of the world would experience when the Almighty truly righted the world.

The birthing was at home, the normal place at the time, even for well-off dairy farmers like the Grahams. The hired hands who hand-milked the dairy herd could hear Mrs. Graham quoting her way through labour and they were impressed. Truly, she was one of God's chosen.

Though he learned his farming from his father, Billy's mother was the real force in his religious life. The Graham side of the family was Scottish by heritage and the Coffey side (the maternal line) was Irish. The family belonged to a small denomination of Presbyterian schismatics, but what counted was that Mother Graham also was in fellowship with the Plymouth Brethren. So, as he learned to read and then to quote scripture, Mrs. Graham gave Billy a spiritual baptism in the doctrines of John Nelson Darby. She spent so much of her own time working out the Dispensations in the Book of Revelation that she hardly lived in the present world. And Billy, throughout his later life, holds on to his mother's vision: when preaching to largely unchurched audiences, he skips the complicated details so that they get the main message – Jesus is Coming Back. The complexities of the Secret Rapture and of the Millennium he keeps to himself.

Mother Graham's prayers are answered when Billy decides to attend Bible College and become a preacher. First he enrolls in Bob Jones Bible College, an institution that is among the most racist in the country and is even less keen on sex: students are expelled for holding hands. Billy does not quite fit in. His family has had black workers and he does not think skin colour damns a person. What should he do? God sent a sign. A Plymouth Brethren elder was staying at the Grahams' farm when Billy returned on school vacation and they prayed and talked and they decided he should withdraw from Bob Jones College – a decision that made possible the rest of Billy's successful career. The Bob Jones label would have been toxic.

Billy attends Florida Bible Institute, an interdenominational evangelical place, and there he first meets the Jeremiah of American Fundamentalism. On his annual winter holiday, William Bell Riley spends a week advising these Florida preachers-in-the-making. Young Graham, Riley decides, has all the markings of a real winner.

WICHITA, KANSAS AND WASHINGTON, D.C.
26 SEPTEMBER-19 NOVEMBER 1919

Self-Determination of Small Nations

A tiny blood clot lodges in the right carotid artery of President Woodrow Wilson. Similar cerebral strokes have occurred in the previous five years, but always he has fought back. The toll it has taken is collective and his courage impressive: quietly, with no fanfare, he has retaught himself after each stroke how to maintain his gait while walking, how to pick up items on his desk without dropping them and, above all, how to talk to politicians and reporters without slurring his words. But, oh, the man is so tired.

Wilson has been campaigning for the passage by the U.S. senate of the Treaty of Versailles and, with it, the Covenant of the League of Nations. It is a hard job, because Wilson had not pressed for the self-determination of Ireland at Versailles; many Irish Catholics have deserted the Democratic Party and are working against him.

Now his political flackman, Joe Tumulty, must tell a waiting crowd that the president cannot speak to them, because he has nervous exhaustion.

The presidential train returns to Washington immediately.

This attack is one stroke too many. Wilson is not able to push himelf back yet again from the abyss; yet, neither does he pitch downward: on the edge. When his cabinet meets in his absence, no one is willing to act. The president manages to receive the King and Queen of Belgium, sitting, swathed in blankets, like a beggar on a chilly street. With his force of will gone, the senate of the United States rejects the Versailles Peace Treaty and kills the hope of many small nations: that a League of Nations, with American backing, would protect them against bullying neighbours.

Woodrow Wilson serves out his term and is awarded the Nobel Peace Prize in 1920.

HUDSON'S BAY, 1920–21; THE ARAN ISLANDS, 1933–34

Reel Power

I wonder what The Fool with the picture box want us to do next – shit on a walrus hide? The words were in one of the Inuit languages and the translator told The Fool that his cast wanted to know if he was happy with their work.

One of Robert Flaherty's blessings was that he was a unilingual American-Irishman from Michigan. He had no ear for languages, and never picked up even broken French though it would have helped him a good deal. Tone deaf to aural culture, yet a genius with visual images. Just as well he never twigged that everywhere he worked in his life, the locals referred to him – in Inuktitut, Samoan, Irish Gaelic, Cajun French – as The Fool, the Big Dick, or God's Bastard.

But what power! Flaherty is the ultimate imperialist, for he is able to convince entire cultures that they actually exist, at their heart, the way he arranges them in front of his motion picture camera.

Ask the Big-Dick if he think we shouldn't make this igloo large enough to hold a whale? says Nanook sarcastically. Flaherty has Nanook and his family constructing an igloo bigger than any the Inuit have ever seen. He needs it that large so that his camera will be able to get inside, and then, when it is completed, Flaherty finds that the structure does not provide enough light for photography, so he has it sliced open. *Tell The Fool that we will freeze our asses to the ice if we're forced to live in this thing! All he'll see is me and my family turning into bear bait.* The translator informs Flaherty that Nanook hopes it will not inconvenience the project if he builds a separate smaller structure, one with the sides closed in.

Flaherty agrees. He already has his vision worked out, the same one that runs through all his work: the noble savage overcoming nature. Flaherty pays Nanook to practise hunting techniques long abandoned (real hunting people are very quick to adapt every new technology; no fools, they), and sets up a taut story line.

And Flaherty makes the same bogus documentary, with a different cast, in the Aran Islands. There they call him God's Bastard or, if they are feeling merely descriptive, the Rich Yank. After receiving whiskey and liberal numbers of ten shilling bills, the local women are convinced to pull their skirts up and go sea-bathing, something their priest would have had them excommunicated for, save he was also on the payroll. In his season, God gives us Rich Yanks, the people of the west of Ireland know.

Flaherty nearly kills half a dozen locals in a poxey harpoon hunt for a giant shark, something that never had been done by Aranmen, at least not in the previous millennium. That sequence cost him enough of those lovely ten shilling notes to paper a gable wall.

The terrifying power of *Nanook of the North*, and of *Man of Aran*, is that they replace reality, not just for outsiders, but for people of the culture itself. That is reel imperialism: the ability to capture whole societies from inside.

DIXON, ILLINOIS. 1922

Mixed Marriage, American Style

The first time Ronald Wilson Reagan found his father flat-out drunk on the front porch was also the year that the young man was baptized as a Protestant – in the Christian Church, which was one of the names of the Disciples of Christ founded by the County Antrim clergyman Alexander Campbell in the nineteenth century. And fair enough: both Jack Reagan and Nelle Wilson, his wife, were second-generation Irish, and a mixed couple. They, like so many American-Irish, had come to the USA by way of Canada (if Canadians were an ethnic group – and they're not, eh? – the Canadians would be tallied as the largest ethnic group in the U.S.). When they married in 1910 in a Catholic rectory (no decent church marriages for mixed couples after the Ne Temere decree of 1908), Nelle had not signed the Pledge to give all children of the marriage to the Catholic faith. And in any case, she didn't feel any promise would hold if her husband was piss-drunk half the time.

So, unlike the Old World's pre-1908 tradition of mixed marriages, with the boys following the father's faith and the girls taking the mother's, the Reagans split the two boys: the older brother, John Neill Reagan, was baptized Catholic and followed that path and Ronald Wilson Reagan, Protestant.

Ronald Reagan spent his life doing what, in his time, one was not supposed to do: cash in on being Irish while praying with the Protestants – and believing with the Darbyites that some day some great man might find it his duty to bring on the Apocalypse.

BOSTON HARBOUR. 1923

Romantic Ireland's Truly Dead and Gone

The future godfather of serious Irish scholarship in the USA, John Kelleher, is a young lad on a boat ride with his father. It's a special thing they do some Saturday afternoons when the half-day's work is done. They like watching Boston harbour from the ferry and Mr. Kelleher points out the waterfront landmarks to his son and tells him how they have changed since his own father's time.

Suddenly Mr. Kelleher is clapped on the back by an old crony, a keen American-Irish nationalist.

"Up de Valera!" the man booms. He is on the anti-treaty side in the expanding Irish Civil War.

"Up your ass," replies Mr. Kelleher, who is not pro-treaty, just disgusted with where the last fifty years of the Irish nationalist struggle have arrived.

And so too is most of the American-Irish Catholic population. It had been generally behind some form of Irish nationalism, ranging from Home Rule through full independence. For them, what the civil war in Ireland did was confirm publicly what the Brits and Anglophiles had been saying sneeringly for so long: give the Irish their own government and the first thing they will do is start killing each other.

From 1923 onwards the bulk of American-Irish Catholics withdraw their interest from events in the old homeland. They join the annual St. Patrick's Day ritual and in a few ghettos where several generations of immigrants and their descendants have failed to make it out into the greater American world – South Boston, and parts of Philadelphia and of New York – they still keep the jar on the bar: coins for Irish freedom. But for the majority, Ireland now is a far country, in equal parts quaint, lovely, and embarrassing.

MERIDIAN, MISSISSIPPI. NOVEMBER 1923

Dumb Name; New Game

The lunatically gifted Ulster poet W.R. (Bertie) Rodgers laconically summarized his own life: "I have had a foot in both graves." He meant that, having served as a Presbyterian minister in Loughgall, County Armagh, he found his way into atheism and to a sort-of version of Irish nationalism.

Jimmie Rodgers, a shambling, disarmingly charming country boy was trying to make a point to Billy Terrell, boss of a travelling tent show that worked its way through the south. Jimmie was trying to describe a new sort of music he was making, based in two worlds.

"And what in hell is your 'blue yodelling?'" asked Terrell, and Jimmie really could not explain. Finally in exasperation, Terrell said, "Well, just do it tonight, and pray that it works."

What Jimmie Rodgers was trying to explain was that he was merging the Irish dance and jigging rhythms of Appalachia and the deep south with the lonesome sort of words he had learned working with black railway gangs.

That night Jimmie knocked out a tent-full of his home towners, the hardest audience in the world, and American Country Music came into existence.

LOS ANGELES, CALIFORNIA. 1923

Menagerie

The Church of the Four Square Gospel was billed as the largest church in the world and probably it was, at least if one discounts all those empty cathedrals all over Europe. This one filled every Sunday with worshippers and with the Holy Spirit.

Also, quite a few animals, since the preacher came from a Canadian-Irish farm background.

She had started out near Salford, Ontario as Aimee Elizabeth Kennedy, the daughter of a farmer and part-time Methodist choir master and of a young lass who had been sent by the Salvation Army to nurse the dying Mrs. Kennedy. Soon Mr. Kennedy was a widower and very quickly this forty-four year old farmer married the fourteen-year-old nurse. People talked, but it was legal.

Aimee, the daughter of the union, married young, to an itinerant evangelist from Magherafelt, County Londonderry, and became Aimee Kennedy Semple. He taught her the preaching business. She was good. Then, when Semple died, she married another gentleman (soon to divorce him) and became Aimee Semple MacPherson.

Her brilliant move was to settle in Los Angeles in 1918, just at the time when it was expanding quickly and filling with people from the midwest and south who wanted the security of old time religion. Aimee gave them an evangelicalism based on everyone's having a conversion experience, upon faith-healing, and on giving a lot of money to the Four Square Gospel Church. Her mother, Minnie Kennedy, moved to Los Angeles and took care of counting the cash.

Excellent family values:, but one especially had to admire the animals. For example, at the Easter 1923 service Aimee featured a lamb and herself as shepherdess, an overaged Little Bo Peep, rescuing the animal. Good theatre in front of a crowd of 5,000, and backed by a fourteen-piece orchestra with harp accompaniment, it was especially nice before the traditional lamb dinner many of her congregation favoured for Easter.

On other occasions, her liturgical creativity was equally impressive: such as the macaw used as a prop for Aimee's sermon on the Garden of Eden (unfortunately, the bird had previously been owned by a sailor). And, the new Californians who flocked to her church loved, just adored, her having the surface of the large baptismal covered with floating rose petals.

Alas, in 1927, Aimee Semple MacPherson and her mother, Minnie Kennedy, clash and they obtain their own divorce: an even split of all the church property, investments, and cash.

Aimee was never the same, though she gained some later admiration for putting her church and its resources into voluntary relief work for the poor of the 1930s. When she died in 1944 her chief assets were an aviary and several pet monkeys.

LAWRENCE, MASSACHUSETTS. 1924

Melting Pot

A *Canadien* named Rochefort is elected mayor of Lawrence, Massachusetts, much to the surprise of the Irish who have controlled the town's politics since it was built. Previously the French-Canadians and the Italians and the East Europeans, who had moved in in ever-increasing numbers since the late 1880s, had kept their place.

In fact, it is a mistake. Many Irish voters had assumed that Rochefort was just a strange form of Roche, a common Catholic name in Munster.

But it is not a mistake, really. The Irish Catholics in the U.S.'s east coast cities are realists and they work out ways to bring the new urban immigrant groups into their system. The most revealing sign of the change in Irish-Catholic America is found on the marriage registers. First the Irish intermarry with the Italians, and then with the French-Canadians and then with the eastern Europeans. It's all within the Catholic Church. These marriages may not make grandmother and grandda happy, but it's not as if they are the real mixed marriages that the Catholic Church condemns, the alliances with Protestants and thus with evil.

THE USA. 1924–1965

Family Limitation

After complaining bitterly about the immigration quotas set in the 1920s, American-Irish leaders become strategically silent. They are shamed.

As of May 1924, the quota of migrants from the Irish Free State was limited to 26,431.

The Irish migration flow never came close to filling the quota and in 1929 was reduced to 17,853: which, again was never approached by Irish immigrants, nor the later quota of 18,700 which held until the rules were changed in 1965.

The whole matter was quietly ignored by American-Irish politicians, because no one wanted to broadcast publicly what informed observers well knew: that from the 1920s onwards, most Irish emigrants preferred to go to England, where, for them, life was better and people were much more like those at home than were the Americans.

NR. COOKEVILLE, TENNESSEE. 1925

More Tolerant Every Day

In the one-room schoolhouses outside of Cookeville, the day always starts with the Star Spangled Banner, followed by the pledge of allegiance to the Stars and Stripes and then a poem is recited that is unique to the Putnam County school system.

Considering that the county had almost no blacks (that part of Tennessee was so dirt-poor that the right to own slaves had been merely a theoretical privilege) and none of the children had ever knowingly seen either a Catholic or a Jewish person, the school board's attempt at inculcating toleration was notable. The daily verse affirmed:

We don't hate the nigger,
The Catholic or the Jew.
They can have their own religion.
Same as I and you.

DAYTON, TENNESSEE. 1925

Strategic Absence

William Jennings Bryan, former U.S. secretary of state under Woodrow Wilson and three-time candidate for the presidency, pleaded with William Bell Riley to be present. Riley was a force and Bryan felt the need of support. The case against John T. Scopes, for teaching an account of creation contradicting that found in the Bible, was dangerous.

Bryan believed in the case: *Evolution is a menace to civilization, and thus should not be taught*, but as an experienced warrior he knew that it would be easy to win the case in court yet lose the battle of public opinion. That would break Bryan's heart, for he personally was convinced that *there is more science in the twenty-first verse of the first chapter of Genesis than in all the scientific books in the world.*

He needs Riley, for as head of the World's Christian Fundamentals Association, he has stature: he photographs well, expresses himself clearly, and his presence would have given Bryan a distinguished northerner to refer the reporters to: mostly they clamp onto the scrum of gap-toothed rural preachers who hang around the courthouse and humiliate Bryan half way to his grave.

Riley refuses. He says he has to attend the Northern Baptist Convention which that year is, oh dear, in Seattle.

Not that Riley is against the Scopes trial. Far from it: he had been chiefly responsible for turning the WCFA away from its unwinnable battle with "modernism" in the old-line Protestant churches to the fight against evolution, but he knew, even more than did Bryan, that the Scopes moment was dangerous. First, there was the matter of Clarence Darrow, as canny a defence lawyer as ever existed and a great man with the reporters.

And, more importantly, the Rev. Dr. Riley dared not be asked where his World's Christian Fundamentals Association had acquired the money to put on such an all-star prosecution in a small town in the mid-south. Granted, there had been plenty of small-envelope gifts from convinced fundamentalist working people, but not anywhere near enough. This was the kind of thing a good reporter would suss out. Grass roots donors could not support such a circus. Riley, as head of the WCFA had promised some large donors – J.C. Penney among others – that if they wrote big cheques, he would keep their names out of it.

Whatever else it was, the trial of John T. Scopes was not a hill billy moment in U.S. history. The fundamentalists on one side and the American Civil Liberties Union on the other, had big silent benefactors behind them, the lawyers were the best in the land at show trials, and each side tried the case in the newspapers more than in the courtroom.

The conviction of John T. Scopes was overturned on a technicality.

The law under which he was prosecuted remained on the Tennessee statute books until 1967.

The Happy Warrior

Al Smith – Alfred Emanuel Smith, to be correct – was the decentest man ever to be humiliated in a presidential election. He did not even carry his home state of New York. And, though he was a Catholic, outside the eastern seaboard he garnered barely half the Catholic votes.

Nobody would have beaten Herbert Hoover in the boom times of the late 1920s; and no one could have done worse than Hoover when the bubble burst: he deepened the Depression by his conservative and seemingly heartless parsimony. Al Smith, in contrast, had already tried out as governor of New York many of the New Deal strategies that eventually dig the U.S. out of the economic doldrums.

But why did Catholics outside the big northern industrial cities turn against one of their own? Because he embarrassed them. He simply did not understand America inland of the east coast. He was against Prohibition at a time when middle America was dry. And the funny, vulgar way he talked – his apprenticeship in the Fulton Fish Market never left him – was so, so common. Middle American Catholics hated that. They were respectable in a way that he never could be. They were scrimping to send their children to parochial schools where they were being taught to pronounce their "d"s and "t"s properly and to speak without waving their arms around, and to avoid making a spectacle of themselves, ever.

Poor, decent Al.

KERRVILLE, TEXAS. 1929

Long Tall Mama Blues

Seventeen-year-old Woody Guthrie is in Kerrville to pay homage to one of the few adults he respects – he fears several, but respect is different – Jimmie Rodgers. The best place he knew to do that was the local barber shop. Hanging around those shops was an art. If you weren't having your hair cut or a shave you sat on a long bench with the old boys and listened, mostly, and then picked up on the rhythm of their conversation. Woody, despite being scrawny and undersized and having a head of hair that looked like a ball of steel wool, fit in by knowing his place and then telling short little stories that made the others laugh. So the barber and the old boys let him sit and wait for the moment Rodgers, pride of the town, came in. Jimmie Rodgers had moved to Kerrville and built a mansion in 1929 because he was predisposed to tuberculosis and the dry air helped him. The old boys in the shop explained to Woody things he already knew: that Rodgers sold more records in the south, and particularly in Texas, than anyone ever had. It was genuine people music. Woody nodded, but did not point out that what made Rodgers unique was not that he sang the Old Country way, bleached by the Appalachians and western plains, but that he added chords and rhythms picked up from blacks. That's why his sound was so good.

At that time, Woody was living with his father in Pampa, Texas. Woody was just down, but his father had been there for a couple of years in refuge from Woody's mother, who had poured kerosene over him while he slept and lit it. Years earlier, she may have killed a younger daughter as well, also by fire. And she was just generally crazy and getting worse. It wasn't her fault, Woody's Da told him one night. It's something that runs in my side of the family too. This was one of the few times he and his father talked about ancestry. Woody's biological and cultural bloodlines were pretty blurred: one-sixteenth Creek, one-eighth frontier-lapsed Irish Catholic (name: Maloney, but that was all Woody's dad could remember), and the rest Appalachian Irish and English Protestants. The Guthries were a widely spread Scottish and Irish clan, but this branch had been planters in the far, and least-safe, salients of the Ulster plantation. Although Mr. Guthrie did not know it, in Ireland they had intermarried with the local population and had a wide cousinhood all over America – including eventually Tyrone Guthrie and Tyrone Power, both distant relatives of Woody's though he never knew it. And it's just as well that Mr. Guthrie did not know about the intermarrying with the Catholics – for not only was he a 33rd degree Mason, but a member of the KKK. "Don't worry, son," his Da told Woody at the end of their talk about family. "That disease of ours only takes one individual a generation. And I'm dead certain your poor late sister was the one what had it."

Woody sat on the barber shop bench for three days and there was no sign of the Blue Yodeler. On the fourth day, Woody said, hell, I'm having a haircut and then I'm going back to Pampa. The shop's owner was pleased to have the custom, but when Woody sat in the chair, the barber surveyed the snaked nest of curls, and said, just a minute, and went out back. He returned with a set of sheep shears. This was a standard joke and the old boys on the bench had been waiting for it and when they saw Woody jump out of the chair, they laughed and slapped each other on the back for a full five minutes.

Woody was just settled back in the chair when Jimmie Rodgers appeared. Everyone stood up; he was a very big deal in town. Woody, no fool, politely offered him his place in the chair and Rodgers took it with grace. He asked Woody about himself and when the young man offered to play a little mouth harp music for him he said, sure lad, love to hear it, although listening to young musicians was the last thing he liked to do. Good manners. Woody did a couple of quick dance pieces, just to show that he could play, and then a sad tune of his own making. "Fine tune," pronounced the father of American country music. "If you're equal good with words, you'll be somebody."

HOLLYWOOD, CALIFORNIA. 1932

What's a Nice Convent Girl Like You ...?

The new Catholic gentry of the Irish Free State raised their children to know their superior status. Major Charles O'Sullivan, a County Roscommon gentleman married to a Scottish wife, made certain his daughter Maureen had all the advantages: Sacred Heart convents in Dublin and, for experience, London and Paris. It paid off handsomely. Maureen, a beautiful, refined eighteen-year-old, met the director of John McCormack's film Song of My Heart. Her career was launched.

Fine career, but it had its ups and downs, for during the 1930s and 40s she was forced to spend endless hours hanging around Holly-wood and vines: Maureen O'Sullivan became Jane to Johnny Weissmuller's Tarzan. Fortunately she was good with animals, even Romanian-born Olympic swimmers who did not respond well to verbal commands.

MCALLEN, TEXAS. 1933

Downward Mobility

Mr. Emmett Dunbar explains to his children why the family is in Texas.

Easy enough. Typical American-Irish Protestants, they had rolled, seemingly without pattern, from Pennsylvania through Appalachia and into Oklahoma. That took generations and along the way some found fortune and stopped moving, while others just faded into dis-ease and death.

The Dunbars became Okies.

These people and their counterparts were the rural heart of the International Workers of the World, the much-feared Wobblies.

Emmett Dunbar had been a young man working for the One Big
Union at a time when one never went into a new county without
someone riding shotgun. Literally.

Klan run us off. Some of them same folks you see in church on Sunday. They're pretty brave when they got sheets over their heads.
Nothing but cowards.

We had to sell out, lock, stock, and barrel.

WASHINGTON, D.C. DECEMBER 1937

Position

He was *from* them, but not *of* them.

That distinction, made by Joseph P. Kennedy, was perfectly accurate: he meant that his family came from the same place and same
sort of people as did most American-Irish Catholics – but that he no
longer was part of that ruck.

The closest to the Kennedy family in previous American history
were the Carrolls of Maryland.

Just as Charles Carroll was the only Catholic signer of the Declaration of Independence so, now, Joe Kennedy becomes a unique Catholic. He is named as U.S. ambassador to the United Kingdom. To be the
first Catholic that the U.S. sends to the court of St. James is a singular
honour. Besides, FDR enjoys sending a Catholic who has sired nine
children to deal with the Brits.

The sign of how far Joe Kennedy has moved from his Irish roots is
that he could have been the American representative to Eamon de
Valera's Eire just by snapping his fingers. He had no such desire.

MINNEAPOLIS, MINNESOTA AND ROYAL OAK,
MICHIGAN. 1935–40

Identify the Speaker

Two separate voices, but their codes are interchangeable:
   – Communism, Bolshevism, and Judaism.

- Conspiracies that threaten our Christian civilization.
- Jews predominate at Communist parades.
- *They are always the worst hecklers of decent Americans.*

Both speakers are clergymen. Both have drunk deeply of the mind-destroying chalice that Henry Ford had spread about so widely in the 1920s and 30s, *The Protocols of the Learned Elders of Zion*, a Russian forgery that purported to be the Jewish plan to take over the world. Both are American-Irish and they both are deeply attached to their own version of the Christian faith.

- the so-called *Kristallnacht* was a minor and just punishment to malefactors.

- There is no question in my mind that Hitler was an instrument of God to save Germany and Europe from the Red Beast.

- The Jews of Germany are not being punished for their religion but for their subversion.

- *Communism and Judaism are too closely interwoven for the national health of Germany.*

The voices are those of Father Charles Coughlin and of Dr. William Bell Riley. Coughlin is the best known Catholic voice in America: he has a weekly radio program that draws over a million listeners. And Riley, "America's Great Pulpit Statesman," is one of the three or four most influential Protestants, a group that is converting the failed program of Fundamentalism into the new, more acceptable package called Evangelicalism. These two men are exceptional only in their ability to be heard.

What is more unsettling is that there are so many millions of U.S. citizens who want to hear their message.

Father Coughlin is driven off the air in 1940 by the combined powers of a new diocesan bishop and of a toughened anti-hate code by the Association of American Broadcasters. Just before Coughlin is silenced, the Rev. Dr. Riley gives him this endorsement. *We have heard Father Coughlin often; we have read many of his printed addresses. He represents the Papacy. I represent its exact opposite – the Baptist denomination ... Yet, I say without apology, that of all the men to whom I have listened on the economic questions of the day, I have found more intelligence in this Priest's deliverances, and more evidence of loyalty to true democracy and to constitutional government ... than I have received from any other orator of the hour.*

Nice to know who one's friends are.

LONDON. OCTOBER 1938

Family Loyalty

Ambassador Joseph Kennedy had cleared his speech with the State Department. Still, trouble.

Kennedy was the first U.S. ambassador to the United Kingdom invited to speak at the Navy League's annual Trafalgar Day dinner. This was not an audience apt to be keen on Kennedy's strong support for Appeasement in general and Neville Chamberlain in particular.

It is true that the democratic and dictator countries have important and fundamental divergencies of outlook, which in certain areas go deeper than politics. Ambassador Kennedy hears the shuffling of chairs and the clearing of throats that indicate that his audience, mostly a bunch of grumpy old men, is becoming grumpier, quickly. *But there is simply no sense, common or otherwise, in letting these differences grow into unrelenting antagonisms. After all, we have to live together in the same world ...* Kennedy glares at his audience in an outright challenge ... *we have to live together in the same world whether we like it or not.*

In the U.S., Kennedy is criticized for being too pro-British in his view of foreign policy. He is comforted to receive a letter from his son Jack, who is starting his junior year at Harvard College. *While it seemed to be unpopular with the Jews etc, [the speech] was considered to be very good by everyone who wasn't bitterly anti-Fascist.*

NEW YORK CITY. 1940

Authenticity

"Just listen to this guy and you'll know he's the real thing." Alan Lomax, son of John Lomax, banker and extraordinary collector of American western music, was trying to sell Woody Guthrie to Lee Hayes, who needed a co-writer in producing worker-and-farmer songs – proletarian ballads – of the sort that Tin Pan Alley would buy.

"He's special?"

Lomax, only twenty-two, was assistant director of the Smithsonian Museum's folksong section. He already had taken Guthrie to Washington, D.C. for a long session. "Pure Gold. He's the best of the entire bunch – he's the American frontier's greatest balladeer."

"He a member?"

"Yes. Strong on the Party."

"Have any musical taste?"

"Only in patches. Dislikes Burl Ives and he absolutely detests 'God Bless America.'"

"All right." Hayes was beginning to be interested. "But I want to see him first."

"No problem there."

"And his wife. And his kids if he's got any. That's how I'll be sure he's authentic."

Woody, who was organizing for the CIO in California didn't mind the drive east. He crossed the country several times a year. As instructed by Lomax, he picked up his wife and children along the way. They all stayed in an apartment Hayes shared with an amiable, if overrun, roommate.

"Yes, he's the real thing, and we're working together," Hayes later reported to Lomax.

"How'd you know he was authentic?"

"Well, he could only be a true-blood shitkicker, he smelled so bad. And then there was the wife, not a straight tooth in her mouth. Kept her hands clasped together and looked at the floor all the time as if she was in a school-room. But it was those three blond kids."

"Authentic?"

"Completely. They spent most of their time flushing the toilet. That to them was a new and magical experience."

"You're kidding?"

"No. Never saw kids so fascinated."

SAN BERNARDINO, CALIFORNIA. 1940

Revenge of the Potato People?

Granted, it took the two McDonald brothers, Richard and Maurice (usually called "Mac") a few years to get their new restaurant idea worked out. Barbecue: that's what they tried at first, and waitresses on roller skates. Nice little business, but people moved in and out too slowly. Old boys could suck on those spareribs forever.

The McDonalds' parents were both Irish immigrants and the one thing mother's cooking had taught the lads was that, when in doubt, do something with potatoes. They decide to serve nothing but French fried potatoes, hamburgers, and to only use disposable plates and throwaway cutlery. Just drive, or even walk, up to a window, order, and you'd get food: fast food, actually.

By the mid-1950s they have twenty franchises and sell their equity in the industry they have invented to a real promoter, Ray Kroc.

The rest is medical history.

HOLLYWOOD, CALIFORNIA. 1940

Win One of Two

To be cast as the legendary George Gipp of Notre Dame in "Knute Rockne – All-American" was a career-making break for Ronald Reagan. Doubly lucky, because he was given one of the best deathbed scenes in any sports movie, ever. *Someday, when the team's up against it, breaks are beating the boys, ask them to go in there with all they've got and win one for the Gipper.*

On the basis of the rough print of this classic, Reagan is offered the second-star role in *The Sante Fe Trail*, something of an Irish production: the Australian-Irish swashbuckler Errol Flynn was signed to play the confederate general Jeb Stuart. Second billing had been offered to John Wayne (né Marion Morrison, son of a Cork woman), but he reckoned that Flynn would have all the good lines and most of the heroic action.

So Ronald Reagan is given his second big film break: he plays Jeb Stuart's foil – George Armstrong Custer. He doesn't talk about that picture much.

WASHINGTON, D.C. 1945–54

Open Season

For many Irishmen and a few women, the House Commitee on Un-American Activities and the Senate Committee on Government Operations were very good for their careers: Congressman Richard Nixon, who parlayed his anti-Communism into the vice-presidency of the U.S.; Senator Joseph McCarthy who for a time was generally recognized as the second most powerful person in the United States; Ronald Reagan, who was a fine witness and showed himself to have the political skills to play in the big leagues; Jean Kerr, the committee staffer and former beauty queen who married Senator McCarthy; and Robert Kennedy, who served as assistant counsel for McCarthy's senatorial Permanent Investigation Subcommitee and who at first followed McCarthy with zealous abandon and later turned on him and wrote the minority report condemning McCarthy's attacks on the U.S. army. All did well in their own way.

The McCarthy era is remembered too clearly to be remembered well – who can forget the newsreels of McCarthy in 1953–54, ill-shaven, heavily medicated, barely coherent, railing at witnesses? Or his chimerical lists – never shown to the public – of hundreds of State Department or Defense employees who were Red agents. The guy was crazy, we say, and try to forget the whole shabby era.

There was something there, and not Commies-under-the-bed. The McCarthy era in its purest form was the revenge of the graduates of Fordham and Marquette and a hundred other Catholic colleges on the alumni of Yale and Princeton and the other eastern citadels of privilege. For the first time, ethnic groups that think they are still being treated as merely second-tier (and especially the Irish) have the chance to stick the boot into what they believe is the old WASP establishment: the State Department, ring-knocking West Pointers, journalists who are too liberal and sneer at religion and patriotism, lawyers in old-line firms who don't employ Catholics. And, come to think of it, having a bash at the Jews who run the entertainment industry is not such a bad idea. It all comes together at the end of a major war where the participation and heroism of the second-tier has been every bit as high as that of the elite – and the elite had held the glory jobs, such as the OSS, while the Irish were platoon leaders with life expectancies of six months.

McCarthyism was wrong, but it was not crazy, except in the specific sense that Joe McCarthy was stark raving mad. But if a nation follows a lunatic, what does it say about the nation?

MINNEAPOLIS, MINNESOTA. 1946–52

Passing the Mantle?

This, in later life, is Dr. Billy Graham's considered judgement concerning Dr. William Bell Riley. *For more than forty years, he had pastored First Baptist Church, a large church in downtown Minneapolis, making it one of the great preaching stations of the Midwest.* Graham, who had met Riley briefly in the late 1930s when he was a student at the Florida Bible Institue, had more recently impressed the now-patriarchal leader of conservative Protestantism. They had shared a pulpit in February 1945, when Graham was just making a stir with his Youth for Christ work. The biggest Youth for Christ operation in the USA was in Minneapolis and that night, Graham and Riley brought forty-four young people out of their seats to dedicate their lives to Christ and to whatever else they might later turn, through proper training.

He was an intellectual, a deep student of the Bible, and a man who spoke with authority and had the respect of liberals and fundamentalists alike. Riley had one problem: he required a spiritual heir. Graham already had learned a lot from Riley's preaching style, which, oratorically florid though Billy's was, followed Riley's example of avoiding the circus excesses like those of Billy Sunday or Aimee Semple MacPherson. The white-haired patriarch had in 1941 resigned his pastorate of First Baptist Church in Minneapolis, but he still ran Northwestern Bible School (and seminary and college, depending on his mood) from that church's capacious parish hall. Billy arrived in Minneapolis in mid-1946 and, after thanking God for helping his team to avoid a near-miss plane incident, preached to the Northwestern Bible School students at a conference on fundamentalist ideas. In private, Dr. Riley told Graham, "Billy, I have chosen you to be my successor."

In vigorous contention with his denomination, then called the Northern Baptist Convention, he battled theological liberalism on many fronts including the educational. Riley and Graham shared the same Darbyite beliefs, that is, County Wicklow Dispensationalism: Jesus will come again; there will be a Secret Rapture of the Church; and Armageddon; and the Millennium. The only difference was that Graham, who was aiming at a larger, younger, less pre-sold audience than Riley, makes the details fairly muddy.

Billy already has the outline for the single sermon he preaches during his long career: world-events-are-threatening-and-are-a-sure-sign-of-JESUSCOMINGAGAIN.

The two preachers get along, in part because they are part of the freemasonry of Irish Protestant theologues and can talk privately about ground-assumptions they cannot ever discuss publicly. "Always milk the Plymouth Brethren; that's what old Dr. Ironside taught me," says Graham, and Riley crackles out a laugh. "And go for the Disciples of Christ, the Campbellites," is his addendum, thus adding Antrim to Wicklow. "You're smart, Billy, to have been ordained Southern Baptist.

That's where the future is. The Presbyterians and Methodists are dropping like flies. Some day, mark my words, the Southern Baptists will be
the only real American Protestants left. Of course they will be in partial
Error." This latter judgement Riley made about quite a few groups.

*William Jennings Bryan was reported to have called him "the greatest
Christian statesman in the American pulpit."* A bit more than a year later,
in August 1947, Billy, who was speaking at a Northwestern Bible
School conference, was summoned to Dr. Riley's bedside. Lying prone,
the old man seemed to levitate, and he said something to Graham that
had a power that went back beyond Christianity. Trouble is, Billy never
remembers it quite right, but then Moses had the same problem on occasion. Either the Rev. Dr. W.B. Riley quotes I Kings 19:19, *So [Elijah] departed thence and found Elisha, the son of Shaphat, who was plowing with
twelve yoke of oxen before him and he with the twelfth; and Elijah passed by
him and cast his mantle upon him.* That version is a touch too rural and
casual (what if the mantle had missed and fallen to earth?) and Billy
also remembers an alternative version, with Riley pointing a bony,
quivering figure at the young evangelist and saying, in paraphrase of I
and II Samuel, *Beloved, as Samuel appointed David King of Israel, so I appoint you head of these schools. I'll meet you at the judgment seat of Christ
with them.* The splendid drama of this second version is slightly under-
cut by Billy's training in the scriptures: he remembers that Samuel had
first appointed King Saul and that had not worked out too well.

All this ends back on earth: Billy Graham agrees to be a vice-presi-
dent of Northwestern Bible Schools and to take over, at least for a
time, if Dr. Riley dies.

Riley dies in December 1947 and soon the Rev. Billy Graham, not
yet aged thirty, is being billed as "the Youngest College President in
America."

The Old Irish Meet the New Irish

Judge Harold Kennedy ran a dignified and firm court. A model:
hadn't even the archbishop recognized this and sent his chancellor
down to observe and to see if there were things that could be
learned from Judge Kennedy that could be applied to his own ecclesiastical court? Judge Kennedy treated his courtroom as if it were a

church and was unbending with the court staff. They had to keep
the place spotless – never mind some silly union rules that laid out
job-demarcations: keep the bench and the seats polished and the
windows clean. Kennedy recessed the court more often than most
judges did and went to his chambers and washed his hands and
checked his white French cuffs. Purity counted.

The judge was one of the new Irish in America: a descendant of
post-Famine Catholics, he was a part of the new establishment.

Judge Kennedy hated to see trash in his court, whether it be a piece
of litter or a morally reprehensible human being. He was a patriotic
American and knew that immorality and everyday slackness threatened the nation. Vigilance was the price of freedom and he did his
best to be vigilant.

So, Woody Guthrie was in trouble the moment, two years earlier,
he had entered Judge Kennedy's court. Guthrie represented the old
American-Irish, in the same way the judge represented the new: he
came from Protestant border-planters in Ulster who had kicked
around the back-country of America forever and had as a group
never made good. The Ulster-Irish of America were now the poorest,
least-educated, lowest-status white social group in the country.

Judge Harold Kennedy saw before his bench not an ethnic specimen, but a piece of litter. Woody Guthrie was tiny. Badly bred in the
literal sense, the judge noted. Hair on him that was tangled and thick
and woolly as a Corriedale, though the judge, never having been
west of the Hudson River, did not know the name of any animal
breeds, so he just settled for "sheep" in his notes. Nicotine stains on
one hand and strangely calloused fingers. And what was this creature
here for, in my pristine court?

For writing dirty letters to decent women.

Worse yet, the man admitted it quite without shame.

And his lawyer claimed that, as Guthrie was a major American writer
of songs, this constituted protected creative expression under the U.S.
constitution; his erotic letters, which, as the judge would see, read like
music: almost as if they were drafts for songs. That argument lasted about
four minutes with Judge Kennedy, who knew that protecting the virtue of
women from indecency was of a higher priority than any such creativity.

In fact, beginning when he was in the military, Woody had been writing sexy letters to lots of women and these notes had gotten riper as time
went on. Mostly the women liked it and returned replies, sometimes coy,
sometimes very detailed. He'd explain in the same rolling prose that

made his stage monologues so seductively illogical how he and the lady in question would fit their bodily parts together and what they would do with their extremities and it was all slightly incoherent, but never with a hint of violence. Amiable erotica. And he would not renounce it.

Besides, he said, the letters in the case, and most of the ones he wrote, were to members or former members of the Martha Graham dance company whom he had met through his second wife ("Divorced," Judge Kennedy carefully noted), and these women understood what he was doing when he wrote about the human body, though one hadn't, he admitted, the one who went to the U.S. attorney in California.

This issue hit the panic-spot of Judge Kennedy – and here he was representative perfectly of middle-class American-Irish Catholics of his generation: they carried from the homeland the fear of sexual expression, the terror of "indecency," the equation of sexlessness with virtue and the expression of sexuality with ... with ... filth.

And now Judge Kennedy has to to listen to this ... to this ... filth read out in his own pure courtroom. He recesses this trial even more frequently than he usually does, and scrubs so furiously that he returns each time to the bench with his hands projecting from his starched cuffs like the claws of a boiled lobster.

Finally, after granting every possible adjournment and delay, Judge Kennedy has to deal with the matter definitively. Both he and Woody, in their own ways, understand each other. *My judge can't even say the word, sex, without thinking the word, maniac,* Woody adjudged. And Kennedy, who had studied up on Woody and knew that he was Communist and a dangerous one because of his songs, did his judging too. He gave Guthrie six months' jail time.

As Woody was being led out, Judge Kennedy showed that he had both done his homework and resurrected a sense of irony.

His last words to the prisoner were, "So Long, It's been Good to Know You."

The Privileged – The "X" Again

The Catholic children of Irish background who enter school from 1950 onwards are one of America's groups of big, big winners. Of course they learn to sing "Faith of Our Fathers," and hear the stories of Catholic martyrdoms, but in the outside world they are among the privileged.

By the time these youths reach full adulthood, the Irish Catholics in the USA will be the second-most privileged group in the country. They will have the highest average family income of any Gentile group; they will have the highest educational level of any Gentile ethnic group: on both these measures of success only Jews will surpass them. And they will be in third place, behind Jews and WASPS in the status-level of the jobs they hold. The Catholic Irish have travelled up the "X" of American life so quickly that they have passed their old bêtes noires, the WASPS, even if the old toffee-noses are not ready to admit the fact.

The Catholic Irish, for all their pain in the Famine era, had hit the wave of the American Industrial Revolution just right. And, from within their own culture came two imperatives that helped the second, third and fourth generations to rise so quickly: they saved money more avidly than any other Gentile group and they were willing to sacrifice, deeply, generation after generation, for the education of their children. That's why, by the 1960s, they were among America's big winners: even if they did not wish to hex their luck by talking about it too loudly.

And the other half of the "X" ran downward. The lowest white group – just above African-Americans – was comprised of Irish ethnicity and Protestant religion: in terms of income, education, job-status. Certainly the American-Irish Protestants produced some wealthy individuals and some finely educated minds. But, if one were born American-Irish Protestant in 1950, the odds were that you would spend your life as one of the forgotten proles of America: rural, small-town, poorly skilled, singing songs not about some imaginary foreign land you had never visited, but about being broke, angry, having little hope and acres of fears.

MINNEAPOLIS, MINNESOTA. 1952

Ditching School

Although it was good publicity being called America's Youngest College President, even Billy knew it was a lie. Northwestern Schools really were not a college. They consisted of a Bible school, a "seminary" and a liberal arts college that was unaccredited. Graham's goal was to follow the example of Wheaton College, from which he had gradu-

ated after attending the Florida Bible Institute, and gain state accredi-
tation for the liberal arts program. But he was making scant progress
and lots of the school's backers considered the changing of anything
from the days of Dr. William Bell Riley to be a sacrilege. Besides, Riley
had left a huge mortgage for a new site for the school, on Loring Park,
Minneapolis, and it was Billy's job to pay it off: probably have to
name the new buildings after Riley too.

Most of the time, Graham was on the road, working from city to
city with his increasingly-successful evangelistic crusades.

And he really did not need any publicity from Northwestern
Schools anymore, for in 1949, during the middle of his Los
Angeles crusade, a miracle had occurred: William Randolph
Hearst, owner of the *Los Angeles Examiner* and sixteen other big-
city papers, had put out the word – puff this guy Graham. He was
great copy, incredibly handsome, and made a nice wholesome balance to the murder stories elsewhere on the front page. By mid-
1950, Billy Graham was big-time and he tried to resign from
Northwestern Schools. The board of trustees begged him to recon-
sider, and he did.

He spent more than a year agonizing over his duty, for the man had
a very deep conscience on some matters.

What finally pushed him to put in an irrevocable resignation in
February 1952 was the continued presence of the Grand Dame of
American Fundamentalism, Mrs. Marie Acomb Riley. Although only
the dean of women, the widow of Dr. Riley treated the Schools as if
they were her own plantation.

A strikingly beautiful woman even in late middle age, she had been
Dr. Riley's assistant and mistress in the days when he was married and
producing six children. The two had married rather swiftly after his
wife's death. This was the result of their having been found in the bap-
tistry of the First Baptist Church taking the waters without any vestal
garments on their persons. The individual who discovered them, a
member of the church's board of trustees, recalled that they were not
doing anything observedly carnal, although he noted that Miss Marie
Acomb, a girl with apparently healthy lungs, showed an impressive
ability to keep her head under water, and this gave Dr. Riley un-
doubted satisfaction.

Billy shut the door on Mrs. Riley, on the memory of Dr. William Bell
Riley, and put a whole new face on the Dispensationalism of the
Wicklow Mountain cleric, John Nelson Darby. He brought it all down
from the mountain.

STRATFORD, ONTARIO, AND MINNEAPOLIS,
MINNESOTA. 1952–63

Kindly Giant

By the early 1950s, Tyrone Guthrie can do in the theatre anything he wishes. He is the world's theatrical Director at Large.

In part this is because he has the advantage of being of Ireland without absolutely having to be there – an inestimable privilege in the 1920–1960s.

And he has won his mid-life freedom by combining immense creativity with an almost total innocence about money. Seemingly, he lives in a long gabardine top-coat which, on his lean and long frame, hangs like the poaching coat of an undernourished countryman.

True upper-middle class Protestant: youth in County Monaghan, then Wellington College and St. John's Oxford; frightened of the cultural policies of the Irish Free State, yet deeply patriotic about Ireland in a vague, non-political way. As a young graduate, he becomes the first really professional presenter for the BBC in Belfast and invents what becomes the usual format for day-time talk radio: experts arguing, professors pontificating, preachers thumping, a bit of poetry, a short story, the news, and, when air-time falls dead, the random thoughts of young Tyrone Guthrie. Then, at the end of the decade, after a season directing in the Scottish National Theatre, he joins the BBC in London and proves that serious drama can be produced on radio. This is not his own invention, but he is there at the start of a glorious tradition.

In the fifties, spending more and more time in North America, he reflects. *All my professional life, I had heard theatre people in Britain and America wishing we had repertory theatres such as exist on the continent of Europe.* By then, he had earned the right to spin his dreams into reality: he had in the 1930s been England's leading experimental director; had directed Olivier at the Old Vic, done opera at Sadler's Wells, and for Rudolph Bing directed several operas at the Met in New York. Guthrie could have cashed in: big.

Instead, he dilutes his remunerative work by preaching his gospel of repertory. Mostly, he argues that it is required on cultural grounds – he has encountered hundreds of badly-trained American actors; *some had majored in something called drama at a university which turned out to be 500 miles from any professional theatre – and* therefore sees professional repertory as a necessity. But, more, Guthrie was a softie. He liked actors and sympathized with the basic condition of good-actors-few-jobs. Repertory: *such a system ... would relieve actors, directors, and technicians of the nightmare anxiety about being out of work, would guarantee them not only security but a wide experience, the chance really to develop both as individual craftsmen and as members of a team.* And, from a director's standpoint, he knows that keeping older professionals in the business is crucial. In fact, their scarcity in America was the hardest thing about directing Broadway theatre: *there seem to be hardly any elderly, or even middle-aged, actors and actresses who have never achieved the top of the ladder, but who nonetheless have behind them a lifetime of professional practice and human experience.*

Thus, when in the summer of 1952 he receives a call at Annagh-ma-kerrig from a self-effacing Canadian businessman, with a wild idea, he listens. Yes, in fact, he will do it: he'll start a Shakespeare Festival in Stratford, Ontario and he'll do it for breakfast money. Guthrie has directed *Oedipus Rex* in Hebrew at the Habimah in Tel Aviv and in Swedish in the State Swedish Theatre in Helsinki, Finland (a rather more sombre performance than in Tel Aviv, he noted), so rural Ontario would be easily within his capabilities. And it was. Beginning in a tent for its first year, the Stratford Festival became a permanent and first-rate repertory company. Then, the people of Minneapolis get the message, and Guthrie somehow works them into his schedule.

By 1963, a superb permanent building houses Sir Tyrone's (he was knighted in 1961) Minnesota repertory company.

Having inherited the Annagh-ma-kerrig estate, Guthrie decides that he owes his homeland something. His first effort is sad and shows that being a Protestant with a big house still has its drawbacks. He funds a small factory to make jam, conserves, preserves, marmalades from local produce. Newbliss, the nearest market town, is dying and needs jobs. Life is so slow that dogs sleep in the road. The biggest hazard to life, besides the remaining keen IRA man, are the local bachelor farmers who drive their lightless tractors down high-hedged boreens at night, after having taken a skinful in town. Guthrie wants to change that, especially to keep the young people at home. Unhappily, the science of accounting is beyond Sir Tyrone's grasp. The factory takes several large annual losses before Guthrie reluctantly permits creditors to close it down.

More successfully, Guthrie tailors his Last Will and Testament to fit the inheritance laws of the Irish Republic. He leaves the house and scenic portions of Annagh-ma-kerrig to the Irish nation to be an artists' colony. With canny idealism, Guthrie specifies that it be overseen by a board representing the arts in both the Republic and Northern Ireland. Nice cultural rep. company, really.

THE USA. 1950S AND 60S

Small Stories

As the American-Irish Catholics become on-average substantial and often wealthy, the church profits: new parish halls, new church buildings, and, above all, parish schools, secondary schools, and colleges are expanded and new ones founded. At their best these schools provide a creche-to-heaven system of spiritual training for both laity and potential-religious.

But they are too tight for many.

Helen Vendler, destined to become the most influential poetry critic in the United States, is admitted from her parish high school to Radcliffe College. Her parents resolutely say no. They accept the word of Boston's Cardinal Cushing that studying at Harvard University could only be done *under pain of mortal sin*, for it was a *godless, atheistic secular university*. Vendler, forced to attend Emmanuel College, eventually settles for a Harvard Ph.D.

Because of the money in the Irish Catholic community and because the self-enclosing educational system was well-funded, the 1950s and 60s are the last era when hundreds and hundreds of young men enter the priesthood. They start early, at age fourteen in minor seminaries and by their late twenties, having been cut off from most of the experiences of young men their own age, they are sent into parishes to be spiritual leaders.

The evidence piles up in the form of small stories, each one an individual tragedy.

What is clear, is that in this generation arises within the American church several hundred (thousands, probably, if all the cases were known) priestly child molesters.

Need it have been like that?

HOLLYWOOD, CALIFORNIA. 1957

The Mark of Zorro

"Silence!"

Tyrone Power is about to do a love scene with an Italian actress. The film is *Solomon and Sheba* and it is schlock, but he knows it is pay-back time: for Twentieth Century Fox has just permitted him to complete an A-film, *Witness for the Prosecution*.

"Action!"

For twenty years, Tyrone Power has been the single highest-drawing Hollywood actor, though Gregory Peck and Cary Grant are now pushing ahead of him. Because of Fox's keeping him in the B-film production line for so long, nobody is sure if he really can act. Alone of actors of his box-office power, he has not been nominated for an Oscar. *Witness for the Prosecution* will change all that, Power knows. An intensely proud man, like an ancient Irish king he knows that much worse than dying is to pass into history without memorable deeds, or, even worse than that, to be remembered for ridiculous ones. *Witness* will put that worry to rest forever.

"Christ, cut! Oh shit, get a doctor!"

After forty takes of a scene in *Solomon and Sheba* in which Power has had to carry up and downstairs the voluptuous Miss Gina Lolabrigida, he has a heart attack.

He dies on the set, while his co-star returns to her dressing room and, spying a tray of fruit on her dressing table, immediately demands a box of chocolates.

DUBLIN. 1958

Those in Peril

My goodness the bed was big. And the bathtub was even bigger: it had to be supported by special steel posts.

Having won a second term as senator for Massachusetts, John F. Kennedy and his wife were celebrating by staying in the best suite in Ireland. John and Jacqueline were emotionally closer than they had been for a long time and they know that this may be the last time they have to relax for a long while: Kennedy does not announce his candidacy for the presidency until early 1960, but he is running already, no mistake about that.

They loved the Tonga Suite in the Shelburne. It had been done up in 1953 for Queen Salote of Tonga (who weighed 325 pounds) and her two cooks and entourage, each of whom was built to Tongan regal scale.

Dangerous, however, for someone with serious back problems. The bathtub was so large that if one slipped from a sitting posture, there was no way to gain purchase to rise from the prone position. John fills the tub half-full, thus depleting the Shelburne's hotwater system for the rest of the day, and sits in luxury. Jackie will join him in a moment. And as well it was a short moment: for John Kennedy, reaching behind himself towards the soap dish, slides downwards and under the water. He tries to float, as if in a swiming pool, but his back hurts so much that he can not stay above water long enough to do anything but take quick gulps of air. Jackie, when she sees what is happening, dangles a towel so that he can catch an edge and pull himself up.

The Kennedys leave a very large tip and a sharpish note to the manager suggesting that he do something about that mantrap of a baptismal font.

KISUMU, KENYA. 1960

Large Figures

After Dwight D. Eisenhower staged the first Presidential Prayer Breakfast for Billy Graham, the evangelist had close to at-will access to every U.S. president for the rest of the century.

Except John F. Kennedy.

And no wonder: in 1960, in Kenya during his African crusade, Graham joined his fellow members of the Southern Baptist convention in a statement that no Roman Catholic should be president of the USA. He preached this in several large meetings.

Kennedy remembered.

That resentment Billy could understand.

What Billy pondered with the mystified mien of a large steer trying to figure out how a cattle-gate worked, was why his friend Richard Nixon had refused his endorsement for the highest office in the land.

The fact that Nixon was going to receive the anti-Catholic vote anyway, and that Nixon's declaring himself to be above such sectarian backwardness might win him some liberal votes, never occurred to Graham.

For all of Nixon's life, Billy takes Dick to be a truly spiritual person and cannot conceive of his acting dishonourably, at least not in God's eyes.

LEWISBURG, PENNSYLVANIA. 24 DECEMBER 1962

Restitution

The warden of the Lewisburg Penitentiary receives a telegram from the attorney general of the United States, Robert Kennedy. He is to free Junius Scales, the only person sent to prison during the McCarthy witch-hunts solely for being a member of the Communist Party.

Robert Kennedy, who for a short time was a slasher for the late Joe McCarthy, was making restitution. He had Scales out of prison in time for Christmas dinner.

DALLAS, TEXAS. 21 APRIL 1963

Satan's Choice

I want to go and have a look. That's what Marina Oswald told the Warren Commission her husband had said. He had just been reading an article in the *Dallas Morning News* and it contained a blistering attack that Richard Nixon had made the previous night in Washington, D.C. on Presidents Kennedy and Castro. It was not entirely clear whom Nixon hated more, but he unambiguously demanded a campaign to force The Reds out of Cuba.

Nixon was planning a trip to Dallas.

I am going to go out and find out if there will be an appropriate opportunity …

Lee Harvey Oswald stuffed a .38 revolver in his belt, buttoned his jacket, and went out.

Richard Nixon did not visit Dallas until 20 November 1963 and by then Oswald had decided on a different target.

THE PHOENIX PARK, DUBLIN. 28 JUNE 1963

Seed Time and Harvest

When President and Mrs. Kennedy visited President and Mrs. de Valera at Arás an Uachtaráin, it was more than a mere courtesy call. The oldest international human icon of Irish heritage was being visited by the youngest.

To mark the event, the American president planted a tree beside the now-mature specimen that Queen Victoria had planted during the Great Famine as a symbol of Ireland's rebirth-to-come.

The Irish newspapers were forbidden by the government to print the news that Kennedy's tree soon died.

DALLAS, TEXAS. 22 NOVEMBER 1963

Beyond Explanation

True tragedy can never be explained, merely observed; over and over again.

That is why the Warren Commission, the in-house FBI and CIA investigations and the thousands of books on the assassination of John Fitzgerald Kennedy are otiose. They would have been unsuccessful even if they were successful.

Much later, an English essayist, Amanda Foreman, using internet dross, produces the most sensible discussion of the event by drawing parallels and contrarities as between Kennedy and Lincoln:

Lincoln: elected to congress 1846
Kennedy: elected to congress 1946
Lincoln: became president 1861
Kennedy: became president 1961
Lincoln: shot on a Friday
Kennedy: shot on a Friday
Lincoln: succeeded by a man named Johnson, born 1808
Kennedy: succeeded by a man named Johnson, born 1908

And more and more. The point of course is that for some things there is no satisfying explanation. Cause-and-effect in the sense used by historians and lawyers becomes evanescent and eventually invisible.

Only pattern remains, the product of the eye of each observer.

WASHINGTON, D.C. 25 NOVEMBER 1963

Class

Jacqueline Kennedy had placed the wife of the Anglophile Paul Mellon in charge of the White House Rose Garden. Mrs. Mellon was an expert horticulturalist, but it nevertheless was a gracious gesture by the Kennedy family. Thomas Mellon, founder of the Mellon banking family, had emigrated from a small holding in County Tyrone to Pittsburgh in 1818. He was well-known not merely for his wealth but for his sectarianism. The Catholics, he said, were "a class trained to a vicious disregard of law and order," and later Mellons had diluted, but not abandoned, their disdain of Irish Catholics.

All that is sealed as forgotten: Jacqueline Kennedy asks Mrs. Mellon to arrange the flowers for the late president's funeral.

EAST WHITTIER, CALIFORNIA. 3 OCTOBER 1967

Solace

Dick and Billy were close, so it was only natural that the evangelist should give a eulogy at the burial of Nixon's mother and comfort him at the graveside. And the man was odds-on to be the next president of the United States.

Hannah Nixon, a deep-dish Quaker, had met Billy Graham in 1949 at one of his crusades, two years before he encountered her son Richard. She was one tough lady, but that is not the sort of thing one says at a funeral.

Indeed, Billy had winced when a local pastor had, as his part of the service, compared Hannah Nixon to the biblical Hannah, one of the two wives of Elkanah. Barren, she had promised to God if she conceived, the child would be dedicated to serving the Almighty.

Unlike the local preacher, Dr. Graham knew his Bible very well. The song of praise that the scriptural Hannah eventually sings in gratitude is actually the text that underpins the Magnificat of the Virgin Mary, something that Graham's branch of Protestantism considers misleading and apt to lead to superstitious veneration of the Blessed Virgin Mary.

Worse, Graham of course knows who Hannah's son was: Samuel: a great leader of the Chosen People, certainly. But his greatest achievement was in his aiding the destruction of his nation's political structure and in abetting its replacement with a monarchy.

For his friend Dick's sake, Billy hopes that the journalists who cover the event do not know their Bible.

QUEEN'S, NEW YORK CITY. 3 OCTOBER 1967

This Land Ain't My Land

He came to Creedmoor State Mental Hospital by inches, and the trip took a decade or more. No one knows when it began. His rambling monologues that always led to a punchline now just rambled. Slurred speech, mostly put down to his heavy drinking. Labile emotions. Increasingly bad temper. Periods of childlike dependence. Minor violence followed by heavy remorse. Sloughs of depression. Bouts of high-energy and immense creativity. Disinhibition. Hands up waitresses' skirts in cafés. Notebooks full of erotic letters to women that now, after his jail-time, he never sent. Logophilia: this the kinder side of his form of Huntingdon's disease, for he produced a massive number of lyrics: until his hands failed him and the pen jumped up and down between the lines without his being able to control it. Until his voice failed him.

Those were the external signs of Woody Guthrie's suffering. Beyond imagining is what it was like inside his mind; what it was to suddenly go dizzy and then, when that stopped, to have his thoughts swirl so quickly that he wished he were back to being dizzy; what it was to be at the mercy of sights that appeared and then left of their own choosing and could not be controlled. They came so often that reality, when it appeared, was only another hallucination; how did a man who always had done what he pleased feel when he found he had the will to do nothing?

Creedmoor Hospital was the right place for him, but its staff could do little more than keep him clean and see that he did not hurt himself.

Near the end, he had a moment of lucidity and it coincided with the arrival of a transcription of his son Arlo's anti-Vietnam war song, "Alice's Restaurant." Woody listened to himself, for Arlo did his father's act perfectly, a seemingly shambling story that contained some tight musical lyrics and a sharp political message. Except, unlike

Woody's political material, it was, damn it, charming. How'd the kid ever figure out how to write a charming anti-war lyric? Woody smiled, proud of a son who had taken the family business just a little bit farther down the road.

Not long after, 3 October 1967, the gods permitted Woody Guthrie to leave the barred-window world and travel to a land where he could ride ponies all the day long, as in the Oklahoma hills where he was born.

KEY BISCAYNE, FLORIDA. JANUARY 1968

Echoes

With his confidant and bagman, Bebe Rebozo, and with his spiritual advisor, the Rev. Dr. Billy Graham, Richard Nixon spends three days in retreat. He is deciding if he will file for the New Hampshire primary and thus begin another run for the presidency: the office that he knows he would now hold were it not for the wretched Irish Catholics of Cook County, Illinois who had corrupted democracy, stolen votes, and put that goddman adventurer ("Beg your pardon, Billy") and his crooked family in control of the most sacred place in our America. ("All places are sacred, Dick; we serve God wherever we are.")

On the first day of Nixon's retreat, the three men talk religion and politics and Graham reads them parts of the book of Romans. And prays aloud. Several times. The second day, Nixon and Rebozo watch football on television and drink; and on the third, Nixon asks America's Protestant Pope for his judgement.

I think it is your destiny to be President.

THE HOMESTEAD, GREENEVILLE, TENNESSEE.
2 JANUARY 1968

Reverence

The lady is sixty-five years of age and healthy, but she is bent nearly double and looks eighty-five. She likes it that way. Most of the time she dresses in nineteenth-century costumes. This is the last living great-grandchild of President Andrew Johnson: Martha Johnson Patterson

Bartlett. For most of her life, she had lived in the house that the then-congressman Johnson had bought in 1851. She had left the Homestead only in 1958, when the United States Parks Service began to restore the house as a presidential site. Wisely, the service has kept her on as a government employee and she gives tours with a panache that no stranger could match. She re-enacts entire episodes of the Civil War and Reconstruction era in a self-composed one-woman show. Every time she mentions The President, she quickly stands straight and then immediately returns to her habitual bent posture: although the body mechanics are different, this is like Roman and Anglo-Catholics genuflecting before the altar. Thousands of school children witness her performance each year and they go away with the clear impression that Andrew Johnson was, if not America's greatest president, very close.

So devoutly does the widow Mrs. Bartlett reverence Andrew Johnson's memory that she has constructed at her own expense in 1968 a perfect replica of the original house. There, when not giving tours in the original Homestead, she continues to live in the world of the most vilified American politician of the nineteenth century.

THE VATICAN. 29 JULY 1968

Not on This Rock

The Curia's nightmare finally has come alive: the one hinted at by Pope Leo XIII in 1899 when he condemned "Americanization" in the church. And, if anything, it is worse than His Holiness had foreseen, for not only were American Catholics – led by the Irish – becoming insufferably chirpy and self-assertive, but the American-Irish Catholic laity now was better educated in secular matters than were the clergy; and several laymen were as adept at abstruse theological arguments as were the most arcane priestly theologues. Along came John Rock.

Irish on both sides (Rock and Murphy were the family names), with immediate post-Famine roots going back to a County Armagh grandfather who had arrived in Marlborough, Massachussetts. A tailor, he did what so many of his generation did: save, save, saved, and bought property and passed it on to his heirs, and they, in turn, transformed the property into more wealth and, crucially, into education for their children. So Irish.

John Rock graduated from Harvard College in the class of 1915 and went on to Harvard Medical School. His Harvard education in no way shook his faith: it deepened it. Along the way, however, he picked up that terribly corrosive American concept of private conscience: do what the inner voice says is right.

By 1950 John Rock is one of the world's experts on human fertility and, perhaps paradoxically, he is a romantic about the sex lives of men and women (he is virtually a poet on the joys of physical intimacy between spouses) and he is not just a practising Catholic, but an expert on dogma. In tandem with his work on human fertility, he masters the Catholic church's immense literature on conception, contra-ception, and related matters.

Rock's breakthrough – The Pill – approved by the Food and Drug Administration of the USA in 1960 revolutionizes human sexual behaviour, worldwide. For Rock, though, the development is a step forward in Catholic moral practice. And he is not being mischievious or insincere when he suggests this, for he is a man of immense Faith. Rock has the high ground. As he argues in a bombshell of a book, *The Time Has Come*, published in 1963, the Vatican had already approved using the Rhythm Method as legitimate. That is, in 1951 the custodians of dogma had finally admitted that sexual relations in a marriage, conducted for purposes other than procreation, were permissable as long as the couple had procreative sex now and again. (Previously, all methods of birth control had been definitively condemned, as recently as 1930.) The Rhythm Method worked according to modern biological knowledge of the monthly period when a woman was sterile. Rock's argument was like that of a good lawyer, arguing upon precedent: if sexual relations were all right during a sterile period in a monthly cycle under the Rhythm Method, they were all right under the sterile period produced by The Pill.

This hit the Vatican at a vulnerable moment. Vatican II was still in session (it continued until 1965) and large ideological shifts were occurring and the Italians in charge of all matters of importance until recently, were losing. Worse yet, Pope John Paul XXIII died in 1963 and was replaced by Pope Paul VI, a very smart ecclesiastical politician. Pope Paul did what smart prime ministers and presidents do the world over – he set up an expert commission, in this case, to report on The Pill and on birth control in general.

Trouble is, the commission was too expert. In mid-1966, the commission submitted its report: medically assisted contraception in certain cases was acceptable.

His Holiness went into shock for two years, consulted in those times only Italian conservatives, and embraced an argument that had nothing to do with human sexuality and everything to do with Papal authority: if The Pill were approved, then the church's 1500-year-old ban on contraception would be reversed and that would show that the Vicar of Christ on Earth was fallible even when speaking on purely dogmatic matters and in magisterium (to use the concepts of the Infallibility Dogma of 1870). Or, as one of the Pope's conservative counselors put it, if the church was wrong about contraception, then God was on the side of the Protestants.

So, totally on his own responsibility, Pope Paul VI in mid1968 banned all forms of artificial birth control in the encyclical *Humanae vitae*.

A big moment in human social history, still being played out throughout the world, and still indeterminate in its demography.

In the USA, however, the results among American-Irish Catholics were definitive. Every survey has shown that they simply decided that they were good Catholics and they were also going to employ birth control: artificial, mostly.

The American-Irish Catholic community had acquired the primary attitude of American Protestantism: that individuals could pick-and-choose what matters of religious belief they wished to accept.

Pope Leo XIII had been right.

RECESSIONAL

Billy Graham's International Presidential Prayer Breakfast

–I wonder how we got here …?

–Me? Took a cab. Walking's just too much trouble these days. All those protestors.

–Well, we made it through 1969.

–And every time I see a sign I have to read it. Then, correct it in my head. Especially the spelling. That's the trouble with being in the print business.

–But we got here.

–One of them spelled out Apart-hate …

–Good phonetics

–Another said: Brits out of Dublin.

–High time, if you ask me.

–High time we had an Irish Pope.

–Really, how'd we get here?

–Oh, yes, I see. I figure I was invited because my secretary was tight with Teddy before his recent underwater driving experiment.

–My invite came from the Leadership Conference. Billy was pretty close to Dr. King and they have a table's worth of tickets set aside.

–Nice you have an Irish name.

–So's half the NBA.

–Kills two birds.

–Good table, you have to admit.

–Good pancakes too.

–Grab the waiter before the coffee disappears.

–Lot better now that all the Big Enchiladas have left. Like a church supper before the Ladies Auxiliary cleans up.

–You filing a story?

–Just the human interest angle. Anything else is off-the-record. Never be invited again.

–Me too: how *did* we get here?

–You know the base line. Saintly Billy sucks up to Ike while he's still in the military. Plays golf with him. Ike pays off when he's elected by attending the first Presidential Prayer Breakfast in 1953 where Billy sells Jesus like he used to sell Fuller Brushes.

–He's smoother now.

–So are Fuller Brushes.

–And pretty soon ...

–Pretty soon we have an annual National Prayer Breakfast and now an International Presidential Prayer Breakfast with half the United Nations' delegations sending their top boys to bend their neck and maybe craw-thump at the Holy Name of Jay-sus.

–All civilization as we gnaw it.

–Entirely. Bit hard on the Jews though.

–Yes. Lieberman looked distinctly uncomfortable.

–Small fish. Big ambition. Wonder how he got on the list? Anyway, Jay-sus was one of theirs.

–Not entirely.

–And Billy's been good on Israel.

–Almost entirely.

–That's why they show. Direct order from Golda Meir.

–That's how *they* got her. What about ...

–Billy wants Israel to burgeon. That's his word, bu-r-g-e-o-n. Then his Jay-sus will come back and kick evil up and down the valley of Megiddo.

–Or is it a plain? Bit hard on the Israelis, I'd say.

–They have Billy sorted out though. Him and Tricky Dick. Israelis know they're peas in a pod on this.

–Really tight with Nixon, isn't he?

–Ever since he was Veep. Play golf. Pray. Crap on the Jews a lot, I'm told.

–Oh?

–You know, love Israel, only democracy in the Middle East and all that, and then make Hymie jokes in private and bitch about Jews running the media and feeding liberal humanism into the school system and being in the pornography industry.

–Not the ones I see. Not much in the way of schlongs and they're missing ...

–No, *behind* the pornography industry.

–Yeh. But Billy's against the old stuff the Jesuits taught you ...

–Christian Brothers actually.

– ... taught you, that the Jews were evil because they killed Jesus.

–Of course. But what have they done for us lately?

–I'm still hungry.

–Grab the waiter. See if he has a Danish for me. Oh, tell him to cut it in half, I can't eat a whole one.

–The other half for me?

–No, I'll take both. Just can't eat a whole Danish.

–Billy surely seems close to Jesus, doesn't he?

–Aren't we all?

–You believe that stuff, that everyone who's ever lived is only six steps removed from Jesus?

–Christ, no. Four max. And, I'd prefer Socrates, or St. Patrick. That's my man.

–So, say we had a string, four or six people, taking you back to St. Patrick. How would you know it was there?

–Wouldn't. Unless you got lucky. Evidence fell at your feet or something.

–Say you did know it was there. Would you feel different, being able to almost touch your Head Mick?

–Yeh … I would. Really.

–You wouldn't worry, maybe, that the whole thing was imaginary?

–You're sounding like a Puritan parson with Doubts.

–Put it another way. Observing anything, anytime, anyplace, past, present future … observing anything changes whatever you're observing. It's the Copenhagen Interpretation.

–Learned that at Howard, did you? Lot in it. A long life in journalism has taught me that if you stare at a congressman in the house men's room, it'll take him forever to take a leak.

–And if you drilled a hole in the wall and waited until he finally …

–Christ on the Cross, what *did* they teach you there? If I waited long enough I'd be so bored, or have such a tight bladder, that I'd write a really pissed-off story. Or none at all.

–Right, so even looking at things from an objective viewpoint …

–If that's what you call a pervert's-hole drilled in a men's room wall …

– … will disturb what you see, even if the disturbance is only within your own head.

–Thanks, Sherlock. On the other hand, any attempt to demonstrate that Truth ain't really true is self-defeating.

–Impressive, isn't it, how sure of things Billy was. About Jesus. And went on, didn't he, about St. Paul?

–Headquarters in Minneapolis, actually …

–The saint. Seems to see himself as the modern St. Paul.

–Well the Cush sees himself as the modern St. Patrick.

–Who's your favourite character in the Bible?

–I'm a Catholic, remember.

–*Roman* Catholic.

–And we didn't read it a lot. But was it ever read *at* us. Selected parts. I'd say my favourite is Joseph of Arimathea.

–Amazing, why?

–His great sense of humour.

–Who's your favourite writer?

–Fiction or non?

–Fiction.

–Arthur Schlesinger.

–Junior?

–There's a senior?

–Was. Nonfiction?

–Oscar Wilde.

–Agree. Truthful. And he understood that there is no such thing as character development. There's only one character in literature and that's the whole human race.

–Yeh. I had to put in ten years at *Reader's Digest* to discover that.

–Except Falstaff of course.

–The beer?

–Kind of. Shakespeare's. Only case of true character development in all of English literature. Everything else is a deceptive motion trick. Like magicians. Look one place, the guy moves when you're not looking. But think you are.

–It's the whole human race.

–Right for once.

–Thanks.

–No human being ever really develops enough to measure. Literature or life. Just changes position in relation to the wallpaper that he's standing in front of.

–Humanity develops, humans don't?

–Spot on. You need the *longue durée* to chart things.

–They really teach you those words at Howard?

–Yes. And concepts. Like that most of your ideas are a pigment of your imagination.

–Easy. No offense meant.

–Yeh. None taken.

–Wonder if Saintly Billy would buy your theory?

–Definitely. Didn't you hear the man? We can do nothing of our own. We're eternally damned. But if we believe. I mean *believe*. Then we're ace. All a gift from God. He just moves the wallpaper behind us and presto, we're in heaven.

–Like an old time photographer with his changeable backgrounds.

–So why *are* we here?

–I'd say Watson and Crick.

–You read Watson's book?

–Just because you're forty years younger doesn't mean I'm totally ignorant.

–No offense meant.

–None taken. But I'd say your long duration has nothing to do with a double helix of proteins or acids or whatever. The real helix is triple, quadruple, more. And it's made up of strands of people and families and communities and tribes and nations and cultures and they all cross each other in a million ways and eventually they make us.

–That's the longest sentence I ever heard you say except when you were up for sentencing.

–I should have pleaded insanity. Woman was crazy to be walking in front of a tavern after dark.

–Doesn't help much to get the story clear to say we're the product of everything. Messy.

–Ah, young genius, that's why you should read Watson again. You only need to get a single cell of the human being sequenced right and you have the whole animal taped.

–So?

–Same way with civilization. And you and me. Only have to get one culture right and you understand them all.

–I'd avoid the Chinese. Never can remember which is the first name.

–And the Swedes. I'm suicidal and alcoholic already.

–On your theory, I'd go with one or two I like. Irish. And the Jews, maybe. Or maybe the Polynesians.

–Polynesians?

–Yeh. They're like Africans without the tragedy. Go with all three maybe.

–Me, I'd stick with the Micks.

–They're taking up the table linens now. We'd better split.

–Hey, don't you want the answer to your question?

–How'd we get here?

–Contingency.

–No kidding.

–Contingency: you believe in it?

–Sure.

–You believe that contingency could have developed the world in any other way than it did?

–Of course.

–Howard University strikes out again.

–Why ...

–Because if the world had developed at all differently than it did, you and I wouldn't be here.

–Ah?

–And *we are* ... Sorry to tell you this my friend, but you and I guarantee that everybody in this room today, every praying, preying, playing pissant pastor, priest and politician is the inevitable sum product of human history.

–Inevitable?

–Would that it weren't so.

–I don't believe in inevitability.

–Suit yourself. You're looking a little pale.

–I'm going to the men's room.

– Don't miss a valuable opportunity. See if you can find a congressman to watch.

POSTLUDE

To Mr. Don Akenson
Front of Leeds and Lansdowne Townships
Nr. the St. Lawrence River
Upper Canada

1 November 2004

Dear Donald Harman Akenson,

I hope that you receive this letter and that you haven't passed
away since writing your book An Irish History of Civilization. It has
near as many funny spellings as your Surpassing Wonder: The Invention of the Bible and the Talmuds, which, also, I purchased on e-bay.
Many things have come up in my life recently, but I was able to read
your latest effort last night and kept at it right until this morning even
though the light here is not too good. I'm not the educated man that
you are (schooling wise), but I do have a strong grasp of the things
you have written about in your recent book because of my family being Irish for quite a long while.

Now DONALD HARMAN AKENSON, it's o.k. for you to see a lot of the
nobility of the Irish as coming from them being in a line of influence
from the ancient Jews, but what about the Milesians? Everybody forgets them these days. And why do you like Paul as being so Irish and
forget Jesus? You do not seem to have a clue as to what the Christian
Gospels are all about and as for the lost letter of Paul being the basis of
St. Padraig's (St. Patrick to you) Confessio, well, do you think that the
Irish would have been converted to the creed of a man who said, "Let
no man judge you in food or in drink?" (Colossians 2:16) Be serious.

We have an annual Prayer Breakfast here and I can see why you
would make such events the anchor points for your narrative, if that
is what it is. Our Prayer Breakfast raises everyone's spirits and is refreshing even to those of us who have trouble with anger management. If you would be willing, I could possibly show you many
places that you seemingly from what I read in your book have actually very partial understanding of even with your great education.

And before I start, why did you end at 1969 (or so)? We're in a new
millennium, you know. Irish history is not like good port is it? Needs
to sit for thirty years to become ripe. Can't face the Troubles, was that
it? or the Church going all wobbly, especially in the homeland? Or
did something big happen about then that makes that the right place
to drop the curtain?

I only ask.

Well, I admit that you are right to include the Protestants as Irish even though lots of them do not want to be. Whole batches of people I know don't want to be what they are and even bigger bunches of what they are do not want to be in the same room with them. So that's all right. No, where you go wrong is being hard on the Rev. Dr. Billy Graham, a great Christian. My reading through our library loan service tells me that you are right that the Irish part of his background – the Coffey grandfather and especially the Plymouth Brethren-keen mother and the blessed Scofield Bible and sainted Dr. William Bell Riley and Irish Dispensationalism and all that – is at the center (or centre as you would spell it in your foreign way) of his soul, like it is at the heart of American Evangelical Protestantism. But DONALD HARMAN AKENSON he is a Man of God, and so what if he had some secret views on the Jews and was close to President Nixon? Besides, his knowledge of the Way to God and of the Future Path of History, with Armageddon and the Rapture of the True Believers, is shared by millions of great Americans, including Mr. Reagan and George Bush (Jr.) two of the finest presidents of the USA I have ever served under, and both of Irish heritage. (You forget that Dr. Graham saved young Bush one summer weekend in Maine and that is why our Commander-in-Chief is so staunchly biblical in his views.)

I also disagree with the way you arrange things so that it appears that the U.S. of A. is not the centre (ah, fooled you that time) of the Irish world, including especially the Diaspora, as you call it. You seem to think that the surface of a globe has no center and that a man (sorry, person) can stand at any place on it and see an infinite horizon in every direction. Technically true, but try selling that one to my grandfather (R.I.P.) in South Boston. An excellent man, he was, and he never lied except once in his entire life. Like me.

So, DONALD HARMAN AKENSON here is the real point and it agitates me quite, quite a bit to say this, and I will anyway, but I think you have written a very lazy history of civilization, as I spell it and you don't, sometimes. You seem to think (if that is the right word) that every human civilization is like a loop of string and that by twisting and pulling any civilization it becomes the same shape as any other. Nice trick, guy. I mean I do read a lot and you are just involved in the NOAM CHOMSKY LAZYASS BY-PASS – the crazy idea that all the rules of human language are found in every language, so a linguist only has to truly crack one to crack them all. Do you really think we are all the same in some way and that we can learn how we operate as human beings by studying just any bunch of people – I should say, any culture?

The more I think about your book, DONALD HARMAN AKENSON, the madder it makes me. The calendar I have access of says this is nearly Guy Fawkes Day and I bet that suits you just fine. Now that you are safely back in the Old Empire. You might enjoy Lewes in Sussex where they burn both the Pope and Fawkes on the same bonfire. People come from miles.

If you are of a mind to do so, you may write me at the following address. Yes, I am in prison and have been for more than 20 years, and I'm on death row.

In Jesus name,
to his glory
[name and address withheld]

P.S. 1 John 4:11

Index

PERSONAL NAME INDEX: VOLUME 2 (BOOKS 3 & 4)

Acomb, Marie. *See* Riley, Marie
Adams, Phoebe, 146
Aiken, Frank, 433–42
Aitkinson, Thomas, 61–2
Albert, Prince, 157
Alexander of Tunis (earl). *See* Alexander, Harold R. L. G.
Alexander, Harold R. L. G. (first earl), 591–2
Alexander, Lady Alexander (*née* Lady Margaret Bingham), 591–2
Alexander, Mrs. William, 45–6
Allen, William O'Meara, 42, 231
Amis, Kingsley, 569
Amundsen, Roald, 488, 491
Anderson, Sherwood, 569
Aquinas, Saint Thomas, 25

Archdale, E. M., 559
Archdall, Mervyn (1786), 177
Archdall, Mervyn (1882), 176–7
Ardagh, John, 484–5
Arensberg, Conrad, 582–3
Arimathea, Joseph of, 664
Arnold, Thomas, Jr., 193–4
Arthur, Chester A., 372–3
Asquith, Herbert H., 407, 414
Augustine, Saint (of Hippo), 598
Austen, Jane, 199
Axson, Ellen. *See* Wilson, Ellen

Baker, Benjamin, 496–7
Balfour, Edward, 267
Ballance, John, 246–8, 250, 251, 254, 449
Barclay, Tom, 532–3

Barnacle, Nora. *See* Joyce, Nora
Barnum, P. T., 279
Baron Shuttleworth of Gawthorpe. *See* Kay-Shuttleworth, James
Barratt, Michael, 94–5
Barry, Redmond, 165–6, 167–9, 172, 173, 175
Barry, William, 227
Bartlett, Martha Johnson Patterson, 655–6
Barton, Robert, 423–4
Bates, Daisy (*née* O'Dwyer *var:* O'Dwyer-Hunt), 178, 183–4, 454–5
Bates, Jack, 183
Bateson, Gregory, 455
Beaslai, Pieras. *See* Beasley, Pierce
Beasley, Pierce, 533
Beauregard, Pierre, 346
Beelzebub. *See* Satan
Benjamin, George, 300, 304–5, 309–10, 312, 319

Benjamin, Isabella, 310

Bennet, Catherine. *See* Meagher, Catherine

Bentham, Jeremy, 42

Bentley, James F., 137–8

Bentley, Mrs. James F., 137

Bentley, Richard, 296, 297, 301, 312

Bergin, Osborn, 404

Bermingham, Patrick, 154

Best, Clyde, 552–3

Best, George, 552–3

Beveridge, Lord William H., 540–3

Biggar, Francis Joseph, 565–6

"Billy the Kid." *See* Bonny, William (aka "Henry McCarty"; "Kid Antrim")

Bing, Rudolph, 546

Bingham, Lady Margaret. *See* Alexander, Lady Margaret

Birkenhead, first Earl. *See* Smith, Frederick

Birrell, Augustine, 611–12

Blackwood, Frederick T. Hamilton-Temple (first marquis of Dufferin and Ava), 448

Blaine, James Gillespie, 375

Blair, Hazel (*née* Corscaden), 548–9

Blair, Leo, 548

Blair, Tony, 548–9

Blake, Catherine Honoria (*née* Hume), 11–12, 319

Blake, Edward, 319–21

Blake, John Filmore, 378

Blake, John, 493

Blake, William Hume, 11–12, 64, 319

Bolton (first Baron). *See* Orde, Thomas

Bonny, William ("Billy the Kid"), 172, 610–11

Borkheim, Sigisimund, 46

Bourke, Edmund (Captain), 249–50

Bouvier, Jacqueline. *See* Kennedy, Jacqueline

Bowen, George Ferguson, 160, 210, 237–8

Bowen-Colthurst, J. C., 413

Boycott, Charles Cunningham, 53

Boyd, Henry, 80–1

Bracken (Sergeant-Major), 214

Bramble, W. H., 518

Breen, Dan, 419–20, 501

Bremner, Elizabeth (*née* Wilson), 217

Bremner, Robert, 216–17

Brett, James, 447

Bright, John, 111

Brookes, James Hall, 371, 612

Brosnahans, family of, 241–2

Brown, George, 302

Brown, J. MacMillan, 462

Brown, John, 331

Browne, Noel, 594–5

Bruce, Edward, 366

Bruce, John, 298

Brugha, Cathal, 416, 419

Bryan, William Jennings, 629–30, 641

Buchanan, James, 325–6, 330–2

Buck, family of, 446–7

Buck, Peter Henry, 446–7, 453–4, 458–9, 463, 464, 466–7, 470–2, 473–4, 475–7

Bunting, Maj. Edward, 41

Buntline, Ned, 380

Buonaparte, Napoleon, 21

Burke, Edmund, 4–5

Burke, John, 380

Burke, Robert O'Hara, 134, 147, 148, 150–1, 483

Burke, T. H., 106

Burns, Joseph, 192

Burns, Lizzie, 43

Bush, George W., 670

Butler, Maire, 391

Butler, Mrs. Frank ("Annie Oakley"), 380

Butler, Robert, 240

Butler, Samuel, 221–2

Butt, Isaac, 118, 165

Byrne, J. C., 259–60

Byrne, Joseph Charles (bushranger), 169–70, 171, 174

Byrne, Myles (guerrilla), 288
Byrne, Myles Emmet (Lt. Col.), 288–9
Byrne, Timothy Anthony, 277

Cahill, Edward, 575
Cairns, William Wellington, 167
Campbell, Alexander, 624, 640
Campbell, Malcolm, 356
Campbell, Mary. See Schadick, Mary
Canavan, William, 461
Carleton, Hugh Francis, 120–1
Carlisle, James, 293–4
Carlyle, Thomas, 21
Carney, Mary, 251–2
Carroll, Charles, 634
Carroll, family of, 634
Carroll, James (N.Z.), 451, 452–4, 470
Carson, Edward, 68–9, 399, 408, 493, 558
Carson, Kit, 326–7, 381
Casement, Roger, 485–7, 495–6, 516–17
Casey, Patrick J., 492
Cashman, Ike, 302
Castro, Fidel, 651
Catlow, family of, 545
Cavendish, Frederick, 106
Chamberlain, Austen, 423
Chamberlain, Neville, 636

Charles I, 348, 407
Chifley, Ben, 473
Childers, Erskine, 408–9, 434
Chiniguy, Charles, 371–2
Chomsky, Noam, 670
Christian, Fletcher (desc. of Fletcher Christian), 221
Churchill, Randolph, 57–8, 111, 401
Churchill, Winston, 401, 423, 430, 431, 491, 529
Clanwilliam, fourth earl, 233
Cleveland, Frances (née Folsom), 376–8
Cleveland, Oscar Folsom, 376
Cleveland, Ruth ("Baby Ruth"), 378
Cleveland, S. Grover, 335, 374–8
Cobden, Richard, 111
Cody, Isaac, 381
Cody, William ("Buffalo Bill"), 361–2, 370, 379–81
Coffey, Benjamin, 347–8, 670
Coffin, Edward Pine, 4–5
Coghlan, Charles Patrick J., 498–9
Cohalan, Daniel E., 620–1
Colborne, John (first Baron Seaton), 13
Coll, Catherine ("Kate"). See Wheelwright, Catherine

Coll, Ned, 63, 70
Collins, Michael, 418, 421, 423–4, 425–6, 427–31, 432, 434–5, 505, 527, 528–30, 557, 558, 559, 567, 593
Combe, George, 316
Comstock, Bill, 380
Connolly, James, 399–400, 407, 413, 414
Conrad, Joseph. See Korzeniowski, Josef Teodor Konrad
"Conroy, Gabriel," 390–1
"Conroy, Gretta," 390–1
Cook, James (Lieut., Cmder, Capt.), 439
Cooney, Detective (N.Z.), 449
Corbett, Jim, 379
Corby, William, 349–50
Corcoran, Timothy, 559–61
Cordner, William, 162
Corkery, Annie (née Reddy), 238
Corkery, Denis, 238
Corkery, family of, 241
Corscaden, family of, 547–9
Corscaden, Hazel. See Blair, Hazel
Cosgrave, William, 571
Costello, John Aloysius, 592–3, 594–5
Coughlin, Charles, 633–4
Cowan, Serg. (N.Z.), 449

Craddock, James, 334
Craddock, Myles, 334
Craig, James, 557, 564–5, 572
Craigavon, Viscount. *See* Craig, James
Crick, Francis H. C., 665
Croke, Thomas, 234
Cromwell, Oliver, 236, 615
Cronyn, Benjamin, 306, 319
Crosby, Fanny, 335
Cuchulainn, 338
Cullen, family of (Castle Robin), 33
Cullen, John (N.Z.), 449, 457–8
Cullen, Paul, 22, 29, 33–4, 36–7, 38, 40, 45, 78–9, 124, 142, 154, 155, 160–1, 234–5, 272, 273, 308, 352, 367–8, 392, 583, 613
Curtin, John, 473
Curtin, Patrick, 140
Cushing, Richard, 648, 663
Custer, George Armstrong, 362–3, 368–70, 638

Dailey, Simon, 23
Daly, James, 496–7
Daly, Robert, 197
Darby, John Nelson, 338–9, 347, 360, 370–1, 609, 612, 613, 621, 625, 640, 645
Darrow, Clarence, 630

Darwin, Charles, 478
Das, Jatindranath, 501
Daughtey, Turner, 348
David (king), 641
Davies, Jefferson, 344
Davin, Nicholas Flood, 503
Davis, Jefferson, 355
Davitt, Michael, 55, 72, 320, 392
Day, Martin, 204–5
Day, Mary Ann (*née* Garvey), 204–5
De Charbonnel, Armand Francis Marie, 307–8
De Valera, Eamon (*var:* Edmund De Valeros, Edmund De Valera), 61–3, 69–70, 72–3, 407, 412, 414, 417–18, 419, 421, 423–4, 425–7, 428, 429, 430–1, 432, 433–4, 451, 462, 505, 506, 513, 522, 536, 538, 539, 540, 558, 566–7, 569–70, 571, 574–80, 581–2, 583, 586–7, 593, 621, 625, 634, 652
De Valera, Juan Vivion, 61–2
De Valera, Sinead (*née* Ni Fhlanagan), 414, 652
De Valero, George, 61, 414
Deacon, H. R. G., 497
Deane, Thomas, 22
Delaney, James, 449
Delaney, William (Fr.), 392–3

Derby, Lord. *See* Stanley, Edward
Devil, the. *See* Satan
Devoy, John, 620–1
Dickens, Charles, 197, 527
Dillon, Constantine, 192
Dillon, John Blake, 320
Dillon, John, 320, 492
Donnelly, Charles, 506
Donnelly, John, 212
Donnelly, Peter, 543–4
Donoghue, Michael, 212
Dougherty, Daniel, 194
Dougherty, Sarah (*née* Macauley), 192–4
Douglas, James, 428
Douglas, Stephen, 332
Dowling, Brigid. *See* Hitler, Brigid
Doyle, Arthur, 527
Dudley, earl. *See* Humble, William
Duff (farrier-major), 213
Dufferin and Ava, first marquis of. *See* Blackwood, Frederick T.
Duffy, Charles Gavan, 14–15, 118, 141–2, 162–3, 179, 180–1, 343, 350
Dujarier, Alexandre, 145
Dumas, Alexandre, 145
Dunbar, Emmett, 633–4
Durham. *See* Lambton, John George
Dwyer, Michael (guerrilla), 169, 185
Dwyer, the Rev. Dean, 169

Dyer, R. E. D., 497

Eaton, Timothy, 302–3
Edward VII, 488
Edward VIII, 572
Eichmann, Adolf, 586
Eisenhower, Dwight D.,
    650, 661
Elijah (prophet), 641
Eliot, George, 111
Elisha (prophet), 641
Emmet, Robert, 182, 288
Engels, Frederick, 32,
    42, 43, 46–7
Eyre, Arthur, 284
Eyre, Herbert, 284
Eyre, Tyler (née Stew-
    art), 284

Fair, James, 375–6
Farrell, James T., 569
Fawkes, Guy, 671
Featherston, Issac, 189
Fergus, Howard, 518
Figgis, Darrell, 409, 428,
    434–5
Figgis, Mrs. Darrell
    ("Milly"), 434–5
Finn, Edmund, 122–3
Fitzgerald, family of,
    212–13
FitzGerald, James Ed-
    ward, 199–200, 251
Fitzgerald, John Patrick,
    203–4
Fitzgerald, Lord Ed-
    ward, 71
FitzGerald, Nicholas, 165
FitzGibbon, Agnes (née
    Moodie), 299–300, 312

FitzGibbon, Charles,
    299–300, 312
FitzGibbon, Col. James,
    12–13
FitzGibbon, Edmund,
    149–50
FitzGibbon, Gibbon
    Carew, 149
FitzGibbon, James, 299–
    300
Fitzpatrick, Alexander,
    168
Fitzpatrick, Ann, 194–5
Fitzpatrick, Patrick,
    194–5
Fitzpatrick, Tom, 327
Flaherty, Robert, 623–4
Flanagan, Tom, 181
Flynn, Errol, 638
Foley, Denis, 223
Foley, Jane. See Te Kiri
    Karamu, Heni
Folsom, Frances. See
    Cleveland, Frances
Folsom, Oscar, 376
Ford, Henry, 606, 635
Ford, Jack. See Ford,
    John
Ford, John (aka Sean
    Aloysius O'Feeney),
    619
Foreman, Amanda, 652
Foster, Vere, 80–1
Franco, Francisco, 505,
    573
Franklin, John, 260–1
Franklin, Lady Jane,
    269–70
Freeman, Edward, 373
Frizell, William, 447

Fyans, Foster, 133

Gabriel (angel), 219
Gabriel, Mary, 235–6
Gallagher, family of,
    445
Gallagher, Kate. See
    O'Malley, Kate
Gallagher, Thomas, 105
Gallaher, David, 243
Galton, Francis, 184
Gandhi, Mahatma,
    500–1
Garfield, James A., 373
Garrett, Patrick, 610–11
Garvey, John, 216–17
Garvin, James Patrick,
    166
Gaskell, Elizabeth (née
    Stevenson), 91–2, 527
Gately, Martin, 611–12
Gawthorpe, first Lord.
    See Kay-Shuttle-
    worth, James (s. of
    James Kay)
George V, 558, 572, 573
George VI, 477
Geronimo, (Chief), 378
Gibbon, Edward, 203
Gipp, George, 638
Gladstone, W. E., 55,
    57–8, 67, 79, 100, 105–
    6, 108, 112, 232, 285,
    319
Glenny, Henry, 172–3
Glynn, Eugene, 182
Glynn, Patrick McMa-
    hon, 182–3
Godley, Charlotte (née
    Wynne), 199–201

Godley, John Robert, 196–8, 199, 200, 201

Gogarty, Oliver St. John, 432

Gonne, Iseult. *See* Stuart, Iseult

Gonne, Maud, 71–2, 287, 396–7, 507, 513

Goold, James Alipius, 154, 158

Gordon, Charles (of Khartoum), 279

Gore-Booth, Constance. *See* Markievicz, Countess Contance

Gosain, 262

Gosset, Ralph, 442

Goulding, William, 528–9

Gowan, Ogle, 313–15

Graham, Dr. Billy, 347, 621–2, 639–41, 644–5, 650–2, 653–4, 655, 661–6, 670

Graham, family of, 621–2

Graham, Marion, 670

Graham, Martha, 643

Graham, Morrow (*née* Coffey), 621–2

Grant, Cary, 649

Grant, Ulysses, 353, 363, 369, 373

Grattan, Henry, 57

Gray, Charlie, 151

Greeley, Horace, 32

Gregg, John A. F., 528–9

Gregory (Lady) Isabella, 180

Gregory, Herbert E., 472, 477

Greig, J. J., 92–4

Grey, George (gov. S. Australia; New Zealand; Cape Colony), 189, 191–2, 193, 199, 202, 203–4, 210, 234, 237–8, 251, 254, 264–5, 268–9

Griffin, Thomas, 158–9

Griffith, Arthur, 390–1, 417, 423–4, 426, 432, 434, 462

Grogan, Cornelius, 286

Grogan, Ewart Scott, 285–6, 514–15, 608

Grogan, family of, 100

Grogan, Nicholas, 100

Grogan, William, 100

Gudgeon, Walter, 440, 441, 442, 450–1

Guinness, Walter Edward, 510–11

Guthrie, Arlo, 654–5

Guthrie, Hannah (*née* Kirk), 341–2

Guthrie, Thomas, 342

Guthrie, Tyrone, 190, 632, 646–8

Guthrie, Woody, 631–3, 636–7, 642–3, 654

Haggard, Henry Rider, 286

Hall, John, 553

Hall, Roger, 409

Halligan, family of, 535–6

Halpin, Maria, 374–5, 376

Ham, 287

Hammarskjold, Dag, 516

Hancock, Dick, 533

Handy, E. C. S., 472

Hannah (w. of Elkanah), 653

Hannan, Paddy, 181

Harcourt, William, 105–6

Hart, Stephen, 169–70, 174

Hartley, Horatio, 216

Hawthorne, Nathaniel, 85–7, 88

Haye, Tom, 288–9

Haye, William, 288–9

Hayes, Timothy, 140

Healy, Alexander, 367

Healy, James Augustine, 367

Healy, Michael, 367

Healy, Patrick Francis, 367

Heam, Marie, 255

Heaney, Seamus, 595–7

Hearst, William Randolph, 608, 645

Heinrick, Hugh, 101–2

Heke (var: Heke Pokai), Hone Wiremu, 191–2, 222

Hemingway, Ernest, 569

Henderson, Robert H., 274–5

Hennessy, Jack, 224

Henry, Albert Royle, 464, 479

Henry, family of, 463–5

Henry, Geoffrey, 464

Henry, R. M., 533

Hercules, 338
Hickey, Patrick, 449
Hickok, William ("Wild Bill"), 362
Higgins, Henry, 177, 184, 468–9
Higgins, Margaret. *See* Sanger, Margaret
Hill, Christopher, 553
Hiller, Walter Patrick. *See* Hitler, William Patrick
Hincks, Francis, 305–6
Hitler (var: Hiller), William Patrick, 526
Hitler, Adolf, 510, 526, 538, 584, 587, 606, 635
Hitler, Brigid (*née* Dowling), 526
Hodgson, George, 294
Hoover, Herbert, 630–1
Houdini, Harry, 429
Hughes, John J., 124
Humble, William (Lord Dudley), 450
Hungerford, Thomas, 149
Hurst, Geoff, 553
Huxley, Aldous, 71, 184, 194
Huxley, Julian, 194
Hyde, Douglas, 65, 66–7, 398

Ireland, James de Courcey, 244–5
Ironside, Rev. Dr., 640
Ives, Burl, 637

Jackel, Miss, 67

Jefferson, Thomas, 612
Jennings, Patrick, 179
Jesus Christ. *See* Yeshua (Jesus) of Nazareth
Jesus-Tangaroa. *See* Yeshua (Jesus) of Nazareth
John Paul XXIII (Pope), 657
John the Baptist, 220, 413
Johnson, "Galley," 525–6
Johnson, Andrew, 348–9, 354–6, 652, 655–6
Johnson, Eliza (*née* McCardle), 348
Johnson, John, 189
Johnson, Lyndon, 652
Johnson, Maggie (*née* McCoy), 526
Johnson, Mollie (*née* McQuire), 525–6
Jones, Stella, 472
Joy, Francis, 41
Joyce, Gertrude Mary, 470
Joyce, James, 74, 388, 389–90, 392, 402–3, 418, 470, 515, 562, 582
Joyce, Nora (*née* Barnacle), 402
Judas Iscariot, 355

Kane, Charles, 224
Kane, Rev. Dr. R. R., 68
Karira, Sergeant (aka "Creed"), 226–7
Kavanagh, Arthur McMorrough, 50–1

Kavanagh, Patrick, 74
Kavanagh, Walter, 51
Kay, Sir James, 77–8, 90–1
Kay-Shuttleworth, James (first Lord Gawthorpe; s. of James Kay), 90
Kay-Shuttleworth, Sir James. *See* Kay, James
Kearny, Stephen Watts, 327
Kehoe, Fr., 240
Kelleher, family of, 241–2
Kelleher, John, 625–6
Kelleher, Patrick J., 455–6, 474–5
Kelly, Dan, 168, 169–70, 171, 174
Kelly, Jane. *See* Te Kiri Karamu, Heni
Kelly, Michael, 461
Kelly, Mrs. Edward (m. of Ned), 167–9, 172–6
Kelly, Ned, 153, 154–5, 159–60, 161, 168–70, 171, 172–6, 182
Kelly, Patrick Jeremiah, 533–4
Kelly, William Thomas, 222
Kelly, Rev. William, 339
Kennedy, Aimee Elizabeth. *See* MacPherson, Aimee Semple
Kennedy, Bridget (*née* Murphy), 340
Kennedy, family of J. F. Kennedy, 18–19, 339–41, 634

Kennedy, Harold, 641–3
Kennedy, Hugh, 428
Kennedy, Jacqueline
    (née Bouvier; later
    Onassis), 377, 649–50,
    652, 653
Kennedy, J. F., 341, 376,
    636, 649–50, 652
Kennedy, Joseph P., 340,
    634, 636
Kennedy, Michael, 169–
    70
Kennedy, Minnie, 627
Kennedy, Patrick Jo-
    seph, 340
Kennedy, Patrick, 18–
    19, 340
Kennedy, Robert, 639,
    651
Kennedy, Theodore, 661
Keogh, Myles, 369–70
Kephart, Horace, 615–
    18
Kerr, Jean. See McCar-
    thy, Jean
Kettle, Mary (née
    Sheehy), 394–5
Kettle, Tom, 387, 394–5,
    402–3, 404, 410, 414–
    15, 515
Kiernan, Thomas, 586
Kilrain, Jake, 378–9
Kimball, Solon, 582–3
"King Billy." See Will-
    iam III
King, John, 150–1
King, Martin Luther,
    367, 661
King, William Lyon
    Mackenzie, 593

Kipling, Rudyard, 494
Kirk, Hannah. See Guth-
    rie, Hannah
Kirkby, Tobias, 33, 37, 40
Kirwan, Daniel Joseph,
    96–8
Korzeniowski, Josef Te-
    odor Konrad, 495–6
Kroc, Ray, 638
Kruger, Paul, 287, 289

Lalor, James Fintan, 139,
    140, 400
Lalor, Peter, 137–41
Lamb, William (second
    Viscount Melbourne),
    341
Lambton, John George
    (first earl of Durham),
    193
Landsfeld, Countess
    Marie von. See Mon-
    tez, Lola
Larkin, James, 399, 404
Larkin, Michael, 41, 231
Laski, Harold, 184
Law, Andrew Bonar,
    402
Lawless, Captain, 271
Leacock, Stephen, 530
Lee, Anthony, 521
Lee, David, 162
Lee, Mary (née Walsh),
    179–80
Lee, Robert E., 353
Lee, William (Lord
    Plunket), 448
Leiberman, Joseph, 662
Leo XIII (Pope), 165,
    607, 656, 658

Leopold II, (Belgium),
    279, 486–7
Lever, Leslie, 540
Lewis, Sinclair, 569
"Liberator." See O'Con-
    nell, Daniel
Liddle, James, 212
Linahan, Timothy, 245–6
Lincoln, Abraham, 332,
    348, 349, 351, 619, 652
Lind, Jenny, 19
Liston, James, 73
Liston, Sonny, 553
Liszt, Franz, 145
Livingstone, David,
    267–8, 500
Lloyd George, David,
    420, 421, 422–4, 431
Lobengula, King (of the
    Matabele), 279
Lolabrigida, Gina, 649
Lomax, Alan, 636–7
Lomax, John, 636–7
Lonigan, Thomas, 170
Lovell, John, 296, 304
Lucey, Cornelius, 590
Lucifer (archangel), 576
Ludwig I (of Bavaria),
    145
Lynch, Arthur, 493
Lynch, Patrick (Bishop),
    352–3
Lyons, Joseph, 473

MacAmhlaigh, Donal,
    541–2
Macauley, Thomas Bab-
    ington, 263–4
MacBride, Iseult Gonne.
    See Stuart, Iseult

MacBride, John (Sean), 287, 378, 396–7
MacBride, Maud. *See* Gonne, Maud
MacBride, Robert, 520
MacBride, Sean (s. of Maud Gonne), 396–7, 493, 513–14, 520, 593–4, 595
MacDonagh, Thomas, 415
Macdonald, John A., 314
Macdonell, Alexander (Bishop), 294
Macdonell, Alexander (educator), 294
MacEntee, Maire. *See* O'Brien, Maire
MacGill, Patrick, 549–50
MacHale, John, 33
Machiavelli, Niccolo, 181
Mackay, John, 375–6
MacManus, Terence Bellew, 14–15, 93, 117–18, 123–4, 126, 128
MacNeill, Eoin, 406–7, 415, 425
MacNeill, James, 428
MacPherson, Aimee Semple (*née* Aimee Elizabeth Kennedy), 626–7, 640
MacRory, Joseph, 505
MacSwiney, Terence, 501
Magennis, Michael, 511
Maguire, James Rochfort, 260–1, 279–80

Maguire, Julia (*née* Wellesley), 280
Maher, Dennis, 233
Maher, Ellen (*née* Walsh), 232–3
Mahon, Bryan, 416
Makea, Queen (Rarotonga), 246–8, 253, 254
Malachy, Saint, 33, 399
Malinowski, Bronislow, 455
Maloney, family of, 632
Mandela, Nelson, 520
Mangan, Peter, 95–6
Manitou, the, 502–4
Mann, Thomas, 569
Manning, Henry, 79, 111, 184
Manning, John, 140, 231
Mannix, Daniel Patrick, 398, 451–2, 458, 461–2, 527–8, 534
Maraea (aka Pikokau), 222
Maretu, 476
Maretua II, 230
Maretua, 228–30
Markievicz, Countess Constance (*née* Gore-Booth), 419
Marsh, Ellen (*née* Moran), 225
Marsh, George, 225
Martin, John, 248
Marx, Eleanor, 43
Marx, Karl, 32–3, 41–2, 43, 600, 606
Mary (BVM). *See* Miriam

Mason, Francis, 184
Massey, Patrick, 511–12
Massey, William Ferguson, 251, 449, 455, 457–8
Matthews, Julia, 148, 150
Matthews, Richard, 478
Maugham, Somerset, 569
Maunsell, Mrs. Susan, 195–6
Maunsell, Robert, 195–6
Mazzini, Giuseppe, 142
McCafferty, James, 93–4
McCafferty, John, 106
McCardle, Eliza. *See* Johnson, Eliza
McCarthy, Jean (*née* Kerr), 639
McCarthy, Joseph R., 614, 638–9, 651
McCarthy, Justin, 111–12
McCarthy, Margaret, 544–6
McCartney, Fr. (Forkhill), 393–4
McCaw, John, 58–9
McClintock, Commodore (s. of Adm. F. L. McClintock), 500
McClintock, Francis Leopold, 483–4, 500
McClintock, Leopold, 270
McCormack ("Widow McCormack"), 16, 118
McCormack, John, 633
McCoy, Frederick, 151–2

McCoy, Maggie. *See*
Johnson, Maggie
McCracken, Henry Joy,
41
McCracken, Mary
Anne, 40–1, 281
McDonagh, Arthur Ed-
ward, 201
McDonald, Maurice,
637–8
McDonald, Richard,
637–8
McDonald, William,
334
Mcdonell, Thomas, Jr.,
213
McDonough, Mary, 348
McDowell, Betty, 550–1
McGee, Thomas
D'Arcy, 307, 308, 317–
18
McGonagall, William
("the Great"), 71, 335
McIntyre, Thomas, 170
McKee, family of, 460–1
McKinley, William, 608
McKinney, family of
(var: McKinstry),
308–9
McKinney, William Fee,
309
McQuaid, John Charles,
564, 575–8, 579–80,
583–4, 585–6, 589,
594–5
McQuire, Mollie. *See*
Johnson, Mollie
Mead (*var:* Meade),
family of, 518–19
Mead, Giles M., 518

Mead, Margaret, 463,
465–7, 469, 471–2,
473–4, 476, 517–19
Meade, family of, 233
Meade, Herbert, 233–4
Meagher, Catherine (*née*
Bennet), 126
Meagher, Thomas Fran-
cis, 345–6, 350
Meagher, Thomas, 111,
117–18, 120, 125–6,
128, 129
Mears (N.Z. draper),
217
Meir, Golda, 662
Melbourne, Viscount.
See Lamb, William
Mellon, family of, 653
Mellon, Paul, 653
Mellon, Rachel (prev.
Lloyd), 653
Mellon, Thomas, 653
Melville, Herman, 8,
87–8
Menzies, Robert, 473
Metraux, Rhoda, 519
Miles, Nelson, 378
Mill, John Stuart, 42–3
Mills, John, 416
Milner, Alfred, 485
Minchin, Richard, 152
Miriam (m. of Yeshua of
Nazareth), 562–3
Mitchel, John, 9, 23, 118,
119, 121, 125, 128,
129–30, 131–2, 135,
141, 174, 342–4, 346
Mitchell, John, 364
Mitiginya, Chief (of
Usongo), 276

Money, Charles, 212–13
Monson, Henry, 207–8
Monteagle, family of,
409
Montez, Lola, 144–5
Montgomery, Bernard
Law, 509–10
Moodie, Agnes. *See*
FitzGibbon, Agnes
Moodie, Donald, 313
Moodie, family of, 283–
4, 296–8
Moodie, George Ben-
jamin Dunbar, 283–4
Moodie, J. A. Dunbar,
311–13
Moodie, John W. D.,
283, 296–8, 301, 303–
5, 309–13, 318–19
Moodie, Robert, 319
Moodie, Susanna (*née*
Strickland), 296, 299–
302, 303–5, 310–13,
318–19
Moody, Dwight L., 371
Moore, Bobby, 553
Moore, T. E. L., 260
Moore, Thomas, 178
Moorehead, Martha. *See*
Power, Martha
Moran, D. P., 74, 559
Moran, Ellen. *See*
Marsh, Ellen
Moran, Patrick (N.Z.
Bishop), 234–5, 240–1
Moran, Patrick Francis
(Aust. Cardinal), 51–
2, 53, 154, 185, 234
Morant, Breaker, 183
Moreland, John, 260

"Morkan, the Misses," 390

Morrow, Catherine (*née* Treahy), 163

Morrow, James, 163

Morrow, William, 469

Mose, 338, 379

Moses, 293, 313, 338

Moss, Frederick J., 253–5, 440, 441, 442

Moyne, Lord. *See* Guinness, Walter Edward

Msiri, King (Congo), 282

Mulgan, John Alan Edward, 478

Mulgan, John, 243

Murphy, Bridget. *See* Kennedy, Bridget

Murphy, Daniel, 155

Murphy, Frances, 155

Murphy, Humphrey, 224

Murray, Daniel, 10, 293–4

Murray, James Patrick, 164

Murray, John, 197

Nanook, 623–4

Napoleon. *See* Buonaparte, Napoleon

Needham, George C., 360

Newman, John Henry, 29–31, 33–4, 37, 194, 273, 387

Ngata, Apirana, 470–1, 476

Ni Fhlanagan, Sinead. *See* de Valera, Sinead

"Nicaragua." *See* Smyth, Patrick J.

Nicholson, John, 262–3, 264, 266–7, 559

Nightingale, Florence, 542

Nixon, Hanna, 653–4

Nixon, Richard, 638, 650–1, 653–4, 655, 662, 670

Noah, 237

Nolan, Dominic, 467–8

Norway, Arthur, 411–12

Norway, Mrs. Arthur, 412

Nugent, James, 288

Nugent, Robert, 351

O'Dwyer, Daisy May (*var*: O'Dwyer-Hunt). *See* Bates, Daisy

Oakley, Annie. *See* Butler, Mrs. Frank

O'Brian, Patrick, 521–2

O'Brien, Conor Cruise, 513–14, 516–17, 522

O'Brien, Edward, 117

O'Brien, Francis Cruise, 393, 402

O'Brien, H. F., 351

O'Brien, Maire (*née* MacEntee), 522

O'Brien, Michael, 42

O'Brien, Patrick Conor Cruise, 522

O'Brien, William Smith, 15, 111, 117–18, 121–2, 128, 134–5, 196, 197, 200, 231, 343, 344

O'Cahan, Sean, 533

O'Callaghan (Dr.), 159

O'Carroll, Achushla, 444

O'Carroll, Anthony, 444

O'Carroll, Colleen, 444

O'Carroll, Dermot, 444

O'Carroll, Kathleen, 444

O'Carroll, Michael, 444

O'Carroll, Mrs. Patrick (*née* Carrington), 444

O'Carroll, Patrick Joseph Felix Valentine O'Neill, 443–4, 453

O'Carroll, Valentine, 444

O'Ceallaigh, Sean T. *See* O'Kelly, Sean T.

O'Connell, Daniel, 6, 14, 108, 118, 120, 139, 166, 317, 345, 408, 614, 615

O'Connell, Edward, 226

O'Connell, Sarah (*née* Russell), 226

O'Connor (Sub-Inspector), 173

O'Connor, Feargus, 82–5

O'Connor, Rory, 433

O'Connor, Standish, 171

O'Connor, T. P., 106–7, 108–9, 534

O'Doherty, Thomas, 591

O'Donnell y Abreau, Carlos, 605

O'Donnell, Cecelia, 255

O'Donoghue, Patrick Denis, 117–18, 121, 128–9

O'Donovan, Jeremiah, 335–6

O'Duffy, Eoin, 504–6
O'Dwyer, Daisy May (var: O'Dwyer-Hunt). *See* Bates, Daisy
O'Dwyer, Michael, 497
O'Farrell, Henry J., 157–8
O'Farrell, Patrick, 460
O'Farrell, Peter, 158
O'Feeney, Sean Aloysius. *See* Ford, John
O'Gorman, Richard, 346
O'Hern, Margaret, 606
O'Hern, Patrick, 606
O'Hickey, M. P., 397–8
O'Higgins, Kevin, 433, 567
O'Kane, Thaddeus, 159
O'Keefe, David, 239–40
O'Kelly, Sean T., 499
O'Leary, John, 56
O'Loughlin, John, 449
O'Malley, Kate (*née* Gallagher), 445
O'Malley, Michael, 445
O'Neill, John, 356
O'Neill, Terence, 600
O'Neill, William Owen, 605
O'Rahilly, Alfred, 428
Orde, Thomas (first Baron Bolton), 491
Orde-Lees, Thomas Hans, 491, 494–5
O'Reilly, John Boyle, 156, 157
O'Reilly, John Robert, 274
Ormonde, Lady, 52
Osborne, family of, 517–19

Osborne, Roger, 517–18
O'Shea, Dan, 181
O'Shea, Katherine (*née* Wood), 64–5
O'Shea, William, 64–5, 106–7, 109
O'Sullivan, Charles, 633
O'Sullivan, Maureen, 633
Oswald, Lee Harvey, 651
Oswald, Marina, 651

Pa, Queen (Rarotonga), 254
Padraig, Saint. *See* Patrick, Saint
Paisley, Ian R. K., 597–8
Palmerston, Viscount. *See* Temple, Henry John
Papehia, 228–30
Park, Mungo, 149
Parke, T. H., 278–9
Parnell, Charles Stewart, 50, 53, 54, 55, 57–8, 59, 64–5, 106–7, 108–9, 111–12, 177, 178, 234, 280, 419
Parnell, Mrs. Charles Stewart. *See* O'Shea, Katherine
Patrick, Saint, 33, 34–5, 44, 162, 272–3, 357–8, 401, 408, 477–8, 506, 565–6, 580, 615, 669
Paul VI (Pope), 657–8
Paul, Saint, 237, 293, 360, 479, 669
Pearse, Patrick, 411

Peck, Gregory, 649
Peel, Robert, 5, 6–7
Pennefather, Edward, 283
Penney, J. C., 630
Perry, Matthew, 88
Persse, De Burgh Fitz-Patrick, 180
Persse, Isabella Augusta. *See* Gregory, (Lady) Isabella
Persse, Mary, 180
Pierce, Franklin, 85
Pigott, Richard, 108
Pius IX (Pope), 44–5, 78–9, 124, 271, 273–4, 353, 369
Pius X (Pope), 395–6
Plunket, 5th baron. *See* Lee, William
Plunkett, Joseph Mary, 416
Polding, John Bede, 154
Polk, George C., 330
Polk, James K., 325–6, 327–9, 335
Polk, Sarah, 328–9
Pore, Heni. *See* Te Kiri Karamu, Heni
Potter (Martha) Beatrice. *See* Webb, Beatrice
Pound, Ezra, 410–11
Power, Henry, 161
Power, Harold, 342
Power, Martha (*née* Moorehead), 341
Power, Tyrone I, 190, 341–2
Power, Tyrone II, 190, 341–2

Power, Tyrone III, 342, 632, 649

Powers, Tom, 611

Powerscourt, Lady. *See* Wingfield, Theodosia

Pringle, Thomas, 310

Quinn, James, 159

Quinn, Patrick, 171, 175

Radcliffe-Brown, A. R., 455

Raleigh, Walter, 226, 539

Ranfurly, Earl of, 439

Rangi Makea Vakatini, 247

Ratan (var: Ratana), Tahupotiki Wiremu, 220

Reagan, Jack, 624–5

Reagan, John Neill, 625

Reagan, Nelle (*née* Wilson), 624

Reagan, Ronald Wilson, 624–5, 638–9, 670

Rebozo, Bebe, 655

Reddy, Annie. *See* Corkery, Annie

Redman, John, 212

Redmond, John, 177–8, 321, 401, 410, 419, 422, 492, 493

Redmond, William, 177–8

Reeves, William Pember, 250

Reilly, Christopher, 216

Rhodes, Cecil, 279–80, 282, 283–4, 285

Riley, Branson Radish, 347

Riley, John, 329

Riley, Marie (*née* Acomb), 645

Riley, William Bell, 347, 609, 622, 629–30, 634–5, 639–41, 645, 670

Roach ("Mear's Irishman"), 217–18

Robb, Nesca, 537–8

Roberts, George, 402–3

Robertson, Thomas, 294

Robinson, Hercules, 170–1

Roch. *See* Rochefort

Rochefort (mayor), 628

Rock, John, 656–8

Rockefeller, family of, 609

Rodgers, Jimmie, 626, 631–3

Rodgers, W. R. ("Bertie"), 626

Rommel, Erwin, 510

Ronan, Jim, 474

Ronan, Tom, 474

Roosevelt, Theodore, 448, 605, 610–11

Ross, Amanda McKitrick, 70–1

Rua Kanana (*var:* Kenan) Hepetipa, 220, 457–8

Russell, Elizabeth, 311–13

Russell, Jane. *See* Te Kiri Karamu, Heni

Russell, Julia, 311–13

Russell, Lord John, 6, 225

Russell, Sarah. *See* O'Connell, Sarah

Russell, Thomas, 311

Ryan, Edward "Ned," 147

Ryan, George Washington (aka William Ryan), 366

Ryan, John Nagle, 147–8

Ryan, Thomas, 216–17

Ryerson, Adolphus Egerton, 293–5, 307–8

Sadleir, John, 127–8, 134, 148, 173

Salote (Queen of Tonga), 650

Samuel (patriarch), 641, 654

Sanger, Margaret (*née* Higgins), 619–20

Sarsfield, Patrick, 15, 72, 181

Satan, 565

Saul (king), 641

Savage, Michael Joseph, 449, 477–8

Scales, Junius, 651

Scanlon, Michael, 170

Schadick, Julius, 252

Schadick, Mary (*née* Campbell), 252

Schlesinger, Arthur, Jr., 664

Schlesinger, Arthur, Sr., 664

Scofield, Cyrus Ingerson, 347, 371, 612–13, 670

Scopes, John T., 629–30
Scott, Andrew, 172
Scott, Dred, 331
Scott, Duncan Campbell, 503
Scott, Robert, 483–4, 487
Scullen, James, 473
Seaton, Lord. *See* Colborne, John (first Baron Seaton)
Seekamp, Henry, 144–5
Selwyn, George Augustus, 231–2
Semple, Robert, 449
Shackleton, Ernest, 483–4, 487–9, 491, 494
Shackleton, Frank, 487–9
Shakespeare, William, 664
Shamir, Yitzhak, 510
Shaphat (f. of Elisha), 641
Shaw, George Bernard, 74, 103, 184, 250, 468–9
Shaw, William, 259
Sheehy, Bessie (Mrs. David Sheehy), 387, 388, 389, 394, 402, 404, 410, 418
Sheehy, David, 59–60, 64–5, 72, 387, 404, 419
Sheehy, Eugene (Fr.), 54, 59–63, 72–3, 407, 414
Sheehy, Eugene, 394, 404
Sheehy, Hanna. *See* Sheehy-Skeffington, Hanna
Sheehy, Mary. *See* Kettle, Mary

Sheehy, Mrs. David. *See* Sheehy, Bessie
Sheehy, Nicholas (Fr.), 54
Sheehy, Richard, 394, 402
Sheehy-Skeffington, Francis, 387–8, 389, 394, 404–5, 412–13, 415
Sheehy-Skeffington, Hanna (*née* Sheehy), 394, 404–5
Shem, 229
Sheridan, Philip Henry, 363, 380
Sherman, William Tecumseh, 363, 369
Sherritt, Aaron, 171
Shield, James, 364
Sidney, John, 189
Sitting Bull (Chief), 380
Skeffington, Francis. *See* Sheehy-Skeffington, Francis
Smith, Alfred Emanuel, 630–1
Smith, Frederick Edwin (first earl of Birkenhead), 423
Smyth, Patrick J., 131–2
Sousa, John Philip, 377
Spencer, Herbert, 184
Spenser, Edmund, 162
Spring-Rice, Mary, 409
Spurzheim, Johann Caspar, 315
Stafford, Edward William, 189
Stafford, Edward, 189, 251

Stafford, Emily Charlotte (*née* Wakefield), 203
Stairs, William, 278–9, 281–2
Stanley, Edward (Earl Derby 1851), 82, 130
Stanley, Henry Morton, 175–6, 279, 281
Stanton, George Henry, 178
Stapleton, William, 518
Steele (Sergeant; RIC veteran), 173, 174
Stephens, James, 34–6, 41
Stevenson, Elizabeth. *See* Gaskell, Elizabeth
Stevenson, Robert Louis, 254
Stewart, George Vesey, 242–4
Stewart, Tyler. *See* Eyre, Tyler
Stockton, Robert F., 326
Stokes, Charles Henry, 276–7, 486
Strickland, Jane, 13, 299–300
Strickland, Susanna. *See* Moodie, Susanna
Stuart, Francis, 507
Stuart, Iseult (*née* Gonne MacBride), 396, 507
Stuart, Jeb, 638
Sullivan, John L., 378–9
Sullivan, John O., 325
Sumner, Edwin ("Bull"), 349
Sunday, Billy, 640

Supple, Gerald, 162

Swift, Jonathan, 21, 32–3

Synge, John M., 404

Talbot, Matt, 563–4

Tapuke (Cheiftainess), 453

Te Awhitu, Wiremu, 478

Te Kere Ngatai-e-rua, 209

Te Kiri Karamu, Heni (aka Heni Pore, Jane Foley, Jane Russell, Jane Kelly), 222–4

Te Kooti Arikirangi Te Turuki, 219, 220

Te Maiharoa, Hipa, 220

Te Rangi Hiroa. *See* Buck, Peter Henry

Te Ua Haumene, 219

Temple, Henry John (third Viscount Palmerston), 269–70

Terrell, Billy, 626

Thant, U, 516

Thoreau, Henry David, 16–17

Thornton, John, 20

Tiberio, 230

Tillet, Ben, 98, 109–11

Tinomana, Queen (Rarotonga), 254

Tobin, Hannah, 334

Tobin, Michael, 334

Tomlinson, John, 535

Tone, Theobald Wolfe, 181, 400

Torpy, James, 153

Torrens, Robert, 149

Treacy, Sean, 419–20

Treahy, Catherine. *See* Morrow, Catherine

Trench, William Steuart, 31–2, 43

Trevelyan, Charles, 115, 263–4

Trevelyan, G. M., 194

Tshombe, Moise, 516

Tumulty, Joseph, 622

Twain, Mark, 530

Updike, John, 521

Vaine, Queen (of Avera), 255

Vendler, Helen, 648

Victor Emmanuel, King (Italy), 273

Victoria, Queen, 21–2, 143, 146, 309, 380, 418

Vogel, Julius, 238, 243

Waddell, Rutherford, 206–7

Wakefield, Arthur, 189, 202–3

Wakefield, Daniel, 202

Wakefield, Edward Gibbon, 196–8, 202–3

Wakefield, Edward Jerningham, 203

Wakefield, Edward, 203

Wakefield, Emily Charlotte, 189

Wakefield, Felix, 202–3

Wakefield, Oliver, 203

Wakefield, William, 189, 202–3

Walker, David, 270

Walsh, Ellen. *See* Maher, Ellen

Walshe, Joseph, 581–2

Walshe, Sean, 162

Ward, Humphry, 194

Ward, Joseph, 251, 450–1

Warren, Earl, 652

Watson, James D., 665

Wayne, John (aka Marion Morrison), 638

Webb, Beatrice (*née* Potter), 184, 250, 443

Webb, Paddy, 449

Webb, Sidney, 184, 250, 443

Weissmuller, Johnny, 633

Wellesley, Arthur, 280

Wellesley, Julia Peel. *See* Maguire, Julia

Wellington, Duke of. *See* Wellesley, Arthur

Wells, H. G., 250

Whately, Henrietta, 193

Whately, Richard, 21, 29, 39–40, 119, 191, 197, 293–4, 484–5

Whatu Kanana Hepetipa, 457

Wheelwright, Catherine ("Kate"; *née* Coll), 61–3, 70

White, R. H., 159

Whitlock, William, 521

Wilde, Oscar, 68–9, 399, 664

William III, 48, 359

Wills, John, 151

Willson, R. W., 126–7

Wilson, Eileen, 396–7

Wilson, Elizabeth. *See* Bremner, Elizabeth

Wilson, Ellen (*née* Axson), 618–19

Wilson, Henry, 559

Wilson, Janet (*née* Woodrow), 330

Wilson, Joseph Ruggles, 296, 330

Wilson, Matt, 474

Wilson, Nelle. *See* Reagan, Nelle

Wilson, Robert, 215–16

Wilson, (Thomas) Woodrow, 330, 608, 618–19, 620, 622–3, 629

Wingfield, Theodosia (Lady Powerscourt), 360

Woodham-Smith, Cecil, 344

Woodrow, Janet. *See* Wilson, Janet

Woodrow, Thomas, 330

Wyman, Jane, 591–2

Wynne, Charlotte. *See* Godley, Charlotte

Wyse, Napoleon Bonaparte, 559

Yeats, William Butler, 56–7, 63–4, 65, 66, 72, 74, 180–1, 389–90, 396, 410–11, 506–7

Yeshua (Jesus) of Nazareth, 219, 229, 230, 237, 361, 641, 663

Young, Brigham, 331

Zaccariah (prophet), 537

STORY TITLE INDEX: VOLUME 2 (BOOKS 3 & 4)

A Big Idea, 150–1

A Bit Missing, 487–8

A Bit of Realism, 270–1

A Catholic Constitution for a Catholic People, 574–8

A Family Matter? 157–8

A Final Nudge, 591–3

A Gentleman's Gifts, 260–1

A Good Irish Boy, 103

A Grateful Nation Remembers, 515

A Great War, 458–9

A Grip on the Future, 356–7

A Head of His Time, 158–9

A Hero's Reward, 511

A Jewel, 469

A Keen Sense, 9

A Man of Principle, 514–15

A Matter of Taste, 445

A Missionary to the End, 275–7

A Nation of Shopkeepers? 274–5

A Necessary Hero, 185

A New and Burning Evangelicalism, 293–5

A Nice Irish Girl, 144–5

A Practical Revolutionary, 399–400

A Question of Values, 121–2

A Rare Sense of Humour, 21

A Real Missionary, 120–1

A Reasonable Assumption, 192

A Revolutionary Agrees With the Protestant Archbishop, 119

A Sense of Reality, 593–4

A Simple Case Study (1), 492–3

A Simple Case Study (2), 493–4

A Strange Duck, 443

A Terrible Weight of Fear, 95–6

A Truly Daft Idea, 151–2

A United Ireland? 421–2

A White Linen Flag, 407–8

Acclimatization, 551–2

Across the Continent, 491

Advance Guard, 5–6

Affirmative Action, 111–12

Alien Abduction, 55–6

All for the Empire? 409–10

All's Ill That Ends Ill, 216–17

Alluvial Deposits, 215–16

Alternate Futures, 154–5

Ambition, 543–4

Amnesia and Exclusion; Retention and Inclusion, 443–4

An Economy of Truth, 4–5

An Equal Distance, 537–8

And, Please, Which Was the Irish Revolution? 558–9

And Proud of It, 544–6

And Still Continuing, 302

And This All Men Call Progress, 225

Animal Magnetism, 146

Anomalies, 367

Another Big Wind, 280–1

Another Hero, 608

Arguably, 597–8

Attention to Detail, 152–3

Authenticity, 636–7

Balance of Power, 246–8

Basic Physics, 498–9

Battle of the Network Stars, 389–90

Before the I.R.B., 14–15

Beginning of the Great Depression, 618–19

Belated Recognition, 478

Benign Difference, 87–8

Benumbed, 607

Better and Better? 595–7

Between the Lines, 346

Beyond Explanation, 652

Big Brandies, 483–4

Big Faith, 29–31

Big Step, 261–2

Bilious Attack, 594–5

Billy Graham's International Presidential Prayer Breakfast, 661–6

Blackbirding, 163–4

Blessed Amnesia, 23–5

Bold Tactics, 416

Book Launch, 473–4

Brand Names, 78–9

Brethren, Pray Without Ceasing, 9–10

Brother, 286

Brotherhood, 299–302

Brown Apostles in Old Age, 228–30

Bruderbund, 103–4

Captive Audiences, 190–1

Caveat, 96–7

Chains, 241–2

Chains, 563–4

Chinese Puzzle, 231–2

Chivalry, 222–4

Christian Socialism, 413

Class, 653

Cleaning House, 432–4

Clear Start, 153

Clerical Judgement, 240–1

Cloudwatcher, 379–81

Code, 47–9

Coins of the Realm, 305–6

Colonial Oppression, 253–5

Comic's Relief, 217–18

Coming of Age, 456–7

Commanding Heights, 417–18

Communication (1), 332–3

Communication (2), 333–4

Communication (3), 334

Complexity, 176–7

Continuing…Continuing, 298–9

Conundrum, 286–7

Corrective Bargaining, 201

Costs, 329–30

Crackers for Christ, 347–8

Critical Awareness, 129–30

Critical Success, 131–2

Cultural Implosion, 568–9

Cut to the Chaste, 271–2

Daft Defamations (1), 363–5

Daft Defamations (2), 371–2

Daft Defamations (3), 373

Days of Devilment, 389

Dead Centre, 509

Deathstar, 63–4

Decline of the Pod People, 202–3

Democracy Warming (1), 566–7

Democracy Warming (2), 569–70

Democratic Impulse, 306

Deserving Survivors, 368–70

Diagnosis, 466–7

Digging With Both Feet, 365–6

Dignity, 191–2

Dining Out, 68–9

Dip, 134

Dirty Pictures, 22–3

Discreet Silence, 147–8

Disillusionment, 462

Dissonance, 442

Distaff Power, 405–6

Ditching School, 644–5

Divine Equation, 273–4

Don't Bait Lions, 180–1

Double, Double, Double-Firsts, 279–80

Downward Mobility, 633–4

Dowry, 227

Dr. Hyde and Miss Jackel, 66–7

Draught Animals, 251–2

Dream Factory, 427–30

Dreams Come True, 250

Dumb Name; New Game, 626

Duty, 86–7

Echoes, 655

Economic Reality, 213–14

Editor's Choice, 46–7

Empathy, 295–8

Endgame, 475–7
Endgames, 266–7
Enthusiasm, 183–4
Epic Modesty, 65–6
Eternal Verities, 97–8
Evangelists, 177–8
Evensong, 45–6
Excrescence? 272–3
Exit Visa, 128–9
Exit Visa, 528–30

Fair Dinkum, 142–4
Fair Effort, 226
Fair Reward, 583–4
Faith and Works, 64–5
Faiths of Our Fathers,
   Living Still, 236–7
Family Cries, 470
Family Force, 155
Family Limitation, 628
Family Loyalty, 636
Famine Relief (1), 16
Famine Relief (2), 16–17
Fascism Has Yet to Be
   Invented, 410–11
Field Control, 264–5
Finding the Hook, 32–3
Fine Name (1), 606
Fine Name (2), 619
Finishing School, 527
Flayed Alive, 310–13
Floating Capital,
   239–40
Full-Time, 463–5

Geology, 341–2
Ghosts (1), 390–1
Ghosts (2), 411
Glorious Things of Thee
   Are Spoken, 570–1

God Save Ireland, Cry
   the Heroes, 392–3
Good Catholic, 141–2
Good Day, 214–15
Googlies All Round, 450
Governmental Effi-
   ciency, 455–6
Great Distances, 538–40
Great Names, 288–9
Grizzly Adams, 578–80

Harbinger, 154
Hard, Silent, 614
Hearing Footsteps,
   450–1
Hedge-Bet, 56–7
Heroes, 404–5
Heroic and Baffling,
   345–6
Holy War, 504–6
Home Rule, 352–3
Honestly? 572
Household Pakeha, 224
Humane Relations,
   130–1
Hybrid Vigour, 109–11

Identify the Speaker,
   634–5
Imperial Moment, 506
Impervious to the Light,
   470–2
In the Blood, 520
In the Image of the Al-
   mighty, 367–8
Information Received,
   92–4
Informed Opinion, 499
In-Gathering of the
   Souls, 25–6

Inhale/Exhale, 19
Inside the Laager, 40
Interior Decoration, 108
Intuition, 161
Invisible Category, 163
Irish Poetic Circles,
   162–3
Irish Politics, 610–11
Irish Revolutionary,
   619–20

James Joyce Wept,
   562–3
John Mitchel's Perfect
   Revenge, 342–4
Joycean Moments,
   461–2
Judge Not, 204–5
Just Recompense, 201
Just Tell Me What Was
   in Their Heads, 315–
   16

Karl Marx Assesses the
   New Brigade, 41–2
Keeping Up Appear-
   ances, 372–3
Kick the Cat, 159–60
Kindly Giant, 646–8
King David's Royal
   Line, 621–2

Land of Peace, 584–5
Large Figures, 650–1
Large Mammals Fight-
   ing, 57–8
Last Ties, 40–1
Lateral Movement, 517
Laughter and Good In-
   tentions, 452–4

Laying the Right Foundation, 647–9
Leader in the Promised Land, 337–8
Leading the Blind, 335
Leaps of Faith, 494–5
Learning Irish Law, 550–1
Legacy, 427
Let's Reflect on This, 339–41
Leverage, 540
Liar's Dice, 80–1
Line Dancing, 330
Listed Species, 361–2
Long Tall Mama Blues, 631–3
Lord, Lettest Now Thy Servant, 327–9
Lord, Suffer Thy Servants, 262–3
Loving Steward of Thy Bounty, 302–3

Make the World Go Away, 513–14
Marriage Lines, 189
Martyred for Their Beliefs, 15–16
"Meet and Right, So to Do," 233–4
Melting Pot, 628
Menagerie, 626–7
Mercy's Voice, 525
Messy Slate, 405–6
Methodist Madness, 207–8
Mild At Heart, 165–6
Minor Ideas, 149–50
Mirrors (1), 401

Mirrors (2), 403–4
Mirrors (3), 406–7
Mirrors (4), 408–9
Missing in Action, 526
Missionary Morality, 479
Mixed Marriage, 225
Mixed Marriage, American Style, 624–5
Moderation, 147
Modern Marriage (1), 395–6
Modern Marriage (2), 396–7
Modesty Forbids, 121
Moneychangers From the Temple, 609
More Calculations, 94–5
More Dominoes Fall, 277–8
More Famine Relief, 91–2
More Renaissance, 73–4
More Room, 326–7
More Songs From Armagh Cathedral, 179–80
More Tolerant Every Day, 629
Mourning Has Broken, 245–6
Museum Conditions, 446–7
My Cousin's Marriage, 598–9

Nature's Dowry, 232–3
Nearly Normal, 115–16
Never in My Life, 303–5
Newtonian Physics, 308–9

Nicely Timed, 419–20
Night Watchman, 148
Nightmares, 532–3
Nightsweats, 485–7
No Accounting, 557
No English Need…, 521–2
No Respecter of Persons, 510–11
No Sale, 155–7
No Sex Please, We're Irish, 588–91
No Surprise, 179
Noah's Ark, 237–8
None Is Too Many, 581–2
"No One Would Wish to Hurt Me." 608
Not According to Script, 520–1
Not on This Rock, 656–8
Not Quite Cricket? 125–6
Not Quite Pur Laine? 552–3
Not So Mysterious a Fact, 10–11
Not the Easter Rising, 457–8
Not Without Resources, 18–19
Not Yet Bloomsday, 391–2
Nuggets, 611–12

Obstacle, 499–500
Obtaining Licence, 136–41
Oedipal Wrecks, 192–4
Oh God, 535

On the Pig's Back, 512
Once Again the Cursed Congo, 516–17
One Domino, 411–12
One Step at a Time, 307–8
One-Celled Life Form, 458
Open Season, 638–9
Opportunity, 605
Opposite Directions, 123–4
Orientation, 269–70
Other Views, 289
Over-Hearing, 460–1

Pacifists Also Bleed, 412–13
Parental Confusion, 100–2
Passing the Mantle? 609–11
Patriotic Messages, 122–3
Patronage, 85–6
Pedagogy, 90–1
Pep Talk, 349
Pet Seminary, 33–4
Poes, 445–6
Political Castles, 251
Poll Book, 514
Pond Scum? or Penicillin? 338–9
Position, 634
Postlude, 318–19
Post-Rationalism, 39–40
Practising for The Bay of Pigs, 366
Press Conference, 509–10

Prevailing Westerlies, 203–4
Pre-Writing History, 172–6
Problem Solving, 170–1
Prophecy (1), 42–3
Prophecy (2), 43
Prosaic, 335–6
Protection, 336–7
Protection Racket, 249–50
Public Policy: A Control Case, 172

Reading the Cards, 209
Real Revolutions, 393–4
Recessional, 418–19
Redeployment, 474–5
Reel Power, 633–4
Reflection, 563
Reflections in a Blood-Red Eye, 268–9
Remember '98, 71–2
Remember This! 492
Remembering Zion, 166
Remittances, 182–3
Repellant Boarderers, 527–8
Repetition, 169–70
Requiem, 549–50
Restitution, 651
Resurgence, 100
Return on Investment, 467–8
Revenge of the Potato People? 637–8
Reverence, 656
Rising Star, 394–5
Romantic Ireland's

Truly Dead and Gone, 625–6
Roofs, 587–8
Royal Progress, 178–9
Rubrics, 522
Rural Reality, 474

Sand Crabs, 211–12
Satan's Choice, 651
Saving Rare Butterflies? 615–18
School Leaving Certificate, 98
Scorecard, 82
Scorecard, 124–5
Scorecard, 227–8
Scrambling Africans, 275
Second Impressions, 167–9
Second Sundays, 387–8
Second Thoughts, 200
Seduction, 196–8
Seed Time and Harvest, 652
Self-Determination of Small Nations, 622–3
Shared Accommodations, 194–5
Short Smiles, 133
Silent Alliance, 536–7
Sing Us Another One, 89–90
Singing Against the Beat, 117–18
Siren Songs, 500–1
Size, 465–6
Slipping the Lead, 496–7
Slow Learner, 533–4

Small Problems, 20

Small Stories, 648

Smartening Up, 572–3

Smiler With a Knife, 430–1

Smoking Kills, 226–7

Socially Transmitted Diseases, 546–7

Solace, 653–4

Solid Sense, 511–12

Something Missing, 244

Something to Count On, 34

Speed Tests, 401–2

Spiritual Reconstruction, 359–61

St. Patrick's Bounty, 477–8

St. Patrick's Day in the Morning, 287–8

St. Patrick's Song, 162

St. Patrick's Well, 33

Steeped in the Faith, 189–90

Sterling's Character, 221–2

Stop Me If You've Heard This One Before, 484–5

Strategic Absence, 629–30

Stringent Self-Control, 31–2

Strong Opinions, 454–5

Such a Damp Desert, 81

Suffer the Little Children, 559–61

Summation, 478

Sunset, 134–5

Sure Thing, 420–1

Surf, 199–200

Swarming, 127–8

Swings and Roundabouts, 267–8

Tall Men Talking, 451–2

Tattered Soles, 313–15

Tennessee Fenians, 355–6

Terribly Thin-Skinned, 397–9

Textual Analysis, 105–6

The Boyne Paradox, 77–8

The Clear Eye, 53

The Constitution of the Irish Free State (1), 317–18

The Constitution of the Irish Free State (2), 319–21

The Constitution of the Irish Free State (3), 422–4

The Curing of Souls, 349–50

The Dark Passions of the Heart, 350–2

The Devil in Sir James, 564–5

The Divine Right to Rule, 34–6

The Era of High Chichi, 439–40

The Establishment, 473

The Ever-Expanding Republic, 325–6

The Fingers of His Hand, 283–4

The First Whenwies, 501–2

The Future Prince, 69–70

The Genteel Touch, 235–6

The Gentry, 98–9

The Glitter, 434–5

The Golden Rule, 561

The Great War, 362–3

The Greatest Place…, 582–3

The Happy Warrior, 630–1

The Hardly United Front, 620–1

The Heart of Darkness, 495–6

The Heyday of Christian Education, 502–4

The Horseman Passes By, 49–51

The Household Cavalry, 535–6

The Imperial War Museum, 517–19

The International Workers of the World, 448–9

The Irish Renaissance, 70–1

The Land League Priest (1), 54

The Land League Priest (2), 59–60

The Land League Priest (3), 60–3

The Land League Priest (4), 72–3

The Last, 565–6

The Last Flash, 357–8

The Liverpool Machine As Portcullis, 77

The Liverpool Machine Grinds On, 530–1

The Liverpool Machine in Operation (1), 3–4

The Liverpool Machine in Operation (2), 8

The Long Road to Irish Unity, 378

The Long View, 353

The Lord's Day, 540–3

The Map Read Lightly, 58–9

The Mark of Zorro, 649

The Missionary Revolution, 490–1

The Most Audacious Task Ever, 612–13

"The New Zealand Wars": Stump the Experts, 209–10

The Old Irish Meet the New Irish, 641–3

The Old Rules, 252

The Old School Lie, 468–9

The Old Ways, 180

The One Remaining Hulk, 126–7

The Pale People Retreat, 221

The Partitionings of Ireland (1), 3

The Partitionings of Ireland (2), 6–7

The Partitionings of Ireland (3), 21–2

The Power of Prayer, 218–20

The Prime Directive, 425–7

The Prisoner's Regimen, 120

The Privileged – The "X" Again, 643–4

The Psychologies of Religious Experience, 37–9

The Rantle-Tree, 238

The Rat Pack, 402–3

The Real Score, 431–2

The Really Old Commonwealth, 447

The Resurrection of the Body, 169

The Resurrection of the Body and the Life of the World to Come, 414

The Second Wave, 13–14

The Shadow of the Future, 448

The South Down Militia are the Terror of the Land, 409

The Tailor and His Shroud, 414–15

The Trinity Ban, 585–6

The Very Man, 370–1

The Virtues of an Ulster Presbyterian Childhood, 206–7

The Wages of Win, 36–7

The Webbs We Weave, 184

The West's Awake, 231

The Word, 106

The Worst Job in the World (1), 348–9

The Worst Job in the World (2), 354–5

The "X," 614–15

Things That Really Count, 200–1

This Land Ain't My Land, 654–5

Those in Peril, 649–50

Thoughts of the Great Gudgeon, 440–2

Three Men in a Tub (1), 106–7

Three Men in a Tub (2), 108–9

Throwback? 378–9

Timing, 181

Timing, 530

Tinting the Gene Pool, 525–6

To Katanga and Part-Way Back, 281–2

Toffs At Work, 212–13

Totally Bad, 244–5

Tourist, 20

Tout Court, 54–5

Traffic Patterns, 248

Trained, 160

Traveling Light, 463

Travels Without My Mother (1), 285

Travels Without My Mother (2), 285–6

Trouble, Right There in River City, 51–2

True Blue and Bruised, 358–9

Truly Enlightened, 488–90

Trust, 459
Try Not to Look, 376–8
Two Irishmen, 234–5
Two-Way Traffic (1), 11–12
Two-Way Traffic (2), 12–13
Tyndale's Disappointment, 195–6

Ulster's Wee Colony, 242–4
Up the Clause, 573–4
Useful? Idiots, 284

Vengeance Is Mine, Saith the Lord, 309–10

Venture Capitalist, 259–60
Very Great Humanity, 586–7
Very Well Trained, 160–1
Vintage Year, 44–5
Vital Fluids, 374–6

War Games, 508–9
Was His an Echo? 506–7
We Shall Never See Their Like, 263–4
Weight of Office, 167
What Counted, 82–5
What's a Nice Convent Girl Like You...? 633

Where He Leads Me, I Will Follow, 278–9
Who Fears to Speak (1), 407
Who Fears to Speak (2), 415–16
Win One of Two, 638
Wisdom? 67–8
Without Resources, 17–18
Wrong Man, Wrong Time, Wrong Place, 330–2

XXXX, 164–5